EXPLORATIONS IN ANCIENT AND MODERN PHILOSOPHY

M. F. Burnyeat (1939–2019) was a major figure in the study of ancient Greek philosophy during the last decades of the twentieth century and the first of this. After teaching positions in London and Cambridge, where he became Laurence Professor, in 1996 he took up a Senior Research Fellowship at All Souls College, Oxford, from which he retired in 2006. In 2012 he published two volumes collecting essays dating from before the move to Oxford. Two new posthumously published volumes bring together essays from his years at All Souls and his retirement. The essays in Volume 4 are addressed principally to scholars engaging first with fundamental issues in Platonic and Aristotelian metaphysics and epistemology and in Aristotle's philosophical psychology. Then follow studies tackling problems in interpreting the approaches to physics and cosmology taken by Plato and Aristotle, and in assessing the evidence for early Greek exercises in optics.

M. F. BURNYEAT was formerly Laurence Professor of Ancient Philosophy at the University of Cambridge and a Senior Research Fellow at All Souls College, Oxford.

CAROL ATACK is a Fellow of Newnham College, Cambridge. She is the author of *The Discourse of Kingship in Classical Greece* (2020) and an associate editor of *Polis*. She previously worked with Myles Burnyeat in the preparation of *The Pseudo-Platonic Seventh Letter* (2015).

MALCOLM SCHOFIELD is Emeritus Professor of Ancient Philosophy at the University of Cambridge and a Fellow of St John's College. He was co-editor with Myles Burnyeat and Jonathan Barnes of *Doubt and Dogmatism* (1980), the first volume of the published proceedings of a series of triennial conferences on Hellenistic philosophy that continues to the present. His most recent book is a survey of Cicero's political thought (2021).

DAVID SEDLEY is Laurence Professor of Ancient Philosophy Emeritus at the University of Cambridge and a Fellow of Christ's College. He was an editor of *Classical Quarterly* and *Oxford Studies in Ancient Philosophy*. His books include (with A. A. Long) *The Hellenistic Philosophers* (Cambridge, 1987) and *Creationism and its Critics in Antiquity* (2007).

EXPLORATIONS IN ANCIENT AND MODERN PHILOSOPHY

VOLUME IV

M. F. BURNYEAT

Prepared for publication by

CAROL ATACK
Newnham College, Cambridge

MALCOLM SCHOFIELD
University of Cambridge

DAVID SEDLEY
University of Cambridge

Shaftesbury Road, Cambridge CB2 8EA, United Kingdom

One Liberty Plaza, 20th Floor, New York, NY 10006, USA

477 Williamstown Road, Port Melbourne, VIC 3207, Australia

314–321, 3rd Floor, Plot 3, Splendor Forum, Jasola District Centre, New Delhi – 110025, India

103 Penang Road, #05–06/07, Visioncrest Commercial, Singapore 238467

Cambridge University Press is part of Cambridge University Press & Assessment, a department of the University of Cambridge.

We share the University's mission to contribute to society through the pursuit of education, learning and research at the highest international levels of excellence.

www.cambridge.org
Information on this title: www.cambridge.org/9781009048675

DOI: 10.1017/9781009049146

© Cambridge University Press & Assessment 2022

This publication is in copyright. Subject to statutory exception and to the provisions of relevant collective licensing agreements, no reproduction of any part may take place without the written permission of Cambridge University Press & Assessment.

First published 2022
First paperback edition 2023

A catalogue record for this publication is available from the British Library

ISBN – Set	978-1-009-04777-7	Hardback
ISBN – Volume I	978-0-521-75072-1	Hardback
ISBN – Volume II	978-0-521-75073-8	Hardback
ISBN – Volume III	978-1-316-51793-2	Hardback
ISBN – Volume IV	978-1-316-51794-9	Hardback
ISBN	978-1-009-04867-5	Paperback

Cambridge University Press & Assessment has no responsibility for the persistence or accuracy of URLs for external or third-party internet websites referred to in this publication and does not guarantee that any content on such websites is, or will remain, accurate or appropriate.

Contents

List of illustrations		*page* vii
Preface		ix
Acknowledgements		x
List of abbreviations		xii
Introduction		1

PART I: ONTOLOGY AND EPISTEMOLOGY — 3

1a *Apology* 30b2–4: Socrates, money, and the grammar of γίγνεσθαι — 5

1b On the source of Burnet's construal of *Apology* 30b2–4: a correction — 41

2 Plato on how not to speak of what is not: *Euthydemus* 283a–288a — 46

3 Platonism in the Bible: Numenius of Apamea on Exodus and eternity — 67

4 *Kinēsis* vs. *energeia*: a much-read passage in (but not of) Aristotle's *Metaphysics* — 93

5 *De Anima* II.5 — 155

6 Aquinas on 'spiritual change' in perception — 213

7 *Epistēmē* — 235

PART II: PHYSICS AND OPTICS — 263

8 ΕΙΚΩΣ ΜΥΘΟΣ — 265

9	Aristotle on the foundations of sublunary physics	286
10	Archytas and optics	305
11	'All the world's a stage-painting': scenery, optics, and Greek epistemology	325

Bibliography   363
Index locorum   384

Illustrations

The plate section can be found between pp 100 and 101

Plate 4.1   Distribution of the Passage in the Stemma Codicum. Red circles mark the presence of the Passage, blue squares the absence of Θ. Stemma Codicum: Dieter Harlfinger, 'Zur Überlieferungsgeschichte der Metaphysik', in P. Aubenque (ed.), *Études sur la Métaphysique d'Aristote*, p. 27. © Librairie philosophique J. Vrin, Paris, 1979. www.vrin.fr.
Plate 4.2   Line of deletion on folio 361^r of Ab = Florence Biblioteca Medicea Laurenziana, ms. Plut. 87.12, f. 361r. Reproduced with permission of MiBACT.
Figure 11.1   House of Augustus, Room of the Perspectival Wall Paintings (Room 11). Drawing by L. Pannuti, from Gianfilippo Carettoni, 'La decorazione pittorica della Casa di Augusto sul Palatino', *Mitteilungen des Deutschen archäologischen Instituts, Römische Abteilung* 90/2 (1983), 373–419, fig. 4 (pp. 386–7).   *page* 355
Figure 11.2   Reconstruction of the Würzburg skēnographia. From Apulian calyx krater fragments in several colours, *circa* 350 BC, Martin von Wagner Museum der Universität Würzburg, inv. H4696+H 4701. Drawing by Brinna Otto, Universität Innsbruck, from E. Simon and B. Otto, 'Eine neue Rekonstruktion der Würzburger Skenographie' *Archäologischer Anzeiger*, 88/1 (1973), 121–31, fig. 3 (p. 125). Reproduced by kind permission of Professor Otto.   359

Figure 11.3 Sketch illustrating Heron, *Catoptrica*, prop. 18.
From *Heronis Alexandrini opera quae supersunt omnia*,
ed. L. Nix and W. Schmidt, ii/1. *Catoptrica*
(Leipzig, 1900), fig. 91a (p. 358).   360

Figure 11.4 Sketch illustrating Heron, *Catoptrica*, prop. 18.
From *Heronis Alexandrini opera quae supersunt
omnia*, ed. L. Nix and W. Schmidt, ii/1. *Catoptrica*
(Leipzig, 1900), fig. 91b (p. 361).   361

Preface

Under the title *Explorations in Ancient and Modern Philosophy* (Cambridge University Press, 2012), Myles Burnyeat published two volumes of those of his collected papers that represented work dating from his periods teaching at University College London (1964–78) and the University of Cambridge (1978–96). He foresaw that a further collection might at some future date assemble publications and perhaps hitherto unpublished papers dating from his tenure of a Senior Research Fellowship at All Souls College, Oxford (1996–2006) and in subsequent retirement. Declining health did not allow him to implement that plan. Without any more specific guidance it was eventually left to his literary executors (Angela Hobbs, Malcolm Schofield, and David Sedley) to propose to the Press two further volumes of his collected papers, representing the philosophical work of this later period. The principles governing their choices are sketched in the Introductions to each of the volumes.

It remains to tender warmest thanks to those individuals and bodies who have facilitated the appearance of Volumes III and IV of *Explorations*: first and foremost Margaret Bent, and for generous financial assistance All Souls College; Oliver Padel; George Boys-Stones, Victor Caston, and James Warren. Michael Sharp at Cambridge University Press has been strongly supportive throughout, and his colleagues Sarah Starkey, Katie Idle, along with Lesley Hay and Franklin Mathews Jebaraj, have been unfailingly helpful in shepherding these volumes through the production process. The editorial work itself was undertaken by Carol Atack, Malcolm Schofield, and David Sedley.

CWA, MS, DNS

Acknowledgements

The chapters in this book were previously published as follows:

1. '*Apology* 30b2–4: Socrates, money, and the grammar of γίγνεσθαι': *Journal of Hellenic Studies* 123 (2003), 1–25 and 'On the source of Burnet's construal of *Apology* 30b2–4: a correction' 125 (2005), 139–42
2. 'Plato on how not to speak of what is not: *Euthydemus* 283a–288a': in Monique Canto-Sperber and Pierre Pellegrin, eds., *Le Style de la pensée: Recueil de textes en homage à Jacques Brunschwig* (Paris, 2002), 40–66
3. 'Platonism in the Bible: Numenius of Apamea on *Exodus* and eternity': in Ricardo Salles, ed., *Metaphysics, Soul, and Ethics: Themes from the Work of Richard Sorabji* (Oxford, 2006), 43–69
4. '*Kinēsis* vs. *energeia*: a much-read passage in (but not of) Aristotle's *Metaphysics*': *Oxford Studies in Ancient Philosophy* 34 (2008), 219–92
5. '*De anima* II 5', *Phronesis* 47 (2002), 28–90
6. 'Aquinas on "spiritual change" in perception': in Dominik Perler, ed., *Ancient and Medieval Theories of Intentionality* (Leiden/Boston/Cologne, 2001), 129–53
7. '*Epistēmē*': in Benjamin Morison and Katerina Ierodiakonou, eds. *Episteme, Etc.: Essays in Honour of Jonathan Barnes* (Oxford, 2011), 3–29
8. 'ΕΙΚΩΣ ΜΥΘΟΣ', *Rhizai* 2 (2005), 143–65
9. 'Aristotle on the foundations of sublunary physics': in Frans de Haas and Jaap Mansfeld, eds., *Aristotle: On Generation and Corruption, Book 1* (Oxford, 2004), 7–24
10. 'Archytas and optics': *Science in Context* 18 (2005), 35–53

11 '"All the world's a stage-painting": scenery, optics, and Greek epistemology': *Oxford Studies in Ancient Philosophy* 52 (2017), 33–75

Note: To give help in following up references, the original pagination of the reprinted articles is indicated at the top of each page on the inner margin, and the original page divisions are marked in the course of the text by a pair of vertical lines, ||.

Abbreviations

DK   H. Diels and W. Kranz, *Die Fragmente der Vorsokratiker*, 10th edn, Berlin 1960–1
DNB   Dictionary of National Biography, Oxford 1885–
EAMP M. F. Burnyeat, *Explorations in Ancient Philosophy*, Vols. I–IV, Cambridge 2012–22
KRS   G. S. Kirk, J. E. Raven and M. Schofield, *The Presocratic Philosophers: A Critical History with a Selection of Texts*, 2nd edn, Cambridge 1983
LSJ   H. G. Liddell and R. Scott, *Greek–English Lexicon*, 9th edn rev. H. Stuart Jones, Oxford 1925–40
OLD   A. Souter, C. O. Brink and P. G. W. Glare, *Oxford Latin Dictionary*, Oxford 1968
RE   A. Pauly, G. Wissowa and W. Kroll, *Real-Encyclopädie der classischen Altertumswissenschaft*, 83 vols., Stuttgart 1893–1980
SIG   W. Dittenberger, *Sylloge Inscriptionum Graecarum*, 3rd edn., Leipzig 1915–24
SVF   *Stoicorum Veterum Fragmenta*, Leipzig 1903–24
TLG   *Thesaurus Linguae Graecae*, Irvine CA 2001–

Classical references are abbreviated according to *The Oxford Classical Dictionary* 3rd edn, with the exception of the following:

M   Sextus Empiricus, *Against the Mathematicians*
PH   Sextus Empiricus, *Outlines of Pyrrhonism*

Introduction

In 1992 Myles Burnyeat published an essay he entitled 'Is an Aristotelian philosophy of mind still credible?', labelling it 'A draft'. As he stated, he did so 'with reluctance'. He had intended it as a working paper only, 'to provoke discussion'. It had provoked not just discussion and as much lively interest as anything he ever wrote, but attempted refutations in print. Hence his own reluctant eventual decision for publication. Many have regretted that in Volumes I and II of *Explorations* he included neither this nor a closely connected article, published in its final English version in 1995 as 'How much happens when Aristotle sees red and hears middle C? Remarks on *De Anima* 2, 7–8'. But as Burnyeat had intended, he continued to work on refining and developing his interpretation of Aristotle's theory of perception, and the main result was the major extended essay of 2002 on *De Anima* II.5, reprinted here in Part I as Chapter 5 (in which he also comments on those earlier publications). Chapter 6 is an allied treatment of the same topic in Aquinas's writings.

Chapter 4 deals connectedly and at length with a much-discussed passage found in some manuscripts of the *Metaphysics* – a 'freak performance', in Burnyeat's view – that presents a very different version of the notion of actuality from that central in *De Anima* II.5. This preoccupation with questions of ontology in his later period (as notably evidenced in the 2001 monograph *A Map of Metaphysics Zeta*) was not confined to Aristotle. Key passages in the *Apology*, *Euthydemus*, and *Timaeus*, all in one way or another concerned with Plato and the verb 'to be', are a particular focus in Chapters 1–3 respectively. Especially striking, perhaps, is Burnyeat's radically novel treatment in Chapter 2 of the puzzle of speaking what is not, as Plato explores it in the *Euthydemus*. Chapter 7 on *epistēmē*, by contrast, represents a return on his part to a quite different topic, first broached by him in the influential 1981 paper 'Aristotle on understanding knowledge' (reprinted as Chapter 5 of Volume II of *Explorations*). Plato as well as Aristotle figures prominently here, too.

Chapters 4 and 5 are both designed in part as studies in 'how to read an Aristotelian chapter', comparable in aim, if not in scale, to *A Map of Metaphysics Zeta*. Reading Plato and Aristotle and their philosophical vocabulary with enhanced textual and philosophical attention is likewise a major preoccupation of other essays on ontological and epistemological themes reprinted in Part I of this volume, as indeed of Chapters 8 and 9 in Part II. Chapter 8, a study of what Burnyeat proposes we should construe oxymoronically as the 'rational/reasonable myth' of the *Timaeus*, already widely considered a classic of Platonic interpretation, here joins in Part II essays on Aristotle's writings in natural philosophy, and on neglected but intriguing evidence for ancient optics.

PART I

Ontology and epistemology

CHAPTER IA

Apology *30b2–4: Socrates, money, and the grammar of* γίγνεσθαι

The problem

οὐκ ἐκ χρημάτων ἀρετὴ γίγνεται, ἀλλ' ἐξ ἀρετῆς χρήματα καὶ τὰ ἄλλα ἀγαθὰ τοῖς ἀνθρώποις ἅπαντα καὶ ἰδίᾳ καὶ δημοσίᾳ.

This sentence is standardly translated, 'Virtue does not come from money, but from virtue money and all other good things come to human beings in both private and public life', *vel sim.* The objection is philosophical. Nowhere else does Plato represent Socrates as promising that virtue will make you rich. Quite the contrary, the promise is that virtue will make you happy whatever fortune brings (*Gorg.* 507c–508b, 522ce, 527cd), for whether you fare well or ill is completely determined by the good or bad character of your soul (*Prot.* 313a, *Gorg.* 470e). And this promise is backed by a warning: the more worldly possessions you have, the more unhappy you will be if you do not know how to use them for the good of your soul (*Meno* 87e–89a, *Euthyd.* 280b–281e; the idea is still going strong at *Laws* 11.661ad). If Socrates was in the habit of promoting virtue as a money-maker, it would be disingenuous of him to say that his words do not recommend pursuing virtue *in order to* make money. Strictly speaking, they do not – but he would know that lots of his listeners would take them that way unless he explicitly corrected a misapprehension which, if left uncorrected, would bring him many more followers.

Some have thought to make the usual translation respectable by quoting the Bible. The first to invoke 'Seek ye first the kingdom of God, and his righteousness; and all these things [*sc.* food, drink, clothing, etc.] shall be added unto you' (*Matthew* 6:33) was Sir Richard Livingstone.[1] The same comparison with Jesus turns up in the recent huge commentary on the *Apology* by De Strycker and Slings.[2] But the Bible, as so often, cuts both ways: 'A rich man shall hardly [i.e. with difficulty] enter into the kingdom of heaven'

---

[1] Livingstone 1938: 26.   [2] Strycker 1994: 140.

(*Matthew* 19:23) is much closer to the Socrates we meet elsewhere in Plato. This is a case where philology should take its cue from philosophy. ||

Alternative translations

Long ago, when contributing to a collection of essays on Socrates edited by Gregory Vlastos, I complained that the standard translation cannot be right. I translated χρήματα more generally as 'valuables' and spoke of 'the Socratic challenge to common notions of what is a valuable possession'.[3] My idea was that Plato meant to leave the sentence open to both a Socratic and a non-Socratic understanding of what counts as a valuable possession, allowing readers to choose for themselves between a philosophical and a non-philosophical interpretation. Vlastos as editor was not convinced, but he printed me nonetheless. He was right not to be convinced.

πλοῦτος ('wealth', 'riches') is the word that lends itself to that kind of figurative extension, not the mundane χρήματα ('money'). Socrates' companion Antisthenes discourses on 'wealth (πλοῦτος) in the soul' at Xenophon, *Symposium* 4.34–44. At the end of Plato's *Phaedrus* (279c) Socrates prays, 'May I consider the wise man rich (πλούσιος). As for gold, let me have as much as a temperate man can bear and carry with him.' Similarly, at *Republic* VII.521a he speaks of the philosopher rulers as those who are really rich (οἱ τῷ ὄντι πλούσιοι), not in gold, but in the wealth that the happy must have: a good and wise life.[4] The pseudo-Platonic *Eryxias* does extend the word χρήματα to cover anything useful (χρήσιμον), including skills (402de), but it takes lengthy argument (cued no doubt by *Rep.* VIII.559c3–4) to make this intelligible, and Plato was dead by the time the dialogue was written.

Even though Vlastos was not convinced, he sympathised with my worry, and later came to endorse a solution we had both shamefully overlooked.[5] The solution had been sitting there all along in Burnet's commentary of 1924:

> 'It is goodness that makes money and everything else good for men.' The subject is χρήματα καὶ τὰ ἄλλα ἅπαντα and ἀγαθὰ τοῖς ἀνθρώποις is predicate. We must certainly not render 'from virtue comes money'! This is a case where interlaced order may seriously mislead.[6]

---

[3] Burnyeat 1971: 210 [Chapter 10 in *EAMP* vol. I].
[4] Cf. the contrast between mortal gold, which the Guards of the ideal city are not allowed to possess, and the divine gold they have in their souls from the gods (*Rep.* III.416e–417a), a contrast echoed later as their being not poor (save financially) but by nature rich (VIII.547b).
[5] Vlastos 1991: 219, with n. 73.   [6] Burnet 1924: 124.

So too, without reference to Burnet, Léon Robin's French translation in the Pléiade series: 'mais c'est le vrai mérite qui fait bonne la fortune' ['but it is true worth that makes fortune good'].[7] But this, like Burnet's rendering, seems not to have caught on. More recently, Luc Brisson in the Flammarion series translates as usual, but in his note to the passage offers a non-standard interpretation (borrowed from a *distinct* point in Vlastos): virtue does get you money, but this is of minor importance compared to the perfection of your soul, which Socrates has just said should be your primary goal.[8]

The story in Germany is much the same. I have found only two exceptions to the rule. Kurt Hildebrandt, in his ominously titled *Platons Vaterländische Reden: Apologie, Criton, Menexenos*,[9] translates as follows: 'Nicht aus dem Gelde Tüchtigkeit entsteht, sondern aus Tüchtigkeit Schätze und alle andere Güter der Menschen, in der Familie und im Staate' ['It is not from money [Gelde] that virtue comes into being, but from virtue valuables [Schätze] and all other human goods, in the family and in the state']. The switch from 'Gelde' to 'Schätze' is a version of my own youthful indiscretion. Later, again without ‖ reference to Burnet, Konrad Gaiser construed ἀγαθά as 'dem Sinne nach prädikativ' ['in a predicative sense'] and offered this translation: 'Nicht aus dem Geld wird einem ἀρετή, sondern aus ἀρετή werden Geld und die anderen Dinge, insofern sie ἀγαθά sind, für die Menschen, für jeden einzelnen wie für die Gesamtheit' ['It is not from money that any ἀρετή comes into being, but from ἀρετή money and the other things – insofar as they are good – for humans, for each individual as for the whole community'].[10] All honour to the French and German scholars who in their different ways have manifested unease with the standard translation.

Sadly, although there have been numerous English-language translators of the *Apology* since Burnet's edition (all of whom will, if they had sense, have worked with Burnet to hand), for a long time they ignored his advice. To my knowledge, only in one short article and a quotation here and there could his influence be discerned. An early example is F. M. Cornford, who in his delightful little book *Before and After Socrates* (1932) found occasion to quote a lengthy chunk of the *Apology*, including this: 'Goodness does

---

[7] Robin 1955.
[8] Brisson 1997: n. 173, referring to Vlastos 1991: 303–8. A similar account of the traditional translation in Brickhouse and Smith 1994: 20 with n. 33.
[9] Hildebrandt 1936. The ominous title [*Plato's Patriotic Speeches*] heralds Hildebrandt's long introduction, where he enlists both Socrates and Plato for the Fascist cause.
[10] Gaiser 1959: 109 with n. 113.

not come from wealth, but it is goodness that makes wealth or anything else, in public or private life, a thing of value for man.'[11] In 1973 John Hammond Taylor published a brief article advocating this construal.[12] A more recent book to quote 30b2–4 in Burnet's translation is C. D. C. Reeve, *Socrates in the Apology: An Essay on Plato's Apology of Socrates*.[13] But of late the situation has changed. Suddenly we have two complete translations of the *Apology* which follow Burnet on the crucial point.

(a) John Cooper, editor of the new Hackett *Plato: Complete Works*,[14] reprinted G. M. A. Grube's translation of the *Apology*,[15] but with the disputed sentence put as follows: 'Wealth does not bring about excellence, but excellence makes wealth and everything else good for men, both individually and collectively.' Grube's original rendering, a version of the standard translation, was relegated to a footnote as 'an alternative'.

(b) In the same year, Michael Stokes brought out a text and translation of the *Apology* in which he adopted the Burnet construal on the grounds that, although linguistically difficult, it is philosophically preferable.[16] In the Anglophone world, the arguments of Burnet and Vlastos are at last beginning to tell.

The only reasoned opposition is that of De Strycker and Slings:

> [Burnet's] construction ... cannot be accepted. The parallelism of the two pointedly antithetical members requires (1) that the sentence could be ended with χρήματα, and that καὶ τὰ ἄλλα κτλ should be considered an afterthought; (2) that γίγνεται should in both members mean 'comes from'. Besides, the collocation of ἅπαντα shows that ἀγαθά cannot be separated from τὰ ἄλλα and ἅπαντα. If Plato had wanted to say what Burnet makes him say, he would certainly not have said it in such an ambiguous and misleading way.[17]

SOCRATES, PLATO, AND ARISTOTLE ON THE VALUE OF MONEY

Let me start from the third point, Burnet's separation of ἀγαθά from καὶ τὰ ἄλλα. Anyone who refuses to allow this has to meet a philosophical (not

---

[11] Cornford 1932: 36; Cornford does not cite Burnet, because he is writing for a non-scholarly audience.
[12] Taylor 1973.   [13] Reeve 1989: 124–5, with n. 21.
[14] J. M. Cooper and Hutchinson 1997. This will be the standard complete works in English translation for a good while to come.
[15] Grube 1975.
[16] Stokes 1997, note *ad loc*. See also Stokes's review of De Strycker and Slings, Stokes 1996.
[17] Strycker 1994: 334.

of course a philological) objection. If χρήματα καὶ τὰ ἄλλα ἀγαθά is a unitary phrase, it implies that Socrates thinks money a good. But where else does Socrates, speaking *in propria persona* as he does throughout the *Apology*, call money or wealth a good? ||

The only pertinent passages I know are ones where he is appealing to his interlocutor's values, not his own (e.g. *Prot.* 353c–354b, *Gorg.* 452c, 467e), or where he is preparing to correct the idea that money is good in itself (*Meno* 78e, *Euthyd.* 279a, *Lys.* 220a).[18] At *Crito* 48c he disdains Crito's readiness to sacrifice money to help him escape from prison; justice is the only value that counts for him, money is simply irrelevant. Again, it is Crito's beliefs he is appealing to when at *Euthydemus* 307a he includes money-making among arts it is fine to have (Crito emphatically agrees that it seems so to him). Contrast *Republic* II.357cd, where money-making is an example given by the aristocratic Glaucon to illustrate the burdensome type of good one pursues only for its consequences, not for itself: Socrates accepts the existence of that *kind* of good, but remains non-committal about the examples.

The *Apology* is a defence of philosophy. Socrates is a philosopher, not a money-maker like his friend Crito, nor an aristocrat like Glaucon. Only philosophical values are relevant to the syntax of our sentence. Given Burnet's construal, *Apology* 30b is in perfect harmony with the famous declaration we meet later at 41d:

> οὐκ ἔστιν ἀνδρὶ ἀγαθῶι κακὸν οὐδὲν οὔτε ζῶντι οὔτε τελευτήσαντι, οὐδὲ ἀμελεῖται ὑπὸ θεῶν τὰ τούτου πράγματα.
>
> For a good man no evil comes either in life or in death, nor are his affairs neglected by gods.

Everyone recognises that Socrates is saying something profound and unusual here. It would be absurd to suppose he means that virtue guarantees a decent income, thereby warding off the evil of poverty. Burnet's construal of the earlier passage allows us to interpret him as saying that virtue will make not only money, but *lack* of money and *everything else* that happens in your life or after death, good rather than bad for you. Both in this life and the next, a virtuous person will make good use of even the

---

[18] Several of these texts are cited by Vlastos 1991: 214–32 to argue that in Socrates' own view wealth is a 'non-moral good' whose value, however, is minuscule compared to the good of virtue. His argument, which has been influential (see nn. 8 above and 25 below), ignores the dramatic contexts within which wealth is called good.

most unfavourable circumstance. The two passages 30b and 4ld stand to each other as positive and negative expressions of the same moral faith.

De Strycker and Slings agree that the two passages should be interpreted together – in their sense. To these they add other texts, notably *Laws* 1.631bc and this passage from *Republic* x, which they describe as 'an authorized commentary' on *Apology* 41d:[19]

> οὕτως ἄρα ὑποληπτέον περὶ τοῦ δικαίου ἀνδρός, ἐάντ' ἐν πενίαι γίγνηται ἐάντ' ἐν νόσοις ἢ τινι ἄλλωι τῶν <u>δοκούντων</u> κακῶν, ὡς τούτωι ταῦτα εἰς ἀγαθόν τι τελευτήσει ζῶντι ἢ καὶ ἀποθανόντι. οὐ γὰρ δὴ ὑπό γε θεῶν ποτε ἀμελεῖται ὃς ἂν προθυμεῖσθαι ἐθέληι δίκαιος γίγνεσθαι καὶ ἐπιτηδεύων ἀρετὴν εἰς ὅσον δυνατὸν ἀνθρώπωι ὁμοιοῦσθαι θεῶι. (613a)

> This, then, must be our conviction about the just man, that whether he fall into poverty or disease or any other *supposed* evil, for him these things will end in some good while he lives or even after death. For a man is never neglected by gods if he is willing to try hard to become just and, by the practice of virtue, to liken himself to god as far as is humanly possible.[20]

On the face of it, Socrates is allowing here that virtue may well fail to ward off poverty. His language also seems incompatible with the standard translation of *Apology* 30b, because if poverty || is only a supposed evil, then wealth is only a supposed good. Most people do suppose that poverty is bad, wealth good. But the Socrates of *Republic* x does not endorse their view.

In order to show that these first impressions are correct, and that neither *Republic* x nor *Laws* 631bc supports the De Strycker–Slings interpretation of *Apology* 30b, I need to track down the mistakes in their reasoning. Admittedly, some scholars are likely to find this superfluous. They would insist that the *Apology* represents the views of Socrates (or: Plato in his early, Socratic period), the *Republic* and *Laws* those of Plato (or: Plato in his middle and late periods), and it is not safe to interpret the *Apology* from the very different dialogues of Plato's maturity. I shall not take that easy way out. On the subject of money, I believe that Plato, who had lots, and Socrates, who did not, are at one. Leaving the *Laws* aside for the moment, let us turn to *Republic* II.

Glaucon has challenged Socrates to show that justice is worth pursuing for its own sake, as an intrinsic good. He insists on postulating a just man

---

[19] Strycker 1994: 234–5; I extend their quotation by one further sentence.
[20] On the nuances of the combination ἢ καί (which De Strycker and Slings render 'or else'), see Denniston 1954: 306: 'Sometimes καί means "also", or marks a climax, "even".'

with a reputation for injustice and an unjust man with a reputation for justice. Which will fare best? Only if the just man fares better, under this radical hypothesis about their respective reputations, will Glaucon be satisfied that justice is to be pursued entirely for its own sake, independently of reputation and its consequences (360e–362c). Adeimantus agrees. He complains that parents, teachers and poets do not recommend the young to practise justice for its own sake, but only for the consequences of a reputation for it (363a). And here he reiterates the consequences of a reputation for justice enumerated by Glaucon earlier at 362bc: people will want you to hold high office in the state and you will be able to marry yourself or your children into any family you wish (362e–363a). In short, a reputation for justice, however unmerited, inspires trust. The question is, how will the postulated unjust man use this trust?

Glaucon supposes that he will abuse it for all he can get, and what he will get is, above all, wealth. Through that will come favours for his friends and damage to his enemies, plus the goodwill of the gods, who will be delighted with his rich offerings and dedications (362bc). The crucial point here that the unjust man's wealth derives, not from his reputation for justice, but from the grasping injustice it conceals: πλεονεκτοῦντα δὲ πλουτεῖν (362b7; cf. 343de, 349c, 366a). If you miss this detail, you will be liable to misconstrue the argument of *Republic* x. I fear that De Strycker and Slings do misconstrue it.

By the end of Book IX Socrates has finished showing that, despite the unpleasant consequences of his reputation for injustice, the just man has the happier life. In Book x, therefore, he feels entitled to drop the requirement that the just man have a reputation for injustice. In fact, he claims, justice *usually* (613c4: τὸ πολύ) and *in the long run* (613c5: πρὸς τὸ τέλος) earns you the esteem of others and, in consequence, it brings the rewards that Glaucon at II.362ac assigned to the unjust man with a reputation for justice: namely, the goodwill of the gods and, from fellow humans, any offices of state you may wish to hold and the opportunity to marry into any family you like (612e–613d). The consequences of a reputation for justice are exactly the same in Book x as they were in Book II. Accordingly, they do not include wealth, which in Book II was the result of the injustice that the unjust man is so good at concealing. On the contrary, the context of the sentence quoted from 613a makes it clear that a just man, unlike the unjust man at 362c (and Cephalus at 1.331b), does not need wealth to win the goodwill of the gods. They respond to his godlike character, not to the offerings that money can buy. De Strycker and Slings are therefore mistaken when they include money among the rewards that usually come from justice in the long run.²¹ All the more are they mistaken when they quote 613a, without attending to the qualification 'supposed', as a promise that the gods will ensure compensation in the after-life for poverty in this.²² ||

Look again at the quote from *Republic* x. It does not say that after death the gods will provide some *other* good to compensate for the awfulness experienced here and now. On the contrary, it is these very things (ταῦτα) – poverty, disease and the like – that will end in some good for those who are virtuous. Virtue will have *made* something good of their trials and tribulations. In that sense, they were all along being cared for by gods. This is a providential universe in which virtue is sufficient for happiness.

Republic x should not be read in isolation. It is the sequel to a lengthy analysis in Books VIII and IX of the forms that injustice takes in city and soul. The degeneration of the ideal city starts with the urge, on the part of one group of rulers, to make money and accumulate private wealth (VIII.547b). Money again is what motivates the next revolution, the forcible imposition of a property-based oligarchy (550c–551b). In due course, the oligarchs' greed for money is the cause of the democratic revolution by which they are overthrown (555bc). The parallel analysis of worse and worse individual personalities is all about the increasing dominance of the lowest part of the tripartite soul: the appetitive (IV.439d: ἐπιθυμητικόν), money-loving (IX.580e: φιλοχρημάτων) part, parallel to the money-making (IV.434c, 441a: χρηματιστικόν) producer class in the ideal city. This is the part of the soul which already in Book IV was described as the largest in our make-up, and the one that by its nature is the most insatiable in pursuing money (442a); money is the means to the satisfaction of bodily desires (IX.580e–581a). The self-inflicted damage that comes to a soul bent on wealth is further emphasised at 589d–590a and 591e. No one who reads Books VIII–IX with care could come away believing that for Plato money in itself is any kind of good.²³ Rather, those Books are an extended demonstration of the thesis of *Meno* 87e–89a and *Euthydemus* 280b–281e that the possession of money is a disaster for all who are not virtuous. They prepare us for the *Republic*'s last word on

---

[21] Strycker 1994: 139.
[22] Strycker 1994: 235. For the qualification 'supposed', cf. also III.406c7: τῶν πλουσίων τε καὶ εὐδαιμόνων δοκούντων εἶναι.
[23] Elsewhere, Plato locates the origin of war in the desire for money and possessions: *Rep.* II.373d–374a, *Phd.* 66cd.

riches: when you go to Hades to choose your next life, beware of 'evils like wealth' (x.619a).

Now for the *Laws*. In the passage cited (1.631bc) the Athenian Stranger distinguishes two classes of goods: 'divine' goods like wisdom and the virtues, 'human' goods like health, beauty and strength. He claims that the divine goods bring with them also the three human goods – plus a fourth, wealth. But to this last he attaches a qualification, which De Strycker and Slings omit to mention: wealth is a good only if it is not blind, but guided by wisdom. That is exactly what Socrates says about wealth at *Apology* 30b, on Burnet's construal (given that for Socrates virtue is knowledge or wisdom), and in the *Meno* and *Euthydemus* passages cited above. It is also what Socrates conspicuously *fails* to say on the standard translation of *Apology* 30b. Again, at *Laws* III.697bc (echoing II.660e–661e), where three types of good are ranked in order of priority, third place is given to the *so-called* (λεγόμενα) goods of wealth and money. The qualification 'so-called' is implied again at IX.870ab, where the Athenian rejects the terms in which wealth is standardly praised among Greeks and barbarians. He insists that wealth is good only as a means to goodness of body and of soul, hence that those who would be happy must conduct their money-making with justice and temperance. *Laws* v.742e–743c goes so far as to argue that the very rich *cannot* be good and therefore cannot be happy; it is not merely difficult, but impossible, for them to enter into Plato's version of the Kingdom of Heaven.

De Strycker and Slings concede that the *Meno* and *Euthydemus* favour Burnet.[24] Let me in turn concede to them that some money might accrue to the just man of *Republic* 613cd when he holds office in the state or contracts an advantageous marriage for himself or one of his children. The *Republic* teaches that the just man and he alone will know how to use that extra money for the good of his soul. An important passage of Book IX (not featured in the discussion of De Strycker and Slings) tells us that a person of understanding (ὅ γε νοῦν ἔχων) will be guided in ‖ their acquisition or disposal of wealth by concern for the constitution (πολιτεία) of their soul, lest it be disturbed by having too much or too little (591ce; cf. IV.443e and X.618be). This is entirely in keeping with Socrates' message at *Apology* 30ab. Virtue guides you to use whatever money you have for the good of your soul; which might mean giving it away to some needy friend. Whereas the standard translation, precisely because it takes χρήματα καὶ τὰ ἄλλα ἀγαθά as a unitary phrase, implies

---

[24] Strycker 1994: 138 n. 39.

that money is a good in its own right, even if, as De Strycker and Slings maintain, it is a minor good compared to virtue.[25] And this, I have argued, runs counter to everything Plato tells us elsewhere about Socrates' attitude to money.

The Platonic texts we have been studying stand at the beginning of a long debate. Some in the later Platonist tradition credit Plato with a standardised triple division of goods into goods of the soul (the virtues), goods of the body (health, beauty), and external goods, amongst which wealth is often included. Thus they agree with De Strycker and Slings in ascribing to Plato the view that external goods such as wealth are genuine goods. These, however, were Platonists who wanted to harmonise Plato and Aristotle. Others such as Atticus, who preferred their Platonism pure, resisted, holding that for Plato the only goods are those of the soul.[26] And Aristotle's own position is more nuanced than appears from the later debate.

Rhetoric I.5, 1360a24–28, b12–25, does count money an external good, and as such a component of happiness, but Aristotle there is rehearsing reputable premises (ἔνδοξα) for orators to use in court or assembly; he does not commit himself to their truth. His own considered view emerges at *Eudemian Ethics* VII.15 (8.3), 1248b26–34 (cf. 1249b12–13): wealth and other supposed (δοκοῦντα) goods are indeed by nature goods, but for some (*sc.* the foolish or intemperate) they are bad – they are good only for those who are themselves good. At *Nicomachean Ethics* I.8, 1099a31–b8, wealth is mentioned among the external goods necessary for happiness, but it is necessary for a particular reason. Aristotle explains that without external goods such as friends, wealth and political power you cannot do certain things your virtues would otherwise lead you to do; the virtues cannot be exercised as widely and grandly as one would wish (cf. VII.13, 1153b17–19).[27] The upshot is that wealth has instrumental value, but only for the virtuous – much as Socrates (on Burnet's construal) maintained! What we find in Aristotle's two *Ethics* is not outright dissent from Plato's view, but a sophisticated development of it.

It remains to consider a passage which De Strycker and Slings might have cited as evidence that Aristotle read *Apology* 30b their way:[28]

---

[25] De Strycker and Slings' position (Strycker 1994) on what they call 'minor goods' is close to that of Vlastos 1991: 200–32 on 'mini-goods'; my objection is indicated at n. 18 above.
[26] See Mansfeld 1997, with a mass of references to the relevant texts.
[27] Here I expand a tiny bit, guided by John Cooper (1985, reprinted in Cooper 1999, ch. 13).
[28] They do cite the passage (Strycker 1994: 140 n. 44), but as a parallel for their understanding of the *Apology*. It was W. L. Newman (Newman 1887, vol. 3 *ad* 1323a36 and 40) who suggested that Aristotle is actually drawing on *Apol.* 30b.

κτῶνται καὶ φυλάττουσιν οὐ τὰς ἀρετὰς τοῖς ἐκτὸς ἀλλ' ἐκεῖνα ταύταις (*Politics* VII.1, 1323a40–1)

People do not acquire and preserve the virtues by the help of external goods, but external goods by the help of the virtues.

Aristotle tells us (1323a21–3) that he is here making use of one of his published works,[29] written for a wider audience than the treatises, and that his treatment of the issues is somewhat superficial || (1323b36–40). That diminishes the authority of this text as a source for Aristotelian doctrine. But it does not rule out the possibility that he is echoing Plato's *Apology*.

The external goods referred to are 'wealth, money, power, reputation, and all such things' (1323a37–8). Does Aristotle mean to say here, what neither *Ethics* maintains, that *all* of these result from virtue – wealth and money included? His conclusion at the end of the chapter will be in line with the *Ethics*, that the best life is a life of virtue equipped with external goods *sufficient for exercising the virtues* (1323b40–1324a2). If the quoted sentence sounds less qualified, that may be because it draws on a popular work where Aristotle works with a broader brush than in the treatises. Moreover, it is embedded in an argument *ad hominem* against people who suppose that, while happiness requires all three types of good, the ideal is to accumulate external goods without limit (1323a38: εἰς ἄπειρον) with enough virtue to get by.[30] To which Aristotle replies that in practice this will lose you the virtues and other goods of the soul, whereas if you go all out for the latter, they will bring you (enough of) the former. It is important here that Aristotle is debating with people who genuinely want (some) virtue as well as money, power and esteem. His point is that if they do not limit their pursuit of external goods, the virtues will fall by the way. Their ideal suffers from *practical* inconsistency, whereas someone who amasses goods of the soul will not thereby be prevented from acquiring (a moderate amount of) the external goods as well.

Nothing in this *ad hominem* argument commits Aristotle to more than Plato said in *Republic* x, that in normal circumstances virtue is likely to win you a good reputation and political office. I see no reason to think that Aristotle has any Platonic text in view, but if he has, to my mind *Republic* x is at least as good a bet as *Apology* 30b. Aristotle at this point claims to be arguing from the facts of practical life (1323a39–40: διὰ τῶν ἔργων), in contrast to some more theoretical arguments to follow (1323b6–7: κατὰ τὸν λόγον). Plato did the same in *Republic* x, after the theoretical arguments of Books II–IX: 'Isn't this how things are, if the

---

[29] Quite possibly the *Protrepticus*: Düring 1961: 254–6.
[30] Here I am indebted to correspondence with John Cooper.

truth must be told?' (613b9–10: ἆρ' οὐχ ὧδε ἔχει, εἰ δεῖ τὸ ὂν τιθέναι;). Socrates at *Apology* 30b speaks in a quite different, exhortatory tone. Of course, if Aristotle meant to echo *Republic* x, it was carelessness or a misunderstanding on his part to list wealth and money with the other external goods. But that is preferable to the supposition that he was remembering *Apology* 30b, taking χρήματα καὶ τὰ ἄλλα ἀγαθά as a unitary phrase, and endorsing the result *in propria persona*. For we have seen that this is not his considered view. Not his view at all.

I have shown that Socrates, Plato and Aristotle all agree that money is not a good in its own right, irrespective of the character of its possessor. As a matter of fact, Plato makes even Cephalus say that wealth is only good for decent types such as (he likes to think) himself (*Rep.* 1.331ab). This should be motive enough to go back to *Apology* 30b in search of a deeper rationale for Burnet's construal.

Being and becoming

First, let me repeat that the objection to the standard translation is philosophical, not philological. Partial parallels for the standard construal are easy to find:

> ὅσα δὲ ἐξ ἐπιμελείας ... οἴονται γίγνεσθαι ἀγαθὰ ἀνθρώποις (*Prot.* 323d6–7)
>
> the goods that people think come about for humans as the outcome of diligence ...

> ἐξ ὧν μάλιστα ταῖς πόλεσιν καὶ ἰδίᾳ καὶ δημοσίᾳ κακὰ γίγνεται, ὅταν γίγνηται (*Rep.* 11.373e6–7)
>
> the sources from which bad things particularly come about for cities, affecting people both individually and collectively

where ἀγαθά and κακά are plainly subject to the verb γίγνεσθαι, not predicate. But any construal which assigns ἀγαθά to the subject-expression at *Apology* 30b2–4 falls to the philosophical ‖ objection that Socrates does not normally consider money a good. Hence Burnet's alternative suggestion that the subject here is χρήματα καὶ τὰ ἄλλα ἅπαντα, with ἀγαθά separated off as predicate; ἐκ remains causal, as in the two passages just cited.[31] My task is to offer a philological explanation of how ἀγαθά *can* be predicate.

---

[31] *LSJ* s.v. III 6.

Both the standard translation and Burnet's alternative need to supply the verb γίγνεται again after the comma. The difference is that the Burnet–Cornford–Vlastos–Cooper–Stokes translation brings it back with a complement it did not have before, separating ἀγαθὰ τοῖς ἀνθρώποις from τὰ ἄλλα. Point (2) of the De Strycker–Slings rebuttal is that this involves an objectionable change in the meaning of the verb γίγνεται. They assume, that is, that the change of *syntax* postulated by Burnet (from γίγνεται without, to γίγνεται with, a complement) entails a change in the *meaning* of the verb. First γίγνεται means 'comes to be', then 'becomes <good>'. The first meaning is existential, the second predicative. It is this assumption I wish to challenge. Burnet's few defenders to date have acknowledged that a change in the meaning of γίγνεσθαι is a difficulty for his construal.[32] I hope to show there is no change of meaning and, consequently, no such difficulty. My argument will involve a lengthy digression, away from the *Apology*, into some of the deeper reaches of Platonic and Aristotelian ontology.

The De Strycker–Slings understanding of γίγνεσθαι is parallel to a standard account of the semantically related verb εἶναι. It is often said that this too is ambiguous between an existential and a predicative meaning. Either '*x* ἐστι' is a complete statement, to be translated '*x* exists', or it is what logicians call an open sentence, '*x* is . . .', where the dots mark a place to be filled by some appropriate predicate: '*x* is *F*'. But recent scholarship has shown that, where Plato is concerned, this view is quite inadequate. It cannot explain, indeed it makes nonsense of, the way Plato handles the Greek verb 'to be' in some of the most important passages of his philosophy.[33] I shall argue that the same holds for his use of γίγνεσθαι.

Let us start with the phenomena. εἶναι is used both with and without a complement. We find both (1a) '*x* ἐστι', and (1b) '*x* ἐστι *F*', where *x* is a subject and *F* some predicate. I leave ἐστι unaccented here and in similar invented sentence forms, because the standard rules for its accentuation purport to differentiate between existence and predication, thereby prejudging the question at issue. In quotations from Greek authors I will treat ἐστι (and Doric singular ἐντι) as enclitic like εἰσί, except when initial and after οὐ. No solution is ideal (why not οὐκ εἰσί?), but for this discussion it is best not

---

[32] Taylor SJ 1973: 51, n. 12; Stokes 1997: 150.
[33] From a voluminous literature, I pick out for their excellence two writers in particular. First, Charles H. Kahn, whose articles Kahn 1976 and Kahn 1981 distil much of his previous work on the subject (listed at his n. 45) going back to his massive study Kahn 1973. And more recently, Lesley Brown, in L. Brown 1994, which generalises the lessons of her pioneering article L. Brown 1986. The idea of extending their approach from εἶναι to γίγνεσθαι is my own initiative.

to encumber what was originally a tonal system of accentuation with a semantic distinction between existence (or possibility) and the copula.[34]

Similarly, γίγνεσθαι is used sometimes with, sometimes without a complement: (2a) '*x* γίγνεται', (2b) '*x* γίγνεται *F*'. Our task is to understand the relation of (2a) and (2b). Thanks to the recent work just mentioned, the better understood relation between (1a) and (1b) should be of help. My argument will be that neither verb is ambiguous. Both (1a) and (2a) are, uncontroversially, complete statements. The more controversial claim is that to pass from (1a) to (1b), or from (2a) to (2b), is not to change the meaning of the verb, but to add a complement to a verb || that was already complete, but further complet*able*. Thus the essential idea is that of a verb which is complete on its own, but which is further completable without change of meaning.

There are many such verbs. Suppose someone rings up and asks what you are doing. You reply, 'I am teaching.' That is a complete answer to the question. But a more complete answer would be 'I am teaching French.' That each of these is a complete statement is shown by the fact that, when you receive the call, the first might be true and the second false (really, you are teaching a subject of which the authorities do not approve). And the first could be known to be true by a person who has no idea what you are teaching. Only a complete statement can be evaluated as true or false. Thus the verb 'to teach' is complete on its own, yet further complet*able* by adding a complement. And no one would say that when a complement is added, it changes the meaning of the verb 'to teach'.[35]

My suggestion is not, of course, that εἶναι or γίγνεσθαι should be construed on the model of 'to teach' as verbs that can take an (accusative) object. I am simply giving a familiar example of a verb which is complete but further completable, in order to help readers understand the less familiar idea that εἶναι and γίγνεσθαι show an analogous pattern. Without a complement they make a complete statement, but one that is further completable by adding a complement – without any change in the meaning of the verb.

To illustrate how this works out Platonic Greek, I adduce two philosophically important passages where the role of εἶναι is crucial.[36]

---

[34] For critical remarks about standard editorial practice, see Barrett 1992: 424–7, and Kahn 1973: Appendix A, 420–5.
[35] The example is gratefully borrowed from L. Brown 1986, but my use of it is more limited than hers. Brown's thesis that 'to teach' is 'a verb of variable polyadicity', in that it can be added to indefinitely ('I am teaching French to small children', 'with enthusiasm', etc.), implies commitments in semantic theory which I do not wish to incur, let alone extend to εἶναι and γίγνεσθαι in ancient Greek.
[36] For obvious reasons, Plato's language is the main focus of this study. Kahn 1973 gives a broader treatment of εἶναι in Homer and authors of the Classical period, which establishes beyond doubt

Being in Plato

At *Theaetetus* 185a8–d1 we find the following stretch of argument, which I translate as best I can word-for-word, using a dash to indicate those places where εἶναι is understood but not expressed in the Greek:[37]

SOCRATES. About a colour and a sound you surely do think about both of them, first, just this: that they both are (ὅτι ἀμφοτέρω ἐστόν)?
THEAETETUS. Yes, I do.
SOC. Consequently also that each – other than the other, and each – the same as itself?
THEAET. Of course.
SOC. And that both – two, each – one?
THEAET. Yes, that too.
SOC. Consequently also you are able to consider whether they – like or unlike each other?
THEAET. Presumably.
SOC. Now through what do you think all these things about them? For you can't grasp what is common about them either through hearing or through sight. Again, this too is evidence for what we are saying: if it was possible to enquire whether both are salty or not (ἆρ' ἐστὸν ἁλμυρὼ ἢ οὔ), you ‖ know you can say by what you would examine them, and this is clearly neither sight nor hearing, but something else.
THEAET. Yes, of course: the power which functions through the tongue.
SOC. Well said. Now, through what does that power function which reveals to you what is common both to everything and to these? I mean that which you express by the words 'is' and 'is not' (ᾧ τὸ 'ἔστιν' ἐπονομάζεις καὶ τὸ 'οὐκ ἔστι'), and the other things mentioned in our questions about them just now. To all these, what organs will you assign through which the perceiving element in us perceives them?
THEAET. You are speaking of being and not-being (οὐσίαν λέγεις καὶ τὸ μὴ εἶναι), and likeness and unlikeness, and the same and different; also one, and any other number connected with them.[38]

Readers will have supplied the verb 'to be', without difficulty, each time a dash indicates that εἶναι is not expressed. But is the verb you supplied the

---

that Plato's use of the verb is typical, however novel the philosophical theory he builds on it. We shall see that the same is true of Aristotle and the other philosophical authors considered below.

[37] In Russian (the language for which this essay on cross-cultural translation was originally written), as in some other Indo-European languages, the present indicative of the verb 'to be' is 'unmarked'. Between two nouns it may be indicated by a dash; in conversation, one simply goes straight from subject to predicate without a word between, just like Plato's Greek in the passage quoted. Note that omission is not restricted to (and so is no criterion for) non-existential uses of εἶναι: Kahn 1973: 264 n. 32, where an example like Hom. *Od.* XIII.102–3 could go over into Russian word-for-word.

[38] I have discussed the philosophical significance of this argument in Burnyeat 1976b [now also Chapter 4 in *EAMP* vol. II], and its place in an overall interpretation of the dialogue in Burnyeat 1990: 52–65.

same verb as you met at the very beginning of the passage, or a different one?

I imagine that many readers will say it is different. They will probably take the verb in 'that they both are' as existential ('they both exist'), but the verb supplied in the sequel as the predicative copula. Notice, however, that in the summing up at the end Socrates' 'is' and 'is not' (τὸ 'ἔστιν'... καὶ τὸ 'οὐκ ἔστι') and Theaetetus' 'being and not-being' (οὐσίαν ... καὶ τὸ μὴ εἶναι) cover both. As if only one verb had preceded. As if for Plato the verb supplied is one and the same with the verb expressed at the beginning. And indeed the argument *requires* a single, unitary verb throughout.

Consider the negative οὐκ ἔστι, which like its positive counterpart expresses something 'common both to everything and to these (*sc.* the colour and the sound we started from)'. If you take οὐκ ἔστι as negated existence, you make Socrates say that the colour, the sound, and everything else both exist and do not exist. Which is absurd. But it is not absurd to understand him to mean, e.g., that the colour *is* the same as itself and *is not* the same as the sound, or that the sound *is* like the colour (in that both are sensible qualities) and *is not* at all salty. As Plato will point out in the *Sophist* (256d–257a, 263b11–12), of everything whatsoever it can be said both that it *is* various things and that it *is not* innumerable other things, where the 'is' expresses predication. Or to put the thesis in its most general and most striking terms, that which is *is not* and that which is not *is* (258d–259b).

Observe how Plato moves in this climactic passage from '*x* οὐκ ἔστι *F* to '*x* οὐκ ἔστι'. (A verb that is complete but further completable is also subject to the reverse process of dropping the further completion: 'I am teaching French' entails 'I am teaching'.) It would clearly be wrong to render '*x* οὐκ ἔστι' here by '*x* does not exist'. And Plato is not the only ancient writer to make such moves:

> καὶ ταὐτὰ ἔστι καὶ οὐκ ἔστι· τὰ γὰρ τῆιδ' ἐόντα ἐν τᾶι Λιβύαι οὐκ ἔστιν, οὐδέ γε τὰ ἐν Λιβύαι ἐν Κύπρωι. καὶ τἆλλα κατὰ τὸν αὐτὸν λόγον. οὐκῶν καὶ ἐντὶ τὰ πράγματα καὶ οὐκ ἐντί. (*Dissoi Logoi* (= DK 90) 5.5)

> And the same things both are and are not. For the things here are not in Libya, nor are those in Libya in Cyprus. And likewise with the rest, by the same argument. So things both are and are not.

Even if the anonymous author, as I suspect, is indebted to Plato,[39] at least he felt no linguistic or logical discomfort at using the same pattern of inference. ‖

---

[39] For scepticism about the standard dating of this tract to around 400 BC, see my entry 'Dissoi Logoi' in Craig 1998: 106–7 [now also Chapter 13 in *EAMP* vol. I].

In sum, there is every reason to think that the ἐστι we supply when Socrates in our *Theaetetus* passage says ἑκάτερον ἑκατέρου μὲν ἕτερον, κτλ is the same verb as the ἐστόν we began with. First it stands on its own, then it joins subject to predicate. It is easy to supply when it joins subject to predicate, because that same verb has already been expressed in the immediately preceding context. Plato brings it back at 185b10 (ἆρ' ἐστὸν ἁλμυρῷ ἢ οὔ) because Socrates began a new line of questioning at 185b7. When εἶναι stands on its own, it is often appropriate to translate with our verb 'to exist', though I would advise against that here.[40] But the possibility of so translating should not deceive us into the idea that 'to exist' reproduces the exact meaning of the Greek verb.

Another philosophically important Platonic passage which requires a unitary understanding of εἶναι is the discussion of knowledge and opinion beginning at *Republic* v.476d. To show the lovers of sights and sounds that they do not have the knowledge they think they have, Socrates takes them through an argument with four steps. They agree (i) that knowledge is always of what is (τὸ ὄν). Then they accept (ii) that each of the many beautiful things they adore will turn out to be ugly as well, hence *not* beautiful, in the same way as each of the many large things will turn out to be no more large than small, hence both large and *not* large; and so on through a series of predicates which apply in one context or comparison only to be replaced in another by their opposites, both contrary and contradictory. From (ii) Socrates infers (iii) that the things conventionally held to be beautiful, large, etc., 'roll around somewhere between what is not and what purely is' (479d4–5: μεταξύ που κυλινδεῖται τοῦ τε μὴ ὄντος καὶ τοῦ ὄντος εἰλικρινῶς), and so concludes (iv) that they cannot be objects of knowledge, precisely because, as agreed at (i), knowledge is always of what is.[41] Here it certainly makes nonsense of the argument to render the participial phrase τὸ ὄν as 'what exists'. That would condemn the beautiful things which turn out ugly and not beautiful to hover, absurdly, between existence and non-existence.[42] If (iii) is to be inferred from (ii), 'what

---

[40] As a case where translation in terms of existence is entirely appropriate, L. Brown 1986: 63–4 aptly cites the *Sophist*'s review of theories about what there is, beginning at 242c.
[41] This is but a brief summary of the points relevant to my discussion. For a fuller treatment of the way τὸ ὄν in (i) unpacks into the explicitly predicative εἶναι of (ii), see Kahn 1981: 112–14.
[42] Just this absurdity is found in the very first English translation of the *Republic* (Spens 1763: 'between existence and non-existence'), and occasionally in its modern successors (e.g. Lee 1955). Some English translators prefer 'between unreality and perfect reality', *vel sim.*, because degrees of reality make better sense than degrees of existence (Cornford 1941, Sterling and Scott 1985, Halliwell 1993, Waterfield 1993). Those who offer 'between nonbeing and pure being', *vel sim.* (Jowett 1875, Bloom 1968, Grube 1974), do so in a context where 'being' need not be understood

purely is' must employ the same 'is' as occurs in predications of the form '*x* is both beautiful and ugly', and 'what is not' the same 'is not' as occurs in '*x* is both beautiful and not beautiful'. Plato moves happily from '*x* is *F*' to '*x* is' and from '*x* is not *F*' to '*x* is not'.

To this unitary verb (and its participial derivatives: τὸ ὄν, τὰ ὄντα, etc.) corresponds, according to Plato in the *Sophist*, a unitary Form: Being. The *Sophist* (252e–260b, 261d) compares Forms like Being and Not-being, Sameness and Difference, to the vowels which join consonants to each other. Every syllable needs a vowel, but that does not make the vowel a mere link (copula). It has a phonetic value of its own. Just so, the 'is' which in Platonic Greek joins subject to predicate has semantic meaning in its own right, such that it can also stand as sole predicate in a complete sentence. ||

A nice illustration for the complete but completable character of Platonic εἶναι is *Laws* x.901c8–d2, where within a single sentence the verb is first complete and then further completed:

> νῦν δὴ δύ' ὄντες τρισὶν ἡμῖν οὖσιν ἀποκρινάσθωσαν οἱ θεοὺς μὲν ἀμφότεροι ὁμολογοῦντες εἶναι, παραιτητοὺς δὲ ἅτερος, ὁ δὲ ἀμελεῖς τῶν σμικρῶν.
>
> Now let the three of us receive an answer from the two parties who agree that gods are – <but are> venal in the view of one, negligent of small details according to the other.[43]

Being in Aristotle

Much the same story can be told of Aristotelian Greek, even though Aristotle is famous for insisting, against Plato's unitary concept of being, that τὸ ὄν λέγεται πολλαχῶς, what *is* is said (*sc.* to be) in many ways. Each of the ten categories (κατηγορίαι, types of predication) imports an irreducibly different genus of being. But none of them are existence in contrast to predication. Being is being a substance, or a quantity, or a quality, etc. As Aristotle explains in *Metaphysics* Z.1 (cf. *Metaph.* Γ.2), each of these is a being (ὄν), but only a substance is a being *simpliciter*

---

as 'existence', because they have used the indeterminate 'what is' and 'what is not' since 476e10. But the two best translations to date (Shorey 1937, Lindsay 1935) stick close to the Greek: 'between that which is not and that which purely is', *vel sim.* (likewise Reeve and Grube 1992, a revision of Grube). This does justice to the fact that που at 479d4 picks up the earlier locative designation of τὸ ὄν as the domain or province (the ἐφ' ᾧ) of knowledge, and of τὸ ὄν as the domain or province of ignorance (477a9–10).

[43] This choice example (later echoed in both content and syntax by Epictetus, *Diss.* 1.12.1) arrived in a letter from Lesley Brown. Earlier in the same discussion, the Athenian undertook to defend the thesis ὡς θεοί τ' εἰσὶν καὶ ἀγαθοί, δίκην τιμῶντες διαφερόντως ἀνθρώπων (887b7–8).

(1028a30–1: οὐ τὶ ὄν ἀλλ' ὄν ἁπλῶς), because a quantity or quality, etc., is always the quantity, quality, etc., *of* some substance. The substance is what it is – it is a dog, a substance, a being – in its own right. The others are beings (ὄντα, things that are) only because they quantify, qualify, etc., some substance. Yet they are beings, albeit dependent ones. So none of this entitles us to equate being ἁπλῶς with existence. That would confine existence to the category of substance, with the result that Aristotle's deliberately generous ontology would be wrecked. Being ἁπλῶς is being a substance. But another way of being is being a quality (of some substance). All of the things that are (as we would say, all of the things that exist) are by being (predicatively) something or other: '*x* ἐστι' implies '*x* ἐστι *F*', for some categorially suitable value of *F*.

Aristotle is more cautious than Plato about the converse implication, from '*x* ἐστι *F*' to '*x* ἐστι'. He acknowledges certain exceptions to the rule that anything which is (predicatively) something or other *is*. For example, 'Homer is a poet' does not imply 'Homer is' (because he is now dead), 'What is not is thought about (δοξαστόν)' does not imply 'What is not *is*' (*Int.* 11.21a25–33, *Soph. el.* 5.167a1–2; 25; cf. 25.180a36–8, *Metaph.* Θ.3, 1047a32–5). But these are exceptions to the general rule that you *can* infer from '*x* is *F*' to '*x* is'; you can unless a particular value of *F* (e.g. being thought about) makes it unsafe to do so.[44] For Aristotle, as for Plato, the 'is' that joins subject to predicate has semantic meaning in its own right. The important difference between the two philosophers is that where Plato recognises just one such 'is', Aristotle insists on ten. Consequently, for Aristotle the meaning that 'is' has varies with the category of the predicate it joins to a subject. ‖

I conclude that Aristotle, like Plato, does not recognise the idea we express by speaking of the verb 'to be' as a mere copula, an empty link. The nearest he gets to it is the difficult and debated passage *De Interpretatione* 3.16b19–25,[45] from which I quote a single sentence:

---

[44] Such exceptions are well discussed by L. Brown 1994: 233–6. The first systematic challenge to the general rule came from the Stoics, who distinguish the class of beings (ὄντα), provocatively restricted to bodies, from the most general class of 'somethings' (τινά), which additionally includes certain incorporeal items like void, place, time and λεκτά ('sayables'). In effect, the Stoics allow '*x* ἐστι *F*' to range more widely than '*x* ἐστι', blocking the inference from the first to the second. For a valuable discussion of this doctrine and its anti-Platonic import, see Jacques Brunschwig, 'The Stoic theory of the supreme genus and Platonic ontology', Brunschwig 1994: 92–157. The inference was defended (question-beggingly) by later Aristotelians (Alex. Aphr. *In Top.* 301.19) as well as Platonists (Plot. VI 1 [42] 25, 9–10).

[45] Weidemann 1994: 178–87 provides an exhaustive account of the debate from antiquity into modern times.

αὐτὸ [*sc.* τὸ ὂν ψιλόν] μὲν γὰρ οὐδέν ἐστιν, προσσημαίνει δὲ σύνθεσίν τινα, ἣν ἄνευ τῶν συγκειμένων οὐκ ἔστι νοῆσαι.

> On its own it [*sc.* bare 'being'] is nothing, but it additionally signifies a certain combination, which cannot be thought of without its components.

Aristotle is often supposed to say here that the 'is' in 'Socrates is wise' has no semantic meaning of its own, but is a mere copula. Yet it fits the context better to take this as a remark about someone uttering the solitary word 'is' all by itself, not about the word 'is' in a standard predication. It is not that in a standard predication the verb has no meaning in its own right, but that *what* its meaning is (what *sort* of being it signifies) is contextually dependent on the subject and/or predicate expressions flanking it; hence without a context it has no meaning at all, whereas an ordinary verb uttered on its own (someone suddenly shouts out 'Sits') does at least put the hearer in mind of its signification.[46] Besides, προσσημαίνει δὲ σύνθεσίν τινα suggests that εἶναι *always* has a copulative function as part (but only part) of its meaning. That would rule out an independent existential meaning. (Once again, to be is to be something or other.) To isolate the copula, it seems, you need to be able to *contrast* it with the 'is' of existence (or, some would add, the 'is' of identity).[47]

The importance of contrast becomes manifest when Galen, writing an elementary logic book for a much later age, lists ten different types of premise, one for each of the Aristotelian categories, but adds an extra. The categorial premises are statements about substance like 'Air is a body', 'Air is not a body', statements about quantity such as 'The Sun is a foot across', 'The Sun is not a foot across', statements about quality and so on (*Inst. Log.* 2, p.5.3–22 Kalbfleisch). But these are preceded, as never happens when Aristotle lists his categories, by this:

> <τῶν δὲ προτάσεων> ἔνιαι μὲν ὑπὲρ ἁπλῆς ὑπάρξεως ἀποφαίνονται, καθάπερ ὁπόταν εἴπῃς 'πρόνοιά ἐστιν· ἱπποκένταυρος οὐκ ἔστιν'. (*Inst. Log.* 2, p.5.1–3)
>
> Of premises, some make an assertion about simple existence, as when you say 'Providence is', 'A hippocentaur is not'.

Thus Galen does isolate what I would call an existential *use* (as opposed to an existential meaning) of the verb 'to be', alongside but distinguished

---

[46] So Whitaker 1996: 55–9 (cf. 30–2), arguing against Ackrill 1963 *ad loc.*
[47] For reason to doubt that the differences between predicative and identity statements are due to different *meanings* of 'is' or ἐστι, see Mates 1979: 216–20.

from predications in the category of substance like 'Air is a body'.⁴⁸ By 'existential use' I mean nothing more than a use that we can translate by our verb 'to exist'. To mark off this use Galen has the noun ὕπαρξις, a word first attested in this role by Philodemus⁴⁹ and increasingly current thereafter in philosophical discussions ‖ about the existence, as we would put it, of this or that controversial item. It was such controversies that he had especially in view when introducing his extra type of premise; he refers to disputes about the ὕπαρξις or οὐσία of fate, providence, gods, and void (*Inst. Log.* 14, p.32.6–11).

Notice, however, that Galen writes <u>ἁπλῆ</u> ὕπαρξις to make the contrast between 'Providence is' and a predication in the category of substance like 'Air is a body'.⁵⁰ The reason is that the root verb ὑπάρχειν can take a predicative complement just like εἶναι.⁵¹ (From Aristotle onwards, logicians canonically rewrite this in reverse form as 'A ὑπάρχει τῷ B', where A is predicate and B subject.) Like εἶναι, ὑπάρχειν is complet*able*. This has implications for the noun ὕπαρξις. It tends to represent uses of ὑπάρχειν which we translate existentially.⁵² Some dramatic examples occur in Philo Judaeus. When he insists that ἔστι τὸ θεῖον καὶ ὑπάρχει, and follows with a reference to God's ὕπαρξις,⁵³ it is tempting to take the καί as epexegetic. At any rate, he often declares that we can (and should) know *that* God exists, but we cannot (and should not aspire to) know *what* he is (his οὐσία, essence) or what he is like (his ποιότης). In saying this, Philo is

---

⁴⁸ Distinguished from it by ἤ at line 3, alongside it because ἔνιαι μέν contrasts with ἔνιαι δέ at line 6, where quantity and other dependent categories come in.

⁴⁹ *De Dis.* 3, col. 10, 35 Diels, *De Pietate* col. 22, 628 Obbink, both about the existence of gods. ὕπαρξις = property comes earlier.

⁵⁰ A different use of the phrase occurs in Galen's near-contemporary Alexander of Aphrodisias, *In Top.* 52.25–53.10, where ἁπλῆ ὕπαρξις is belonging to something *simpliciter* as opposed to belonging as its genus; it contrasts with the different ways of being or belonging to a subject (τρόποι ὑπάρξεως) determined, not by the theory of categories, but by the *Topics* doctrine of predicables. In general, ἁπλοῦς and ἁπλῶς are devices for setting aside whatever qualifications are relevant in a given context.

⁵¹ Examples: Arist. *Meteor.* 2.8.365b24, *Part. an.* 4.10.688a 21; Sext. Emp. *Pyr.* 2.5, *Math.* 8.305, 9.182; Alex. Aphr. *In APr.* 275.21; Plot. 1 4 [46] 3, 28–9, II 1 [40] 2, 27–8.

⁵² For the good reason that 'being there already' is what the verb expresses on its second extant occurrence (Pind. *Pyth.* 4.205) and frequently thereafter. In a valuable (and humorous) article, 'The origin of ὑπάρχω and ὕπαρξις as philosophical terms' (Glucker 1994), John Glucker classifies the various uses of ὑπάρχειν in both philosophical and non-philosophical authors of the fifth and fourth centuries BC, and shows how they all relate in one way or another to the idea of being there already. He speaks more readily than I would of different 'senses' of the verb, overestimates the extent to which its range narrows later under Stoic influence, and wrongly assigns the first existential use of the noun ὕπαρξις to Philo Judaeus. But these minor disagreements still leave me in debt to his helpful contribution.

⁵³ *Opif.* 170. Cf. *Opif.* 172; *Spec.* 1.41, 2.225; *Aet.* 53 and 70.

helped by being able to gloss the verb εἶναι with the noun ὕπαρξις, to make clear that he means being *simpliciter*, not being (predicatively) something or other. Thus 'The fact that He *is* can be apprehended under the name of existence' (τὸ δ' ὅτι ἔστιν ὑπάρξεως ὀνόματι καταληπτόν).[54] Or again, God says ἴδετε, ἴδετε, ὅτι ἐγώ εἰμι (*Deuteronomy* 32:39), and Philo interprets: ὅτι ἐγώ εἰμι ἴδετε, τουτέστι τὴν ἐμὴν ὕπαρξιν θεάσασθε.[55]

Yet in principle a verbal noun might represent any use of its root verb. And in practice the form '*x* ὑπάρχει *F*' allows the noun ὕπαρξις to signify the obtaining of a whole state of affairs, *x*'s actually being *F*, just as τὸ ὄν does in the *Republic* x passage (613b9–10) cited above (p. 8).[56] ὕπαρξις also serves as the noun (a) for the construction ὑπάρχειν τινί which || expresses a predicate's belonging to a subject,[57] (b) for the generic being *of* something,[58] and (c) for the specific οὐσία of any item in any category.[59] Eventually it becomes a noun of divided reference, so that Simplicius, for example, can treat all ὄντα as ὑπάρξεις.[60] Evidently, the import of ὕπαρξις varies with, and depends upon, its larger context. It nominalises whichever use of ὑπάρχειν is in play. Certainly, it has a use, as οὐσία does, which corresponds to our 'existence' and is most naturally translated that way. But if this use is a function of context, it should not be represented as a prior lexical meaning brought *to* the context. One should be cautious

---

[54] *Praem.* 40, reading ὀνόματι with Colson and all MSS except A, against Cohn, who prints A's ὄνομα.
[55] *Post.* 168.
[56] Examples: Plut. *De E* 387c; Apollonius Dyscolus, *Conj.* 216.11–16 (where ὕπαρξις contrasts with ἀναίρεσις, something's not being the case); Sext. Emp. *Pyr.* 2.5, *Math.* 8.304. So too in Galen himself ὕπαρξις (without ἁπλῆ) sometimes represents the use of ὑπάρχειν to signify the obtaining of a whole state of affairs: *Inst. Log.* 3, p.7.13; p.8.8–9; 4, p.9.21; 5, p.12.17. In the Stoic definition of a true proposition under attack at Sext. Emp. *Math.* 8.85–6 (φασὶ γὰρ ἀληθὲς μὲν εἶναι ἀξίωμα ὃ ὑπάρχει τε καὶ ἀντίκειταί τινι) ὑπάρχειν *cannot* mean 'to exist' because there are false propositions as well as true. The truth of a Stoic ἀξίωμα (a non-linguistic item expressible by a sentence) is something's being the case, a whole state of affairs obtaining; Gal. *Inst. Log.* 15, p.35.12 and 17, or Sext. Emp. *Pyr.* 1.14 may serve to illustrate ὑπάρχειν used in accordance with this definition. There is even a word ὑπαρκτικός, glossed by Ammonius, *In Int.* 27.12–13 as 'expressive of one thing's belonging or not belonging to another', which corresponds (for subject–predicate propositions) to the modern logician's 'having truth-value'. It is then no surprise to find that in modal logic ὑπάρχουσα πρότασις is an 'assertoric' premise of the form '*x* belongs to *y*' (with ὑπαρχόντως, not in LSJ, the associated adverb), as opposed to an 'apodeictic' one of the form '*x* necessarily belongs to *y*': e.g. Alex. Aphr. *In APr.* 124.21–8.
[57] A very clear example is Alex. Aphr. *In Top.* 375.16–17, 23–4.
[58] Porph. *ap.* Simpl. *In Cat.* 34.21–3; Ammon. *In Cat.* 20.26–21.1.
[59] Alex. Aphr. *In Metaph.* 399.14–16: ἡ γὰρ ἑκάστου οἰκεία ὕπαρξις οὐσία ἐκείνου.
[60] *In Cat.* 67.27–36, where it is handy to have a term which is neutral between the various Aristotelian categories in a way that ὄντα cannot officially be.

about saying, as many scholars have done, that ὕπαρξις *means* existence.[61] One should be equally hesitant to claim that Galen's extra type of premise establishes an existential meaning for εἶναι. Rather, he has singled out a use to which the verb can be put in a given context. Which is not enough to yield an 'is' meaning 'exists' to contrast with the bare copula.

Compare ὕπαρξις in the sense of 'property'. That is a genuinely distinct meaning, in need of its own dictionary entry, which ὕπαρξις shares with οὐσία. At *Theaetetus* 144cd Plato introduces Theaetetus as a talented youth whose trustees have wasted the οὐσία (property) he inherited from his wealthy father. In the ensuing discussion Socrates' midwifery will help him give birth to a theory of knowledge which does away with οὐσία (being) and leaves only becoming: ἔστι μὲν γὰρ οὐδέποτ' οὐδέν, ἀεὶ δὲ γίγνεται (152d).[62] Such word-play is typical of Plato. A pun is clear evidence of distinct meanings. It is hard to imagine a comparable pun on the predicative and existential uses of either οὐσία or ὕπαρξις.

At this point we should return to Aristotle. When at *Posterior Analytics* II.1, 89b31–5 he points to a certain priority attaching to the question whether e.g. a centaur or a god is or is not ἁπλῶς (as opposed to: is white or not), he immediately adds that once we know *that* the thing is, we inquire '*What*, then, is a god?' (τί οὖν ἐστι θεός). One cannot in English ask *'*What*, then, exists a god?' Aristotle treats a statement of the form '*x* is', which we would naturally (and for many purposes not wrongly) render '*x* exists', as prelude to the question 'What is *x*?' (hence the οὖν). For him, to be *is* to be something or other (in one of the ten categories), so if a centaur or a god is, *what* (predicatively) is it? He regards the 'is' of 'is *simpliciter*' as complete but further complet*able* – by a predicate in the category of substance.[63] I have little doubt that this Aristotelian text, together with *De Interpretatione* 10.19b12–15 (discussed below), is Galen's cue for adding his extra premise. Aristotle's pupil Eudemus of Rhodes had already spoken of Σωκράτης ἐστι and Σωκράτης οὐκ ἔστι as

---

[61] On the importance of distinguishing the 'input question' (what meaning a word brings to its sentential context) from the 'output question' (what meaning it has in that context), see Wiggins 1971.
[62] From a paragraph which is itself a vivid illustration of the impossibility of distinguishing an existential as opposed to copulative meaning for either verb.
[63] Here again I follow L. Brown 1994. Compare Kahn 1976: 333: 'Thus for Aristotle, as for Plato, existence is always εἶναί τι, being something or other, being something definite. There is no concept of existence as such, for subjects of an indeterminate nature... Platonic Greek for "X exists" is "X is something", εἶναί τι.' For examples of this use of εἶναί τι, see *Phd.* 74a9–12, 102b1, *Rep.* IX.583c5, 584d3, *Tht.* 157a3 and 5, *Soph.* 246e5, 247a9, *Tim.* 51b7–8, *Phlb.* 37a2–9. The idiom is less frequent in Aristotle, because of his technical contrast between εἶναί τι and εἶναι ἁπλῶς, but examples abound in his discussion of place at *Phys.* v.1–5 (210a12, etc.).

'simple premises' (ἁπλαῖ προτάσεις).⁶⁴ He is likely to be systematising, not dissenting from, his master. The same holds for Galen. In which case the ἔστι of his extra premise will be as completable as the ὑπάρχειν of his ἁπλῆ ὕπαρξις. ||

About the other side of the missing contrast I can venture further. Were Aristotle to start thinking in terms of a copula without semantic meaning of its own, he would lose not only the theory of categories, but also other philosophical theses centred on that all-important verb εἶναι. There would be little or no content to the distinction between a thing's essential and its accidental *being* (*Metaph*. Δ.7), which would reduce to the distinction between its essential and accidental *predicates*. There would be little or no sense to the idea that potential being is as much a type of being as actual being (*Metaph*. Δ.7; E.2, 1026a33–b2; H.1, 1045a32–4). Worst of all, there would be no subject matter for first philosophy, which is the study of *being qua being* (*Metaph*. Γ.1–2, E.1).

BECOMING IN ARISTOTLE

Now for a parallel account of γίγνεσθαι. The close relation between εἶναι and γίγνεσθαι is recognised by Aristotle at *De Interpretatione* 10.19b12–15, where he groups γίγνεσθαι with ἔστιν, ἔσται, ἦν and the like. All these count as verbs by the definition of ῥῆμα laid down in *Int*. 3, because they additionally signify time. Hence, when combined with a subject, they suffice, without further complement, to make an assertion, e.g. ἔστιν ἄνθρωπος; or (I add) γίγνεται ἄνθρωπος. Aristotle goes on to consider the case where ἔστιν – or (I add) γίγνεται – is 'predicated additionally as a third thing' (τὸ ἔστι τρίτον προσκατηγορηθῇ).⁶⁵ His example is the predicative assertion 'A human is just' (19b19–22: ἔστι δίκαιος ἄνθρωπος) – to which I add 'A human becomes just' (γίγνεται δίκαιος ἄνθρωπος). But he says nothing to show that in his eyes this is a different ἐστι/γίγνεται, or a different meaning, from before.⁶⁶

In other contexts, however, Aristotle distinguishes γίγνεσθαι ἁπλῶς from γίγνεσθαι τι, where ἁπλῶς indicates a use of the verb without complement and τι its use with a complement from one of the three

---

⁶⁴ *Fr*. 27 Wehrli = Schol. In Ar. *APr*. 1 cod. 1917 *in margine* p.146a24–7 Brandis.
⁶⁵ Cf. *APr*. 1.l.24b16–18; 3.25b22.
⁶⁶ Weidemann's lengthy review of rival interpretations of the passage (Weidemann 1994: 327–38) nowhere pauses to defend the assumption (written into his translation) that Aristotle switches from ἐστι as 'Existenzprädikat' to ἐστι as 'Kopula'; nor does he record anyone else doing so. About γίγνεται both he and Ackrill 1963 remain silent.

non-substantial categories (quality, quantity and place) in which he holds change can happen. (Recall the parallel treatment of εἶναι in the phrase quoted from *Metaph.* Z.1, 1028a30–1: οὐ τὶ ὂν ἀλλ᾽ ὂν ἁπλῶς.) It is not that ordinary speakers are likely to say ἄνθρωπος γίγνεται ἁπλῶς. They say ἄνθρωπος γίγνεται and *Aristotle* uses ἁπλῶς to mark the difference between that use of the verb and its use when someone says ἄνθρωπος γίγνεται δίκαιος or τρίπηχυς or ἐν Λυκείῳ.[67]

Aristotle's most extended discussion of the contrast between γίγνεσθαι ἁπλῶς and γίγνεσθαι τι is *De Generatione et Corruptione* 1.2–5.[68] The task he sets himself is twofold. First, he will vindicate the coherence of the idea that things come to be *simpliciter*. Then he will defend the distinction between (a) coming to be *simpliciter* (substantial change) and (b) change of quality (ἀλλοίωσις) or quantity (αὔξησις καὶ φθίσις). In (a) a subject comes to be from another subject which perishes in the process, as when the water in your kettle disappears into steam or air. In (b) a single subject remains while new properties replace the old. Note the symmetry.[69] In (b) a subject remains while one property is exchanged for another. In (a) a property remains (according to Aristotle, both water and air are wet) while one subject is exchanged for another. ||

This is not the place for a detailed analysis of Aristotle's arguments, which are among the most difficult in the corpus. Rather, I am interested in the way some commentators react to them philosophically. Take C. J. F. Williams, who explains very clearly in his Introduction why Aristotle's distinction between γίγνεσθαι ἁπλῶς and γίγνεσθαι does not match our distinction between coming into existence and coming to be something or other.[70] Aristotle treats the contrast between (2a) '*x* γίγνεται' and (2b) '*x* γίγνεται *F*' as a case of categorial ambiguity. He associates (2a) with a predication in the category of substance (the γένεσις results in the truth of e.g. 'Socrates is a human', 'Cerberus is a dog'), (2b) with a predication in one of the non-substantial categories (the γένεσις results in the truth of e.g. 'Socrates is wise', 'Cerberus is sleepy'). Thus Williams reads (2a), as I do, in terms of a predicative rather than an existential meaning of εἶναι. But then

---

[67] This last is the use that Aristotle invokes for a list of the three types of non-substantial change at *Cael.* 1.7, 274b15–16 (εἰ ἀδύνατον γενέσθαι λευκὸν ἢ πηχυαῖον ἢ ἐν Αἰγύπτῳ), so please do not think that γίγνεσθαι ἐν Λυκείῳ would have to mean 'be born in the Lyceum'. At Hdt. v.33 Megabates set sail and in due course ἐγένετο ἐν Χίῳ. Against the idea that 'to be born' is the root meaning of γίγνεσθαι, see Kahn 1973: 384–5.

[68] At 317a33 Aristotle uses κυρίως as a synonym for ἁπλῶς; at 317a17 he speaks of ἡ ἁπλῆ καὶ τελεία γένεσις. Briefer treatments of the contrast can be found at *Phys.* v.1.225a12–17, *Metaph.* 8.1.1042a32–b8.

[69] Here I am indebted to Sarah Broadie.   [70] Williams 1982: ix–xv, cf. p. 83.

he argues that Aristotle did not have the philosophical resources to analyse (2a) adequately. No one did until Frege in the nineteenth century had the insight that 'exists' is a second-order, not a first-order predicate; it is a predicate of concepts, not of objects, and what e.g. 'Tame tigers exist' says is that the concept 'tame tiger' has at least one instance, can be truly predicated of at least one object which is both a tiger and tame.[71] Not having the modern logical analysis of the verb 'to exist', Aristotle inevitably failed to make adequate sense of (2a). He lacked insight into his own language.

I wish to argue, on the contrary, that it is Williams who lacks insight – not into his own language, English, but into the Greek that Aristotle spoke, read and wrote in the fourth century BC. In Aristotle's Greek (2a) makes a complete statement which, like (1a) '*x* ἐστι' but *unlike* our modern '*x* exists', can be further completed by adding a complement without any change in the meaning of the verb. You cannot pass from '*x* exists' to *'*x* exists tame/ a tiger'. But the texts adduced earlier from Plato's *Theaetetus* and Aristotle's *Posterior Analytics* show that in their Greek you can pass from '*x* ἐστι' to '*x* ἐστιν ἥμερος/τίγρις'. Now for the parallel case of (2a) and (2b).

Consider this sentence at *Metaphysics* Z.7, 1032a13–14: πάντα δὲ τὰ γιγνόμενα ὑπό τέ τινος γίγνεται καὶ ἔκ τινος καὶ τί. If you are surprised at the syntax, please note that variants with the same syntax are found elsewhere (*Metaph.* Z.8, 1033a24–8; Θ.8, 1049b28–9; *Gen. an.* II.1, 733b24–6; cf. also *Phys.* I.7, 190b10–13). We are dealing with a formula dear to Aristotle's heart, not a piece of careless writing. The problem is how to render it into a modern language.

A word-for-word translation would be this:

> Everything that comes to be comes to be (i) by the agency of something and (ii) from something and (iii) something.

But that feels ungrammatical in English. One would be uncomfortable reading it aloud to an audience, because we incline to understand clauses (i) and (ii) as existential, clause (iii) as copulative. To ease the transition to (iii), W. D. Ross in the Oxford Translation[72] finds it necessary to repeat the verb 'comes to be':

---

[71] Frege 1953, §53; my example 'Tame tigers exist' comes from an often-cited debate between W. Kneale and G. E. Moore on the question 'Is existence a predicate?' (Kneale and Moore 1936; Moore 1959: 115–26).

[72] Ross 1928a.

Everything that comes to be comes to be by the agency of something and from something and comes to be something. ||

This is exactly parallel to the way English has to render Burnet's construal of *Apology* 30b. Would De Strycker and Slings object to Ross's translation of Aristotle? If so, Aristotle would object to their objection, since it would be philosophically disastrous for him to admit that the transition to (iii) involved a change of meaning.

Immediately after the sentence quoted, Aristotle explains point (iii):

τὸ δὲ τὶ λέγω καθ' ἑκάστην κατηγορίαν· ἢ γὰρ τόδε ἢ ποσὸν ἢ ποιὸν ἢ πού.

I mean 'something' in accordance with each category: <everything comes to be> either a so-and-so or so much or so qualified or somewhere.

He has (iii) cover all four categories in which change can occur, including the category of substance. All are γίγνεσθαι τι, because what he usually calls γίγνεσθαι ἁπλῶς is now a special case of γίγνεσθαι τι. Ross's English captures the whole formula with the single verb 'comes to be', but he has to write the verb twice because his *Sprachgefühl* tells him (rightly, I am sure) that 'comes to be something' is a different meaning from 'comes to be' *simpliciter*.[73] But ancient Greek allows Aristotle to write γίγνεται once only to produce a formula that will cover all the four types of change he recognises. In the next chapter of *Metaphysics* Z, restating the doctrine quoted (1033a24–7), Aristotle himself repeats the verb γίγνεσθαι for (iii), just like Ross. Evidently, it makes no difference to him how the point is expressed.

Can we give a concrete example to show how Aristotle conceives the structure of substantial coming to be? There is no problem in the case of non-substantial change: 'Socrates comes to be musical from being unmusical, by the agency of his teacher Damon' can be said while the process is

---

[73] Much less happy is H. Tredennick's Loeb translation (Tredennick 1933: 'Everything which is generated is generated by something and from something and becomes something.' The best German translation, that of Michael Frede and Günther Patzig (Frede and Patzig 1988), has 'Aber alles, was entsteht, entsteht unter Einwirkung von etwas, wird aus etwas und wird zu etwas.' They too find it necessary to change the verb. The most widely cited French translation is Tricot 1964, where we read 'Tout ce qui devient, devient, par quelque chose et à partir de quelque chose, quelque chose.' This mirrors the Greek nicely, thanks to the fact that 'devenir' is rarely existential in meaning (here I am indebted to advice from Francis Wolff). A similar effect can be achieved in English by changing the word-order: 'Everything that comes to be comes to be something, from something, by the agency of something', which, like the French, is most naturally heard as confined to non-substantial change. The drawback is that this English, like that French, fails to capture the whole of what Aristotle intends.

going on. But 'Socrates comes to be a human from the menses of Phainarete, by the agency of Sophroniscus', if said while the process is still going on, makes it sound as if Socrates pre-exists himself. For the name 'Socrates' has no application until Socrates has come to be. The solution is to put it in the past tense, as we usually do: 'Socrates came to be (was born) in 469 BC'. Aristotle will now ask, '*What* did Socrates come to be?', and will answer 'a human being' (*Metaph*. Z.7, 1032a18), or perhaps 'a rational two-footed animal'. Sometimes he will change the subject and speak of matter coming to be a human being, or more abstractly, of a potential human coming to be an actual one. But these philosophical technicalities do not belong in the grammatical analysis of an ordinary Greek verb. The fact remains that Aristotle's use of εἶναι ἁπλῶς and γίγνεσθαι ἁπλῶς does not correspond well to our use of 'exist' and 'come to exist'. It would be nonsense to add 'unqualifiedly' (ἁπλῶς) to 'exists' or 'comes to exist' in an attempt to English εἶναι or γίγνεσθαι ἁπλῶς. Aristotle's addition of ἁπλῶς implies that in his vocabulary it is one and the same verb that is used, first without, and then with, a complement.

Now given that (iii) covers the predicates acquired in all four categorially different types of change, the quoted formula is, by Aristotle's lights, quadruply ambiguous. γίγνεσθαι is πολλαχῶς λεγόμενον (*Phys*. 1.7, 190a31–b1), so the meaning of γίγνεσθαι varies with the category ‖ of predicate acquired through the change. What the compendious formula teaches us, however, is that for Aristotle the ἁπλῶς use of γίγνεσθαι, like the ἁπλῶς use of εἶναι, is further completable – by a predicate in the category of substance.

I can now offer a formal argument. Premise (1): Ross's unease with the transition to (iii) shows that Williams is right about his own language, English – when 'comes to be' is used without a complement, 'to be' has an existential meaning which resists further completion. Premise (2): Aristotle is right about his own Greek – 'x γίγνεται' is a complete statement which is yet further completable, even when the subject is a newly created substance. That is, even when *x* γίγνεται ἁπλῶς, the result of the process is not to be expressed by a statement '*x* ἐστί' in which ἐστι has an existential meaning that resists further completion. When Socrates ἐγένετο ἁπλῶς, he ἐγένετο ἄνθρωπος and both ἔστιν ἁπλῶς and ἔστιν ἄνθρωπος became true of him. Conclusion: between Aristotle and Williams, language changed.

This need not mean that Greek changed, or any natural language. Maybe all that happened was that philosophy and theology came to be pursued in modern European languages instead of Latin and Greek. The question turns on whether either ancient language acquired a verb for existence that is grammatically uncomplet*able* in the manner of our '*x* exists'. ὑπάρχειν fails the test, because (as already noted) it retained a predicative use parallel to copulative εἶναι.[74] So too, for that matter, did *ex (s)tare* and *ex(s)istere* in Latin.[75] Certainly there are contexts in which ὑπάρχειν demands an existential translation. But the same is true of εἶναι. Consider this example of post-classical Greek:

> ὥστε εἴπερ εἰσὶ θεοί, φθαρτοί εἰσιν. οὐκ ἄρα θεοί εἰσίν. Εἴγε μὴν ἔστι θεός, ζῷόν ἐστιν ... (Sext. Emp. *M.* ix.141–2)

> The result [*sc.* of the preceding argument] is that if there are gods, they are perishable. Therefore there are not gods. Again, if there is a god, it is an animal ...

The arguments are undoubtedly about (what we call) existence, but Sextus continues to treat εἶναι as complete but further completable, adding and dropping predicates at will. He could have substituted ὑπάρχουσι for εἰσί throughout.[76] The best candidate in ancient Greek for existence pure and simple is ὑφίστασθαι, ὑφεστηκέναι and the associated noun ὑπόστασις. A passive verb cannot take a predicative complement.

Yet even if Galen is wrong when he remarks that the Greeks have recently come to use ὑφεστηκέναι for the same conception (ἔννοια) as they have long used εἶναι and ὑπάρχειν (*Inst. Log.* 3, p.7.19–22),[77] it may be doubted whether uncompletability is enough to make ὑφεστηκέναι correspond to modern verbs for existence. Epicurus tells his followers that in all their actions they should reckon with τὸ ὑφεστηκὸς τέλος (*KD* 22): he is not referring to whatever actual end they have in view, but to the *real* or underlying purpose (the avoidance of pain and disturbance) that should control all their conduct.[78] Again, the three neo-Platonic ὑποστάσεις are not the only things that exist, but different levels of *reality* to which various existing things may be assigned. In principle, one class of things could be more of a reality (ὑπόστασις μᾶλλον) than another ‖

---

[74] And continued to do so into late antiquity, beyond the authors cited n.51 above: witness Hesychius s.v. σῶς: ὁ ὁλόκληρος καὶ τέλειος. ὁ σωζόμενος καὶ <u>σῶς ὑπάρχων</u> (example owed to Michael Frede).
[75] Examples: Lucr. III.97; Cic. *De Orat.* II.54.217.
[76] As at *M.* x.4 he substitutes predicative ὑπάρχειν for the εἶναι he used in virtually the same sentence at *P.* III.124. For this and other examples of the interchangeability of the two verbs in Sextus, see Janáček 1948: 42–4.
[77] Is Galen updating Aristotle's statement (*APr.* 1.36, 48b2–4) that ὑπάρχειν is said in as many ways as εἶναι?
[78] Cf. the translations 'real purpose' in Bailey 1926, and 'il fine realmente dato' in Arrighetti 1973.

(Plotinus VI.1 [42] 29, 18).[79] Existence, by contrast with reality, is an all-or-nothing concept. A thing either exists or it does not,[80] and it is nonsense to say that one thing exists *more* than another.

Another problem with the group ὑφίστασθαι, ὑφεστηκέναι, ὑπόστασις, is how far they differ significantly from ὑπάρχειν, ὕπαρξις. In discussion of this issue much weight – too much weight, I believe – has been put on a celebrated claim by Chrysippus to the effect that the present alone can be said to ὑπάρχειν, not the past and the future, which should be allowed only to ὑφεστηκέναι.[81] Whichever of the conflicting translations and interpretations of this precious testimony we prefer,[82] we must agree that the two verbs stand here in contrast to each other. But elsewhere, and often, they do not. Sextus argues (*M.* VIII.338) that if the human species does not exist, nor does Socrates: ἀνθρώπου μὴ ὑπάρχοντος οὐδὲ Σωκράτης ὑφέστηκεν. Alexander emphasises (Alex. Aphr. *In APr.* 4.9–11) the importance of grasping when things that differ in their essential being (κατ' οὐσίαν), such as form and matter, are nonetheless inseparable in actual existence: τῇ ὑποστάσει τε καὶ ὑπάρξει. It would be no easy matter to fix the range and nuances of the ὑπόστασις group.[83]

Rather than pursue these complications further, I close with a suggestion. Perhaps it is a mistake to expect *any* ancient Greek verb to match our 'to exist'. Perhaps what needs explaining is not the absence of a specialised verb for existence in ancient Greek and Latin, but its presence in modern European languages. Even in English 'to exist' was a late-comer: the earliest citation in the OED is 1602, with the comment: 'The late

---

[79] Admittedly, Plotinus is attacking the Stoics here, not expounding his own philosophy, and I know no other place in Plotinus where ὑπόστασις admits of degrees. But compare, in the same treatise, μᾶλλον ὄν (26, 8), μᾶλλον οὐσίας (27, 37), μᾶλλον εἴη (28, 16), μᾶλλον οὐκ ὄν (29, 24). My concern is with language, not philosophy, and one case is enough to establish the grammatical *possibility* of grading ὑπόστασις in the same way as οὐσία.

[80] Cf. n. 42 above.

[81] Stob. *Ecl.* 1.106.18–23W = *SVF* 2.509 = LS 51B (4); Plut. *Comm. not.* 1081f = *SVF* 2.518 = LS 51C (5).

[82] For a judicious treatment of the texts and the debate they have prompted, see Schofield 1988.

[83] The basic study (Dörrie 1955) is not superseded by the essays in Romano and Taormina 1994, which mostly focus on what the words are applied *to* rather than on the prior issue of the meaning in virtue of which they can be so applied; in Fregean terms, on reference instead of sense. As a result, they deliver much arcane metaphysico-theological doctrine, but (apart from Glucker) scant linguistic analysis; doctrinal differences are one thing, semantic differences another. More promising is the approach taken by Damascius, *De Principiis* 2.74.23–77.24 Westerink (= Ruelle vol. 1, ch. 62): he compares εἶναι with six other Greek verbs for 'to be' (ὑφεστάναι, ὑπάρχειν, τελέθειν, πέλειν, σῴζεσθαι, τυγχάνειν), arguing that they differ in meaning both from εἶναι and from each other even though they share uses, including an existential use, in common. Better still would be treatment by the methods of transformational grammar, which replace (and thereby illuminate) ontology in Kahn 1973 and epistemology in Lyons 1963.

appearance of the word is remarkable: it is not in Cooper's Lat.–Eng. Dict. 1565, either under *existo* or *exto*.'[84] Similarly, Étienne Gilson in his classic work *L'Être et l'Essence* speaks of the French 'exister' taking root only in the seventeenth century.[85] Given the anti-Scholastic mood of the early modern period, an uncompletable verb might have been welcomed as a neat way of blocking Aristotelian questions before they could arise.

None of this impugns Frege's great insight. That is independent of the way one language or another expresses (what we call) existence. From his point of view, any language that can express inferences involving propositions of the form 'Some *F* is *G*' (is there any language that cannot?) is talking about existence, even if it lacks a word specifically devoted to its expression. For 'Some *F* is *G*' on his analysis means 'There exists at least one *x* such that *x* is both *F* and *G*'. In logical notation, $(\exists x)(Fx \wedge Gx)$. Frege's is a logic of thought, not of language. ||

BECOMING IN PLATO

Now imagine Plato reading the *Metaphysics*. He will not see quadruple ambiguity in the formula we examined from Z.7 (p. 30 above), because he does not subscribe to the Aristotelian theory of categories. When he distinguishes types of change (*Tht.* 181cd, *Laws* x.893c ff.), this has no semantic consequences. They are species of change in the same way as dogs and horses are two species of animal, in one and the same sense of 'animal'. So in principle Plato can accept Aristotle's formula as unambiguously true.

He certainly accepts point (i): see *Timaeus* 28a4–6. He seems to accept (ii) as well, at least sometimes: see *Phaedo* 70c ff. There is no need to discuss these texts in detail, because for our purposes the interesting question is his attitude to (iii). Does he agree that everything that comes to be comes to be something?

The place to start is the well-known Platonic contrast between the sensible world as the realm of becoming (γένεσις) and the ideal world of Forms as the realm of being (οὐσία). There is a straightforward statement of the contrast at *Timaeus* 27d–28a, but this presupposes readers who already understand what it amounts to. So let us go back to the *Republic*, where the contrast is first introduced at the beginning of Book VI, with direct reference to the argument from Book V we discussed earlier, which

---

[84] OED (2nd edn, Oxford 1989) s.v.
[85] Gilson 1948: 15. I thank Michael Screech for checking French lexicographical resources to confirm that Gilson's claim is substantially correct.

has just reached its conclusion that the lovers of sights and sounds lack knowledge and are not philosophers (479d–480a).[86] By way of introduction to the next point, Socrates sums up the preceding argument with a long 'since'-clause (484b3–6) which explains why the lovers of sights and sounds are not philosophers. The reason is that philosophers are those who are able to grasp 'that which is always identically the same' (οἱ τοῦ ἀεὶ κατὰ ταὐτὰ ὡσαύτως ἔχοντος δυνάμενοι ἐφάπτεσθαι), whereas the lovers of sights and sounds 'wander among things that are many and that vary in every sort of way' (οἱ ... ἐν πολλοῖς καὶ παντοίως ἴσχουσιν πλανώμενοι). Already, 'that which is always identically the same' fills out and clarifies Book v's (deliberately) indeterminate phrasing 'what is' or 'what purely is'.[87] A page later (485a10–b3), Socrates characterises philosophers as passionately keen on any study that will show them something of 'that being which always is and does not wander under the influence of becoming and destruction' (ἐκείνης τῆς οὐσίας τῆς ἀεὶ οὔσης καὶ μὴ πλανωμένης ὑπὸ γενέσεως καὶ φθορᾶς). This is clearer still. But it leaves us with an important question: what kind of becoming and destruction is he talking about?

It is true that the Forms are eternal. They neither come into existence nor pass away. But it is equally true that they never change in any respect. In the Book v argument, which Socrates is summarising, there was not a word about sensibles coming into existence and passing away. It was all about their changing from beautiful to ugly, large to small, and so on. We should hold on to this relation with the Book v argument as we read through Books vi and vii, where Plato gradually builds up the contrast between, on the one hand, the unchanging intelligible Forms, and on the other, the sensible world understood as the realm of γένεσις or τὸ γιγνόμενόν τε καὶ ἀπολλύμενον.[88] Plato is not just emphasising that the things around us come into being and pass away. He is as much or more – I believe more – concerned with their predicative changeability.[89] We cannot make sense of a basic theme of Plato's philosophy unless we see

---

[86] The Theory of Forms itself was first introduced earlier in Book v at 475e–476d. But that passage has none of the subsequent emphasis on the changeability of sensible things.

[87] I say 'deliberately' because the Book v argument was designed to soothe the lovers of sights and sounds and persuade them that they lack knowledge, without blatantly telling them that, from an epistemological point of view, they are sick (476d8–e2). To this end, Socrates kept his hand close to his chest, not revealing until later the full import of the various admissions he secured from his interlocutors, who refuse to accept the existence of Forms. For a pioneering account of what the argument with the lovers of sights and sounds does and does not presuppose, see Gosling 1968.

[88] vi.508d7, vii.521d4, e3, 525b5, 526e7, 527b5–6, 534a3.

[89] For more on this subject, from a different angle, see Frede 1988.

that his generalising use of γένεσις and γιγνόμενα is as compendious as the Aristotelian formula discussed above. For both philosophers, the verb γίγνεσθαι treats all forms of change alike.

Indeed, when Plato wants to be crystal clear that he is speaking of what Aristotle calls γίγνεσθαι ἁπλῶς, he is prepared to write it out in full as γενέσθαι ὄν (*Soph.* 245d1–2): just as to be is to be (predicatively) a being/something that is (εἶναι ὄν), so to come to be is to come to be a being/something that is. To which he adds (245d4) that whenever something comes to be, at that moment it has come to be a whole (τὸ γενόμενον ἀεὶ γέγονεν ὅλον). Never mind the philosophical import of these strange remarks.[90] My interest is in their grammar and the way predicates like ὄν and ὅλον can be added on to γίγνεσθαι even in places where our inclination would be to translate existentially.

A final passage to pit Burnet against his critics, this time on text as well as translation, is *Phaedrus* 245d1–3. In his OCT it reads as follows:

> ἀρχὴ δὲ ἀγένητον. ἐξ ἀρχῆς γὰρ ἀνάγκη πᾶν τὸ γιγνόμενον γίγνεσθαι, αὐτὴν δὲ μηδ' ἐξ ἑνός· εἰ γὰρ ἔκ του ἀρχὴ γίγνοιτο, οὐκ ἂν ἔτι ἀρχὴ γίγνοιτο.
>
> A first principle cannot come into being. For everything that comes to be necessarily comes to be from a first principle, but a first principle necessarily does not come to be from anything – for if it were to come to be from something, it would no longer come to be a first principle.

The crux is the last five words, where the leading MSS have οὐκ ἂν ἐξ ἀρχῆς γίγνοιτο. Editors who follow the MSS have a hard time explaining the logic,[91] whereas Burnet's text is logically pellucid: by definition, a principle that comes to be *from something* can no longer count as a first principle.[92] Fortunately, the nominative ἀρχή or ἔτι ἀρχή is vouched for by Cicero (*Rep.* vi.27, *Tusc.* 1.54), Iamblichus (*In Nic.* 79.3–4 Pistelli), and 'Timaeus Locrus' (*ap.* Theodoret. *Therap.* 2.108 Raeder), all of them earlier than any extant support for ἐξ ἀρχῆς.[93] I offer the OCT version as

---

[90] There are parallels at *Parm.* 153c7–e3. My construal of the *Sophist* passage follows Cornford 1935: 225 nn. 2 and 26.

[91] Compare the varying translations and notes in, e.g., Léon Robin's Budé edition (Paris 1947); Vries 1969: 122–3; Rowe 1986.

[92] The context makes clear that the principle we are discussing is the ultimate first principle of all movement.

[93] See Burnet's *apparatus*, or the fuller one in Robin, which quotes several proposed emendations. Cicero translates, *nec enim esset id principium, quod gigneretur aliunde*. Note how he puts the consequent of the conditional first, because the passive *gigneretur* cannot take a complement to match Plato's ἀρχὴ γίγνοιτο.

another example of Burnet rightly recognising a Platonic sentence in which γίγνεσθαι appears complete on its own, only to be further completed in the next clause.

THE TRANSLATION AGAIN

I conclude that the ambiguity of which De Strycker and Slings complain would be lost on Plato. Quite simply, the addition of a complement to γίγνεται in the second member of the antithesis at *Apology* 30b2–3, as required on Burnet's construal, would not strike Plato as a change in the meaning of the verb. Like εἶναι, γίγνεσθαι is open to further completion. My point is not that Plato needs to be consciously aware of this fact, but that *we* have to be consciously aware that our categories may fail to apply to ancient Greek. Of all anachronisms, anachronism in grammar is the most insidious. ‖

Thus point (2) of the De Strycker–Slings objection fails. It is an anachronistic retrojection of our own grammatical structures. Point (1) was the claim that the parallelism of the two pointedly antithetical members requires that the disputed sentence could be ended with χρήματα, and that καὶ τὰ ἄλλα κτλ. should be considered an afterthought. But on its own this is mere assertion, which carries no weight without the support of the other two objections. Burnet's new construal leaves the sentence as antithetical as it was before. It simply offers a different, and philosophically more significant, antithesis than the traditional translation. Socrates has just said that all he ever does is go around Athens urging people to change their priorities. Instead of giving their attention to the accumulation of money, neglecting their own soul, they should put the state of their soul ahead of the state of their bodies or their bank accounts (29d–30b). On either translation, our sentence explains why people should take him seriously. But Burnet's version, I have argued, is both linguistically unimpeachable and philosophically superior. Unlike the standard translation, it fits Plato's overall portrait of Socrates.

HYPERBATON

It remains to address the separation of ἅπαντα from its noun phrase χρήματα καὶ τὰ ἄλλα. Hyperbaton, a disruption of the expected order of words, is common enough in Plato not to need illustration here.[94] Quantifiers like ἅπαντα and numerical adjectives (e.g. τριττά in my next

---

[94] There is a section on hyperbaton in the 'Digest of Platonic idioms' affixed to the Rev. James Riddell's edition of the *Apology* (Riddell 1877; repr. *separatim* Amsterdam 1967), and many

quotation) are especially liable to be displaced from their expected position. All we need now is a *reason* for delaying ἅπαντα at *Apology* 30b. I suggest it is the rhetorical emphasis gained by juxtaposing ἅπαντα to καὶ ἰδίᾳ καὶ δημοσίᾳ: 'Virtue does not come from money, but from virtue money and other things come to be good for human beings – yes, *all* other things, both in private and in public life.'

On this construal, the emphatic ἅπαντα delivers its strongest punch in the final phrase, 'and in public life'. So far from καὶ τὰ ἄλλα κτλ. being an afterthought, as De Strycker and Slings describe it, those words lead to a climax that will sound deeply offensive to the Athenian demos, whom Socrates will soon counter-charge with rampant injustice in their public life (31d–32c).[95] To this charge he adds another: Athenian politics does not follow the Socratic order of priorities, which would mean putting the wisdom and moral character of the community ahead of its wealth and power (36cd). These later passages help to establish the *tone* of the disputed sentence. Imagine the sentence delivered aloud with a pause just before ἀγαθά to begin the final crescendo.[96] The meaning would be clear, and clearly insulting, to all lovers of democracy. Very different from the bland and implausible message of the standard translation, that cultivating virtue will make you better off in worldly terms.

The diagnosis of hyperbaton leaves ἀγαθά free to serve as predicate to the subject τὰ ἄλλα ... ἅπαντα. The row of neuter plurals should not disturb. The TLG reveals no other instance in Plato of the collocation τὰ ἄλλα ἀγαθά, whereas hyperbaton amid neuter plurals is not unique. Witness *Republic* IX.581c3–4: ||

διὰ ταῦτα δὴ καὶ ἀνθρώπων λέγομεν τὰ πρῶτα τριττὰ γένη εἶναι, φιλόσοφον, φιλόνικον, φιλοκερδές;

where Adam translates 'And for this reason we say that the primary classes of men are also three in number, etc.?', and comments,

> I take τριττά as predicative: the hyperbaton is not, I think, a difficult one, because the stress of the voice falls on τριττά, and to my ear it sounds more idiomatic than τὰ πρῶτα γένη τριττὰ εἶναι would be.[97]

---

examples from Plato in Denniston 1952, ch. 3, 'The order of words'; a recent, more theoretical treatment, again with numerous examples from Plato, is Devine and Stephens 2000. From antiquity we have a superb account of the rhetorical effectiveness of hyperbaton in Longinus, *On the Sublime* 22. The technical term ὑπερβατόν occurs already in Plato, *Prot.* 343e3, in a context which assumes that readers need no elaborate explanation of what it is.

[95] On the *Apology* as both defence and counter-accusation, see my 'The impiety of Socrates' (Burnyeat 1997b, reprinted as Brickhouse and Smith 2002: 133–45 [now also Chapter 11 in *EAMP* vol. II]).

[96] So Taylor SJ 1973: 51.   [97] Adam 1963, *ad loc*.

Or *Laws* VII.798d1–2:

τὰ μὲν οὖν ἄλλα ἐλάττω μεταβαλλόμενα κακὰ διεξεργάζοιτ' ἄν

where the subject of the verb is τὰ ἄλλα μεταβαλλόμενα, the object ἐλάττω κακά: 'Other changes would produce lesser evils.' A neat example of what Burnet meant by 'interlaced order'.[98]

---

[98] As already intimated (n. 37 above), this essay was originally designed for a Russian audience more familiar with the standard rendering from the translation by Michail Solov'ev than with Burnet's commentary or recent scholarly literature on the philosophically all-important Greek verb 'to be'. I owe a very great debt to my translator, Irina Levinskaya, for making me explain each unfamiliar point as clearly as possible, to produce an argument that would be satisfactory to us both in either language. (The Russian version, attentive to their translations of all the crucial texts, is due to appear in 2003 in a collection of articles put out by the Philosophy Faculty of St Petersburg University. [Published as Burnyeat 2005b in the journal of the St Petersburg Plato Society]) At a later stage I benefited from discussion and correspondence with J. N. Adams, Susanne Bobzien, Luc Brisson, Lesley Brown, David Charles, John Cooper, Bruce Fraser, Jaako Hintikka, Edward Hussey, Charles Kahn, Calvin Normore, Dominic Scott, Lucas Siorvanes, Michael Stokes and William Taschek, and from M. L. West's lectures on Greek accentuation; from the opportunity to present the sections on Aristotle at the Fifteenth Symposium Aristotelicum (devoted to *Gen. corr.* 1) in Deume, Holland in 1999; from a wide-ranging discussion the same year in the Classics Department at Toronto, followed up by a vigorous letter from Brad Inwood; and from a friendly exchange of views with S. R. Slings.

CHAPTER IB

On the source of Burnet's construal of Apology 30b2–4: a correction

In a recent issue of this journal I wrote on behalf of John Burnet's construal of the sentence οὐκ ἐκ χρημάτων ἀρετὴ γίγνεται, ἀλλ' ἐξ ἀρετῆς χρήματα καὶ τὰ ἄλλα ἀγαθὰ τοῖς ἀνθρώποις ἅπαντα καὶ ἰδίᾳ καὶ δημοσίᾳ at Plato, *Apology* 30b.[1] Burnet argues that ἀγαθά does not go with τὰ ἄλλα ἅπαντα, but is predicate to the verb γίγνεται which we supply from the previous clause. The result may be translated as follows: 'Virtue does not come from wealth, but it is virtue that makes wealth or anything else, in private or public life, a good thing for human beings.' Contrast the standard translation, 'Virtue does not come from money, but from virtue money and all other good things come to human beings in both private and public life,' which claims that virtue will make you rich – a claim that is both implausible in itself and contrary to everything we know about Plato's Socrates. Burnet's construal yields a quite different and philosophically superior interpretation:

> [T]his splendid utterance is not to be confounded either with the Biblical exhortation, 'Seek ye first the kingdom of God and His righteousness, and all these things shall be added unto you', nor with the Stoic doctrine of the self-sufficiency of the 'wise man' (cf. Hor. *Ep.* 1 i. 106: *sapiens uno minor est Iove, dives, liber, honoratus, pulcher, rex denique regum*): the lesson here taught is 'that without ἀρετή the so-called good things of this life are nothing worth: it is the possession of ἀρετή that gives them their quality of goodness'.

These, however, are not the words of Burnet. They appear in a school edition of the *Apology* published by Harold Williamson in 1908, sixteen years before Burnet's well-known edition.[2] I should not have credited the better construal to Burnet.

---

[1] M. F. Burnyeat, '*Apology* 30b 2–4: Socrates, money, and the grammar of ΓΙΓΝΕΣΘΑΙ', *JHS* 123 (2003), 1–25 [Chapter 1A in this volume]. I owe deep thanks to Paul Kalligas for pointing me to Williamson's anticipation of Burnet's construal.
[2] Burnet 1924; Williamson 1908.

Yet I hesitate to claim it should be credited to Williamson. His frontispiece describes the author as Assistant Master at Manchester Grammar School, Late Tutor and Lecturer of Balliol College, Oxford. Born in 1872, educated at Manchester Grammar School, Williamson went up to Balliol in 1891 and graduated in 1895 with Firsts in Mods and Greats. He won the Craven Scholarship in 1893. He was Lecturer and Tutor at Balliol from 1895 to 1898, but not a Fellow. Then he went back to be a master at his old school. We might expect to have heard more from him if he had the capacity to see how to solve a philosophical crux by exploiting a syntactical possibility undreamed of by generations of earlier scholars. ||

Now according to Balliol records, when Williamson was a student his tutors were W. H. Hardy and J. A. Smith.[3] This latter was exactly the sort of grammatical virtuoso I am looking for. His little-known 1917 article 'On general relative clauses in Greek'[4] was a powerful blow to the (still widespread) belief that Plato posited a Form corresponding to every general term in the language. The sole evidence in the corpus for Plato wishing to extend the realm of Forms that far is *Republic* x.596a6–8:

εἶδος γάρ πού τι ἓν ἕκαστον εἰώθαμεν τίθεσθαι περὶ ἕκαστα τὰ πολλά, οἷς ταὐτὸν ὄνομα ἐπιφέρομεν.

Shorey translates,

> We are in the habit, I take it, of positing a single idea or form in the case of the various multiplicities to which we give the same name.

Without exception, the same effect is conveyed, in one set of words or another, by the twenty-one other translations of the *Republic* on my shelves, from the very first English rendering by Spens (1763) to the most recent by Griffith (2000).[5] They all say that there is to be a Form for every general term.

What Smith pointed out in his article is that the sentence is ambiguous. The syntax can equally well be parsed to mean: 'for we are, as you know, in the habit of assuming [as a rule of procedure] that the Form which corresponds to a group of particulars, each to each, is always one, in which case we call the group, or its particulars, *by the same name as the Form*' (italics mine). The standard translation just assumes that 'the same name' means 'the same name as each other'. But Plato's words allow both

---

[3] Kinch Hoekstra kindly took the time and trouble to search the Balliol records on my behalf and send me this and other information used below.
[4] Smith 1917.   [5] Ferrari and Griffith 2000; Spens 1763.

construals. And Smith's claim was that the standard rendering, which takes the relative clause at the end as general, would normally require either a different relative pronoun instead of the simple ὅς, or ἄν plus subjunctive instead of the indicative verb that Plato wrote.[6] Never mind whether readers find this effort as successful as Burnet's construal of *Apology* 30b2–4. I think it considerably more relevant to its context than the standard rendering, and its mere possibility blunts the case for supposing there to be a Form for every general term. But the point I am urging here is that Smith's proposal reveals the same cast of mind as Burnet's construal of *Apology* 30b2–4.

The title of Smith's article has ensured that to this day very few people are aware of it. To the best of my knowledge, the first published reference to it is in an article of my own dating from 1989.[7] It is never mentioned by Harold Cherniss, who aspired to read everything on Plato and who regularly cited *Republic* 596a to bolster his belief in a Form for every concept.[8] But it seems to have survived by word of mouth in Balliol tradition. I first learned of it from Jonathan || Barnes, then teaching at Balliol. He got it from his Balliol tutor R. M. Hare, who insisted on the importance of Smith's construal. Hare was taught by Cyril Bailey (editor of Epicurus and Lucretius), who in turn was taught by J. A. Smith. I shall suggest a similar, though shorter, chain of influence for the case of *Apology* 30b2–4.

A somewhat better known article of Smith's, under the characteristically untempting title 'Aristotelica',[9] includes a definitive account of the difference between the prepositions κατά and μετά as they are used when Aristotle at *Nicomachean Ethics* VI.13, 1144b24–30, discusses the question whether virtue should be conceived as κατὰ τὸν ὀρθὸν λόγον or as μετὰ τοῦ ὀρθοῦ λόγου. To readers of this journal Smith will be most familiar as co-editor with W. D. Ross in the initial stages (1908–12) of the magnificent Oxford translation of Aristotle, to which he contributed an excellent rendering of the *De Anima*, where he often sees subtleties that other translators miss.[10] Ross wrote of him,

---

[6] For this last point he cites Goodwin 1897, §§532, 534. The same construal is advocated, independently of Smith and on philosophical rather than grammatical grounds, by John M. Rist (Rist 1984, reprinted as Rist 1996, ch. 2). Rist has confirmed to me that he did not know of Smith's article.
[7] Burnyeat 1989 at n. 4; more easily available as Burnyeat 1992a and Burnyeat 2000a.
[8] See, for example, Cherniss 1944: 244.   [9] Smith 1920.
[10] Smith 1931. In Burnyeat 2002 [Chapter 5 in this volume] I point to several examples, especially at n. 63.

He was deeply versed in philology (and, as became a Highlander, not least in Celtic philology) and acquired with extraordinary facility at least a reading knowledge of many languages. He had a very acute feeling for the precise meaning, and the development of the meaning, of words.[11]

To confirm the picture formed so far, I cite two examples from the large quantity of Smith's unpublished notes and discussions preserved in Balliol College Library. The first is a short but subtle note written in September or October 1930 to decide exactly what sort of dative is involved at Aristotle, *Nicomachean Ethics* III.5, 1114b2: ἕκαστος ἑαυτῷ τῆς ἕξεώς ἐστί πως αἴτιος. The second, dating from October 1929, favours taking διὰ τὸ λογικῶς ζητεῖν at *Metaphysics* Λ.1, 1069a26–8 with the main clause rather than joining Ross and everyone else in the view that it goes with what immediately precedes. All eight *Metaphysics* translations on my shelf agree with Ross, and I have no doubt that they are right to do so.[12] But, as before, my interest is in the cast of mind that sees a combinatory possibility in the syntax that no one else has dreamed of, either before or since.

Now Smith became a Fellow of Balliol in 1891, the very year that Williamson arrived, and remained there until 1910, when he moved to Magdalen on being elected Waynflete Professor of Moral and Metaphysical Philosophy. In this latter capacity he taught a version of Idealism strongly influenced by Croce and Gentile, and wrote in a lyrical style markedly different from his contributions to classical studies.[13] The question is whether he could have influenced Burnet as well as Williamson.

Easily, for Burnet was a Balliol man too. Admittedly, he graduated in 1887, before Smith became a teaching Fellow. He became a Prize Fellow at Magdalen College in 1889, but in 1890/91 was away on temporary professorial stints in Scotland, and he took up the Chair of Greek in St Andrews in 1891. So he was out of Oxford when Smith was elected to his

---

[11] *DNB* 1931–40, 819–20.
[12] Ironically, it was Ross's punctuation in his edition of 1924 that made Smith's conjecture feasible. For Ross put parentheses round τὰ γὰρ γένη ... ζητεῖν, whereas previous editors had printed a high stop after τιθέασιν in line 27, which enforced the standard construal. Now all Smith had to do was close the parenthesis four words earlier, after μᾶλλον.
[13] Both style and content are illustrated by his autobiographical contribution 'Philosophy as the development of the notion and reality of self-consciousness' in Muirhead 1925: 227–44. Readers of this journal may like to know that Smith's interest in Croce and Gentile was shared by his successor in the Waynflete Chair, the philosopher and ancient historian R. G. Collingwood, who graduated from University College, Oxford, in 1912. I conjecture that Collingwood attended Smith's lectures. At any rate, they became good friends: Collingwood 1970: 18.

Fellowship. On the other hand, Smith went up to Balliol as a student in 1884, only one year after Burnet. They were contemporaries. ||

I conclude that, if I am right to hail J. A. Smith as the most likely originator of Burnet's construal, there are two possible routes of transmission. The first possibility is that the construal, together with an explanation of its philosophical significance, passed from Smith to Williamson in an undergraduate tutorial, and then in written form to Burnet, who consulted Williamson's edition of the *Apology* when preparing his own. This would help to explain why Williamson's note on 30b2–4 conveys the philosophical moral of the passage in fuller and clearer terms than Burnet's note on the same text. Williamson was closer to the source.

But a second possibility is that Smith conceived the idea in his undergraduate days and told Burnet directly, while Williamson got the same message from Smith later. If in their respective editions Williamson expressed it better than Burnet, well, we have it on Smith's authority that as an undergraduate Burnet 'showed no particular interest in philosophy'.[14] The interest in Plato for which we know him began after graduation when he went to St Andrews to serve as private assistant to Lewis Campbell, to whose Chair he would soon succeed.

On the whole, I favour the second, simpler solution to the mystery.

---

[14] *DNB* 1922–30, 138.

CHAPTER 2

Plato on how not to speak of what is not: Euthydemus 283a–288a

THE QUESTION

Aristotle says that a person who gets annoyed by fallacious arguments without being able to diagnose the faults rouses a suspicion that their annoyance is due, not to appreciation of the truth, but to their inexperience (*SE* 175a14–16).

The question I address here is whether Plato shows this kind of inexperience when, in dialogues earlier than the *Sophist*, he confronts the fallacious argument that false statement is impossible because to speak falsely is to say what is not, and to say what is not is not to say anything, not to speak at all. Likewise, according to the same pattern of argument, false judgement is impossible because to judge falsely is to judge what is not, and to judge what is not is simply not to judge, or to think anything, at all.

We meet this argument in Plato's *Euthydemus*, in the *Cratylus*,[1] in the *Theaetetus*, and finally in the *Sophist*. But only || in the *Sophist* is the fault diagnosed. The earlier dialogues get annoyed with the argument. They tell us it is absurd to deny the possibility of false judgement or statement. Socrates in the *Euthydemus* (287e–288a) argues very effectively that the

---

[1] I shall not discuss the *Cratylus* here, save to observe that, while at 429cd Cratylus maintains both (a) that there is no such thing as an incorrect name, and (b) that there is no such thing as false statement, it is Socrates who brings out that (a) implies (δύναται) (b). Cratylus seems not to have seen the connection between two paradoxes he enjoys teasing people with. Note his puzzlement at 429c10 and the terms in which he endorses (b) at 429c4–6: not because it is implied by (a), but on the independent ground that false statement is τὸ μὴ τὰ ὄντα λέγειν – not saying things that are. The last point is pertinent to the subject of this essay, but the way it is developed hardly adds to our understanding of the fallacious argument I am concerned with. This is not a criticism. The *Cratylus* has its own agenda to pursue. So does the *Republic*. If, unlike many scholars, I do not include *Rep.* 478b as an occurrence of the same fallacy, that is because, instead of concluding that opinion can only be of what is, the argument starts from the premise that opinion *cannot* be of what is, otherwise it would be knowledge. Fallacious or not, the argument is different from the one I want to discuss.

denial is (dialectically) self-refuting, because if there is no such thing as false judgement, it cannot be false or wrong to judge that there is; hence if it is true there is no false judgement, but Socrates thinks it is false, then it is false that there is no false judgement.[2] But to show that the conclusion of a fallacious argument is absurd or self-refuting is not yet to show what is wrong with the fallacious argument itself. Only the *Sophist* does that.

Hence my question. Was Plato too inexperienced earlier in semantics and the philosophy of language to be able to give the diagnosis? Does the *Sophist* make the triumphant announcement that Plato can at last solve the problem he has been grappling with, unsuccessfully, for years?

The majority of scholars who have considered this question answer 'Yes'. Much of the reverence felt towards the *Sophist* is due to the belief that here at last the hard problem is successfully solved. Earlier – so we are told in countless books and articles – Plato was not yet clear about how to deal with the puzzles of false judgement and false statement.

My answer is 'No'. This is not because I make the *a priori* assumption that Plato was omniscient and omnipotent, and could never have been perplexed or in a muddle about anything. Rather, it is because when I read the earlier texts, they seem to me to show unmistakable signs that they were written by an author who knows, at least in outline, the solution he is going to provide in the *Sophist*, and who is concerned to stimulate his readers to start working out certain elements of that solution for themselves. ||

This is the point at which to acknowledge that the question I have raised is an Anglophone obsession. The countless books and articles I have just referred to are nearly all in English. The case is similar to the Anglophone obsession with the Third Man argument, which not long ago Jacques Brunschwig undertook to explain to a French audience.[3] It has meant much to me over the years to have known and admired such a friend as he is of our ways of doing the subject. But I too, like him, have sought enlightenment across the water. Only to a friend would I offer the following deconstruction of an attitude to texts which has long – too long – shaped Anglophone writing about Plato's development. I dedicate it to a wonderful reader and subtle logician.

The attitude I have in view can be illustrated by a single sentence from an influential paper by Gilbert Ryle:

---

[2] On dialectical self-refutation, see my 'Protagoras and Self-refutation in Later Greek Philosophy', Burnyeat 1976a [now also Chapter 1 in *EAMP* vol. 1].
[3] Brunschwig 1985.

At least in the *Sophist* he saw that what it is for a sentence to say or tell something cannot be explicated merely in terms of what it is for expressions to be the names of things.[4]

It is the first two words I wish to probe.[5] ||

Judging what is not in the *Theaetetus*

Let us begin with the *Theaetetus*. At 188cd Socrates introduces for discussion the idea that false judgement occurs when someone thinking about something or other (ὁτουοῦν) judges about it things which are not (τὰ μὴ ὄντα). Theaetetus finds the suggestion plausible (εἰκός), so our first duty as readers is to look for an interpretation that does indeed offer a plausible account of false judgement. Forget about the subsequent refutation with its scandalous analogy between judging and perceiving. Socrates' suggestion should be considered on its own merits first. We can assess the refutation later.

There are two elements in Socrates' account: that about which the judgement is made and the things judged about it. I propose the following interpretation. That about which the judgement is made is the subject of the judgement, the things judged about it are the predicates. It is the predicates, not the subject, which are described as things which are not. So Socrates' suggestion amounts to this: false judgement is judging about some subject predicates which are not (the case), i.e. ascribing to the subject predicates which do not belong to it, features it does not in fact possess.

This certainly merits Theaetetus' response, 'That's very plausible.' Provided we restrict ourselves to subject–predicate judgements, Socrates' account of false judgement is simple, straightforward and, so far as it goes, correct. As such, it reappears unmodified as part of the much fuller account

---

[4] Ryle 1990: 43. This paper, though not published until after Ryle's death, has been a significant presence in Anglophone scholarship since Friday 16th February 1952, when it was read to a distinguished audience at the Oxford Philological Society. [See the Foreword I prepared for the posthumous publication, and note that the blank space in the middle of p. 42 should be filled with the words 'Wittgenstein's – I cannot even claim that it was Plato's. (I *do* now, 1959.)'] Of course, its influence was boosted by Ryle's justly famous article 'Plato's *Parmenides*' (Ryle 1939), p. 129–51, 302–25, reprinted as Allen 1965: 97–147, and his 'Letters and Syllables in Plato' (Ryle 1960). But it is the 'Logical Atomism' paper that makes clear how much Ryle's picture of a radical change in Plato's thought owed to debates in nineteenth- and twentieth-century philosophy about the complexity of propositions.

[5] Needless to say, none of the above should be read *either* as a general certificate of innocence for scholars writing in languages other than English, *or* as disparagement of Ryle's work on Plato, for which I have the greatest admiration.

of false statement in the *Sophist*. I must now say something to make this interpretation as plausible to my readers as the account itself is to Theaetetus.

The phrase 'about something' is notoriously vague. In the *Sophist* (263a) 'Theaetetus is sitting' is taken to be about (περί) Theaetetus – the same thing as 'Theaetetus is flying' is about. It is not about the whole fact or state of affairs constituted by Theaetetus' sitting. I make the same choice here in the *Theaetetus*, on the grounds that it fits the preceding context better. We have just been through the argument that || one cannot judge one thing to be another, where the 'things' in question are things we know or do not know as illustrated by Socrates and Theaetetus. Someone who knows neither Socrates nor Theaetetus could not possibly take it into their head to judge that Socrates is Theaetetus or Theaetetus Socrates. The premise on which the overall argument depends is restated at 188c6, just before our section begins: 'for everything whatsoever, we either know it or we do not know it'. Here 'everything' (πάντα) ranges over all *terms* comparable to Socrates and Theaetetus. That makes it natural to take 'something or other' at 188d3 to refer to things of the sort we have been talking about, not complete states of affairs.

The second phrase 'things that are not' is equally vague. It could refer to the predicate part of the false statement 'Theaetetus is flying', as it does in the *Sophist* (263b), or to the whole statement 'Theaetetus is flying'. The description 'judging what is not about something' could apply not only to someone who thinks 'Theaetetus is flying' about Theaetetus, but also to someone who thinks 'Theaetetus is flying' about seated Theaetetus or the state of affairs constituted by Theaetetus' sitting. But once again the context in the *Theaetetus* gives grounds for the same choice as in the *Sophist*: the things that are not are such things as the predicate term flying.

Consider the 'other-judging' (ἀλλοδοξία) suggestion, introduced at 189bc to rescue false judgement after Socrates has argued, by analogy with perceiving, that one cannot judge what is not. The point he emphasises when he expounds the idea of judging one thing *instead* of another is that both items are 'things that are'. This is his response to the (supposed) failure of the account of false judgement as judging about something things that are not. And his examples are predicate terms: beautiful and ugly. Theodorus judged Theaetetus ugly instead of beautiful.[6] That fits

---

[6] The example is clearly inspired by Socrates' recent correction (185e) of the opinion Theodorus expressed at 143e.

very well, it seems to me,[7] || with the hypothesis that it was predicate terms he had in view before, when talking of things that are not.

One *caveat* before turning to the refutation. I have not claimed that the *Theaetetus* gives any hint of the grammatical or syntactic distinction drawn in the *Sophist* between the part of an assertoric sentence that refers to the subject and the part that ascribes to that subject a predicate such as flying or sitting.[8] The distinction I am interested in is the distinction between the subject of a judgement or statement, however that subject is picked out or referred to, and what is said or judged about it. And that distinction is no more than we find Plato equipped with already in the *Phaedo* (102bd), where he distinguishes between Simmias and the largeness or smallness Simmias has, which earns him the description (ἐπωνυμία) 'large' or 'small'.

Now for the refutation. With the two flanking proposals for explaining false judgement, the refutation is initiated by Socrates himself. In our passage, the trouble stems from an imaginary questioner who sets about examining us. This awkward fellow complicates Socrates' original suggestion by inserting a distinction between (i) judging what is not about one of the things that are and (ii) judging what is not just by itself (αὐτὸ καθ' αὑτό). Elsewhere I have proposed that (i) is a restatement of the account of false judgement that Socrates has just put forward, while (ii) represents the idea that the object of a false judgement is nothing at all – there is nothing for the judger to judge. (ii) leaves out, while (i) takes care to mention, that the false judgement judges what is not *about something* (one of the things that are – περὶ τῶν ὄντων του); therein lies the crucial difference between them.[9] ||

The basis for this interpretation is that the phrase αὐτὸ καθ' αὑτό standardly serves to remove some qualification or relation previously mentioned: here the qualification 'about some one of the things that are'. The result is that the false judger is left judging what is not without reference to anything at all.[10] And this is the cue for Socrates to develop

---

[7] As also to John McDowell (McDowell 1973: 198).
[8] A further *caveat*: the *Sophist*'s distinction between (roughly) nouns and verbs is a helpful means to understanding the possibility of falsehood, and one well suited to the syntax of a natural language like Greek or English, but it is not in fact essential. This has been clear since Wittgenstein's *Tractatus*, but seldom surfaces in Platonic scholarship; the only two examples I know are McDowell 1973: 233–4 and Denyer 1991: 117–27, 46–64.
[9] Burnyeat 1990: 77–8.
[10] From the same understanding of αὐτὸ καθ' αὑτό McDowell (1973: 199) derives a different conclusion: that the item judged αὐτὸ καθ' αὑτό, i.e. not about something that is, is a subject such as Theaetetus. McDowell thus reads 188d8–10 as the question whether any *term*, subject or predicate, in a false judgement can be a thing which is not. But the big difference between us is how

the analogy between judging what is not and seeing or touching what is not there to be seen or touched. Touching/judging what is not ⊨ touching/judging nothing ⊨ not touching/judging at all. The argument uses only (ii), as if (i) had not been mentioned. Hence the conclusion, that there is no judging what is not, is a *reductio ad absurdum* of (ii) presented as a refutation of (i) as well. In case we miss the point, we are reminded of the distinction between (i) and (ii) at the end of the argument (189b1–2), where Socrates explicitly claims to have refuted both (i) and (ii).

The usual view of this passage is that it shows Plato still unclear about how to solve the problem of false statement and false judgement.[11] When the elements of the puzzle are reassembled in the *Sophist* (237be), the distinction between (i) and (ii) will play an important role in disarming the Eleatic challenge. In the *Theaetetus* the distinction is ignored or overridden, the result being impasse and confusion. Plato, on this view, shows inexperience.

I propose a very elementary reply. Confusion in the text is not necessarily confusion in the author of the text.[12] A little || later in the *Theaetetus* (190e–191a) Socrates says that he and Theaetetus should be ashamed of the way they have let this argument, and the other two arguments against the possibility of false judgement, trample over them, like sailors trampling over seasick passengers in a storm. I think this implies that readers of the *Theaetetus* should be ashamed of themselves, if they lie down under the argument we have been looking at and do not stand up to find a way out of the difficulty for themselves.

Let us then return to the argument. Plato has provided the materials for a solution, as the *Sophist* will show, precisely in the distinction between (i) and (ii). The difference between (i) and (ii) is that (i) discerns a *structure* in the false judgement – a structure in which a predicate is attached to a subject – whereas (ii) treats the judgement as an unstructured whole. A model on which judgements relate to the world in the same sort of unstructured way as touching, seeing or (we may add) naming, will tie anyone in knots when it comes to the question 'What is a false judgement

---

to explain the fact that the subsequent argument for a negative answer completely ignores the distinction between subject and predicate (cf. next note).

[11] So e.g. McDowell 1973: 201: 'One of the objects of Plato's criticism in the *Sophist* is, I believe, Plato himself, in such passages as the present one.'

[12] For an exemplary illustration of this principle, see the first section (pp. 16–23) of Richard Robinson's well-known article 'Plato's Consciousness of Fallacy' (Robinson 1942, cited from Robinson 1969, ch. 2). Unfortunately, the second section (pp. 23–38) proceeds on the principle that no more clarity can be ascribed to the author than is made explicit in the text; the hints and nudges that counted in the first section are discounted in the second.

the judgement (name) for'. The only available answer, when a judgement like 'Theaetetus is flying' is taken as an unstructured whole, appears to be: Nothing. There is nothing in the world for the judgement to name or latch on to, for there is no such thing as Theaetetus-flying. And finding oneself in knots is the best way to appreciate the importance of the qualification 'about something' which (i) includes and (ii) leaves out. The qualification points to a structural complexity within the false judgement which the scandalous *reductio* ignores.[13] It is true of perceiving, as of naming and mentioning, that without something to perceive/name/mention the act does not come off at all. But once you have ‖ succeeded in perceiving or mentioning Theaetetus, who is something that is, you can go on to misdescribe him as old or stupid. That is what it means to judge things that are not about something that is. Precisely because there is a distinction between what a judgement is about and what is judged about it – a distinction with no parallel in perceiving and naming – there is a difference between judging what is not about something and judging without anything to judge.

Suppose, however, the imaginary questioner comes back[14] with the rejoinder that the story just told does not remove the difficulty, but merely confines it to the predicate part of the judgement. Instead of a blank nothing for the whole judgement to be of, we are now contemplating an equally unintelligible attempt to predicate a blank nothing of something that is. Why should a small blank count as an improvement on the larger one?

A fair question, to which the answer is 'Read the *Sophist*.' My claim is not that the story is already told in the *Theaetetus*, but that a puzzle is set to make the reader start thinking about the significance of the distinction between subject and predicate. In the *Theaetetus*, the Wax Block model discerns structure in judgements of identity like 'That [referring to the person seen at a distance] is Socrates' (191b). Identity judgements combine two terms of the same type, and may be mistaken even though each term is something that is. But the more complex structure of subject and predicate in descriptive statements is postponed to the *Sophist*, which picks up and develops (i)'s phrase 'things that are not about (περί) something'. In the sequel-dialogue it becomes clear that our imagined rejoinder is

---

[13] A rare case of someone noticing the pointer is Denyer (1991: 110–11); earlier, in ch. 2 on the *Euthydemus* arguments I consider below in a rather different translation, he gives a superb account of what is wrong with treating a statement or judgement as analogous to a name.

[14] As have actual questioners in audiences to whom I have presented this essay.

misconceived. 'What is not about something' is not the designation of a blank nothing (albeit a small one). For it presupposes a complete predicative structure, such as Theaetetus not being ugly or his not flying.

The distinction between (i) and (ii), and the appreciation of structural complexity that goes with it, is not of course the whole of the *Sophist*'s contribution to the understanding of || how we can and should speak of what is not. But it is part of it, and the relevant part if one wishes to charge Plato himself with failing earlier to distinguish between names and sentences, between speaking of something and saying something. The charge is often made, e.g. by G. E. L. Owen,[15] who goes on to explain it by reference to certain 'primitive assumptions about language' which retard Plato's progress until they are modified in the *Sophist*. These assumptions 'have been too often studied in Plato to need expansion here', but a bare summary is provided:

> Words are given their purchase on the world by being used to name parts of it, and names, or the basic names to which others are variously reducible, are simple proxies for their nominees.

Such is Owen's basis for suggesting that what goes wrong in the *Theaetetus* is that the predicate word (which says what is not *about* something) is treated as a name that misfires: 'where there should be the flight ascribed to Theaetetus, there is no such object for the word to hit'. This is simultaneously to acknowledge, and to trample down, that little word 'about' – like someone who, when told to look in the sky for 'the flight ascribed to Theaetetus', searches for a flight without a flier. It is the small blank objection again, now imputed to Plato himself rather than his imaginary questioner.

I reply that Plato's text invites such an explanation only if it is taken as an unstructured whole, a straightforward argument to defeat the sensible proposal it begins from.[16] || Certainly, Owen's charge fits the refutation. The analogy between judging what is not and touching what is not does obliterate the distinction between speaking of something and saying something, as it obliterates the distinction between (i) and (ii). But Plato wrote both parts of this text, the part that makes the distinction and the part that

---

[15] In his seminal essay 'Plato on Not-Being' (Owen 1970b: 244–5, also Owen 1986: 120, with n. 39).
[16] Likewise, David Wiggins (1972: 75–7) takes the analogy between judging and touching as a sign that *Plato was* 'seized by a mental cramp' which needs an elaborate hypothesis to explain it. In striking contrast, Owen's account of the second part of the *Parmenides is* a paradigm of how to read, and respond to, Plato when he is in challenging mode: Owen 1970a: 341–72, also published as Owen 1986: 85–103.

tramples it down. I conclude that the passage is not written by an author lacking in experience of semantics and philosophy of language. Its author is out to challenge *readers*, who may be lacking in experience of semantics and philosophy of language, to reflect on the point that the structural relation between subject and predicate is the key, not only to understanding how false judgement is possible, but through that to much bigger questions about the relation of thought and language to the world in general. It may even contribute something, I shall suggest, to the understanding of love.

Saying what is not in the *Euthydemus*

But before talking about love, a word about laughter. Everyone knows the *Euthydemus* is funny.[17] Everyone agrees that the arguments put forth in this dialogue by the sophists Euthydemus and Dionysodorus are an exhibition of how not to argue. It is evident, too, that, as Socrates keeps complaining, the sophists themselves are not seriously trying to teach the boy Cleinias. But from none of this should we conclude that Plato is not seriously trying to teach his readers. 'Of || opposites there is a single science' (τῶν ἐναντίων μία ἐπιστήμη). An exhibition of bad argument and bad thinking can teach us a lot about good argument and good thinking – provided we are prepared to think ourselves as well as to laugh. As with the *Theaetetus*, I shall suggest that Plato's text provides the materials we need to think with.

A full appreciation of these materials requires some knowledge of an elusive associate of Socrates called Antisthenes, who notoriously maintained that contradiction is impossible, meaning that it is impossible to contradict what someone else has said. We learn from Aristotle (*Met.* Δ.29, 1024b26–34 with *Top.* I.11, 104b20–1) that Antisthenes inferred the impossibility of mutual contradiction (and then the impossibility of falsehood) from the prior thesis that nothing can be spoken of except by its own proprietary account (οἰκεῖος λόγος). Why did Antisthenes hold that nothing can be spoken of except by its own proprietary account?

Aristotle's curt diagnosis is that Antisthenes failed to distinguish statements of essence from statements ascribing an accidental feature.[18] It is true in a way that Socrates and musical Socrates are the same thing, but if

---

[17] The following editions, commentaries, and translations are referred to by author's name alone: Canto-Sperber 1989; Decleva Caizzi 1996; Dodds 1959; Edwin Hamilton Gifford 1905; Hawtrey 1981; Sprague 1965.
[18] There is no reason to think this was mere oversight. In Burnyeat 1990: 164–73, I speculate about a deeper motivation, having to do with the conditions for reference and identification.

the qualification 'in a way' is omitted or ignored, this truth is liable to turn into the falsehood that it is not Socrates you are talking about unless you speak of him as musical. In which case it is not Socrates you are talking about if you attempt to describe him, falsely, as unmusical. Hence it is not Socrates you are talking about if you attempt to contradict someone who says truly that he is musical.

The *Euthydemus* shows how the argument goes:

> 'There are accounts (λόγοι) for each of the things that are?'
>
> 'Certainly.'
>
> 'An account of how each is, or of how it is not?'
>
> 'Of how it is.' (285e–286a)

This premise is a slightly disguised version of Antisthenes' slogan that each thing has its own proprietary account.[19] The ensuing argument spells out the consequences of supposing that the only way to speak of a thing is to use its proprietary account, which describes it as it is:

> 'Would you and I contradict each other if we both spoke an account of the same thing?[20] In that case we would surely say the same.'
>
> He agreed.
>
> 'But if neither of us speaks the account of the thing, would we then contradict each other? Or in this case would neither of us have mentioned (μεμνημένος) the thing at all?'
>
> This too he admitted.
>
> 'Well, then, when I speak the account of the thing, and you give another account of another thing, do we then contradict each other? Or do I speak (of) the thing while you do not speak (of) it at all? How could someone who does not speak (of) a thing contradict someone who does?' (286ab)

As my brackets reveal, the argument forces the account (λόγος) of a thing to function as an unstructured whole. No distinction is allowed between speaking of something and saying something, so there is no room for the idea that speaking of or mentioning something is only part of what is involved in saying something true or false.

Credit is due to Aristotle for seeing this and expressing it in his own terminology of essence and accident. But what of Plato? Is he simply

---

[19] It should be permissible to recognise the allusion to Antisthenes, here and at *Theaet.* 202b3, without being accused of succumbing to the Antisthenes-mania denounced by Hermann Keulen (1971: 82–4). For sanity on this matter, see Canto-Sperber 1989: 203–4.

[20] I follow the text of Burnet, not that of Gifford, who accepts Heindorf's addition of τόν before τοῦ. The τόν in the sequel is justified by the present exchange.

retailing the argument for our amusement, or does he prod us to see the point for ourselves? I shall suggest that by the time Dionysodorus propounds the Antisthenean argument, the materials for its solution have been put before us by Plato not once only, but several times.

Go back to 283e. The argument Euthydemus is about to present for the conclusion that falsehood and lying are impossible is really just another version of the slide from a structured to an unstructured model of false statement which || Dionysodorus exploits later for the Antisthenean conclusion that contradiction is impossible. (This is not the first time in the dialogue that Dionysodorus repeats his brother's argument in more detail and so with the trick less cleverly disguised: it happens in the first eristic scene with the arguments equivocating on μανθάνειν.) Euthydemus starts off with a clear reference to that about which the statement is made (τὸ πρᾶγμα περὶ οὗ ἂν ὁ λόγος ᾖ – 283e9). That subject, he argues (284a1–4), must be one of the things that are, and it must be that thing, no other, that the speaker λέγει, where λέγει can still be read as 'speak of or about'.[21] But then the preposition περί 'about' disappears and at 284a5–6 speaking of something that is becomes speaking of, saying, or stating what is, in a sense that amounts to stating a whole fact or specifying a whole state of affairs, i.e. speaking the truth. In other words, Euthydemus at 284a5–6 passes from a structured to an unstructured model of statement.[22]

In case we miss the point, Plato makes him do something rather similar in the next paragraph, beginning at 284b. At 284b5 Euthydemus gets Ctesippus to agree that one cannot do anything about or act towards things that are not. Both text and translation are tricky.[23] As I struggle through with it || as best I can, notice how the περί of 284b5 disappears. This time it is περί plus accusative, not genitive as before. Περί plus accusative can mean 'about',[24] but it probably does not mean that here.

---

[21] No doubt πρᾶγμα is as slippery a term as τὸ ὄν, but if the πρᾶγμα here was the whole state of affairs (as perhaps just before at 283e4), rather than the subject, Ctesippus would not assent without demur. It should be emphasised that λέγειν plus accusative (as in λέγοντα τὸ πρᾶγμα at 283e9) is quite ordinary Greek for 'speak of something' (cf. e.g. 300b3–4, *Phdo* 94d7–8, *Smp.* 221e4–5, *Prm.* 137c2, *Theaet.* 202a2). Hence there is no need to invoke (with Gifford and Canto) an ambiguity between 'speak of some existing object' and 'speak existing words'.

[22] Contrast the well-known argument of *Rep.* V, where the unstructured εἶναι τε καὶ μὴ εἶναι of 477a6 (corresponding to the unstructured τὸ ὄν of 476e10–477a4) unfolds into the predicative structure, 'each of the many is and is not what one says it is', of 479b9–10. No fallacy there, as is made clear by Charles Kahn (1981: 112–14).

[23] I am fairly confident about the text (see nn. 27 and 28), but the difficulty of capturing its meaning is evident from the translations cited in n. 17 (to which add Denyer 1991: 8–9): they vary so widely when they reach this passage that one begins to suspect Euthydemus (as portrayed by Plato) of deliberate obfuscation. A translator has no option but to chance their arm.

[24] Despite Dodds' note *ad Gorg.* 490c8, see *Soph.* 232b2–3, *Plt.* 277e8.

Nevertheless, it implies a relationship to something, a relationship which drops out when the περί disappears.²⁵ The result is that Euthydemus can argue that, just as doing or making something that is not is not doing or making anything at all, so saying something that is not is not saying anything at all:

> And Euthydemus asked, 'Things that are not simply are not?'
>
> 'Correct.'
>
> 'Absolutely nowhere, then, are things that are not things that are?'
>
> 'Nowhere.' (284b3–5)

At first sight, this emphasis on the spatial is puzzling. All becomes clear when we reach the example of orators speaking in the Assembly. Moral: a fallacious argument may contain false clues ('red herrings'), where the fallacy does not lurk.²⁶

> 'Is there any way, then, to perform an action (πράξειεν ἄν τίς τι) in relation to (περί) these things that are not, with the result that the agent (whoever it may be) makes them – makes those things that nowhere are things that are?'²⁷
>
> 'It does not seem so to me,' said Ctesippus. (284b5–8) ||

The issue is not whether one can make something which was not and now is. Any craftsman can do that.²⁸ The issue is whether the product of making can be something that is not.

> 'Well then, when orators speak in the Assembly, do they perform no action?'
>
> 'Certainly, they act,' he said.
>
> 'Then if they act, they also make (ποιοῦσι)?' 'Yes.' (284b8–c1)

---

²⁵ A possible comparison (but I hesitate) might be with *Cratylus* 429ce. After Cratylus denies that one can say, falsely, 'This is Hermogenes' of someone who is not properly so named, Socrates moves on from εἰπεῖν to προσειπεῖν and asks 'whether one can address Hermogenes by that name ('Hello, Hermogenes') if it is not in fact his name.

²⁶ Compare Aristotle, *SE* 24, 179b17–26.

²⁷ Read ὥστ' ἐκεῖνα with Burnet, following the marginal corrections in T and W, not Hermann's emendation ὥστε καὶ εἶναι (accepted by Gifford, Sprague, Hawtrey, Canto). In the interests of clarity I would remove the commas Burnet prints around τὰ μὴ ὄντα in b5–6 and add a comma before τὰ μηδαμοῦ ὄντα at b7. My translation of the resulting text agrees with that of Caizzi, except that I take τὰ μηδαμοῦ ὄντα to be pregnant with the sense given to the phrase at b4–5.

²⁸ Thus Hermann's emendation is to be rejected on philosophical as well as philological grounds; all the more so Hawtrey's claim that, *whatever* the text, the argument is about bringing what is not into existence. Parmenides-mania is no better than Antisthenes-mania. If only scholars would heed the wise warning issued long ago by Hermann Bonitz, 'Euthydemos' [1860], in Bonitz 1886, 126–8 n. 17, against treating Euthydemus and Dionysodorus as minor epigoni of Heraclitus and Parmenides, Protagoras and Gorgias, or any other substantive theory. The brothers undertake to refute any thesis, false *or true* (272ab). They have no philosophical beliefs at all.

Another red herring: the verb ποιεῖν means both 'do' and 'make', but it is not obligatory to assume that Ctesippus is tricked by the ambiguity.[29] Maybe he agrees that to act is to make something, viz. the action 'performed' (as we say) or 'accomplished'. Any action adds to the sum total of events in history.

> 'So speaking is acting and making?'
>
> He agreed.
>
> 'Then,' he said, 'No-one speaks things that are not – for that would already be making something, but you agreed that no-one can make what is not. So on your account no-one speaks falsehoods. Quite the contrary, if Dionysodorus speaks, he speaks things that are true and things that are.' (284c1–6)

Having set out from the idea of an action περί things that are not – an action that somehow relates to things that are not – the argument is now contemplating an absurd attempt to do or make things that are not. The action is a non-action, the making of nothing at all. Recall how the *Theaetetus*, once || the vital περί of (i) was lost from view, argued similarly that, just as touching something that is not is not touching, so judging something that is not is not judging at all.

Compare also 287a: when someone performs an action (ὅταν τίς τι πράττῃ), it is impossible to miss or fail in the action (οὐκ ἔστιν ἁμαρτάνειν τούτου ὃ πράττει). One either performs the action with success or one performs no action at all. It would sound plausible for Euthydemus to say that non-performances exist nowhere. But then he will make it seem impossible to achieve a non-performance by trying to jump over a wall and falling flat on one's back.

I hope that by now you may be prepared to agree that this section of the *Euthydemus* is not merely a riot of fallacies. There is a pattern to the confusion, a pattern which is repeated, with variations, in each of the three bad arguments we have looked at so far. None of them attend to the distinction between subject and predicate. I ask: Why should Plato so design the discussion that the same or similar trick is played several times, if not to get us, the readers, to notice the common pattern? The essence of logic is the effort to abstract for study the structures and patterns which are common to different forms of words and different arguments. In the first eristic scene we were given two pairs of opposed arguments, each pair much the same though dressed up differently,[30] and each effecting their

---

[29] *Pace* Hawtrey, Canto, Caizzi.
[30] As Socrates remarks at 276e9–277a1: διὰ τῶν αὐτῶν ὧνπερ τὸ πρότερον.

refutation of Cleinias by equivocation on the verb μανθάνειν. At the end (278a) Socrates pointed out that it was one and the same equivocation that had been exploited twice over.[31] The discerning of sameness is as important for the understanding of bad argument and bad thinking as it is for the understanding of good argument and good thinking. On the other hand, it is characteristic of Socratic-Platonic pedagogy not to teach the truth in a treatise like Aristotle's *Sophistici Elenchi*, but to stimulate readers to work out the truth for themselves. In the first eristic scene of the *Euthydemus* Socrates shows us how to do it. Thereafter we are expected to manage for ourselves, with such help as the author may provide.

This help comes by a variety of ways and means. A notable example is the hilarious scene at 295b–296d, where Euthydemus rails against the qualifiers (παραφθέγματα) that Socrates keeps adding to his answers to stop the sophist inferring that Socrates knows everything. Plato does not explain the fallacy of *secundum quid*. He displays it in action, so vividly that an alert reader will catch the point on their own.[32] The later Platonist Alcinous has it exactly right when he says that in the *Euthydemus* the study of sophisms is sketched (ὑπογεγραμμένην) by Plato in the following sense: *provided we read the book carefully*, we will find indicated (ὑποδεδεῖχθαι) therein which sophisms depend on language, which on things, and how to diagnose the faults (*Didaskalikos* 159.38–42). Alcinous' double use of the prefix ὑπο-, implying incompleteness and indirection, would not be appropriate if he was reporting on the clear and explicit statement of this division of sophisms in Aristotle's *Sophistici Elenchi* 4.165b23–24. It is perfectly matched to the *Euthydemus*' style of pedagogy, which expects readers to complete the lesson for themselves.

Returning then to the second eristic section of the dialogue, consider Ctesippus' objection at 284c7–8, directly after the conclusion of the argument just quoted about saying and doing:

> 'Bloody hell, Euthydemus!' said Ctesippus, 'He [Dionysodorus] speaks *in a way* of things that are, but he certainly does not speak of them as they are.'

---

[31] Commentators are seldom satisfied with Socrates' explanation: see the debate on 'Plato's Sophistry' between Michael Stewart and Rosamond Sprague (Stewart and Sprague 1977). But before joining in the search for extra fallacies (e.g. a fallacy of composition at 276e–277b), one needs some criterion to detect red herrings.

[32] Cf. Bonitz 1886: 109: 'Nachdrücklicher kann wohl kaum bei solcher Kürze der schlagenden Antworten bezeichnet werden, dass die unter einander *verschiedenen* Objecte des Wissens und des Nichtwissens, diese nothwendig hinzuzudenkenden Glieder der Relation, weggelassen werden müssen, um den Schein des Widerspruches herzustellen.'

The structured model of statement returns for a moment, only to be misinterpreted and abused by Dionysodorus in the sequel. Ctesippus contrasts speaking of a subject and speaking of it as it is, where 'as' (ὡς) introduces an *oratio obliqua* clause. Speaking of something as it is is saying how it is, describing it correctly, attributing a predicate that truly belongs to it. Dionysodorus understands this perfectly well, as his paraphrase reveals (284d1: λέγουσι τὰ πράγματα ὡς ἔχει). But then he and Euthydemus seize on the 'as' construction and turn it into a series of adverbial comments about speaking badly of bad things or people, bigly of big ones and hotly of hot ones. Their grossness helps the reader to see the significance of Ctesippus' original formulation. Ctesippus did not mean speaking hotly of hot things, but speaking of hot things as hot, describing them as hot.

Once again, remember that Plato is the author of both parts. He wrote Ctesippus' words as well as the sophists' mishandling of them. I reiterate the point because even the best readers of Plato need reminding from time to time. Here is a lovely quotation from George Grote's famous defence of the Sophists in his *History of Greece*:

> We continually read from the pen of the expositor such remarks as these – 'Mark how Plato puts down the shallow and worthless Sophist' – the obvious reflection, that it is Plato himself who plays both games on the chess-board, being altogether overlooked.[33]

But later in the same chapter Grote remarks, with reference to the *Theaetetus* passage on judging what is not,

> Plato was long perplexed before he could solve the difficulty to his own satisfaction.[34]

So to continue on the same note, Plato is also the author of the third part of the exchange we are considering, where Ctesippus, outraged by the sophists' mishandling of his formulation, grabs their weapon and turns it abusively || against them: 'They [the good] speak frigidly of frigid people and say they argue frigidly' (284e4–5). The Greek construction (τοὺς γοῦν ψυχροὺς ψυχρῶς λέγουσί τε καὶ φασὶν διαλέγεσθαι) zeugmatically combines the two 'as' constructions in one insult. Ctesippus' lack of cool is a portent of his imminent corruption by the sophists.[35] Meanwhile, I infer that Plato knows pretty well what is going on in the fallacious arguments we are examining. He does not suffer from inexperience.

---

[33] Grote 1888, vol. VII, p. 43. Sprague (Stewart and Sprague 1977: 46–7) makes the same point by insisting that 'Plato's dialogues were written by Plato.'
[34] Grote 1888, vol. VII, p. 75 n.   [35] A theme beautifully handled by Robin Jackson (1990).

The corollary is that Plato expects active participation from his readers. Consider the words with which Socrates at 274c7–d1 calls upon the sophists to demonstrate their wisdom. Referring to the assembled company, he says: 'They are all ready to μανθάνειν.' At first reading we naturally (and properly) take μανθάνειν as 'learn'. But on re-reading the dialogue for the second (third, fourth ...) time, a bell should ring: this is the word whose ambiguity is about to become the focus of the whole first scene. We may then notice that at 274c4–d1 Socrates points (δεικνύς) to *two* groups of people ready to μανθάνειν. Having already at 274b2–6 pointed (δεικνύς) to the lovers of Cleinias as ready to μανθάνειν, he now conjoins them with the pupils of Euthydemus and Dionysodorus (ἑταῖροι = μαθηταί at 273a2). Are the two groups ready to μανθάνειν in the same sense? Not if the sophists' teaching is at all effective. At least some of the pupils will be watching to *understand* better how the trick is played. In a different spirit, alert re-readers of the dialogue should learn to do the same.

The difference of spirit is crucial. The pupils will be watching to understand better how to use the tricks for their own ends, my alert readers to understand how the tricks can be detected and exposed. As for Socrates, not only does he include himself among those who wish to μανθάνειν at the beginning (274b3), but even after the reported discussion has ended he persists in wanting to go with Cleinias, Crito, ‖ and his sons to school with the brothers (272bd, 304bc).[36] I shall suggest that he wants both to understand the tricks and to use them for good ends instead of bad. What is clear is that Plato himself, in writing the dialogue, has appropriated the sophists' method of teaching by example[37] and turned it to *his* own purpose. Aristotle thought Plato's purpose would be best served by a didactic treatise like the *Sophistici Elenchi*, but in a famous passage at the end of the work he testifies that teaching by example is the method sophists like Euthydemus would have used:

> Where this discipline is concerned [*sc.* dialectic, in contrast to rhetoric], it was not the case that part of the work had been done before, while part had not. Nothing existed at all. For the training given by the paid professors of

---

[36] Michael Narcy (Narcy 1984, ch. 2) denies that Socrates' desire to study with the sophists is ironical, on the grounds that at 272bd and 304bc Socrates is talking to Crito, not (as at 274b3) to the brothers: 'Pourquoi de l'ironie à l'égard de Criton?' (p. 40). A partial answer may be found at 290e–291a and *Phaedo* 115c: Crito is always good for a tease. But Narcy's claim could have been partially vindicated against the *communis opinio*, had he attended to the different senses of μανθάνειν.

[37] Cf. Robinson 1942, p. 23: 'the *Euthydemus* as a whole, just because it is so *concrete*, does not solve the question what *abstract* consciousness Plato had of fallacy'.

eristic argument was like the teaching of Gorgias. For he[38] used to hand out rhetorical speeches, while they handed out speeches in the form of question and answer, for their pupils to learn by heart. Both parties supposed that these would usually cover the arguments on either side.[39] This made the teaching they gave their pupils rapid,[40] but unsystematic. For their idea was to train people by giving them the products of their art, rather than the art. (*SE* 24, 183b34–184a4)

Remember those pictures in children's magazines which invite you to say what is wrong: you look, and eventually you see that the giant is shown wearing his boots backwards. Children quickly learn the sort of fault to search for. Grown-ups could easily learn to produce such pictures for themselves. ||

Love in the *Euthydemus*

To complete my own picture, I turn to the very first argument of this section of the dialogue (283cd). It is about love and learning, not falsehood or contradiction, but that makes it all the more interesting and significant that the root of the fallacy is the same: inattention to the subject–predicate distinction.[41] This time, moreover, we have some comments by Socrates to help us see it is the same.

The argument begins just after Socrates has demonstrated (282ab) that what young Cleinias should be trying to get his family, friends and lovers is wisdom, for wisdom is the only thing good in itself. Very well, says Dionysodorus, if Socrates and the rest of you want Cleinias to become wise, you want him to cease to be what he now is, viz. ignorant, and become what he now is not, viz. wise. From this truth Dionysodorus infers the falsehood that Socrates, Ctesippus and the rest want the person who Cleinias now is to perish. What fine friends and lovers Cleinias has, if their chief concern is that he should die (283cd)!

In the Greek the fallacy depends on the relative phrase ὃς νῦν ἐστίν (283d5), which can express either what Cleinias is, i.e. a predicate such as being ignorant (cf. 293c8–d1: ὃς εἶ = ἐπιστήμων), or *who* he is, his identity

---

[38] Reading ὁ μέν (Solmsen, Barnes) for οἱ μέν.
[39] ἐμπίπτειν suggests a tacit typology, or at least that the arguments handed out are to serve as paradigms for generating others like them: cf. ἔστι γὰρ στοιχεῖον καὶ τόπος εἰς ὃ πολλὰ ἐνθυμήματα ἐμπίπτει (*Rhet.* ii.25, 1403a 19).
[40] As Euthydemus boasts (273d) and Ctesippus demonstrates in practice.
[41] As so often, the one to perceive this most clearly is Bonitz 1886: 106–8. Compare the Antisthenean-sounding argument against change at *Parm.* 162d5–8: If the one altered from itself, the account (ὁ λόγος) would no longer be about the One, but about something else.

as a subject for predicates like ignorance or wisdom.[42] A translator might appeal to two construals of the phrase 'cease to be the person he is'. Socrates wants Cleinias to cease to be the ignorant person he is and become a wise person instead. Dionysodorus infers that Socrates wants Cleinias to cease to be the person we call Cleinias. The gap between premise and conclusion is marked by Socrates getting anxious or disturbed (ἐθορυβήθην – 283d4).[43] || He sees what is coming. But it is not until 285ab that he has a chance to offer a calming comment.

It is a splendid mode of destruction the sophists have discovered if they can replace a bad self by a good one.[44] By all means let them destroy the bad, if that signifies making him wise. Socrates volunteers to serve as the test case by letting the sophists play Medea on him, boiling him up in their wonderful new recipe for wisdom. Ctesippus, not to be outdone in the presence of his beloved Cleinias, volunteers to be flayed like Marsyas as well (285cd).

Socrates' comment implies a distinction between the destruction of Cleinias and the destruction of ignorant Cleinias, hence a distinction between Cleinias and ignorant Cleinias which parallels Aristotle's distinction between Socrates and musical Socrates.[45] They are the same in a way, but not unqualifiedly so, otherwise Dionysodorus' inference would be sound. This is a point of logic which Ctesippus had failed to appreciate earlier. Ctesippus' furious indignation at 283e, which initiates the arguments about falsehood, shows him insensitive to the difference between a verbal blow and a real argument (cf. also 284e6–285a1). His annoyance certainly fits Aristotle's diagnosis that it is due to inexperience rather than appreciation of the truth. By contrast, Socrates' distinction between Cleinias and ignorant Cleinias is the cool reaction, not only of reason, but of genuine love. For Ctesippus' fury suggests that, emotionally, he does not in fact distinguish Cleinias from ignorant Cleinias. Unlike Socrates, Ctesippus does not think of the boy as someone who could and should be changed from ignorance to wisdom. Nor does his kind of || love express itself in a desire to accomplish that educational change.

---

[42] For this diagnosis, see Gifford, p. 36, and L. Brown 1986: 57–8. On ὅς = οἷος, see LSJ sv, B IV 5.
[43] Not 'thrown into confusion' (Sprague), if that implies logical confusion: compare 275d7.
[44] Note the *alienans* τινά at 285b1.
[45] The parallel is developed by Pierre Aubenque (Aubenque 1962: 448–51), who aptly cites Aristotle's statement *(Met.* [Γ.2], 1004b1–2) that the philosopher is the proper person to deal with the question whether Socrates is the same as Socrates sitting. Aubenque appreciates Aristotle's sense of the potential ramifications of the question, but Plato's contribution he dismisses as 'railleries faciles'.

Still less does he appreciate that there is a deeper Platonic sense in which to be changed from ignorance to wisdom is to become dead: dead to this world and its bodily concerns. This is the meaning of the thesis advanced in the *Phaedo* (64a ff.) that to practise philosophy seriously is to practise being dead. It is an aspect of the fallacious argument about love which readers can appreciate if (and only if) they have read the *Phaedo*, where Ctesippus will be present (59b). Of course, at the dramatic date of the *Euthydemus* Socrates' death still lies in the future. But anyone who reads the *Euthydemus* together with the *Phaedo*[46] can see what keeps Ctesippus from appreciating the affinity between philosophy and death. He lacks what the *Phaedo* teaches, a keen sense of the real distinction of soul and body. Thus Ctesippus' thoroughly emotional response to Dionysodorus' fallacy is a failure in logic which betrays, as the remainder of the dialogue will confirm, a failure of love. ||

THE MORAL

We should not be surprised by Plato's offering a lesson in love at the same time as a lesson in logic. The *Euthydemus* does not isolate logic as a discipline on its own, still less does it anticipate the insights to be gained from a study of logical form. What links logic and love is that both are aspects of the use of argument in discussion, especially discussion directed to educating the young. It is the whole spirit of argument, one might say, that the dialogue is about. The *Euthydemus* shows us how many more ways there are for an argument to go wrong than are dreamed of in the logic books.[47] By the same token, it shows us how much more is required for

---

[46] A useful exercise even if, as standardly assumed, *Phaedo* is the later dialogue. But no-one is entitled to be confident that this is so – for an eye-opening explanation of what stylometry has *not* established, see Keyser 1992, concluding 'And the chronology of Plato? – I know no more than Campbell; nor does anyone.' Accordingly, the only chronological assumption made in this essay derives from Campbell: that the *Sophist* is later than the other dialogues discussed. I will concede that the *Euthydemus* is probably earlier than the *Theaetetus*, but on literary rather than stylometric grounds: the qualifier-dropping argument which constitutes the ἄφυκτον ἐρώτημα of *Theaet.* 165ad (cf. *Euthyd.* 276e5) strikes me as written for the enjoyment of readers who know the *Euthydemus*. But once literary considerations are allowed, *Euthyd.* 290c–291a cries out for attention. Plato wrote both Cleinias' remarks about mathematicians and dialecticians, generals and politicians, and the fifteen-line paragraph where Crito refuses to believe that such advanced thinking could have come from anyone but a superior being (e.g. Socrates). Like Narcy 1984: 183, I read this as a deliberate cross-reference to the *Republic*, presupposing readers who know that work. Conversely, an allusion to Euthydemus and Dionysodorus would have been appropriate at *Rep.* 495b–496a, but none appears. But to turn conviction on this matter into argument is a task for another occasion.

[47] Including logic books devoted (in whole or part) to fallacy, with the splendid exception of C. L. Hamblin, *Fallacies* (Hamblin 1970).

good argument, good reasoning, than appropriate premises and valid inference. These are only the raw materials.

In bad reasoning, similarly, equivocation and qualifier dropping are only the raw materials. They are not by themselves enough to vitiate an argument, as can be seen from the first protreptic scene of the *Euthydemus*. At 279c–280b Socrates appears to equivocate on good fortune (εὐτυχία),[48] and at 281de he undoubtedly drops the qualifier as he passes from:

(1) ordinary goods like wealth, honour and courage are in *themselves* neither good nor bad (since they acquire value or disvalue depending on whether wisdom or ignorance controls their use),

to the conclusion,

(2) such things are neither good nor bad – wisdom is the only good, ignorance the only evil.

But it is clear at each stage what Socrates is saying.[49] Nothing is concealed. There is nothing for the sophistic party ‖ to laugh at (cf. 278e1–2); even when Socrates has a bit of fun at Cleinias' expense (279d6–8), he does it gently, without the sexually charged sadism of the sophists' booby traps.[50] The materials from which arguments are constructed can be used for good or bad, depending on the spirit which controls their use.[51]

The materials of argument are of course much easier to abstract and theorise about than the virtues and vices which control their use in live discussion. One advantage of the pedagogic indirection of the *Euthydemus* is that the relevant virtues and vices can be displayed in action. Plato is

---

[48] Stewart (Stewart and Sprague 1977: 23) fulminates against the equivocation; Sprague (Stewart and Sprague 1977: 59–60) replies that it is benign.
[49] It is instructive to study Gregory Vlastos' painstaking vindication of the argument (Vlastos 1991: 228–30). On the one hand, he is entirely correct that the argument is sound, for the reasons he gives. On the other hand, it never occurs to him that Plato may have an ulterior purpose in letting Socrates drop the qualifier. Such is the danger of extracting the passage from its context in the dialogue and treating it as a straightforward exposition of Socratic moral philosophy; it would be hard to take the second protreptic scene that way.
[50] The atmosphere of sex and aggression is established by Socrates' suggestion (272d) that Crito's sons could serve as bait (δέλεαρ) to persuade the sophists to teach the oldies too: 'I feel sure that their desire to get the boys will make them give us lessons, too' (Sprague's English neatly matches the ambiguity of the Greek ἐφιέμενοι ἐκείνων).
[51] Compare Aristotle, *Met*. Γ.2, 1004b22–5 (also *SE* 1, 165a28–31): sophistic and dialectic range over the same subject matter as philosophy, but philosophy differs from dialectic in its cognitive power, from sophistic in its choice of life (τοῦ βίου προαιρέσει).

perfectly capable of laying out the truth in didactic mode. The *Sophist* gives a straightforward presentation of the puzzles of false statement and their solution.[52] The *Euthydemus* prepares us for this, without competing with the *Sophist*, by showing two people in action controverting the possibility of false statement in the presence of the young. In that context, their bad reasoning verges on the wicked. An understanding of why the arguments are fallacious might help save a vulnerable soul. A generous reader of the *Euthydemus* will therefore welcome the rigours of the *Sophist*. Tough going as that dialogue may be, it offers both a more theoretical understanding of who the sophist is, and an explicit account of falsehood. ||

The starting point for the *Sophist*'s analysis of false statement is the distinction between subject and predicate. If the suggestions made in this essay have hit the mark, the fallacious arguments about love and speaking of what is not in the second eristic scene of the *Euthydemus* are designed by an author who wants his readers to start thinking about the distinction between subject and predicate – and who wants them at the same time to realise that the significance of the distinction goes far beyond the sphere of logic. Such is the central scene of a dialogue that opens with Crito asking for the identification of a subject ('Who was it you were discussing with, Socrates, yesterday in the Lyceum?', 271a), and closes with Crito worrying whether to entrust his sons to any of the people who call themselves philosophers. To which Socrates replies that, if he cares about the education of his sons, he should distinguish the predicate philosophy (αὐτὸ τὸ πρᾶγμα) from the subjects who practise it (306e–307c).[53]

---

[52] They are called puzzles (ἀπορίαι – 237d7–238a2, 238d6) and the presentation explicitly sets aside the use of 'not being' as an instrument of eristic or play (237b10: μὴ τοίνυν ἕνεκα μηδὲ παιδιᾶς, ἀλλ' εἰ σπουδῇ ...).

[53] This essay was first conceived for a conference on 'me-ontology' in memory of Henri Joly, organised by Curzio Chiesa at Geneva in 1989. The other contributions, including one by Jacques Brunschwig, were published in *Revue de Théologie et de Philosophie* 122 (1990); my dilatoriness allowed me to benefit from the discussion of successive drafts at Amherst College, Chicago, Galway, Lille, Oxford, Paris, Pomona College, and Princeton.

CHAPTER 3

Platonism in the Bible: Numenius of Apamea on Exodus and eternity

Dedicated to Richard Sorabji

Let me begin with the customary modest disclaimers. About the Book of *Exodus* I have nothing to say. I shall refer to the narrative, but on scholarly matters my ignorance is total. About Numenius my ignorance is extensive, but compensated for by some opinions – opinions about how he responded to a famous passage in *Exodus*, where God reveals his name to Moses from the burning bush: 'I am that I am.' The Greek of the Septuagint translation is ἐγώ εἰμι ὁ ὤν, 'I am He who is.' That Greek is my starting point here, for Numenius' interpretation of it encourages me to persevere in a view of eternity I have maintained since the memorable time, years ago in the 1960s and 70s, when Richard Sorabji and I used regularly to lecture together in the University of London. We argued amicably against each other for two hours every week, about eternity and much else, before and with a large audience of seventy or more students drawn from several of the London Colleges. Numenius did not feature in those debates. Neither of us was much aware of him yet. If I now claim Numenius[1] as an ally in an old dispute, it is to reinforce the message that Sorabji has made vivid, in so many ways, to the intellectual community today: the voluminous writings of the ancient Platonist philosophers are a treasury of acute, challenging philosophy.

I

Perhaps the best introduction to Numenius is his most quotable line (Frag. 8, 13), 'What is Plato but Moses talking Attic?' (τί γὰρ ἐστι

---

[1] Whom I cite from the Budé edition by Édouard des Places (Des Places 1973), where 'fragments' include testimonia. The translations are my own, but most of the fragments I quote derive from Eusebius' *Praeparatio Evangelica*, which is helpfully translated into English by E. H. Gifford (1903); his rendering often strikes me as more accurate than that of des Places.

Πλάτων ǁ ἢ Μωσῆς ἀττικίζων;).[2] Let this quip serve notice that we are to discuss a writer of wit and verve – the only witty Platonist after Plato himself, whose deep understanding of the Platonic philosophy is set forth in prose of high literary sophistication.

I shall come to the importance of Attic shortly. The importance of Moses for Numenius is that by tradition he was author of the Pentateuch, the first five Books of the Bible, not just a hero of the story.[3] That made him a star witness in a project announced in Frag. 1a, carefully copied out by Eusebius from Book 1 of Numenius' dialogue *On the Good*:

> On this question [*sc.* the incorporeality of God],[4] having cited and sealed the testimonies of Plato, we should go back further and bind these testimonies together with[5] the teachings of Pythagoras, and then summon the peoples of good repute, adducing their rites and doctrines and the traditions they celebrate in agreement with Plato (τὰς τελετὰς καὶ τὰ δόγματα τάς τε ἱδρύσεις συντελουμένας Πλάτωνι ὁμολογουμένως), such as those ordained by the Brahmans and Jews and Magi and Egyptians. (Frag. 1a)

For Eusebius, Bishop of Caesarea in the fourth century AD, this and other texts he quotes from *On the Good* support the idea that Plato had somehow come to know the philosophy of Moses. Either he heard about it when he travelled to Egypt, or he reached the same results by his own reflection on the nature of things, or he was inspired by God (*PE* XI.8.1). Platonism is thus shown to derive from, or to embrace the same truths as, the Judaic tradition.[6] Numenius' thesis is unambiguously about agreement ǁ on the truth (cf. Frag. 1b, 2–3: δόγματα ... ἀληθῆ), not about historical

---

[2] So quotable that apparently it circulated on its own. Eusebius quotes it twice. (i) at *PE* IX 6, 9 (followed by frags. 1a and 9) he has it from Clement (*Strom.* I 22.150, 4), who assures us that his near-contemporary Numenius did write the words but does not say where. Then again (ii) at XI 10, 14, just after quoting Numenius' account of eternal being in frags. 5, 6, 7, and 8 to confirm the claim he made at XI 9, 4–5 that Plato reworked Moses' words into the *Timaeus*. (Later appearances of the saying in Theodoret, *Therap.* II 114 and the Suda *sv.* 'Numenius' presumably derive from Eusebius.) This *rapprochement* between Plato and Moses on the subject of eternal being leads Eusebius to comment that Numenius' well-known saying (ἐκεῖνο τὸ λόγιον) is reasonably attributed to him. We should agree, even if we cannot know which work the saying comes from. Such doubts about authenticity as have been expressed are effectively rebutted by John G. Gager (1972: 66–8).
[3] Frag. 30, 5–6 treats *Gen.* 1:2 as the words of 'the prophet'.   [4] A safe inference from frag. 1b, 4–6.
[5] For Numenius' use of συνδέομαι, cf. frags. 18, 8 and 24, 59.
[6] The idea that Plato's philosophy, and Pythagoras' too, derives from the Jews goes back to a commentary on the Pentateuch (standardly dated second century BC) by the Jewish Peripatetic Aristobulus, who claims they studied the *Exodus* story and 'our' law in translation (Euseb. *PE* IX.6.6, followed by Numenius' λόγιον; XIII.12.1). Pythagoras' borrowing of Jewish (and Thracian) ideas is already found in the third-century biographer Hermippus *ap.* Josephus *Ap.* 1.165. Such claims are but one symptom of a widespread ancient tendency (anxiously combatted in the opening chapters of Diogenes Laertius) to find foreign origins for Greek philosophy. By the early modern period some were ready to believe that Pythagoras was himself a Jew: Schneewind 1998: 536–40.

derivation. All these peoples, not only the Jews, agree with Plato that the divine is incorporeal.[7] Not of course that they express it as clearly as he does, but the agreement discernible in their teachings and cults – coming as it does from other places and times – corroborates the truth of Platonism. They are all independently responding to the same truth as he did. As a modern philosopher might put it, they all 'tracked the truth'.[8]

But why Attic? No quotable quote could be made of the trite point that Moses did not speak Greek at all. The contrast is not between Greek and Hebrew, but between two dialects of Greek, the Attic used by the Athenian Plato and the Doric of the Pythagorean writings. Modern scholars regard the extensive corpus of Pythagorica as Hellenistic forgeries, leaving only a few fragments of Philolaus and Archytas to represent earlier Pythagoreanism in written form. For later antiquity, that corpus was simply 'the Pythagorean writings'. Numenius, writing in the second century AD, would know that neo-Pythagoreans of the previous century like Moderatus had adduced three disabling factors to explain the extinction of the good old Pythagorean philosophy: (i) τὸ αἰνιγματῶδες, the enigmatic form in which it was presented, (ii) *the inherent obscurity of the Doric dialect* (ἐχούσης τι καὶ ἀσαφὲς τῆς διαλέκτου), plus (iii) the fact that the really fruitful ideas were filched and propagated as their own by Plato, Aristotle and the Academy, who made things worse by collecting the sillier-looking stuff (i.e. the ἀκούσματα) and publishing it as the distinctive teaching of the Pythagorean school.[9] Moral: Attic is the language of clarity. ||

By contrast, the Greek of the Septuagint is not Attic, and it is often unclear. The same may be said of the supposed hexameters of Musaeus (DK 2 B), whose name Numenius uses to speak of Moses in frag. 9.[10]

---

[7] On my understanding of frag. 1a, which is indebted to Michael Frede's ground-breaking study, 'Numenius' (Frede 1987: 1048), the non-Greek peoples are commended for agreeing with Plato, who sets the standard of truth jointly with Pythagoras. Contrast G. R. Boys-Stones (2001: 114–18), who has frag. 1a commend Plato for his skill in deriving ancient wisdom from non-Greek sources. That derivationist line was taken by many other thinkers discussed in Boys-Stones' interesting book, but Numenius is importantly different. Even Eusebius allows for the possibility of Plato reaching the truth on his own. An even more derivationist reading appears in Arnaldo Momigliano, *Alien Wisdom: The Limits of Hellenisation* (Momigliano 1978: 147), who cites the question 'What is Plato but Moses talking Attic?' as typifying later antiquity's subordination of reason to revelation, Greek thought to Oriental wisdom. That is quite unjust to Numenius, in whose thought Greek confidence remains as strong as it was in the days of Hippias.

[8] See Nozick 2003: 172–96. Roughly, to track the truth is to be reliably receptive to truth and, in addition, reliably unreceptive to what is false.

[9] Porph. *VP* 53. Although the source is usually taken to be Moderatus himself, this is not certain and (c) is cited as a complaint of 'the Pythagoreans' generally.

[10] It is clear from Eusebius' commentary before and after frag. 9 that he has no doubt that Numenius does mean Moses when he writes 'Musaeus', and Origen confirms in frags. 1b, 1c, and 10a that

However Numenius understood the identification of Moses with Musaeus, he undertakes to show that the Jews and other peoples of good repute share an understanding of God which is most clearly expressed in Plato's Attic prose. Hence his pointed exclamation, 'What is Plato but Moses talking Attic?'[11]

Now already in the fifth century BC the sophist Hippias (DK 86 B6) had included Musaeus, Orpheus and poets like Homer, together with prose writings of Greek and barbarian authors, in a doxographical miscellany designed to bring out the underlying kinship between wildly different expressions of the same idea. For example, he relates Thales' choice of water as the origin of things to the role of Oceanus as progenitor of the gods in Homer and Orpheus, and probably also to the figure of Nun, the primeval waters, in Egyptian mythology.[12] A certain amount of allegorising is inevitable in such a programme. You show that your non-philosophical sources, however venerable, poetic or foreign, contain obscurely condensed expressions of thoughts which the philosophers articulated in more adequate form. Most Greek philosophers were happy to continue the practice that Hippias began.[13] Numenius is thus || a relative late-comer in a long tradition, and he too is devoted to the art of allegorising:

> I am also aware [writes Origen] that Numenius the Pythagorean, a man who expounded Plato with very great skill and maintained the Pythagorean

---

Numenius did quote Moses and recount his adventures in Egypt. The identification of Moses with Musaeus is otherwise attested only in the romancing Jewish historian Artapanus (probably second century BC), who says that when Moses reached manhood the Greeks called him Musaeus; he became the teacher of Orpheus and the inventor of numerous things including philosophy (Euseb. *PE* IX 27, 3–4). Gager (1972: 139) doubts that Numenius would endorse much of this (but see below) and diagnoses 'a simple adjustment of the orthography to the common Greek name'. I find that unlikely and suggest two alternatives. (i) 'Moses' could easily oust an original 'Musaeus' as the λόγιον circulated on its own, for reasons both of clarity and of Christian propaganda. (ii) Although in the other surviving fragments 'Musaeus' occurs once (frag. 9, 4), 'Moses' not at all, Numenius might still have used 'Moses' in some work other than *On the Good*.

[11] Since by Numenius' day Plato had become a model (albeit a disputed model) in the war of styles between the 'Atticists' and 'Asianists', one might suspect further word play on ἀττικίζων = 'Atticising'. Although Numenius' own style is a vigorous, often picturesque Asiatic, the virtue claimed for Atticism was its naturalness and lucidity, a virtue in which Plato excels, at least for much of the time: 'When he expresses himself in plain, simple and unartificial language, his style is extraordinarily agreeable and pleasant; it becomes altogether pure and transparent, like the most pellucid of streams' (DH *Dem.* 5; tr. Usher). Once again, Attic is the language of clarity.

[12] See Patzer 1986, especially ch. 2. Patzer builds here on the pioneering work of Bruno Snell.

[13] Aristotle, for example, is reported (D.L. 1.18) to have written in the first Book of his *De Philosophia* about the Magi and their dualism of good and bad principles, Oromasdes (Zeus) and Areimanios (Hades); cf. *Met.* N.4, 1091b4–12, where the Magi are cited alongside the ancient poets, Pherecydes, Empedocles and Anaxagoras. His pupil Eudemus collected the cosmo-theological views of the early Greeks and the Near East.

doctrines, quotes Moses and the prophets *in many passages* in his writings, and gives them no improbable allegorical interpretation, as in the book entitled *Epops* and in *On Numbers* and in *On Place*. In Book III of *On the Good* he even quotes a story about Jesus, though without mentioning his name, and interprets it allegorically ... He also quotes [cf. frag. 9] the story about Moses and Jannes and Jambres. (Frags. 1c and 10a recombined, from Origen, *Contra Celsum* IV.51.14–24; tr. Chadwick, slightly altered. Emphasis mine.)

The novelty Numenius brings to this tradition is his detailed attention to the Bible and the Jews.[14] The shock value of his question 'What is Plato but *Moses* talking Attic?' can be gauged by comparing another Platonist of the second century AD, contemporary with or somewhat later than Numenius, the Celsus against whom Origen wrote his *Contra Celsum*. Celsus agrees with just about everything I have ascribed to Numenius so far, with one exception: Moses and the Jews. According to Celsus, Moses was a corrupt Egyptian priest, not one of the wise men of old who tracked the truth. The Jews were a band of rebellious slaves who escaped with him, not one of the peoples who expressed in their cults and institutions the Ἀληθὴς Λόγος, the one true account which Celsus finds independently witnessed to, not only by the non-Jewish peoples Numenius cites in frag. 1a, plus the Assyrians, Odrysians, and Samothracians, but even by the Druids, Getae, Hyperboreans and Galactophagi. To exclude the Jews Celsus is prepared to go to the limits of the known world and beyond.[15]

By contrast, Numenius not only includes the Jews and their prophet Moses. He also appears to exclude the Doric Pythagorica. Frag. 1a, quoted above, puts Pythagoras on a par with Plato as a wise man who tracked the truth,[16] but not once in the extant remains does Numenius ‖ appeal to a

---

[14] I am not bothered if someone prefers to postulate that Numenius got his knowledge of the Bible second-hand from a compendium of some kind. It must have been pretty detailed, to judge by Origen's report, with quotations included. But I do reject the outright disbelief in Origen manifested by M. J. Edwards (1990a: 64–75), who urges that Eusebius would have quoted more if there had been more to quote in *On the Good*.

[15] For a helpful detailed account of Celsus' philosophical outlook, see Frede 1994.

[16] Frag. 24, 18–20 counts Plato 'no better than Pythagoras, and doubtless (ἴσως) no worse either'. Is Numenius hesitating to rank Plato with Pythagoras? Although some have read frag. 7, 4–7 as allowing that Plato could have missed a truth that Pythagoras knew, this is merely the concession of an abstract possibility to pacify (παραμυθήσεσθαι) a trouble-maker, followed up at once by a quotation which shows Plato tracking the truth at issue. Accordingly, I suspect that frag. 24, 18–20, is not hesitation, but rather a recherché mathematical joke to affirm the equality of the two sages. In Eudoxus' theory of proportions two magnitudes A and B are equal if, and only if, A exceeds and is exceeded by the same magnitudes as B, whether the magnitudes (so long as they are homogeneous) are commensurable *or* incommensurable. Plato and Pythagoras are both philosophers (homogeneity), but in such different styles that no unit of magnitude will measure both

Pythagorean source to determine what Pythagoras taught. He proceeds as if the best and only way to find that out is by careful interpretation of Plato.[17] His sole attested reference to 'certain Pythagoreans' (frag. 52, 15–24) is a contemptuous dismissal of their claim that matter and the Indefinite Dyad derive from the One. As one of the last Platonists to abide by the correct dualist interpretation of the *Timaeus*, he is sure that Plato's doctrine on matter agrees (*concinere*) with that of Pythagoras (frag. 52, 3–4). Frag. 1a proposes that we go back to Pythagoras from Plato, implying that Plato is the one true exponent of Pythagoras' philosophy. Plato's writings need the careful interpretation Numenius provides because, mindful of the fate of Socrates (cf. frag. 23), he did not think it safe to be completely open about theological topics. Instead, his exposition of the Pythagorean philosophy took the middle way between clarity and unclarity (frag. 24, 57–62), striking a mean between Socrates and Pythagoras (frag. 24, 73–4). Plato is clearer than the Pythagorean writings, and clearer than Moses, but still not as clear as Numenius endeavours to be. For he undertakes to give us Plato 'himself in himself', separated like the Forms (χωρίζειν ... αὐτὸν ἐφ' ἑαυτοῦ) from Aristotle, the Stoic Zeno, and the New Academy, so that we may see his Pythagorean essence (frag. 24, 66–70).[18]

Question: if while expounding the Pythagorean philosophy Plato is at the same time Moses talking Attic, does that not imply a rather special status for Moses too? I shall argue that in Numenius' eyes Moses did indeed excel other foreigners as a Pythagorean/Platonist *avant la lettre*, and that the *Exodus* account of his receiving the revelation of the divine name is deliberately echoed in Book 11 of *On the Good*. ||

II

Having sketched a context for Numenius' interest in Moses, I can turn to my next task, which is to make it plausible that Numenius has Moses in mind when he discusses eternity. Remember the conversation with the

---

(incommensurability). Nonetheless, they are equal to each other if Plato is neither better nor worse than Pythagoras, because this means that Plato does not exceed anyone in wisdom that Pythagoras does not also exceed, and he is not exceeded by anyone who does not also exceed Pythagoras. We will meet more examples of Numenius' remarkable even-handedness (p. 74 and n. 25 below).

[17] This point is forcefully argued in Frede 1987: 1044–8. I follow Frede in declining to describe Numenius either as a Pythagorean or as a Middle Platonist.

[18] My last four references do not relate to *On the Good*. Frag. 23 is cited by Eusebius from a work entitled *On the Secrets of Plato*, frag. 24 from Numenius' scintillating *On the Academics' Infidelity to Plato*.

burning bush. In the King James translation Moses asks, 'Who am I that I should go unto Pharaoh, and that I should bring forth the children of Israel out of Egypt?' Then, when he has been reassured that the Lord will be with him in this undertaking, he asks, 'When I come unto the children of Israel, and shall say unto them, The God of your fathers hath sent me unto you; and they shall say to me, What is his name? what shall I say unto them?' *Exodus* 3:14 gives the answer to these questions (I insert the Septuagint Greek at the crucial points): 'And God said unto Moses, I AM THAT I AM (ἐγώ εἰμι ὁ ὤν): and he said, Thus shalt thou say unto the children of Israel, I AM hath sent me unto you (ὁ ὤν ἀπέσταλκέν με πρὸς ὑμᾶς)'.[19]

It is often thought that Numenius has this Biblical text in mind when in frag. 13 he calls the First God of his version of Platonism ὁ ὤν. Eusebius, our source for frag. 13, had no doubts, but some modern scholars have hesitated to follow, and a number have resorted to emendation of the MSS reading ὁ ὤν. Eusebius can be vindicated, I believe, by independent evidence of Numenius' detailed interest in the *Exodus* narrative.

The scene with the burning bush comes at the beginning of the narrative of the Israelites' escape from Egypt. Numenius frag. 9 (already cited from Eusebius) is about the sequel, the story of how Moses–Musaeus led the Jews out of Egypt after defeating Pharaoh's magicians. Except that in Numenius' retelling Pharaoh's magicians are a match for Moses and are able to disperse even the most violent of the plagues. And they have names: Jannes and Jambres. Numenius did not get those names from the Book of *Exodus*. Their first appearance in the Bible is II *Timothy* 3:8 (*circa* 120 AD), which assumes they will be familiar to its readers from earlier Jewish tradition.[20] Evidently, Numenius has not only studied the *Exodus* narrative. He has also done some back-up research.

There were plenty of sources to draw upon. Pro-Egyptian versions of the story had been written by Manetho (third century BC), Lysimachus (second ‖ century BC), Apion (first century BC), and the Stoic philosopher Chaeremon (first century AD).[21] Josephus (first century AD) in his *Contra Apionem* took up arms on the other side, as had Ezekiel (perhaps second century BC), who gave a pro-Jewish presentation of the events in the form of a Greek tragedy on the Aeschylean model, from which extensive

---

[19] The Vulgate has: 'Ego sum qui sum. Ait: Sic dices filiis Israel: Qui est, misit me ad vos.'
[20] References to Jewish literature in Stern 1980: 213. Jannes at least had been heard of at Rome, being coupled with Moses as known magicians by Pliny *NH* xxx.11 and Apuleius *Apol.* 90.
[21] For discussion of this anti-Semitic historiography, see Boys-Stones 2001, ch. 4.

fragments survive.[22] As Michael Frede has shown,[23] there was a philosophical issue at stake in these polemics about how and why the Israelites left Egypt. Did the Jews qualify as an ancient people in their own right, with a wisdom of their own? Not if they originated as a rabble of Egyptians, either slaves on the run (Celsus) or expelled lepers (the more usual view). If, on the other hand, they were a genuine people, their wisdom would be worthy of an allegorising elucidation to show its affinity with the latest modern philosophy, whether Stoic or Platonic. Chaeremon, like Celsus later, was happy to do this for the Egyptians, but not for the Jews. What is most interesting about Numenius' version of events is that he treats both sides with an even hand.[24] In striking contrast to the Bible, frag. 9 reports that Jannes and Jambres were equal to Moses in their powers of magic.

Philosophically, this fits the programme of frag. 1a, where the Egyptians track the truth no less than the Jews.[25] *Ergo*, they had better be equally skilled in applying their knowledge to work wonders. Yet wonders are worked within the created realm. According to frag. 17 (from *On the Good* Book VI), while the Divine Craftsman is generally known among the peoples of the world, the First Mind is altogether unknown. This First Mind, the First God of Numenius' version of Platonism, senior to (πρεσβύτερος)[26] and more divine than the Demiurge, is Being itself (αὐτοόν). Could it be that in the scene with the burning bush, where Moses writes of a God called ὁ ὤν, Numenius found an exception to the general ignorance of the divinity of Being itself?

Let me repeat here that I know nothing about the Book of *Exodus*. I am not discussing the merits of ὁ ὤν as a translation of the Hebrew.[27] Let || me add that we have no evidence that Numenius read Philo Judaeus, who does of course have a great deal to say about ὁ ὤν in *Exodus* 3:14.[28] My

---

[22] Text, translation and commentary in Jacobson 1982. What survives of the scene with the burning bush does not include 'I am that I am.'
[23] Frede 1989, esp. 2072–5. [24] Cf. n. 16 above.
[25] Cf. the equable juxtaposition of Moses, the Egyptians, and Heraclitus in frag. 30.
[26] As the Good is superior πρεσβείᾳ at *Rep.* 509b9–10.
[27] Those as ignorant of Hebrew as I am may be interested in a variant translation given by Hippolytus in his account of a self-styled Gnostic sect, the Naasenes: γίνομαι ὃ θέλω καὶ εἰμί ὃ εἰμί (*Haer.* v 7.25, p. 84 Wendland). The first clause comes close to 'I will be what I will be,' which knowledgeable colleagues tell me is the meaning of the original. (I owe the reference to Christopher Stead.)
[28] *Aet.* 53 and 70; *Mos.* I 75; *Opif.* 170 (cf. 172); *Post.* 168; *Praem.* 40; *Spec.* I 41, II 225. Philo does not connect the name with eternity, but explains it as designating nothing but God's ὕπαρξις in contrast to his οὐσία or ποιότης, which are beyond our comprehension. Conversely, *Quod Deus* 32 denies past or future to eternity without mention of ὁ ὤν (though cf. τὸ ὄν in 33).

sole concern is what a Platonist philosopher of the second century AD would make of the information that the name of the Jewish God is ὁ ὤν.[29] It might, for instance, remind him of Plutarch's *On the E at Delphi*, where the highest-level interpretation of the inscription *E* is εἶ = 'Thou art', which in turn is explicated in terms of the Platonic contrast between being and becoming, eternity and time. The message is that Apollo is to be worshipfully addressed 'Thou art' – an utterance complete in itself (392a: αὐτοτελὴς προσαγόρευσις) without any complement after the verb 'to be' – because his being is an eternal present, with no trace of past or future. Plutarch could easily have called the God at Delphi ὁ ὤν, meaning He whose eternal being transcends time.[30]

This brings me back to frag. 13, where Numenius' First God is called ὁ ὤν and distinguished from the Demiurge. If the First God is Being itself, there is no call for Dodds' emendation of the phrase ὅ γε ὤν ('He who is') to ὅ γε ἁ (= πρῶτος) ὤν ('He who is first').[31] Dodds argued that the received text 'cannot be defended as a Hebraism'. There is no need to do so, for in itself the phrase is impeccable Greek. The issue is not whether Numenius borrowed it from the Septuagint,[32] but whether the Septuagint expression struck him as an exceptionally advanced point of agreement with Plato's conception of the first principle of everything. Did he find Moses agreeing with Plato that it is a principle whose being is an eternal present without trace of past or future? ‖

III

But surely, you may protest, Plato's first principle is the Good, which we all know is 'beyond being' (*Rep.* 509b9: ἐπέκεινα τῆς οὐσίας). It is bad enough having to endure these later Platonists' predilection for treating as Mind and God a principle which for Plato was the supreme *object* of the mind's quest for a kind of knowledge that God, the divine mind, already

---

[29] Frag. 56 shows Numenius responding to the commandment 'Thou shalt have no other gods before me' (*Exod.* 20:3).

[30] Plutarch also exhibits the shift between masculine and neuter designations of God which some have urged against ὁ ὤν as an alternative to the αὐτοόν of frag. 17: εἷς ὤν ... ὄντως ὄν (393ab).

[31] See Des Places 1973 *ad loc.* and Dodds 1960: 15–16, with a parallel emendation of frag. 16 to boost the suggestion. More recently, John Dillon (1977: 368 n. 1) would read ὁ γεωργῶν, picking up the image of the First God as farmer in line 1. This and other emendations are firmly rebutted by John Whittaker (Whittaker 1978).

[32] Although in his excellent defence of the MSS reading John Whittaker (Whittaker 1967) shows that the phrase travelled from the Septuagint into quite a spread of later ancient literature. Frag. 13's designation of the Demiurge, Numenius' Second God, as lawgiver derives not from the Bible, but from Plato's *Timaeus*: νόμους τε τοὺς εἱμαρμένους (41e), διαθεσμοθετήσας (42d).

has. Is it not a travesty of Plato to ascribe eternal (or any other kind of) being to his first principle, and to identify the Good with Being itself?

Not at all. From a philosophical point of view, Numenius' interpretation is quite defensible. In frags. 19 and 20 he argues that if the Demiurge is good, it must be because, like any other good thing, he participates in the Form of Good.[33] Quite generally, he continues, anything which is F (a human, horse, ox, etc.) is so because it is modelled after and participates in the corresponding Form, the F itself. Now apply this causal principle to the famous passage in *Republic* 509b where Socrates proclaims that the Good is cause of the being (τὸ εἶναί τε καὶ τὴν οὐσίαν) of the Forms which are the objects of knowledge. If Plato's first principle, whether we call it the Good or the One,[34] is itself good and itself one, because it is the cause of goodness and unity throughout the intelligible realm, must it not also, as cause of the Forms' being, *be* in its own right too? Must not the first principle be Being itself, just as Numenius holds, as well as Goodness and Unity? When Socrates says that the Good is beyond being, perhaps his meaning is that, like any Form in its causal role, it is beyond and distinct from the being it explains.

That Numenius read the passage this way seems to be confirmed by frag. 16, 8–10, which argues that if the Demiurge of becoming is good, the Demiurge of being must be the Good itself, which is by nature one with Being (αὐτοάγαθον σύμφυτον τῇ οὐσίᾳ). Frag. 16, 15–16, then distinguishes the being (οὐσία) of the First God from that of the Second. Nor is Numenius the only Platonist to take such a view of 'beyond being'. Both the view and the argument for it are found in an anonymous commentary on Plato's *Parmenides* which Hadot attributed to Porphyry, || but which some people think could be earlier.[35] The commentator is discussing the

---

[33] Cf. also frag. 16, 8–10 and 14–15; frag. 19, 8–11.

[34] Numenius frag. 54 derives Apollo's epithet 'Delphian' from an old Greek word δέλφος (unknown to LSJ) meaning 'one'! A strange twist on the then common etymology of 'Apollo': α privative + πολλά (e.g. Plut. *De E* 393c). The identity of the Good and the One is unambiguously expressed at frag. 19, 12–13, echoing Aristoxenus' report of Plato's Lecture on the Good: τὸ ἀγαθὸν ὅτι ἐστὶν ἕν; see Des Places 1973 *ad loc.* Numenius also equates his First God with the *Timaeus*' Form of Animal (frag. 22).

[35] Hadot 1968. The ascription to Porphyry is powerfully questioned in M. J. Edwards 1990b. Gerald Bechtle (Bechtle 2000) asserts, not without reason, a pre-Plotinian date. The best ground for the earlier date is given by Michel Tardieu (Tardieu 1996), who shows that a lengthy passage of Victorinus, *Adversus Arium* (1.49.9–50.21), corresponds closely with material in a Gnostic *Apocalypse of Zostrianus*, now preserved in Coptic translation from the lost Greek original which Plotinus got Amelius to refute (Porph. *VP* 16). The correspondence is so close as to indicate that Victorinus and the Gnostic author used a common source, which Tardieu suggests was none other than Numenius himself. In reply, Hadot (Hadot 1996b) rightly doubts that Numenius would speak of the first principle as Pneuma (*spiritus* in Victorinus). Still, the source has to be from around his time, the time of so-called Middle Platonism. Hadot remains disinclined to backdate the

second deduction of Part II of the *Parmenides*, the positive deduction about the One which is. He claims that this One which is derives its being from the One 'beyond being' of the negative first deduction, by participating in it. (After all, it is the *second* One in the dialogue and where else could its being come from?) In that case, he argues, the first One must be Being as well as One, a Being beyond the being that Socrates was talking about in the famous passage of the *Republic*. Plato was riddling (αἰνισσομένῳ) when he spoke of the One beyond being simply as the One which is not.[36]

But whatever the date of this Anonymus, already in the first century AD Seneca's *Epistle* 58 records a Platonist division in which the supreme genus is that which is, *quod est*.[37] In Aetius, Plato's God is that which really is (τὸ ὄντως ὄν) as well as the One (*Dox. Gr.* 304.24). We have already seen that the same holds for Plutarch, who expressly declares that what is must be one even as the one must *be* (*De E* 393b: ἓν εἶναι δεῖ τὸ ὄν, ὥσπερ ὂν τὸ ἕν). Another representative of such views is Alcinous, author of a *Handbook of Platonism* usually dated around || 150 AD, which would make him Numenius' contemporary. Alcinous' line is that God, the first principle of Platonism, is not totally inexpressible as Moderatus had claimed, and as Plotinus and many others will insist later, but only nearly so (*Did.* 164.8). Rather like the elements of the *Theaetetus*, God can be named but not described, and among his names we find not only 'Good(ness)', 'Proportion', 'Truth', and 'Divinity', but also: οὐσιότης, Beingness (164.33–4).

All in all, around this period a significant group of Platonists maintain that the *Republic* should be interpreted in such a way that, if the Good is beyond and explanatory of the being of the Forms, it must itself be Being.[38] And this is hardly surprising if we recall that long ago Aristotle had said that much the hardest and most puzzling problem for first philosophy was whether or not unity and being (τὸ ἕν καὶ τὸ ὄν) are the

---

Anonymous Commentator as well, though it was he who spelled out the parallels between him and Victorinus, which include the primacy of Being. An alternative to a predecessor of Plotinus is a conservative contemporary, reluctant to deny being to the First God of Platonism. One such, according to a suggestive paper by Paul Kalligas (2001: 594–5), was Longinus, who may even have followed Numenius in appealing to Moses and ὁ ὤν. S. Pinès (Pinès 1971) adduces three Arabic texts which cannot derive from Plotinus because they state or imply that the first principle is itself Being.

[36] Anon. *In Plat. Parm.* (in Linguiti 1995) XII.23–35; cf. IV.8–9, 27, V.4–5, X.16–25. Linguiti himself ends his thorough review of previous scholarship by proposing a fourth-century date (p. 91).

[37] Discussion in David Sedley's contribution to this volume ['Stoic Metaphysics at Rome', Sedley 2005].

[38] Cf. also Proclus, *In Rep.* I.281.11–12, citing unnamed persons who ask why the Good cannot be both οὐσία and ὑπερούσιον.

very substance of the things that are (οὐσία τῶν ὄντων), as 'the Pythagoreans and Plato maintain'(*Met.* B.1, 996a4–7). The ground he reports for this claim is that unity and being are the highest genera, predicated of everything whatsoever, hence principles of everything whatsoever (B.3, 998b17–21; cf. Z.16, 1040b16–19). Half a millennium later, we find Origen (third century AD) confessing that the issue of whether the highest principle of Platonism is Being or not remains hard to decide (δυσθεώρητος).[39]

I do not myself undertake to defend Numenius' and others' interpretation of 'beyond being'. But I do defend the *question*, 'Is the Good also Being itself as well as Unity itself? If not, why not?', as a question that any thoughtful Plato scholar should consider today. What I find so admirable in Numenius and later Platonists is the way they can force us to notice aspects and problems in Plato that we moderns have long lost sight of. We have lost sight of them because we no longer approach Plato's writings in the way they did, as repositories of sacred truth. When faced with the phrase 'beyond being' in *Republic* VI, modern scholars tend to respond like Glaucon does. He says Ἄπολλον, δαιμονίας ὑπερβολῆς (509c1–2), which is Greek for 'Wow!' Like him, they do not feel impelled to ask what 'beyond being' actually means. Geoffrey Lloyd cites the phrase as a paradigm Greek paradox to compare with the Nuer belief that 'twins are birds' and mysterious Pythagorean injunctions such as 'Abstain from beans,' 'Do not stir the fire with a knife.'[40] How many modern scholars have bothered to confront the phrase 'beyond being' with later passages of the *Republic* which describe the Good as 'the brightest part of being' (518c9: τοῦ ὄντος τὸ φανότατον), 'the most blessed part of being' (526e3–4: τὸ εὐδαιμονέστατον τοῦ ὄντος), and 'the best among beings' (532c5–6: τοῦ ἀρίστου ἐν τοῖς οὖσι)?[41]

IV

On the Good came out in at least six Books. Since Aristotle and the early Academy, Περὶ τἀγαθοῦ had been a standard title for discussing the fundamentals of Platonism – *die Prinzipienlehre* as our German colleagues put it. In Book 1 Numenius raised the question 'What is being?' (frags. 2, 23; 3, 1; 4a, 7–9: τί ἐστι τὸ ὄν), already equating this with the good (frag. 2, 5: τἀγαθόν). He argued in familiar Platonic style that what is,

---

[39] *Contra Celsum* VI.64.14–28.   [40] Lloyd 1990, 16–17.
[41] An admirable exception is Baltes 1997, reprinted in Baltes 1999: 351–71.

properly so called, cannot be matter or anything bodily such as earth, air, fire or water, nor even all these elements taken together, because all such things are subject to change (frag. 3). Consequently, only the incorporeal can qualify as being (frag. 4a, 25–32). Alongside these philosophical arguments he ranged the testimony of peoples of good repute who agree that God is incorporeal (cf. frag 1a, quoted above).[42] No details of Numenius' ethnographical survey have come down to us, but I surmise that Moses and the Jews will have stood out because they alone got so far in tracking the truth as to *identify* God with being. The others will have earned praise for expressing allegorically in their myths and ceremonies the less abstract doctrine proved in frag. 4a, that material things must be held together and governed by some changeless incorporeal entity.

On now to Book II, where Numenius introduced his positive philosophical account of being. As a Platonist, he naturally turned to the *Timaeus*, where Plato himself raises the question 'What is being?', presupposing (on the strength of other dialogues containing arguments like those Numenius rehearsed in Book I) that this means: 'What is it that always *is* and never comes to be?' (27d6: τί τὸ ὂν ἀεί, γένεσιν δὲ οὐκ ἔχον). Numenius' interpretation of Plato's answer to this question exploits not only the *Timaeus*' initial dichotomy between being and becoming at 27d–28a, but also its subsequent elaboration in terms of the contrast between eternity and time at 37d–38b. Here is how he summons his readers to the task:

> 'Come then, let us mount up as close as our power permits to what is (τὸ ὄν), and let us say this:- What is never was, nor will it ever come to be. Rather, it always *is*, || in a definite time, the present only (ἔστιν ἀεὶ ἐν χρόνῳ ὁρισμένῳ, τῷ ἐνεστῶτι μόνον). If anyone wants to call this present 'eternity' (αἰών), I join them in that wish. But time past, now that it has fled away, we should think to have fled away and escaped into not being any longer, while time future as yet is not, but professes that it will be able to have made its way into being. It is not therefore reasonable to suppose what is, at least in one sense of the phrase (ἑνί γε τρόπῳ),[43] either not to be, or to be no longer, or not yet to be. For when it is put that way, the statement contains a single mega-impossibility, that the same thing both is and is not, all at once.'

---

[42] Where note the legal overtones of σημηνάμενον, μαρτυρίαις, ἐπικαλέσασθαι, προσφερόμενον.

[43] An acknowledgement, and dismissal, of the ordinary language usage of the verb 'to be' in connection with changeable material things, e.g. 'There is a fire burning in the hearth which is hot and yellowish-red.'

– 'In that case, any other thing could hardly be, seeing that what is itself is not, in respect of its very being (τοῦ ὄντος αὐτοῦ μὴ ὄντος κατὰ αὐτὸ τὸ ὄν).'[44]

– 'So what is is eternal (ἀΐδιόν) and is stable always in its character and identity (κατὰ ταὐτὸν καὶ ταὐτόν).' (Frag. 5, 1–20)

The special mark of being is that it can only be expressed in the present tense, and must always be expressed in the present tense. A thing that *is*, in the sense that it enjoys true being, has no past or future; nothing can be said of it in the past or future tense. You cannot even say, as Melissus did (frag. 2), that it always was and always will be, for that would imply its enduring through the whole of ordinary time in the same way as a flower lasts through a small part of ordinary time and an Oxford college through a somewhat larger part of ordinary time. Epicurus' atoms and Aristotle's God do last in that way for all time, but being as Plato understands it is eternal in a different sense. It does not *last through* time at all.

The question is, What does that mean? It is a question that stirs fond memories of the London lecture hall where I first heard Sorabji air his controversial answer, subsequently written up in *Time, Creation and the Continuum*.[45] He holds that a being, in the sense relevant to eternity, does not last through time because true being, according to Plato, simply has no temporal dimension. It not only has no past or future, it has no present either. Eternity, on Sorabji's view, is just *timelessness*, the absence of all aspects of temporality. Consequently, the 'is' of Plato's true being is the tenseless 'is' that many philosophers find in mathematical statements like '2 + 2 = 4' or in trivial tautologies like 'Justice is justice', 'A bachelor is an unmarried man'. According to Numenius, on the other hand, the 'is' of Platonic being is still tensed: it is *present* tense.[46] The reason why a Platonic being does not last through time is that eternity is present time which stays fixed and never becomes past. A Platonic being always *is*, in a definite time, the present only.

---

[44] The first quotation in this paper to bring on an interlocutor. In frag. 14, 16 he is addressed ὦ ξένε, but in truth there are few signs of the dialogue form as we find it in Plato, or even Cicero. Frede, 'Numenius', 1050, points out that *On the Good* fits better into a genre which became popular in later antiquity, that of exposition enlivened by the occasional question and answer, such as Maximus *On Matter*, quoted *in extenso* at Euseb. *PE* VII 21–64. We can be reassured by this parallel that the interlocutor's role is not a casualty of Eusebius' transcription of Numenius, but was as intermittent in the original as in the surviving fragments.

[45] Sorabji 1983, chs. 8–9, where he gives his own translation and interpretation of the texts of Plato, Plotinus, and Boethius discussed below.

[46] The Greek χρόνος was used for 'tense' as well as 'time'.

This is an extraordinarily difficult idea to grasp. It is very hard to see how 'always in the present' is not a contradiction in terms or, as Hobbes would have it, unintelligible nonsense:

> [T]hey will teach us, that Eternity is the Standing still of the Present, a *Nunc-stans* (as the Schools call it;) which neither they, nor anyone else understand, no more than they would a *Hic-stans* for an Infinite greatnesse of Place. (*Leviathan*, chap. 46)

Yet however difficult, the idea of an eternal present is a vital ingredient in the long history of responses to *Exodus* 3:14. When Aquinas came to discuss the divine names, the present tense of the verb 'to be' was one of several reasons he gave why the *Qui est* of God's answer to Moses is the most appropriate of all names for the deity. 'Est' signifies 'esse in praesenti', which is maximally appropriate to a being whose *esse* knows neither past nor future (*ST* Ia qu. 13, art. 11).

Aquinas cites Augustine for this conception of eternity,[47] which points us back towards the Platonic tradition. I believe that the entire tradition, from the *Timaeus* onwards, understands eternity as present being with no past or future, not as mere timelessness. But let me start with Parmenides, for both parties to the debate agree that the history of eternity begins with Parmenides frag. 8, 5–6: 'It never was nor will be, since it now is, all together, one, continuous'.

Many students of Presocratic philosophy have taken Parmenides to be speaking of what is as something with a present but no past or future. Given this interpretation, some find themselves puzzled, others ready to embrace the idea with enthusiasm. I count Plotinus among the enthusiasts, since his treatise 'On Eternity and Time' is full of Eleatic echoes, including 'all together as one' (III.7 [45] 3, 12), as in a point (3, 18),[48] 'unextended' (2, 33; 3, 15; 6, 46–7; 11, 54; 13, 44 and 63), 'always all present' (3, 17), 'partless' (3, 18; 6, 48–50), 'unshakeable' (5.21; 11, 3), 'whole' (4, 33–4; 5, 4; 11, 54–6), 'full' and 'not lacking' (6, 36). But Sorabji rejects the interpretation outright, for both Parmenides and Plotinus. Parmenides may seem to speak of a detached present without a past ‖ preceding it or a future to follow, but a more charitable interpretation is to see him as 'groping for the concept of timelessness'.[49] And what Parmenides groped for, Plotinus will grasp.

---

[47] See *Conf.* XI.13 (*semper praesentis aeternitatis*), *Trin.* V.2.
[48] Sorabji 1983: 118 rightly observes that this need not mean it *is* a point or instant.
[49] Sorabji 1983: 120–1; cf. 50–1, 99, 128. An important Whiggish influence here, I take it, is G. E. L. Owen's brilliant paper, Owen 1966, also from his *Logic, Science and Dialectic* (London 1986), ch. 2.

Sorabji's argument for his reading of Parmenides is purely philosophical, not textual. All he says is that the idea of something 'always in the present' is incoherent. 'How are we to understand *endurance* without a past or future?' Indeed, 'the enduring present ... appears so baffling that argument would be needed to establish not its incoherence, but its coherence'.[50] He then proceeds to survey a large number of later accounts of eternity, beginning with Plato's *Timaeus* and going on to Plotinus and subsequent Platonists. But however suggestive of a detached present their language may be, he declines to admit that any of them could believe that the 'is' of eternity is genuinely present tense.

Numenius is absent from the survey, for the good reason that in those days neither of us was aware of his contribution to our debate. It is an important contribution because he comes relatively early in the Platonic tradition. His clear testimony, and his well-known influence on Plotinus, make it a live possibility that later Platonists will have shared his understanding of eternity. In some cases at least, that suggestive language is to be taken at face value. The most celebrated example is Boethius' definition of eternity as 'the complete possession all at once of an infinite life' (*interminabilis vitae tota simul et perfecta possessio*), a definition he immediately relates to Plato:

> Some people who hear that Plato held that this universe had no beginning in time and will have no end wrongly think that in this way the created world is coeternal with its creator. It is one thing to be extended through an infinite life, which is what Plato ascribed to the world, quite another to encompass all at once the whole presence (*totam pariter ... praesentiam*) of an infinite life, which is manifestly a property peculiar (*proprium*) to the divine mind. (*Cons. Phil.* v.5)

Mere timelessness is hardly the prerogative of God.[51]

This is not the place to reopen the passage-by-passage debate on Platonist texts we used to enjoy. Having put a question-mark against the lot, I propose to concentrate here on the crucial sentences of the *Timaeus* from which Numenius begins. That will fortify me to broach the underlying issue in this disagreement, namely: How far is it legitimate to allow ourselves, when interpreting philosophical texts from traditions || other than our own (be they past or contemporary), to be guided by what 'we' can make sense of?

---

[50] Sorabji 1983: 100, criticising unpublished early work of mine on Parmenides.
[51] Sorabji 1983 ch. 8 considers whether timelessness is plausibly attributed to universals, numbers, or truth.

V

If eternity was mere timelessness, as Sorabji holds, the creation of time would require the creation of the present as well as the creation of past and future. But that is not what we find in *Timaeus* 37e–38a:

> There were no days and nights, months and years, before the Heaven came into being, but he planned that they should now come into being at the same time that the Heaven was framed. All these are parts of time, and 'was' and 'will be' are forms of time that have come to be; we are wrong to transfer them unthinkingly to eternal being. For we say that it was and is and will be, but 'is' alone really belongs to it and describes it truly; 'was' and 'will be' are properly used of the becoming that proceeds in time, for they are changes (κινήσεις γάρ ἐστον), whereas that which is always changelessly in the same state cannot become older or younger by the lapse of time – it neither became so ever, nor has it become so now, nor will it be so hereafter. (Tr. after Cornford and Zeyl)[52]

Only 'was' and 'will be' have come to be (37e4). Only they are changes (note the dual ἐστόν at 38a2) – as Plutarch put it (*De E* 393a), 'They are displacements and deviations of a nature unfitted for constant being'.[53] Unlike 'was' and 'will be', the present tense 'is' is not said to have come to be and is not characterised as change (κίνησις). It should be perfectly clear that the 'is' which really belongs to the realm of true being is the very same 'is' as occurs in the mistaken pronouncement 'It was and is and will be' (37e6). It is also the same 'is' as occurs in a list of supposedly 'inaccurate' statements with which Timaeus rounds off the paragraph: 'What came to be *is* a thing which came to be,' 'What comes to be *is* a thing which comes to be,' and again 'What will come to be *is* a thing which will come to be,' || plus 'What is not *is* something that is not.' Timaeus defers for a more

---

[52] The discussion of this text in Sorabji (1983: 109) concentrates on the word 'always' at 38a3, a topic I shall come to later. For as Sorabji tells the story of eternity, Plato's use of this and other terms implying duration set a problem for Plotinus and his successors when they grapple with the *Timaeus*.

[53] ἐγκλίσεις τινές εἰσι ... καὶ παραλλάξεις τοῦ μένειν ἐν τῷ εἶναι μὴ πεφυκότος. The phrase κινήσεις γάρ ἐστον is usually translated 'for they are motions'. That would be correct for days and nights; as parts (μέρη) of time, they are units measured by the Sun's motion around the Earth. But 'was' and 'will be' are contrasted with such parts and called forms or types (εἴδη) of time. *Tht.* 181cd distinguishes local motion (φορά) and alteration (ἀλλοίωσις) as two forms or types (εἴδη) of κίνησις, where 'alteration' covers growing older as well as change of quality. Given the focus in 38a3–5 on becoming older or younger (first brought out properly, to my knowledge, by Owen (1966: 39), and now reflected in Zeyl's translation), it seems best to take our cue from Plutarch and read κινήσεις γάρ ἐστον in terms of the *Theaetetus*' generic notion of change (Plot. III.7 [45] 3. 35 writes μεταβάλλειν εἰς τὸ ἔσται). A close association between being in time and becoming older and younger can be observed at *Parm.* 141ad, 151e ff.

suitable occasion the task of picking over these sentences to expose their faultiness, but at least in the first three it seems clear that his analysis would turn on the point that 'is' is *present* tense[54] – exactly the point which Numenius insists upon.

Once again, the admirable Platonist Numenius can force our jaded modern eyes to notice a feature of Plato's text – only past and future are created – which has not been sufficiently emphasised in modern attempts to understand Plato's doctrine of eternity. It is true that Plato does not echo Parmenides' emphatic 'now', still less does he anticipate the later Platonist distinction between the 'now' of eternity and the 'now' of ordinary time (Boethius' *nunc stans* and *nunc fluens*). But throughout the passage he is plainly thinking in terms of the present tense use of 'is', not of some detensed alternative. All honour to Numenius for confronting us with a particularly forthright statement of the idea that eternity is genuinely *present* being. Let that serve as prelude to his equally interesting account of *being*.

VI

For all these remarks about eternal being, Numenius tells us at the start of frag. 6, have been by way of introduction. Frag. 5 on eternity led immediately to the great revelation:

> '... I will not make any more pretences, nor claim not to know the name of the incorporeal. Perhaps this is the point at which it is more agreeable to say it than not to say it. So then – I say that its name is the very thing we have long been inquiring into (λέγω τὸ ὄνομα αὐτῷ εἶναι τοῦτο τὸ πάλαι ζητούμενον). Let no-one laugh if I say that the name of the incorporeal is 'substance and being' (οὐσίαν καὶ ὄν).
>
> The reason why 'being' (ὄν) is its name is that it has not come to be and will not perish, nor can it undergo either any other change or any better or worse development. Rather, it is simple and unalterable and constant in its form, neither voluntarily departing from its sameness nor being forced to do so by anything else. Then again[55] Plato said in the *Cratylus* that names themselves are applicable to things by virtue of their likeness to them. So let it be granted and decided thus: the incorporeal is that which is.[56] ||

---

[54] If the second example seems innocuous, because τὸ γιγνόμενον is present tense like ἐστί, turn to *Parm.* 153c7–e3 and *Soph.* 245d1–4 (cf. Ar. *Top.* IV.5, 128b6–9): only at the end of the process does τὸ γιγνόμενον come to be ὄν and ὅλον.

[55] This use of δὲ καί (Denniston 1934: 305) adds a further reason for the name; a reason based on the nature of the name supplements a reason based on the nature of its nominatum.

[56] So E. H. Gifford 1903 translates εἶναι τὸ ὄν ἀσώματον. Des Places 1973 has it the other way round: 'l'être est incorporel', which he admits is not the conclusion we have been led to expect. He cites the

Appropriately for a climactic moment, this passage is dense with allusions to other texts. It will take time to spell them out in detail. I shall proceed in chronological order.

First, the Book of *Exodus*. There is no parallel in Plato or any other Greek philosopher I know for such a revelation of the divine name, let alone for the revelation to consist of so common or garden a name as 'being'. Given that Numenius' First God has already been called ὁ ὤν,[57] and given that the *Exodus* narrative has already been used to show the Jews agreeing with Plato, I trust that readers will find it overwhelmingly likely that Numenius' own revelation scene in frag. 6 was meant to recall Moses' encounter with the burning bush.

Second, Plato. At first sight, he may seem to yield precedence to Moses here, with only a supplementary argument from the *Cratylus* expressly attributed to him. But a work *On the Good* can hardly neglect the famous simile of the Sun in Plato's *Republic*. The link is the words 'Let no-one laugh', which take us back to Glaucon's reaction on being told that the Good is 'beyond being, surpassing it in dignity and power'. Socrates reports, 'And Glaucon said μάλα γελοίως, "Apollo, what daemonic excess"' (509c1–2). Translators divide over μάλα γελοίως. Is Socrates laughing at Glaucon ('Glaucon very ludicrously said')[58] or the other way round ('with much amusement Glaucon said')?[59] The Greek could mean either, but the second alternative is a better match for 506d, where Socrates feared that if he tried to say what the Good is, even at the level of his earlier account of the virtues, he would disgrace himself and incur laughter. He plays safe by

---

same formula in the first sentence of frag. 7, which followed closely after frag. 6, but this reports what the speaker has just said and so is not independent evidence for what he meant to say in frag. 6. The solution is to read Plato as closely as Numenius did, for there one can find definitions stated in this form, with the definiendum lacking an article and seemingly in predicate position: e.g. *Rep.* 332b9–c2 with d7–8, 335c1–5 with 336a9–10. Des Places gets it right at frag. 19, 12–13: τὸ ἀγαθὸν ὅτι ἐστὶν ἕν.

[57] More than once, it would seem from the resumptive γε in ὃ γε ὤν. The πάλιν in frag. 13, 1 introduces a *second* proportion to explain the relation between the First God and the Demiurge. This disposes of the confident assertion of M. J. Edwards (Edwards 1989), that it is 'sufficiently plain' that Numenius had done nothing earlier in *On the Good* to prepare his readers for the unusual nomenclature ὁ ὤν. Edwards therefore goes back to Gifford's construal: ὤν as copula with σπέρμα its predicate. In reply to the usual objection that a sower cannot sow himself, he cites texts on the consubstantiality of parent and offspring. But then, in a construction he admits to be difficult, to secure an object for the verb σπείρει he detaches χρήματα σύμπαντα (understood as a periphrasis for the soul mixture of the *Timaeus*) from εἰς τὰ μεταλαγχάνοντα αὐτοῦ. The complications soon multiply *praeter necessitatem*.

[58] So Shorey, in line with Proclus (*In Rep.* 1.274.5, 286.1), Jowett, Adam, Lindsay, Bloom. Lee has 'to the general amusement'.

[59] So, in effect, both Grube and Reeve. *Rep.* 398c7 shows that it is not out of character for Glaucon to laugh at what Socrates says.

offering a likeness of the Good instead of a || definition – and still incurs laughter. Numenius' speaker has even more reason to fear being laughed at when, like Moses, he announces that the name of the incorporeal is just 'being'. All that palaver building up to the revelation of the divine name, and then, when the revelation arrives, as in *Exodus* it is more of a puzzle than the question it answers. The name of the incorporeal, the name that is to say of God, is ὄν. But surely we have all along been arguing that only the incorporeal is ὄν. Are we not now being told the utterly trivial truth that τὸ ὄν is named ὄν? Besides, as the most unspecific word in the language ὄν would seem to be the least revelatory name you could come up with.

This is the point at which to note a third allusion threaded into frag. 6. For anyone familiar with Aristotle's *Metaphysics* the phrase τοῦτο τὸ πάλαι ζητούμενον should leap off the page as a semi-quotation from Z.1, 1028b2–4,[60] where Aristotle states that the question everyone has been asking and puzzling over since philosophy began, the question τί τὸ ὄν; ('What is that which is?') is the question τίς ἡ οὐσία; ('What is substance?'). The allusion explains why the word οὐσία ('substance') suddenly appears alongside ὄν in frag. 6, 7. Already in Book 1 Numenius was asking τί τὸ ὄν and treating it precisely as an old, old question on which ancient peoples agreed with Plato. He does not need Aristotle's support for going back to the distant past. His reuse of Aristotle's phrase τὸ πάλαι ζητούμενον is more likely to point a way forward from the seemingly laughable conclusion that the name of the incorporeal is the very name we have been puzzling over all along, τὸ ὄν. Numenius, I suggest, follows Aristotle in thinking that the question τί τὸ ὄν; can usefully be recast as the question τίς ἡ οὐσία; Let me explain why this would be a helpful way forward.

In a much-cited passage of his classic study *L'Être et L'Essence*,[61] Étienne Gilson claimed Z.1, 1028b2–4 as proof that Aristotle made no distinction between essence and existence. To this interpretation there are two important objections.

The first objection is to Gilson's understanding of οὐσία in this text as essence rather than substance. Aristotle's view is that the Presocratics did not have, save for a few fumbles, the concept of essence,[62] so they could not possibly have been asking 'What is essence?'. When read in its entirety, *Metaphysics* Z.1 shows that the question Aristotle conceives himself to share with the older philosophers is the question, 'What are the

---

[60] So too Frede (Frede 1987: 1051), but no sign of recognition from des Places.
[61] Gilson 1948: 59. [62] *Ph.* II.2, 194a18–21; *Met.* A.6, 987b3–4; M.4, 1078b17–29.

fundamental underived constituents of the universe? What are the things that exist and are what they are independently and in their own right, such || that everything else owes its being to them?' To *that* question Numenius as a Platonist quite naturally replies that what exists and is what it is independently and in its own right is: Being with a capital B, Being itself, the αὐτοόν of frag. 17.

Like Aristotle's *Metaphysics*, *On the Good* is written as an arduous journey which starts from the principles needed to explain the sensible world and ascends to a divine first principle very different from the gods of popular religion, different even from the Divine Craftsman of the *Timaeus* (frag. 12, 7–14). It is easy to see how the question 'What is it that everything else owes its being to?' would fit the context of God's speaking from the burning bush in *Exodus* 3:14. The God of the Old Testament is precisely that to which everything else owes its being. But a Platonist can understand this in two ways, one as efficient causation by a Divine Craftsman, the other as imitative participation in Being itself, whether directly or by way of less exalted Forms which themselves derive from Being. Numenius could well have been encouraged to take 'I am that I am' in this second way by the fact that Aristotle speaks of 'What is the primary, fundamental being?' as the old, old question which everyone has been grappling with since philosophy began. Numenius would not be the first to count Moses the discoverer of philosophy itself.[63]

The second objection to Gilson is that Aristotle does not mean that there is no difference at all between his two questions τί τὸ ὄν; and τίς ἡ οὐσία; On the contrary, precisely because οὐσία signifies that which is in the primary way, that which explains the being of everything else, if we can answer the second question we will have the key to answering the first. There is a difference between the two questions because the highest level of being, whatever it may be, is the one that explains the rest. And it seems to me that, as against Sorabji on Plato on eternity, so against Gilson on Aristotle Numenius has it right.

Finally, Plato's *Cratylus*. The speaker has already explained (frag. 6, 7–12) why the name ὄν is appropriate to the incorporeal, viz. because the incorporeal, and only the incorporeal, is immune to change. This explanation of the name, based on the nature of its nominatum, is a straightforward corollary of the thesis argued at length in Book 1 that nothing corporeal can be ὄν, because all bodily things are subject to change. We now expect a supplementary explanation based on the nature

---

[63] See n. 10 above on Artapanus.

of the name ὄν itself,[64] which should display some likeness to its incorporeal nominatum. But our expectation is frustrated. Numenius moves at once to trumpet his conclusion ('So let it be granted and decided thus: the incorporeal is that which is') without stopping to specify any resemblance || between name and bearer.[65] He is as much of a tease as the God of *Exodus* 3:14.

Since we are left to speculate on our own, I suggest we recall the etymology of ὄνομα ('name') as 'search for a being' at *Cratylus* 421ab: τοῦτ' ἔστιν ὄν, οὗ τυγχάνει ζήτημα ὄν, τὸ ὄνομα. I cannot help thinking that Numenius' strangely worded sentence λέγω τὸ ὄνομα αὐτῷ εἶναι τοῦτο τὸ πάλαι ζητούμενον (frag. 6, 5–6: 'I say that its name is the very thing we have long been searching for') is a transposition of this etymology into a context where it can be fused with Aristotle's τὸ πάλαι ζητούμενον to suggest that the name of the incorporeal signifies *the* object of search, the being which, once found, will explain everything else. Its name is Name itself, from which all ordinary names derive as all beings derive from Being itself.[66]

VII

But enough of speculation. The ancient obsession with etymology does not appeal to modern philosophers trained in the analytic tradition. But please put up with it a little longer, for etymology can provide a useful focus on the debate I began from.

Here is Plotinus on the etymology of αἰών, 'eternity':

> When we use the expressions 'always' (τὸ ἀεί) and 'not a thing which at one time is and at another is not' (τὸ οὐ ποτὲ μὲν ὄν, ποτὲ δὲ μὴ ὄν), it is *for our own sake* (ἡμῶν ἕνεκα)[67] that we put it that way. No doubt 'always' is not used in its proper (κυρίως) sense. When applied to the incorruptible it might mislead the soul into imagining an extension of something becoming more, something indeed which is never going to fail. It would have been better perhaps just to say 'being' (ὄν). But even though 'what is' (τὸ ὄν) is a satisfactory name for being (οὐσία), since people tended to think that becoming is in fact [or: is also] being (οὐσία), to grasp <the difference>

---

[64] Cf. n. 55 above.
[65] Des Places 1973 *ad loc.* seems oblivious to the difficulty, merely referring us to *Crat.* 430a10 for a general statement of the likeness theory of names.
[66] Another route to the same conclusion would be a different etymology: ὄνομα = ὄν + ὁμοιώσει.
[67] In their *editio maior* (Henry and Schwyzer 1951) Henry-Schwyzer put a comma between ἡμῶν and ἕνεκα to join ἕνεκα with τῆς σαφηνείας. Their *editio minor* (Henry and Schwyzer 1964) accepts, as does Armstrong 1967, Dodds' proposal to excise τῆς σαφηνείας as a gloss on ἡμῶν ἕνεκα.

they needed the addition of 'always'. For it is not the case that being (ὄν) is one thing and *always* being another, any more than a philosopher is one thing and the true philosopher another. It is because there is such a thing as putting on a pretence of philosophy that 'true' got added. Just so, 'always' (ἀεί) was added to 'being' (τῷ ὄντι), i.e. to ὄν, so that the word αἰών ['eternity'] means 'always being'. For this reason, the 'always' should be taken to mean 'truly' being (ἀληθῶς ὄν), and it should be contracted into an extensionless power which in no || way needs anything besides what it already has. Rather, it has everything there is (ἔχει τὸ πᾶν). (III.7 [45] 6, 22–36; tr. after Armstrong)

The etymology αἰών = ἀεί + ὄν may come from Aristotle (*DC* 1.9, 279a22–8), but Plotinus gives it a pedagogical twist towards Platonism. 'Always' is said from the point of view of ordinary people immersed in the sensible world of becoming, to guide them to a higher perspective. Sorabji takes a different view of this 'crucial passage'. Its purpose is to introduce a novel, non-temporal sense of 'always' in which the word 'merely has the function of denoting *true* being as opposed to coming to be'.[68] This makes it sound as if Plotinus bids us disregard the usual meaning of 'always' and substitute a quite different, unrelated sense, which only the philosophically enlightened will understand. For anyone else – for anyone, that is, unacquainted with the Platonist concept of true being – the etymology of 'eternity' will be more of a hindrance than a help.

In ancient theories of language the 'proper' (κυρίως) sense of a word may contrast with a variety of 'improper' extended, figurative, or catachrestic uses, not all of which would call for a separate entry in the dictionary. For example, when Homer speaks of the 'ten thousand noble deeds' accomplished by Odysseus (*Il.* 2.272), that grand hyperbole counts for Aristotle (*Poet.* 1457b11–13) as 'metaphor' (μεταφορά), i.e. as an 'improper' (οὐ κυρίως) meaning of the number word. The example is pertinent because Plotinus clearly wants people to keep in mind some part, but not all, of the ordinary meaning of 'always', otherwise he would not warn them against extrapolating to an infinite extension. (We would not ask Odysseus to tell us about deed no. 9,997.) The helpful force of the etymology αἰών = ἀεί + ὄν is negative: an eternal thing is *not* a thing whose being has a beginning and end in time – hence Plotinus' addition of the phrase 'not a thing which at one time is and at another is not' (τὸ οὐ ποτὲ μὲν ὄν, ποτὲ δὲ μὴ ὄν). What we must resist is the temptation to infer (with Aristotle) the positive conclusion that an eternal thing *endures forever*

---

[68] His phrase (Sorabji 1983: 112) where in translating the passage he renders ἡμῶν ἕνεκα 'as a concession to ourselves'.

throughout an infinity of time. Only so will the etymology of 'eternity' help us transcend the temporal order to renew contact with the extensionless present of true being.

We live, Plotinus goes on to say (7, 1–6), in both time and eternity. We have a share of both. This calls attention to the 'we' who read and respond to his treatise. Is it the 'we' who grew up Here in the sensible world of time or the 'we' who most truly belong There in the realm of eternity? Plotinus answers 'Both'. He is writing for those who attempt the ‖ journey of thought from Here to There. The phrase 'always in the present' joins the view from Here with the view from There to express, not a contradiction in terms, but the termini of an arduous transition from one all-encompassing perspective to another. Remember Boethius' comparison: God sees the whole of history in his eternal present as a traveller on a high mountain sees things far and near all at once, in a single temporal present (*Cons. Phil.* v.6). A more mundane comparison would be with a novelist's synoptic grasp of all the events and life-histories in their story. Such analogies offer a many-one mapping from the infinitely numerous successive times of ordinary experience to the unitary present of the divine (authorial) perspective. As *homo viator* 'we' are on the way to that height. 'Always in the present' is meant to help us upwards, not to fix in a formula the perspective we are struggling to achieve. Sorabji's disambiguation would frustrate Plotinus' pedagogic aim. To repeat, 'It is *for our own sake* that we put it that way'.

Let me concede that Plotinus' more scholastic successors do make formulaic use of two senses of 'always'.[69] But this concession offers less than Sorabji wants, because when they speak of the 'always' of ordinary time and contrast it with a non-temporal (ἄχρονος) 'always' belonging to eternity, the question arises whether the second term of this contrast is the bare contradictory of the first, as Sorabji holds, or the richer notion of an eternal present. For any follower of Plato, time is a likeness (εἰκών) of eternity, its moving image (*Tim.* 37d). Time's model is non-temporal in the sense that it is other than time,[70] but it can hardly be a mere absence or negation of time. Without a strong positive notion of eternity Platonic metaphysics would collapse.

---

[69] See Procl. *In Tim.* 1.239.2–6 and other passages cited by Sorabji (Sorabji 1983) – where, however, note the beautifully fluid treatment of 'always' quoted from the Christian Origen, fellow-student with Plotinus in the school of Ammonius Saccas. It does credit to their teacher.

[70] So already, long before Plotinus, Plut. *De E* 393a: κατὰ τὸν αἰῶνα τὸν ἀκίνητον καὶ ἄχρονον καὶ ἀνέγκλιτον, where the last epithet picks up the description of 'was' and 'will be' as ἐγκλίσεις (n. 53 above) and in the very same sentence God is assigned to a single 'now' for always.

VIII

There is much in Platonism that does not make sense to a mind content with the conceptual framework of ordinary experience. Plato speaks frequently of the bafflement and hostility that philosophy arouses, in intellectuals as well as others. His word for what philosophy – his type of philosophy – is up against is δόξα, inadequately || translated 'opinion', by which he intends the full range of beliefs, assumptions, values, and habits of mind we acquire, largely without realising it, by being brought up to live in the sensible world.[71] The dialogues record many confrontations between Opinion and Philosophy, but the refutation of Opinion is less an end in itself than a means of opening our minds to the possibility of an alternative perspective. That is why the dialogues are full of images as well as arguments. Opinion is so deeply rooted in our soul that it tends to be intransigent, blind to alternatives, resistant to argument. An image like the Ship of State in the *Republic*, or the Charioteer with his two horses in the *Phaedrus*, can liberate us from the familiar chains of Opinion to the realisation that alternative perspectives are available, which provide novel starting points for argument. And the famous similes of Sun, Line and Cave offer the prospect of progressing, gradually, from the temporal perspective of ordinary life in the sensible world towards the godlike perspective which the *Timaeus* identifies with eternity in contrast to time. Such progress, a turning *of the whole soul* from the realm of Becoming to that of Being (*Rep.* 518c), will transform everything: our understanding of the world, our values, the way we live – *and thereby our standards of what makes sense*.

This transformative intent is characteristic of all ancient philosophy,[72] but the other-worldly leanings of Platonism take it to extremes and thereby set a problem for historians of philosophy, especially those like Sorabji and myself whose background in the analytic tradition encourages a critical engagement with the views and arguments of past philosophers.[73] The problem is this. From what standpoint are we to judge the coherence of the

---

[71] Cf. Numenius frag. 52, 53–5: Pythagoras did not hesitate to defend the truth with assertions that go against people's opinion and expectations.

[72] See my 'The Sceptic in his Place and Time' (Burnyeat 1984a, also Burnyeat 1997a) [Chapter 12 in *EAMP* vol. 1].

[73] I do not mean that critical engagement is bound to be hostile. On the contrary, Eleanor Stump and Norman Kretzman (in Stump and Kretzman 1981) give an admirable display of how analytic techniques, sympathetically applied, may be used to rescue the eternal present from over-quick dismissal.

idea of an eternal present? Who are the 'we' who write the history of this long-lived notion? I suspect that Plotinus would hear in Sorabji's objections the voice of a 'we' who insist, with Aristotle, that the temporal framework we grew up with Here – the framework which shaped our language and thought – is the only one there is, hence the only one we can make sense of. From this perspective a present tense without past or future connections is 'a kind of logical torso',[74] a defective || remnant of ordinary time. Which is to say, with Borges, that 'eternity is an image wrought in the substance of time'.[75] But does not that inversion of Plato simply beg the question?[76]

---

[74] Owen 1966: 40.   [75] Borges 1999: 123.
[76] This paper began as a pagan contribution to a memorable inter-faith (Jewish, Christian, Muslim) conference on 'The Great Tautology', organised by myself, Alexander Broadie and George Steiner at Robinson College, Cambridge on Friday 22–Sunday 24 May 1992 to discuss the centuries-long reception of *Exodus* 3:14 by philosophers of the three religions. Subsequent versions benefited from discussions at Cambridge (the Patristic Seminar and the B Club), Cornell, Dublin, London, and Princeton. For advice and help I am most grateful to John Dillon and Michael Frede, for usefully critical comments to Paul Kalligas, Ricardo Salles and David Sedley. I sign off on 1 May 2003, soon after the fall of Baghdad to the US and British invasion, which gravely damaged the prospects for any renewal of such inter-faith philosophical dialogue.

CHAPTER 4

Kinēsis *vs.* energeia: *a much-read passage in (but not of) Aristotle's* Metaphysics

In memoriam Michael Frede

We are to discuss what is now one of the most famous passages in Aristotle: *Metaphysics* Θ.6, 1048b18–35, on the distinction between κίνησις and ἐνέργεια.* The Passage, as I shall capitalise it, has been endlessly analysed by philosophical enthusiasts. It is a particular favourite with those trained in analytic philosophy.[1] But || few of these enthusiasts have attempted to explain how it fits into the overall programme of Θ.[2] Ignoring context is usually a fault. But not here, for the good reason that the Passage does not fit into the

---

* This paper began as a contribution to a seminar on *Metaphysics* Θ held in Cambridge during the Spring Term of 1995. Acknowledgements for critical comments and many other kinds of help are owed to Peter Adamson, Gwenaëlle Aubry, David Charles, Alan Code, Michel Crubellier, Sten Ebbesen, Doug Hutchinson, Stephen Makin, Wolfgang Mann, Terumasa Okhusa, Jan Saif, Anna-Maria Schiaparelli, Bob Sharples. Very special acknowledgements are due to Michael Frede and David Sedley for their continuing support over the long period of gestation and for the important substantive contributions their expertise has made to its eventual outcome. To Francesco Ademollo I owe thanks for help (both philological and administrative) in connection with the manuscript in Florence, plus comments at various stages in the growth of the paper. In addition, I thank audiences in Berlin, Florence, Lille, Munich, Oxford, and Toronto for their sympathetically critical discussions.
[1] In part because of the use made of it in modern discussion by Ryle (1954: 102–3, cited and criticised by Ackrill (1965: 123, 25–6, reprinted as Ackrill 1997: 142–62) and Kenny 1963. Thus Penner: 'It was Ryle who first showed analytical philosophers the gold mine there was in Aristotle' (Penner 1970: 395). On the other side of the Channel, the view can be rather different: 'C'est à lui [the Passage] que je m'attacherai, à cause de sa valeur philosophique considérable, et aussi – l'avouerai-je? – par ce souci sportif de venir en aide aux passages quelque peu laissés-pour-compte, et relégués dans les notes et les subordonnés concessives des ouvrages savants . . .' ['It is this [the Passage] on which I will focus, on account of its considerable philosophical importance, and also – if I may be so bold – in the interests of fair play here, to give a helping hand to paragraphs that have found themselves slightly forlorn, and relegated to the notes and to concessive parentheses in works of scholarship'. . .]. So wrote Brague 1988: 454 (the 'points de suspension' are [the ellipse at the end is] his), twenty-three years after Ackrill's seminal paper on the Passage, 'Aristotle's Distinction between Energeia and Kinesis' (Ackrill 1965). In the sequel Brague cites Ackrill, but none of the articles that poured out in the lively controversy he prompted. I am grateful for Brague's unanalytic discussion, despite numerous textual disagreements signalled below. The anti-analytic discussion of Dufour 2001, by contrast, is a thicket of confusion.
[2] An honourable, even heroic, exception is Kosman 1984.

overall programme of Θ, was not written for Θ, and should not be printed in the place we read it today. So I shall argue.

If I am right, the analysts can legitimately keep analysing the Passage on its own, as an isolated fragment of uncertain origin. I will join in myself. For nothing I say here is meant to impugn the philosophical interest and importance of the Passage, or to deny that it is authentic Aristotle. But I will suggest that its focus is rather different from what it is usually taken to be. I will also argue, controversially, that the Θ.6 distinction is unique in the corpus and should not be imported into other Aristotelian contexts such as *Nicomachean Ethics* x or *De Anima* II.5.

To speak, as I have just done, of 'the overall programme of Θ' is to take a lot for granted. This is not the place to elaborate a detailed interpretation of Θ. Let me simply acknowledge that my thinking about Θ has been much influenced by Michael Frede's 1994 paper on potentiality in *Metaphysics* Θ.[3] So far as I am concerned, that is the starting point for all future discussion of Θ's contribution to the Aristotelian philosophy.[4] ||

Part I: Text

1. To motivate the textual enquiry that follows, I begin with a philosophical complaint. The main business of Θ.6 is to contrive an analogical extension. Θ began by studying the contrast between δύναμις and ἐνέργεια in the sphere of change. But Aristotle made it clear from the outset that for his current project, which is to explain potential and actual *being*, change is not the most useful sphere to consider (Θ.1, 1045b27–1046a4). We begin there in order to arrive somewhere else, where the contrast is between δύναμις as ὕλη and ἐνέργεια as οὐσία. That transition is the task of Θ.6, as Aristotle explains both at the start of the chapter (Θ.6, 1048a25–30) and when the extension has been completed (1048b6–9). I use C to mark cases of change, S for the cases of substantial being that Aristotle wants to reach:

> Since we have discussed the kind of potentiality which is spoken of in connection with change, let us determine what, and what sort of thing, actuality is. In the course of our analysis it will become clear, with regard to the potential, that besides ascribing potentiality to that whose nature it is to change something else or to be changed by something else, either without

---

[3] Frede 2001. In Burnyeat 2001b, especially ch. 6, I do have things to say about the role of Θ in the larger context of the *Metaphysics*.
[4] This sentence was written years before Frede's sudden death at Delphi in August 2007.

qualification or in a certain manner, we also use the term in another sense, which is what we have been after in discussing these previous senses.

Actuality [ἐνέργεια] is the thing being present [ὑπάρχειν], but not in the way we speak of when we say it is potentially present; (S) we say that potentially, for instance, a Hermes is in the block of wood and the half-line in the whole, because it might be separated out, and (C) even someone who is not exercising knowledge [μὴ θεωροῦντα] we call knowledgeable [ἐπιστήμονα] if they are capable of exercising knowledge. The other case [*sc.* when they are exercising it] is <knowledge> in actuality.

Our meaning can be seen by induction from particular cases. We should not seek to capture everything in a definition, but some things we should comprehend [συνορᾶν] by analogy. Thus as (C) that which is building is to that which is capable of building, so is the waking to the sleeping, and that which sees <something>⁵ to a sighted thing with its eyes shut, and (S) that || which has been shaped out of the matter to the matter, and that which has been wrought to the unwrought. Let actuality [ἐνέργεια] be distinguished as one part of this antithesis, the potential [τὸ δυνατόν] as the other. Not everything is said to be in actuality [ἐνέργεια] in the same sense, but only by analogy – as A is in B or to B, so is Γ in Δ or to Δ; for (C) some are related as change [κίνησις] to capacity [δύναμις], while (S) others are related as substance to some matter. (Θ.6, 1048a25–b9)⁶

Notice that in this text building is listed, alongside exercising knowledge, being awake, and seeing, as an example of ἐνέργεια, while all four are classed as κίνησις in relation to δύναμις. In the Passage, by contrast, building is not ἐνέργεια, but κίνησις (1048b29–31), while seeing is not κίνησις, but ἐνέργεια (1048b23, 33–4).

No problem yet. The Passage introduces a new distinction. Some actions (πράξεις) have an external goal, some do not, because the goal is the action itself.

---

⁵ Throughout this paper I am faced with translation difficulties arising from the fact that the morphology of ancient Greek verbs does not distinguish, as English morphology does, between the continuous and the non-continuous present. Since I am translating, I write whichever form strikes me as the most natural way, in the given context, to put Aristotle's verbs into *English*. Consequently, I feel no obligation to follow Ross and other English translators who write 'is seeing' here to match the previous 'is building'. I write 'sees', with the accusative 'something' || inserted to stop 'sees' being equivalent to 'has sight'. The fact is that 'is seeing' is relatively rare in English, for reasons not unconnected with the philosophical content of the Passage. It is in part because Greek morphology lacks an equivalent to our distinction between two forms of the present that Aristotle has a phenomenon to analyse. Read on.

⁶ My translation here borrows freely from Barnes 1984 and Irwin and Fine 1996, but I decline to follow them in translating ἀφωρισμένη (1048b5) as if it referred to the definition Aristotle has just said we should not seek. For reasons given by Burnyeat 1984b: 125–6 I agree with Jaeger's decision to read τῷ with EJ at 1048a37, rather than Aᵇ's accusative, and θάτερον μόριον with Alexander at 1048b5–6 rather than the manuscripts' datives (Jaeger 1957), but I reject Jaeger's supplement <ἡ> (from Alᶜ) at 1048b5.

Building aims at the production of a house, which will last for years to come. Seeing, by contrast, does not aim at a further product. Its goal is internal to itself, to see what is there to be seen.[7] The new distinction divides the previous list of C-type ἐνέργειαι into two groups: those like seeing which are ἐνέργειαι in the new, more tightly defined sense that they aim at nothing beyond themselves, and those like building which aim at a further product. The latter become κινήσεις in a sense of the word more specific than ‖ at 1048b8, where it covered seeing and the exercise of knowledge as well as building.

But now move on to Θ.8, 1050a23–b2:

> And while in some cases the exercise [χρῆσις] is the ultimate thing (e.g. in sight the ultimate thing is seeing, and no further product besides this results from sight), but from some things a product follows (e.g. from the art of building there results a house over and above the act of building), yet none the less in the former type of case the exercise is the end [τέλος], and in the latter more of an end than the potentiality [δύναμις] is. This is because[8] the act of building is in what is being built, and it comes to be, and is, simultaneously with the house.
>
> Where, then, what comes to be is something apart from the exercise, the actuality [ἐνέργεια] is in the object being produced, e.g. the actuality of building is in what is being built and that of weaving in what is being woven, and similarly in other cases, and in general the change [κίνησις] is in what is being changed;[9] but where there is no further product apart from the actuality [ἐνέργεια], the actuality is in the subjects themselves, e.g. the seeing is in the one who sees and the theorizing [θεωρεῖν] in the one who theorizes, and life is in the soul (which is why happiness is too; for it is a certain sort of life). (1050a23–b2, trans. after Ross–Barnes)

This text develops a distinction like that drawn in the Passage between seeing, which is its own end, and building, which aims at a further product, but the distinction is presented as a distinction between two kinds of ἐνέργεια. *Not* as a distinction between ἐνέργεια and κίνησις. In Θ.8 ἐνέργεια contrasts with δύναμις, not with κίνησις.

Similarly, ἐνέργεια contrasted with δύναμις before the Passage, when Θ.1 opened the enquiry by announcing that the first topic to consider would be potentiality and actuality (δύναμις and ἐνέργεια) in the sphere of

---

[7] This should not mean that seeing is not useful to us, or that it cannot be valued as a means as well as an end. That would be inconsistent with e.g. *Met.* A.1, 980a21–6, and *NE* I.6, 1096b16–19 (cf. III.10, 1118a22–3). *Protrepticus* B70 D says: 'One would choose to have sight even if nothing other than sight itself were to result from it.' The means–end relation extends further than the relation of action to product.

[8] The γάρ explains why the house being built is more of an end than the building of it; cf. Ross 1924, *ad loc.*, and the translation of M. Furth (Furth 1985).

[9] 'Change' here includes substantial change.

change (κίνησις), where the relevant potentialities are (first and primarily) the capacity to bring about change (μεταβολή) in another or in oneself *qua* other, and (second and derivatively) the correlative capacity to undergo change by the agency of another or oneself *qua* other (1045b35–1046a13). The corresponding actuality (ἐνέργεια) is the change (μεταβολή or κίνησις)[10] taking place. || (As *Physics* III.1–3 explains, the two potentialities issue in a single actuality, which is active change when viewed from the side of the agent, a passive undergoing when viewed from the side of the patient.) Editors who print the Passage in its usual place owe us an account of why, when he makes his all-important distinction, Aristotle does not alert us to the difference between his present and his previous use of ἐνέργεια. In his previous use ἐνέργεια does not contrast with κίνησις, but includes it. Indeed, Θ.3, 1047a30–2, tells us that, historically, κίνησις is the primary case of ἐνέργεια, the case from which the term ἐνέργεια was extended to cover the actuality of being as well as the actuality of change.

The text quoted from Θ.8 is another challenge for editors to explain. Why, having introduced the distinction between ἐνέργεια and κίνησις, should Aristotle proceed to ignore it? Not only Θ.8, but all the rest of Θ is written without the slightest regard for the terminological innovation which is the main burden of the Passage.

Time for philology.

2. Let me start with three different presentations of the manuscript evidence for the Passage:

(a) Christ (1895)   18 ἐπεί–35 κίνησιν om E Alex.... 28 τούτων–35 κίνησιν linea perducta delenda significat A^b.

(b) Ross (1924)   18 ἐπεί–35 κίνησιν A^b, codd. plerique, Philop., cod. F Alexandri: om EJΓ, codd. ceteri Alexandri ... 28 τούτων–35 κίνησιν expunxit A^b.

(c) Jaeger (1957)   18 ἐπεί–35 κίνησιν A^b et recc. plerique: om. Π Al (add. unus Alexandri cod. F); additamentum ut vid. ab ipso Ar. ortum (cf. 35 λέγω), oratio est admodum dura et obscura et in libris corrupta; verba 35 τὸ μὲν οὖν ... 36 ἔστω recapitulatio sunt, sed eorum quae hoc additamentum praecedunt (!) ... 28 τούτων–35 κίνησιν delenda notat A^b.

The three versions send rather different signals to the reader.

It is well known that the *Metaphysics* is an open tradition, going back to two different ancient editions of the text. It survives in two independent

---

[10] μεταβολή is the word used in Θ.1, but κίνησις takes over from Θ.2, 1046b17.

branches, which in Harlfinger's ground-breaking study are dubbed α and β.[11] Plate 4.1 [between pages 100 and 101] gives the overall picture. You can see, very clearly, the double pattern of transmission. ‖

The primary manuscripts for α are E (tenth century) and J (ninth century); Jaeger's Π denotes their consensus. For β the primary manuscript is A^b, written in the twelfth century, although from Λ.7, 1073a1 to the end a fourteenth-century hand takes over and follows the EJ tradition. The Passage is found in A^b, not in EJ. Should the apparatus criticus start from the absence, as Christ does (J was unknown to him),[12] or, with Ross and Jaeger, from the presence?

I believe it is the *absence* of the Passage from one entire branch that should be underlined. Ross gives a table of the main lacunae (his word) in E, of which the Passage is by far the longest. He estimates that around 750 letters are missing (the precise number depends on how one emends a badly damaged text). The next largest omission is only 61 letters.[13] (The largest lacuna in A^b, which editors say is highly lacunose by comparison with EJ, is 169 letters.)[14] Such an exceptionally large lacuna is hard to explain by mechanical damage or the usual types of scribal error. The Passage appears to be a coherent textual unit, with beginning, middle, and end, so one possibility is a learned excision from the α branch; in due course we will be looking at evidence of an attempted excision in A^b. But a more economical suggestion is that A^b preserves what Jaeger calls an 'additamentum' of considerable length.

Jaeger had a keen nose for detecting additions made by Aristotle himself when revising or updating a treatise. In his OCT of the *Metaphysics* he uses double square brackets to mark (what he judges to be) additions of this nature, additions by Aristotle himself. Since he prints the Passage within double square brackets, we must suppose that by 'additamentum' he means an addition by Aristotle himself, which was subsequently lost or excised from the ‖ EJ tradition.[15] But Jaeger's expression 'additamentum ut vid. ab Ar. ipso ortum' could equally well suggest that the addition

---

[11] Harlfinger 1979 introduces the idea of two different ancient editions (Ausgaben) in his very first paragraph, with acknowledgement to Christ 1895 and Jaeger 1957. The section on 'The Text of the Metaphysics' in Ross 1924, vol. i: clv–clxvi, contains further useful information.

[12] Gercke 1892 was the first announcement of the importance of J, Ross 1924 the first edition to use it for constituting the text. Both Bekker 1831 and Schwegler 1847 side with Christ 1895 in highlighting the absence of the Passage from the α tradition as they knew it from E.

[13] Ross 1924, vol. i: clx.   [14] Ross 1924, vol. i: clix.

[15] See his explanation of the brackets at Jaeger 1957: xviii. Jaeger's hypothesis about the origin of the Passage was anticipated by A. Smeets (Smeets 1952: 56–7).

stems from someone *other* than Aristotle, reproducing words written by Aristotle for some *other* context. That is the line I shall eventually pursue.

For the moment, however, let me stress that 'additamentum' is the *mot juste*, for the reason Jaeger gives when in his apparatus he says of lines 1048b35–6, 'recapitulatio sunt, sed eorum, quae hoc additamentum praecedunt (!)' ['[these words] are a recapitulation, but of those which precede this addition']. Θ.6 began by proposing to determine 'what, and what sort of thing, actuality is' (1048a26–7: τί τέ ἐστιν ἡ ἐνέργεια καὶ ποῖόν τι). It ends, echoing these very words, by saying that the job is now done: 'What, and what sort of thing, "in actuality" is may be taken as explained by these and similar considerations' (1048b35–6: τὸ μὲν οὖν ἐνεργείᾳ τί τέ ἐστι καὶ ποῖον, ἐκ τούτων καὶ τοιούτων δῆλον ἡμῖν ἔστω). The main body of Θ.6 wants to know what it is for something to be *in actuality* (note the dative ἐνεργείᾳ at 1048a35, b6, 10–11, 15), i.e. to be something actually, as contrasted with what it is for something to be *in potentiality* (δυνάμει, 1048a32, b10, 14, 16), i.e. to be something potentially. The Passage is about what it is to be *an actuality* (ἐνέργεια in the nominative), as opposed to a mere change (κίνησις): an entirely different question. As Jaeger remarked, the last sentence of Θ.6 ignores this second question and links back to the topic proposed at the beginning of the chapter; note EJ's dative ἐνεργείᾳ again at 1048b35.[16] What is more, ἐκ τούτων in the last sentence (1048b36) can hardly refer to the Passage immediately preceding, because that is on the second question, not the first.[17] ||

So far, then, I agree with Jaeger that the Passage is an addition which interrupts the main argument of Θ.6. And I am inclined to agree also that the Passage is authentic Aristotle, both in style – Jaeger cites the first-person verb λέγω (1048b35), which is indeed a feature of Aristotle's prose[18] – and in thought. Who else would have such thoughts? More on that later.

Let me also make it clear that I do not take the fact that the Passage interrupts the argument of Θ.6 as a reason for doubting that the addition was made by *Aristotle*. Such awkwardness is fairly common in other places

---

[16] A^b has ἐνεργεῖν here: unsatisfactory, since the verb has not featured in the chapter so far, but it too links better with the opening question than with the narrower question of the Passage.

[17] Christ 1895, Ross 1908 (translation, but not his edition), and Tricot 1964 print the last sentence of Θ.6 as the first of Θ.7. The chapter divisions have no ancient authority, of course (they derive from Bessarion's Latin translation, which did not have the Passage [Bessarion and Argyropoulos 1515], and first appear with a Greek text in Michael Isingrin's 1550 reissue of Erasmus' edition, [Erasmus 1550]), but for that very reason ancient readers would expect ἐκ τούτων to refer to what immediately precedes. The move cures nothing. (References: Ross 1908 ('Ross Tr.¹' translated from Christ's edition'); (2) Ross 1928a ('Ross Tr.²', done from his own edition).

[18] 465 hits in the *TLG*, including one just a couple of pages back at Θ.5, 1048a10–11.

where Jaeger and others find reason to diagnose additions from Aristotle's own hand.[19] My argument for someone else's intervention will come later, on different grounds.

3. Meanwhile, a brief word about the infinite in 1048b9–17. This section is a supplement to what precedes. It applies the main question of the chapter, 'What is it to be in actuality?', to a case that does not fall under either of the headings '(C) as change [κίνησις] to capacity [δύναμις]' or '(S) as substance to some matter'. The infinite has a different way (ἄλλως) of being in potentiality and actuality. It does not have the potentiality to be actual as an infinite magnitude existing on its own (χωριστόν). Rather, it has the potentiality to be actual *for knowledge* (1048b15: γνώσει). This is difficult – difficult both to translate and to interpret.

First, the problem of translation: how much to supply with γνώσει from the preceding clause? Ross Tr.² supplies the minimum: 'It exists potentially only for knowledge.' Barnes restored Ross Tr.¹: 'its separateness is only in knowledge'. (Similarly Furth.) My ‖ paraphrase of the received text, 'it has the potentiality to be actual for knowledge', is motivated by 1048b10–11, which leads us to expect an account covering *both* what it is for the infinite to be in potentiality *and* what is it for it to be in actuality.

But none of these versions is easy to understand. Certainly, we know that, however many divisions are made, more are possible.[20] But how can that knowledge of ours ensure the potential *being* of the infinite? Or its separateness? Or its actuality? The reality of the infinite ought to be prior to knowledge, not posterior. And how to square this text with *Phys.* III.6, 207a25–6 (cf. I.6, 189a12–13; *Post. An.* I.22, 82b–83a1), where Aristotle claims that the infinite *qua* infinite is unknowable? I offer a simple emendation to remove the difficulty.

At *Metaph.* Z.13, 1038b28, there is much to be said for Lord's emendation of γενέσει to γνώσει to bring the text into line with what was said about the priority of substance in Z.1, 1028a32–3.[21] The converse

---

[19] Two cases which I endorse are (i) the hypothesis of Ross and others that *Met.* Z.7–9 began as a separate essay which Aristotle later incorporated into its present context (I discuss the resulting awkwardnesses in Burnyeat 2001b: 29–38), and (ii) the Solmsen–Barnes hypothesis that Aristotle added two sections of syllogistic analysis to the otherwise topic-based treatment of argument in his *Rhetoric* (this too creates awkwardness, which I discuss in Burnyeat 1994: 35–8, [= Chapter 7 in *EAMP* vol. 1]).

[20] Such is the explanation offered by Burnyeat 1984b: 127, and (if I understand him) Ross 1924 *ad loc.* Bonitz 1848 is surprised at the almost frivolous way ('mira levitas') Aristotle tackles the question of how the infinite is in potentiality and actuality.

[21] In their recent edition (Frede and Patzig 1988) M. Frede and G. Patzig print γνώσει and give convincing reasons in their note *ad loc.*

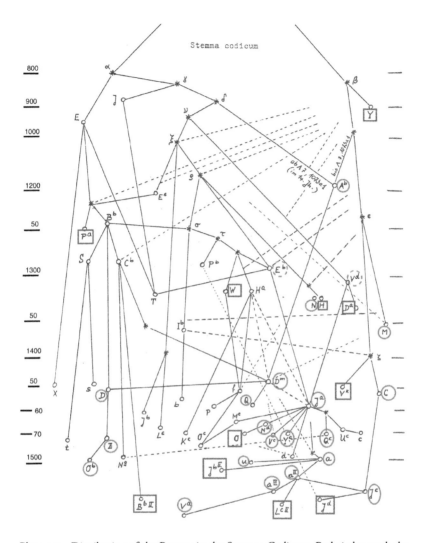

Plate 4.1 Distribution of the Passage in the Stemma Codicum. Red circles mark the presence of the Passage, blue squares the absence of Θ. Stemma Codicum: Dieter Harlfinger, 'Zur Überlieferungsgeschichte der Metaphysik', in P. Aubenque (ed.), *Études sur la Métaphysique d'Aristote*, p. 27. © Librairie philosophique J. Vrin, Paris, 1979. www.vrin.fr.

Plate 4.2 Line of deletion on folio 361ʳ of Ab = Florence Biblioteca Medicea Laurenziana, ms. Plut. 87.12, f. 361r. Reproduced with permission of MiBACT.

emendation here (γνώσει→γενέσει) would bring Θ.6 into line with *Phys.* III.6, 206a21–5, where the infinite is said to be in actuality in the same way as a day or a contest, τῷ ἀεὶ ἄλλο καὶ ἄλλο γίγνεσθαι. As one hour or one race succeeds another, so a magnitude's potential for continuous division is actualised by successive cuts, one after another. The infinite has a potentiality to be actual not as a separate entity but γενέσει, in a process which may go on and on without limit.[22]

4. Now let me turn to Ross and his account of the positive testimony in favour of the Passage in the direct and indirect traditions. His commentary ad loc. is even more gung-ho than his apparatus:

> This passage occurs in most of the manuscripts (including A[b]), and a paraphrase of it occurs in a good manuscript of Alexander (F). It is omitted by EJTΓ and Bessarion, and is very corrupt in the other manuscripts. But it contains sound Aristotelian doctrine and terminology, and is quite || appropriate to its context, and there is no apparent motive for its introduction, so that on the whole it seems safe to treat it as genuine.[23]

Clarifications: T, a fourteenth-century manuscript, is one of just two 'codices recentiores' listed among Ross's sigla.[24] Γ is the Latin translation of Aristotle's *Metaphysics* by William of Moerbeke (*circa* 1265–72), which was based on J and another manuscript from the α tradition.[25] A version of Cardinal Bessarion's Latin translation of *circa* 1452 may be found in volume iii of the Berlin Academy's classic edition of the works of Aristotle.[26] None of these antedates A[b]. That said by way of clarification, I take up Ross's several points in order:

(i) 'This passage occurs in most of the manuscripts (including A[b])'. Understandable at the time it was written, long before Harlfinger's stemma gave us a clear picture of how the *recentiores* relate to the primary manuscripts and to each other. This stemma was based on a collation of four stretches of text (book Α.980a21–982a3, all of α, Κ.1059a18–1060a20, Ν.1092a9–1093b28), followed by a collation of Η.1045a1–Θ.1045b36 for some fourteen manuscripts which the first collation had revealed to be

---

[22] This proposal has already been accepted by S. Makin (Makin 2006, *ad loc*).
[23] Ross 1924, ii. 253.   [24] For its affiliations (pretty mixed), see Harlfinger 1979.
[25] Vuillemin-Diem 1995: 165–99; Vuillemin-Diem 1976: lxii–lxvii. Gudrun Vuillemin-Diem suggests that the Translatio Anonyma sive 'Media', dating from before the start of the thirteenth century, is based on a manuscript with affinities to both the α and the β traditions; nevertheless, the Passage is missing there too.
[26] The Latin version of the Passage at 513b17–34 is in square brackets, because it is not the work of Bessarion but an addition to cater for Bekker's Greek text in volume ii of the Berlin edition [Bekker 1831]. No name is attached to the translation, which differs markedly from Strozza's version (n. 44 below).

wholly or partly independent of each other. In none of this was the Passage included. But Christian Brockmann kindly looked on my behalf at the photographic collection in the Aristoteles-Archiv in Berlin and discovered that the important manuscripts containing the Passage are all ones which Harlfinger had independently shown to belong to the β tradition or to have been contaminated by it. Thus the Passage confirms the correctness of Harlfinger's stemma.

In a letter dated 26 June 1995 Brockmann writes:

> Nach Prüfung der wichtigsten Handschriften läßt sich die Frage 'Wie ist der Passus *Met.* Θ.6, 1048b18–35, überliefert?' zunächst einmal klar || beantworten und hier bestätigt sich eindeutig das Stemma von Dieter Harlfinger.
>
> Der Passus fehlt im Überlieferungszweig α: fehlt in Vind. phil. 100 (J), Par. 1853 (E), Esc. Y 3.18 (E^s), Vat. 255 (V^d), Laur. 87, 18 (B^b). In Vat. 255 (V^d) ist der Text von einem zweiten Schreiber, einem Korrektor, am Ende der *Metaphysik* ergänztworden, wobei er an der Stelle, wo der Text fehlt, einen Hinweis auf die Ergänzung eingetragen hat: ζήτει τὸ τοιούτον [ ]χ[ ]α ἐν τῷ τέλει τοῦ βιβλίου (wahrscheinlich σχῆμα).[27]
>
> Der Passus ist vorhanden im Zweig β: vorhanden in Laur. 87, 12 (A^b), Ambr. F 113 sup. (M), Taur. B VII 23 (C), Marc. 205 (D^m). Der Text ist außerdem vorhanden in Par. 1850 (D) und Oxon. N.C. 230 (O^b). Wenn man in Harlfingers Stemma schaut, erklärt sich dieser Befund: Vermittler ist der Marc. 205 (D^m), der auf A^b zurückgeht. Diese Handschriften sind also in diesem Punkt nicht unabhängig von A^b.[28] Im Marc. 205 (D^m) gibt es zur Stelle einen Hinweis von jüngerer Hand, daß dieser Passus sich in manchen Büchern nicht finde, und dass es mit dem Text τὸ μὲν οὖν ἐνεργείᾳ τί τέ ἐστι bei dem Zeichen weitergehe.

[Examination of the most important manuscripts makes it now possible once and for all to answer clearly the question: 'How has the passage *Met.* Θ.6, 1048b18–35 been transmitted?', and Dieter Harlfinger's stemma is unambiguously established.

The passage is missing in manuscript tradition α: in Vind. phil. 100 (J), Par. 1853 (E), Esc. Y 3.18 (E^s), Vat. 255 (V^d), Laur. 87, 18 (B^b). In Vat. 255 (V^d) the text has been added at the end of the Metaphysics by a second scribe, who is making corrections. At the point where the text is missing, he has a note on the addition: ζήτει τὸ τοιούτον [ ]χ[ ]α ἐν τῷ τέλει τοῦ βιβλίου (apparently σχῆμα).

---

[27] The σχῆμα is a plain circle, which duly reappears right at the end of the manuscript, where the Passage is written out.

[28] In a later letter Brockmann reported that the Passage is also present in the fifteenth-century Taur. C I2. 5 (Z), *as was to be expected* given that Harlfinger's stemma places it between D and O^b.

The passage is found in tradition β: in Laur. 87, 12 (A^b), Ambr. F 113 sup. (M), Taur. B VII 23 (C), Marc. 205 (D^m). In addition, the text is found in Par. 1850 (D) and Oxon. N.C. 230 (O^b). If one takes a look at Harlfinger's stemma, the explanation is clear: the intermediary is Marc. 205 (D^m), which goes back to A^b. So these manuscripts are at this juncture not independent of A^b. In Marc. 205 (D^m) there is a note at that point by a later hand, to the effect that in many books this passage is not included, and that the text continues with the words τὸ μὲν οὖν ἐνεργείᾳ τί τέ ἐστι.]

Jaeger's annotation 'A^b et recc. plerique' was wiser than Ross's bold 'codd. plerique', though 'plerique' is false in either case.

What is most interesting about these findings is that the Passage occurs in M (fourteenth century) and C (fifteenth century), the two *recentiores* which Harlfinger singled out as worthy of attention from future editors of the *Metaphysics*, because they witness to the β tradition independently of A^b.[29] We may thus conclude that the Passage was already in the β branch before A^b, in some common ancestor it shared with M and C. Brockmann's collation of the Passage in M and C is printed for the record as Appendix 1 below.

The next step was taken during my time as Fellow of the Wissenschaftskolleg zu Berlin in 2004/5, when over a number of visits to the Aristoteles-Archiv Brockmann kindly took me through a survey of the remaining *recentiores*. The results, which confirm and strengthen the findings of his original letter, are best seen in Plate 4.1, where my red circle marks a manuscript we found to contain ‖ the Passage, my blue square a manuscript which does not include book Θ. I put a dotted red circle around Marc. 211 (E^b) to indicate that the Passage is absent from the main text but a fourteenth-century hand has written it in the margin.[30] The dotted red circle around Vat. 255 (V^d) also indicates a corrector's activity, as explained in Brockmann's letter. The majority of the manuscripts have no mark from me because they transmit Θ without the Passage.

Before continuing my response to Ross, let me note that the investigation summarised in Plate 4.1 amounts to a complete collation of the relevant manuscripts for a passage of the *Metaphysics* which did not figure in Harlfinger's original project. The results of this independent research uniformly confirm his stemma. All the more reason for me to express my deep gratitude to Christian Brockmann for help over many hours staring at

---

[29] Harlfinger 1979: 32–3. In response, C. Luna (Luna 2005) has shown what can be gleaned from collating M and C for *Metaphysics* M–N, where A^b no longer represents the β tradition.

[30] On this hand, which made extensive corrections in E^b and may have affiliations with C, see Harlfinger 1979: 14.

microfilm in the Aristoteles-Archiv: time and again his trained eyes understood what mine could only see.

(ii) 'and a paraphrase of it occurs in a good manuscript of Alexander (F)'. True, but the situation is more complicated than Ross reveals. In Hayduck's Berlin Academy edition of Alexander, which Ross is using, the siglum F denotes a copy of the so-called Alexander commentary written in the margins of one of the *recentiores* just mentioned, Ambr. F 113 sup. (M). I say 'so-called' because by the time the commentary gets to Θ – in fact from book E onwards – we are no longer reading Alexander of Aphrodisias (second century AD), but a Pseudo-Alexander who can safely be identified as Michael of Ephesus, who wrote early in the twelfth century.[31] Now another good text of the Alexander commentary, Hayduck's L, is found in the margins of A^b itself (thus L = A^b as F = M) – and here the paraphrase is missing. Furthermore, F's paraphrase begins by ‖ saying τοῦτο κεφάλαιον ἐν πολλοῖς λείπει: 'this chapter is missing in many copies'. Hayduck prints the feeble paraphrase that follows in a footnote, not in his main text, which implies that in his judgement (to be confirmed below) its author is not even Pseudo-Alexander. It is someone else's addition to the commentary, a supplement designed to make up for the fact that Pseudo-Alexander himself said nothing about the Passage, because he did not know of its existence. Hence the absence of the paraphrase in L, despite the presence of the Passage in A^b where L is written. The paraphrase is an anxious response to the presence of the Passage in M, not independent evidence in favour of reading it there.

(iii) 'But it [the Passage] contains sound Aristotelian doctrine and terminology'. Where exactly does Ross find his proof of soundness? The issue is important enough to claim our attention later. I will argue that Ross is right about the *doctrine* (witness Θ.8 as just quoted, or *NE* I.1), but that the *terminology* is unique to the Passage. Even *NE* x.3–5, often cited as parallel, will not serve.

(iv) 'and is quite appropriate to its context'. Not really, as Jaeger helped us see. Readers from the USA please note that 'quite' here does not mean 'very'. That would be an absurd claim.

(v) 'and there is no apparent motive for its introduction'. I agree. The motive remains to be discovered.

---

[31] The identity of Pseudo-Alexander with Michael, proposed by S. Ebbesen (Ebbesen 1981), is now thoroughly confirmed by Luna 2001. Michael's commentaries were convincingly redated by R. Browning to the period 1118–38 (Browning 1962, reprinted as Sorabji 1990: 393–406); previously, his date was standardly given as *circa* 1070.

One further item, from Ross's apparatus: 'Philop.' An unwary reader could easily be reassured by this: at least the Passage was known to Philoponus in the sixth century AD. Not at all. The commentary in question was wrongly ascribed to Philoponus, as is proved by its containing references to Michael of Ephesus.[32]

Two further facts about Pseudo-Philoponus are relevant here. The first is that it was he who composed the paraphrase added in F. The Greek text of his commentary remains unpublished; for a long time it was known only through a sixteenth-century Latin translation by Francesco Patrizzi (= Frane Petrić, the founding father of Croatian philosophy).[33] But Michael Frede showed me || photographs of the two known complete Greek manuscripts of this commentary: the paraphrase occurs on folios 105^v–106^r of cod. Vat. Urb. gr. 49 (fourteenth century) and folio 150^v of cod. Vind. gr. Phil. 189 (sixteenth century).[34] In both the paraphrase is plain to see.

The second relevant fact is that it has recently been revealed that what Ross called 'a good MS of Alexander (F)' is not all by Alexander and Pseudo-Alexander. From book K onwards it is Pseudo-Philoponus, and the manuscript ascribes this portion of the commentary to George Pachymeres (1242–*circa* 1310).[35] There can be little doubt that the scribe who wrote F in Ambr. F 113 sup. (M) had access in the Bibliotheca Ambrosiana to the commentary of Pseudo-Philoponus, i.e. Pachymeres, who is a century later than A^b. For the end of the Pseudo-Philoponus commentary is also found at fos. 27^v–30^r of Ambr. I 117 inf. (sixteenth century).[36] When the scribe noticed that Pseudo-Alexander had nothing to say about the Passage, he compensated by borrowing the paraphrase from a nearby copy of Pseudo-Philoponus.

5. Finally, the curious and highly unusual line drawn through the latter part of the Passage in A^b, most clearly described by Christ: '28 τούτων–35 κίνησιν linea perducta delenda significat A^b'. Plate 4.2 [facing p. 101] shows a thin vertical line starting just above the middle of τούτων, near the

---

[32] See Ebbesen 1981, appendix 8: 'Ps.-Philoponus, in Metaphysicam'.
[33] Now reprinted with an introduction by Lohr as Lohr 1991. Already Bonitz in his 1847 edition of the Alexander commentary was led by the Latin to suspect that Pseudo-Philoponus might be the author of the paraphrase, which Bonitz knew in the incomplete citation of Brandis's collected scholia (Bonitz 1847: 551; Brandis 1836, 781a47–b12).
[34] These two manuscripts are, respectively, nos. 1999 and 2214 in Wartelle 1963.
[35] Alexandru 1999: 350, n. 11, and 351. Eleni Pappa (Pappa 2002: 21–2 n. 74) is puzzled and sees numerous similarities with Pseudo-Alexander, but this cannot hold for the paraphrase of the Passage now under discussion. Pachymeres' own *Metaphysics* ignores Θ (Pappa 2002: 30).
[36] See Wartelle 1963 no. 1022 with annotation.

centre of the first line of fo. 361ʳ, which then proceeds downwards to the fourteenth line of writing. The last words of the fourteenth line are ἐκείνην δὲ κίνησιν. The line stops under the ε ‖ of ἐκείνην, where it meets the circumflex accent over ἐνεργεῖν (Aᵇ's variant for ἐνεργείᾳ at 1048b35)[37] – again roughly in the centre of the line of writing. This the editors interpret as marking for deletion all of 1048b28–34 plus the first four words of 35.

Now the reddish-brown ink used for the line is the same colour as the ink used for L, the version of the Alexander commentary written in the margin of Aᵇ. The Aristotelian text in Aᵇ is also reddish-brown but noticeably darker, often almost black. This is clear evidence that the line was drawn by the scribe who wrote L, not by some later corrector. There was no such line in the ἀντίγραφον, otherwise it would have been copied (if copied at all) in the darker ink of the main text. This is confirmed by the fact that there is no such line in either M or C.[38]

But the scribe who wrote the bulk of L, including the part under discussion, also wrote the corresponding part of the main text of Aᵇ up to Λ.7, 1073a1.[39] The two inks flow from two pens (the letters in the text are thicker than those in the margin) held in turn by a single hand.[40] As one page succeeds another, you see each ink oscillating independently between darker and lighter, as each pen is dipped into the ink or its inkbottle is refilled. But what matters here is that the Passage is a different tint from the surrounding commentary and the line of deletion. This suggests that the scribe would first write a chunk of Aristotle, leaving space for the commentary above, below and alongside the main text, and only later go back to enter the relevant portion of commentary. One can almost see it happening.

Across the top of fo. 361ʳ, above the first line of the main text (1048b18, where the vertical line begins), run two lines of the commentary (581.16–19 in Hayduck's edition: καὶ εἰπὼν τὸ μὲν οὖν ἐνεργείᾳ τί ἐστι καὶ ποῖον ... νῦν λέγει, ὅτι πότε δυνάμει), which belong to the transition that Pseudo-Alexander is now making from Θ.6 to Θ.7. He has finished with Θ.6. Not so the main text below, ‖ in which Θ.7 only starts near the bottom of the page at the seventeenth of nineteen lines of writing, because

---

[37] n. 16 above.
[38] Which puts paid to the fantastic suggestion of P. Gohlke (Gohlke 1961: 455 n. 77), that the line was drawn by Aristotle, once he had committed himself to the *Physics* III doctrine that κίνησις is after all a kind of ἐνέργεια, and faithfully transmitted in the Aᵇ tradition.
[39] Harlfinger 1979: 32 with n. 62, hesitates over whether to assign responsibility for *Metaph.* A–Λ.7 to one scribe or two contemporary ones. That is irrelevant here since, if they are two, the change-over comes at fo. 456ᵛ, nearly a hundred pages after Θ.6.
[40] The same situation in M: both text and commentary are one and the same hand throughout.

the Passage is still in full flow. Whether or not the scribe noticed this extra material earlier, he cannot help noticing it now. And that puts him in exactly the situation that led to the paraphrase from Pseudo-Philoponus being added to F in the margin of M. What to do about a large chunk of Aristotelian text to which nothing in the commentary corresponds? The same situation but a different response. Instead of adding to the commentary, the scribe of L pauses to subtract some of the Aristotelian text. At least, that is what he does if editors are right to interpret the line as a mark of deletion.

I shall assume that they are right, because the result of deleting exactly the words τούτων ... κίνησιν would be to restore the balance between the main text and the accompanying commentary. The last sentence of Θ.6 would begin on the first line of the main text, just below the last line of the upper portion of commentary where ὅτι πότε δυνάμει starts elucidating Θ.7. Delete the first part of the Passage as well and the commentary would run a full page ahead of the Aristotelian text. Keeping text and commentary in step with each other is something any scribe might care about, but this one more than most – because he got it so disastrously wrong before.

All through the first five books of the *Metaphysics* A^b is full of blank white spaces. Evidently, the scribe began what was meant to be an *édition de luxe* by copying out the whole of books A–Δ on their own, often only a few lines per page, leaving much more space than would turn out to be needed for the Alexander commentary in the margin. Perhaps he did not have the Alexander commentary to hand and assumed it would be more expansive than it is.[41] When he did get hold of the commentary, all he could do was trail it down the margin in lines of irregular length, at times writing as few as two or three words in a space that could take many more. The effect is pretty, like a cascade of pink water each side of the page, but wasteful of expensive parchment. By contrast, from book E onwards the layout is efficiency itself. The white margin separating commentary and text can stay reasonably constant, because text and commentary keep more or less in step with each other – until we reach the Passage on fo. 361^r. At which point the scribe signals the need to take action. ||

The action is twofold. First, the deletion of exactly the words τούτων... κίνησιν, no more. Second, adjusting the balance of text and commentary in the following pages in order to restore correspondence between the two. This takes a while. When chapter 8 begins on fo. 363^v the main text

---

[41] In that case Harlfinger 1979: 32 would not be right to suggest that the ἀντίγραφον of A^b included both main text and commentary.

(a smaller chunk than usual) is still running some 10 cm. ahead of the commentary. But by the beginning of chapter 9 on fo. 371^v exact parity has been achieved, allowing Θ to end as neatly as it began. Iota then begins a new page of its own.

This is a thoroughly 'physical' explanation of the line of deletion.[42] There is simply no need to wonder why the scribe did not turn back a page to delete the earlier part of the Passage (1048b18–27) as well. He is not objecting to the content, but dismayed to find his text and commentary out of sync again.

6. To sum up: the Passage is well attested in branch β, not at all in α. Harlfinger's investigations, which postdate the editions of Ross and Jaeger, underline the difficulties that both confronted. The Passage is better confirmed than before in β, eliminated entirely from α. What is an editor to do?

We are so familiar with the Passage that most of us find it hard to imagine a *Metaphysics* which simply leaves it out. But there have been such versions. As already noted (Section 4 above), it was not in Cardinal Bessarion's Latin translation (*circa* 1452), done from H^a,[43] which Plate 4.1 shows as lacking the Passage. It was neither in the Latin translation/paraphrase of the first twelve books of the *Metaphysics* by Argyropoulos (*circa* 1415–87) nor among the lemmata Latinised by Sepúlveda for his translation of the Alexander commentary (1527). Tracking back further, none of the medieval Latin translations includes the Passage. In particular, its absence from the Moerbeke translation used by Aquinas ensured that we have no comment on its subtleties from the Angelic Doctor. No comment from Averroes either: the Passage did not get into Arabic.[44] ||

The ancient commentators on Aristotle speak frequently enough of τελεία ἐνέργεια or of ἐνέργεια κυρίως, contrasting this with ἐνέργεια ἀτελής,[45] but to my knowledge not one of them uses the single word

---

[42] In reaching which I have been helped by discussion with Michel Crubellier.
[43] So Mioni 1968: 78.
[44] In the Venice 1562 edition of the *Metaphysics* in Bessarion's Latin translation, accompanied by a Latin text of Averroes' commentary, although not in the earlier edition of 1552, the Passage is presented (without comment from Averroes of course!) in a Latin version which, the reader is told, was prepared for teaching purposes by Kyriacos Strozza.
[45] Samples, all of them commenting on passages where modern scholars are tempted to invoke the narrow meaning given to ἐνέργεια in the Passage: Them. *In DA* 55.6–12, 112.25–33 Heinze; Philop. *In DA* 296.20–297.37 Hayduck; Simpl. (?) *In DA* 126.2–3, 264.25–265.16 Hayduck. A particularly clear account of the difference between τελεία ἐνέργεια and κίνησις, which is ἀτελής ἐνέργεια, is Philop. *Aet.* 64.22–65.26 Rabe. In a work that long-windedly dots every possible I and crosses every possible T, it is hard to believe that the author would not have drawn on, or at least mentioned, the Passage – had he known of its existence. I infer that he did not.

ἐνέργεια in the sense of the Passage, as equivalent to τελεία ἐνέργεια. The only clear echo of the Passage I have been able to discover comes from medieval Byzantium. Michael of Ephesus, commenting on Aristotle's account of pleasure in *NE* x.2, obviously knows the Passage, and uses it to good effect. But given that Michael is the same person as Pseudo-Alexander, we have just seen both A^b and M = F testifying that he did not find it in the copy of the *Metaphysics* he used when writing his commentary! I shall return to Michael in a final Postscript (Section 16 below).

Meanwhile, let me simply mention here that there is scholarly dispute about whether, when Plotinus in *Enneads* VI.1 [42].16ff. criticises the Aristotelian account of change as ἐνέργεια ἀτελής, he has the Passage in view as well as *Physics* III.1–3, from which he quotes.[46] The issue is best reserved for Appendix 2 below, where I argue, controversially, that Plotinus' remarks and the discussion they inspired among later Platonists show a striking absence of acquaintance with the Passage. There is certainly no sign of the Passage in *Enneads* II.5 [25], a treatise which starts from the question ‖ whether τὸ ἐνεργείᾳ εἶναι is the same as, or different from, ἐνέργεια. Nor in two treatises on happiness, 1.4 [46] and 1.5 [36].

A good way to appreciate how contingent were the factors that brought the Passage into our editions is to study the route by which it got into the Aldine. Sicherl has shown that the 'Druckvorlage' of the Aldine was Par. 1848 (Q^c, circa 1470).[47] Q^c is a descendant of Vind. Phil. 64 (J^a), and J^a has the Passage, presumably by 'contamination' from D^m, which was one of Brockmann's positive results. Now J^a is one of the most copied manuscripts of all time,[48] as can be seen from the stemma. What is interesting is that, while four of its descendants have the Passage, three of them do not. Why the difference?

---

[46] Henry and Schwyzer 1951–73, *ad loc.* cite the Passage, but A. H. Armstrong (Armstrong 1988), does not. Brague 1988: 454 with n. 2, is sceptical. I agree with him that ch. 16 can be understood without reference to the Passage. If ch. 18 seems to operate with some sort of contrast between κίνησις and ἐνέργεια, that can be explained as the product of Plotinus' own dialectic in chs. 16 and 17. The recent discussion of this dialectic in Chiaradonna 2002, ch. 2, does appeal to the Passage. So too I. Croese (Croese 1998), ch.4, entitled 'The Late NeoPlatonic interpretation of the motion–*energeia* distinction'. Yet Damascius is a late Neoplatonist who can write as if it is a matter of course that ἐνέργειαι are either τέλειαι or ἀτελεῖς (*In Phileb.* 191 Westerink). Returning to 6.1.16ff., Gwenaëlle Aubry points out to me that the absence of the term πρᾶξις, in a Plotinian text which is bent on distinguishing ἐνέργεια from ποίησις, makes it doubtful that its author has the Passage in mind.

[47] Sicherl 1976: 1–90; acknowledged by Harlfinger 1979: 26 n. 56 bis, too late to redraw the lower right-hand quarter of his stemma (Plate 4.1), where a, a^{II}, a^{III} designate successive editions of the Aldine.

[48] Harlfinger 1979: 25.

Go back to D^m (written for Bessarion around 1443) and the annotation by a later hand mentioned at the end of Brockmann's letter (above, p. 102–3). Attached to the beginning of the Passage, the annotation reads: ση(μείωσ)αι ὅτι ἔν τισι βιβλίοις οὐκ εὑρίσκεται ἕως τὸ μὲν οὖν ἐνεργείᾳ ('Note that up to τὸ μὲν οὖν ἐνεργείᾳ is missing in some books'). The identical annotation, with the identical sign ≏ linking annotation to the relevant part of the text, is found not only in D^m's direct descendant Marc. 200 (Q), but also in J^a.[49] In J^a, moreover, the annotation is in the same hand as the main text and there is a line drawn in the left vertical margin to clarify the reference of the annotation. This line has been mistaken in modern times for a mark of deletion.[50] It is presumably a similar mistake that leads Ambr. L 117 sup. (M^c), Salm. M 45 (d), and Paris. Suppl. 204 (U^c) to omit the Passage without indicating the fact. By contrast, Paris. Suppl. 332 (Y^c) at fos. 313–14 neatly copies Passage, sign, and annotation exactly as it appears in J^a but without the marginal line; Vat. 257 (V^c) inserts Cηαι at the beginning and end of the Passage without specifying what is to be noted; while Neap. III D 35 (N^d) includes the Passage in its main text with no trace of annotation. Had the scribe of Q^c thought along the same lines as the scribe of U^c, the Passage would not have appeared in the Aldine and the || world might well not have known what it was missing until Brandis collated A^b for his school edition of the *Metaphysics* (1823) and for Bekker's Berlin Academy edition of 1831.[51] As it is, Q^c is like N^d in that it simply transmits the Passage as part of the main text with no indication that it has ever been questioned. Aldus would have seen no reason to worry.

Let us dwell a moment on contingency. The manuscript tradition now before you in Plate 4.1 shows that not all ancient readers of Aristotle's *Metaphysics* (I suspect, rather few) would meet the Passage. Its quiet entry via Q^c into the tradition of modern publication ensured that lots of us would come to find it familiar, hard to think away, hence hard to suppose it might have been unavailable to many ancient students of Aristotle. None the less, not all moderns have succumbed.

---

[49] Thereby providing yet another independent confirmation of Harlfinger's stemma.
[50] Bernadinello 1970: 70.
[51] Brandis 1823: vii looks forward to Bekker's big edition, the preface to which (Bekker, vol. i: iii) makes it clear that they shared the task of travelling around Europe to inspect the 101 manuscripts there listed (Bekker 1831, vol. i: iii– vi) and divided the responsibilities of preparing the final product on behalf of the Berlin Academy. Both note in their apparatus criticus that the Passage is omitted in certain manuscripts, although only Bekker specifies these as ET and only he records the crossing out in A^b; both note A^b's ἐνεργεῖν for ἐνεργείᾳ at 1048b35. Brandis's apparatus ascribes F's τοῦτο τὸ κεφάλαιον ἐν πολλοῖς λείπεται to 'Alex.'!

Once the Passage was included in the first Aldine (1498), it was printed in the Greek text of editions by Erasmus (1531, 1539; reissued 1550), Turrisanus (1552), and Sylburg (1585).[52] But not in the Basel Latin translation of 1542. In 1590 Isaac Casaubon put the Passage in square brackets, on the grounds that, although it is in the manuscripts (*sc.* the manuscripts he knows or knows of), it was unknown to the old Latin translators and to Alexander; his brackets and note reappear in a series of editions by W. du Val (1619, 1629, 1654), the brackets alone in Mauro's Latin version with commentary (1658) and in Weise's edition of the Greek (1843). The Passage is completely omitted in Thomas Taylor's English translation of 1801.[53] Barthélemy-Saint-Hilaire (1879), having had the benefit || of Bonitz's emendations when translating the Passage, still found the result so unsatisfactory that he complained in his note *ad loc.*, 'peut-être eût-il mieux valu le passer tout à fait sous silence, comme l'ont fait Alexandre d'Aphrodise et Bessarion' ['Perhaps it would have been better to pass over it entirely, in silence, as Alexander of Aphrodisias and Bessarion did']. We should prepare to think the unthinkable.

Ross writes:

> It is perfectly clear that neither EJ nor A^b should be followed exclusively. But the weight of the Greek commentators and of the medieval translation is decidedly on the side of EJ, and I have accordingly followed this group of manuscripts, except where the evidence of the Greek commentators, or the sense, or grammar, or Aristotelian usage ... turns the scale in favour of A^b.[54]

For the particular case of book Z, this judgement has recently been strengthened by Michael Frede and Günther Patzig. They have produced a Greek text of Z which aims to follow the α tradition of EJ, not exclusively, but wherever possible. The result, in my view, is a triumph. The text is harder to read than Jaeger's, to be sure, but that is the point. For A^b, as they put it, systematically smoothes out the crabbiness of Aristotle's treatise style, sometimes as the result of misunderstanding.[55]

---

[52] Schwegler 1847: i. xv–xx gives a helpful history of *Metaphysics* editions since the Aldine, brought up to date by Hecquet-Devienne 2000: 105–33 (reprinted with slight alterations in Goulet 2003: 245–9).

[53] T. Taylor 1801: 210 n.: 'Several lines follow this word [γνώσει] in the printed text which are not to be found in the Commentary of Alexander, and are not translated either by Bessarion or Argyropoulos, the most antient translators of Aristotle. I have, therefore, omitted them in my version, as undoubtedly spurious.'

[54] Ross 1924, vol. i, pp. clxiv–clxv.

[55] Consult their introduction, Frede and Patzig 1988, vol. i, ch. 1, 'Zum griechischen Text'.

Z is only one book of the *Metaphysics*. We may not infer from one book to the rest. But we should, none the less, take note of a possibility: in Θ too the balance in favour of the α branch may be even stronger than Ross described. Let this be the cue for my alternative to Jaeger's suggestion that the Passage originated as an addition by Aristotle himself, which must therefore have been lost or excised from the EJ tradition (branch α) at a fairly early stage.

Look at the emendations all over the Passage in your Greek text. As Bonitz said, before he applied his magic touch,

> Sed librariorum error, ex quo omissus est in quibusdam exemplaribus universus hic locus, idem ad singula videtur verba pertinuisse; ea enim tot scatent corruptelis, ut non alia Metaphysicorum pars cum iis possit comparari.[56]||

> [But scribal error, which was responsible for the omission of this whole passage in some manuscripts, seems to have extended to individual words; for they are brimming with so many corruptions that no other part of the *Metaphysics* can be compared with them.]

As Ross said afterwards, 'The text has been vastly improved by Bonitz.'[57] An obvious hypothesis to explain the extent of corruption is that the Passage began as an annotation in the β tradition, written in a margin where it was cramped for space or liable to damage (fraying, finger wear, moisture, etc.).[58] That is why so many vitally important words now appear as supplements, in angled brackets. They were missed out when, at some later point in the β tradition, the annotation was mistakenly copied into the main text.

On this hypothesis, the Passage is a fragment of Aristotelian philosophy from some work now lost to us.[59] The annotator could be quite late, as late as such works were still around to be consulted. There is no need at all to

---

[56] Bonitz 1848: 397. Brague 1988: 456–7, would minimise the extent of corruption by hypothesizing that the Passage began as a hastily scribbled note from Aristotle to himself. But then why was it not transmitted in the α tradition?

[57] Ross 1924: ii. 253. To verify this observation, try making sense of the Passage as printed in Bekker. Schwegler 1847 made a noble effort with both text and translation, but the strain is evident on nearly every line. Yet it should be added that in Bonitz's apparatus every single emendation is marked 'fort.', i.e. 'perhaps'; his commentary is similarly modest and hesitant about restoring the Passage.

[58] An important, well-known case of this kind is A.5, 986a29–30, where a marginal note about the relative dates of Pythagoras and Alcmaeon has been written into the text of E, but is unknown both to Alexander and to the A^b tradition.

[59] Cf. Kirchmann 1871, ii: 50–1 n. 815, who rightly finds the Passage so irrelevant to its context in Θ that he suggests it may have been interpolated into the text 'aus einem anderen Werke des Aristoteles'.

think of ancient editors, let alone of an addition signalled somehow by Aristotle himself for inclusion in the next copying out of Θ. Aristotle is the last person to have reason for writing the aberrant terminology of the Passage into the main text of Θ.

7. This brings us to the question of motive. What was the annotation meant to explain or illuminate? Several possibilities come to mind:

(i) The text it best explains is Θ.8, 1050a23–b2, already quoted. The distinction there between ἐνέργειαι which aim at a further product and those which are their own end is parallel to the distinction drawn in the Passage between πράξεις which aim at a further product and those which are their own end. The motive for a marginal note would be to tell readers of Θ that elsewhere Aristotle marks the distinction with special terminology.

The snag is that Θ.8 is over two Bekker pages on from Θ.6. How would a note on Θ.8 get written into the text of Θ? Either (a) by carelessness or (b) by design. (a) is not impossible. For example, a learned reader thinks the Passage should be in the main text of Θ.8, but his copyist misunderstands the directions he has been given. (b) supposes a learned reader who thinks that the Passage is genuinely relevant to Θ.6 and has it written there. Why not, if an outstanding scholar like Ross finds it 'quite appropriate to its context'?

(ii) Alternatively, the annotation was a comment on Θ.6. Either (a) by someone who failed to see, as have many others since, that the Passage addresses a different question from the rest of Θ.6, or (b) by someone who knew that very well and wished only to point out that elsewhere Aristotle takes a different tack from the one he follows in the earlier part of Θ.6.

A different tack on what? On a sentence in Θ.6 that might well disturb a reader who knows the Passage, or *NE* 10, or *Metaphysics* Λ. The sentence, quoted above, p. 95, is 1048b8–9:

τὰ μὲν γὰρ ὡς κίνησις πρὸς δύναμιν, τὰ δ' ὡς οὐσία πρός τινα ὕλην.

Some are related as change to capacity, while others are related as substance to some matter.

Once the analogical extension is completed, these are the two headings under which all instances of the contrast between δύναμις and ἐνέργεια are subsumed: some are contrasted (C) as δύναμις to κίνησις, others (S) as ὕλη to οὐσία. Examples under the second heading, the one Θ is really interested in, are the Hermes in the wood, the half-line in the whole (1048b32–3), the matter as opposed to what is separated out of it, and the unworked up as opposed to what it is worked up into (1048b3–4).

The disturbing bit is the examples Aristotle cites under the first head, as δύναμις to κίνησις: knowledge vs. contemplation, the craft of building vs. building, sleeping vs. waking, sight vs. seeing (1048a34–b2). Subtract building, and in each case the second term is the sort of item which the Passage calls ἐνέργεια in *contrast* to κίνησις. Subtract waking and seeing, and what remains is an activity that Aristotle in *NE* x and *Metaphysics* Λ ascribes to God: contemplation, theorising, the exercise of knowledge.

Now in Θ.6, 1048b8, the noun κίνησις is used broadly to cover a builder's active agency as well as the passive change undergone ‖ by the bricks: it picks up both κινεῖν and κινεῖσθαι from 1048a28–9. We know that Aristotle's God κινεῖ ὡς ἐρώμενον. But that describes God's relation to the rest of the cosmos. Contemplation is what he is, his οὐσία (Λ.6, 1071b19–20), his life (Λ.7, 1072b26–8), his pleasure (1072b16). Contemplation is what makes him the most excellent of all beings (Λ.9, 1074a18–21). Any student of Aristotle could think it misleading to say that God is κίνησις or that his contemplating is κίνησις. Especially since κίνησις usually refers to passive change (κινεῖσθαι), which would imply that God, the great Contemplator, undergoes change. A Byzantine cleric might well agree with Philoponus (*Aet.* IV.4) that the very thought is blasphemous. Someone who knew the Passage might well think to write a marginal note to show that Aristotle knew better, that elsewhere κίνησις is not κίνησις but ἐνέργεια.[60]

This last suggestion, (ii[b]), would be my preferred choice for a story about how the Passage began its journey into the text of Θ.6. But let imagination be reined in here. It is enough that once the marginal note hypothesis is accepted, to account for extreme textual disrepair in the Passage, plausible stories can be told about how it got into the main text. The next question is what to say about our newly discovered fragment of Aristotle.

8. The style is that of the treatises rather than the published 'exoteric' works: no connecting particle in 1048b25, neither verbs nor connectives in 29–30. As Jaeger says, 'oratio est admodum dura et obscura'. The best clue

---

[60] Indeed, C. Natali (Natali 1991: 70, 76, reprinted as Natali 2004: 31–52), suggests that the Passage is 'una glossa di Aristotele a 1048a34–5': Aristotle wanted to clarify the status of θεωρῆσαι in those lines. But I suspect that by 'glossa' Natali means 'explanation', not a marginal note, in which case my previous objection stands: why does Aristotle in the sequel continue to use ἐνέργεια in the same broad sense as it had before the Passage? The same objection tells against two other attempts to make the Passage fit into Θ.6: (i) Menn 1994: 106–7 has it 'repair the damage' done by the broad (and, he claims, chronologically early) use of κίνησις at 1048b8; (ii) Irwin 1988: 565 n. 19 suggests that the actualities that Aristotle identifies with forms also meet the present-perfect test, e.g. '*x* is a statue' and '*x* has been a statue' are both true if either is.

as to its original context is the word πρᾶξις, which does not occur elsewhere in Θ. This has a wide spread of meanings, but not endlessly wide. In biology almost any function || of living things, from heavenly bodies down through animals to plants, may count as a πρᾶξις: *De caelo* II.12, 292b1–2; *DA* II.4, 415a18–22; *De sensu* 1, 436a4; *HA* VIII.1, 589a3; VIII.10, 596b20–1; *PA* 1.5, 645b14–35; *GA* I.23, 731a25; cf. *NE* VII.14, 1154b20.[61] But the word does not consort easily with inanimate things. When we turn to the first chapter of the *Nicomachean Ethics*, we find that some πράξεις aim at an end beyond themselves, others just at the ἐνέργεια, the doing of the action itself. But the *Ethics* also has a narrower use of πρᾶξις, confined (as the Passage confines it) to things done for their own sake: VI.2, 1139a35–b4; VI.5, 1140b6–7; cf. 1.8, 1098b18–20; *Pol.* VII. 3, 1325b16–21. A good example is the second of the passages just listed:

> τῆς μὲν γὰρ ποιήσεως ἕτερον τὸ τέλος, τῆς δὲ πράξεως οὐκ ἂν εἴη· ἔστι γὰρ αὐτὴ ἡ εὐπραξία τέλος.
>
> For while making has an end other than itself, action cannot; for good action itself is its end. (trans. Ross)

If Aristotle is going to restrict πρᾶξις, or πρᾶξις τελεία, or the more general term ἐνέργεια, to things done for their own sake, the most likely context is an ethical one. That would fit the inclusion of εὖ ζῆν and εὐδαιμονεῖν among the examples in Θ.6 (their perfects, not previously attested, may have been dreamt up by Aristotle for the purpose) and give relevance to the statement that with these you don't have to stop, as you do when you are slimming someone (1048b26–7). I shall reinforce this suggestion later with an argument to show that the Passage *cannot* have started life in a physical treatise.

But of course there may be ethical stretches, long or short, in || non-ethical writings. One remarkable example is *De caelo* II.12, 292a22–b25,

---

[61] The inclusion of plants in the *De caelo* and of recuperation in the *Nicomachean Ethics* passage respectively should alleviate the concern of M.-T. Liske (1991: 161), that Aristotle would hardly count recuperation and becoming something as 'Handlungen'. R. Polansky (Polansky 1983, reprinted in Anton and Preus 1992: 211–25) correctly points out that all the ἐνέργειαι exemplified in the Passage are psychical, since all involve soul, but incorrectly (n. 18) allows this to be equivalent to P. S. Mamo's claim (Mamo 1970) that they are all mental processes, which living is not. Polansky's exclusion of plant life (pp. 165, 168), which would narrow the range of ἐνέργειαι yet further, is a non sequitur from the premise that nutrition and reproduction are not themselves ἐνέργειαι in the narrow sense. To his credit he does, however, point out (p. 164) that most of the κινήσεις mentioned (being slimmed, learning, being cured, walking, building) are equally 'psychical', being confined to animate things. Only coming to be and movement have wider scope.

where value theory is brought in to solve problems about the motion of the heavenly bodies. A small-scale example is Θ.8, 1050b1–2, the parenthesis about happiness at the end of the passage quoted earlier, which Ross wrongly describes as a 'digression'.[62] Even the *Physics* finds it relevant at one point to say that happiness is a sort of πρᾶξις.[63] Ethical considerations are seldom far from Aristotle's mind, whatever he is writing on. All we can say at this stage is that the Passage looks ethical in character, and leave future editors of *Aristotelis Fragmenta* to decide where to print it. I will propose a more positive location later.

Part II: Meaning

9. Now for the philosophical content. The discussion in the scholarly literature is largely focused on the so-called 'tense test': φing is an ἐνέργεια if, and only if, from the present tense (whether Englished as '*x* φs' or as '*x* is φing') we may infer '*x* has φed'. If we may not infer the perfect from the present, φing is a κίνησις. Thus seeing is an ἐνέργεια because 'Theaetetus sees Socrates' implies 'Theaetetus has seen Socrates', but building is a κίνησις because 'Ictinus is building a temple' does not imply 'Ictinus has built a temple'; on the contrary, it implies that the temple he is presently building (which may be his first) is not yet built. There is much to say, much has been said, about this test as a criterion for distinguishing ἐνέργειαι from κινήσεις. But why suppose that *inferences* are what Aristotle has in view?

On the face of it, all we find in the Passage is a string of conjunctions:

> At the same time we see *and* have seen, understand *and* have understood, ... while it is not true that at the same time we are learning *and* have learnt, or are being cured *and* have been cured. (1048b23–5; trans. after Ross)

It takes argument to show that these and other expressions of the form 'at the same time *p* and *q*' indicate entailments from *p* to *q*.

So far as I know, the first to appreciate this point was J. L. Ackrill ‖ in his pioneering article on the Passage.[64] The argument he provided was

---

[62] Ross 1924 *ad loc.*: 'The reference to εὐδαιμονία is a digression.'
[63] *Phys.* II.5, 197b5: ἡ δ' εὐδαιμονία πρᾶξις τις· εὐπραξία γάρ; cf. *Pol.* VII.3, 1325a32.
[64] The alternative interpretation he was arguing against has it that 'at the same time *p* and *q*' expresses the logical *compatibility* of *p* and *q*. This idea is taken up by S. Waterlow (Waterlow 1988: 183ff.), and endorsed by T. Potts (Potts 1965: 66–7, while Russo actually translates 'è possibile nello stesso tempo vedere e aver già visto' (Russo 1992), etc. But surely 'at the same time *p* and *q*' asserts actual joint truth, not just the possibility of joint truth. When Aristotle, in a related context, does want to

convincing (see below), with the result that the main focus of subsequent debate has been on inference from the present to the perfect. What few[65] have remarked upon is this. In nearly all Aristotle's instantiations of 'at the same time p and q', p is present and q perfect. But just once it is the other way round:

ἑώρακε δὲ καὶ ὁρᾷ ἅμα τὸ αὐτό, καὶ νοεῖ καὶ νενόηκεν.

One has seen and sees the same thing at the same time, understands and has understood <the same thing at the same time>.[66] (1048b33–4)

If the second limb of this chiasmus is treated as licence to infer 'x has understood' from 'x understands', by parity of reasoning the first should license inferring from 'x has seen' to 'x sees'.

This suggestion has one advantage. If 'at the same time p and q' asserts a biconditional, not just a one-way entailment, then Aristotle's putting the point as a conjunction is logically less sloppy than it would otherwise appear. If he has a two-way connection in mind, it no longer matters that he does not spell out whether it is p that entails q or vice versa. His thought could be put as follows: 'For all times t, p and q are true together at t or false together at t.'

A second advantage is that it helps to explain why Aristotle should make a point of saying that, where κινήσεις are concerned, present and perfect are different (1048b30–3: ἕτερον).[67] If in the case of ἐνέργειαι, by contrast, present and perfect are the same, they had better be mutually entailing.

The obvious objection is that from Theaetetus' *having* seen || Socrates it does not follow that he sees him now. This objection assumes that the perfect refers to the past, either directly or indirectly. Direct reference to the past is characteristic for the perfect in Latin ('Veni, vidi, vici'), and in spoken French or spoken Italian, where the perfect is often a simple past tense (like the past definite in literary French and Italian) which would go over into English as an aorist of the form 'x φed': '[Hier] j'ai lu votre livre et puis ...', 'Io sono arrivato [due mesi fa] e dopo ...'. In spoken German

---

speak of the possibility of joint truth, he uses the modal verb ἐνδέχεσθαι (*SE* 11 178a9–28, discussed below).

[65] The one exception I have noted is Potts 1965: 66.

[66] I take τὸ αὐτό as the object of the verbs in this sentence, not their subject. All the other illustrative examples in the Passage are verbs with no subject expressed, this being an idiom Aristotle often uses (especially in *Topics* and *Rhetoric*) to indicate that it does not matter what the subject is; in the felicitous terminology of J. Brunschwig (1967: lxxxix and 138 n. 2), the absence of a subject may be regarded as 'un variable en blanc'.

[67] On construing ἕτερον as predicate, not with Ross 1924 as subject, see n. 89 below.

too the perfect is a past tense: '[Gestern] habe ich Brot gekauft.'[68] But English preserves a distinction between '*x* φed' and '*x* has φed', the perfect being a tense of *present* time. Consider the difference between 'I lost my passport' and 'I have lost my passport.' The second implies, as the first does not, that at the time of speaking the passport is still lost. This is *indirect* reference to the past. Rather than referring directly to a past event, the perfect in English commonly expresses the continuing present relevance of some past event. 'I have come, I have seen, I have conquered' would sound bizarre unless we imagine Caesar still in Britain. And it is now much too late for you or me to say, in the third person, 'Caesar has invaded Britain'.[69] As Goodwin's *Syntax of Greek Moods and Tenses* put it long ago in 1897, 'The perfect, although it implies the performance of the action in past time, yet states only that it *stands completed* at the *present* time. This explains why the perfect is classed with the present as a primary tense, that is, as a tense of *present* time.'[70]

In ancient Greek the so-called resultative perfect behaves very || much like the perfect in English.[71] But there is also another, more ancient type of perfect which survives into the fourth century BC and beyond. Consider the following: γέγονα, δέδοικα, εἴωθα, ἔοικα, ἕστηκα, λέληθα, μέμνημαι, οἶδα, πέφυκα, πέπονθα, συμβέβηκα, τέθνηκα. They are or can be wholly present, with no past reference at all. They are best analysed in terms of aspect rather than tense. Or consider a famous line of Empedocles: γαίη μὲν γὰρ γαῖαν ὀπώπαμεν, ὕδατι δ᾽ ὕδωρ, 'With earth do we see earth, with water water' (fr. 109.1). ὀπώπαμεν is a perfect formation, but it functions as the sort of timeless present one finds in 'The Sun sets in the

---

[68] The bracketed time-references are of course optional.
[69] Here I am indebted to Stephen Makin. Interestingly, the Stoics reported by Sextus Empiricus, *M.* VIII.254–6, treat constructions with the verb μέλλειν (not as future but) as present tense with indirect reference to the future, in parallel to their analysis of the Greek perfect as, like the English, present tense within direct reference to a past event. Were it to be correct, as claimed by M. J. White, that '*x* has φed' is true if, and only if, at some earlier time '*x* φ's' or '*x* is φing' was true, English would lose the difference between perfect and aorist (M. J. White 1980: 254). We could say, both truly and appositely, 'Caesar has invaded Britain.' The fact is, we can't.
[70] Goodwin 1897: 13–14. Plato, *Parmenides* 141de, lists γέγονε as a verb both of past (when coupled with ποτέ) and of present time (coupled with νῦν, as e.g. at Plato, *Rep.* 354c). Ignored by philosophical commentators on the Parmenides, this interesting feature is discussed by P. Chantraine (1927: 159–62), following the seminal contribution of A. Meillet (Meillet 1924). Proclus, *In Tim.* i.290.23–6 Diehl, combines past and present when, to explain πῶς γενητὸν τὸ πᾶν, he writes of the cosmos as ἀεὶ γιγνόμενον ἅμα καὶ γεγενημένον.
[71] For a nice trio of examples see Plato, *Grg.* 508e6–509a7. At least in English the resultative perfect should be treated in terms of tense, not aspect, since it has both imperfective and perfective forms, e.g. 'I have been reading *War and Peace*' vs. 'I have read *War and Peace*,' the first of which is true rather more often than the second. This tells against Bauer's counsel of despair (Bauer 1970: 196): 'the English perfect can neither be regarded as a tense nor as an aspect, but is a category in its own right'.

West,' 'Lions are mammals'; no competent translator would render 'With earth have we seen earth...'[72] Occasionally, English has a form to match: 'I am persuaded', 'I am called' could in a given context translate πέποιθα and κέκλημαι better than 'I have been persuaded', 'I was called', while the Tailor of Gloucester's 'Alack, I am undone!' might on occasion do justice to the Greek οἴμοι.

Tense locates an event or situation in time: past, present, or future. (Pluperfect and future perfect are no exception, since they locate an event or situation before a previously specified past, or after a previously specified future.) Aspect, by contrast, views an event or situation as complete or incomplete.[73] Past, present, and future || may each be expressed in two different ways: an imperfective way that talks of an ongoing process, divisible into stages, or a perfective way that presents something whole and complete, without regard for internal temporal divisions. For an English example, contrast the imperfective 'Next year I will be writing a book on Aristotle' with the perfective 'Next year I will write a book on Aristotle': same tense, different aspect.[74] It could matter a lot which form you used on your grant application.

For a Greek example, we may turn to Plato's *Protagoras*, 316b3–4, where Protagoras asks whether Socrates and Hippocrates would like to

---

[72] Many more examples of the two types of perfect, and a wonderful discussion of the evolution of the Greek perfect from aspect into tense, in Chantraine 1927, ch. 7.

[73] Comrie 1976 is a helpful general introduction to this subject; Duhoux 1992: 138ff. is nice and clear on aspect in ancient Greek. For a monograph devoted to ways in which aspect is expressed in English, see Brinton 1988. One scholar of the Passage who has seen that the issue is aspect, not tense, is Kosman (1984: 123–7). He too infers the sameness of present and perfect in the case of ἐνέργεια, but he misses his best evidence by translating 1048b33–4 the wrong way round: 'At the same moment one sees and has seen' (similarly Tredennick 1933). And he persists in trying to make the English perfect convey the purely aspectual meaning he wants, without even indirect reference to the past. Others who have shifted attention from tense to aspect are Potts 1965, Penner 1970, Mourelatos 1978, reprinted in Tedeschi and Zaenen 1981: 191–212, Graham 1980, Furth 1985, Jansen 2002, Linguiti 2000, M. J. White 1980, and Frede 1993, this last being a paper in which the Passage is seen as the stimulus (direct or indirect) for discussions of aspect in Diodorus Cronus, the Stoics, and later grammarians. While hailing all these, especially Frede for his demonstration that the ancients themselves distinguished between tense and aspect, I maintain that, apart from Hope 1952 and Graham, no one has appreciated what drastic measures are required (see below) to produce an English version that highlights aspect rather than tense.

[74] Recall n. 71 above. Faced with Aristotle's statement at *Met.* Δ.7, 1017a27–30 (cf. *De int.* 12, 21b9–10), that there is no difference between τὸ ἄνθρωπος ὑγιαίνων ἐστί and τὸ ἄνθρωπος ὑγιαίνει, or between τὸ ἄνθρωπος βαδίζων ἐστὶν ἢ τέμνων and τὸ ἄνθρωπος βαδίζει ἢ τέμνει, R. A. Cobb (Cobb 1973) supposes that it puts all Greek present-tense statements on a par with the *English* present-progressive periphrasis '*x* is φing'. This would require English translators to go in for nonsensical locutions such as 'He is knowing...', 'We are believing...', not to mention that Cobb has to follow Ross in rendering ὑγιαίνων ἐστί by 'He is recovering' rather than 'He is in good health', for which the only parallel offered by LSJ comes from the Book of Ezekiel! On the contrary, Aristotle's message is that, while being is involved in every category, it is a *different* kind of being in each.

hold their discussion with him (διαλεχθῆναι) in private or in company. Socrates replies that it makes no difference to him. Let Protagoras decide how he wishes to discuss (διαλέγεσθαι) the matter of young Hippocrates' education (316c3–4). In Greek, the ‖ dependent moods of the verb (subjunctive, optative, infinitive, imperative) generally differ in aspect, not tense,[75] and this enables Plato to mark a subtle difference between Socrates and the sophist. Protagoras' aorist infinitive already envisages a definite end to the discussion, which he eventually declares at 361e6: 'Now it is time to turn to something else'. Socrates' present infinitive is characteristically open-ended: he will go on for as long as the interlocutor is willing.[76] A less 'studied' Platonic example[77] is the contrast between the imperfect and the aorist of one and the same verb at *Ion* 530a8: 'Were you competing [ἠγωνίζου] and how did the competition go for you [ἠγωνίσω]?'

True, Aristotle is not interested in verbs as such, but what they stand for; if he was interested in the verbs themselves, he would hardly treat living well and living as distinct examples (1048b25–7). But if we do translate into linguistic terms, to help our own understanding, then Aristotle's contrast between κινήσεις and ἐνέργειαι comes out as a contrast between verbs whose present tense has imperfective meaning, e.g. 'to slim' or 'to build', and verbs whose present tense has perfective meaning, e.g. 'to see'.[78] We shall later (pp. 128–9) find Aristotle remarking on the fact that the difference is purely semantic, not a difference which is grammaticalised in the morphology of the relevant Greek verbs.

All this makes it difficult to translate the Passage into English. In English we cannot eliminate the perfect's (indirect) reference to the past. Therefore we must insert a counteracting phrase.[79] ‖

---

[75] The exceptions involve indirect discourse or the presence of ἄν. For a full elucidation, see Goodwin 1897: 22–47. Although he does not use the term 'aspect', that is what he is describing.

[76] The dramatic difference between the two infinitives was first brought to my attention by Heda Segvic. I discuss this and other character-revealing aspectual contrasts in the *Protagoras* in Burnyeat 2013.

[77] Borrowed from Mourelatos 1978: 195.

[78] With Ackrill 1965: 127: 'The perfect [sc. of an ἐνέργεια verb] can always be used of the period preceding a moment at which the present can be used', and the phrasing 'X has (just) φed Y' in Waterlow 1988: 188–9, compare Frede 1993: 146: 'Aristotle clearly does not think that the fact that somebody who grasps something has grasped it, shows that somebody who grasps something must have grasped it at some previous time.' While agreeing with Frede, I add that, equally clearly, as Ackrill stresses, Aristotle thinks that, in the case of κίνησις, someone who is moving something has moved it earlier! This is his thesis that there is no first moment of motion, set out in *Physics* v.6.

[79] Compare Brague 1988, 460–1, 468–9, 471–2, on the 'acrobaties' required when translating the Passage into French.

Two of Aristotle's examples may help: εὖ ζῇ καὶ εὖ ἔζηκε ἅμα, καὶ εὐδαιμονεῖ καὶ εὐδαιμόνηκεν. Translate: 'at the same time *x* lives well and has achieved the good life',[80] '*x* is happy and has achieved happiness'. For these cases at least, the objection is overcome. The entailment runs both ways: not only from '*x* lives well' to '*x* has achieved the good life', and from '*x* is happy' to '*x has* achieved happiness', but also from '*x* has achieved happiness/the good life' to '*x is* happy/living well'. The counteracting phrase 'has achieved' enforces perfective meaning and makes the past irrelevant. It does not matter when happiness/the good life started. The assertion is that it is going on now,[81] complete at every moment. That is, there is no moment at which its goal is not (yet) achieved. Happiness, the good life, is continuing success. And so indeed is life itself (1048b27). Living things for Aristotle are self-maintaining systems. It is thanks to the threptic soul, whose function is nutrition and reproduction, that throughout life, be it long or short, they succeed in staying alive. A splendid example of perfective meaning. Present and perfect are indeed the same.

So much for the examples of ἐνέργειαι expressed by intransitive verbs. The other examples of ἐνέργειαι in the Passage involve transitive verbs,[82] for which we must supply, not only an object, as we did for slimming – the same object for both the present and the perfect – but also a phrase to counteract the English perfect's reference to the past. Here goes: '*x* sees *y*' implies, and is implied by, '*x* has got sight of *y*' or '*x* has (got) *y* in view'; '*x* understands *y*' implies, and is implied by, '*x* has understood *y*'; '*x* knows *y*' implies, and is implied by, '*x* has achieved knowledge of *y*'.

I now offer a rendering of the whole Passage which attempts to convey its full meaning in plausible English. At this stage I keep to Jaeger's text, except that at 1048b33 I prefer Ross's solution: ἕτερον, καὶ κινεῖ καὶ κεκίνηκεν.

> Since of actions which have a limit none is an end, but all belong to the class of means to an end, e.g. slimming, and since the things themselves, when one is slimming them,[83] are in process of changing in this sense, that

---

[80] Modern readers are at liberty to substitute 'a good life' for 'the good life'.
[81] Note the impropriety of coupling '*x* has achieved happiness' with '*x* died last month', which goes quite properly with '*x* achieved happiness'.
[82] Similarly, the κίνησις verbs include both transitive examples (learning, building) and intransitive ones (being cured, walking).
[83] In taking αὐτά as the object of some agent's slimming, I follow Ross and the *communis opinio* against Brague 1988: 458, who construes αὐτά as the means of slimming and translates, 'ces moyens, chaque fois que l'on fait maigrir, sont en mouvement de façon telle [οὕτως referring forwards] qu'ils ne sont pas en eux-mêmes [ὑπάρχοντα in its copulative use] les résultats en vue de quoi le mouvement (se produit)'. If this makes sense at all, it seems to be tautological. On the other

what ‖ is aimed at in the change is not yet present, these[84] are not cases of action, or not at any rate of complete action. For none of them is an end. Action properly speaking[85] is one in which the end is present. For example, at the same time one sees <a thing> and has <it> in view, and one is wise and has achieved wisdom, and one understands <something> and has understood <it>, but it is not the case that <at the same time> one is learning <something> and has learned <it>, or that <at the same time> one is being cured and has been cured. One lives well and has achieved the good life at the same time, and one is happy and has achieved happiness <at the same time>. If that were not so, the action would at some time have to cease,[86] as when one is slimming <someone>. But as it is, this is not the case: one lives and <at the same time> has stayed alive.

Of these <actions>, then, we should call one set changes, the other actualities. For every process of change is incomplete: slimming, learning, walking, building. These are changes, and they are certainly[87] incomplete. For it is not the case that at the same time one is walking and has taken a walk,[88] nor that one is building <something> and has built <it>, nor again that one is becoming <something> and has become <it> or is being changed ‖ <in some way> and has been changed <in that way>, but they are different;[89] as are one's changing and one's having changed <something>. But one has got in view, and one sees, the same thing at the same time, and one understands <something> and has understood <it>. The latter type <of action> I call actuality, the former change.

---

hand, for translating I prefer Ross Tr.[1], 'the things themselves when one is making them thin', to Ross Tr.[2], 'the bodily parts themselves when one is making them thin', which forgets that the target of a slimming course may be the whole person, not just their tummy.

[84] ταῦτα must pick up 'actions which have a limit', not the nearer αὐτά.
[85] 'Properly speaking' renders the intensifying καί before πρᾶξις in 1048b23; Penner 1970: 454 uses italics to the same effect: 'that in which the end inheres *is* an action'.
[86] Ross translates 'would have *had* some time to cease', followed by 'as it is, it *does* not cease' (emphasis added); likewise Furth 1985 and Makin 2006. But ἔδει ἄν is the sole main verb in the sentence, which continues in the present tense. For this reason I take the unfulfilled condition to be present, not past. 'Does not cease' comes dangerously close to implying that happiness and life never cease at all. I take it that Aristotle means living to be an obvious example to buttress the less obvious claim about living well. The point is well put by Makin 2006: 142 (despite his translation): 'It would not make sense to ask whether Candy has *finished* living, seeing, or understanding the theorem (as opposed to having *stopped* doing those things).'
[87] Emphatic γε (Tricot 1964: 'certes'), to be contrasted with the limitative γε of 1048b22: Denniston 1954, 114–16 and 157.
[88] Or: 'has walked <to where one is going>'. Scholars commonly feel the need to supply a destination, as found at *NE* x.4, 1174a29–b2. But 'has taken a walk' has perfective meaning even if the walking was merely a postprandial stroll.
[89] Taking ἕτερον, with most translators, as predicate, not subject to the verbs. By contrast, in his note *ad loc.* Ross renders, 'It is not the case that a thing at the same time is being moved and has been moved; that which has been moved is different from that which is being moved, and that which has moved from that which is moving': three falsehoods in a row! The versions in his Tr.[1], Tr.[2], and Ross–Barnes hardly fare much better. Casting ἕτερον as subject only makes for trouble.

Call this Version A. Its sole purpose is to give readers a sense of how the Passage runs when the focus shifts from tense to aspect.

Part III: A revised text

10. But prior to translation is establishing the text. Version A sticks closely to the printed text we are all familiar with. That text needs to be re-examined in the light of the hypothesis that the Passage began as a marginal annotation. For the hypothesis changes the ground rules for resolving difficulties of text and translation. The two recommendations that follow are a gift from David Sedley, very gladly received.

(i) When writing the Passage into the main text from a cramped margin, a scribe might well lose words, even important words, but it is much less likely that he would make additions. Additions, if any, would be due to subsequent attempts to clarify the obscurities of the Passage once it had entered the main text of branch β, as attested by A^b, M, and C. Conclusion: let us try to eliminate as many editorial square brackets from the printed text as is feasible, on the grounds that they presume to diagnose an unwanted addition to the original text as it stood in the margin. (a) Jaeger's bracketing of καὶ κινεῖ καὶ κεκίνηκεν at 1048b33 is plainly unnecessary. I have already chosen to read, with Ross, ἕτερον, καὶ κινεῖ καὶ κεκίνηκεν. (b) In Version B below, an annotated rendering of the first few sentences of the Passage (1048b18–23), I insist on retaining the 'abstraction operator' αὐτό, deleted by Christ on the grounds, hardly compelling, that 'αὐτό et αὐτά variae lectiones esse videntur'. This decision was accepted by Ross without further explanation, and by Jaeger, who said 'vel οὕτως abundat', which I simply do not || understand. One might alternatively diagnose dittography. I shall defend αὐτό.[90] Finally, only one, easily explicable pair of square brackets will remain.

(ii) An inserted portion of text may contain anaphoric pronouns whose reference in the original context was to something no longer visible in the new environment. A nice illustration is the masculine pronoun οὗτοι at

---

[90] Brague 1988: 457–8 too would keep αὐτό, but in predicate position: 'la cure d'amaigrissement est, par rapport au fait de faire maigrir, justement cela'. This is his translation of the manuscripts' text τοῦ ἰσχναίνειν ἡ ἰσχνασία αὐτό, ignoring Bywater's emendation τό for τοῦ and citing Δ.2, 1013a35–b1 (the only other occurrence of ἰσχνασία in Aristotle), as warrant for taking ἡ ἰσχνασία to cover all the means – instruments as well as activities – to the completed action ἰσχναίνειν; αὐτό he construes as a reference to τῶν περὶ τὸ τέλος, so that 'justement cela' means 'is a member of the class of means to an end'. That strikes me as an awfully long-winded way to secure the same result as Jaeger gets by simply deleting ἡ ἰσχνασία αὐτό, and Δ.2 hardly justifies so distinguishing ἰσχνασία from ἰσχναίνειν, since the verb does not appear in the chapter.

Met. Λ.8, 1074b3, usually taken to pick up the neuter θείων σωμάτων at 1074a30–1. Elsewhere I have argued that 1074a38–b14 was originally written as the immediate sequel to 1073a3–b38, so that οὗτοι picks up the planets (Venus, Mercury, Jupiter, etc.) named at 1073b31–8. This is a case where the context preceding the pronoun has not vanished. It has merely been separated so that Aristotle can stop to do his calculation of the number of intelligences needed to move the spheres postulated by the astronomical systems of Eudoxus and Callippus; for which purpose he reverts to his usual staccato style, in striking contrast to the literariness of the preceding and following sections.[91] A rare glimpse of a process we cannot usually observe.

No wonder the most serious difficulties of text and translation are located in the first portion of the Passage. That is the portion most likely to become obscure as the result of being separated from an earlier discussion we can no longer read. Accordingly, I now offer Version B, an annotated rendering of the first few sentences, to try out the possibilities opened up by the conclusions reached under (i) and (ii). As with those conclusions, so too much of the detail to follow is owed to David Sedley. All of it should be read as tentative exploration, not a set of firm proposals. Changes to Jaeger's text ‖ are marked with an asterisk. Bold type marks a phrase discussed in the relevant numbered annotation.

> Since of actions which have a limit **none** is an end, but all **belong to the class of means to an end** (1), e.g. slimming in the sense of the slimming process considered in itself [οἷον τὸ ἰσχναίνειν [ἡ ἰσχνασία] αὐτό*] (2), and since the things themselves one is slimming, when one is slimming them, are in process of changing **in this sense, that** the results aimed at in the change are not yet present (3), these are not cases of action, or not at any rate of complete action. For none of them is **in itself** (4) an end. It is in that former thing [ἐκείνῃ* without <ἡ>*] (5) that the end and **the** [retaining ἡ*] **action are present** (6).

(1) The partitive genitive τῶν is appropriate because κινήσεις are not the sole members of that class; if they were, nothing could be both an end and means to some further end. On the other hand, the emphatic 'none' excludes from present consideration actions which are both means and ends, in accordance with what appears to be a semi-technical meaning of

---

[91] Burnyeat 2001b: 141–5. The argument takes off from Friedrich Blass's suggestion (Blass 1875) that, since both stretches of text (1073a3–b38, 1074a38–b14) avoid hiatus (a mark of literary style), they were copied out by Aristotle from his lost *De philosophia*. That they were not originally written for Λ is further confirmed by the backwards-referring δέδεικται of 1073a5, for no such proof has preceded in the text of Λ as we have it.

πέρας, exemplified at *DA* 1.3, 407a23–5: τῶν μὲν γὰρ πραγματικῶν νοήσεων ἔστι πέρατα (π̄ᾶσαι γὰρ ἑτέρου χάριν), αἱ δὲ θεωρητικαί ..., 'Practical thoughts have limits, for they are all *for the sake of something else*, whereas theoretical thoughts ...'.

(2) One could remove the square brackets by printing ἤ *if*, but *only* if, ἤ ἰσχνασία αὐτό is a plausible Aristotelian phrase. On this, see below. Bonitz made αὐτό pick up τέλος, so that ἡ ἰσχνασία is the τέλος of τὸ ἰσχναίνειν: 'So ist z. B. das Zieldes Abmagerns die Magerkeit'. Ross Tr.[1] proposed to read just οἷον ἡ ἰσχνασία αὐτό: '"the process of making thin" is of this sort', which reappears (without the inner quotation marks) in Ross–Barnes, but in his edition and Tr.[2] he favours τὸ ἰσχναίνειν ἢ ἰσχνασία [αὐτό], αὐτά ..., crediting τό and ἤ to Bywater.

(3) With Ross Tr.[1] I take the accusative absolute μὴ ὑπάρχοντα ... κίνησις to elucidate οὕτως, the way they are changing. To Ross's note, 'αὐτά is curious, and some corruption may be suspected', I respond that the word is curious, but might cease to be so if we could access its original context. Alternatively, it emphasises the transition from the slimming process considered in itself to the items under treatment.

(4) Line 20's αὐτό is still in force.

(5) ἐκείνη was printed in the Aldine and every subsequent edition || until Bonitz emended,[92] as well as by Christ after him; iota subscript, often omitted in papyri and manuscripts, scarcely counts as an emendation.[93] I propose that the pronoun picks up an earlier but now lost designation of the kind of thing that will soon be dubbed ἐνέργεια. The Berlin Academy's bracketed Latin version (on which see n. 26 above) renders the sentence thus: 'nec enim ea finis est, sed in illa inest finis et actio', where 'ea' corresponds to ταῦτα but 'illa' has no visible reference at all. Full marks to the unnamed translator!

(6) Since Bonitz this sentence has been doubly emended to yield the meaning 'that movement in which the end is present is an action' (Ross), with πρᾶξις in predicative position. Version B puts ἡ πρᾶξις in subject position alongside τέλος, in line with the transmitted text. The idea of the

---

[92] Both Ross 1924 and Jaeger 1957 cite Bonitz 1848 as proposing ἐκείνη ᾗ (misprinted in Jaeger's apparatus as ἐκείνη ῇ). True enough for Bonitz's apparatus, but in the commentary *ad loc.* he prints ἐκείνη ἐν ᾗ.

[93] Ross's apparatus does in fact report 'ἐκείνη codd.', and Jaeger probably means to do the same (the iota subscript in his apparatus has mistakenly migrated to the immediately preceding ἐκείνη), but this has to be (correct) inference from the grammar of ἐνυπάρχει, not autopsy, for no subscript is visible in A^b. Christ 1895: vii–viii reports that E is punctilious in writing iota subscript, whereas A^b hardly bothers. Brockmann's collation of the Passage in M and C (Appendix 1 below) found no iota subscript in either.

action itself being present when the end is[94] may be compared with *NE* x.4, 1174a19–21: an instance of building is complete either at the moment it is finished or in the whole time *up to and including* that finish. In the Passage αὐτό abstracts from the finish, so that τὸ ἰσχναίνειν cannot count as action, or at any rate not as a complete action; cf. αὐτῇ τῇ βαδίσει at *NE* x.4, 1174a32. Aristotle shifts from speaking of the act as *being* or not being the *telos* (1048b18 and 22) to saying that it *contains* the *telos* (1048b22).

In Version B the key to the whole passage is the retention of what I would call the 'abstraction operator' αὐτό at line 20. The manuscript text, found in M and C as well as A[b], is τοῦ ἰσχναίνειν ἡ αὐτό. Bekker, Schwegler, and Christ all print the transmitted τοῦ,[95] but Bywater's τό for τοῦ is accepted by both Ross and Jaeger. As a result, they have a problem with ἡ ἰσχνασία αὐτό. Ross opts to follow Bywater in printing ᾗ for ἡ at 1048b19, while Jaeger brackets ‖ ἡ ἰσχνασία as a reader's gloss on τὸ ἰσχναίνειν. Restoring αὐτό, as I propose to do, makes it essential to delete the two preceding words. Let me explain why.

Plato frequently couples the neuter αὐτό with a feminine or masculine noun, and not just in contexts involving the Theory of Forms. At *Rep.* 363a Adeimantus complains that the poets do not praise δικαιοσύνην αὐτό, but the consequences of a reputation for it; he does not mean they fail to praise the Platonic Form of Justice. At *Smp.* 199d a question about αὐτό τοῦτο πατέρα is a question about a father – any father – in so far as he is a father.[96] But the only Aristotelian examples of this usage recorded in Bonitz's *Index Aristotelicus* s.v. αὐτό are references to Platonic Forms. My *TLG* search through the corpus under αὐτό, αὐτοῦ, αὐτῷ confirmed his finding: several thousand examples, but the only relevant ones are semiquotes from Plato. On the other hand, it is Aristotelian usage to couple αὐτό with article plus infinitive:

GA v.8, 789a4–6: Suckling as such [τὸ θηλάζειν αὐτό] contributes nothing to the growth of teeth.

NE ix.11, 1171a35–b1: The very act of seeing one's friends is pleasant [αὐτό ... τὸ ὁρᾶν τοὺς φίλους ἡδύ].

---

[94] Similarly Brague 1988: 459 on both text and meaning.
[95] Which Schwegler 1847, ii. 155 (cf. iv. 383), equates with τὸ τέλος: 'so ist die Magerkeit Zweck des sich Abmagerns'. A similar rendering in Lasson 1907, who would print οἷον τοῦ ἰσχναίνειν ἡ ἰσχνασία, αὐτό δε ὅταν... (p. xv).
[96] For a more general discussion, with examples, of the 'abstraction operator' αὐτό in Plato, see Burnyeat 2000b: 35–7 [now also Chapter 1 in *EAMP* vol. III].

EE VII.12, 1244b29–30: If one were to cut off and abstract mere knowledge and its opposite [εἰ ... τις ἀποτέμοι καὶ ποιήσειε τὸ γινώσκειν αὐτὸ καθ' αὑτὸ καὶ μή].

Pol. VIII.3, 1338a1–3: Leisure of itself [τὸ σχολάζειν ... αὐτό] is thought to give pleasure and happiness and a blessed life.

I conclude that the phrase τὸ ἰσχναίνειν αὐτό is well chosen to concentrate our minds on the slimming process as such, excluding its end and completion.

If this is accepted, ἡ ἰσχνασία becomes a reader's gloss – a correct gloss guided by ἰσχνασία at 1048b29 – not, as Jaeger supposed, on τὸ ἰσχναίνειν, but on the full phrase τὸ ἰσχναίνειν αὐτό. Without much preceding context to clarify the point of the phrase, it was understandably found obscure. And once the gloss got copied into the main text between ἰσχναίνειν and αὐτό, the two successive nominatives led a scribe or reader who decided for η as ἡ, not ᾗ or ἤ, to change τό to τοῦ. ||

So much for the square brackets. Doug Hutchinson has urged in correspondence that two pairs of angled brackets could go as well if we adopt Fonseca's emendation of 1048b23: ὁρᾷ ἅμα καὶ ἑώρακε καὶ νοεῖ καὶ νενόηκεν.[97] Reducing Bonitz's three verb pairs to two leaves a neat parallel with the pairs of contrasting pairs that follow in lines 24–6. I am mildly favourable to this idea.

Someone may say I have now cut the ground from under my feet, in that, if Version B is accepted, and Fonseca's restoration of 1048b23 preferred to Bonitz's, the Passage is no longer so corrupt as it was when I argued from its extreme textual disrepair to the marginal annotation hypothesis (pp. 112–3 above). Certainly, it is less corrupt. But removing a quantity of brackets leaves plenty of emending still to do. Bonitz's emendation ἅμα for ἄλλα at lines 23 and 25 must certainly stand; in the manuscripts only lines 30 and 33 have ἅμα. Whatever the fate of φρονεῖ in line 23, we must supply ἑώρακε to twin with ὁρᾷ. Bonitz's <δεῖ> after δή at 1048b28 is extremely plausible too, rather more so than Schwegler's λέγω/λέγομεν – unless it is thought sufficient to follow Brague in attributing imperatival force to the bare infinitive λέγειν.[98] Then there is

---

[97] Fonseca 1613, *ad loc.* Fonseca does not explain how he arrives at this proposal, but Hutchinson's suggestion is that 1048b23's φρονεῖ originated when the ἑώρακε needed after ὁρᾷ got corrupted into φρονε and was later 'corrected' into φρονεῖ. Alternatively, φρονεῖ might have originated as a gloss on νοεῖ.

[98] Brague 1988: 456 n. 9. While Plato quite often uses the infinitive that way, Bonitz 1955, 343a22–5, cites for such usage only the inauthentic *Rhet. ad Alex.* 23, 1434b18–19. Yet then he

Bywater's crucially important τό for τοῦ at 1048b19, not to mention the iota subscript for ἐκείνῃ at 1048b22. Further doubts, worries, and improvements are recorded in the apparatus of Ross and Jaeger, but not endorsed by them.[99] The Passage is still a highly damaged stretch of the *Metaphysics*. ||

Part IV: Uniqueness

11. Let me now return to Ross and his confidence that the Passage 'contains sound Aristotelian doctrine and terminology' (p. 101 above). Ross offers no proof of this assertion, but he always had Bonitz's commentary in front of him as he wrote, and Bonitz does offer proof. He lists parallels in other works from which, he claims, the Passage 'cum placitis Aristotelicis optime concinere ... apparet' ['... seems to agree very well with Aristotelian principles']. I shall take his proof texts one by one, to show that, while each features some element also found in the Passage, none of them contains everything we find there. Most importantly, none of them contains or requires the *terminological* distinction between κίνησις and ἐνέργεια. Nor, to be fair, does Bonitz, unlike Ross, assert that they do.

What is at stake in this section of the enquiry is whether the distinction drawn in the Passage between κίνησις and ἐνέργεια occurs anywhere else in the corpus. If, as I shall argue, it does not, scholars should stop treating it as a central theme of Aristotle's philosophy and stop importing it into their exposition of his other works. It is a unique, problematic intrusion into the text of the *Metaphysics*.

(a) We begin with one of Aristotle's logical treatises. *SE* 22 is a study of a type of fallacy which depends on the fact that linguistically similar expressions can stand for categorially different things. The example I am interested in is developed at 178a9–28. You are asked, 'Is it possible to act and to have acted on the same thing at the same time [ἆρ' ἐνδέχεται τὸ αὐτὸ ἅμα ποιεῖν τε καὶ πεποιηκέναι]?'[100] 'No.' 'But it is possible surely to see

---

proceeds to a row of impeccably Aristotelian infinitives which have, he says, the force of a verbal noun in -τέον. Nearly all are from logical works, which will be relevant in section 14 below. A striking example, given the subject matter of this paper, is *Top.* VI.8, 146b13–16: σκοπεῖν δὲ καὶ εἰ γένεσίς ἐστι πρὸς ὃ ἀποδέδωκεν, ἢ ἐνέργεια· οὐδὲν γὰρ τῶν τοιούτων τέλος· μᾶλλον γὰρ τὸ ἐνηργηκέναι καὶ γεγενῆσθαι τέλος ἢ τὸ γίνεσθαι καὶ ἐνεργεῖν.

[99] Although Jaeger 1957 speaks *in propria persona* when his apparatus says that the sentence ἀλλ' οὐ μανθάνει ... ὑγίασται at 1048b24–5 belongs after εὐδαιμόνηκεν in line 26.

[100] W. A. Pickard-Cambridge (in Ross 1928b), writes, 'Is it possible to be doing and to have done the same thing at the same time?', which makes τὸ αὐτό an internal accusative. But the follow-up question demands that it be an external accusative, as does the solution in terms of categories. Of

and to have seen the same thing at the same time and in the same respect/ at the same angle [ἀλλὰ || μὴν ὁρᾶν γέ τι ἅμα καὶ ἑωρακέναι τὸ αὐτὸ καὶ ταὐτὸ ἐνδέχεται].'[101] You can accept that, without being refuted, provided you insist that seeing belongs in the category of undergoing (πάσχειν), not the category of action (ποιεῖν).

Now this is about the *possibility* of seeing and having seen, not about the *necessary* conjoint truth of present and perfect, but it is still interesting that the argument under discussion presupposes respondents who will find themselves inclined both to answer 'No' to the opening question and to accept the apparent counter-example. Despite the linguistic similarity between the verbs ποιεῖν and ὁρᾶν, there is a difference to which a native speaker of Greek will be sensitive, even though it may take a sophism to jolt them into thinking about it and a philosopher to provide a theory of categories which can explain it.

Aristotle provides the theory, but he writes in terms which suggest that anyone might propound the sophism in an attempt to trick their opponent.[102] The scenario envisaged is a dialectical exchange. He treats the simultaneity of seeing and having seen as a commonplace of dialectical debate, not his own discovery.[103]

(b) In *De sensu* 6, 446b2–6, Aristotle comes closer to asserting the necessary conjoint truth of present and perfect for verbs of perception:

> Now, even though it is always the case that at the same time one hears a thing and has heard it,[104] and in general perceives and has perceived, || and they [perceptions] involve no becoming, but exist [*sc.* when they do]

---

course, the ambiguity of ποιεῖν can give rise to fallacy (Plato, *Euthd.* 284bc), but that is not the sort of fallacy Aristotle wants to illustrate here. Poste 1866 translates, 'Can we be making and have made one and the same thing?' (similarly Ackrill 1965: 123, and, in French translation, Dorion 1995), but no one would be tempted to class seeing something as a case of making something, whereas Platonic accounts of vision do involve the perceiver's acting on the object: *Theaet.* 153e–154a; *Tim.* 45bd.

[101] 'At the same angle' is a nice suggestion by Brague 1988: 462.
[102] Michael of Ephesus [alias Pseudo-Alexander], In *SE* 149.29 Wallies, is explicit that it is sophists who put the questions. Goldschmidt 1982: 172 agrees.
[103] Brague 1988: 462–3 agrees, as does Graham 1980: 121. If the point is indeed a commonplace, we can reject outright the claim of A. Rijksbaron (Rijksbaron 1989: 45), that it 'cannot possibly be seen as reflecting actual Greek usage', in which ἑώρακε always involves a past reference. Of course ἑώρακε does often have past reference (Plato, *Soph.* 239e1, is a nice example signalled to me by Lesley Brown), but Chantraine's message is that the perfect evolved over time with successive forms continuing to coexist.
[104] ἅπαν can be taken either as the subject of the verbs (Ackrill 1965) or as their object. I prefer the latter, in line with n. 100 above. But either way, a universal generalisation results, which can equally well be conveyed by the 'always' I have borrowed from Barnes's revision of the Oxford translation. As for καὶ εἰ, it suits the context well to take it as 'even though', introducing an admitted fact: Denniston 1954: 301–2.

> without undergoing a process of coming to be, nevertheless, just as, when the blow has been struck, the sound is not yet at the ear ...

There is little point to this (incomplete) sentence unless Aristotle wants to affirm the antecedent of its opening conditional 'even though ... nevertheless ...'. The antecedent presents a 'logical' truth which might seem hard to reconcile with the evident physical truth that sound and smell take time to travel to the perceiver. It was the quantifier 'always' that Ackrill adduced as evidence that in this text, and so also in the Passage, the form 'at the same time *p* and *q*' is meant to indicate an inference from *p* to *q*, not just a conjunction.[105] I agree, but add that the quantifier serves even better as evidence for an inference going both ways at once.

(c) We now move fully into physics. At *Phys.* III.2, 201b31–3, we find this:

> ἥ τε κίνησις ἐνέργεια μὲν εἶναί τις δοκεῖ, ἀτελὴς δε· αἴτιον δ'ὅτι ἀτελὲς τὸ δυνατόν οὗ ἐστιν ἐνέργεια.
>
> Change is thought to be a sort of actuality, but an incomplete one; the explanation is that the potential thing whose actuality it is is incomplete.

The thesis that change is a sort of actuality, but an incomplete one, is no passing remark. It is part of Aristotle's definition of change, which has a foundational role in his physics. In the wider argumentative context of *Physics* III.2, to deny that change is incomplete actuality would be to reduce it to not-being, the status the Platonists assign it. In effect, Aristotelian physics, which is the study of things with an internal principle of change and stability, would have no real subject matter to investigate.[106]

The thesis that change is incomplete actuality reappears in *DA* II.5, 417a16–17, this time without the qualification 'is thought to be' and with a back-reference to *Physics* III.1–3 as the place where the thesis was explained (καὶ γὰρ ἔστιν ἡ κίνησις ἐνέργεια τις, ἀτελὴς μέντοι, καθάπερ ἐν ἑτέροις εἴρηται). Another comparable text is *DA* III.7, 431a6–7: ||

> ἡ γὰρ κίνησις τοῦ ἀτελοῦς ἐνέργεια,[107] ἡ δ' ἁπλῶς ἐνέργεια ἑτέρα, ἡ τοῦ τετελεσμένου.
>
> For change is the actuality of the incomplete; actuality unqualified, the actuality of what is complete, is different.

---

[105] Ackrill 1965: 124, except that in his translation the quantifier is 'everything' taken as subject of the verbs: 'everything at the same time hears and has heard'.
[106] This is one of the places where Frede 2001 is especially relevant to my discussion.
[107] Some editors add C's ἦν here.

262–263]   *Part IV: Uniqueness*   131

Here Aristotle makes explicit what the other two physical texts imply, that incomplete actuality contrasts with another sort of actuality: actuality unqualified, actuality *simpliciter*, or, as he might equally well have said, complete actuality.

But this is still not the doctrine of the Passage. ἐνέργεια still contrasts with potentiality (as it does in the rest of *Metaphysics* Θ), not with κίνησις. On the contrary, κίνησις is explained as ἐνέργεια: ἐνέργεια which is incomplete. I conclude that the original home of the Passage was not a physical treatise. For its exclusive distinction between κίνησις and ἐνέργεια runs counter to a foundational thesis of Aristotelian physics. In the Passage being a κίνησις entails not being ἐνέργεια at all.

12. To say this is not to deny the Aristotelian provenance of the distinction. The Passage shows how easy it is to pass from '*x* is only qualifiedly *F*' to '*x* is not *F* at all, but something else'. Thus, by way of preparing for its terminological innovation, the Passage says that actions (πράξεις) which are not their own end *either* do not count as action, *or* at any rate they are not complete action (1048b21–2: οὐκ ἔστι ταῦτα πρᾶξις ἢ οὐ τελεία γε). In the sequel the first disjunct is chosen, with ἐνέργεια substituted for πρᾶξις. κινήσεις, because they are incomplete, are not ἐνέργειαι at all. It is the second disjunct that prevails in the physical treatises. Yes, κινήσεις are ἐνέργειαι, subject to the qualification that they are incomplete ἐνέργειαι. To motivate the terminological innovation of the Passage, we should look for a (non-physical) context where the first disjunct would be philosophically more appropriate than the second, where there are grounds for saying that a πρᾶξις or ἐνέργεια which is not its own end is not πρᾶξις or ἐνέργεια at all.

Which brings me, of course, to the *Nicomachean Ethics* and to Aristotle's critique of the theory put forward in Plato's *Philebus* that pleasure is a process of becoming (γένεσις). *NE* x.3–5 is the text most often, and most confidently, cited as parallel for the κίνησις– ‖ ἐνέργεια distinction in the Passage.[108] Before tackling it, it will be helpful to review our findings so far.

Go back to *Met.* Θ.6, 1048b8–9: τὰ μὲν γὰρ ὡς κίνησις πρὸς δύναμιν, τὰ δ' ὡς οὐσία πρός τινα ὕλην ('some are related as change to capacity, while others are related as substance to some matter'). In his note *ad loc.* Ross writes:

> At one time Aristotle includes ἐνέργεια in κίνησις (*Rhet.* 1412a9); at another he includes κίνησις in ἐνέργεια (*Phys.* 201b31, *De An.* 431a6,

---

[108] In dealing with book x I have been helped by testing discussion with David Charles.

EN 1154b27); at another he speaks of the two as mutually exclusive (1048b28). κίνησις is said to be an ἐνέργεια but ἀτελής (*Phys.* 201b31), or to differ from ἐνέργεια because it is ἀτελής (1048b29). The variations of language need not disturb us. κίνησις and ἐνέργεια are species of something wider for which Aristotle has no name, and for which he uses now the name of one species, now that of the other. The difference is brought out as well in ll. 18–35 [i.e. the Passage] as anywhere in Aristotle.[109]

It is correct that both κίνησις and ἐνέργεια have what one may call a generic use; in Section 1 above we noted generic κίνησις in Θ.6, generic ἐνέργεια in Θ.8. It is correct also that κίνησις has a specific use for processes directed towards an end-state external to themselves, as laid down in *Physics* III.1–3. Such variety should not surprise. κίνησις and its parent verb had already had a long history in ordinary Greek. But ἐνέργεια and the associated verb ἐνεργεῖν are first attested in Aristotle himself. Probably his invention, they start off as terms of art.[110] Furthermore, while it is correct – I emphasised the point earlier (above, p. 95–6) – that at Θ.6, 1048b8–9, κίνησις is generic in that it covers both building and seeing, nowhere does Aristotle expressly divide κινήσεις into those which are their own goal and those that aim at a further product. He does so divide ἐνέργεια, as in *NE* I.1, 1094a16–17, and in Θ.8 as quoted above, but the nearest he gets to a parallel division of κίνησις is *NE* X.3, 1174b4: 'Most κινήσεις are incomplete' (αἱ πολλαὶ ἀτελεῖς). Nor does he ever acknowledge the idea of κίνησις unqualified, or complete κίνησις.[111] In the philosophical language of the time that would sound bizarre.[112]

I conclude that the generic uses of κίνησις and ἐνέργεια are not on a par. They should not be regarded as alternative extensions to the generic level of the terminology for two parallel species. Ross's account is not only too simple. He goes wrong at the start by making the Passage his point of departure. The Passage is the only text he cites – I have been arguing it is the only text he can cite – for κίνησις and ἐνέργεια as parallel species of a

---

[109] Quoted with approval by Smeets 1952: 108 n. 37, Goldschmidt 1982: 176, and Linguiti 2000: 59 n. 149. Contrast Skemp 1979: 244: 'we are all dissatisfied with the complacent remark of Ross in his note on *Metaph.*, 1048b8 that "the variations of language need not disturb us"'.

[110] At *NE* VII.12, 1153a15–17, the persons who wrongly think that ἐνέργεια is γένεσις are clearly philosophers. On Aristotelian word formation, Fritz 1938, esp. 66–9 on ἐνέργεια and ἐντελέχεια, is most interesting.

[111] The phrase κίνησιν τελείαν at *NE* X.3, 1174a28, denotes a thing you cannot find at any time prior to arrival at the (external) goal: a completed change rather than one that is intrinsically complete.

[112] Contrast Proclus, much later, on τελεία κίνησις at *In Parm.* 797.32–8 Cousin. Ross's use of the phrase in his note on *Metaph.* Θ.6, 1048b18–21, is illicit.

wider but nameless genus.¹¹³ But even here he ignores two important facts. First, in the Passage the genus does have a name: πρᾶξις. Second, its subdivision into κινήσεις and ἐνέργειαι is presented as a terminological innovation. Ross's procedure is methodologically back to front.

The truth is that, when Aristotle says in *DA* II.5 that κίνησις is ἐνέργεια τις, ἀτελὴς μέντοι ('change is a sort of actuality, but an incomplete one'), he is not locating specific κίνησις in a wider class. 'Change is a sort of actuality' does not mean 'Change is one species of actuality alongside others,' but 'Change is an actuality of a sort, not a mere nothing.' Aristotle is reminding us of how in *Physics* III.1–3 he rescued κίνησις from the oblivion of unreality and not-being to which the Platonists would consign it. The τις in ἐνέργεια τις has an *alienans* function. The difference between ἡ ἁπλῶς ἐνέργεια and ἐνέργεια ἀτελής is not the difference between two species of a genus (like the ἐνέργειας διαφερούσας τῷ εἴδει at *NE* x.5, 1175a25–6), but the difference between an ἐνέργεια in the full sense of the term and one from which you cannot expect everything you would normally expect from an ἐνέργεια.¹¹⁴

Thus the relation of specific κίνησις to generic ἐνέργεια is not a species–genus relation like that of deer to animal. Only in the Passage do κίνησις and ἐνέργεια appear as parallel species of a common genus, πρᾶξις. That requires a change in the meaning of the term ἐνέργεια, such that being an ἐνέργεια entails not being a κίνησις, which || is enough to make it the case that, by contraposition, being a κίνησις entails not being (in the new, narrowed sense) an ἐνέργεια. To produce the exclusive contrast between κίνησις and ἐνέργεια there is no need for the term κίνησις to change meaning as well. κίνησις in the Passage keeps to the specific use it has elsewhere, for changes (active or passive) intrinsically directed at an end-state outside themselves. In that case it can still be called ἐνέργεια τις in the *Physics* sense of that phrase. In view of what the Passage does with the generic term πρᾶξις, one might say that κίνησις is now not ἐνέργεια, *because* it is only ἐνέργεια τις in the old sense.

I conclude that what we should look for in the *Nicomachean Ethics* is evidence that the term ἐνέργεια is being used in the exclusive sense of the Passage. Then, provided κίνησις has its standard specific sense, each term will exclude the other.

---

[113] Similarly, in his *Physics* commentary (Ross 1936, *ad* 201b31–2, Ross refers to the Passage as a fuller statement of the doctrine of *Physics* III.2!

[114] See Appendix 2 for an exemplary ancient explanation of this point by Iamblichus.

13. The place to start is Aristotle's report of the *Philebus* account of pleasure:

τέλειόν τε τἀγαθὸν τιθέντες, τὰς δὲ κινήσεις καὶ τὰς γενέσεις ἀτελεῖς, τὴν ἡδονὴν κίνησιν καὶ γένεσιν ἀποφαίνειν πειρῶνται. οὐ καλῶς δ' ἐοίκασι λέγειν οὐδ' εἶναι κίνησιν. (*NE* x.3, 1173a29–31)

> Postulating that the good is something complete, whereas changes and becomings are incomplete, they try to show that pleasure is change and becoming. But they seem to be wrong when they say this. Pleasure seems not to be change at all.

The word Plato used is γένεσις, not κίνησις.[115] γένεσις, not κίνησις, is the word Aristotle himself uses when criticising the *Philebus* theory in *NE* VII.12, 1153a7–17. If the book X discussion brings in κίνησις as well, Aristotle must have a purpose in mind. I suggest that the purpose is to translate what Plato means by γένεσις into his own terminology.[116]

After all, γένεσις in Aristotle standardly refers to the coming to be of a new substance, in contrast to the alteration, growth, or spatial movement of an existing substance. The *Philebus* announces a compendious, exclusive dichotomy between γένεσις and οὐσία, where γένεσις covers, not only the building of ships (54b), but also || the body's being restored to its natural state by food and drink (54e). When Aristotle needs a compendious noun to cover all types of change, he chooses κίνησις or μεταβολή.[117] So what more natural than to gloss Platonic γένεσις as Aristotelian κίνησις? In its standard specific sense κίνησις is directed towards an end-state outside itself, and this fits the *Philebus* characterisation of γένεσις as always 'for the sake of' the οὐσία that results.

Problem: the *Philebus* understands 'for the sake of' in an *exclusively* instrumental sense. Goodness is confined to the οὐσία for the sake of which any particular γένεσις occurs (54c–d). Then, if pleasure is γένεσις, it is altogether excluded from the class of things that are good. If Aristotelian κίνησις does duty for Platonic γένεσις, it too must be completely severed from the class of things that are good. This is not Aristotle's normal view: the text from *Metaphysics* Θ.8 quoted earlier (p. 96) has it that the exercise of a capacity to build is *more* of an end than the capacity, although

---

[115] So far as I know, the only place where Plato uses κίνησις of pleasure and pain themselves is *Rep.* 583e9–10, where the point is to contrast them with the ἡσυχία of the intermediate state in which one feels neither pleasure nor pain.

[116] Cf. *Top.* VI.8, 146b13–19, a curious passage where γένεσις is glossed by ἐνέργεια (broad sense).

[117] *Cat.* 14; *Phys.* III.1, 200b33–201a9; V.1, 224b35–225a20; and n. 10 above. But for a strikingly compendious use of the verb γίγνεσθαι, see *Met.* Z.7, 1032a13–15.

it is less of an end than the ultimate thing, the resulting house (1050a23–8).[118] In the *Philebus* the activity of shipbuilding is not an end at all, because it is *entirely* for the sake of the resulting ship.

To see how this could lead to an exclusive contrast between κίνησις and ἐνέργεια, as in the Passage, turn to the other place where the *Philebus* account of pleasure comes under fire, *Nicomachean Ethics* VII.12:[119]

> ἔτι οὐκ ἀνάγκη ἕτερόν τι εἶναι βέλτιον τῆς ἡδονῆς, ὥσπερ τινές φασι τὸ τέλος τῆς γενέσεως· οὐ γὰρ γενέσεις εἰσὶν οὐδὲ μετὰ γενέσεως πᾶσαι, ἀλλ' ἐνέργειαι καὶ τέλος· οὐδὲ γινομένων συμβαίνουσιν ἀλλὰ χρωμένων· καὶ τέλος οὐ πασῶν ἕτερόν τι, ἀλλὰ τῶν εἰς τὴν τελέωσιν ἀγομένων τῆς φύσεως.

> Again, it is not necessary that there should be something else better than pleasure, as some say the end is something better than becoming; for pleasures are not in fact becomings, nor even do they all accompany some becoming. *On the contrary, they are actualities and themselves each an end.* Nor do they occur when we are becoming something, but when we are exercising a capacity already possessed. And not all have an end distinct from themselves, only the pleasures of people who are being led to the perfection of their nature. (1153a7–12) ||

The last sentence quoted is proof that ἐνέργεια in this text does not have the exclusive sense of the Passage. It speaks of pleasurable ἐνέργειαι directed towards a further, external goal, the perfecting of our nature: these will be, or at least they will include, the pleasures of learning in theoretical, ethical, or practical domains (cf. *Phys.* VII.3, 246a12–b3, 247a2–3). The pleasures of learning are expressly mentioned at 1153a22–3; the pleasures of κινήσεις more generally feature in the next chapter, alongside those of ἕξεις, at 1154a13–15. In *Physics* III.1–3 learning was both κίνησις and thereby ἀτελὴς ἐνέργεια, and so it must be here if, however delightful in itself, it is an ἐνέργεια in pursuit of an external goal. But in the Passage learning is a paradigm example of κίνησις as *opposed* to ἐνέργεια. QED. More on the pleasures of learning and progress below.

Meanwhile, pursuing his polemic with Plato Aristotle here puts γένεσις and ἐνέργεια in exclusive contrast, as again at 1153a15–17, although the penultimate sentence in the quotation just given (οὐδέ ... χρωμένων) implies that ἐνέργεια retains its standard contrast with δύναμις or ἕξις (cf.

---

[118] Cf. ὧν κίνησις τὸ τέλος at 1050a17 and the comparative formulation at *NE* I.1, 1094a5–6. Remember that, besides producing a house, the exercise of the builder's art helps to preserve it for future use (*DA* II.5, 417b3–5).

[119] In studying which I have been greatly helped by discussion with Christof Rapp.

1153a24–5). Still, once γένεσις is glossed as κίνησις, which does not happen in the book VII discussion, we might expect a corresponding exclusive contrast between κίνησις and ἐνέργεια.

Many scholars find that expectation fulfilled in book x, where γένεσις is indeed glossed as κίνησις (x.3, quoted above; cf. 4, 1174b10 and 13) in the initial statement of the *Philebus* theory.[120] But so far as I can see, the critique that follows nowhere forces us to abandon Aristotle's usual understanding of κίνησις and ἐνέργεια. He does not take up the opportunity to make ἐνέργεια incompatible with κίνησις. Let me track through the arguments one by one.

(a) x.3, 1173a32–b4: It is a feature of all κίνησις that it can be qualified by the adverbs 'quickly' and 'slowly'. We can walk quickly or slowly, but we cannot enjoy something quickly or slowly. True enough, and an effective argument against the *Philebus* account of pleasure as κίνησις. But since the term ἐνέργεια does not occur, the argument cannot help our enquiry.

The next argument (1173b4–7) is couched in terms of γένεσις, not κίνησις. In the string of arguments that rounds off the chapter ‖ γένεσις comes up once more (1173b19), κίνησις not at all. κίνησις does not return until x.4.

(b) x.4, 1174a14–b14: all κίνησις takes time to reach its form and completion, whereas pleasure, like seeing, is complete at any moment. Aristotle does not say that κίνησις is incomplete ἐνέργεια, but he insists that it is incomplete (1174a22, 27–8, b4), and he refers us elsewhere for an accurate, scientific account of κίνησις (1174b2–3). If, as some think, the reference is to *Physics* v.1–4, note this remark at v.1, 224b10: 'We have defined κίνησις previously', which presupposes III.1–3. So the term κίνησις retains its standard specific sense, as defined in those crucial chapters. Other scholars (beginning with Michael of Ephesus, In *EN* x.4, 552.17 Heylbut) suppose the reference is to *Physics* VI–VIII, but this changes nothing since VIII.1, 251a8–10, also draws on III.1–3. As for ἐνέργεια, it simply does not occur in the lines we are discussing. Once more, the enquiry draws a blank.

Some may protest that even if the word ἐνέργεια does not occur, Aristotle is presupposing the narrow use defined in the Passage when he contrasts the idea that pleasure is κίνησις or γένεσις with his own view that it is a whole and wholly present at every instant (1174a17–19, b9).[121]

---

[120] Ackrill 1965 set the pattern and many followed suit. A rare sign of caution is Bostock 1988: 260–1: *NE* x argues 'at least roughly' along the same lines of thought as the Passage.

[121] Liske 1991, after acknowledging (p. 161) that the Passage is the sole explicit presentation of the distinction, goes on to describe *NE* x.4 as the text where 'Aristoteles die κίνησις-ἐνέργεια-

I reply that what this contrast shows is that Aristotle can make his point in other words, without calling on the term ἐνέργεια in either the broad or the narrow sense. To say that pleasure does not require a stretch of time, because it is a complete whole in the present now, is enough to refute the claim that pleasure is γένεσις or κίνησις, which do require a stretch of time, but it does not impose the narrow meaning of the Passage on the word ἐνέργεια for the simple reason (to repeat) that that word is neither used nor mentioned.

(c) x.4, 1174b14–17, launching Aristotle's own account of pleasure, does use ἐνέργεια, but qualifies it as τελεία, which would be redundant if the term had the narrow sense defined in the Passage:

> αἰσθήσεως δὲ πάσης πρὸς τὸ αἰσθητὸν ἐνεργούσης, τελείως δὲ τῆς εὖ διακειμένης πρὸς τὸ κάλλιστον τῶν ὑπὸ τὴν αἴσθησιν (τοιοῦτον γὰρ μάλιστ' εἶναι δοκεῖ ἡ τελεία ἐνέργεια ...)

> Since every sense is active in relation to its object, and a sense which is ǁ in good condition acts completely in relation to the most beautiful of its objects (for complete activity seems to be especially of this nature ...) (trans. Ross–Urmson)

Even those like myself who would prefer to translate τελεία ἐνέργεια here as 'perfect activity' should acknowledge that Aristotle begins in a way which positively discourages taking ἐνέργεια in the narrow meaning of the Passage. Compare τελειοτάτη ἐνέργεια at 1074b20 and 22.

(d) From x.4, 1174b14, to the end of x.5 Aristotle expounds his own theory that pleasure completes an ἐνέργεια as a supervenient end. Since he states that there is no pleasure without ἐνέργεια (1175a20–1), it is not surprising that the words ἐνέργεια and ἐνεργεῖν occur again and again. The main examples often remind scholars of the Passage: perceiving, thinking, contemplating, living.[122] But there is nothing to show that ἐνέργεια is

---

Unterscheidung *zwar nicht explizit* thematisiert, aber doch die genauste Charakterisierung von ihr gibt, die sich in seinem Werk findet' (p. 166).

[122] So, influentially, Ackrill 1965: 128: 'Aristotle does not say that he is here talking of the distinction between energeiai and kineseis. But he likens pleasure or enjoyment (ἡδονή) to seeing, and contrasts both with kineseis, using as examples of kineseis house-building and walking – which were also used as examples of kineseis in the *Metaphysics* passage. Both the choice of examples and the general account of the contrast leave no doubt that it *is* the energeia–kinesis distinction that he is using.' As if building and (if not walking) rolling and jumping were not both κινήσεις and ἀτελεῖς ἐνέργειαι in the *Physics* (III.1, 201a16–19; b8–13). As if Θ.8 (quoted above) does not contrast seeing with building while counting both as ἐνέργειαι. Only Croese 1998: 122 n. 3 has the grace to say that she accepts Ackrill's conclusion because 'To our knowledge this claim has not been questioned.' Others just follow suit, although I. M. Crombie, in his review of Bambrough (Crombie 1967: 32) was an early dissenting voice, spot on: '[Ackrill] says that Aristotle

being used in the exclusive sense defined in the Passage, and at least one of Aristotle's examples should give us pause. This is x.5, 1175a30–5:

> The pleasure proper to a given ἐνέργεια helps it forward. For those who enjoy that ἐνέργεια do it with more discernment and with greater accuracy. Thus those who are fond of geometry become proficient in it, and grasp its problems better, and similarly those who are fond of music *or of building* or of other arts make progress towards their proper function [ἐπιδιδόασιν εἰς τὸ οἰκεῖον ἔργον], because they enjoy it.[123]

Building, as we have seen, is a standard example of incomplete ἐνέργεια. What are these lovers of building (φιλοικοδόμοι) doing here if Aristotle means to confine ἐνέργεια to the restrictive meaning ‖ of the Passage?[124] Sophisticated answers have been offered, to the effect that a κίνησις such as building may be looked upon as an ἐνέργεια in so far as at each and every moment the builder can be said to exercise, and to have exercised, the art of building.[125] But in the absence of any positive indication that in book x ἐνέργεια and κίνησις exclude each other, it seems better to suppose they do not.[126] We then have to admit that the Passage is the sole place in the corpus where Aristotle's now famous distinction between κίνησις and ἐνέργεια can be found.

And it is not just lovers of building who make difficulty for the view I am opposing. All the people in this text are learners. The ἐνέργεια helped forward by their keen enjoyment is that of learning some knowledge or skill, not the exercise of finished expertise. Certainly one learns to build by building, though not in the fully skilled way a qualified craftsman does. But this is a point made in *Metaph.* Θ.8, 1049b29–1050a3, in the very chapter I quoted earlier to illustrate the generic use of ἐνέργεια, which covers both seeing and building. There Aristotle suggests that a practising apprentice must at each stage have acquired, and be exercising, some part of the body of knowledge (1050a1: τι τῆς ἐπιστήμης) they are learning. So we have two options for what it is that the lovers of building enjoy. It is

---

"classifies enjoying on the energeia side of the energeia–kinesis distinction". But what Aristotle says is simply that enjoying is not a κίνησις.'
[123] Translation indebted to Rackham 1934.
[124] Another example most naturally taken as incomplete is writing (x.5, 1175b19).
[125] Owen 1971–2: 143 (reprinted with the original pagination as Barnes et al. 1977: 92–103) and Owen 1986: 334–46; Kosman 1969 at nn. 21 and 32 (cf. Waterlow 1988: 186–9); Gill 1980: 136; Liske 1991: 176–8. Gosling and Taylor 1982: 312–14 is to my mind a crushing critique of this solution.
[126] Owen 1971–2: 147 and 150, agrees, while being equally confident (cf. 139) that in book VII (which Ackrill 1965 does not discuss) ἐνέργεια *does* carry the exclusive sense of the Passage; Owen's book VII claim was refuted earlier, p. 135.

either (i) the (active) exercise of partial productive knowledge or (ii) the (passive) process of acquiring more and more of the full body of knowledge. The two are compatible, even extensionally the same, and could each be highly enjoyable. Both are intrinsically directed towards a product or end-state outside themselves. According to Θ.8, (i) is an ἐνέργεια directed at a further product; according to *Physics* III.1–3, (ii) is an incomplete ἐνέργεια. The Passage would say || that both are κίνησις, not ἐνέργεια at all. But nothing in *Nicomachean Ethics* x.5 requires, or even hints, that we should understand ἐνέργεια in the exclusive sense of the Passage. Nothing requires, or even hints, that we should understand Aristotle's theory of pleasure to exclude the possibility of enjoying those ἐνέργειαι (generic) which are κινήσεις (specific) as well as those which are their own goal.[127] What he insists on is that pleasure is complete at every moment, from which it hardly follows that the activity enjoyed must itself be complete at every moment. Every child knows that making things is fun. A crossword puzzle offers adult pleasures – until you have completed it! Why shouldn't a keen apprentice delight in each and every moment of the process of slowly carving out the flutes of a column? Aristotle is undoubtedly right to say that their enjoyment will hone their skill.

This last point is worth dwelling on. A very good reason to avoid reading the narrow Passage meaning of ἐνέργεια into *NE* x.3–5 is that it would saddle the work with a monstrously distorted account of what we can enjoy. It would also make those chapters clash, not only with VII.12, 1153a7–12, discussed above, but also with VII.14, 1154b26–8:

> ... God always enjoys a single and simple pleasure; for there is not only an activity of movement [κινήσεως ἐνέργεια] but an activity of immobility [ἐνέργεια ἀκινησίας], and pleasure is found *more* in rest than in movement [μᾶλλον ἐν ἠρεμίᾳ ἐστὶν ἢ ἐν κινήσει]. (trans. Ross, emphasis added)

Which surely implies that there can be pleasure in κίνησις, even if it is less, or less satisfying, than pleasure in rest or pleasure in action undertaken for its own sake.[128] I propose, therefore, that in x.3–5 ἐνέργεια has the same generic meaning as it has in *NE* I.1 and *Metaphysics* Θ.8, not the narrowed meaning of the Passage.

(e) For confirmation, read on to the end of book x. Aristotle twice insists that happiness involves ἐνέργειαι from which no further end is

---

[127] Here I agree with Waterlow 1988: 187 n. 19, and Owen 1971–2: 151, against e.g. Bostock 1988: 260.
[128] Compare Michael of Ephesus, *In EN* x, 555.20–9 Heylbut, for the view that τέλειαι ἐνέργειαι are the most pleasurable, but ἀτελεῖς ἐνέργειαι can be pleasurable too.

sought beside the ἐνέργεια itself (x.6, 1176a35–b7; x.7, 1177b1–26). In both cases the context makes it clear that this is a substantive requirement, not a mere tautological expansion of (in the terminology of the Passage) 'Happiness involves ἐνέργειαι'.|| From beginning to end, *NE* x is innocent of the restrictive sense of ἐνέργεια defined in the Passage.[129]

14. Finally, *DA* II.5 again. I have already quoted from it the statement that change is incomplete actuality (417a16). The chapter proceeds to make distinctions 'concerning potentiality and actuality' (417a21: διαιρετέον δὲ καὶ περὶ δυνάμεως καὶ ἐντελεχείας), but none of the distinctions involves withdrawing the statement that change is incomplete actuality. The main distinction put before us is the one that tradition knows as the distinction between first and second potentiality, a distinction entirely absent from the Passage. Conversely, throughout *DA* II.5 actuality contrasts with δύναμις, not with κίνησις. Ackrill was right when he denied that the *De anima* has any truck with the κίνησις–ἐνέργεια distinction as presented in *Metaphysics* Θ.6.[130]

None the less, there are two very interesting disjunctions in *DA* II.5 which can illuminate the disjunction at Θ.6, 1048b21, 'either these are not action [πρᾶξις], or at any rate they are not complete action'. About the Θ.6 disjunction I said that it would depend on the context of enquiry which disjunct was appropriate. The same is true, I believe, of *DA* II.5, 417b6–7, '[the transition to exercising knowledge] is either not alteration or it is a different kind of alteration', and 417b13–15, '[learning] is either not to be described as being affected or there are two kinds of alteration'. In the case of the transition to exercising knowledge, Aristotle immediately opts for the first alternative: not alteration at all (417b8–9). And this despite the fact that the transition to exercising knowledge serves him as a model for the transition to perceiving, which he insists on continuing to call alteration (417b29–418a3). Learning, on the other hand, the acquisition of knowledge as opposed to || its use, he continues to treat as a special type of alteration, even while acknowledging the legitimacy of a perspective from

---

[129] This blocks an argument to the effect that the account in *Metaph.* Λ.7 and 9 of God's changeless activity of contemplation and its enjoyment 'provides us with Aristotle's philosophical motivation' for the distinction drawn in the Passage (Kahn 1985: 333). The claim is premised on the assumption that *NE* x treats both pleasure and contemplation as ἐνέργειαι in the narrow sense of the Passage. God is indeed changeless, but in Λ as in Θ.8 ἐνέργεια contrasts with δύναμις, not with κίνησις.

[130] Ackrill 1965: 140–1, endorsed by Burnyeat 2002: 49 n. 56 [Chapter 5 in this volume]. Contrast the free use made of the Passage for the elucidation of *DA* II.5 by Kosman 1984, and others too many to list.

which it too is not alteration. I have argued elsewhere[131] that his motive for treating perception and intellectual learning as special types of alteration, different from the alteration by which fire heats the surrounding air, is to keep some (but not all) psychology within the scope of Aristotelian physics, which is defined as the study of things that have an internal principle of change and stability. That enables him to use the analysis of alteration worked out in the *Physics* and *De generatione et corruptione* I, and now refined in *De anima* II.5, to explain the cognitive accuracy of both perception and intellectual learning. If perception and intellectual learning did not fall within Aristotelian physics, this project would abort.

If that is correct, it confirms, I submit, my earlier claim that it cannot have been in a physical context that Aristotle opted to say that change is not actuality at all. The most likely context is ethical, and more specifically a critique of the account of pleasure in Plato's *Philebus*. Earlier it transpired that, contrary to standard expectations, *NE* VII gets closer to the restrictive language of the Passage than *NE* X. But book VII still does not quite make it. That leaves the lost works. We should look for a suitable title in the ancient catalogues of Aristotle's numerous writings.

15. Diogenes Laertius twice lists a one-book work *On Pleasure* (Περὶ ἡδονῆς).[132] The first such title keeps company with a number of Aristotle's dialogues. The Passage is hardly in the polished prose for which the dialogues were known. The second, however, goes with a group of works that one would classify as 'logical': Περὶ ἡδονῆς α´ or, more probably, Περὶ ἡδονῆς προτάσεις α´.[133]

Nothing but the title is known of it, yet it is just possible that one fragment survives:

> καὶ περὶ ἡδονῆς δ' εἴρηται ποῖόν τι καὶ πῶς ἀγαθόν, καὶ ὅτι τά τε ἁπλῶς ἡδέα καὶ καλὰ καὶ τά τε ἁπλῶς ἀγαθὰ ἡδέα. <u>οὐ γίνεται δὲ ἡδονὴ μὴ ἐν πράξει·</u> διὰ τοῦτο ὁ ἀληθῶς εὐδαίμων καὶ ἥδιστα ζήσει, καὶ τοῦτο οὐ μάτην οἱ ἄνθρωποι ἀξιοῦσιν.
>
> Concerning pleasure, too, it has been said what sort of thing it is and how it is a good, and that the things pleasant without qualification are also fine, || and the things good without qualification are pleasant. *But pleasure does not occur except in action*; for that reason, the truly happy man will also live most pleasantly, and it is not vainly that people believe this. (*EE* VIII.3, 1249a17–21; trans. Woods)

---

[131] Burnyeat 2002 [Chapter 5 in this volume].
[132] D.L. v.22 and 24; cf. Hesych. no. 15; Ptolemy el-Garib no. 17.
[133] On text and context I follow Moraux 1951: 93–5.

This fragment does not fit into its wider context. It concludes a discussion ('Concerning pleasure, too, it has been said ...') which is not in fact to be found earlier in the chapter, with the result that we have been given no means of understanding 'for that reason'.[134] But we are clearly in the presence of an Aristotle who in some ethical context wants to connect pleasure, πρᾶξις, and happiness.

Nor is Aristotle alone in having written a monograph *On Pleasure*. So too, apparently, did Speusippus (D.L. IV.4: one book), Xenocrates (D.L. IV.12: two books), Heracleides Ponticus (Athen. 512a), Strato (D.L. V.59), and Theophrastus, who is credited (D.L. V.44) with one book, Περὶ ἡδονῆς ὡς Ἀριστοτέλης (*On Pleasure According to Aristotle* or *On Pleasure in the Style of Aristotle*),[135] plus another entitled simply *On Pleasure*,[136] and – last, but would that we had it! – *On False Pleasure* (D.L. V.46: one book). It would seem that the *Philebus*, like Plato's Lecture on the Good, aroused a furore of discussion.

Ethics, however, is not the only branch of philosophy which the Aristotelian scheme of things kept apart from physics. Another is theology or first philosophy. David Sedley has urged me to consider this intriguing fragment:

> ἀπαθὲς γὰρ ὁ νοῦς, φησὶν ὁ Θεόφραστος, εἰ μὴ ἄρα ἄλλως ᾖ τὸ παθητικόν, οὐχ ὡς τὸ κινητικόν (ἀτελὴς γὰρ ἡ κίνησις) ἀλλ' ὡς ἐνέργεια. ταῦτα δὲ διαφέρει, χρῆσθαι δὲ ἀναγκαῖον ἐνίοτε τοῖς αὐτοῖς ὀνόμασιν ... (Thphr. fr. 307d FHS&G)

> 'For *nous* is unaffected', Theophrastus says, 'unless of course "capable of being affected" has a different sense: not "capable of being changed" (for change is incomplete), but "*energeia*". These are different, but sometimes it is necessary to use the same names ...'

Could Theophrastus be suggesting that all would be clear if we used the language of the Passage when speaking about νοῦς, giving ἐνέργεια its exclusive sense? In which case, we might propose his crisp, Aristotelian

---

[134] See Woods 1982, *ad loc*. I owe thanks to Doug Hutchinson for directing my attention to the fragment.

[135] For the idiom, compare Aristotle's Πολιτικῆς ἀκροάσεως ὡς ἡ Θεοφράστου α' β' γ' δ' ε' ϛ' ζ' η' (D.L. V.24) and the (hardly enlightening) commentary of Moraux 1951: 95–6 with n. 3.

[136] R. Bodéüs (Bodéüs 2001: cv–cvii) proposes (i) that these two Theophrastus titles are identical with Aristotle's two Περὶ ἡδονῆς titles, while (ii) the absence of a *Politics* in the list of Theophrastus titles to correspond to ἡ Θεοφράστου in my preceding note suggests hesitation over the authorship of a single eight-book *Politics*. The first proposal is less likely than the second, given that Theophrastus did not write dialogues.

style (which includes frequent use of the first-person verb λέγω) as a possible originator for the Passage itself.

I think not. The quoted fragment is still in the field of physics, more specifically in the triple scheme of *De Anima* II.5 and its careful, qualified extension to νοῦς in III.4, especially 429a13–18.[137] Aristotle wants to say that the intellect's taking on an intelligible form is not a change so much as the fulfilment of its nature, the actualisation of the inherent potentiality for knowledge which he counts as part of our biological make-up, our matter (II.5, 417a22–8). The qualification is necessary because he too, just like Theophrastus at the end of the quoted fragment, considers it necessary to go on using the language of change when speaking of the intellect (417b28–418a3). The intellect's taking on of form is a change or, if you prefer, a switch to *first* actuality, not second. Second actuality is the using of what one has learnt.[138]

16. Now look at Jaeger's apparatus criticus to the last sentence of Γ. In A^b the sentence is followed by a doublet of the first three words of Δ. The same thing happens at the transition from E to Z and from I to K. Again, Ross records that in A^b the end of H duplicates the first words of Θ. Ambr. F 113 sup. (M) shows the same phenomenon at the end both of Γ and of H.[139] Such 'reclamantes', as they are called, or (less correctly) 'custodes', are designed to help readers identify with confidence which papyrus roll comes next in the edition they are studying. Evidently, each roll contained two books. A^b also shows traces of uncial stichometric numerals. The β tradition must ‖ go back to a papyrus edition from pre-codex days,[140] when lots of Aristotle was available. The Passage could have begun as a marginal annotation quite early.

But the marginal annotation hypothesis is no less compatible with a codex edition. For at least some of Aristotle's lost works survived into late antiquity. In the fifth and sixth centuries AD we find Damascius reporting from Aristotle's three-book treatise on the philosophy of Archytas,[141] Simplicius quoting verbatim from Aristotle's *On Democritus* and his

---

[137] On this point I am in agreement with Huby 1999: 124–5.
[138] Further clarification in Burnyeat 2002. I address Aristotle's theory of the intellect in my Aquinas Lecture, 'Aristotle's Divine Intellect' [Burnyeat 2008b].
[139] The information about M comes from S. Alexandru (Alexandru 2000), who also reports unspecified examples of the same phenomenon in Vat. 115 (V^k, 15th cent., containing only books A–E).
[140] As Christ 1895 was the first to note. See now Harlfinger 1979: 29.
[141] Damasc. Pr. 306 (ii.172.20 Ruelle) = Arist. fr. 207 Rose³. For the title, see D.L. v.25.

Epitome of the *Timaeus*.[142] Harlfinger's stemma shows the α and the β traditions of the *Metaphysics* starting, independently, in the ninth century, the period when masses of ancient literature were lost as crucial choices were made about which uncial manuscripts should be transcribed into the new minuscule script. Often, the transcription would be made from a single uncial manuscript which was then discarded.[143] The corruption of ἅμα to the nonsense-making ἀλλά at 1048b23 and 25 (common to A^b, M, and C) would have happened in an uncial manuscript: AMA can be mistaken for AΛΛA much more easily than αμα for αλλα.[144] We can safely conclude that the Passage was already present in the hyparchetype β itself.

The question I must perforce leave unanswered is this: How many copies of the *Metaphysics* circulating in antiquity would have had the Passage? How typical, in other words, was the β tradition? My failure to find a single ancient author who knows the Passage may be just that, my failure; my search was very far from exhaustive. Yet it is telling that scholars as widely read as Philoponus and Simplicius (see Appendix 2) remain ignorant of its existence, as do the medieval Arabic and Latin traditions.

A more important lesson to learn from this investigation is that present-day scholarship should stop citing the Passage as a source of standard Aristotelian doctrine. It is a freak performance. ||

Postscript on Michael of Ephesus

17. Volumes 19–20 of the Berlin Academy *Commentaria in Aristotelem Graeca* contain the surviving paraphrases of, and commentaries on, the *Nicomachean Ethics*. Look up the passages that deal with Aristotle's discussion of pleasure in *NE* VII or X. In volume 19 no one has anything of interest to say, and there is a total absence of echoes from the Passage in *Metaphysics* Θ.6. They simply talk of ἐνέργειαι as either τέλειαι or ἀτελεῖς. The same is true of volume 20 until one reaches the last commentary, by Michael of Ephesus. Suddenly, the overall intellectual quality improves and – lo and behold – at 543.22 Heylbut, commenting on *NE* x.2, he writes οὐ γάρ ἐστι γένεσις, ἀλλ' ἐνέργεια … αἱ δ' ἐνέργειαι τέλη εἰσὶν ἀλλ' οὐχ ὁδοὶ πρὸς τέλη. The subject he is speaking of is pleasure. What follows is this:

---

[142] *In De caelo* 294.33–295.22 Heiberg = Ar. fr. 208; 296. 16–18 (cf. 379. 12–17) = Arist. fr. 206. For the titles, see D.L. v.25 and 27.
[143] See Reynolds and Wilson 2000: 58–61. Harlfinger 1979: 29–30, argues against Jaeger's proposal (Jaeger 1957: viii) that E and J came from two distinct transcriptions.
[144] So Jaeger: 'idem error est frequens in script. unciali'.

ὅτι δὲ τέλος ἐστιν ἡδονὴ καὶ οὐχὶ γένεσις, μάθοιμεν ἂν ἐντεῦθεν. ἐπὶ μὲν γὰρ τῶν γενέσεων οὐχ ἅμα γίνεται, οὐδὲ ὅτε γίνεται. οὐ γὰρ ἅμα γίνεται σὰρξ καὶ σάρξ ἐστιν ὅτε γίνεται, οὐδὲ ὅτε γίνεται ἡ οἰκία τότε ὅτε γίνεται καὶ ἔστιν. ἐπὶ δὲ τῶν ἐνεργειῶν, οἷον τοῦ ὁρᾶν, ἅμα τε ὁρᾷ καὶ ἑώρακε· καὶ ἐπὶ τῶν ἡδονῶν ἅμα τε ἥδεται καὶ ἥσθη, ὥστε ἐνέργεια ἐστι καὶ οὐ γένεσις. εἰ δὲ ἐνέργεια, καὶ τέλος ἀλλ' οὐχ ὁδός τις καὶ μεταβολὴ πρὸς τέλος. (*In EN* 543.22–30 Heylbut)

> That pleasure is an end and not a becoming, we may learn from the following. In the case of becomings, it is not the case that something is at the same time both becoming <something> and already being <that something> while becoming it.[145] For it is not the case that, at one and the same time when flesh is coming to be, it both is flesh and is coming to be flesh, nor that when a house is coming to be, at the same time as it is coming to be a house it also is a house. But in the case of actualities like seeing, at the same time one sees and has seen. So too with pleasures: at the same time one enjoys <something> and has enjoyed <it>,[146] so that pleasure is an ‖ ἐνέργεια, not a γένεσις. And if it is an ἐνέργεια, it is also an end, not a journey or change towards an end.

This is almost a *Rückübersetzung* into Byzantine Greek of Ackrill on the same Aristotelian text, with both construing the perfect as a tense with past reference. Neither Ackrill nor Michael found the equivalence of present and perfect in the *NE* passage they were commenting on. As we have seen, the equivalence is noticed in the *Sophistici elenchi* and the *De sensu* as well as Θ.6, but only Θ.6 uses it as a criterion for being an ἐνέργεια in the special narrowed sense that Michael is temporarily using here.[147] There can be little doubt that Michael knows the Passage. He is indeed the sole ancient or medieval writer I have been able to find who clearly reveals that he does know it.[148] But we also saw that Michael, alias Pseudo-Alexander,

---

[145] This sentence and the next look to be indebted to Alexander's commentary on the *De sensu* passage which I quoted in sect. 11(b) above: Alex. *In De sensu* 125.3–9 Wendland.

[146] Translation problem: ἥσθην is aorist, not perfect. As Owen 1971–2: 150, remarked, the verb ἥδεσθαι 'had no known perfect tense'. Answer: at *In SE* 149.31–2 Wallies, while commenting on the passage of Aristotle's *Sophistici elenchi* discussed above, pp. 128–9, Michael explicitly casts ἑώρακε as past tense, doubtless because that was what by his day the perfect had become (Mihevc 1959: 120–30; cf. n. 103 above. Compare the way Plotinus, *Enn.* I [42].16.13–14 (from the part of this treatise discussed in Appendix 2 below), puts κεκίνηται parallel to ἔτεμε, a verb which also has a normally formed perfect.

[147] I say 'temporarily' because already at 545.7 Heylbut, after the very next lemma, he has gone back to the normal broad use of ἐνέργεια, which continues in the sequel: see esp. 545.20–30, 562.34–6, 568.35–569.2 Heylbut.

[148] No sign of the Passage in, for example, Alexander's *Ethical Questions*, despite his having plenty to say about pleasure. Appendix 2 below casts doubt on the common view that the Passage was known in Neoplatonist circles.

did not read the Passage in the *Metaphysics* when composing his commentary on that work. He knows it, but not from the *Metaphysics*; or at least, not from the manuscript he used when writing his *Metaphysics* commentary. He must have read it, or a text making the same or a similar point, somewhere else.

A couple of comments on Michael's methods of work are pertinent here:

> Michael ... was remarkable among Byzantine scholars for the scope of his interests. He commented on Aristotelian works which were all but ignored by other commentators as well as on those which were studied traditionally.[149]

> ... Michael vacuumed old manuscripts to find notes for his *Elenchi* commentary. Indeed his whole method of work consisted in gathering whatever ancient materials he could lay hands on, putting them together, mending them and supplementing them, so as to produce something that could be ‖ a companion to a whole work by Aristotle. He put together commentaries on the *Metaphysics* and *Ethics* in this way too.[150]

Even if in the libraries of twelfth-century Constantinople he is rather unlikely to have come across an old uncial manuscript containing Aristotle's Περὶ ἡδονῆς, Michael could well have read a report of its exclusive distinction between ἐνέργεια and κίνησις. More must have happened than that one day he stumbled upon a *Metaphysics* manuscript from the β tradition which did contain the Passage, for his remarks contain material (e.g. about the coming to be and being of flesh and house) which do not echo either the Passage or the Nicomachean chapter he is commenting upon.[151] The one thing we may be sure of is that he would not have used such material unless he had reason to believe it represented, directly or indirectly, the Philosopher's thoughts.

My argument has not tried to deny that they are the Philosopher's thoughts. Only to affirm that they derive from some very, very special context about which we can only speculate.

Appendix 1: The Passage in M and C

The collation was kindly carried out by Christian Brockmann, using Jaeger's OCT as the work of reference. All differences from this edition are noted, except missing accents and differences in the use of accents in connection with enclitics; there is no iota subscript in either manuscript.

---

[149] Mercken 1973: 3–29, reprinted as Sorabji 1990: 407–43, at 433. [150] Ebbesen 1990: 451.
[151] Cf. n. 145 above.

Appendix 1: The Passage in M and C

M (Ambr. F 113 sup.)

1048b19–20	οἷον τοῦ ἰσχναίνειν ἡ ἰσχνασία αὐτό. The words occur in the last line of fo. 151ᵛ. The page turns after ἰσχναν. Later, in 1048b29, the scribe writes ἰσχνασία and not ἰσχνανσία.
1048b20	δ' ὅταν
1048b22	ἐκείνη ἐνυπάρχει
1048b23–4	καὶ ἡ πρᾶξις. οἷον ὁρᾷ· ἀλλὰ καὶ φρονεῖ καὶ νοεῖ
1048b25	ἀλλά instead of ἅμα ‖
1048b27	ἔζηκε (no nu ephelkystikon)
1048b28	no δεῖ (of course)
1048b31	It seems that he writes ᾠκοδόμησεν, but the sigma is not clearly visible on the photograph
1048b31(?)	The manuscript has καὶ κινεῖ καὶ κεκίνηκεν
1048b34	νενόηκε· (no nu ephelkystikon)

C (Taur. B VII 23)

1048b19	ἀλλὰ τὸ περὶ (τὸ instead of τῶν)
1048b19–20	οἷον τοῦ ἰσχναίνειν ἡ ἰσχνανσία αὐτό.
1048b20	δ' ὅταν
1048b21	ὑπάρχοντος οὗ ἕνεκα
1048b21	ταύτη (?)
1048b21	ἡ πρᾶξις (add ἡ)
1048b21	Between ἡ πρᾶξις and ἦ there might something, but the photograph does not permit precise determination of whether there really is something meaningful and what it is.
1048b22	ἐκείνη ἐνυπάρχει
1048b23–4	καὶ ἡ πρᾶξις· οἷον ὁρᾷ ἀλλὰ καὶ φρονεῖ καὶ νοεῖ καὶ νενοημένα μανθάνει (!) <u>νενοημένα and no ἀλλ' οὐ</u> In the margin *varia lectio*, but the margin is damaged. The sign (two dots) seems to refer back to ὁρᾷ. *First line of the note:* γρ(άφεται) and the beginning of a word, three letters more or less visible: καλ (?) *Second line of the note:* φρονεῖ (it seems)
1048b25	ἀλλά instead of ἅμα
1048b27	omits οὖ
1048b28	no δεῖ (of course)
1048b28	λέγει instead of λέγειν
1048b29	ἰσχνανσία
1048b31	The manuscript has καὶ κινεῖ καὶ κινεῖται (!)

Postscript on C
A number of C's unusual readings (ἀλλὰ τὸ περὶ; ἡ before πρᾶξις; omission of ἀλλ' οὔ; καὶ νενοημένα μανθάνει as an independent sentence) are shared by N and by the fifteenth-century hand (very similar to Bessarion's) which has written the Passage into the margin of E^b (twelfth century). Bessarion owned E^b as well as D^m, which has the Passage, plus three more *Metaphysics* manuscripts: H^a, f, and Q. ||

APPENDIX 2: DID PLOTINUS, *ENNEADS* VI.1 [42].15–22, START A DEBATE ABOUT THE PASSAGE?

Enneads VI.1.16 opens an interesting critique of Aristotle's definition of κίνησις as ἐνέργεια ἀτελής. There is no doubt that Plotinus has *Physics* III.1–3 in mind, since he starts with an abbreviated quotation of the definition at *Physics* III.2, 201b31–2.[152] Where Aristotle writes:

ἥ τε κίνησις ἐνέργεια μὲν εἶναι τις δοκεῖ, ἀτελὴς δε· αἴτιον δ' ὅτι ἀτελὲς τὸ δυνατόν, οὗ ἐστιν ἐνέργεια.

Change is thought to be an actuality of a sort, though incomplete, because the potential thing whose actuality it is is incomplete,

Plotinus rehearses no more than this:

εἰ δε τις λέγοι τὴν κίνησιν ἀτελῆ ἐνέργειαν εἶναι ...

If someone were to say that change is incomplete actuality ...

Whether deliberately or because he is quoting from memory, he omits Aristotle's explanation of just why the actuality which change is is an incomplete actuality. He proceeds, as will emerge shortly, to substitute a quite different account of his own.

The critique of Aristotle's definition which then follows elicited comments and replies from Porphyry, Iamblichus, and finally Simplicius, who wrote up the debate in his commentary on Aristotle's *Categories* 303.32ff. Kalbfleisch. An impressive body of modern literature treats this many-sided encounter as a debate about the Passage as well as about *Physics*

---

[152] The definition is repeated at *DA* II.5, 417a16–17, without further explanation, just a back-reference to *Physics* III.2.

III.1–3. Both Croese chapter 4 and Chiaradonna 2002 chapter 2 are such contributions, as is Natali, 'La critica', which I recommend as a helpful guide for reading through Plotinus' text.[153] I shall argue that, on the contrary, no contestant in this ancient discussion reveals knowledge of the Passage. Since one or another of them would probably have mentioned it had they ‖ been aware of its existence, the debate is evidence that the Passage remained as little known in antiquity as it is in our manuscript tradition.

To put the issue in a nutshell: in annotating *Enneads* VI.1.16 Henry-Schwyzer cite the Passage alongside *Physics* III, Armstrong mentions only the latter. I shall argue (as promised above, p. 109 n. 46) that Armstrong's choice was the canny one. The double tradition displayed by Harlfinger's *stemma codicum* guarantees that not all ancient readers of the *Metaphysics* would find the Passage in the copy before them. The Arabic and Latin translators clearly did not. The burden of proof must now be on anyone who maintains that Plotinus or his critics did know the Passage. Meanwhile, congratulations to Gwenaëlle Aubry for writing a considerable book on δύναμις and ἐνέργεια in Aristotle and Plotinus[154] which mentions the Passage only once – to set it aside. *Ab esse ad posse valet consequentia.*

Plotinus starts out by treating 'Change is incomplete actuality' as a straightforward definition *per genus et differentiam*, the genus being ἐνέργεια and ἀτελής the differentia. The immediate result is that incompleteness becomes a straightforward attribute of the ἐνέργεια which is κίνησις and Plotinus can argue, against Aristotle as thus construed, that walking, for example, is walking, in the completest possible sense, from the walker's very first steps. What remains incomplete after a step or two is not the walker's walking, but his walking a certain distance (16.5–12).

---

[153] Natali 1999. The only justification I have found offered for coupling the Passage with *Physics* III.1–3 in discussion of the debate between Plotinus and his critics is Croese 1998: 122: 'The way in which motion is described in the two passages shows that Aristotle has in mind *more or less* the same concept as in the *Physics*' (emphasis added). E. Emilsson's recent *Plotinus on Intellect* (Emilsson 2007: 56) is properly cautious about bringing in the Passage.
[154] Aubry 2006.

True, but the purported criticism of Aristotle's definition is in fact an elucidation of the point Aristotle is making when he grounds the incompleteness of the walking on incompleteness as an attribute of the walker (τὸ δυνατόν). The walking, for Aristotle, is the actuality of the walker's potential to be in another place (not a potential to *walk*). Accordingly, it remains an incomplete actuality throughout the period of a walker's walking right up to their arrival at the place they have the potential to be in.[155]

I conclude that, as so often, two great minds are talking past each other. Aristotle does not deny what Plotinus affirms, that walking is walking all along, from the start, or that κίνησις is already ἐνέργεια, already therefore actual κίνησις, before it reaches its goal. On the contrary, ἀτελής expresses what *sort* of ἐνέργεια it has been (actually) all along, namely, one that manifests and seeks to realise the walker's potentiality for being at a certain place (which may never be reached).

Since the very concept of κίνησις as ἀτελής ἐνέργεια is excluded by the Passage, Plotinus is most unlikely to have the Passage in view. His subsequent ‖ argument (16.14–39) that ἐνέργεια is no more 'in timelessness' (ἐν ἀχρόνῳ) than κίνησις is is expressly indexed to *Phys*. 1.3, 186a15–16 (cf. VIII.3, 253b25; *Pol*. 1307b35) on ἀθρόα μεταβολή, not to *Metaphysics* Θ.6.[156] Nowhere does he allude to the relation of present and perfect tenses. Nor does anyone in the debate recorded by Simplicius, which ranges widely through the merits and demerits of the Aristotelian category ποιεῖν καὶ πάσχειν.

The best contribution comes from Iamblichus (ap. Simpl. *In Cat.* 303.35–304.10 Kalbfleisch). He attacks Plotinus' assumption that 'Change is incomplete actuality' is a straightforward definition *per genus et differentiam*, the genus being ἐνέργεια and ἀτελής the differentia. Instead, he says we should read ἀτελής as an *alienans* qualification. Rather than placing κίνησις within the wider class of ἐνέργεια, it indicates that κίνησις barely counts as ἐνέργεια at all: 'it falls away into some altogether inferior nature' (303.37–8 Kalbfleisch). But at least it has a

---

[155] For clear elucidation of this point, see the now classic article Kosman 1969.
[156] Likewise, J. C. De Groot's very interesting article 'Philoponus on *De anima* II 5, *Physics* III 3, and the Propagation of Light' (De Groot 1983) fails to show that Philoponus knows the Passage as well as the ἀθρόα μεταβολή passages in Aristotle's *Physics*. Cf. n. 45 above on the striking absence of the Passage from Philoponus, *De aeternitate mundi*.

nature of sorts. The definition allows Aristotle to insist that κίνησις is not the nothing, the not-being, to which some Platonists of the Academy would condemn it.[157]

This acute piece of commentary brings me back to Plotinus. If he says in VI.1.16.6–7 that κίνησις is ἐνέργεια μὲν πάντως, ἔχει δὲ καὶ τὸ πάλιν καὶ πάλιν, he cannot be using ἐνέργεια in the sense defined in *Metaphysics* Θ.6, which is such that κίνησις is not ἐνέργεια at all. He casts κίνησις as a proper species of the genus ἐνέργεια, substituting ἔχει δὲ καὶ τὸ πάλιν καὶ πάλιν[158] for what he took to be Aristotle's differentia ἀτελής. Accordingly, when he ‖ proceeds to say that κίνησις is already ἐνέργεια, he cannot mean ἐνέργεια in the sense of *Metaphysics* Θ.6. In general, no one who predicates ἐνέργεια of κίνησις or κίνησις of ἐνέργεια is following the exclusive distinction we find, uniquely, in the Passage.

Now to pull back the curtain. Simpl. *In Cat.* 307.1–6 Kalbfleisch cites ἐνέργεια μὲν πάντως, ἔχει δὲ καὶ τὸ πάλιν καὶ πάλιν, plus the words that follow down to the end of Plotinus' sentence at 16.8, as a quotation from Iamblichus recording a Stoic objection to Aristotle's account of κίνησις as ἐνέργεια ἀτελής. Everything I have found in Plotinus so far is borrowed from Stoics. This shows some Stoics – whether of Hellenistic or Imperial vintage we need not decide – responding to Aristotle's *Physics*. It does not and cannot show them aware of the Passage,[159] which eliminates the very possibility of ἐνέργεια ἀτελής.[160]

---

[157] Here again, as at the very beginning of this project, I refer readers to Frede 2001.
[158] Whatever that means: neither Bréhier's 'un acte qui recommence de nouveau à chaque instant' (Bréhier 1924–36), nor Armstrong's 'has also the "over and over again"' (Armstrong 1967), nor Linguiti's 'si presenta come un di nuovo e poi di nuovo' (Linguiti 2000: 73 n. 200) is helpful. Wagner 1996: 140 is just baffling: 'embraces its completeness recursively'. MacKenna, as usual, strives for a definite meaning: 'It entails repetition (lacks finality). It repeats, not in order that it may achieve actuality – it is that already – but that it may attain a goal distinct from itself and posterior' (Mackenna 1956). A better guide, perhaps, is *Enn.* III.7 [45].8.37–41, where the πάλιν καὶ πάλιν of κίνησις is likened to the πάλιν καὶ πάλιν of water flowing πάλιν καὶ πάλιν and the distance it is observed to cover. This rather suggests that the phrase τὸ πάλιν καὶ πάλιν simply refers to κίνησις being something that is essentially extended through time, as opposed to a thing which is complete ἐν τῷ νῦν. In other words, πάλιν καὶ πάλιν conveys the idea of going on and on. Cf. πάλιν ἐφεξῆς in the discussion of time itself at III.7 [45].11.36–7 and the contrast with eternity at 3.15ff. Why can't Plotinus translators give us something that makes sense?
[159] *Pace* Frede 1993: 146. The Stoic origin of Plotinus' words is not signalled by Armstrong 1988, although Kalbfleisch as editor of Simplicius is scrupulously detailed in his source citation.
[160] In preparing this Appendix I have been helped by the knowledgeable advice of Riccardo Chiaradonna, Paul Kalligas, and Lucas Siorvanes. It is more important than usual to add that they are not responsible for my conclusions.

METAPHYSICS: MODERN EDITIONS; ANCIENT, MEDIEVAL, AND MODERN COMMENTARIES; MEDIEVAL AND MODERN TRANSLATIONS

Academia Regia Borussica, *Aristoteles Latine*, interpretibus variis edidit (Berlin, 1831); Nachdruck herausgegeben und eingeleitet von Eckhard Keßler (Munich, 1995).

Alexander of Aphrodisias. *In Aristotelis Metaphysica Commentaria*, (1) ed. H. Bonitz (Berlin, 1847); (2) ed. M. Hayduck (CAG 1; Berlin, 1891).

Aquinas, Thomas, *In duodecim libros Metaphysicorum Aristotelis expositio*, editio iam a M.-R. Cathala, O.P. exarata retractatur cura et studio P. Fr. Raymundi M. Spiazzi, O.P. *(Turin and Rome, 1964)*.

Argyropoulos, J., *Aristotelis ... opus metaphysicum a ... Bessarione ... Latinitate ... donatum ...cum adiecto in XII. primos libros Argyropyli ... interpretamento*, ed. J. Faber (Paris, 1515).

Averroes, *Aristotelis Metaphysicorum libri XIIII, cum Averrois Cordubensis in eosdem commentariis, et epitome, etc.* (Venice, 1562; photographic repr. Frankfurt am Main, 1962).

Barnes, J.: see Ross and Barnes.

Barthélemy-Saint-Hilaire, J., *Métaphysique d'Aristote*, traduite en français avec des notes perpétuelles (3 vols.; Paris, 1879). ||

Bekker, I., *Aristoteles Graece, ex recensione Immanuel Bekker*, edidit Academia Regia Borussica (2 vols.; Berlin, 1831).

Bessarion: see Argyropoulos.

Bonitz, H., *Aristoteles: Metaphysik, übersetzt* (ed. Eduard Wellmann, 1890), mit Gliederungen, Registern und Bibliographie herausgegeben von Hect‹o›r Carvallo und Ernesto Grassi (Munich, 1966).

Aristotelis Metaphysica, recognovit et enarravit (2 vols.; Bonn, 1848–9; vol. ii. Commentarius, reprinted Hildesheim, 1960).

Brandis, C. A., *Aristotelis et Theophrasti Metaphysica*, ad veterum codicum manuscriptorum fidem recensita indicibusque instructa in usum scholarum edidit ['Brandis ed.'] (Berlin, 1823).

Casaubon, I., *Operum Aristotelis Stagiritae philosophorum omnium longe principis, nova editio Graecè et Latinè* (Lyon, 1590).

Christ, W., *Aristotelis Metaphysica, recognovit, nova editio correctior* (Leipzig, 1895 [1st edn. 1886]).

Du Val, W., *Aristotelis opera omnia, Graece et Latine* (Paris, 1629, 1654, etc.).

Erasmus, D., *Aristotelis ... opera ... omnia* (Basel, 1531, 1539, 1550).

Fonseca, Petrus da, *Commentaria in Metaphysicorum Aristotelis Stagiritae libros* (4 vols.; Cologne, 1615–29 [1st edn. of Θ: 1604]).

Frede, M., and Patzig, G., *Aristoteles: Metaphysik Z, Text, Übersetzung und Kommentar* (2 vols.; Munich, 1988).

Furth, M., *Aristotle: Metaphysics Books Zeta, Eta, Theta, Iota* (VII–X), translated (Indianapolis, 1985).

Gemusaeus, H., *Aristotelis Stagiritae, philosophorum omnium facile principis, opera quae in hunc usque diem extant omnia, Latinitate partim antea, partim nunc*

primum a viris doctissimis donata, et ad Graecum exemplar diligenter recognita (Basel, 1542).
Gohlke, P., *Übersetzung der Metaphysik des Aristoteles*, 2nd edn. (Paderborn, 1951).
Hope, R., *Aristotle: Metaphysics, translated* (New York, 1952).
Irwin, T., and Fine, G., *Aristotle: Selections, translated, with introduction, notes, and glossary* (Indianapolis, 1995).
Jaeger, W., *Aristotelis Metaphysica, recognovit brevique adnotatione critica instruxit* (Oxford, 1957).
Kirchmann, J. H. von, *Die Metaphysik des Aristoteles, übersetzt, erläutert und mit einer Lebensbeschreibung des Aristoteles versehen* (2 vols.; Berlin, 1871).
Lasson, A., *Aristoteles: Metaphysik, ins Deutsche übertragen* (Jena, 1907).
'Londinenses', *Notes on Eta and Theta of Aristotle's Metaphysics*, recorded by Myles Burnyeat and others (Oxford, 1984).
Makin, S., *Aristotle: Metaphysics, Book Θ, translated with an introduction and commentary* (Oxford, 2006). ||
Mauro, S., *Aristotelis opera omnia . . . brevi paraphrasi et litterae perpetuo inhaerente expositione illustrata* (Rome, 1658; repr. Paris, 1885).
Moerbeke: see Vuillemin-Diem.
Pappa, E., *Georgios Pachymeres, Philosophia Buch 10: Kommentar zur Metaphysik des Aristoteles, Editio Princeps. Einleitung, Text, Indices* (Corpus Philosophorum Medii Aevi, Commentaria in Aristotelem Byzantina, 2; Athens, 2002).
Pseudo-Philoponus, *Expositiones in omnes* XIV *Aristotelis libros Metaphysicos*, übersetzt von Franciscus Patritius, Neudruck der ersten Ausgabe Ferrara 1583 mit einer Einleitung von Charles Lohr (Commentaria in Aristotelem Graeca: Versiones Latinae temporis resuscitatarum litterarum, herausgegeben von Charles Lohr, 2; Stuttgart–Bad Cannstatt, 1991).
Ross, W. D., *Aristotle's Metaphysics: A Revised Text with Introduction and Commentary* ['Ross'] (2 vols.; Oxford, 1924).
   Metaphysica (The Works of Aristotle Translated into English under the Editorship of J. A. Smith and W. D. Ross; Oxford, 1908) ['Ross Tr. 1', done from Christ's edition].
   Metaphysica (The Works of Aristotle Translated into English under the Editorship of W. D. Ross (Oxford, 1928) ['Ross Tr. 2', done from his own edition].
Ross, W. D., and Barnes, J., *Metaphysics*, in J. Barnes (ed.), *The Complete Works of Aristotle: The Revised Oxford Translation*, vol. ii (Princeton, 1984).
Russo, A., *Aristotele: opere, vol. vi. Metafisica* (Rome and Bari, 1973).
Schwegler, A., *Die Metaphysik des Aristoteles*, Grundtext, Übersetzung und Commentar nebst erläuternden Abhandlungen (4 vols.; Tübingen, 1847–8; repr. Frankfurt am Main, 1960).
Sepúlveda, Juan Ginés de, *Alexandri Aphrodisiei commentaria in duodecim Aristotelis libros de prima philosophia*, interprete J. G. S. (Paris, 1536 [1st edn. Rome, 1527]).

Sylburg, F., *Aristotelis et Theophrasti Metaphysica* (Frankfurt am Main, 1635).
Taylor, T., *The* Metaphysics *of Aristotle, Translated from the Greek* (London, 1801).
Tredennick, H., *Aristotle: The* Metaphysics, *with an English translation* (2 vols.; Cambridge, MA, and London, 1933–5).
Tricot, J., *Aristote: Métaphysiques, traduction nouvelle et notes* (2 vols.; Paris, 1933).
Vuillemin-Diem, G., *Metaphysica Lib. I–X, XII–XIV*, Translatio Anonyma sive 'Media' (Aristoteles Latinus, xxv.2; Leiden, 1976).
Metaphysica Lib. I–XIV, recensio et translatio Guillelmi de Moerbeka, edidit (Aristoteles Latinus, xxv 3.1–2; Leiden, New York, and Cologne, 1995). ||
Weise, C. H., *Aristotelis opera omnia*, editio stereotypa (Leipzig, 1843).

CHAPTER 5

De Anima *II.5*

INTRODUCTION

The negative message of *De Anima* II.5 is easy to state. This is the chapter in which Aristotle informs us of his view that, although perceiving is traditionally thought to be a case of being affected by something, an alteration || caused by the object perceived, it is only in a refined sense of being affected or altered that this is true. In the ordinary sense of these terms they signify the loss of a quality and its replacement by another (opposite or intermediate) quality from the same range (417a31–2; 417b2–3; 15; *Ph.* v.2, 226b1–8; *GC* I.7, 324a5–14). That is not what happens in perception, which is a different way of being affected and altered. Aristotle concludes by saying that, for the discussion of perception now beginning, we must go on using the language of being affected and altered, but understand it in the light of the distinctions he has put before us in the main body of the chapter (418a1–3).

In other words, *De Anima* II.5 is the chapter in which Aristotle expressly denies that perceiving is the sort of alteration or change of quality which a cold thing undergoes when it is warmed or a green thing when it is coloured red.

The negative message of II.5 is of some significance for current controversies about Aristotle's theory of perception. Richard Sorabji has defended,[1] and continues to defend,[2] an interpretation whereby the alteration Aristotle has in view, when he speaks of perceiving as alteration, is an ordinary qualitative alteration that would be observable by scientists who, unlike Aristotle, had instruments giving access to the inside of the relevant organ.[3] Better equipped than Aristotle himself, these scientists could observe one quality replacing another. They could measure the change of

---
[1] In his 'Body and Soul' (Sorabji 1974); cf. Ross 1949: 136–7.
[2] In his 'Intentionality' (Sorabji 1992); cf. also Sorabji 1991.
[3] Sorabji 1974: 49–50 with n. 22 and p. 64; Sorabji 1992: 209–10.

temperature involved in feeling warmth; they could see or film the change of colour involved in seeing red; they could hear or record the noises sounding in a listener's ear. On Sorabji's account, what goes on inside the organ is an alteration – a replacement of one sensible quality by another – of the same kind as the alterations that occur outside when a cold thing is warmed or a green thing coloured red. My objection[4] is that this is the sort of alteration that in II.5 Aristotle *contrasts* with the sort that perceiving is, where the altered state is not lost (like the cold and the green in the ordinary examples) but preserved (417b3–4).

So much for the negative message of II.5. The positive alternative is harder to grasp. If perceiving is not an ordinary alteration of the type familiar from other Aristotelian writings such as the *Physics* and *De Generatione et Corruptione*, what sort of alteration can it be?

One possibility is suggested by certain details in Aristotle's account of the sense organs. Let us be clear that when Sorabji's scientists observe red replacing green within a perceiver's eye, that is not the replacement to concentrate on. Distinguish change of perception from the change which is perception. When the eye sees first green, then red, on Aristotle's theory its seeing green is one alteration, its seeing red another, and in each case Aristotle will say that the alteration is the taking on of a colour (first green, then red) by something *transparent*. But now, transparency is not a quality on the same range as green and red. It is a neutral state, which enables the eye to be receptive to all the differences in the colour range. So perhaps the alteration which is seeing can be the literal coloration Sorabji claims it to be and yet differ from ordinary alteration as defined in the *Physics* and *De Generatione et Corruptione*. It differs because what is lost in the alteration is not an opposite or intermediate quality from the same range as the colour replacing it.[5]

But this cannot be the positive message of II.5 either. Even if it were true that perceiving is an alteration that differs from ordinary alteration only in that it starts from a neutral, rather than from a contrary state, II.5 says nothing about the neutrality of the sense organs. Neutrality is first mentioned in II.8 (hearing depends on still air walled up inside the

---

[4] Burnyeat 1992b: 19 (a paper originally composed and circulated in 1983). But I went too far when I denied that perceiving is alteration in any sense at all. Read on.

[5] Sorabji himself, I should emphasise, does not in the writings cited above dwell on the difference between altering from green to red and altering from transparent to red (cf. Sorabji 1992: 212). I owe thanks to David Sedley for insisting that I do so. But see now Sorabji 2001, preceded by Broackes 1999.

ear – 420a9–11), and becomes a major theme in II.10 (esp. 424a7–10).[6] I have argued elsewhere that the neutrality of the sense organs is a vital clue for understanding what happens when Aristotle sees red and hears middle C.[7] But it is not relevant to II.5, which is a general introduction to the study ‖ of animal perception.[8] In Aristotle's order of presentation, refining the notion of alteration comes before his detailed account of the five senses and their organs. We should respect that order, not grab pieces of evidence indiscriminately from all over the treatise. Otherwise we destroy the integrity of one of Aristotle's most carefully organised works. We may hope that II.5 will eventually help us understand the role of neutrality. But first we must get clear about the positive meaning of 'alteration' in the Aristotelian theory of perception; in particular, we need to understand what Aristotle means by saying that in perception the altered state is not lost, as happens in ordinary alteration, but preserved. And the best way to do that, I propose, is by a close scrutiny of the actual process of refinement undertaken in *De Anima* II.5.

It is a long chapter. By following it from beginning to end, we can see the refined notion of alteration emerging from the careful elaboration of distinctions that went before. As often in philosophy, the meaning of the conclusion is determined by the arguments, the message by the medium.

But I also have an independent interest in the medium. There is much discussion nowadays about the problems of reading a Platonic dialogue, but none about the problem: How should one read a chapter of an Aristotelian treatise? Many of the doctrines, claims and distinctions found in *De Anima* II.5 can just as easily be found elsewhere in the corpus. Some of them – the distinction between potentiality and actuality is a prime example – are so familiar that scholars seldom stop long enough with the chapter to inquire, What are they doing here? How, in detail, do they contribute to the final result? To my knowledge, II.5 has never received the kind of close scrutiny I offer here. I offer it not only in the hope of settling some controversial questions about Aristotle's theory of perception, but

---

[6] This claim presupposes rejection of Hutchinson's proposal that III.12–13 belong between II.4 and II.5, for the neutrality of the organ of touch is mentioned at III.13, 435a21–4 (Hutchinson 1987). But I do reject the proposal anyway, for two reasons. First, because Hutchinson's transposition would have the result that the crucial idea of receiving form without matter would make its initial appearance without context or explanation at III.12, 434a29–30, not as II.12's generalisation from the preceding study of individual senses. Second, because III.12–13 serve well enough where they are to round off the treatise with a teleologically grounded sketch of relationships and dependencies between faculties that have so far been analysed on their own.
[7] Burnyeat 1995.   [8] Cf. n. 14 below.

also with the aim of drawing my readers into wider issues about how an Aristotelian discussion works on the page.

In particular, I am interested in the function of the cross-references to other parts of the chapter, to other parts of the treatise, and to other treatises like the *Physics* and *De Generatione et Corruptione*. These cross-references are not to be dismissed as due to a later editor. That may be a plausible account for some of the cross-references in the corpus, but not for those in II.5. Here they are woven too closely into the texture of the discussion to be the work of anyone but Aristotle himself. Even if you ‖ think the cross-references in the corpus do not in general contain the clues scholars once hoped to find for the chronological ordering of the treatises, some of them may still offer guidance as to how a particular stretch of writing should be read. If, as I shall argue, this is indeed the case for the cross-references in *De Anima* II.5, the same may be true elsewhere.[9]

Finally, the text. Compared with other Aristotelian works, the *De Anima* has a higher than average number of textual problems, and not only in the third Book. It is all too easy to get used to Ross's OCT (or whatever edition you normally work with) and forget how many philological-cum-philosophical decisions are presupposed by the neatly printed page. Martha Nussbaum writes,

> The philosopher/scholar should be especially attentive to the critical apparatus when working on the *De Anima*, and should think with more than usual care about the alternatives that have been proposed, using, if possible, more than one edition.[10]

I agree; there is much to ponder in the apparatus to II.5.[11] The same holds, I would add, for the nuances of alternative translations. Accordingly, my footnotes will regularly call attention to differences of interpretation that may result from one choice or another in matters of text and translation. In addition, the two Appendices attempt to undo the effects of an emendation by Torstrik which, even when it is not printed, has so skewed the translation, and hence the interpretation, of the key lines 417a30–417b7 that a central Aristotelian doctrine is widely misunderstood.

---

[9] In Burnyeat 2001b, ch. 5, I argue that the network of cross-references which link the many treatises of the corpus to each other should be read non-chronologically, as indications of the order of argument and exposition and hence of the appropriate order of reading. Burnyeat 2004b [Chapter 9 in this volume] is a particular case study of how this approach applies to the physical works.

[10] Nussbaum and Rorty 1992: 2.

[11] The most convenient account of the complicated manuscript tradition of the *De Anima* is Barbotin and Jannone 1966: xxiv–xlv; Ross 1956 is no longer adequate.

SETTING OUT THE *ENDOXA*

I shall approach the chapter as a model example of Aristotelian dialectic working to refine the reputable opinions (*endoxa*) – in this case the opinions that surround the idea that perception is some sort of alteration. To grasp the positive message of II.5 we need first to ask what preliminary || understanding of 'perception' and of 'alteration' we should bring to our reading of the chapter, and then watch carefully to see how, by the end, that preliminary understanding is transformed. The transformation is dramatic. Its implications reach far beyond the controversy I began from.

We are to speak generally about all perception (416b32–3). Book I of the *De Anima* has reviewed a number of previous philosophers' accounts of perception. Aristotle's highly schematised roll-call of reputable opinions on the nature of soul sets out from the two great distinguishing marks by which, he claims, earlier thinkers separated animate (ensouled) things from inanimate ones: perception and movement (1.2, 403b20–8). Perception, in this discussion, is the basic *cognitive* capacity of soul.[12] Those who looked to perception to explain the nature of soul were saying, in effect, that to be animate is to have the means of getting information about the world – a view Aristotle will endorse in his own terms when he makes the power of perception definitive of what an animal is (II.2, 413b1–4; cf. *GA* 1.23, 731a24–b5).

Some of these philosophers distinguish perception from other, higher types of cognition; most according to Aristotle do not.[13] But it is common ground between Aristotle and everyone else that the lowest level of cognitive interaction with the environment is the level at which the senses operate. In what manner the senses operate, what explains their operation, how much information about the world they can deliver and in what form it comes – all of that is moot, to be discussed and determined between now and the end of III.2.[14] It is the first two of these questions that II.5 will address.

---

[12] The conjunction of knowing and perceiving at 404b9 (τὸ γινώσκειν καὶ τὸ αἰσθάνεσθαι τῶν ὄντων) is echoed by the cognitive vocabulary which predominates in the sequel: 404b17; 28; 405a23; 28; 405b8; 13–16; 21. The critical assessment in 1.5 starts with the same conjunction at 409b24–5 (ἵν' αἰσθάνηταί τε τῶν ὄντων καὶ ἕκαστον γνωρίζῃ) and continues with a similar predominance of cognitive vocabulary: 409b26; 30–1; 410a8; 18; 24–6; 29; 410b2–4; 9–10; 16; 411a4–6; 24.

[13] The Platonists do (1.2, 404b25–30); the older philosophers do not (1.2, 404a27–b6, discussed below; III.3, 427a21–2; cf. *Met.* Γ.5, 1009b12–13).

[14] The last sentence of III.2, 'So much, then, by way of discussion of the principle by which we say that an animal is capable of perception' (427a14–16), closes the discussion begun at the beginning of II.5

As in Book 1, so here we start from the reputable opinions on the subject: ||

> [1][a] Perception consists in[15] being changed[16] and affected, as has been said; for it is held [b] to be some sort of alteration. In addition, some say [2] that like is affected by like.[17] (416b33–5)

That these claims are not yet endorsed in Aristotle's own voice is confirmed by the back-reference 'as has been said', which reports Aristotle's *report* in 1.5 of what had been supposed by reputable thinkers in the tradition:

> They suppose (*titheasin*) that perceiving is some sort of being affected (*paschein ti*) and changed. (410a25–6)

[1][b] has also been said before, but in a very different context (II.4, 415b24) where it is clear that the word 'alteration' (*alloiōsis*) carries a technical Aristotelian sense 'change of quality', presupposing his theory of categories, which no previous thinker could have intended.[18] Aristotle's doctrine that, besides generation and destruction, there are just three categorially distinct types of change – locomotion (change of place), alteration (change of quality) and growth/diminution (change of

---

and thereby credits all the intervening material (including III.2's account of perceptual self-awareness) to the power of perception.

[15] Translations of συμβαίνει ἐν vary between 'consists in' (Hicks 1907; Hett 1935; Ross 1961 in his summary; Hamlyn 1968; Barbotin and Jannone 1966) and expressions like 'depends on', 'results from' (Rodier 1900; Smith 1931; Tricot 1959; Wallace 1882). The causal implications of the latter are certainly premature so early in the chapter. 'Consists in' can be misleading in a different way, as we shall see (p. 200 below), but it is vague enough to mean no more than that perception belongs within the wider class of passive changes. I argue later for this understanding of [1][a] as a statement of classification.

[16] The usual translation 'moved' (Hamlyn 1968; Hett 1935; Hicks 1907; Smith 1931) is misleading for several reasons, the most immediate being that [1][b] will subsume alteration under κινεῖσθαί τε καὶ πάσχειν. κινεῖσθαι must therefore correspond to κίνησις in the generic usage exemplified at I.3, 406a12–13, not to κίνησις meaning 'spatial movement'.

[17] How to translate καί in the last sentence? Usually, it is taken as 'also': 'Some add' (Hicks 1907; Ross 1961), 'Some say too' (Hamlyn 1968; cf. Barbotin and Jannone 1966). But this tends to suggest that the thinkers who propounded [2] did so in conjunction with [1][a] or [b]. I hope to leave readers feeling that that is unlikely and irrelevant; for the dialectic of the chapter, Aristotle needs only to have these opinions in play, not to have any one thinker subscribe to the lot. Smith 1931 and Hett 1935 translate, 'Some say that like is affected only by like', with καί intensifying the emphasis on likeness; this is what [2] amounts to, as we shall see. Alternatively, my 'In addition' is designed to keep καί as 'also' but give it wider scope: 'Another opinion in the field is [2].'

[18] Some scholars (Hamlyn 1968; Rodier 1900) propose this passage as the target of the back-reference 'as has been said' attached to [1][a]. I hope to show that the shift from [1][a] to [1][b] is not as innocent as they presume. But at least they stay within the treatise, unlike Hutchinson 1987: 376, who targets *Ph.* VII 2, 244b10–245a2.

quantity) – was introduced without argument early in the treatise at 1.3, 406a12–13. ‖ The conclusion to draw is that, whereas our preliminary understanding of 'perception' comes from reading the *De Anima*, our understanding of 'alteration' should have been formed already by studying works like the *Physics* and *De Generatione et Corruptione*.[19]

This creates a problem for our reception of [1][b]. [1][a] looks vague and general: they suppose that perception consists in some change or other in which the perceiver is passive. [1][b] makes this more precise, specifying the change they have in view as alteration or change of quality. Both statements present a reputable opinion from the tradition. With what right does Aristotle substitute 'alteration' for 'passive change' when reporting what other people think? Even if those earlier thinkers used *alloiōsis* or related words in writing about perception,[20] why should their meanings be confined in his categories?

The relevant group of thinkers has been associated from the start with the principle that like is known or perceived by like (1.2, 404b17–18; 405b15; 1.5, 409b26–8). Their position is summed up in the passage already cited from 1.5, where they are said to combine [1][a] with the epistemological thesis,

> [3] Like perceives like and knows like by virtue of being like it. (410a24–5)

Likeness for Aristotle tends to mean 'same in quality'.[21] Once we join [1][a] with [3] we realise that the qualitative bias made explicit by [1][b] was present all along. Yes, but the two most prominent named members of the group, Empedocles and Plato in the *Timaeus*,[22] both account for perception by the movement of microscopic effluences and particles. In their case at least, for Aristotle to explain [1][a] 'Perception consists in some sort of passive change' by [1][b] 'Perception is some sort of qualitative alteration' is to insist that, for the purposes of the present discussion, the meaning of their ideas is to be fixed by his physics, not theirs.[23] ‖

---

[19] See *Ph.* III.1, esp. 200b32–201a3; v.1–2; *GC* I 4; also *Cat.* 14.
[20] See the quotations in III.3, 427a23–6, and *Met.* Γ.5, 1009b18–25.
[21] *Cat.* 8, 11a15–19; cf. *Met.* Δ.9, 1018a15–18; 15, 1021a11–12.
[22] They were named at 1.2, 404b8–18, as thinkers who make the soul out of their favoured elements in order to explain perception and cognition; Aristotle returned to them at 5, 409b23–4.
[23] There is a neutral use in which the family of terms πάσχειν, πάθος, πάθημα does not select for any category, and a narrower use in which they select for attributes in respect of which a thing can alter and hence for the category of quality; cf. Ross 1924 *ad Met.* Δ.21. [1][b] reads πάσχειν in [1][a] more narrowly than Empedocles or Plato are likely to have intended. A further narrowing takes place at *Ph.* VII.2–3, 244b2ff., where alteration is confined to changes in *sensible* quality and perception is included under alteration (for discussion, see Wardy 1990: 139ff.) To read this narrowest notion of alteration into [1][a] from the start would be outrageously unfair to the

We need not be shocked to find the reputable opinions served up already cooked in an Aristotelian stew. It is well known that the same is true of Aristotle's treatment of his predecessors in the first book of the *Metaphysics*. My interest is in his presentation of the reputable opinions, not their historical accuracy. Aristotle has objections of principle against those who account for perception, or for other cases of being affected, by appeal to what happens at the microscopic level (*GC* I.8), and he is taking those objections for granted here. *That* is the point to emphasise. From page 1 of the *De Anima*, where knowledge of soul is introduced as one of the most important and certainly the most difficult of the tasks *of natural philosophy* (I.1, 402a1–11), Aristotle's physical theory is presupposed. His psychology is designed to be the crowning achievement of his physics.[24]

A good example of psychology's intimate relation to the rest of Aristotelian physics is coming up next. But first, I want to pick out another feature of [1][b]: the careful vagueness of the phrase 'some sort of alteration' (*alloiōsis tis*), which echoes and preserves the careful vagueness of the phrase 'some sort of being affected' (*paschein ti*) in I.5's version of [1][a] (410a25, quoted above).[25] 'Alteration' may carry its technical meaning 'change of quality', but Aristotle intends to leave plenty of room for the question what sort of change of quality perception is. The answer could be that perception is a certain kind of alteration, a subspecies marked off from others by an appropriate differentia. Alternatively, rather than 'a kind of alteration', *alloiōsis tis* could mean 'an alteration of a kind', the *tis* ‖ being an *alienans* qualification to signal that perception is an alteration only in an etiolated sense.[26] I shall argue for the second: perception is an alteration from which you cannot expect everything you would normally expect from alteration.

---

thinkers [1][a] reports. Yet it is the notion that Aristotle will obtain in II.5 by analysing perception *of* a sensible quality as alteration *by* it.

[24] The programme is mapped out in *Meteor.* I.1 (discussion in Burnyeat 2004b, [Chapter 11 in this volume]). By 'physics' in this paper I mean the Aristotelian study of nature (φυσική), not the deeply anti-Aristotelian physics we have inherited from the seventeenth century; correspondingly, the adjective 'physical' means 'pertaining to Aristotelian physics' and imports no contrast with the mental. (In Burnyeat 1992b I confusingly switched back and forth between this and the modern usage of 'physical' in contrast to 'mental'; for amends and clarification, see Burnyeat 2001a [Chapter 6 in this volume]).

[25] This is the place to note Hicks's comment (Hicks 1907 *ad* 410a25) that the τι in πάσχειν τι agrees with the infinitive taken as a noun; it is not an accusative governed by the infinitive. There need be no significance in the variants τε for τι at 410a25 and τι for τε at 416b33, but they are interesting nonetheless.

[26] A nice illustration of *alienans* τις in *DA* is III.10, 433a9–10: εἴ τις τὴν φαντασίαν τιθείη ὡς νόησίν τινα, where the very next sentence makes clear that φαντασία is not really νόησις. Cf. I.1, 403a8–9; II.5, 417b3 (echoing Pl. *Euthd.* 285b1); III.3, 427a19–20; 12, 434b18.

Developing the *aporia*

After the reputable opinions, we expect a puzzle (*aporia*) to show that they cannot all be true as they stand; some modification is required. In fact, we know that already. To quote yet again, this time in full, from 1.5:

> Further, it is absurd for them to maintain, on the one hand, [*2] that like is unaffected by like and, on the other, [3] that like perceives like and knows like by virtue of being like it, while at the same time[27] they suppose [1][a] that perceiving is some sort of being affected and changed, and so too is conceiving and knowing. (410a23–6)

Never mind whether any one philosopher ever held this seemingly inconsistent triad of opinions; we are dealing with a dialectical construct, not the stuff of history. The inconsistency is produced by adding in the principle [*2] that like is *un*affected by like. This has not been mentioned in the *De Anima* so far. It comes from *De Generatione et Corruptione* 1.7, 323b1–15, which ascribes it to all previous thinkers except Democritus.[28] ||

De Generatione et Corruptione 1.7, 323b1–15, is also the source of the opposite (Democritean) opinion [2] that like is affected by like, which makes its first appearance in the *De Anima* at the beginning of 11.5. It is entirely appropriate, then, that Aristotle's next move in 11.5 (417a1–2) is to send us to *De Generatione et Corruptione* 1.7 for a general (*katholou*) account of what [2] gets right and what wrong. The cross-reference to *De Generatione et Corruptione* 1.7 identifies the place where [2] and its contrary [*2] met head on and their conflict was resolved. The point of the cross-reference is not to say 'If you are interested in this topic, you will

---

[27] At 410a25 Rodier 1900 reads γάρ instead of the usual δ', and Smith 1931 translates 'for'. γάρ has poor manuscript support, but at least it recognises that *[2] and [3] on their own, without [1][a], make no absurdity. If you translate the δ' adversatively as 'but' or 'yet' (Hamlyn 1968; Hett 1935; Hicks 1907; Ross 1961), you are liable to suggest that Aristotle supposes *[2] and [3] do make an absurdity on their own. My rendering of δ' is modelled on Siwek 1965's 'cum tamen'.

[28] This enables Hicks 1907 and Ross 1961 *ad* 410a23 to agree that, if we go by Aristotle's testimony, the charge of inconsistency holds against everyone except Anaxagoras, who denied that like knows like (1.2, 405b14–15; 19–21), and Democritus. True enough, if 'affected' has the same meaning in [*2] and [1][a]; for example, if in both it means simple qualitative alteration. But that only underlines once more how artificial it is to leave out microscopic events when reviewing earlier theories of perception. Again, Joachim 1922 *ad* 323b10–11 finds it strange that [2] should be attributed to Democritus alone, given that Empedocles and others subscribe to [3] and Aristotle treats [3] as a special case of [2]. But [3] does not instantiate [2] without [1][a] and a parallel assurance that 'affected' has the same meaning in both premise and conclusion. From the point of view of historical accuracy, the chief victim of distortion is perhaps Plato: he does at *Tim.* 57e5–58a1 propound a version of [*2], but for that very reason (and others) he should not be treated as a straightforward adherent of [3]. For intellectual knowledge, if not for perception, he has his own version of the assimilation story by which Aristotle solves the ἀπορία (*Tim.* 90cd).

find more about it in *GC* 1.7,' but 'You need to bear *GC* 1.7 in mind as you read *DA* 11.5.'[29]

Both the conflict and the resolution presuppose the previous chapter of *De Generatione et Corruptione*, which isolated a narrow meaning of 'being affected' (*paschein*) and a correspondingly narrowed meaning of 'acting on' (*poiein*) – meanings that apply only to alteration or change of quality (1.6, 323a16–20).[30] The chapter we are supposed to bear in mind as we read *DA* 11.5 is narrowly concerned with alteration. Aristotle speaks in *GC* 1.7 of agent and patient, acting on and being affected. But he means agent and patient of qualitative change, altering and being altered. Small wonder it has been hard to find an explanation or justification in the *De Anima* for Aristotle's tendency to construe his predecessors in qualitative terms, as when he gives [1][b] as his gloss on [1][a]. The decision to concentrate on qualitative change was made elsewhere, outside the *De Anima*.

It was not of course an arbitrary decision. *De Generatione et Corruptione* is a work about the lowest level of Aristotle's world, where the elements change into each other (elemental generation and destruction), act on each other and on other things, and combine by mixture to form more complex stuffs like bronze or flesh. At this level quality is all-important. Quality determines the elemental natures and explains their transformations and interactions. For the primitives of the theory are not 'the so- || called elements', earth, air, fire and water, but rather the four elementary qualities – hot and cold, wet and dry, hot and cold being active powers, wet and dry passive – which (a) explain the other tangible qualities that differentiate bodies as bodies (*GC* 11.2, cited at *DA* 11.11, 423b29), and (b) determine through their four compatible combinations the essential natures of earth, air, fire and water (*GC* 11.3). It is this qualitative physics that Aristotle invokes for the study of perception. The lower is to help us understand the higher. How?

What we should have learned from GC 1.7 is that [*2] 'Like is unaffected by like' and [2] 'Like is affected by like' each capture one part of a larger truth. For an agent *A* to affect a patient *P*, *A* must *assimilate P* to itself (*homoioun heautōi*, 324a10–11), as when fire makes a cold thing hot or warmer than it was before. *A* and *P* start off characterised by contrary predicates from the same range; they are thus generically alike, specifically

---

[29] This was well understood in the ancient tradition. Witness the extra words λεκτέον δὲ καὶ νῦν (*vel sim.*) sometimes found added after πάσχειν at 417a2 (details in Philop. 290, 25–8; Rodier 1900 *ad loc.*; the apparatus of Barbotin and Jannone 1966).
[30] Cf. n. 23 above.

unlike. When they meet, A is bound to act on P, and P is bound to be acted upon by A, just because they are contrary to each other; that is the nature of contrariety. So A and P end up with the same or closer predicates of the range.

Two curious arguments support this analysis (323b18–29). One is that there could be no interaction between whiteness and a line, which confirms the requirement of generic likeness. The second argument is that, if likeness rather than contrariety was the explanation of A's affecting P, both P and every other thing would continually affect itself (each thing is always as like itself and as close to itself as anything could be!), and nothing would be indestructible or unchangeable. This supports the requirement of specific unlikeness. Combine generic likeness and specific unlikeness, and qualitative contrariety emerges as a fundamental explanatory principle of Aristotelian physics (323b29–324a14).[31]

My theme is the dependence of Aristotle's psychology on (the more elementary parts of) his physics. What interests me, therefore, is to see the second of the arguments just mentioned reappearing in *DA* II.5, 417a2–6, as the puzzle which will show that the reputable opinions need modification. Why are the senses not self-activating? They would be self-activating if P perceives A because of the likeness between them: P, which is always like itself, would continually perceive itself without needing an external stimulus. It was *GC* I.7, 323b1–15, which made clear that 'Like $\parallel$ is (un)affected by like' is to be read causally: 'Like is (un)affected by like because they are alike.' All the *De Anima* has to do is take perceiving as a special case of being affected and find suitable values for P and A.[32] The puzzle

---

[31] Corollary: an organic unity cannot be affected by itself (*Met*. Θ.1, 1046a28; cf. *Ph*. VIII.4, 255a12–15).

[32] (i) Editors standardly remark that for P Aristotle writes αἰσθήσεις (417a3) but means the organs rather than the faculties of sense, since it is the former that consist of the same elements as external objects. Parallels can of course be found (see Hicks 1907 *ad loc*.), but it seems important to add that there may be a philosophical reason for the language used here. Aristotle's target is a view he originally characterised (I.2, 404b8ff.; 5, 409b23ff.) by saying that those who explain soul by cognition of like by like make the soul consist of their favoured elements, whether these are material (Empedocles, etc.) *or immaterial* (the Platonists). They make the cognitive faculties out of elements too (410b22), and fail to give reasons for denying that the soul is nothing but the elements it consists of (410b10–12). I suggest, therefore, that for P Aristotle writes αἰσθήσεις because that is what he means; it is his opponents who equate αἰσθήσεις with the elements (cf. Plutarch of Athens *apud* Simplic. 118.8–10).

(ii) For A Aristotle writes 'the elements in virtue of themselves or their accidents' (417a5–6). Ross 1961 is right, against Rodier 1900 and Hicks 1907, that συμβεβηκότα here must cover essential as well as accidental qualities of the elements, but wrong to see the disjunction as Aristotle hedging on which disjunct is more correct. It is not his doctrine either that perception is always of the elements (which in Aristotelian compounds have only potential existence), or that elements are ever perceived in virtue of themselves (*per se*); the classification of sense-objects in II.6 would have them perceived

about the senses perceiving themselves is then a complete and conclusive refutation of the initial set of reputable opinions, [1][a] and [2]. They cannot both be true as they stand.

But we already know from 1.5 (above, p. 163) that if [1][a] is combined with the opposite principle [*2] that like is unaffected by like, we must give up or modify the reputable opinion which gave rise to this whole discussion: [3] like perceives like. This is the moment for Aristotle to reveal the truth that does justice to the truth in each of [1][a], [2], [*2], and [3].

A PRELIMINARY *LUSIS*

The solution (*lusis*) which points the way forward is the assimilation story from *De Generatione et Corruptione*. For *P* to perceive *A*, *P* and *A* must be unlike to begin with, so that *A* can affect *P* (because of the unlikeness between them) and make *P* like itself. The perceiving is an assimilation in which *P* becomes like *A*.

With [3] thus modified, the reconciliation of [2] and [*2] in *GC* 1.7 allows [1][a] to stand – unmodified but now unambiguously explicated by [1][b]. For the upshot of the dialectic we have just been through is to confirm that perceiving is an alteration in the technical Aristotelian sense 'change of quality'.

However, it is not until the end of the first paragraph of II.5 that Aristotle sums up the assimilation story:

> [A] For this reason, in one way a thing is affected by like, and in another by unlike, as we said;[33] for it is the unlike which is affected, although when it has been affected it is like. (417a18–20)

As the initial 'For this reason' (*dio*) indicates, the lesson learned from *De Generatione et Corruptione* 1.7 is now embedded in a wider explanatory

---

accidentally, in virtue of their sensible qualities, whether essential (earth's dryness) or accidental (its colour). I conclude that the clause ὧν (...) τούτοις at 417a5–6 states the doctrine of Aristotle's opponents, and that the disjunction recalls the problem posed for Empedocles at 1.5, 409b31–410a13, about how he can explain the perception of compounds (which in his physics, as viewed through the Aristotelian eyes of *Ph.* II.1, 193a21–8 and *GC* II.7, 334a25–b2, are accidental assemblages of elemental bits).

[33] Hicks 1907 and Ross 1961 *ad loc.* refer to II.4, 416a29ff., where [*2] makes its second appearance in the treatise (line 32) and the dialectical treatment of conflicting opinions on nutrition exactly parallels the treatment of perception, the outcome being that in nutrition a feeder assimilates food to itself and the food takes on the form of the feeder. Hicks also entertains, but considers less probable, the idea that 'as we said' simply reiterates the reference to *GC* 1.7. The question scarcely matters, since any reader who has followed up the earlier cross-reference to *GC* will realise that *DA* II.4 itself rests on *GC* 1.7, as well as the lengthy analysis of growth in *GC* 1.5.

context. The wider context is furnished by the all-pervasive Aristotelian concepts of potentiality and actuality.[34] Aristotle's immediate response to the puzzle about why the senses are not self-activating was to conclude that a perceiver as such is a potential being, not yet an actuality. That is why it needs an external cause to start one perceiving – exactly as combustible fuel needs an actual fire to set it blazing (417a6–9). It is only after perceiving and the senses have been connected to potentiality and actuality (417a9–18) that Aristotle reaches [A] and shows us he is prepared to endorse [1][b] in his own voice. [1][b] is simply [A] applied to perception.

This wider context for the assimilation story [A] does not come from *De Generatione et Corruptione* 1.7.[35] The work to which Aristotle's cross- ‖ referencing now sends us (417a16–17) is *Physics* III.1–3 on the nature and definition of change itself.[36]

What we should have learned from *Physics* III.1–3 is that alteration, by virtue of being a kind of change, is 'a sort of actuality (*energeia tis*), though an incomplete one' (417a16–17). The point is even more technical than it sounds.[37] Alteration, as a kind of change, is the actuality of the alterable *qua* alterable (*Ph.* III.1, 201a11–12): what alters does so because it has a potentiality to be qualitatively unlike its present self, and the process of alteration is the exercise or actuality of that potentiality, its fullest manifestation. At the end of the process, when the subject has become unlike it was, the potentiality which existed before and (more fully) during the alteration is no more. It is exhausted, used up. A new quality, which is a new potentiality for change, has replaced the old.

This is the reason why alteration is essentially incomplete. It is defined by and directed toward an end-state outside itself. Cold is a potentiality for

---

[34] Hett 1935 begins a new paragraph at πρῶτον μὲν οὖν (417a14). Hardly obligatory, but he is right that the argument takes a new turn here.

[35] The only hint of potentiality and actuality there is the reference to τὸ δυνάμενον θερμὸν εἶναι at 324b7–8. Then silence until the equally brief reference at *GC* I.9, 326b31.

[36] 417a16–17 virtually quotes *Ph.* III.2, 201b31–2. But obviously the quotation makes little sense without III.1 to explain it. Moreover *Ph.* III.3, on the identity of changing and being changed and the location of both in the changed, will supply a key doctrine for the theory of perception in *DA* III.2, 425b26–26a26. Note also the supergeneralisation of which [A] is one instance at *Ph.* III.2, 202a9–12. Accordingly, I take the cross-reference to be Aristotle's way of announcing that *DA* presupposes *Ph.* III.1–3 as the unitary discussion it was written to be. That might explain why in *DA* III.2 he feels no need to add a second cross-reference to the text he has already told us to bear in mind.

[37] For help with the technicalities I recommend Kosman (1969: 40–50, 56–8), followed by Waterlow 1988, ch. 3 and Hussey 1983: 58–65. These authors all agree that the traditional charge that Aristotle's definition of change is circular can be blocked if we understand the relevant potentialities as potentialities for being, not as potentialities for changing. I have not been persuaded by critics like Heinemann who continue to prefer the latter. An obvious objection is that the actuality of a potential *for changing* should be complete as soon as change begins.

being warm. Being warmed, the actuality of that potentiality, is the process of changing from cold to warm. But once a thing *is* warm, it is no longer manifesting and no longer even possesses the potentiality for being warm.[38] It has the actuality of warmth instead. The cold has been destroyed and replaced by its contrary. Alteration really alters.

The notion of incomplete actuality suggests a contrast with complete actuality. This would be a process or activity which is not defined by and || directed towards an end-state outside itself. Rather, it is defined by and directed towards itself; its end is to engage in the activity itself, for its own sake. In ethical and metaphysical contexts Aristotle often contrasts activities which are their own end with those aiming at a further product (e.g. *EN* I.1, 1094a3–5; X.6, 1176b6–7; *Met.* Θ.8, 1050a23–b2), but nowhere, so far I as know, does he call the former 'complete actuality'. The ancient commentators contrast change (*kinēsis*) with complete actuality (*teleia energeia*),[39] but the closest Aristotle gets to doing so is in three places, one far better known than the others.

(i) In *Metaphysics* Θ.6, 1048b18–35, actions which are their own end are classed as actualities (*energeiai*) in a sense that *excludes* change (*kinēsis*). Change, being incomplete, is not *energeia* at all, not even incomplete actuality. This terminological restriction on the scope of the term '*energeia*', unique in the extant corpus,[40] suggests that the passage was written as a contribution to metaphysics (first philosophy) or ethics, not physics. For in Aristotle's physics the idea that change is (incomplete) actuality has a foundational role. Thus (ii) he worries in *Physics* III.2, 201b33–5, that the notion of change is elusive, difficult to grasp, because it cannot be classified either as privation or as potentiality – or as actuality un-qualified (*energeia haplē*). Yet if change is nothing real at all, physics will have no subject matter to study. The one possibility remaining is that change is a qualified sort of actuality. So it becomes part of Aristotle's official definition of change (reaffirmed as such at VIII.5, 257b8–9) that change is a qualified actuality, intrinsically other-directed and incomplete. But the

---

[38] See *Ph.* II.1, 201a19–22; b10–11, with Kosman 1969: 57–8, Waterlow 1988: 115. Does this commit Aristotle to denying that if a thing is warm, it can be warm (*ab esse ad posse valet consequentia*)? No. What it shows is that the concept of potentiality on which Aristotelian physics is founded is not the bare concept of possibility.

[39] So e.g. Themistius 18.20–37, 112.28–32; Philoponus 296.21–297.10; Simplicius (if it be he) 264.23–6; Sophonias 66.14–17.4.

[40] Or so I argue in Burnyeat 2008a [Chapter 4 in this volume], where I also show that the passage was not written for *Metaphysics* Θ, even if (as I assume here) it is authentic Aristotle.

Physics does no more than mention the contrasting idea of unqualified actuality.

(iii) *De Anima* III.7, 431a6–7, contrasts change, as the actuality of something incomplete, with the actuality of something complete or perfected, and calls the latter 'unqualified actuality' (*hē haplōs energeia*). In (ii) and (iii), unlike (i), change remains actuality – subject to the qualification that it is incomplete. It is incomplete because (as explained already at *Ph.* III.2, 201b32–3) the potential thing it is the actuality of is itself incomplete; the latter is incomplete, I take it, because it is not yet what it has the potentiality to be. (ii) and (iii), because they do at least mention an || unqualified actuality that contrasts with the incomplete actuality of change, offer a line of thought to which I must certainly return. Not so (i), which rules itself out of the repertoire of passages relevant to the idea of change as incomplete actuality. If from time to time in the sequel I mention (i), I do so only to keep it at bay. Its influence on interpretations of II.5 has been a hindrance, rather than a help, to understanding the positive message of the chapter.

Back now to alteration. After reminding us that change is incomplete actuality, Aristotle adds that the agent of alteration must already have in actuality the quality the patient will acquire (417a17–18, from *Ph.* III.2, 202a9–13). This would allow him to reformulate the assimilation story [A] for perception in terms of potentiality and actuality, as follows:

> [P/A] The perceiver[41] is potentially what the sense-object is actually, e.g. warm or red, so perceiving is being assimilated to that object, altering to become actually warm or red.

Just that is the conclusion Aristotle states at the very end of II.5, 418a3–6, where 'as has been said' refers back to the context we are discussing.[42] So this is a good place to review the results of the dialectic so far. At the end of the first paragraph of II.5 Aristotle has assembled all the equipment he

---

[41] I write 'perceiver' here for two reasons. First, to bracket the question whether a perceiver is potentially *F* by virtue of having a sense which is potentially *F* or by virtue of having an organ which is potentially *F*; since my opponent presses hard for [P/A] to be a thesis exclusively about organs (Sorabji 1974: 52–3, 1992: 212–13; cf. Hamlyn 1968: 104, 13), it is only fair to keep my language as clean as I can. (For what it is worth, *EN* x.4, 1174b17–18, implies that at least in that context it does not matter which we say.) But second, 'perceiver' may well be the best translation for τὸ αἰσθητικόν in II.5. Thus at 418a1 and 3, instead of a reference to 'the perceptive faculty' (Barbotin and Jannone 1966; Hicks 1907; Ross 1961; Theiler 1959; Tricot 1959), a reference to the subject capable of perceiving (Hett 1935; Rodier 1900; Smith 1931) would match the preceding neuters τὸ ἔχον τὴν ἐπιστήμην (417b5–6), τὸ φρονοῦν (417b8), τὸ μανθάνον (417b12); a similar translation at 417a6 would match the following neuters τοῦ καυστικοῦ (417a8), τὸ δυνάμει ἀκοῦον καὶ ὁρῶν (10–11); 417b16 and 418a1 will fall into line later. II.3, 415a6–7 is a nice example of a single sentence where both meanings of the -ικόν ending are displayed.

[42] So Rodier 1900 and Ross 1961; Hicks 1907 is needlessly hesitant.

needs for a full formulation of [P/A]. Had he provided it at once, without pausing to add the refinements of 417a21–418a3, we would still have a remarkable account of perception.

The most remarkable feature is a causal scheme which explains why one cannot perceive warmth or red unless something actually warm/red is ‖ present to stimulate the appropriate sense. It is not just that some external cause is needed for perception. Perceiving something is being assimilated to it, e.g. being warmed or reddened, and the whole weight of Aristotelian physics stands behind the demand that the cause of this alteration be something actually warm or red.

What is more, the warm or red object acts as cause in virtue of being warm or red. Not for Aristotle the modern idea that the object acts on the perceiver in virtue of some non-phenomenal feature (molecular motion, light reflectancy) on which its appearing warm or red depends. Aristotle's is a world in which, as I have emphasised before,[43] colours, sounds, smells, and other sensible qualities are as real as the primary qualities (so called by us). They are real in the precise sense that they are causal agents in their own right.[44]

An immediate corollary, to be announced in the next chapter, II.6, is that perception of such qualities as red and warmth is always true (418a14–16; cf. III.3, 428b18–19; 21; 27–8; 6, 430b26–30; *Met.* Γ.5, 1010b2–3). This doctrine has provoked much puzzled discussion. It is seldom recalled that, if seeing red is being reddened and assimilated to something actually red, there is bound to be a match between the qualitative content and the qualitative cause of sight.[45] In causing the perceiver to become warm or red, sensible qualities cause themselves to be perceived

---

[43] Burnyeat 1992b: 21–2.
[44] Essential reading on this topic is Broadie 1992, interestingly (but in my view unsuccessfully) challenged by Broackes 1999.
[45] We should not make too much of the solitary qualification ἢ ὅτι ὀλίγιστον ἔχουσα ψεῦδος at 428b19; Aristotle himself ignores it at 21 and 27–8. Since Aristotle assumes his readers will understand the qualification, we should look for help within the chapters between II.6 and III.3. There we find II.9, 421a9–26, on the 'inaccurate sense-organs' that make hard-eyed animals bad at discriminating colours and humans bad at discriminating smells, though we do brilliantly with objects of touch. No need to look ahead to the types of perceptual illusion discussed in *De Insomniis* 2, which are hardly examples of 'the least possible error'. No need to join the sophisticated revival by Charles 2000: 118–24 of Block 1961's teleological interpretation of proper object perception as true whenever all is functioning well. II.9's cases are genuine perceptions, not mere illusory appearance, for they are appropriately caused (as illusions are not) by the sensible form of the object perceived. Yet to hard-eyed animals that form appears less bright, or less distinctly orange, than it actually is. Again, *PA* II.2, 648b12–17, mentions a case where the cause of a hot thing's feeling hotter than it should is the perceiver's condition, not their sense-organ. This is an exaggerated response to real heat out there, not just the illusory effect of fever within.

as the qualities they are. Conversely, to perceive is to be altered *by* the sensible quality one has a perception *of.* ||

This result sets the framework for the *De Anima*'s theory of perception. All the talk of perceivers becoming by sensible forms and taking on the colour or smell perceived – all this derives from applying the assimilation story [A] to the special case of perception, as spelled out in [P/A]. But perception is a very special case, as we are about to see.

For Aristotle in 11.5 does not proceed directly to a full formulation of [P/A]. First comes a lengthy and complex analysis (417a21–418a3) of different types of potentiality. When we do reach [P/A], at the very end of the chapter, our understanding of what it means to say that the perceiver is *potentially* what the sense-object is actually is quite different from what it would have been had Aristotle derived his conclusion immediately from [A].[46] The difference brings with it, as a direct consequence, a new and radically different understanding of 'alteration' in our starting point [1][b]. In one fell swoop all the evidence for the Sorabji interpretation is turned to evidence for a different view. The rest of the *De Anima* must be read in accordance with that different view, as must its sequel *De Sensu*, which starts by announcing, 'All that has already been said about soul is to be assumed' (1, 436a5; tr. Hett).

THE DEMAND FOR DISTINCTIONS

We have learned a lot from *De Generatione et Corruptione* 1.7 and *Physics* III.1–3. But it is not enough for more than a preliminary solution. Aristotle's directions to the reader are loud and clear:

> *To begin with* let us speak[47] as if being affected and being changed and actual exercising (*energein*)[48] are the same thing; for change is indeed a sort of actuality (*energeia tis*), though an incomplete one … ||

---

[46] Both Themistius 54.3–20 and Philoponus 289.31–2 have a sound appreciation of the point.

[47] Editors generally print λέγωμεν, both here and at 416b32; an exception is Barbotin and Jannone 1966, who print λέγομεν each time. λέγομεν makes reasonable sense: by speaking in the simple way we are now (since 417a6) speaking about potentiality and actuality, we are ignoring the distinctions embarked upon at 417a21ff. Correspondingly, ἁπλῶς at 417a22 refers to the way potentiality and actuality are spoken of in the preceding paragraph. Nonetheless, I prefer λέγωμεν in both places. The chapter is full of more or less imperative expressions: 417a21; b8; 11–12; 14; 30; 418a2. They are important guides to an intricate discussion.

[48] 'Actual exercising' is a compromise translation meant to bring out the connection, essential to this context, between actuality (ἐνέργεια) and the exercise (ἐνεργεῖν) of an active or passive δύναμις; cf. *Met*. Θ.8, 1050a22–3. As a case of πάσχειν, perceptual sentience is passive, so I avoid the word 'activity'.

> At the same time, however,[49] distinctions should be made concerning potentiality and actuality (*entelecheia*). For *at the moment* we are speaking[50] about them in a simple way.[51] (417a14–17 ... 21–2)

The discussion that follows sets out from a distinction between two types of potentiality (417a22–8; cf. 417b30–2).[52] A distinction between two types of potentiality implies a corresponding distinction between two types of actuality. We will find Aristotle unwilling to tell us as much as we would like to know about the actuality side of the distinction.

His reticence on this point shows up already in the provisional assumption that 'being affected and being changed and actual exercising (*energein*) are the same thing'. In effect, he is asking us to suppose that there is no such thing as complete or unqualified actuality,[53] and *a fortiori* no such thing as *energeia* in the exclusive sense of *Metaphysics* Θ.6. There is only the incomplete actuality exhibited by a process of change which is defined by and directed towards an end-state outside itself. An extraordinary request. What can it mean?

Putting that puzzle on hold for later, let us note that the 'simple' way of speaking which Aristotle refers to here is the way he introduced ‖ potentiality and actuality in response to the puzzle about why the senses are not self-activating. The puzzle shows that a perceiver as such is a potential being, not yet an actuality (417a6–7, p. 167 above). The moral is that we must recognise two meanings of nouns like 'sense', 'sight', and 'hearing', corresponding to two meanings of the verbs in such sentences as '*P* perceives', '*P* sees', '*P* hears'. In one meaning they signify a potentiality or capacity for perceiving (*P* is a seer or hearer even when asleep), in the other its actuality or exercise

---

[49] δέ and καί function separately here (Denniston 1954: 305). δέ contrasts the distinctions to follow with the simple way we have been speaking about potentiality and actuality so far, while καί (for which the manuscript evidence is overwhelming) links to the previous imperative λέγωμεν in 417a14–16. We will distinguish different types of potentiality and actuality as well as continuing to speak as if being affected and being changed and actual exercising are the same thing.

[50] Torstrik's emendation ἐλέγομεν ('Just now we were speaking'), adopted by Ross 1956, is not only unnecessary, but wrongly suggests that 417a21 makes a complete break with the previous paragraph's 'simple' way of speaking. We shall see that the gradual process of refinement begun at πρῶτον (417a14) is still not completed when we reach εἰσαῦθις at 417b29–30.

[51] Hamlyn's translation 'in an unqualified way' (Hamlyn 1968) suggests that the contrast is potentiality and actuality *simpliciter* vs. potentiality and actuality in some respect or with some qualification, as e.g. ὂν ἁπλῶς vs. τὸ ὂν at *Met.* Z.1, 1028a31, or ἐνέργεια ἁπλῆ vs. ἐνέργειά τις at *Ph.* III.2, 201b33–202a3 (cited above). But here, as at 417b2 and 30, to speak of *X* ἁπλῶς is to speak of it without distinguishing kinds of *X* (cf. III.2, 426a26; *EN* II.7, 1108b7–8); Philoponus 299.4 glosses the word as ἀδιορίστως. Aristotle enjoins us to make distinctions, not to add qualifications to what has already been said.

[52] The parentheses that Ross 1956, following Torstrik 1862, prints around 417a26–8 are unnecessary and serve to obscure rather than to clarify the message.

[53] Well appreciated by Themistius 55.6–12 and Simplicius 120.13–14.

(417a9–13).⁵⁴ But 'To begin with' (*prōton*) marks all this as a preliminary formulation. And it is easy to see why Aristotle should wish us to be aware of the preliminary character of his remarks so far.

For if the potentiality here is the type discussed in *Physics* III.1–3, its exercise will be the incomplete actuality of real alteration. The sense of sight will be the eye's potentiality to *be* red instead of transparent or the green it presently is. In short, the Sorabji interpretation will be correct.

'But distinctions should be made.' The sense of sight is not that type of potentiality. Nor, consequently, is its exercise the incomplete actuality of real alteration. The Sorabji interpretation stops with the preliminary solution. Aristotle does not.

THE TRIPLE SCHEME

More technicalities – but this time Aristotle will lay them out on the pages of the *De Anima*. We are to be introduced to the distinction that tradition knows as the distinction between first and second potentiality. This is not a case where the lower is invoked to help us understand the higher (cf. p. 164–5). On the contrary, the distinction developed here for knowledge and perception is invoked in *Physics* VIII.4, 255a30ff., to explain the natural motions of earth, air, fire, and water. That indeed is the only other work outside the ambit of the *De Anima* where the triple scheme, as I shall call it, is on display.⁵⁵ ||

Physics VIII.4 does not refer to the *De Anima*. It treats the distinction between first and second potentiality as a piece of conceptual equipment available for use when needed: 'Since the potential is spoken of in more than one way' (255a30–1). Yet the distinction is not explicitly marked in *Metaphysics* Δ, Aristotle's philosophical lexicon (compare Δ.12 with Δ.7, 1017a35–b9). Nor, more strikingly, does it receive attention in *Metaphysics* Θ.6, 1048b18–36, despite the connection scholars sometimes draw between that text and the topics of *De Anima* II.5.⁵⁶ Conversely, there is no reference in II.5 to the distinction in *Metaphysics* Θ.6 between actuality (*energeia*) and change (*kinēsis*). Let us read on.

⁵⁴ On the problematic sentence 417a13–14, see Hicks 1907 *ad loc*. His hesitations about adopting αἰσθητόν from Alexander *Quaest*. III.3, 83.6 (with Förster 1912; Ross 1956; Torstrik 1862) seem to me unsound, as does the defence of the MSS αἰσθάνεσθαι by Welsch 1987: 103–4 with n. 3. Better still, I incline to think, is the solution offered by Rodier 1900: read αἰσθητόν and delete the whole sentence as a marginal note to the effect that the potential/actual distinction applies also to the objects of perception. Alternatively, emend to αἰσθητικόν.
⁵⁵ The brief allusion at *Sens*. 4, 441b21–3, is clearly within the ambit of *DA*, presupposing the careful elaboration of II.5.
⁵⁶ See especially Kosman 1984: 128–32. Ackrill 1965: 160–2 was quite right to disassociate the two texts.

Last time Aristotle set out from two meanings of perception verbs (417a9–13). His new distinction is modelled on two meanings of the nouns and adjectives which figure in such sentences as '*P* is a knower' (*epistēmon*), '*P* has knowledge', and in more specific attributions like '*P* has the art of literacy',[57] '*P* is a builder'; the knowledge verbs come in later.[58] In one meaning, any member of the species *Homo sapiens* is thereby and from birth a knower, because the capacity for thought and reasoning, which differentiates human from beast, is also a capacity for knowledge.[59] In ‖ the other meaning, someone who has acquired a sound knowledge of letters is a knower, by virtue of having an ability they can exercise at will (417a22–8).

Both types of potentiality contrast with the actuality of someone exercising their knowledge of letters. This last is the person who knows in the proper sense of the verb (417a29–30).[60] So there are three cases:

(1)	(2)	(3)
potentiality	*potentiality*	*actuality*
P is a knower	*P* is a knower	
	P knows[61]	*P* knows

---

[57] I.e. *P* is able to read and write (Theiler 1959 translates 'wer das ABC inne hat'). This, rather than the more highbrow achievements of Alexandrian scholars, is the standard meaning of γραμματική in Aristotle's day; LSJ sv aptly cite the definition at *Top.* VI.5, 142b31–4. It makes good, simple sense of the example at 417a29: actively knowing this A means using one's knowledge to recognise the A one is reading or to create the right shape when writing A. And it fits the suggestion in n. 73 below that the passage we are embarking on echoes the Aviary section of Plato's *Theaetetus*, where reading letters is precisely what ὁ γραμματικός is described as doing (198e).

[58] At 417a29 and b8–11. *Ph.* VIII.4 also starts with the adjective. Aristotle might well feel the verb ἐπίστασθαι to be inappropriate for first potentiality.

[59] For thought (διάνοια) and reasoning (λογισμός) as the differentia of human, see II.3, 414b18; 415a7–11 (cf. I.5, 410b24; II.2, 413b12–13; 30; 414a13; 3, 414a32; *Met.* A.1, 980b27–8). My word 'also' is intended to pass lightly over the problem of fixing the exact relation of thought and reasoning to the intellect (νοῦς); that, as Aristotle keeps saying (415a11–12 echoes I.4, 408b13–29; 5, 410b12–15; II.2, 413b24–31) is another subject, for another discussion. Aristotle's καί in τὸ γένος τοιοῦτον καὶ ἡ ὕλη at 27 is equally delicate. He cannot be alluding to the analogy between genus and matter that he sometimes mentions but never firmly endorses (*Met.* Δ.28, 1024a36–b 9; Z.12, 1038a6–8; I.8, 1058a1, 23–4), since γένος here is human nature in its fully differentiated specificity (for the usage, cf. *Met.* Δ.28). The potentiality for knowledge is intrinsic to the actuality that makes us human. From this some will infer that the potentiality must be grounded in the ὕλη of *DA* II.1, 412a9–11 (cf. Philop. 305.34–306.7); they can render καί 'and so'. Others will be happy to leave ὕλη in its abstract meaning 'potentiality' (Bonitz 785a46–56). Themistius 55.20–1 paraphrases ὁ μὲν ὅτι τὸ γένος τοιοῦτον καὶ ἡ φύσις τοῦ ἀνθρώπου, ὡς εἶναι δεκτικὴ ἐπιστήμης.

[60] The reason why this is the proper (κυρίως) meaning of the verb is doubtless that, as actuality, it is definitionally and teleologically prior to the correlative potentiality (II.4, 415a17–20; *Met.* IX.8, 1049b10–17; 1050a7–12).

[61] The implication that '*P* knows' can be entered under (2), with the verb in a potential sense, is confirmed by the more specific verbs at 417b8–11.

No reader of the *De Anima* can fail to notice that we have met this scheme before. In II.1, however, the emphasis was on (2) and (3) as two types of actuality, not on (1) and (2) as two types of potentiality. As knowledge possessed is to knowledge in use, so is soul, i.e. the organised set of functional capacities which comprise the form or 'life' of a living thing, to the actual exercise of those capacities. Knowledge possessed was the model used to help us understand the definition of soul as 'the *first actuality* of a natural body which is potentially alive' (412a22–8). But nowhere in II.5 is (2) clearly called actuality.[62]

Another innovation in II.5 is that the model of knowledge is explicitly extended to (1). This would not have suited the earlier context, where the explanandum was life as such and Aristotle intended to assert that the only body which is potentially alive is one that is actually alive (II.1, 412b15–17; 25–6). It is certainly not true that '*P* is a knower' in sense (1) implies '*P* is a knower' in sense (2).

It is important to appreciate these differences between II.1 and II.5, and the reasons for them, before adopting the technical terminology that tradition has devised for the triple scheme:

(1)   (2)   (3)
first potentiality   second potentiality
                      first actuality   second actuality

Of the four labels, 'first actuality' is the only one found in Aristotle himself, and that only in *DA* II.1 (412a27; b5). But there is ample justification for the others and they make it easier to give a crisp statement of the issue before us: Which type of potentiality does [P/A] refer to, first or second?

Aristotle's answer will be 'second' (417b17–18). But first he explains why it matters. It matters because there is an important difference between the type of change or alteration involved in passing from (1) to (2) and the type involved in passing from (2) to (3). That is why the emphasis in II.5 is on first and second *potentiality*. Change is the actuality of the potential *qua*

---

[62] The two places where one might think to find (2) so called are debatable. At 417a30–2 ἐνέργεια is written into the text by the Torstrik–Ross emendation I reject in Appendix 1. At 417b13 τοῦ ἐντελεχείᾳ ὄντος may in fact correspond to ἐντελεχείᾳ ὄντος at 417a29 and refer to the exercise of knowledge involved in the activity of teaching (cf. *Ph.* III.3, 202b7; Philop. *De aeternitate mundi* 71.4–7; *Soph.* 67.5). *Ph.* VIII.4, 255a35–b1, does put actuality and potentiality together: γίγνεται ἐνεργείᾳ τὸ δυνατόν, οἷον τὸ μανθάνον ἐκ δυνάμει ὄντος ἕτερον γίγνεται δυνάμει. Another passage I would cite for the combined description is *DA* III.4, 429b5–9, but not everyone recognises that this is about knowing in sense (2).

potential (*Ph.* III.1, 201a10–12, p. 167 above). So to understand a change one has to understand what sort of potentiality it is the actuality of. The difference between first and second potentiality will be spelled out in terms of the difference between passing from (1) to (2) and passing from (2) to (3). We shall then know all that II.5 has to tell us about the difference between the actualities corresponding to the two types of potentiality.

A WARNING

As just hinted, the long intricate process of refinement that lies ahead will not reach completion within II.5. Aristotle's directions to the reader are again loud and clear:

> But there may ['will' in most translations] be an opportunity *another time* for a full clarification (*diasaphēsai*) of these matters; *for the present*, let it be enough to have got this far in drawing distinctions[63] <that we can say the following:>||
>
> Since we do not in fact speak of the potential in a simple way, but would say that a boy is potentially a general in one meaning, and that an adult is potentially a general in another meaning, so it is [i.e., in both ways; most translations have 'in the latter way'][64] that we speak of the perceiver.[65] (417b29–418a1)

---

[63] The sentence νῦν δὲ διωρίσθω τοσοῦτον implies that the process of distinguishing could be taken further, although we will not do that now. Accordingly, I take περὶ μὲν τούτων in the preceding sentence to refer to the distinctions called for at 417a21–2 and elaborated in the sequel. These have been the main subject of the preceding discussion, but on another occasion they could be more fully clarified than they have been so far; after all, we are still speaking 'as if being affected and changed and actual exercising are the same thing'. The language fits this suggestion: διωρίσθω echoes διαιρετέον at 417a21, οὐχ ἁπλοῦ here picks up ἁπλῶς there. I thus reject Simplicius' influential note (125.11–12), which refers περὶ τούτων to the last section of the previous paragraph: 'Concerning how the universal and contemplation is up to us: he will speak more clearly about them in Book III'. Following Simplicius, translators commonly render εἰσαῦθις as 'later' (*sc.* in *DA*), treat γένοιτ' ἄν as future indicative (only Smith writes 'may'), and send us to III.4 or III.4–5 for the promised clarification. An additional reference (Philop. 308.20–2, Soph. 69.37–9) to the little that Aristotle has to say about the practical intellect in III.7 is presumably motivated by the immediately preceding remark (417b26–8) about ἐπιστῆμαι (probably arts such as literacy or building) that deal with sensible things. The difficulty is that nothing in Book III could really be described as a full clarification of the issue Simplicius is interested in. When he reaches III.4, Simplicius does not remind us of the promise he made at II.5, for the good reason that III.4 does not explain the point that contemplation is up to us, but merely states once again that this is so (429b7). Given Simplicius' gloss on περὶ τούτων, the only reasonable comment is that of Ross: 'It may be doubted whether A. has any particular passage in mind; he perhaps never gave the elucidation he intends to give'. The references in Bonitz 358a28–33 (to which add *Ph.* I.9, 192a34–b1, looking forward to first philosophy) show that καιρός alludes to an unspecified occasion outside a given treatise more often than to a definite place within it.

[64] The minority of translators (Ross 1961; Smith 1931; Wallace 1882) who refer οὕτως to both meanings of 'potential', not just the last, would of course agree that what an animal is born with and lives by is a second potentiality. But before birth comes the πρώτη μεταβολή of 417b17, and we shall find that this passage from being a first to being a second potentiality perceiver has a role of its own in the refinement process.

[65] On translating τὸ αἰσθητικόν, see n. 41 above.

417a21 called for distinctions 'concerning potentiality and actuality'. But by the end of II.5 only the potential has been properly dealt with. Indications and implications for a corresponding contrast between two types of actuality have been plentiful, as we shall see, but they have not been fully clarified. Concerning actuality, the discussion remains incomplete.

The essential incompleteness of II.5 has not been appreciated. Since antiquity scholars have felt free to draw on all they know about Aristotle to expound his meaning here. This paper will be more circumspect. ||

Because I am interested in the question how to read an Aristotelian chapter, I propose to take Aristotle at his word: II.5 does not contain everything he has to say about the triple scheme. And when I do draw on other works, it will often be to contrast what they say with Aristotle's meaning here.

TWO TYPES OF POTENTIALITY, TWO KINDS OF TRANSITION

Aristotle continues in terms of the model. A knower in sense (1) has a potentiality to be a knower in sense (2), viz. someone who 'has been altered through learning and has repeatedly changed from a contrary condition' (417a30–2).[66] The second conjunct of this specification brings out a point which is more fully analysed elsewhere, in the discussion of the priority of actuality to potentiality at *Metaphysics* Θ.8, 1049b29–50a2. Just as an apprentice learns to be a builder by building, though not yet with the finished skill of the master, so pupils learn arithmetic or literacy by gradually acquiring, and exercising themselves in, bits of knowledge they were ignorant of before. It is true that one cannot exercise an art one does not have, but it is sophistry to infer from this that one cannot learn. By 'a contrary condition', therefore, Aristotle means ignorance of this or that aspect of the knowledge to be learned. The second conjunct explains that learning is a stage by stage process, a *growth* of knowledge.[67]

By contrast, a knower in sense (2) has a potentiality to be someone who knows in sense (3), viz. someone who has changed 'in another way': from

---

[66] This is construal (B) of the sentence 417a31–2, defended in Appendix 1.
[67] Thus καί is epexegetic of διὰ μαθήσεως (Smith 1931 translates 'i.e.'); this construal makes intelligible the variant μεταβάλλων for μεταβαλών. Cf. *EN* II.4 for the parallel point about acquiring a virtue.

having and not exercising the art of arithmetic[68] or literacy to exercising it (417a30–b2).[69] ||

This explanation of the difference between the two potentialities (1) and (2) continues the pattern we are familiar with. A potentiality is defined by what it is a potentiality to be – in the present case a knower in sense (2) or a knower in sense (3). At the same time, the difference between being someone who knows in sense (2) and being someone who knows in sense (3) is articulated as that between having been altered through learning and having changed in a different way. Senses (2) and (3) of 'P knows' are specified as the results of two types of change. Ultimately, then, the two potentialities we are interested in are differentiated as potentialities for being the result of two types of change.[70] That is why Aristotle's next move (417b2) is to say, 'Being affected is not simple either.'[71] The distinction between two types of potentiality leads into a corresponding distinction between their actualities: two types of being affected or altered, one of which might be said not to be alteration at all (417b5–7). Aristotle will deny that the exercise of knowledge is alteration (417b8–9). But he will refuse that option for perception, preferring to speak in terms of two types of alteration (418a1–3). Let us do the same.

At this stage the first type of alteration is assumed to be the ordinary alteration we studied in the *Physics*, where indeed learning is a standard example of alteration;[72] modern readers have to suspend their post-Cartesian inclinations and accept that Aristotelian physics puts learning on a par with being warmed. That done, we can focus in *DA* II.5 on how the second type of alteration diverges from the first. The second is the novelty we need to understand.

---

[68] Read ἀριθμητικήν for the MSS αἴσθησιν (following Themistius' paraphrase 55.28, Torstrik 1862 and Ross 1956, against Rodier 1900, Hicks 1907, and most scholars since), or perhaps accept Theiler's ingenious suggestion ἀρίθμησιν (Theiler 1959). Despite the majority preference, and despite Philoponus testifying to αἴσθησιν as early as 529 AD (*De Aet. Mundi* 69.26), conservative policies are indefensible in this case, for two reasons. (a) The MSS illogically (as Hicks concedes) anticipate in the model the thing the model is designed to illuminate, thereby making αἴσθησις an instance of ἐπιστήμη (!) and wrecking the step by step articulation of Aristotle's argument. (b) A marginal note inspired by 417b18–19 could so easily cause corruption. A third ground for the emendation is canvassed n. 73 below. Alternatively, just delete τὴν αἴσθησιν ἤ.

[69] This is construal (B) of the sentence 417a32–b2, defended in Appendix 1.

[70] Not, please note, as potentialities for two types of change, on pain of the circularity that Kosman 1969 showed the way out of.

[71] οὐδέ picks up ἁπλῶς at 417a22.

[72] *Ph.* III.3, 202a32ff. is the most conspicuous case, but there are many others; cf. the miscellany of changes listed at III.1, 201a18–19.

We have already seen that ordinary alteration involves the loss of one quality and its replacement by another opposed quality from the same range. Aristotle makes the point vivid here by calling it 'a sort of destruction by the opposite' (417b3).[73] As one learns, ignorance gives way to ‖ knowledge like cold to warmth. At the end of the process the ignorance, like the cold, is extinguished and destroyed. It has been replaced by its opposite, knowledge in sense (2).

But it is obvious that knowing in sense (3) is not opposed to knowing in sense (2) as the latter is to ignorance. Linguistically, the termini of the transition between (1) and (2) are marked by contrary descriptions: 'ignorant' vs. 'knows'. The termini of the transition between (2) and (3) are both marked by the same word 'knows'. We have been told that (3) is the proper meaning of the word (417a29). That establishes a difference in meaning between (2) and (3), but not an opposition. On the contrary, Aristotle insists that the termini of the transition between (2) and (3) are like each other: both are to be described as knowing, save that one is knowing potentially, the other actually (417b4–5). Rather than a destruction, the second type of alteration is better called a preservation (*sōtēria*, 417b3) of the state it starts from. Whereas learning destroys ignorance, as warming something destroys its potentiality to be warm, knowing in sense (3) preserves the knower's sense (2) potentiality to be someone who knows in sense (3).

Much more is in play here than the common observation that knowledge – be it of languages, sciences, or skills – is kept up and perhaps even strengthened by exercise and use.[74] No doubt Aristotle has that in mind, but he is also applying a fundamental principle of his physics: no alteration without contrariety.

Then why call the transition from (2) to (3) an alteration at all? Preservation sounds more like the opposite of alteration than a species of

---

[73] Such language is for obvious reasons not common in Aristotle's discussions of non-substantial change (*Ph.* 1.9 and *GC* 1.4 are exceptions motivated by their context). In n. 26 I suggested that φθορά τις is an echo of Pl. *Euthd.* 285b1 (cf. 283cd), where φθόρον τινά refers to the 'destruction' involved in becoming wise and good, i.e., to μανθάνειν in one of the two senses ('learning' and 'understanding') which the sophists confuse and Socrates distinguishes in the dialogue. Well might Aristotle recall the *Euthydemus* here, for his model for the two senses of 'alteration' tallies exactly with Plato's two senses of μανθάνειν. In the related passage from the Aviary section of the *Theaetetus* (198d–199a) the examples are ὁ ἀριθμητικός and ὁ γραμματικός, which may support the emendation defended in n. 68. Unlike Aristotle, Plato in the *Theaetetus* does not distinguish senses of 'know' (only senses of 'have'), but he does, as in the *Euthydemus*, anticipate Aristotle's two types of transition with the διττὴ θήρα of 198d.
[74] Pl. *Smp.* 208a; *Theaet.* 153b.

it. The answer is again to be found in a fundamental principle of Aristotelian physics.

Epistemic states like knowing arithmetic and being literate are dispositional states (*hexeis*) which belong to the category of quality.[75] Standardly in Aristotle, any change in the category of quality is an alteration.[76] As Alexander drily remarks, the transition from (2) to (3) is certainly not growth or spatial movement.[77] Then it must be an alteration of some kind. For it is the firm doctrine of Aristotle's *Physics* (III.1, 200b33–201a3, repeated *DA* I.3, 406a12–13) that there are no (non-substantial) changes besides change of quality, quantity and place. Aristotle, it appears, has a compelling reason of theory to say that the transition from (2) to (3) is an alteration, as well as a compelling reason (the absence of contrariety) for saying it is not.

This should help explain why at 417b5–7 he offers two alternative ways of describing the transition from knowing in sense (2) to knowing in sense (3).[78] Either (a) it is not an alteration at all, or (b) it is a different kind of alteration. In favour of (a), he amplifies the point just made about the similarity of the termini by saying that the knower's transition to knowing in sense (3) is an 'advance into itself and into actuality' (417b6–7) – a surprisingly lyrical phrase, which I shall take up when we return to perception. In favour of (b), he adds nothing, and hardly needs to: that preservation is different from ordinary alteration is plain to see.

There is of course one way Aristotle could escape the dilemma. He could deny that the transition from (2) to (3) is a change of any kind. But already at II.4, 416b1–3, we read that a carpenter is not affected by the material he works on; he merely changes (*metaballei monon*) from inactivity to activity. Merely changing, without being affected, is not the same as not changing. So the same choice applies: either (a) the builder's switch to activity is not alteration, but 'an advance into himself', or (b) it is a different kind of alteration. When *Metaphysics* Θ.6 presents its distinction between actuality (*energeia*) and change (*kinēsis*), seeing and the exercise of

---

[75] In *Cat.* 8 knowledge-terms are a main focus of attention.
[76] Particularly relevant here are the definition of alteration at *GC* I.4, 319b6–14, and the use of learning as a prime example of alteration at *Ph.* III.3, 202a32ff. (n. 72 above). Not relevant (yet) is the non-standard passage *Ph.* VII.3, 247b1–248a9, which argues not only that the transition from (2) to (3) is not alteration, but also, contrary to II.5's assumptions so far, that the transition from (1) to (2) is not alteration either.
[77] *Quaest.* III.2, 81.25–6; cf. III.3, 84.16–17, where ποιόν must be a slip (by scribe or editor) for ποσόν.
[78] For defence of the usual view that this transition is what Aristotle means to be describing, see Appendix 2.

knowledge appear as paradigm examples of actuality in contrast to change. But, to repeat, there is no hint of *that* distinction anywhere in II.5. On the contrary, the distinction between the two transitions is introduced as a distinction between two kinds of being affected (*paschein*, 417b2) – in keeping with the provisional assumption of 417a14–15 that the only actuality there is is the incomplete actuality exhibited by a process of change which is defined by and directed towards an end-state outside itself. ||

It is critically important that we respect Aristotle's reticence here. Remember the warning I gave earlier. The question to ask is: Why does II.5 *not* announce that perceiving and the exercise of knowledge are examples of unqualified actuality, which is its own end, hence not examples of change, which is defined by and directed towards an end-state outside itself? On the one hand, Aristotle will shortly say it is not good to call it alteration when a knower exercises their knowledge (417b8–9). On the other hand, for perception he ends up saying that, due to the lack of specialist vocabulary, we have to go on using the language of alteration and being affected, so please remember not to give those verbs their standard meaning (418a1–3). Why tolerate for perception the unclear language rejected for knowledge? What would Aristotle lose if he simply gave up the language of alteration and found new terms to characterise perceiving?

These questions would be pressing even if we did not know that elsewhere Aristotle distinguishes between unqualified actuality and the qualified (incomplete) actuality of change, and once offers special terminology (*energeia* vs. *kinēsis*) to mark the difference. Readers who have that knowledge must be especially careful to let Aristotle not use it here.

Fortunately, some materials for answering our questions are given in II.5, 417b19–28 – the passage which leads up to Aristotle's final decision on how perceiving is best described. After expounding the triple scheme, with its several morals, Aristotle returns to perception. In terms of the triple scheme, the passage from (1) to (2) – from lacking to possessing the power of perception – is effected as part of the embryological development initiated by the male parent. Consequently, we and other animals are born with the power of perception already at second potentiality. Hence actual perceiving, the exercise of our sensory powers, is to be ranked with (3), the exercise of knowledge (417b16–19). But, Aristotle continues (19–20), there is a difference (*diapherei de*). A difference, that is, between using one's senses and using one's knowledge.

DIFFERENCES BETWEEN KNOWING AND PERCEIVING

The difference has to do with the causality of the two cases. Exercising knowledge is something we can do at will (417b19–26), but perceiving is not 'up to us'; it depends on an external agent, the particular object perceived (417b20–6).[79] This difference implies another. For the *knower*, the || transition between (2) and (3) is not a passive change, hence not a change at all as change is understood in *Physics* III.1–3. For the *perceiver*, on the other hand, the transition between (2) and (3) is a passive change, as [1][a] proposed, and within the framework of Aristotelian physics the only change it can be, as [1][b] explained, is alteration. If the external objects of perception are agents (*ta poiētika*, 417b20), perceivers must be patients in something like the sense of *De Generatione et Corruptione* I.7.[80]

We can now see what Aristotle would lose by giving up the language of alteration. He would cut the links with the dialectic of *De Generatione et Corruptione* I.7 and the categorial analysis of change in *Physics* III.1–3. He would be set adrift, not merely from the reputable opinions he began with, but from the entire project of comprehending perception within the framework of the physics he develops in the *De Generatione et Corruptione* and *Physics* by analysis, systematisation and refinement of reputable opinions from the earlier tradition. He would have to tear up the *De Anima* and start again.

There would also be an epistemological loss. Perception is a power of *receptivity*, not of autonomous activity. To perceive is to submit to being in-formed (as we still say) about the particular objects around us, by the agency of the very objects we receive information about. Such receptivity is necessary for perception's content to be objective truth. It is objective because it is determined by the particular external object which causes the perception, rather than by factors internal to the perceiver. Ultimately, the role of [P/A] is to account for the cognitive accuracy of perception by treating the determination of perceptual content by the object perceived as a special case of assimilation or alteration. And for this it is essential to retain the idea that perception is some sort of passive change with a particular external cause.

---

[79] Both points featured earlier in the chapter (417a7–8; 27–8), but only now are they brought together to make the contrast.

[80] Contrast Rodier 1900 *ad* 417b20: 'Les sensibles ne sont pas, à proprement parler, les agents de la sensation, puisque celle-ci n'est point une passion, mais le passage à l'acte des facultés du sujet' ['Sensibles are not properly speaking the agents of sensation, since quite simply sensation is not a patient, but the process culminating in the activity of the subject's faculties']. That is not Aristotle but Plotinus, e.g. *Enn.* III.6.1, IV.6.2.

Aristotle's solution is to keep the language of alteration, without which perception would no longer be covered by the pattern of explanation expounded in *De Generatione et Corruptione* 1.7 and *Physics* III.1–3, but to refine the meaning of 'alteration' so that it signifies a (2)–(3) transition rather than the ordinary change it signifies elsewhere. To prepare for this, he must introduce the triple scheme without giving the impression that a (2)–(3) transition is incompatible with dependence on a particular external cause. That, I propose, is (part of the reason) why he makes no use of ‖ the distinctions he draws elsewhere between unqualified and incomplete actuality, *energeia* and *kinēsis*. (More on this later.)

But the triple scheme is introduced in terms of knowledge. This may be in deference to its Platonic ancestry,[81] but the fact remains that from 417a22 to 417b16 the focus is exclusively on knowledge and how to describe the two transitions involved in its acquisition and use.[82] Now if the point of the exercise is to elaborate a model that can be applied to perception (from 417b16 onwards), then the knower's two transitions must themselves be described in terms compatible with an external cause.

This makes for strain. Aristotle issues several caveats about the language he finds himself using: it is not really appropriate to knowledge. But the chief sign of strain is the tortuous prose. I have already written two appendices and numerous footnotes to extricate his meaning from various textual and grammatical thickets. This is one of the densest stretches of the corpus. I hope that my readers will be encouraged to push on by the suggestion that the difficulty of Aristotle's writing is due to the difficulty of the philosophical task he has undertaken.

HOW NOT TO SPEAK OF KNOWING

It is 'not good' (*ou kalōs echei*) to call it alteration when a knower (*to phronoun*) exercises their knowledge (417b8–9). 'Teaching' is not the right (*dikaion*) word to describe what brings a second potentiality knower to the actuality of knowing in sense (3) (417b9–12).[83]

---

[81] Cf. n. 73 above. [82] Recall n. 68 above.
[83] At Pl. *Tht.* 198e 'learning from oneself' is not right either. Whether we keep the MSS ἄγον or change it to ἄγειν and then delete κατά (Ross 1956; Torstrik 1862), the verb suggests – without quite entailing – a causal agent distinct from τὸ νοοῦν καὶ φρονοῦν and parallel to the causal agent in the contrasting description at 12–13. What could the non-teaching causal agent be that brings a knower to the actuality of knowing in sense (3)? Torstrik suggested a geometrical figure (cf. 'this A' at 417a29), Philoponus 304.7 τὸ ἐπιστητὸν ἢ τὸ αἰσθητόν. Other scholars tactfully refrain from asking the question. Torstrik 1862 also thought it mad to describe τὸ ἄγον as διδασκαλία (hence his emendation τὸ ἄγειν). I prefer the tortuosity of the MSS.

There is a background to this rather muted criticism. In Aristotle's book lots of people do speak of knowing as alteration. *Metaphysics* Γ.5 quotes Empedocles, Democritus, Parmenides, Anaxagoras, and Homer to illustrate the claim, 'In general, because they suppose that knowledge (*phronēsis*) is perception, and that perception is alteration, they say that what appears ǁ to perception is necessarily true' (Γ.5, 1009b12–15).[84] *DA* III.3 cites similar evidence for the even more tendentious statement, 'The ancients say that knowing (*to phronein*) and perceiving are the same' (427a21–2). III.3 itself harks back (427a17–19; 28–9) to the roll-call of earlier opinions in Book I, and at I.2, 404a27–b6, we find Democritus and Anaxagoras attacked for equating *nous* with soul generally, which implies that they see no difference between perception and higher forms of cognition. In sum, if perception is alteration, and perception is not different from higher forms of cognition, all cognition is alteration.

Now the aim of Aristotle's review of previous opinions about soul is to profit from what was well said (*kalōs eirēmena*) by his predecessors and to guard against what was not well said. In the course of Book I several highly reputable opinions are rejected as 'not well said' (I.3, 407a2–3; 5, 411a24–6). The audit continues in Book II (2, 414a19–20; 4, 415b28–6a3; 416b8–9). The criticism at 417b8–9 is thus the latest in a sequence, couched in similar language to the rest. For knowledge, it seems, the language of alteration is ruled out.

This is confirmed by the argument. In full, what Aristotle says is, 'For this reason [*sc.* because of the preservative character of (2)–(3) transitions] it is not good to call it alteration when a knower exercises their knowledge *any more than* when a builder builds.' Contrary perhaps to modern expectations, and against the grain of ancient prejudice, the builder functions here as the more obvious case of non-alteration. If the builder does not alter, but merely changes from inactivity to activity, then the knower's passage to activity is not alteration either. The premise was laid down in the previous chapter (II.4, 416b1–3). The new conclusion extends the lesson from productive skills to higher cognition generally.[85]

---

[84] Truth follows alteration because Aristotle assumes his own causal scheme (pp. 170–1 above). Hence he must restrict 'alteration' in its refined meaning to the perception of proper objects, otherwise all perception whatsoever would be true, contrary to *DA* III.3, 428b18–30. The restriction hardly needs to be made explicit because common sensibles like size and motion do not belong to the category of quality and so cannot be agents of Aristotelian alteration. For a valuable discussion of these matters, see Caston 1996.

[85] It is instructive to compare the clear appreciation of the argument's structure in Waterlow 1988: 187, n. 19, with Alexander *Quaest.* III.2, 81.27–82.7, and Simplicius 123.10–14, whose prejudices

Such scrupulosity about the language appropriate to exercising knowledge serves to highlight the contrast with Aristotle's treatment of the language appropriate to perceiving. At 417b5–7 he gave us a disjunction: ‖ either (a) not an alteration at all or (b) a different kind of alteration. He has now shown that for knowing he prefers (a). But throughout the *De Anima* and related works perception is classified as a sort of alteration (*alloiōsis tis*). I infer that the point of the disjunctive formulation was to make (b) available for the special case of perception. Perceiving is to be different both from the exercise of knowledge, which is not alteration at all, and from the ordinary alterations with which Sorabji and the Presocratics have confused it.

A FURTHER REFINEMENT

Although 'teaching' is not the right word to describe what brings a second potentiality knower to the actuality of knowing in sense (3), it is the right word to describe what brings a first potentiality knower to the state of knowing in sense (2). But even here the implication that to teach someone is to alter them can be misleading. For the pupil, whom we have hitherto considered under the description 'ignorant', is also a knower in sense (1).[86] When the pupil is so considered, the termini of the (1)–(2) transition are no longer marked by contrary descriptions, but by the same word 'knower', in different but compatible senses. Just this was Aristotle's ground for saying that the (2)–(3) transition is either not an alteration or a different kind of alteration. By parity of reasoning he can repeat the move for the (1)–(2) transition: either (a) learning ought not to be called being affected at all, or (b) there are two types of alteration (417b12–15).

These are not the same two types of being affected or altered as the two distinguished at 417b1–7.[87] There ordinary alteration, due to contrariety, served as foil to preservation. Here it is foil to what I shall call *development*. ‖

---

show in their taking the builder to be the less obvious case – because he uses his body. Themistius 56.5 has it right.

[86] At 417b12 ἐκ δυνάμει ὄντος (*sc.* ἐπιστήμονος) refers to first potentiality, whereas at b10 the same phrase signified second potentiality. Torstrik 1862 excised the later occurrence as ungrammatical, a scribe's erroneous repetition. He was right that τὸ ἐκ δυνάμει ὄντος μανθάνον is oddly phrased, wrong to apply the knife. The oddity confirms Aristotle's determination to treat the two potentialities and the two transitions as parallel.

[87] Hence the textual crux at 417b14: Should ὥσπερ εἴρηται be printed, or left out on grounds of falsehood? Hayduck was the first to say, 'delenda videntur, quoniam diserte quidem nihil tale supra scriptum videmus' ['It looks as though they should be deleted, since we clearly see nothing like that written above'](Hayduck 1877: 11). But this is to understate the case for omission. Not only has Aristotle not previously said, or even hinted, that the (1)–(2) transition is not πάσχειν, but 417a30–b3 deliberately treats it as πάσχειν in contrast to the (2)–(3) transition. Some respectable MSS omit

Ordinary alteration Aristotle now describes, less vividly than at 417b3, as 'change towards negative conditions' (417b15). What he means is the familiar story we read before. Alteration is coming to be qualitatively unlike one's present self. At the end of the process, what was e.g. cold is not cold, but warm: the negation 'is not'[88] signifies that one quality has been replaced by another. Alteration, as we saw earlier, really alters.

Such alteration may well be temporary. Warmth, being a potentiality of the same type as the cold which preceded it, is a potentiality to be cold again. In normal circumstances you can expect a warm thing to change back to cold. That is why, when Aristotle formulates the contrast between two types of alteration at 417b15–16, the results of ordinary alteration like warmth or cold are termed *diatheseis* (his word for temporary conditions), but the results of the (1)–(2) transition to knowing in sense (2) are called *hexeis* (his word for firmly fixed dispositional states).[89] In normal circumstances you can expect a knower *not* to change back to ignorance. This is not to deny that knowers can lose their knowledge – through disuse, forgetfulness, disease, etc. – but to insist that knowledge is not a potentiality to be ignorant as before in the way warmth is a potentiality to be cold again.[90] Knowledge, like virtue, like life itself, is a potentiality of a different type.

That, of course, is the thought with which we started drawing distinctions 'concerning potentiality and actuality'. What we are now discovering || is that the difference extends to first potentiality as well. That too is a different type of potentiality from the warmths and colds of ordinary

---

the words, as do Rodier 1900, Hicks 1907, Ross 1961; Siwek 1965; Smith 1931. No commentator witnesses for them until Sophonias 67.24 in the fourteenth century, long after the MSS they appear in. The only published defence I know for printing ὥσπερ εἴρηται is De Corte 1932: 193–4 (followed in the translations of Tricot 1959 and Barbotin and Jannone 1966), according to whom the phrase applies, not to the whole thought 417b12–4, but more narrowly to ἤτοι οὐδὲ πάσχειν φατέον and most especially to οὐδέ: the (1)–(2) transition also is a case where it is appropriate to say, as was said about the (2)–(3) transition earlier, 'This is not being affected either.' The outcome is much the same as it would be if ὥσπερ εἴρηται could be paraphrased 'by parity of reasoning'. But I find it hard to take οὐδέ here otherwise than as 'not at all' (note the variant οὐδέν), and easy to imagine a reader writing ὥσπερ εἴρηται in the margin in an effort to chart the course of an intricate argument. After all, Ross remains unclear enough to suppose that ὥσπερ εἴρηται would change from false to true if, following a suggestion of Förster 1912, ἤ was put before instead of after the words.

[88] στερητικός in its standard logical meaning = ἀποφατικός (see Bonitz *sv.*). στέρησις as that from which change begins is not to the point, nor, *pace* Them. 56.6–12, Philop. 304.16–22 and Rodier 1900, is change to στέρησις in the sense of a bad condition like blindness or disease. What is needed is a calm version of 417b3's φθορά τις.

[89] The contrast between διάθεσις and ἕξις is most fully developed at *Cat.* 8, 8b26–9a13.

[90] Recall n. 38: Aristotelian potentiality is more than bare possibility.

alteration. Aristotle does not spell out the implications of the difference. We must do it for ourselves.

If being a knower in sense (2) is not the 'negative' of being a knower in sense (1), the latter potentiality does not have to be lost, used up or 'destroyed' when knowledge is acquired. Nor can it be lost in the ordinary way if being a knower in sense (1) is an intrinsic part of human nature (417a27); otherwise, it would be death to gain knowledge.[91] Hence, as the ancient commentators saw, if gaining knowledge is a change at all, it should be described as developing or perfecting the nature one already has.[92] Whereas ordinary alteration involves attributes accidental to a thing's nature, Aristotle speaks of the type of alteration that results in epistemic states (*hexeis*) as 'a change towards nature' (417b16). There is a sense in which the learner, as well as the fully formed expert, qualifies for that lyrical phrase 'an advance into itself'.[93] Indeed it is Aristotle's view that the potentialities a biologist has to deal with are in general such that a thing can be nearer or further from itself – rather as, if you are a sleeping geometer, you are further from yourself than you are when awake but not theorising (*GA* II.1, 735a11–17).

So much for option (b): distinguishing ordinary alteration and development. The alternative (a) is to say that gaining knowledge is not an alteration, not a case of being affected at all. Elsewhere, at *Physics* VII.3, 247b9–8a9, this is the option Aristotle prefers.[94] He prefers it on the ground that gaining knowledge is in truth a coming to rest, i.e. a cessation of change, rather than a change. Let me pause to wonder what this might mean.[95] ||

At first sight the idea seems bizarre, especially if the example to hand is an individual item of knowledge such as knowing that 7 + 5 = 12 or knowing how to spell 'Theaetetus'. Why not keep to the view we met

---

[91] Recall n. 73 and Dionysodorus' threat to Cleinias. That a knower's first potentiality is preserved was appreciated by Plotinus, *Enn.* II 5.2.23–6. In general, if first potentialities were not preserved, Aristotle could not say that the only body which is potentially alive is one that is actually alive (II.1, 412b25–6).

[92] 'Perfecting' is standard in the ancient commentators, implying that καὶ τὴν φύσιν is epexegetic of τὰς ἕξεις: Alex. *Quaest.* III.2, 82.13–17; 3, 84.27; Them. 56.12; Philop 304.24. For the reverse epexegesis, cf. *Met.* Λ.3, 1070a11–12: ἡ δὲ φύσις τόδε τι καὶ ἕξις τις εἰς ἥν.

[93] Philoponus 304.26–8 agrees.

[94] Accordingly, Simplicius 123.34–5 assumes a licence to draw on *Physics* VII in interpreting this part of *DA* II.5.

[95] For antecedents, see Pl. *Phd.* 96b, *Crat.* 437ab. For help with the peculiarities of the argument in *Physics* VII.3 and its wider context, see Wardy 1990: 209–39. Like him (pp. 86–7 et passim), I do not make the standard assumption that *Physics* VII is an early work.

earlier at 417a31–2, that learning is a series of changes from ignorance to knowledge of this or that aspect of the subject under study?

But consider the examples used to illustrate the triple scheme: knowing arithmetic and knowing one's letters. The question 'When did you acquire the ability to read and write?' or 'When did you get to know the multiplication table?', like the question 'When did you form the habit of drinking tea in the mornings?', could be answered 'When I was five' or 'In 1994', but not, as could be the case with individual items of knowledge, 'On my fifth birthday', let alone 'At 8.00 a.m. on Tuesday 13 September, 1994'. Just as a habit begins when you stop doing things differently, so knowledge of the whole subject begins when you stop making mistakes, when the last bit of ignorance is changed to knowledge. While the last mistake and its correction are determinate, exactly datable events, that they are indeed the last can be verified only in retrospect some indeterminate time later. When knowledge is conceived as the mastery of a whole complex domain, it becomes reasonable to invoke the dictum 'There is no coming to be of being at rest' (*Ph.* VII.3, 247b12) to support the claim that gaining knowledge is not a change but the cessation of change.

But now it seems unreasonable not to say the same about individual bits of knowledge: knowing that 7 + 5 = 12, knowing how to spell 'Theaetetus'. They are *hexeis* too (417a32) – *habitus* as the Latin translators say. They too begin when you stop making mistakes, when the last false judgement on the matter gives way to a consistent pattern of correct judgement. In this case what is true of the whole domain of knowledge is true of its parts: the passage from (1) to (2) is not an alteration, because it is not a change but the cessation of change.

None of this is on display in *De Anima* II.5. All more reason to infer, as before, that the point of the disjunctive formulation 'Either (a) not a being affected at all or (b) there are two types of alteration' is to make (b) available for the special case of perception. The considerations I put together to help explain why (a) might be Aristotle's preferred option for the passage to knowing in sense (2) could not possibly be applied to an animal's acquisition of sensory powers in the period between conception and birth.[96] That is undeniably the result of change. It is the end-result of || the series of changes by which the form of the male parent is taken on by the female material so as to constitute an animal, i.e. a perceiver. It is the

---

[96] *EN* II.1, 1103a26–b2, expressly forbids applying the model of knowledge-acquisition to the acquisition of sensory powers; cf. also *Met.* Θ.5, 1047b31–5.

'first change' (*prōtē metabolē*, 417b17) in the strong sense that the embryo 'is first an animal when perception first occurs' (*GA* v.1, 778b33–4). The previously plant-like organism was a first potentiality perceiver. The transition to being a second potentiality perceiver is not the coming to be of a new entity, but neither is it a straightforward case of an existing subject exchanging one quality for another. Rather, the subject arrives at a new phase of its own existence. Such a 'change towards nature', a real 'advance into itself', is no ordinary alteration.[97]

RECAPITULATION

It is time to take stock again. *De Anima* II.5 has separated three different things under the title 'alteration'. I shall give them numbers and names:

(Alt¹) ordinary alteration is the replacement of one quality by a contrary quality from the same range;
(Alt²) unordinary alteration is the development of the dispositions which perfect a thing's nature;
(Alt³) extraordinary alteration is one of these dispositions passing from inactivity to exercise.

Aristotle first distinguished (Alt¹) and (Alt³), with learning as his example of (Alt¹). Then he distinguished (Alt¹) and (Alt²), with learning now an example of (Alt²). The ultimate aim was to exhibit an animal's acquiring of sensory powers as a case of (Alt²), their exercise as a case of (Alt³). Neither is the ordinary alteration (Alt¹) that we studied in *De Generatione et Corruptione* I.7 and *Physics* III.1–3. Biology often requires more refined notions of alteration than were needed for the elemental level of *De Generatione et Corruptione* I.7 and the very general discussion of *Physics* III.1–3.

But if we are as mindful of the lessons of those chapters as Aristotle expects us to be, we will see that a distinction between three types of alteration implies a corresponding distinction between three different types of potentiality. Alteration is the actuality of the alterable *qua* alterable (*Ph.* III.1, 201a11–12; p. 167 above). If there are three such alterations,

---

[97] The definition of alteration at *Ph.* v.2, 226a26–9, explicitly excludes change involving τὸ ποιὸν ἐν τῇ οὐσίᾳ, i.e. the differentia. Is Aristotle thinking ahead to the unordinary alterations involved in generation? Burnyeat 2004b [Chapter 9 in this volume] offers several examples where *GC* I thinks ahead to the conceptual needs of other physical works, including those of *DA* II.5.

there must be three types of potentiality for the three alterations to be the actualities of:

> (Pot¹) the ordinary potentiality of a hot thing to be cold or of a cold thing to be hot;
> (Pot²) the first potentiality, grounded in a thing's nature, to be a fully developed thing of its kind, capable of exercising the dispositions which perfect its nature;
> (Pot³) the second potentiality of a developed thing to remain a fully developed thing of its kind by exercising, and thereby preserving, the dispositions which perfect its nature.[98]

Pulling all the threads together, we could draw up the following schedule of actualities:

> (Act¹) is the actuality of (Pot¹), and proceeds towards the replacement of (Pot¹) by a contrary potentiality of the same kind;
> (Act²) is the actuality of (Pot²), and develops the dispositions which perfect the subject as a thing of its kind;
> (Act³) is the actuality of (Pot³), and contributes to the continued preservation of the dispositions which perfect the subject as a thing of its kind.

Aristotle does not pull all the threads together in this way. Having distinguished different types of potentiality, he does not move on to different types of actuality, but asks us to be content with the distinctions he has drawn so far (417b29–30). Thereby he avoids a number of complications which would delay his getting into the detailed study of perception that II.5 is meant to introduce. In particular, he avoids having to take cognisance of the fact that we are still speaking 'as if being affected and being changed and actual exercising (*energein*) are the same thing' (417a14–16). We have made distinctions, but in terms which leave unchallenged the idea that (Alt¹), (Alt²), and (Alt³) are all examples of change (*kinēsis*) in the sense of *Physics* III.1–3: actuality (*energeia*) which is incomplete in the sense that it is directed towards a result beyond itself (417a16; p. 167 above). The very words 'alteration' and 'being affected' imply as much, especially when II.5 is read in proximity to *De Generatione et Corruptione* I.7 and *Physics* III.1–3. ‖

---

[98] To the texts already mentioned add II.4, 416b14–17, on the preservative function of the nutritive soul.

Recapitulation

Now elsewhere Aristotle insists that seeing, for example, is not incomplete in the sense just given. It is complete at every moment, i.e. it is not intrinsically directed towards any result besides and beyond itself; its goal is simply to see what is there to be seen (*Met.* Θ.8, 1050a23–5; *EN* x.4, 1174a13–b14; *EE* II.1, 1219a16). On several occasions he cites a logical rule that holds for perception verbs like 'to see' and 'to hear', as well as for verbs like 'to contemplate' which refer to the exercise of theoretical knowledge: at the same time one φs and has φed (*SE* 22, 178a9–28; *Sens.* 6, 446b2–6; *Met.* Θ.6, 1048b23–34). The idea is that there is no moment of φing at which the goal of φing is not achieved.[99] This does not immediately show that seeing is a counter-example to II.5's provisional assumption that being affected, being changed and actual exercising (*energein*) are the same thing. For (Alt³) is the transition to seeing, not seeing as such. But it does show there are a number of issues in II.5 that further distinctions might address. In particular, we would like to know more about the relation between seeing and the transition to seeing.

Meanwhile, Aristotle offers the alternative of saying that (Alt³) is not alteration at all (417b6). He offers the same alternative for (Alt²) (417b13–14), where the illustrative example is learning. But in *Metaphysics* Θ.6 learning is classed as change or *kinēsis*: it is as incomplete, because intrinsically directed to a result beyond itself, as slimming and building (1048b24–5; 29). As already mentioned (p. 173), *Metaphysics* Θ.6 is innocent of the distinction between first and second potentiality and so has no basis for separating (Alt²) from ordinary alteration (Alt¹). It is safe to conclude that *Metaphysics* Θ.6 is not the place where Aristotle undertakes the further analysis that would complete the process of refinement begun in *De Anima* II.5.

Nor is *Metaphysics* Θ.8, 1050a23–b2, where seeing, an activity that contains its own goal, is contrasted with building, which aims at a product beyond itself. That too is innocent of the distinction between first and second potentiality. Remember that *Physics* VIII.4 is the only other place in the extant corpus where the distinction between first and second potentiality can be found (p. 173 above). If there are any further refinements, they must be sought within the ambit of the *De Anima*. ‖

---

[99] More accurately, there is no moment at which the immediate goal of φing is not achieved. Aristotle does not deny that the goal of seeing and other cases of perceiving may itself be the means to some further goal: *Met.* A.1, 980a2–6, *EN* I.4, 1096b16–19.

In search of more

This brings me back to *De Anima* III.7, 431a4–7, mentioned earlier (p. 169). III.7 is a collection of fragmentary scraps often thought to have been put together by an early editor.[100] I prefer to treat it as a sort of 'folder' kept by Aristotle himself for storing bits and pieces which might in due course be integrated into the treatise.[101] But whatever its origin and status, the passage in question shows how Aristotle may once have thought to continue the process of refinement begun in II.5:

> In the case of sense, on the one hand,[102] clearly the perceiver already was potentially what the object perceived makes it to be actually; for it [the perceiver][103] is not affected or altered. This must therefore be a different kind of change (*kinēsis*) [or: some kind of thing different *from* change].[104] For change is [or: was agreed to be][105] the actuality of the incomplete. Actuality unqualified, the actuality of what is completed/perfected (*tetelesmenou*), is different.

Here, as in *Physics* III.2, Aristotle makes explicit what other texts merely imply, that incomplete actuality contrasts with a different sort of actuality: actuality unqualified, actuality *simpliciter*, or, as the ancient commentators put it, complete actuality. In effect, he takes up the option of || saying that the transition to perceiving is not an alteration at all, but 'an advance into oneself', a perfected disposition springing to its proper actuality. The

---

[100] So Torstrik 1862, followed by Ross 1956, who is in turn followed by Hamlyn 1968.
[101] Burnyeat 2001b, ch. 3 introduces the concept of an Aristotelian 'folder' to help account for the peculiarities of *Met.* Z.3–5.
[102] There is no δέ to answer this μέν. The fragment is itself a torso.
[103] Menn 1994: 110 n. 49 is exceptional in taking the αἰσθητόν as the subject of the verbs, not the αἰσθητικόν, so that Aristotle argues from the object's not changing to the conclusion that the perceiver is the passive partner in the encounter. It is true that the object does not change (otherwise perception would always mislead), but the fact that the perceiver is changed is not in dispute and needs no argument. The dispute is about the manner of its changing, which our fragment (as traditionally understood) begins to clarify. Smith's translation best captures the direction of inference indicated by γάρ: from the absence of alteration to the reason why no alteration is needed, viz. the sense is already potentially what the object makes it to be actually. Hicks 1907 and the French translators get much the same effect by saying that the object *merely* brings the potential into actual exercise. (As before, I render τὸ αἰσθητικόν by 'perceiver': nn. 41, 65 above.)
[104] So, rather plausibly, Ross 1961 and Hamlyn 1968.
[105] A number of MSS omit ἦν after ἐνέργεια at 7. It is very wrong if editors who print the word (= all editors save Ross 1956) then cite II.5 as the implied back-reference (so Hett 1935; Rodier 1900; Smith 1931). There is nothing in II.5 about the incompleteness of the subject of change. Supposing ἦν does refer to another text, not just to established doctrine, a better candidate is *Ph.* III.2, 201b32–3, to which (as we saw) II.5 itself refers. That does mention the incompleteness of the subject of change.

transition may still (depending on how we translate) count as some sort of change (*kinēsis*), but if it does, it is a different kind of change from those of *Physics* III.1–3 because a perceiver is not altered when they perceive something; like the builder of *De Anima* II.4, they merely switch from inactivity to exercise, from potentiality to the actuality of the power of perception. One commentator hails this passage as Aristotle discarding at last much of what he had said earlier about perception being some sort of alteration. Another denounces it, for that very reason, as an interpolation.[106] Both reactions are too quick. We do not know what Aristotle would have done with the option he is beginning to develop. All we have is the one brief fragment, either because Aristotle wrote no more or because the continuation was lost. In the extant corpus, II.5's process of refinement is nowhere carried to completion.[107]

In this situation all we can do is observe Aristotle at work in II.5 and speculate about why he takes the refinement no further. He *asks* his readers to join with him, initially, in speaking 'as if being affected and being changed and actual exercising are the same'.[108] This is an invitation to cooperate, not an attempt to deny, or to disguise, the difference between complete and incomplete actuality. It is a request to readers who do have some sense of what would be involved in a full clarification to keep that knowledge in abeyance for a while, so that II.5 can set out such distinctions as are relevant for the purpose to hand. I have already proposed that the immediate purpose is to do justice to the receptivity of perception (p. 170, p. 182). On that, more shortly. I want first to add a more distant goal.

Look again at the passage (417b29–418a1) where Aristotle warns that the process of refinement is to remain incomplete. Two types of potentiality are mentioned. Clearly, they are the two potentialities of the triple scheme: (Pot²) and (Pot³). A boy's eligibility for being a general is confirmed, not cancelled, when he reaches the age at which he can actually be elected.[109] (Pot¹) has been left behind. When Aristotle says that we

---

[106] Hamlyn 1968 *ad loc.*; Webb 1982: 27 n. 14.
[107] I suspect that a stronger statement is in order: it was not carried further in any work available to Simplicius and Philoponus but not to us. Cf. n. 63 above.
[108] Recall n. 47's defence of the reading λέγωμεν.
[109] I suppose this to be a genuine analogy in which νόμος is invoked to illustrate φύσις and δύνασθαι refers to legal capacity. This gives force and point to the phrase τὸν ἐν ἡλικίᾳ ὄντα. The age in question is not known for certain, but at Athens it was probably at least 30 (Rhodes 1981: 510–11). Thus the analogue for a first potentiality perceiver (i.e. a newly conceived embryo in the womb prior to 'the first change' of 417b15–16) is a newly born male whose legal standing is such that, if and when he reaches the stipulated age, he will acquire the further capacity for a passive change, being elected, into a busily active office. A non-legal acquired capacity for generalship would presumably be some skill or experience such as Nicomachides boasts of at Xen. *Mem.*

must ‖ go on speaking of the perceiver as being affected and altered (418a2–3), Sorabji's ordinary alteration is not even a candidate for being the sort of alteration he has in view. Only (Alt²) and (Alt³) are pertinent, the one for the acquisition of sensory powers, the other for their exercise.

They continue to be pertinent until *De Anima* III.4, where perception becomes the model for knowing, instead of the other way round, and the acquisition of knowledge is treated as a special case of being affected (*paschein ti*, 429a14–15; b24–6; 29).[110] The word 'alteration' is not used, but learning is analysed, in terms strongly reminiscent of [P/A], as an assimilation in which the intellect comes to be actually, instead of potentially, like its object; in other words, as the unordinary alteration (Alt²) it was said to be in II.5.

Thus II.5 sets the framework for studying both the most basic cognitive capacity of soul and its highest. At birth perception is a second potentiality, intellect a first potentiality. Both are to be included in Aristotelian physics. However, unlike modern proponents of 'naturalised epistemology', Aristotle is acutely concerned to fix the limits of physical science, lest no scope be left for first philosophy.

The *locus classicus* for the worry is *De Partibus Animalium* I.1, 641a32–b12, where Aristotle argues that if intellect (*nous*) falls within the scope of physics, so too do its objects, the intelligibles (*ta noēta*), and physics will aspire to be a theory of *everything*. His response is that physics, natural science, does not deal with all soul, but only with soul that is a principle of change: 'Not all soul is nature, *phusis*' (641b9–10).[111] Physics extends as far as change extends and no further (*Met.* E.1; cf. ‖ *Ph.* II.2). For nature, the object of physics, is a principle of changing and resting (*Ph.* II.1, 192b21–2).

I can now present the hypothesis which explains, I believe, both the intricacy of II.5 and its reticences. The reason why II.5 takes the refinement process no further than it does, why only incomplete actuality is considered, why the discussion is full of qualifications and alternatives, why the writing is so tortuous, and finally, why this paper has to be so

---

III.4.1; being of a certain age is no doubt a necessary condition for that sort of qualification, but it is hardly sufficient.

[110] On πάσχειν τι Hicks 1907 *ad* 429a14 rightly recalls his note *ad* 410a25, cited above, n. 25. Aristotle's addition ἤ τι τοιοῦτον ἕτερον (429a14–15) confirms that it is a very special case.

[111] Does this exclude all νοῦς, or only the active exercise of second potentiality νοῦς? If the former, *PA* is inconsistent not only with *DA*, but also with the *Physics*' attitude to learning. The related worry at *GA* II.3, 736b5–8, is answered by the famous statement that νοῦς enters θύραθεν (27–9), from outside: a statement which can perfectly well refer, not to a magic baptism, but to second potentiality νοῦς acquired through the agency of a teacher.

long, is that Aristotelian physics is by definition the science of things that change. If physics is to study the (2)–(3) transition involved in perceiving and the (1)–(2) transition involved in learning, it must treat them as types of change, where 'change' means passive change. That, I propose, is why II.5 distinguishes two special types of alteration, (Alt³) and (Alt²), while acknowledging, in the disjunctions of 417b6–7 and 12–15, the legitimacy of perspectives from which neither would be alteration or any kind of passive change.

I do not mean that physics cannot study the active agency which brings change about. Of course it can, and must, do that. But Aristotle has good epistemological reasons for putting the two transitions on the passive side of this correlation. He wants both second potentiality perception and first potentiality intellect to be powers of *receptivity*, rather than of autonomous activity.[112] Both are capacities for being in-formed by an object, a sensible form in the first case, an intelligible form in the second. Both perceptual content and conceptual content must be determined from outside if the content is to be objective truth.[113] Aristotle holds strong views on this determination being something that occurs *naturally* as part of the life cycle of animate beings, both the rational ones and the non-rational perceivers. His task in II.5 and III.4 is to refine the basic explanatory notions of his physics to the point where the attainment of truth, by sense-perception or by intellect, can be accounted for as some sort of natural physical change.

But the further refinements undertaken in III.4 are another subject, for another and more controversial discussion.[114] All I need say here is that || for the highest, as for the lowest, types of cognition Aristotle intends to make serious use of the assimilation story to explain the cognitive accuracy of sense and intellect. The word 'must' (*anagkaion*) in 'We must go on using "being affected" and "being altered"' (418a2–3) is the 'must' of hypothetical necessity: those verbs really are needed for the explanatory goals of the *De Anima*. Aristotle is not normally shy of inventing new

---

[112] The key terms are δεκτικόν, δέχεσθαι, linked to the notion of 'form without matter' first introduced at II.12, 424a18–19; cf. 424b1–2; III.2, 425b23–4; 12, 434a29–30. The parallel is drawn for the intellect at III.4, 429a15–18. Remember that it is proper (ἴδιον) to a human to be ζῷον ἐπιστήμης δεκτικόν, an animal receptive of knowledge (*Top.* v.4, 132b2–3, et al.).

[113] For the parallel, see III.6, 430b27–30, disregarding the daggers in Ross 1956.

[114] Note especially πάσχειν ὑπὸ τοῦ νοητοῦ (429a14) instead of the teacher normally presupposed as the agent of assimilation (cf. the surprising suggestion at *Met.* A.1, 980b21–5, that animals without hearing do not learn). *Ph.* VII.3, 248a2–3 is a partial exception: ἠρεμίζεται πρός ἔνια μὲν ὑπὸ τῆς φύσεως αὐτῆς, πρός ἔνια δ' ὑπ' ἄλλων. More considerable is *DA* III.4, 429b9: μαθεῖν ἢ εὑρεῖν. The difference between teacher and intelligible form disappears when we view the teacher, in the perspective of *Ph.* III.1–3, as bringing the form to the learner as the builder brings the form of house to the bricks.

terminology. If he refrains from invention here, preferring to refine existing notions, it is for a reason. New words could not draw on the explanatory power of the familiar theorems from *De Generatione et Corruptione* 1.7 and *Physics* III.1–3.

This takes us back to the problem raised earlier (p. 191) about how the transition to seeing, an example of (Alt³), relates to seeing as such, which is complete at every moment. Seeing is the end-state without which the transition would not count as any sort of alteration. But it is an end-state instantaneously achieved. When Aristotle says there is no coming to be (*genesis*) of seeing, any more than of a geometrical point or arithmetical unit (*Sens.* 6, 446b3–4; *EN* x.4, 1174b12–13), he means that there is no time-consuming *process* that precedes the seeing. What precedes is nothing but the animal's enduring *capacity* to see: in II.5's terms, a second potentiality. (Alt³) is as limiting a case of alteration as ingenuity could devise.

But I hope to have made clear that Aristotle has theoretical reasons for devising it. The language of alteration directs attention to the causal agent responsible for getting itself perceived. Perception is not 'up to us', and it is cognitive of sensible qualities in our environment precisely because it is not 'up to us'. II.5's careful analysis of the transition to perceiving helps to ensure that from now on, when we meet simpler statements which ignore the transition and describe perceiving itself as alteration or being affected,[115] we hear them as: 'Perception is special sort of qualitative change induced by the actual quality it is a perception *of*.' Provided this is understood, the (instantaneous) transition to perceiving and perceiving ‖ can be allowed to merge. And it can be left to other works (*Ethics* and *Metaphysics*), where the causality of perception is less important, to make capital of the point that there is no moment of perceiving at which its goal is not achieved.

Conclusion

We may now return to perception for the decisive announcement at 418a1–3:

> Since we have no names to mark the difference between them [*sc.* first and second potentiality],[116] but our distinguishing has shown that they are

---

[115] Examples from later within *DA*: II.11, 424a1–2; 12, 424a22–4; III.12, 435a1 (cf. *Insomn.* 2, 459b4–5). Examples from elsewhere (to be discussed below): *MA* 7, 701b17–18; *Ph.* VII.2, 244b10–11.

[116] What is missing is not one name for the difference (Hicks 1907: 'as this distinction has no word to mark it'), but two names, one for each of the items distinguished (Barbotin and Jannone 1966:

different and in what way they are different, we must go on using 'being affected' and 'being altered' as if these words <still> had their standard meaning.[117]

The long-delayed statement of [P/A] follows immediately (418a3–6), linked by the back-reference 'as has been said' to the original formulation of the assimilation story [A] at 417a18–20.[118] But what it means for the perceiver to be *potentially* such as the sensible object is actually, to be *affected* and *altered* by the sensible object, so as to be *assimilated* to it – all of that is dramatically different from what it would have been before. New meanings of 'potentiality' have been distinguished, and we have seen how they bring with them new, non-standard meanings of 'being affected' and 'being altered'. Hence there will be new meanings also for 'assimilation' and its specific varieties: 'being made red', 'being warmed', || 'sounding Middle C'. By the end of II.5 the familiar theorems from *De Generatione et Corruptione* I.7 and *Physics* III.1–3 have been filled with a whole range of new meanings undreamed of in earlier philosophy.

The result is that perception is *alloiōsis tis* in the *alienans* sense, 'an alteration of a sort': an alteration from which you cannot expect everything you would normally expect from alteration. You cannot expect the perceiver to be really altered, really reddened at the eye; seeing red is not at all like a case of internal bleeding. You cannot even expect the alteration to take time, as ordinary changes do (*Ph.* V.1, 224a35).

Nevertheless, you can still expect from perceiving some of the things you would normally expect from alteration. The term has not lost all connection with the lessons of the other physical works. You can expect this type of alteration to be caused by a sensible quality, which determines the qualitative character of the effect in the perceiver in such a manner that the perceiver is in some new sense assimilated to it. To see a red object is to

---

'puisque ces différentes acceptations n'ont pas reçu de noms distincts'). Presumably, this remark of Aristotle's was the cue for the later tradition to come up with the terms 'first' and 'second potentiality'. Carteron 1926–31 translates *Ph.* VIII.4, 255b9–10, as if that (admittedly suggestive) text already had the terms, but to my knowledge they are first attested in Alexander (cf. *Quaest.* III.3, 84.34–6; 85.25–6).

[117] ὡς κυρίοις ὀνόμασιν is usually translated 'as if these words were the proper terms'. But the references in Bonitz 1955, sv. κύριος show that a κύριον ὄνομα is a word used in its ordinary, standard, or accepted meaning, as opposed to a word that requires explanation (γλῶσσα) or a word used in a transferred meaning (μεταφορά). Either way the implication of ὡς, as earlier at 417a14, is negative: perception is *not* properly called πάσχειν and ἀλλοιοῦσθαι, or (on the rendering I prefer) is so called only in a non-standard meaning of the verbs. I write 'go on using' to bring out the point that the novelty is not the verbs, which have been in use since the beginning of the chapter, but (as the ancient commentators agree) their non-standard meaning.

[118] Cf. n. 42 above.

be reddened by it *in a way* (cf. the *alienans* qualification *estin hōis* at III.2, 425b2–3).[119] To feel the warmth of a fire is to be warmed by it, but not in the way the cold room or your chilled hands are warmed by it.[120]

Naturally, readers will ask: But what are these new ways of being reddened and warmed? II.5 does not say. Our chapter is a general introduction to the study of perception and cognition. It distinguishes between the two non-standard types of alteration that are pertinent to the *De Anima*, (Alt³) and (Alt²), by contrasting each in turn with ordinary alteration (Alt¹). The main positive message of II.5 is that the new meanings exist: [P/A]'s description of perceiving as assimilation is to be understood as referring ‖ to extraordinary alteration (Alt³), a (2)–(3) transition, and hence to a new way of being reddened or warmed. If you want to know more about what such assimilations amount to, read on. Many of the answers are in II.7–11, where Aristotle studies the individual senses one by one, with II.12 the general summing up. But he continues to add to the picture in Book III (III.3, 428b10ff., on appearance, *phantasia*, is a vital contribution) and in the *De Sensu*. If we respect the author's order of presentation, we will learn soon enough.

In a study of II.7–8,[121] I have argued that according to the Aristotelian theory of perception the effect that colours and sounds have on the relevant sense-organ is the same as their effect on the medium. Suppose Aristotle sees a red object. The effect of the red colour is a 'quasi-alteration', as I there call it, in which neither the medium (obviously) nor the eye (*pace* Sorabji) turns red, but red *appears* to Aristotle through the medium at his eye. All Sorabji's scientists would see, given an instrument for looking into the transparent jelly of Aristotle's eye, is: the red object Aristotle sees (if they look from behind) or the flesh around the

---

[119] Webb 1982: 38 with n. 101 resists the *alienans* interpretation here and translates 'it is true that it is coloured', on the grounds that LSJ and Bonitz cite no case of ἔστιν ὡς = πως in a genuine Aristotelian work. Evidently, he wants a case of ἔστιν ὡς by itself, like ἔστιν ὅπου at *Pol.* IV.5, 1299b28, as opposed to ἔστι μὲν ὡς ... ἔστι δ' ὡς οὔ). An unreasonable demand, but easily met by reading Aristotle, e.g. *Met.* Z.10, 1035a14 with 2–4; l.9, 1058b16.

[120] The idea that perception of hot and cold is intuitively a favourable, perhaps the most favourable case, for the Sorabji interpretation should dissolve on inspection of *PA* II.2, 648b11–649b8, where Aristotle's discussion of the many meanings of 'hot' begins (648b12–15) with a distinction between imparting heat and being hot to the touch (= τὴν ἁφὴν θερμαίνειν, 649b4–5). This text establishes beyond question that in Aristotle's mind 'heating the room' and 'heating the touch' are two quite different things; Johansen 1998: 276–80 has a good discussion of the point, while Burnyeat 2001a [Chapter 6 in this volume] presents Aquinas as an Aristotelian thinker who accepts that perceiving heat is always accompanied by actual warming, but not that the warming underlies the perception as matter to form.

[121] Burnyeat 1995.

transparency. Just as the power of vision is preserved by its exercise, so the eye preserves its neutral state of transparency when Aristotle sees first green, then red.[122] Precisely because transparency lies outside the colour range, transparent stuff is the ideal material base for a second potentiality which is to be preserved, not lost, on each and every occasion of perceiving. Precisely because transparency is a standing material condition for eyes to have the power of sight, and analogous conditions apply to the other sense organs, these organs must remain *perceptibly* neutral throughout. Thus the transparent stuff within the eye would not even exhibit to scientific observation the sort of borrowed colours one sees on a TV screen, a white wall illuminated by red light, or a sea whose surface viewed from a distance shows a tinted sheen; borrowed colours are no easier to see through than inherent colours.[123] All that happens when Aristotle sees red is that (to use ‖ a more recent jargon) he is 'appeared to redly' and is so appeared to because the object is red. This gives the sense in which he is reddened by the red object, and comes (instantaneously) to be like it. The object's redness appears to him. He is aware of red.

We should be careful not to think of Aristotle's awareness of red and the red's appearing to him as two events, one of which causes the other. *Physics* III.3 lays it down that correlative cases of acting on and being affected (e.g. teaching and learning) are one and the same event, taking place in the patient, described from different points of view. And this physical principle is invoked in the key doctrinal passage *DA* III.2, 425b26–426a26, to give the result that Aristotle's seeing red is identical with the red object's action of appearing to him. The cause of this doubly described but single event is the object's redness.

Of course, Aristotle might be appeared to redly because of some internal condition or disease; this might happen even when he has a red object in view. But that would not be seeing red: 'Appearance is not the same thing as perception' (*Met.* Γ.5, 1010b3). Seeing red is being appeared to redly by a red object in the external environment, because it is actually red.[124] Proper object perception is always true. Extraordinary alteration is an

---

[122] In both sense and intellect ἀπάθεια is a condition of receptivity: III.4, 429a15–18; 29–31. With σωτηρία at 417b3 compare σωζόμενον in the description of the organ of taste at II.10, 422b4, and Magee 2000: 318–19 in contrast to Broackes 1999: 66–7.

[123] Thus II.5 does, as I hoped p. 31, help us to understand the importance of the neutrality of Aristotelian sense-organs. The TV analogy has often been put to me as an example of (Alt³) compatible with literal coloration. The sea's sheen, discussed at *Sens.* 3, 439b1–5, is Sorabji's starting point for his new approach in Sorabji 2001.

[124] The 'because'-clause could be used to rule out the case of a white object appearing red because it is bathed in a red light, or grey because it is seen at a distance. Aristotle touches on such issues at *Met.*

accurate awareness of objectively real sensible qualities in the environment. That is how the refinements of II.5 allow the general principles of Aristotelian physics to account for the basic *cognitive* function of soul.

Two controversial morals

The Sorabji interpretation combines two claims: (i) that ordinary alteration is what Aristotle requires for perception, (ii) that its role is to stand to awareness as matter to form.[125] I have shown that a careful reading of II.5 makes (i) untenable. I then went beyond II.5 to argue, with the help of a previous study of II.7–8, that the alteration relevant to perception, extra- || ordinary alteration (Alt³), is itself the awareness of sensible qualities in the environment. From this it follows that (ii) is untenable as well: extraordinary alteration is not the underlying realisation of awareness, but awareness itself. My final point is that the untenability of (ii) can be established from within II.5, without the extra illumination from later chapters of the *De Anima*.

Let us go back to the beginning:

> [1][a] Perception consists in (*sumbainei en*) being changed and affected, as has been said. (416b33–4)

The translation 'consists in'[126] may suggest that the change in question is the underlying realisation of perception. But the back-reference 'as has been said' is to I.5, 410a25–6, 'They suppose that perceiving is some sort of being affected and changed', where the 'is' sounds more like the 'is' of classification than the 'is' of composition. The same goes for [1][b], 'Perception is some sort of alteration'. But this is not decisive. Considered on their own, both the I.5 and the II.5 versions of [1][a] could be taken either way.

Considered in the full context of II.5, however, [1][a] and [b] are unmistakably statements of classification. The whole business of the chapter is with types of alteration. Learning, the transition from (1) to (2), is unordinary alteration (Alt²), and this is a distinct *type* of alteration because it is the development of a firmly fixed dispositional state (*hexis*) which perfects the subject's nature. Aristotle's example is learning to be

---

Γ.5, 1010b3ff., but he nowhere specifies further conditions external to the perceiver (besides the presence of light) for seeing red.

[125] References for (i) in n. 3 above; for (ii), see Sorabji 1974: 53–6; Sorabji 1992: 208–9. (i) is a position that Sorabji shares with Slakey's well-known paper, (ii) an addition which avoids Slakey's conclusion that ordinary alteration (the eye's going literally and visibly red, etc.) is all there is to perception on Aristotle's account.

[126] For the alternatives, please reread n. 15.

literate, which culminates in being able to read and write. It would be nonsense to say that developing the ability to read and write, an unordinary alteration (Alt²), stands to learning one's letters as matter to form. It is what learning to be literate *is*. In the statement 'Learning is some sort of alteration', the 'is' is clearly the 'is' of classification, not the 'is' of composition.

By parity of reasoning, it should be nonsense to say that extraordinary alteration, a (2)–(3) transition, stands to perceiving as matter to form. Extraordinary alteration is what perceiving is, not some underlying realisation for it. The 'is' in [1][b] is like the 'is' in 'Alteration is a sort of change', not like that in 'Anger is boiling of the blood around the heart'. It is the 'is' of classification, not the 'is' of composition.[127] ||

This conclusion does more than complete my refutation of the Sorabji interpretation of Aristotle's theory of perception. It bears also on a wider controversy, of larger philosophical significance.

Martha Nussbaum and Hilary Putnam have defended,[128] and continue to defend,[129] the thesis that Aristotle's psychology is an ancient version of what modern philosophers know as the functionalist solution to the mind–body problem. For the solution itself, as a solution suited to modern physics for the mind–body problem bequeathed to us by Descartes, I have much admiration. My objection to the Nussbaum–Putnam thesis[130] is that Descartes' problem presupposes Descartes' rejection of Aristotelian physics, a rejection we all share today. Aristotle's account of the soul–body relation cannot be resurrected to help in the modern war against Cartesian dualism because, as I have emphasised throughout this paper, Aristotle's psychology is designed to be the crowning achievement of his physics, and his physics is irretrievably dead and gone. I am all in favour of setting up comparisons between ancient and modern philosophy. But what I think we learn from comparing Aristotle and modern functionalism is how deeply Descartes' influence has settled in ordinary consciousness today.

So large a claim is obviously not one I can take further here.[131] But it so happens that the Sorabji interpretation of the 'is' in [1][b] is a main prop for the Nussbaum–Putnam thesis. They need an underlying realisation for

---

[127] Cf. Philoponus 290.4–5: ἡ οὖν αἴσθησις ἀλλοίωσις, ἡ δε ἀλλοίωσις κίνησις, ἡ αἴσθησις ἄρα ἐν τῷ ἀλλοιοῦσθαί τε καὶ κινεῖσθαί ἐστι.
[128] Putnam 1975: xiii–xiv; Nussbaum 1978: 69 with n. 14 et passim.
[129] Nussbaum and Putnam 1992.   [130] Burnyeat 1992b: 16, 26.
[131] But see Burnyeat 2001a [Chapter 6 in this volume]. Nussbaum and Rorty 1992 is a splendid symposium on the issues involved. For an introduction to functionalism and its varieties,

perception if perception in Aristotle's theory is to conform to, and confirm, the general functionalist pattern: constant form in variable matter. [1][b] is the star witness for their case. So if, as just argued, II.5 makes Sorabji's point (ii) untenable, the Nussbaum–Putnam thesis is seriously undermined.

Admittedly, Nussbaum and Putnam do not cite [1][b] from the *De Anima*. They adduce the same proposition as it appears (in the plural) at *De Motu Animalium* 7, 701b17–18: 'Perceptions are in themselves alterations of a sort (*alloiōseis tines*)'.[132] But it is the same proposition, and I ‖ have been arguing that *DA* II.5 is Aristotle's official account of how it is to be understood.[133] So if Sorabji falls on claim (ii), Nussbaum and Putnam fall with him.[134] The (extraordinary) alterations which perceptions are do not serve as the underlying material realisation of perception. They belong on the side of form rather than matter. As Aristotle will put it in the well-known passage II.12, 424a17–24, the alterations are the receiving of sensible form without matter.[135] That is what Aristotelian perception essentially is.

I recommend Ned Block's 'Introduction' (Block 2002), in which the idea of Aristotle as the father of functionalism achieved textbook status, citing Hartman 1977: 131–66 at 171, 177.

[132] Nussbaum and Putnam 1992: 39, the key item in their 'Exhibit A' but in my own translation, to be compared with Nussbaum's in her *De Motu*: 'sense-perceptions are at once a kind of alteration' (Nussbaum 1978: 42), '*aistheseis* are a certain type of qualitative change' (147), 'perceptions just are some sort of alteration' (151). Nussbaum and Putnam paraphrase the first of these as 'perceptions just *are* (*ousai*), are realized in, such *alloiōseis*'. The crux is εὐθύς, which I take to mean 'directly', 'in their own right', in contrast to the alterations caused by perceptions mentioned in the previous sentence. (A good illustration of this logical sense is *Met.* H.6, 1045a36–b6; more in Bonitz 1955 sv.) A helpful parallel is *Poet.* 10, 1452a12–14: εἰσὶ δὲ τῶν μύθων οἱ μὲν ἁπλοῖ οἱ δὲ πεπλεγμένοι· καὶ γὰρ αἱ πράξεις ὧν μιμήσεις οἱ μῦθοί εἰσιν ὑπάρχουσιν εὐθὺς οὖσαι τοιαῦται. λέγω δὲ ἁπλῆν μὲν πρᾶξιν κτλ.

[133] Nussbaum 1978: 151–2 agrees that we are dealing with a 'clear recapitulation of the *DA* position on perception'. The cross-references between the two treatises support this. While *DA* III.10, 433b19–30, looks forward to the account of animal movement in *MA*, *MA* 6, 700b4–6, looks back to *DA* on the question whether the soul is itself moved (Bonitz 100a45 refers us to II.2–3; Nussbaum 1978 ad loc. to 1.3–4; Burnyeat 2001b, ch. 5, n. 72, to III.9–11) and if so, how, while b21–2 looks back to *DA* III.3 on the differences between appearance, perception, and intellect. Nussbaum 1978: 9–12 draws the chronological conclusion that *MA* is a late work. I prefer to emphasise that, whatever the dating of individual works, readers of *MA* are expected to have studied *DA* as carefully as readers of *DA* are expected to have studied *GC* and *Ph*.

[134] Nussbaum argues for reading [1][b] with the 'is' of composition in Nussbaum 1978: 146–52 (cf. pp. 256–7). Nussbaum and Putnam 1992: 36 distance themselves from Sorabji's account of perceptual assimilation (previously accepted by Nussbaum), but at p. 40 they endorse his (i) and (ii), merely substituting a different set of underlying ordinary alterations to make them true. Their substitute alterations (heating and chilling and resultant changes of shape in the bodily parts) cannot, as Sorabji's ordinary alterations can, provide a material account of the difference between seeing red and feeling warmth – for the good reason, I believe, that Aristotle invokes heating and chilling to explain how perceptions produce animal movement (see below), not to explain the initial perceiving.

[135] Notice πάσχει (i.e. ἀλλοιοῦται) at 424a23.

The *De Motu Animalium* version of [1][b] does, however, add something important to the picture we have formed so far. The question at issue in the context is, How do animals get moving? Aristotle cites automatic puppets and other mechanical systems as analogies to illustrate how a small initial change can produce a variety of larger changes further on in the causal chains for which the mechanisms are designed (701b24–6) – ‖ 'just as, if the rudder shifts a hair's breadth, the shift in the prow is considerable' (701b26–8, tr. Nussbaum). The key idea is the incremental power of certain types of causal chain.

When Aristotle comes to apply this idea to animal movement, he mentions several alterations. The first alteration is (a) the heating and cooling of bodily parts, which causes them to expand, contract, and change their shape (701b13–16).[136] He then adds that such alterations[137] may in turn be caused by any of three things, each of which either is or involves alteration. (b) 'Perceptions are in themselves alterations of a sort' (701b17–18), and (c) there are the alterations which, he now argues, are involved in (i) the appearing or (ii) the conceiving of something hot or cold, either pleasant or painful (701b18–23).[138] The novelty is to see extraordinary alterations (b) listed alongside ordinary alterations (a) as members of the same causal chain.[139]

Another place where this happens is *Physics* VII.2. *Physics* VII.3 was mentioned earlier for its claim that gaining knowledge is not an alteration, because it is not a change but the cessation of change. In the previous chapter, by contrast, Aristotle insists that when an animate thing perceives, no less than when an inanimate thing is warmed or cooled, this is an

---

[136] I agree with Nussbaum 1978 *ad loc.* that in 16 ἀλλοιουμένων is epexegetic of διὰ θερμότητα καὶ ... διὰ ψύξιν.

[137] ἀλλοιοῦσι with no object specified at 16 because Aristotle is moving to the causes of the alterations (a) just mentioned.

[138] At line 20 Nussbaum excises θερμοῦ ἢ ψυχροῦ ἢ on the grounds that it is hard to make sense of the words: 'Aristotle nowhere suggests that the hot and the cold have, in themselves, any particular motivating power as objects of thought. Their inclusion probably originated in a gloss by a scribe anxious to indicate that θερμόν went with ἡδύ, ψυχρόν with φοβερόν (Nussbaum 1976: 152). A reasonable excuse for the editorial knife, but one that can be rebutted by making sense, as follows. Precisely because the hot and the cold have no motivating power in themselves, but only in relation to the agent's situation (θερμόν does not go with ἡδύ in a heatwave), Aristotle makes separate mention of the cognitive content and the emotional aspect. (The claim in Nussbaum and Putnam 1992: 43 that Aristotle nowhere separates the cognitive and the emotional in this way is falsified even for perception by *DA* II.9, 421a7–16; III.7, 431a8–17.) Since hot and cold are opposites, one might paraphrase, 'hot or cold, whether it be the hot which is pleasant and the cold frightful or the other way round'.

[139] I suppose that alterations (c) are to be understood in the light of the doctrine that thinking, the exercise of intellect, requires φαντάσματα (*DA* III.7, 431b2–9; 8, 432a8–10), (φαντάσματα in turn being likenesses of the perceptual alterations from which they derive (III.2, 429a4–5).

alteration – of a sort: 'The senses too are altered *in a way*' (244b10–11).[140]
|| It is scarcely an exaggeration to say that the Aristotelian universe would collapse if perception could not legitimately be treated as alteration alongside ordinary alterations like heating and cooling; for perception so characterised has a pivotal role in the *Physics*' grand argument for the existence of a first, unmoved cosmic mover.

I take these two texts (*MA* 7, *Ph.* VII.2) as some confirmation for my hypothesis that it is the needs of physics that lead Aristotle to classify perception as alteration and (passive) change. To return briefly to *De Motu Animalium*: if Aristotelian physics is to account not only for perception, but for the role of perception in determining animal movement, perceptual awareness must itself be a physical change – one of the small initial changes that set the series going. Nowadays the favoured alternative would be to treat 'perception' as a place-holding term for *whatever it is* in the animal's physiology (let the scientists find out) that starts it moving. That is functionalism. It is not Aristotle, for it rests on the post-Cartesian assumption that terms like 'perception' and 'awareness' belong to our mental vocabulary *in contrast to* the vocabulary of the physical sciences.[141] No wonder modern scholars have had difficulty translating [1][a] and [b]. 'Perception is some sort of alteration' seems to subsume the mental under the physical. But for Aristotle the physical does not contrast with the mental in the way we are used to.[142] His psychology, to say it for the third time, is the crowning achievement of his physics.

FINALE

Before I stop, a word about an objection often put to me: 'Even if perceiving as such is not ordinary alteration, it might still involve ordinary alterations in the body, or other changes of a non-qualitative kind. After all, neither the builder's transition to activity nor his building is alteration or passive change, but that does not exclude his getting hot and bothered on site.'

---

[140] ἀλλοιοῦνται γάρ πως καὶ αἱ αἰσθήσεις. For discussion, see Wardy 1990: 144–9. But I prefer Ross's translation of αἰσθήσεις as 'senses' to Wardy's 'sense-organs', which allows him to interpret the statement as referring, albeit vaguely, to ordinary alterations in the body.

[141] Readers may like to compare my remarks on the Ramsey sentence at Burnyeat 1992b: 22 with the assumption at Nussbaum and Putnam 1992: 40 that committing Aristotle to reductive materialism is the only alternative to understanding the 'is' of [1][b] as the 'is' of composition.

[142] More on this in Burnyeat 2001a [Chapter 6 in this volume].

I agree that *De Anima* II.5 shows only that the Sorabji interpretation is ‖ wrong. Claim (i) is wrong because the assimilation that perceiving is is not ordinary alteration (Alt¹). Claim (ii) is wrong because the extraordinary alteration (Alt³) that perceiving is is not its underlying material realisation. From this it obviously does not follow that no underlying realisation is needed for extraordinary alteration (Alt³) itself. The extraordinary alteration which perceiving is does require certain standing conditions in the organ – transparency for example. Why not material processes as well? II.5 on its own does not rule out the involvement of some (as yet unspecified) ordinary alteration, or some non-qualitative change, which stands to the extraordinary alteration (Alt³) that perceiving is as matter to form. What II.5 shows is that the assimilation refined in the course of the chapter cannot itself play such a role; the perceiver's becoming like the object perceived is not a material process but belongs on the side of form. This leaves *logical* space for a material realisation of perception, a space that commentators can fill with coded messages, vibrations, or any other processes they fancy.¹⁴³

But Aristotle goes on speaking of perception as alteration and not speaking of it as anything else. We have just seen him still at it in *De Motu Animalium*. He leaves no *textual* space for anything but alteration – and remember that in his physics alteration is an irreducible type of change, one of the only four types there are.¹⁴⁴ We have watched Aristotle extending his notion of alteration, originally defined in *De Generatione et Corruptione* I for cases like a fire's heating a cold room, to fit the alteration by which a perceiver sees red. He has taken care to specify the refinements needed for the purpose. The presumption is that in other respects the analogy between heating and perceiving holds good.

Let me push this point a little further. Aristotle's story about the heating action of fire is *logically* compatible with an underlying process in ‖ terms, say, of molecular motion. But it is perfectly clear that heating for Aristotle

---

¹⁴³ Sorabji 1992: 210 lists various suggestions that have been made, with references. Two cautions are in order. First, anyone who chooses a process that Aristotle would count as κίνησις had better not combine it with the idea that perceiving is ἐνέργεια in the sense which *Met.* Θ.6 contrasts with κίνησις, lest they countenance a matter-form marriage between logically incompatible partners. Second, there is a widespread illusion that Aristotle's methodological remarks in *DA* I.1 positively demand some concomitant material change underlying perception. Nussbaum and Putnam 1992 appreciate that the claim has to be argued for, not assumed. I argue the contrary in Burnyeat 1995: 433 with n. 38.
¹⁴⁴ *Cat.* 14, 15a17–27, expressly rejects the idea that alteration necessarily involves some non-qualitative change. The only place to suggest otherwise is *Ph.* VIII.7, 260b7–13, disarmed by Furley 1989: 134.

is a primitive, elemental process which needs no further material changes to explain it. Anyone who proposed otherwise, to bring Aristotle nearer to modern views, would violate the spirit of his texts. The same is true, I submit, of Aristotle's theory of perception, which takes up more pages in the *De Anima* (not to mention *De Sensu*) than any other topic. If so extended a treatment leaves no textual space for further material changes underlying the alteration which is perceiving, we should take the author at his word. He has said what he has to say about perception. Extraordinary alteration (Alt³) is where he means to stop.

The merit of the Sorabji interpretation is that it accounts for Aristotle's continuing use, throughout the *De Anima* and related works, of the qualitative language of alteration as the *lowest level* description of what happens in perception. Anyone who claims to interpret Aristotle, not just to make up a logically possible theory inspired by Aristotle, must match Sorabji's achievement over the same range of texts. No responsible interpretation can escape the question this paper has been discussing: Given that perception is to be *wholly* explained as some sort of alteration, which sort is it? Sorabji's ordinary alteration, or the extraordinary alteration I have laboured to bring to light in *De Anima* II.5? Within the text as Aristotle wrote it, *tertium non datur*.[145]

APPENDIX 1: 417A30–B2

ἀμφότεροι μὲν οὖν οἱ πρῶτοι κατὰ δύναμιν ἐπιστήμονες, ἀλλ' ὁ μὲν διὰ μαθήσεως ἀλλοιωθεὶς καὶ πολλάκις ἐξ ἐναντίας μεταβαλὼν ἕξεως, ὁ δ' ἐκ τοῦ ἔχειν τὴν ἀριθμητικὴν ἢ τὴν γραμματικήν, μὴ ἐνεργεῖν δέ, εἰς τὸ ἐνεργεῖν, ἄλλον τρόπον.

30 οἱ [πρῶτοι] κατὰ δύναμιν ἐπιστήμονες <ἐνεργείᾳ γίνονται ἐπιστήμονες> Torstrik: οἱ πρῶτοι κατὰ δύναμιν ἐπιστήμονες <ὄντες, ἐνεργείᾳ γίνονται ἐπιστήμονες,> Ross 32 On preferring ἀριθμητικήν to the MSS reading αἴσθησιν, see n. 68. ||

Modern discussion of this densely concentrated passage begins with Torstrik. On the received text, ἀμφότεροι οἱ πρῶτοι is the subject of the

---

[145] This paper originally took shape in seminars at Princeton (1989), Harvard (1991), and Pittsburg (1992); to the senior and junior members of those audiences, many thanks for helping me clarify my ideas and improve my arguments. Thanks also to later audiences in St Petersburg and at a conference in Basel on ancient and medieval theories of intentionality. Individuals who gave challenging criticism and useful comments include Sarah Broadie, Victor Caston, David Charles, Dorothea Frede, Michael Frede, Thomas Johansen, Geoffrey Lloyd, Martha Nussbaum, Ron Polansky, Malcolm Schofield, David Sedley, Richard Sorabji, K. Tsuchiya, Robert Wardy.

sentence at 30, bifurcating into ὁ μέν as the subject of the sentence at 31, ὁ δ' the subject of the sentence 31–b2. To this Torstrik had two objections.

To begin with, he said, the first sentence is ridiculously repetitive: we have just been told not only that but how (1) and (2) are potential knowers. Then, more damagingly, with ὁ μέν as subject (referring to first potentiality) διὰ μαθήσεως ἀλλοιωθείς is in predicate position, but it is absurd to say of a newly born infant ὁ μέν (sc. ἐστι) διὰ μαθήσεως ἀλλοιωθείς. The future perfect ἠλλιοιωσόμενος would fit, but not ἀλλοιωθείς. (Theiler 1959 does in fact read and translate ἀλλοιωθησόμενος ... μεταβαλών.)

After much thought (*diu haec animum sollicitum habuerant: sentiebam corruptelam, medela in promptu non erat*), Torstrik found a solution: *desideratur notio transeundi*. If διὰ μαθήσεως ἀλλοιωθείς is what the infant *becomes*, instead of what the infant already *is*, the difficulty disappears.

Torstrik proceeded to write the idea of transition into the text by emendation. Ross does the same, rather more neatly in that he does not have to excise πρῶτοι or shift κατὰ δύναμιν ἐπιστήμονες to subject position. Most editors and translators suppose that the Torstrik–Ross *meaning* can be got out of the text as it stands, without emendation.

But how? The only scholar to explain is Hicks:

> There is no verb in this sentence (sc. ἀλλ' ὁ μὲν κτλ.). We cannot supply κατὰ δύναμιν ἐπιστήμων ἐστί from the last sentence because of the participles ἀλλοιωθείς and μεταβαλών. The effect of these participles is best shown if we supply γίγνεται ἐπιστήμων, 'but the one [becomes possessed of knowledge] after modification ... the other ...'

Call this construal (A). It has been followed, without further discussion, by nearly every translator since. It can also claim ancient precedent: both Alexander *Quaest.* III 3, 83.27–30 and Philoponus 300.8–30 take this line, which Philoponus expounds again with especial clarity at *De Aeternitate Mundi* 69.4ff., dating from 529 AD (our earliest MS of *DA* is E, tenth century); his quotation of our passage at 69.22–70.1 and 71.17–20 confirms that he read it in the form in which it has come down to us, without supplementation.

The other ancient commentators are less definite. Themistius 55.25 writes ἀλλ' ὁ μὲν δεῖται μαθήσεως καὶ τῆς κατὰ τὴν μάθησιν ἀλλοιώσεως, but this is paraphrase (inexcusably adopted by Rodier for his translation). Simplicius 121.29–30, ἀλλ' ὁ μὲν τελειούμενος ἀλλοιώσει τῇ διὰ τῆς μαθήσεως, seems to fall to a version of Torstrik's second objection: even the present participle τελειούμενος is inappropriate to a newly born infant.

Sophonias 66.38–67.4 is interestingly obscure: ἀμφότεροι μὲν οὖν οἱ πρῶτοι κατὰ δύναμιν ἐπιστήμονες, ἀλλ' ὁ μὲν πρώτως, ὁ δὲ δευτέρως, καὶ ὁ || μὲν διὰ μαθήσεως ἀλλοιωθεὶς καὶ πολλάκις ἐξ ἐναντίας μεταβαλὼν ἕξεως, ὁ δὲ ἐκ τοῦ ἔχειν τὴν αἴσθησιν τελείαν ἢ τὴν γραμματικὴν μὴ ἐνεργεῖν δέ. It is time to reopen the issue.

I agree that Hicks was right to say we cannot supply κατὰ δύναμιν ἐπιστήμων ἐστί. But he was also right to expect the missing verb to be carried forward from the previous sentence; that would be more normal than leaving readers to supply a wholly new verb like γίγνεται. Hence what I propose we supply after ὁ μέν is: κατὰ δύναμίν ἐστιν. κατὰ δύναμίν ἐστιν ἀλλοιωθείς is a perfectly proper thing to say of Torstrik's infant. The child is now *potentially* (not of course actually) someone who has been altered through learning.

Next, I supply after ὁ δ' not just κατὰ δύναμιν ἐστιν, but κατὰ δύναμίν ἐστι μεταβαλών. Hicks ad 417a32 already saw the need to supply a participle from the ὁ μέν sentence as well as a main verb. He chose μεταβαλών, rather than ἀλλοιωθείς, but without explaining why. Three reasons can be given: (a) the construction ἐκ ... εἰς is standard for μεταβάλλειν (*Ph.* III.5, 205a6; V.1, 224b7–10; VI.5, 235b6, etc.), and already in 417a31 ἐκ goes with μεταβαλών; (b) the emphasis on opposition in the immediate sequel (417b2–3) implies that what the ἄλλον τρόπον is other than is (not learning but) changing from an opposite state; (c) μεταβαλών, as the more general term, gives a better lead-in to the disjunction 'either not an alteration or a different kind of alteration' (417b6–7) – it would be odd to say of a transition introduced as an alteration that either it is not an alteration or it is a different kind of alteration.

Such is the construal adopted in the main text of this paper. Call it construal (B). Here is a translation to fit:

> Both the first two are potentially knowers, but the former <is potentially> someone who has been altered through learning, i.e. someone who has repeatedly *changed from an opposite state*, the latter <is potentially someone who has changed> *in another way*, viz. from having knowledge of arithmetic or letters without exercising it to the actual exercise.

It is just possible that this is what Sophonias is saying. It is quite probable that Themistius construed the same way before paraphrasing (legitimately enough) potentiality as lack or στέρησις.

Let me now list the differences between construal (A) and construal (B). (A) spotlights the changes, (B) the results which the two potentialities are potentialities for; (B) articulates the two potential senses of '*P* is a knower' in terms of two different things the knower has a potentiality to be, (A) describes the two types of transition that take *P* from (1) to (2) and from (2) to (3). Neither construal makes for elegant Greek, but to understand Aristotle's Greek philology must ascend to the condition of || philosophy, and the central philosophical point about potentiality is that it is a potentiality to *be*, not to become, unlike one's present self (p. 169, p. 178 above). Until Kosman 1969 this was seldom recognised. Once the point is taken, construal (B) may be recommended on philosophical grounds, as well as because it is more economical (I submit) in its philological demands.

There is a second philosophical reason for preferring construal (B). From a technical point of view the predicate at 30 is ἐπιστήμονες, not κατὰ δύναμιν ἐπιστήμονες. The correct parsing of the sentence is not 'Both are potentially-knowers', but 'Both are-potentially knowers', with κατὰ δύναμιν modifying the copula (εἰσίν understood). Not only does Aristotle in his logic standardly treat the modal adverbs 'necessarily' and 'possibly' as copula-modifiers, but metaphysically (to come closer to present concerns) potentiality and actuality are for him modes of *being* (*Met.* Δ.7, 1017a35–b2; E.2, 1026b1–2; Θ.1, 1045b33–4; Λ.5, 1071a3–5). The triple scheme presents three different ways of *being* a knower, and it is the two ways of being-potentially a knower that our passage distinguishes. Accordingly, κατὰ δύναμιν εἰσίν should be treated as a unit and carried forward as a unit from 30 to 31 and 31–2. If this means allowing the adjective ἐπιστήμων to extend to knowing in sense (3), Aristotle implies that it may so extend when he writes λέγομεν ... ἐπιστήμονα καὶ τὸν μὴ θεωροῦντα, ἂν δυνατὸς ᾖ θεωρῆσαι (*Met.* Θ.6, 1048a34–5; cf. Θ.8, 1050b34–1051a2, perhaps *EN* VII.3, 1147b6, and Alex. *Quaest.* III.25–6, Them. 55.23–4, Philop. *De Aet. Mundi* 71.12–13).

My third reason for advocating construal (B) is structural. It offers a steadily developing exposition. First the triple scheme with its two types of potentiality (417a22–9); then a further articulation (not a mere repetition, as Torstrik 1862 complained) of the two potentialities as potentialities for being the results of two types of alteration (417a30–b2); finally an account of the alterations themselves which are the actualities of these potentialities (417b2–7). Construal (A) merges the second stage with the third and thereby misses one of the finer details in Aristotle's gradual unfolding of his contrast.

The only other scholar to have seen that the passage requires rethinking in the light of the point that potentiality is potentiality to be is Mary Louise Gill. She translates (Gill 1989: 176) as follows:

Now both of the first are potential knowers, but the one, having been altered through learning and often changed from an opposite state <is a potential knower in one way>, the other from having arithmetical or grammatical knowledge but not exercising it to the exercise <is a potential knower> in another way. ‖

Construal (C), as this may be called, starts by challenging Hicks' claim that we cannot supply κατὰ δύναμιν ἐστιν ἐπιστήμων. Hicks' objection is met by shifting ἀλλοιωθείς and μεταβαλών to subject position, agreeing with ὁ μέν (it remains unclear whether ὁ δ' also has a participle attached). The result is interpreted by Gill to mean that both ὁ μέν and ὁ δ' have the potentiality to be knowers *in sense (2)*; they have the same potentiality but in different ways. In consequence, Gill denies (Gill 1989: 178–80) that the first potentiality is lost when the learner becomes a knower in sense (2).

Aristotle denies it too, according to my account in the main text – but later at 417b12–16 and not (*pace* Gill) for all potentialities whatsoever. In any case, the objection to construal (C) is that, once the past participle ἀλλοιωθείς is moved to subject position, Torstrik's infant causes trouble again. The newly born have the potentiality to be knowers in sense (2), but the alteration that achieves this goal should be in the future, not the past tense.

Appendix 2: 417b5–7

θεωροῦν γὰρ γίνεται τὸ ἔχον τὴν ἐπιστήμην, ὅπερ ἢ οὐκ ἔστιν ἀλλοιοῦσθαι (εἰς αὑτὸ γὰρ ἡ ἐπίδοσις καὶ εἰς ἐντελέχειαν) ἢ ἕτερον γένος ἀλλοιώσεως.

Hicks 1907, followed by Tricot 1959 and Barbotin and Jannone 1966, would supply ἐπιστῆμον as complement to γίγνεται, with θεωροῦν denoting the manner of becoming: 'For it is by exercise of knowledge that the possessor of knowledge becomes such in actuality'. The more usual construal takes θεωροῦν as complement to γίγνεται: 'the possessor of knowledge in sense (2) comes to be actively knowing in sense (3)'. Hicks says that γίγνεται is 'an odd verb to use, if we bear in mind ἅμα νοεῖ καὶ νενόηκεν'. Indeed it is. The oddity is part and parcel of a deliberate strategy whereby II.5 *refrains* from invoking the idea of unqualified (complete) as opposed to incomplete actuality, or of ἐνέργεια in a sense that excludes κίνησις. Instead, Aristotle intends to keep both perception and intellectual learning within the scope of physics by refining the ordinary scheme of *De Generatione et Corruptione* 1.7 and *Physics* III.1–3.

Gill 1989: 222–6 departs further from the usual construal of these lines by denying that Aristotle makes any reference to the transition from (2) to (3). Taking as the antecedent of ὅπερ not γίγνεται understood as referring to transition, but either θεωροῦν or θεωροῦν γίγνεται understood as mere periphrasis for θεωρεῖ, she holds that the activity itself (3), not the transition to it, is what is here said to be either not an alteration or at least another kind of alteration. My objection is that on anyone's account of || the earlier lines 417a30–b2 (see Appendix 1), they include a contrast between the transition from (1) to (2) and that from (2) to (3). In which case it is strained not to let θεωροῦν γίγνεται refer to the latter transition.

BIBLIOGRAPHY: *DE ANIMA*: MODERN EDITIONS, ANCIENT AND MODERN COMMENTARIES, MODERN TRANSLATIONS

Barbotin, E. See Jannone, A.

Forster, Aurelius. *Aristotelis De Anima Libri III*. Budapest: Academia Litterarum Hungarica, 1912.

Hamlyn, D. W. *Aristotle's De Anima Books II, III (with certain passages from Book I). Translated with Introduction and Notes*. Oxford: Clarendon Press, 1968.

Hett, W. S. *Aristotle On the Soul, Parva Naturalia, On Breath*. With an English translation. Loeb Classical Library. London: Heinemann and Cambridge, MA: Harvard University Press, 1935.

Hicks, R. D. *Aristotle: De Anima. With Translation, Introduction and Notes*. Cambridge: Cambridge University Press, 1907. Reprinted New York: Arno Press, 1976.

Jannone, A. and Barbotin, E. *Aristote, De l'Ame. Texte établi par A. Jannone, traduction et notes de E. Barbotin*. Paris: Les Belles Lettres, 1966.

Philoponus. *In Aristotelis De Anima Libros Commentaria*, ed. Michael Hayduck. CIAG Vol. XV. Berlin: Reimer, 1897.

Rodier, G. Aristote: *Traité de l'Ame. Traduit et annoté*. 2 vols. Paris: Ernest Leroux 1900. Reprinted Dubuque: William C. Brown, n.d.

Ross, W. D. *Aristotelis De Anima. Recognovit brevique adnotatione instruxit*. Oxford: Clarendon Press, 1956 (editio minor).

Aristotle De Anima. Edited, with Introduction and Commentary. Oxford: Clarendon Press, 1961 (editio maior).

Simplicius (?). *In Libros Aristotelis De Anima Commentaria*, ed. Michael Hayduck. CIAG Vol. XI. Berlin: Reimer, 1882.

Siwek, Paulus. *Aristotelis Tractatus de Anima. Edidit, versione latina auxit, commentario illustravit. Collectio philosophica lateranensis*. Rome: Descle, 1965.

Smith, J. A. *De Anima*. The Works of Aristotle Translated into English under the general editorship of W. D. Ross. Vol. III. Oxford: Clarendon Press, 1931.

Sophonias. *In Libros Aristotelis De Anima Paraphrasis*, ed. Michael Hayduck. CIAG Vol. XXIII. Berlin: Reimer, 1883.

Theiler, Willy. *Aristoteles uber die Seele. Ubersetzt.* Berlin: Akademie Verlag, 1959.
Themistius. *In Libros Aristotelis De Anima Paraphrasis*, ed. R. Heinze. CIAG Vol. v. Berlin: Reimer, 1890.
Torstrik, Adolfus. *Aristotelis De Anima Libri III*. Berlin: Weidmanni, 1862.
Tricot, J. *Aristote De L'Ame. Traduction nouvelle et notes.* Paris: Vrin, 1947.
Wallace, Edwin. *Aristotle's Psychology. In Greek and English, with Introduction and Notes.* Cambridge, 1882.

CHAPTER 6

Aquinas on 'spiritual change' in perception

One of the pleasures that Aquinas offers a student of ancient philosophy like myself is a sense of recognition. Here is a thoroughly Aristotelian mind at work, even though the world he lives in and its cultural assumptions are entirely different from those of the fourth century BC. Nowhere is this more true, I believe, than in Aquinas' theory of perception and his remarks about spiritual change. Yet in the scholarly literature on Aristotle's theory of perception the terms 'spiritual change' and 'spiritualism' have come to stand for a view of perception which departs radically from Aristotle.[1] Hence this inquiry: What does Aquinas mean when he speaks of spiritual change?

The phrase certainly does not render any expression in Aristotle's Greek. So how did it get into the scholarly literature on Aristotle's theory of perception? Here I must confess to having written the following:

> All these physical-seeming descriptions – the organ's becoming like the object, its being affected, acted on, or altered by sensible qualities, its taking on sensible form without the matter – all these are referring to what Aquinas calls a 'spiritual' change, a becoming aware of some sensible quality in the environment.[2]

I wrote that in an attempt to sum up my reasons for disagreeing with an influential interpretation of Aristotle's theory of perception put forward by Richard Sorabji, who holds that Aristotle's talk of receiving sensible form without matter refers to a physiological process.

When one perceives red, the eye-jelly quite literally turns red (on the inside), a process which stands to the awareness of red as matter to form. The Sorabji interpretation makes perception comparable to anger, in which Aristotle discerns two components: boiling blood as matter, desire for revenge as form (*DA* 1.1, 403a25–b12). Underlying perceptual

---

[1] Sorabji 1991; Everson 1997: 58–60 *et passim*.   [2] Burnyeat 1992b: 21.

awareness there is a material change in the sense-organ – the organ of sight becomes red, the organ of touch || becomes cold, and so on – which could in principle be observed if scientists had the appropriate instrumentation.[3] My view, by contrast, is that Aristotle treats perception as importantly different from anger.[4]

In this polemical context I was greatly impressed by Aquinas' commentary on the *De Anima*. I found him a helpful ally (along with Philoponus and Brentano), whose idea of spiritual change encouraged me to put forward what was thought to be a shocking proposal, to the effect that Aristotle believes that, when he sees red or hears middle C, nothing happens save that he sees red and hears middle C. Contrary to modern preconceptions, there is no material process underlying perception, none at all. Just the perception.[5]

I still hold to this interpretation of Aristotle and I still find Aquinas an ally, at least for the case of vision, which he describes as the most spiritual of the senses. My task here is to find out what exactly he means by this, with a view to determining how close his theory of perception is to Aristotle's. For spiritual change has also been debated in the scholarly literature on Aquinas. Writing about Aquinas' theory of perception, D. W. Hamlyn had this to say:

> Aquinas believes, therefore, that corresponding to the physical change in the sense-organ there is a spiritual change resulting in a *phantasma*, which is a particular mental entity.[6]

To which Sheldon M. Cohen replied with a mass of evidence to show that the mind–body dualism of Hamlyn's account (which has a long scholarly tradition behind it) is foreign to Aquinas. When he speaks of the reception of sensible form without matter as a spiritual change, he does not mean it is a mental event in any sense that contrasts with 'physical', but that it is a peculiar kind of physical event.[7] I think Cohen is right about this.[8] But he has difficulty explaining just what kind of physical event it is. Perhaps Aristotle, and an Aristotelian scholar, can help.

To my mind, both the debate about Aristotle and the debate || about Aquinas illustrate how difficult it is for us to think our way back into the framework of Aristotelian physics, so deeply has our conception of the

---

[3] Sorabji 1979, esp. 49–50; further defended in Sorabji 1992.
[4] Burnyeat 1995: 433, with n. 38, explains why *DA* I.1, carefully read, does not put perception on a par with anger.
[5] Burnyeat 1992b, backed up in detail for sight and hearing by Burnyeat 1995, and in still greater detail for all five senses by Johansen 1998, [cf. Brentano 1977].
[6] Hamlyn 1961: 47–8.   [7] Cohen 1982.   [8] Pasnau 1997: 35–6 agrees.

physical been affected by Descartes and the seventeenth century. But that is a conclusion I must argue for.

Meanwhile, I ask readers to pardon the autobiographical elements in this essay. As one party to the debate about Aristotle, I can hardly avoid them. Since, moreover, Richard Sorabji is also writing in this volume, I should explain that on Aquinas we are basically at one.[9] The main disagreement between us is about whether Aquinas is as good an interpreter of Aristotle as I think he is. Sorabji offers a dramatic narrative of how later Aristotelians (ancient and medieval) 'dematerialised' the theory of perception, denying that it always requires a material process; in particular, already in antiquity it became common to hold, as Aquinas does, that the eye does not become coloured when one sees red. On Sorabji's view, Aquinas and his predecessors have rejected an important part of Aristotle's theory.[10] In my narrative, Aquinas has read Aristotle, as a commentator should, with insight and integrity.

A HIERARCHY OF THE SENSES

Let us, then, start with Aquinas in his role as commentator. The first place in his *De Anima* commentary where he says that vision is more spiritual (*spiritualior*) than the other senses is § 417. You will not find any such thesis in Aristotle's *De Anima*,[11] nor Aquinas' argument for it, although the argument is constructed from impeccably Aristotelian premises about the objects of the several sense-modalities. At one extreme, things are visible in virtue of a property that || earthly bodies share with celestial ones (transparency).[12] At the other extreme, touch is of properties (hot, cold, and the like) which differentiate the elements as such. In between come taste, smell and sound. The first two of these depend on the mixture

---

[9] [Sorabji 2001].   [10] Sorabji 1991.
[11] Although *Nicomachean Ethics* x.5, 1175b36–1176a1, does rank the senses in respect of their purity (καθαρειότης), with sight the most pure and touch the least so, as preparation for a parallel ranking of the pleasures of exercising them. Aristotle does not explain what he means by 'purity' in this context, but the explanation is likely to be ethical, not physical. In Plato, a pure pleasure is one unmixed with pain and the satisfaction of felt needs like hunger and thirst. In Aristotle, seeing is a standard example of something we value and enjoy for its own sake, rather than as the means to some further goal; this is less true, he adds, of the other senses (*Met.* A.1, 980a21–6; Θ.6, 1048b23 and 33–4; Θ.8, 1050a24–5 and 35–6; *EE* II.1, 1219a16; *EN* 1.6, 1096b16–19). Aquinas sets up his hierarchy in quite different terms, which in his *Ethics* commentary, § 2056, he proceeds to impose on Aristotle's brief remarks about purity.
[12] Aristotle holds that transparency is required both in the medium of sight and in the objects seen, whose colour depends on the transparent elements in their material composition. But for his present purpose Aquinas does not go into details.

of hot and cold, wet and dry in a body's composition, while the cause of sound is local (rectilinear) motion: the striking of one body against another to start the sound, then its transmission to the ear of a perceiver.[13] Since motion, like transparency, is a property shared with celestial bodies (even if theirs is a circular motion), Aquinas can hint at a hierarchy of the senses to mirror the arrangement of the cosmos. Sight is the most spiritual sense, followed by hearing, because they both have something in common with the heavens. Touch comes lowest because it consorts with the elements.

The next paragraph (§ 418) contains a second, quite different argument for the greater spirituality of vision:

> Secundo apparet quod sensus visus est spiritualior ex modo immutationis. Nam in quolibet alio sensu *non est immutatio spiritualis sine naturali*. Dico autem immutationem naturalem prout qualitas recepitur in patiente secundum esse naturae, sicut cum aliquid infrigatur vel calefit aut movetur secundum locum. Immutatio verum spiritualis est secundum quod species recipitur in organo sensus *aut in medio* per modum *intentionis*, et non per modum naturalis formae. Non enim sic recipitur species sensibilis in sensu secundum illud esse quod habet in re sensibili. Patet autem quod in tactu et gustu (qui est tactus quidem) fit alteratio naturalis; calefit enim et infrigatur *aliquid* per contactum calidi et frigidi, et *non fit immutatio spiritualis tantum*. Similiter autem immutatio odoris fit cum motu quadam fumali evaporatione, immutatio soni cum motu locali. Sed in immutatione visus *est sola immutatio spiritualis*. Unde patet quod visus inter omnes sensus est spiritualior, et post hunc auditus.

> Secondly, it is evident from the kind of change it involves that the sense of sight is more spiritual. For in the case of the other senses *there is no spiritual change without natural change*. I call a change natural when the quality is received in the patient in accordance with its natural being, as when something is cooled or warmed or moved in space. But a spiritual change is one whereby the form is received in the organ || of sense, *or in the medium*, as an *intentio*, not as a natural form; that is, the sensible form is not received in the sense in accordance with the being it has in the sensible object. Now it is obvious that in the case of touch and taste (which is a sort of touch) there is a natural alteration. *Something* is warmed or chilled due to contact with a thing that is hot or cold, and there is *not only a spiritual change*. Similarly, the change induced by smell is associated with a certain smoky vapour, and the change induced by sound is associated with local

---

[13] The closely related passage at *ST*, 1a, q. 78, a. 3 mentions both stages: 'sonus ex percussione causatur et aeris commotione'. The commentary is less explicit, but I incline to think that § 417 has the first stage in view, § 418 the second.

movement. But in the change of sight *there is nothing but spiritual change.* Whence it is clear that of all senses sight is the most spiritual, with hearing next in line.[14]

It will take time to disentangle the various points I have italicised.

First, the contrast between spiritual change and natural change. It is perfectly clear that Aquinas is denying that any part of the eye turns red when one perceives red. The sensible form of red does not colour the eye in the way it colours the object perceived. It is in the eye not as a natural form, but as an *intentio*. About *intentio*, of course, a concept derived from Islamic philosophy, there is a large literature. But origins are less important than the use to which Aquinas puts the idea. And clearly he means to pick out the manner in which a sensible form is present either in the perceiver or in the medium between perceiver and object perceived. The red of a red flag does not colour the medium, or the eye, in the way it colours the flag. In neither the medium nor the eye do we have to do with a natural change.

In my view, this is entirely Aristotelian. For Aristotle holds that perception always involves indirect contact through a medium. The sensible form affects the medium, which in turn affects the organ of sense, and the way it affects the medium is the same as the way it affects the organ. That is why the eye has to be composed of transparent liquid and why the ear must contain still air, so that colours and sounds can make themselves appear, via the medium, in the organ of sense. Both the medium and the eye are said to be coloured – but in a way that contrasts with the way flags and fruit are coloured.[15] It is this special way of being coloured that Aquinas aims to capture by his contrast between spiritual and natural change. ||

All perception requires a spiritual change, but in the case of senses other than sight this is associated with natural change as well. It would be a mistake, however, to suppose that what is meant is Sorabji-type physiological change *in the organ*. For it turns out that hearing involves a natural change *in the medium* rather than the organ (sound is produced in the medium and travels through it to the organ), while odours are associated with a smoky vapour produced by a natural change (evaporation) *in the object smelled.*[16] Only touch and taste (a sort of touch) involve natural change *in the perceiving subject*, as when the stove warms your hand at the same time as you feel its heat. I postpone comment on

---

[14] My translation is at several points indebted to that in Sorabji 1991: 256–7.
[15] See *DA* II.7, 418b4–6 and 11; *Sens.* 3, 439a19–21; *DA* III.2, 425b22–3; Burnyeat 1995: 425–9. Aquinas at §§ 589–90 gives an excellent account of what it means for the eye to be coloured 'in a way'.
[16] *ST*, 1a, q. 78, a. 3 adds that evaporation is the effect of heating (a natural change) in the object smelled.

the studied vagueness of the phrase by which this change is introduced: '*something* is warmed or chilled'. For already an interim conclusion can be drawn. Aquinas holds that the organs of sight, hearing, and smell undergo a spiritual change in perception, nothing more.

A nice question now arises.[17] Does the natural change involved in touch and taste stand to the spiritual change (awareness of cold or sweetness) as matter to form? Does the natural change underlie the spiritual one or is it a mere accompaniment? Aquinas nowhere suggests the former. I shall argue for the latter.

It is Aristotelian doctrine that when two bodies are in direct contact, the hotter is bound to warm the colder and be cooled by it, the colder is bound to cool the hotter and be warmed by it (*GC* 1.6–7). Aristotle does not mention this when discussing touch and taste in the *De Anima* because there he is concerned to characterise perception, and perception is always indirect contact through a medium. Direct contact between eye and a coloured object makes vision impossible, and Aristotle extends this thesis to all the senses, with the result that the hand which warms up when I feel a hot stove is not the organ of touch but its medium; the organ is deep within the body, near the heart. Aquinas knew what he was doing when he wrote that touch is accompanied by natural change in 'something'.[18] The something is not the organ of touch but its fleshy medium, so the warming or cooling are not Sorabji-style material changes in the || organ. Aquinas is doing no more than acknowledge, commonsensically, that a hot thing felt will produce other effects on the perceiver, effects which have nothing to do with the perceiving. Likewise, ice-cream cools the tongue regardless of whether its taste is strawberry or peppermint. Aristotle would not wish to disagree.

I recognise a thoroughly Aristotelian mind at work here, because, when I compare Aquinas with the Aristotelian treatise he is interpreting, I too find a total absence of material processes standing to perceptual awareness as matter to form. The chief difference between Aristotle and his commentator is that Aquinas uses the various kinds of natural change connected with senses other than sight to arrange the five senses in a hierarchy descending from the most to the least spiritual: sight, hearing, smell, taste, touch. This had been done before,[19] but the natural changes Aquinas invokes for the purpose are either changes that Aristotle mentions himself,

---

[17] A question not squarely faced, so far as I can see, by Sorabji 1991.
[18] At § 496 (cf. §§ 433, 437, 526–8, 542 *et alibi*) he acknowledges the general thesis that direct contact with the organ prevents perception.
[19] Especially by Philoponus. See the very interesting narrative, with illustrative texts, in Sorabji 1991.

when explaining the operation of the several senses (e.g. the travelling of sound),[20] or they are changes he would accept (e.g. my hand warming up) but find irrelevant to a scientific account of perception. None of them are changes in the organ itself.

THE HIERARCHY IN THE *SUMMA THEOLOGICA*

We should check this finding against the closely related passage *ST*, 1a, q. 78, a. 3,[21] where Aquinas offers a new, slightly different version of the hierarchy of senses. In the *Summa* he is free from the constraints of the Aristotelian text he was commenting on before, and he allows himself to speak of the hand as an organ of touch:[22]

> Ex parte autem organi, est immutatio naturalis in tactu et gustu: nam et manus tangens calida calefit, et lingua humectatur per humiditatem || saporum. Organum vero olfactus aut auditus nulla naturali immutatione in sentiendo, nisi per accidens.
>
> So far as concerns the organ, natural change is involved in touch and taste; for the hand that touches hot things is warmed, and the tongue is moistened by the wetness of flavours. But the organs of smelling and hearing are not affected in perceiving by any natural change, except accidentally.

This last sentence is welcome confirmation of the interim conclusion just drawn about the organs of sight, hearing, and smell. But at the same time it implies that in perception by touch and taste the hand's warming up and the tongue's being moistened are non-accidental natural changes. Does that cast them as material processes which underlie the spiritual change as matter to form?

No. First, wetness is not a flavour, but an object of touch. The moistening of the tongue is *non*-accidental because, just as colours can only be perceived in light, so flavours can only be perceived in liquid – and liquid is bound to moisten things it is in contact with. But that moistening is accidental *to the perceiving*. Likewise, I suggest, the warming of the hand

---

[20] A complication: from Aristotle's point of view celestial motion is movement properly so called, the travelling of a body or substance, whereas a sound is a sensible form audible first here, then there. Its travelling is what I call a quasi-movement, because Aristotle does not recognise the movement of a wave or vibration as movement properly so called (Burnyeat 1995: 429–30). Consequently, Aristotle might not approve Aquinas' comparison between sounds and stars, which treats both types of travel as natural change, distinguished only as rectilinear vs circular.

[21] Already cited nn. 13 and 16 above.

[22] Thanks to the Galenic tradition, Aquinas knew about nerves and the centrality of the brain. Aristotle knew neither.

is a non-accidental effect of contact with a hot stove, which is nonetheless accidental to the perception of heat.

I make this suggestion because, when Aristotle distinguishes meanings of 'hot' by listing the different effects of heat, among them being hot to the touch, he treats the perception of warmth as a relatively autonomous effect. *A* may be hotter than *B*, in the sense that it burns things more powerfully, without its imparting more heat to them or feeling hotter to the touch.[23] Aquinas does not go into such detail. He merely acknowledges a double effect of heat on perceivers: a spiritual change accompanied by a natural change. He nowhere suggests that the natural change underlies the spiritual one as matter to form.

I conclude that *none* of the natural changes Aquinas mentions in connection with senses other than sight stand to the spiritual change as matter to form. They are a necessary part of the total process, whether as causal antecedents (sound and smell) or concomitant effects (touch and taste). They are not constitutive of perceiving as such. It is not only the organs of sight, hearing, and smell that ‖ undergo a spiritual change and nothing more (save accidentally). Even when hand and tongue are treated as the organs of touch and taste, the awareness of their proper objects is a spiritual change without any underlying material process. The difference between the lowest two senses and the others is that touch and taste are inevitably accompanied by a variety of natural changes which have nothing to do with perceiving. The inevitability of these irrelevant natural changes is to be explained, not by the theory of perception, but by the omnipresent causal role that Aristotelian physics assigns to the elemental qualities hot and cold, wet and dry.

Aquinas says as much himself at q. 78, a. 3, r. 4:

> Sensus gustus, secundum dictum Philosophi, est quaedam species tactus quae est in lingua tantum. Non autem distinguitur a tactu in genere, sed a tactu quantum ad illas species quae per totum corpus diffunduntur. Si vero tactus sit unus sensus tantum, propter unam rationem communem obiecti, dicendum erit quad secundum rationem diversam immutationis distinguitur gustus a tactu. Nam tactus immutatur naturali immutatione, et non solum spirituali, quantum ad organum suum, *secundum qualitatem quae ei proprie obiicitur*. Gustus autem organum non immutatur de necessitate naturali immutatione secundum qualitatem quae ei proprie obiicitur, ut scilicet lingua fiat dulcis vel amara, sed secundum praeambulam qualitatem, in qua fundatur sapor, scilicet secundum humorem, qui est obiectum tactus.

---

[23] See the elaborate discussion in *PA* II.2, 648b11–649b8. Aquinas refers to *PA* in §§ 1 and 5 of his *De Anima* commentary.

The sense of taste, the Philosopher says, is a certain kind of touch found only in the tongue. It is distinguished not from touch in general, but from those kinds of touch that are distributed throughout the body. If, however, touch is a single sense, not several, because there is a single account of its object, then the thing to say is that taste is distinguished from touch by reason of a difference in the kind of change involved. For touch is changed, in respect of its organ, by a natural change, not only by a spiritual one, in accordance with the quality which is its proper object. Whereas there is no necessity for the organ of taste to undergo natural change *in accordance with the quality which is its proper object*. That is, there is no necessity for the tongue to become sweet or bitter. What is necessary is that it should undergo natural change in accordance with the quality which is the prerequisite for and basis of flavour, namely, wetness, one of the objects of touch.

THE HIERARCHY IN THE MEDIA OF PERCEPTION

We may now return to the *De Anima* commentary to consider what Aquinas has to say in §§ 493–5 about spiritual change in the ‖ medium. Here too there is a hierarchy. The visible qualities of things have a more formal and more noble being (*esse formalius et nobilius*) than other sensible features, because transparency links them to the incorruptible bodies in the heavens. Consequently, spiritual change in the medium is effected more by *visibilia* than by other *sensibilia* (§ 495: *spiritualis immutatio fit a visibili magis quam ab aliis sensibilibus*). This could mean either that colours produce spiritual change in the medium more frequently than smells do, or that the change they produce is more spiritual than that effected by other *sensibilia*. The second meaning is indicated by the larger context and by the categorical statement at § 493 that only the medium of sight undergoes spiritual change without natural change; the media of the other senses undergo natural change as well. The evidence for this claim is that contrary colours can be seen simultaneously from different angles through the same body of transparent air, whereas contrary smells diffusing at the same time in the same space tend to interfere with each other. Smells and sounds are also liable to interference by winds. The implication is that both types of interference are due to the natural changes that accompany the spiritual change in the medium.[24] Only the medium of sight undergoes a purely spiritual change, nothing more.

As before, the question arises whether the natural changes stand to the corresponding spiritual ones as matter to form. As before, the answer is

---

[24] Cf. § 420 (*quae habent solum esse intentionale, non faciunt transmutationem naturalem*), *ST*, 1a, q. 67, a. 4 (*intentiones autem non causant transmutationes naturales*).

'No'. This is clear from Aquinas' remarks about vultures. Vultures scent their prey from a vast distance – too far away for the smell to have reached them in smoky vapour from the decaying corpse. The corpse could not produce enough vapour for that without being reduced to nothing, which is not what we observe to happen. Two assumptions are at work here. First, the vapour would have to stretch continuously all the way from corpse to vulture, so that the corpse could be scented at any point along the path of diffusion; Aquinas does not consider the possibility of an isolated cloud of vapour, like a puff of spray from a scent-bottle, drifting on its own from one place to another. Second, and deeply revealing of the mind-set of Aristotelian (as opposed to Atomist) physics, even an elephant's corpse could not give off enough material for the job, || because that presupposes particles or portions of matter (the unit of vaporisation, so to speak) too small for the imagination to grasp.

Aquinas' solution is that the smoky vapour does not reach as far as the vultures, but the spiritual change in the medium extends beyond the point where the vapour is exhausted. If the spiritual change extends further than the natural change, the former does not need the latter as its underlying material process. In which case, even when both are present it cannot be said that the one is (hypothetically) necessary for the other. Nor does Aquinas suggest a different material substratum to replace the smoky vapour. Within the framework of Aristotelian physics it follows that the two changes, the natural and the spiritual, were never related as matter to form. They were merely concomitant.

Receiving form without matter

De Anima 11.12 is the chapter in which Aristotle, having gone through the five senses one by one to explain how each is affected by its proper objects, generalises to an account of perception as such. It is in this generalisation that we encounter, for the first time in the treatise, the celebrated formula 'receiving sensible forms without matter':

> The generalisation we should make about all perception is that a sense is what is capable of receiving sensible forms without matter, as wax receives the marking of the ring without the iron or gold; it takes on the golden or brazen marking, but not insofar as it is gold or insofar as it is bronze. Likewise, the individual sense is affected by some thing that has colour or taste or sound, but not by these insofar as each is said to be such and such a thing; it is affected by them insofar as each is of a certain quality and according to its form. (424a17–24)

In commenting on this text at §§ 551-3, Aquinas gives what I believe to be the obviously correct interpretation of Aristotle's contrast between receiving a sensible form with, and receiving it without, matter. The Sorabji interpretation has it that the eye-jelly is reddened, the organ of touch is warmed, without any red or warm matter being transferred from the object perceived.[25] On Aquinas' reading, the point is not about the transfer of matter from agent to ‖ patient (that is not required even in ordinary natural change, e.g. when fire warms the air around it), but about how the matter of the patient comes to be disposed as a result of interacting with the agent. The patient receives a sensible form with matter when its matter becomes disposed to that form in the same way as it is already disposed in the agent; the patient, in other words, becomes like the agent both in matter and in form, so that both agent and patient are red or warm in the same way. The patient receives a sensible form without matter when it becomes like the agent in form without becoming similarly disposed in its matter. The patient is red or warm in a way, but not in the way the agent is. The sensible forms red and warmth are present in the perceiver in a different manner from the manner they are present in the object perceived.

Fine, you may say, but what manner is that? So far the characterisation is negative. We are told that the sensible form is not present in the perceiver in the way it is present in the object perceived, which echoes Aquinas' earlier statement that the form is not received in the sense in accordance with its natural being, the being it has in the sensible object (§ 418, quoted above). These negative phrases are no better than Aristotle's vague talk of the eye or the medium being coloured in a way. Should not a commentary find something more positive to say? Our attention may quicken when at the end of § 553 we meet this:

> ... alterius modi esse habet forma in sensu et in re sensibili. Nam in re sensibili habet esse naturale, in sensu autem habet *esse intentionale et spirituale*.
>
> ... the form has a different mode of being in the sense and in the sensible object. In the latter it has natural being, but in the sense it has *intentional and spiritual being*.

But it is not clear that this tells us more than we know already.

Both 'intentional' and 'spiritual' are much-used terms of art from previous medieval philosophy. Do they illuminate the present context by

---
[25] Sorabji 1979: 52, with n. 28, further defended in Sorabji 1992: 217-18.

importing from outside an independently established positive meaning to fill out the negative characterisations that we have made do with so far? Or do they simply replace those characterisations with a handy positive label?[26] Aquinas gives no gloss on either term, || and we have already rejected Hamlyn's idea that 'spiritual' equates with 'mental'. On occasion, knowledge of the previous history of a term may be a hindrance as much as a help to understanding.[27] Origins, to repeat, are less important than the way Aquinas *uses* 'intentional' and 'spiritual' to elucidate the Aristotelian text he is commenting on. They pick out the very same thing as Aristotle expresses by 'form without matter'.

Accordingly, I suggest that they helpfully emphasise the aspect of Aristotle's meaning which Sorabji's interpretation denies, namely, that receiving form without matter is not a physiological process underlying perceptual awareness. It *is* perceptual awareness of something, a mode of cognition. From the beginning of his *De Anima* Aristotle treats perception as the most basic cognitive capacity of soul; he regularly couples 'perceiving' with cognitive verbs like γιγνώσκειν, γνωρίζειν.[28] No medieval reader would be surprised to find the terms *intentionalis* and *spiritualis* at work in a discussion of cognition.

For an Aristotelian, both sensible and intelligible forms are present to the world in two irreducibly different ways, one of which is cognitive of the other. The form of tiger, for example, is active in the forests as the organising principle of the life of tigers, but it may also be present, differently, in the intellect of a zoologist who has reached a principled understanding of that kind of life. Similarly, the orange and black colouring of a tiger's striped coat will also be present, differently, in the eye of its mate as they hunt together, watching each other's movements. Both intellect and the senses are powers of *receptivity*. In both intellectual understanding and (proper object) perception we submit ourselves to being in-formed (as we still say) by the very objects we receive information about. When a cognitive state is wholly determined by its object, sensible or intelligible, the result is objective truth.

To express this idea of determination by a sensible or intelligible object, Aristotle adapts the language of assimilation which he develops in *De Generatione et Corruptione* 1.7 to analyse the kind of alteration that occurs

---

[26] This is the view taken by Pasnau 1997: 37–41: *all* Aquinas means by 'intentional' is 'not natural'.

[27] This, I am sorry to say, is the lesson to be learned from Tellkamp 1999: 56–129. The lesson the author would wish us to learn is that Aquinas' concept of spiritual change is an incoherent amalgam of irreconcilable philosophical traditions.

[28] 1.2, 404b9ff.; 1.5, 409b24–5ff.

when a fire is lit to warm a cold room. Agent and || patient start out with contrary qualities from the same range, and the first makes the second qualitatively like itself, or more like than it was before. This is a case of what Aquinas calls natural change, involving both form and matter. Aristotle in *De Anima* II.5 announces that he will apply the *GC* schema to perception, but he spends much of that chapter on a complicated account of the ways in which perceptual assimilation is not like the case of fire warming a cold room. Perceiving warmth, he suggests, is either not alteration at all or it is alteration of a different kind from becoming warm in the way the air in the room does.[29] Aristotle's explanation is as negative as Aquinas'. The formula 'receiving sensible forms without matter', introduced in *DA* II.12, is equally negative. Both philosophers take a negative route to reach a concept of change applicable to perception. More on this later. Meanwhile, even if Aquinas' terms 'intentional' and 'spiritual' do little more than remind us that perceptual cognition is what we are discussing, they are good labels, and we should be glad to have them. For remember that Aristotle makes the power of perception definitive of what an animal is. To be an animal is to have a cognitive capacity for acquiring information about the world through the senses – by receiving forms without matter.

As for *intentiones* in the medium, while they are not themselves cognitions (for a reason to be clarified later), their sole function is to bring about cognition.[30] When Foster and Humphries come to § 418 of the commentary, where I translated 'But a spiritual change is one whereby the form is received in the organ of sense, *or in the medium*, as an *intentio*, not as a natural form', with *intentio* left in the original Latin, they translate *intentio* by 'as a form causing knowledge'. Inelegant, no doubt, but a shot in the right direction.[31]

BODILY CHANGE

So far I have argued that there is no sign in Aquinas of the view that perception requires an underlying material process. In this respect || perception is importantly different from anger, which requires boiling

---

[29] Elucidation and discussion in Burnyeat 2002 [Chapter 5 in this volume]. [30] Cf. n. 24 above.
[31] Foster and Humphries 1951. They are attacked for their effort by Pasnau 1999: xxii–xxiii, who in § 418 writes simply 'in the manner of an intention'. This connects with his view that the meaning of *intentio* is purely negative (n. 26 above). But in general Pasnau is right that their translation lacks the precision needed for philosophy. Their persistent rendering of *immutatio naturalis* by 'material change' (e.g. at the start of § 418 itself) is deeply wrong, as will appear.

blood to serve as matter to the relevant form, desire for revenge. Aquinas goes into various natural changes associated with perception, but on perception itself he remains thoroughly Aristotelian.

This brings me back to the intersection of the debate about Aristotle's theory of perception and the debate about Aquinas' theory of perception. A key text here is *ST*, 1a, q. 75, a. 3:

> Aristoteles posuit quod solum intelligere, inter opera animae, sine organo corporeo exercetur. Sentire vero, et consequentes operationes animae sensitivae, manifeste accidunt cum aliqua corporis immutatione, sicut in videndo immutatur pupilla per speciem coloris; et idem apparet in aliis. Et sic manifestum est quod anima sensitiva non habet aliquam operationem propriam per seipsam, sed omnis operatio sensitivae animae est conjuncti.
>
> Aristotle held that, of the functions of the soul, understanding alone is exercised without a corporeal organ. Sensation, however, and the attendant operations of the sensitive soul manifestly involve some change of the body, as when in seeing the pupil of the eye is changed by the form of colour. The same thing is apparent in the case of the other senses. Hence it is clear that the sensitive soul has no operation peculiar to itself, but every operation of the sensitive soul belongs to the composite.

This text has featured in both debates, both the debate about Aristotle and the debate about Aquinas. I shall call it text T.

It was one of the texts that Cohen cited to rebut Hamlyn's idea that a spiritual change is a mental event. According to Cohen, with whom I agree, the bodily change that Aquinas refers to is not distinct from the seeing. It *is* the seeing, which occurs when the pupil is changed by the form (*species*) of colour. This change, the seeing, is not a mental event *in any sense that contrasts with 'physical'*:

> If by 'a mental event' we mean an awareness, then under certain conditions the spiritual reception of a sensible form is both a mental event and a physical event, but it is never not a physical event. (Aquinas allows for acts of awareness that are not physical events, but only in intellection and volition, not in sensation.)[32] ||

A decade later Martha Nussbaum and Hilary Putnam brought up text T to show I was wrong to borrow Aquinas' notion of spiritual change to help articulate my shocking interpretation of Aristotle.[33] But Nussbaum and Putnam read T very differently from Cohen. They take Aquinas' 'change

---

[32] Cohen 1982: 195.
[33] Nussbaum and Putnam 1992: 53; Burnyeat 1992b: 21, (quoted above). Our translations of T differ, but not on any point of substance.

of the body' to refer to some (unspecified) material changes in the eye *concomitant* with the seeing. Seeing is becoming aware of a sensible quality such as red, but this cognitive achievement requires material changes in the eye. Unlike Hamlyn and Sorabji, whose Aquinas diverges markedly from their respective Aristotles,[34] Nussbaum and Putnam agree with me that Aquinas' theory of perception is close to Aristotle's. The issue between us is whether either philosopher invokes material processes to underlie the seeing. They say both do. I have argued elsewhere that Aristotle does not,[35] and I hope to have persuaded readers of this essay that Aquinas does not do so either. At least not in his *De Anima* commentary or in the passages from question 78 of the *Summa Theologica* discussed earlier. So the issue is whether T presents a radically different view.

Let us, then, look more closely at the Nussbaum–Putnam reading of T:

> Aquinas never, in fact, adopted the entirety of the Burnyeat position. For although in his commentary on *De Anima* he does interpret the reception of form without matter in much the way Burnyeat says he does – awareness of red being a non-reducible intentional item – he consistently holds that each act of perceiving has material necessary conditions, and that these material conditions are *changes in the sense-organs*: 'For as things exist in sensation they are free indeed from matter, but not without their individuating material conditions,[36] nor apart from a bodily organ' (*In* II *De Anima*, Lect. 5, § 284). Free from matter, in that I become aware of red without my sense-organ literally going red. But there is none the less some concomitant material change in that organ. The *Summa* asserts this repeatedly, and unequivocally. ||

And then follows text T, with some further supporting references.[37]

The proper medieval thing to say at this point is *Distinguo*. I distinguish, as indeed Nussbaum and Putnam do in their second sentence, the claim (a) that there are material necessary conditions for perception, and the claim (b) that these necessary conditions are material changes in the sense-organ. With Aquinas, I accept (a), but not (b):

---

[34] Compare ch. 3 of Hamlyn 1961 with ch. 1 and with the more detailed account of Aristotle in Hamlyn 1968; and compare Sorabji 1991: 228, with 241–4.

[35] Burnyeat 1992b, 1995.

[36] This part of the quotation is irrelevant to the debate about what happens in the sense-organ, because it concerns the contrast between intellect and perception, and the point that perception is of external particulars, not universals: see the surrounding context, §§ 282–5.

[37] 1a, q. 75, a. 4 ('sensing is not an operation of the soul by itself'); 1a, q. 76, a. 1, *'et saepe'*. (The emphases in the quotation are theirs, not mine.) It is hard to know how to respond to *et saepe*. Q 76, a. 1, like q. 75, a. 4, only says that perceiving requires a bodily organ, as do q. 77, a. 5 and q. 78, a. 3 (quoted earlier), and *Quaestiones De Anima*, 19. But that, I am about to argue, is beside the point.

> Est autem alia operatio animae infra istam [*sc.* operatio animae rationalis], quae quidem fit per organum corporale, non tamen per aliquam corpoream qualitatem. Et talis est operatio animae sensibilis, quia etsi calidum et frigidum, et humidum et siccum, et aliae huiusmodi qualitates corporeae requirantur ad operationem sensus, non tamen ita quod mediante virtute talium qualitatum operatio animae sensibilis procedat; *sed requiruntur solum ad debitam dispositionem organi.*
>
> Below this [*sc.* the operation of the rational soul] there is another operation of the soul, which is indeed performed through a corporeal organ, but not through some corporeal quality. Such is the operation of the sensitive soul. For although hot and cold, wet and dry, and other such corporeal qualities are required for the operation of a sense, they are not required in such a way that the operation of the sensitive soul proceeds by means of the power of such qualities. *They are required only to ensure the proper disposition of the organ.* (*ST*, 1a, q. 78, a. 1)

There are indeed material conditions necessary for a given sense-organ to be capable of functioning. According to Aristotle, the eye must contain transparent liquid, the ear still air, and the organ of touch must be at a mean of temperature and hardness. But these are static, standing conditions, not processes or events underlying the act of perception.[38] Aquinas is as usual less detailed on physiological matters, but he clearly takes the same line. Provided the sense-organ has the proper disposition, it is ready for the spiritual change which is perception. Like Aristotle, he stops at claim (a), as he did in the *De Anima* commentary, § 200, where the sensitive soul is contrasted on the one hand with the vegetative, which does work through the active and passive powers of sensible qualities, and on the other ‖ hand with the intellect, which lacks even the sensitive soul's dependence on a bodily organ.[39]

And it is the spiritual change that Aquinas describes in text T. The 'change of the body' is none other than the change immediately specified: 'as when in seeing the pupil of the eye is changed by the form of colour'. It is the receiving of form without matter. No amount of force can extract from T a reference to a material process underlying the taking on of form without matter. The taking on of form without matter is, as Putnam and Nussbaum agree, my becoming aware of red without my sense-organ

---

[38] For more on this point, see Burnyeat 1995: 422–3, and Johansen 1998.
[39] Pasnau 1997: 41–2 and 78, is another modern scholar unwilling to give up claim (b). Aquinas, he says, reasonably leaves open the details or 'mechanisms' of how spiritual alteration happens. In other words, Pasnau assumes there *must* be material changes underlying spiritual alteration, even though he is aware that Aquinas nowhere even hints at any. And the image he uses to express that assumption derives from 'the mechanical philosophy'.

literally going red. But for Aquinas, that spiritual change (perceptual awareness) is itself a kind of bodily change.

THE MEANING OF 'PHYSICAL'

This is the hard point to convey to modern readers. When I wrote that Aristotle's 'physical-seeming' descriptions (the organ's becoming like the object, its taking on form without matter, etc.) refer to the animal becoming aware of some sensible quality in the environment, Nussbaum and Putnam took me to have said that perception is not one of the doings of the body, while Sorabji supposed I had denied that any physical change at all is needed in perception.[40] I do plead guilty to having written in a misleading way. Because I was moving to and fro between ancient and modern, I several times used the word 'physical' as a synonymous variant for 'material', in accordance with modern rather than Aristotelian usage.[41] But Aristotelian physics includes form as well as matter. That is why Aquinas has no qualms || about citing a spiritual change (perception of colour), which involves form *without* matter, to make the point that the operations of the sensitive soul all involve a bodily change.

Conversely, Cohen, after establishing that a spiritual change is a physical event, casts about for a way to characterise it in non-cognitive terms. Perhaps, he wonders, 'the *species sensibilis* spiritually received is the reflection of a colour in the pupil of the eye', the pupil being a sort of mirror. He admits that Aristotle at *De Sensu*, 2, 438a5–12, expressly rejects the view, attributed to Democritus, that seeing is mirroring.[42] He should also have mentioned that in his commentary on the *De Sensu*, §§ 48–52 Aquinas explains very clearly why Aristotle is right. He concludes that the reflection of yourself which you see in the eye of someone looking at you has nothing to do with that person's seeing; this is explained rather by the power of sight (*virtus visiva*) in their eye. I would add a further point. The spiritual change in the medium of sight is an *intentio* too, the receiving of form without matter. But the air does not reflect colours. Something has gone badly wrong with Cohen's account.

---

[40] Nussbaum and Putnam 1992: 37 and 45; Sorabji 1992: 220–1. Sorabji's words are echoed by Everson 1997: 85, even though soon afterwards (pp. 103–5) he explains, correctly, that for Aristotle psychological capacities and activities are themselves physical capacities and activities.

[41] Burnyeat 1992b: 16, 18, 19, 21 (quoted above), 22. Let me signal here the subtitle of my paper, 'A Draft', and the preface explaining why I was reluctant to see it published in its current rough form, which dates from 1983. In Burnyeat 1995, where I am concentrating on Aristotle, I observe his distinction between 'physical' and 'material', as explained pp. 11–22.

[42] Cohen 1982: 207.

I suspect that the root of the trouble is the word 'physical' and its modern meanings. Reflection is a phenomenon which a modern philosopher can comfortably accept as 'wholly physical', even if they would hesitate to say the same about seeing or the awareness of colour. 'Wholly physical' is indeed how Sorabji characterises the sensory process depicted by Cohen, against which he proposes that *intentio* in Aquinas should be understood as non-physical information (a 'message') physically housed in eye or medium.[43] While Cohen seems to be uncomfortable with the idea of a physical or bodily event in which nothing happens save that an animal becomes aware of red, Sorabji includes a non-physical message in Aquinas' account of perceiving. But Aquinas himself, as we have seen, happily insists that seeing red is (i) a purely spiritual change, nothing more and (ii) a bodily change to the eye where the form of red is received without matter. And I take it that all parties – ancient, medieval, and modern – would agree that 'bodily' implies 'physical'.

The problem is that they might not be agreeing to quite the same thing. Let 'physical' cover anything within the scope of physics. Then ‖ it will depend on one's physics what 'physical' implies and what it contrasts with. Since Descartes and the seventeenth century, 'physical' has tended to contrast with 'mental', a word that cannot be traced further back than Augustine.[44] In the Aristotelian scheme of the sciences, psychology – the study of soul, which includes a good deal of (what we now call) our mental life[45] – is part of physics. Aristotle's *De Anima* opens by saying it is the most valuable part, both because it admits of the greatest precision and because soul is the best and most wonderful object that physics can study.

This is not mere hand-waving. I have already mentioned that the analysis of perception in *DA* II.5 is a refined version of the account of alteration developed in *GC* I.7 for action and passion in general. The schema which explains what happens when a fire warms your room is adapted to explain what happens when you notice the red colour of the

---

[43] Sorabji 1991: 243. His reason: 'This would be in line with the sense of "intention" we found in Avicenna and Albert.'

[44] The earliest citation in the *Thesaurus Linguae Latinae* is Augustine, *De genesi ad litteram* XII, vii, 16 [*PL*, 34, 459], which names three kinds of *visio: corporale, spirituale, intellectuale*. The third is so called *ab intellectu, quia mentale a mente ipsa vocabuli novitate nimis absurdum est, ut dicamus*. (Aquinas refers to this text at *ST*, 1a, q. 78, a. 4, but only for its use of the word *spirituale*.) *Mentalis* here is a synonym for *intellectualis*. Much philosophy will have to go by before the word approximates to our present-day use of 'mental'.

[45] Only a good deal of it, because 'Not all soul is nature' (*PA* I.1, 641b9–10). Physics extends as far as change extends and no further (*Met.* E.1). Intellectual learning falls within its scope (see my next paragraph), but other aspects of the intellect are reserved for first philosophy (metaphysics).

chair you are sitting in. Add some more refinements and it will also explain what happens when you learn enough Latin to read Aquinas in the original (*DA* III.4). All three happenings are examples of assimilation. Cognitive assimilation, whether it be perception or intellectual learning, falls under the same overall schema as ordinary physical alteration. The task of Aristotelian psychology is to differentiate it from ordinary alteration while staying within the framework of Aristotelian physics. Hence the negative approach that both Aristotle and Aquinas adopt to demarcate two types of *unordinary* physical alteration. For perception they subtract the underlying material process. For intellectual learning they go further and deny dependence on a bodily organ. Cognition becomes a limiting case of alteration, one of the four types of change defined in *Physics* III.1–3,[46] and its analysis the crowning achievement of an ambitious || theory of action and passion whose foundations were laid in *GC* I.7.[47]

After all, the form which the sense-organ receives without matter is the very same form as exists with matter in the object perceived. If it was not the same, perception would not reveal objective truth. Form and matter are basic principles of Aristotelian physics. Form's presence in the sense-organ without matter is therefore as physical a fact as its presence with matter in the object perceived. If its presence in the sense-organ is awareness, and awareness is a mental phenomenon in the modern sense, then for Aristotle and Aquinas perception is both physical and mental. Just this, of course, was what Cohen had so effectively shown, before he went off after reflections.

Thus both natural and spiritual change fall within the realm of physics, because both involve form. The contrast between them is not that spiritual change is (wholly or partly) non-physical, but that it is a change of form alone. It is a physical, but not a material change.

THE POWER OF PERCEPTION

Finally, we may return to spiritual change in the medium. What is the difference between an *intentio* in the medium, which is not awareness, and an *intentio* in the eye of a perceiver, which is? Cohen asks a similar

---

[46] Where intellectual learning (hardly the sort of example you would expect to find in a modern introduction to physics) is still on a par with ordinary alteration.

[47] Aristotle starts his account of perception in *DA* II.5 with cross-references to both *GC* I.7 and *Ph*. III.1–3 (417a1–2, 16–17). For detailed discussion of the connections between these three texts, see Burnyeat 2002 [Chapter 5 in this volume]. Aquinas' *De Anima* commentary contains numerous references to the *Physics* and five to *GC*: §§ 351, 439, 539, 546, 720.

question. Having decided that the *intentio* in the eye is some sort of reflection, he wants to know why this reflection is a sensation, given that reflections elsewhere (in a mirror, on a bald man's head) are not. Not finding any text where Aquinas addresses this issue, he suggests an answer in terms of desire. Reflection in a person's eye, unlike a reflection on their bald head, is apt to produce in them a desire for (or aversion from) the thing reflected.[48]

But this makes matters worse, since, to repeat a point I made earlier, an *intentio* in the medium is not a reflection at all. In fact, ‖ Aquinas does tell us why an *intentio* in a sense-organ is a perception whereas the same *intentio* in the medium is not:

> ... odorare est sic pati aliquid ab odore quod sentiat odorem. Aer autem non sic patitur ut sentiat, *quia non habet potentiam sensitivam*; sed sic patitur ut sit sensibilis, inquantum scilicet est medium in sensu.
>
> Smelling is what happens when something is affected by a scent in such a way as to smell it. Air is not affected in the same way, *since it has no power of perception*. It is affected in such a way as to become perceptible, inasmuch as it is a medium for perception. (§ 563, commenting on *DA* II.12, 424b14–18)[49]

What a very simple answer! I have the power of perception, the air around me does not. A modern reader could be forgiven for thinking it no answer at all. But within the framework of Aristotelian physics it is complete and conclusive.

Aristotelian physics makes frequent use of explanations that appeal to a power or capacity (δύναμις in Aristotle, *potentia* in Aquinas). The power of perception is just one of many examples where a power defines an essence or nature, in this case what it is to be an animal, and, for an Aristotelian, reference to an essence or nature is frequently a terminus of explanation. That is where explanation gets back to a first principle and comes satisfactorily to an end, in psychology as in other fields of inquiry (*DA* I.1, 402a7–8, b25–6). Thus when we are told that an animal's power of perception is what makes the difference between what scent does to the air and what it does to the perceiver, we should not ask for more. The explanation does not add to what happens, which in both cases is a receiving of form without matter. What it adds is a difference in *where*

---

[48] Cohen 1982: 207–9.
[49] For debate about the original Aristotelian context, see Burnyeat 1992b: 25–6, and Sorabji 1992: 218–19.

it happens: in a being which has, or a being which does not have, the power of cognition. End of explanation.

A true Aristotelian is one who is content with this appeal to a power or potency, who resists the demand for underlying material processes to activate the power or a categorical (non-dispositional) base to explain it.[50] That demand, in its strongest ancient version, should have been quashed by the detailed critique in *GC* 1.8 of the || theory of imperceptible pores which the Atomists posit to explain what happens in medium and sense-organ alike.

But crude as ancient Atomism may look to us now, one of its key tenets has become an important part of the modern scientific outlook, namely, the idea that life came relatively late in the formation of the world we inhabit. For a long time this world contained only inanimate things. In due course these inanimate things gave rise to living creatures of ever increasing complexity. At some stage in this evolutionary process, a new power came into being: the power of perception. It is difficult to treat a power that has emerged in this way from simpler antecedents as a terminus of explanation, a fundamental fact which needs no accounting for, not even in historical or evolutionary terms. Aristotle can treat such powers as first principles of explanation because he is vehemently opposed to the idea that life came late. For him the species are eternal, as is the world itself. The power of perception never emerged from anything. Aquinas can do the same, despite the Christian doctrine that the world was created by God. For it was created complete with the whole *scala naturae*. The power of perception was there from the outset, by God's *fiat*.[51]

THE MORAL

It is hard for anyone today to lay aside the mind–body contrast we have inherited from Descartes and the seventeenth century, harder still to think oneself back into the framework of Aristotelian physics, where the physical does not contrast with (what we call) the mental, but includes (some of) it. Such is the moral to draw, it seems to me, from this review of two debates, one about Aristotle, the other about Aquinas. None of the parties to these debates would sign up to the philosophy of Descartes. Yet all have been so

---

[50] Pasnau fails this test: recall n. 39 above on 'mechanisms'. As a result, he is led to think that the difference between air and animal is just a matter of degrees of receptivity to sensible form: Pasnau 1997: 47–57.
[51] Details in *ST*, 1a, q. 74.

influenced by him that his distinction between mind and matter, which excludes the mental from the realm of physics, insinuates itself into their language, and thereby into their thought, making it difficult for them to read the ancient and medieval texts they are debating. The result is confusion, unclarity, argument at cross-purposes.[52] I include myself in the indictment. I should not have used the phrase 'physical-seeming' to characterise Aristotle's talk of the sense-organ becoming like the object, its being affected, acted on or altered by sensible qualities, its taking on sensible form without matter. These are both physical (in Aristotle's sense) and mental (in the modern sense). My lack of clarity, together with my borrowing Aquinas' phrase 'spiritual change', led critics to think I meant to deny that perception for Aristotle is a physical or bodily event. Perhaps I was not distinctly aware, way back in 1983, of what I meant.[53] Still, as philosophers, we should all have known that some things are what they seem.[54]

---

[52] In the Aquinas debate, the critique of Cohen in Haldane 1983 is vitiated by his conflation of 'material' and 'physical'. In the Aristotle debate as presented in Nussbaum and Rorty 1992, only Frede 1992: 104 and Code and Moravcsik 1992: 130–1, are totally clear that 'physical' does not equate with 'material'.

[53] Recall n. 41 above.

[54] I should like to thank Dominik Perler for the stimulus of his 1997 seminar in Oxford on 'Medieval Theories of Intentionality', in which we discussed a number of the texts referred to here.

CHAPTER 7

Epistēmē

For Jonathan Barnes

Once upon a time in the Anglo-Saxon world there was a great debate among students of Plato. Did he, or did he not, become clear about the distinction between knowledge *that*, knowledge *how*, and knowledge *by acquaintance*? The time – as Jonathan Barnes will remember, and others will know by testimony, reading or hearsay – was the 50s, 60s, and early 70s of the last century: the twentieth century of the Christian era.

There was a reason why the debate occurred then, not earlier, and scarcely since. The reason was Gilbert Ryle, whose influence on the study of ancient philosophy in Anglophone countries was deeper and more long-lasting than his influence on philosophy at large. By 'influence' I do not mean that Ryle had a school of followers. Any such suggestion would be injustice to a man who said, deploring the very idea of schools and followers in philosophy: 'There could, in my view, be nothing more unwholesome than unanimity among philosophers.'[1] Rather, the measure of Ryle's influence is the extent to which *the agenda for discussion* in Anglophone Platonic scholarship was for some considerable time set by his work.[2] It is certainly due to him that high on the agenda in the 50s, 60s, and early 70s of the twentieth century was the 'epistemic troika', as I shall call it, of knowledge that, knowledge how, and knowledge by acquaintance. At the same time, in the same years, the very same topic was central to mainstream epistemology.

The epistemic troika can be viewed as a codification of two contrasts that Ryle originally exploited in quite different contexts. The first of these, the contrast between knowledge by acquaintance and knowing that, derived from Bertrand Russell and was important to Ryle in his reflections

---

[1] Ryle 1937. Cited from Ryle 1971a: 153–69, at p. 156.
[2] For more detail on Ryle and classical studies, see Burnyeat 2004a.

on Russell and on Wittgenstein's *Tractatus*. It features importantly in Ryle's seminal paper 'Plato's *Parmenides*', published in *Mind* (1939),[3] and in the famous unpublished paper on Socrates' dream in the *Theaetetus*, ‖ read to an amazingly distinguished audience of classicists and philosophers at the Oxford Philological Society on 15 February 1952.[4]

The contrast between knowing how and knowing that, on the other hand, was important to Ryle in his reflections on Descartes and the myth of the ghost in the machine. First broached under the now familiar title 'Knowing How and Knowing That' in a Presidential Address to the Aristotelian Society (1945–6), it features strongly in *The Concept of Mind* (1949), and it entered into the study of ancient philosophy through John Gould's highly original but now largely forgotten book *The Development of Plato's Ethics* (1955), which attracted a sternly critical review from Gregory Vlastos.[5] Gould invoked Ryle in an attempt to make sense of the Socratic paradox 'Virtue is knowledge' by construing the knowledge in question as knowledge how rather than knowledge that. At the same time, he summoned Bruno Snell as witness to his claim that knowing how had been the basic meaning of Greek knowledge vocabulary since Homer. Scholars had misunderstood Socrates 'in the misleading light of a later attachment to intellectual or contemplative theories of the mind, which stem in the main from the subsequent work of Plato and Aristotle'.[6]

Place Ryle's two contrasts together and you have the epistemic troika with which it soon became obligatory for modern books on epistemology to begin: so A. J. Ayer, *The Problem of Knowledge* (1956), Israel Scheffler, *Conditions of Knowledge: an Introduction to Epistemology and Education* (1965), D. W. Hamlyn, *The Theory of Knowledge* (1970), David Pears, *What Is Knowledge?* (1971), Keith Lehrer, *Knowledge* (1974), and many more.[7] They all deal with knowledge that, knowledge how, and knowledge by acquaintance – usually in that order. Place the two contrasts together in the context of ancient philosophy and you produce the question, much discussed when Barnes and I were young: 'How far did Plato arrive at a

---

[3] Ryle 1939. See especially pp. 36–41 in the reprint in Ryle 1971b.
[4] The Minute Book entry recording those present is reproduced in my introduction to the posthumous printing: Ryle 1990: 21–46. On p. 42 after line 22, readers should supply the missing words 'Wittgenstein's – I cannot even claim it was Plato's'; to which Ryle later added '(I *do* now, 1959)'.
[5] Ryle 1945; Gould 1955; Vlastos 1957, reprinted as Vlastos 1981: 204–17.
[6] Gould 1955: 7, citing Snell 1924 and Snell 1953.
[7] Ayer 1956; Scheffler 1965; Hamlyn 1970; Pears 1972; Lehrer 1974.

distinction between knowledge that, knowledge how, and knowledge by acquaintance?'[8]

So much by way of a preliminary 'historicising' of the epistemic troika and its place in twentieth-century intellectual life. My aim, of course, as with much historicising, is to raise the suspicion – at this stage it can be no more than a suspicion – that the troika lacks universal validity. It belongs to its time and place, and tells us more about our own local past than about the language and thought of distant cultures.

This suspicion is strengthened by recent challenges within contemporary philosophy to the very idea of a categorial distinction between knowing that and || knowing how. Impressive arguments have been produced for the thesis that knowing how to do something is as propositional as knowing that such-and-such is the case or knowing when something happened. Needless to say, these arguments have not passed unchallenged.[9] In effect, a post mortem on the epistemic troika has begun.

But what strikes me most when looking back over these discussions, old and new, is their insufficient attention to languages other than English.[10]

---

[8] The first book-length treatment of the issue so formulated was W. G. Runciman's *Plato's Later Epistemology* (Runciman 1962), written while he was attending G. E. L. Owen's graduate seminars at Harvard during the academic year 1958–9.

[9] Leading prosecutors are Stanley and Williamson 2001, followed – more persuasively, in my view (although he spends pages proving the correct but irrelevant point that being *able* to do something on some occasion is not a sufficient condition for *knowing* how to do it) – by Paul Snowdon (Snowdon 2004). For the defence, and gaining my vote: Ian Rumfitt (Rumfitt 2003).

[10] Rumfitt is an impressive exception. His recommendation (Rumfitt 2003: 165) that 'this is an area where a trawl through cross-linguistic data might be of real philosophical interest' is backed by revealingly disparate data from French, ancient Greek, Latin, and Russian. I agree, and will add Italian and German. But first, a word about his Russian examples – in particular about their use of the verb уметь, which Rumfitt, like all my dictionaries, renders as 'know how to'. One case discussed is 'Он умеет плавать' ('He knows how to swim'), said of a man with a broken leg who therefore is currently *unable* to swim. The complication is that if we switch the verbal aspect from imperfective to perfective, as in 'Он сумел убежать из тюрьмы', it is only if the escaping subject has the talents of a Houdini that we can render 'He knew how to escape from prison'. (In the Houdini Museum at Niagara Falls one can learn [come to know, to understand] quite a lot about how [by what skills and devices] it was *that* he made his escapes, but this is far from coming to know how *to do* the same or similar things oneself.) Of anyone else one would translate with something like 'He contrived to escape from prison', which carries no promise that they could do it again. I conclude that уметь *overlaps* with English 'know how to' without *coinciding* with it. I gather that the French 'Il a su (faire quelque chose)' is found in a similar use. This is consistent, I believe, with Edward Craig's impressive defence, in *Knowledge and the State of Nature* (Craig 1990), sections xvi–xvii, of the claim that there needs to be, and is, some point to counting at least certain capacities and/or certain cases of acquaintance as *knowledge*, be it in English or other languages: namely, that such capacities and cases have in common with knowing that the potential to serve as sources of information – for the transmission of knowledge – *for others*. Craig's wonderful book is curiously absent from recent discussion of knowing how.

Brief, oversimplifying contrasts are drawn between *savoir* and *connaître*,[11] *wissen* and *kennen*, *sapere* and *conoscere*, but no attention is paid to differences between, or complications within, the several languages. Typically, the first item in each of these three foreign pairs is twinned with knowing that, why, when, and so on, and the second with knowledge by acquaintance of a person or thing – and there the matter is left. The challenge of ancient Greek is that it has *three* verbs for knowing, *none* of which can be exclusively assigned to one or other member of the epistemic troika.

The usual way to begin the epistemic troika is linguistic. We are invited to contrast three types of grammatical construction which the English verb 'to know' can admit: ||

(1) I know that the sun is shining: K + that-clause.
(2) I know how to ride a bicycle: K + how + verbal infinitive clause.
(3) I know John Smith: K + direct object noun phrase.

But these linguistic criteria are not firm enough to deliver the philosophical goods. If I gesture at someone riding a bicycle and say:

(1)# I know that *that* (pointing) is how to ride a bicycle

what I attribute to myself is somewhat ambiguous. Is it knowledge 'how' or knowledge 'that'? And while

(2)# He knows how to find her

might on occasion ascribe skill in games of 'hide and seek', it would usually amount to

(3)# He knows the answer to the question 'Where is she?'

in which the construction 'knows' + noun phrase indicates something that a philosopher would wish to count as knowledge that – for example, 'He knows that she is in her counting house.'

---

[11] Here I quote Pierre Pellegrin's translation of *APo.* 1.2, 71b9–13 (Pellegrin 2005). Under the section heading 'Le *savoir* scientifique' [Scientific knowledge [*savoir*]], he writes: 'Nous pensons *connaître scientifiquement* chaque chose ... lorsque nous pensons *connaître* la cause du fait de laquelle la chose est, *savoir* que c'est bien la cause de la chose et que cette chose ne peut pas être autrement qu'elle n'est. Il est donc clair que le *savoir scientifique* est quelque chose de cette sorte' ['We think we know each thing scientifically [*connaître scientifiquement*] ... when we think that we know [*connaître*] the cause why the thing is so, i.e. that we know [*savoir*] that this is indeed the cause of the fact that the thing is so, and that the thing could not be otherwise than it is. So it is clear that scientific knowledge [*savoir scientifique*] is something of this sort']. It seems clear that the two verbs differ more in the grammatical constructions they admit than they do in meaning. As Craig notes, the French call epistemology *la théorie de la connaissance*, while the Germans call it *Erkenntnistheorie* without restricting its scope to the direct object constructions standard for *connaître* and *kennen* (Craig 1990: 140–1).

I am well aware that a more subtle grammatical analysis would show that the syntax of (3) # is different from that of (3). Whereas 'John Smith' is a plain proper name, a phrase like 'the answer to the question' is the nominalisation of a complex propositional clause. But that is my point. The characterisation '"knows" + direct object' does not suffice to pick out the kind of knowledge that *philosophers* wish to classify as acquaintance-knowledge. Only some noun phrases will do.[12]

Likewise, the characterisation 'K + how + verbal infinitive clause' does not suffice to pick out the skills, capacities, and flairs in which Ryle was philosophically interested. Only some uses of 'knows how' will do. The passage from superficial linguistic features to substantive philosophical distinctions is neither quick nor easy.

All the more problematic is the attempt to base the epistemic troika on superficial linguistic features of a distant dead language such as ancient Greek. In the 50s, 60s, and early 70s of the twentieth century the attempt might begin from an assumption that γιγνώσκειν/γνῶσις could be glossed as knowledge by acquaintance, and ἐπίστασθαι/ ἐπιστήμη as knowledge that.[13] The idea was that if the author of Plato's || later dialogues could be found distinguishing between γνῶσις and ἐπιστήμη, and γιγνώσκειν and ἐπίστασθαι, he could be patted on the back for at last distinguishing between knowledge by acquaintance and knowledge that.

More commonly, it was taken for granted that any coupling of a knowledge verb with a noun phrase in direct object construction signals knowledge by acquaintance. All that talk in the *Republic* about the philosopher knowing the Forms – this proved that when he wrote the *Republic*, Plato was hopelessly and confusedly attached to an acquaintance model for knowledge.[14] He was in the grip of the idea that knowledge, or the best

---

[12] I italicise *philosophers* because we will later meet a linguist who would admit as knowledge by acquaintance any case of 'knows' plus direct object, even 'knowing the fact that . . .' The effect is to empty the notion of acquaintance of all epistemological import.

[13] So Lesher 1969. Encouragement for such thoughts could perhaps be sought in the LSJ (new ninth edn, 1940) entry for γιγνώσκω: 'as dist. fr. οἶδα *know by reflection*, γιγνώσκω = *know by observation*'. But where Plato is concerned, this latter distinction is illusory: see Lyons 1963: 179, n. 2; 206.

[14] An especially refined version of this charge is John McDowell, citing *Tht.* 147b2–5, 196d8–10 as evidence that Plato tends to treat (1) 'know *x*' (*connaître*) and (2) 'know what *x* is' (*savoir*) as interchangeable, and then diagnosing a slide from (2) to (1) via the Greek idiom, equivalent to (2), which (he says) 'can be *literally* represented by (3) "know *x* what it is"' (my italics) McDowell 1969: 190–1. One might as well say that a literal translation of German into English would put the verb at the end of subordinate clauses or that a literal translation of Latin into English would eschew both definite and indefinite articles! For a properly principled analysis of the structures created when the subject of a Greek subordinate clause is attracted into a main clause containing a verb of knowing or saying, see Lyons 1963: 107–10.

kind of knowledge, is a sort of spiritual vision.[15] No one stopped to ask whether a noun phrase such as αὐτὸ τὸ ἀγαθόν might not be more like 'the answer to the question' in (3)# than it is like the proper name 'John Smith' in (3). Instead, they rushed to the *Theaetetus* and *Sophist* in order to find what Ryle had promised they would find: Plato liberating himself from the confusions of the *Republic* and becoming clear about the all-important difference between knowledge by acquaintance and propositional knowledge that such-and-such is the case.[16]

Some found what they were looking for, but most did not – in which case they said: 'So much the worse for Plato's progress in these matters: he did not get as clear as he should have done.' They never said: 'So much the worse for the twentieth-century English scheme through which we have been trying to understand him.' Still less did they attend to Plato's express indication at *Phaedo* 75cd that the phrase 'αὐτὸ τό such-and-such' is (to be understood as) a nominalisation of the propositional form αὐτὸ ὅ ἔστι such-and-such' – and here I quote David Gallop's exemplary translation: ||

> Our present argument concerns the beautiful itself, and the good itself, and just and holy, no less than the equal; in fact, as I say, it concerns everything on which we set this seal, *'what it is'* in the questions we ask and in the answers we give.[17]

---

[15] And not only Plato. In 1967, Jaakko Hintikka appealed to Snell 1924 and Snell 1953, Bluck 1961, Runciman 1962, and others, to support a far-reaching claim that it is characteristic of Greek epistemology in general, Aristotle included, 'to think of knowledge in terms of some sort of direct acquaintance with the objects of knowledge, e.g. in terms of seeing or witnessing them' (Hintikka 1967: 72). He even follows Snell's misreporting of *Iliad* 11.484–7 as saying that the Muses know everything because they are *always* at hand to see what goes on (Hintikka 1967: 74, reporting Snell (1953), p. 136). The word 'always' is not in the Greek, nor in its translation as presented by Snell and Hintikka. Worse still, ancient readers would remember from their Hesiod that the Muses can tell of much that happened before they were sired by Zeus (*Theog.* 25, 36, 53ff.).

[16] Runciman 1962 gives the flavour of the times. Yet Ryle's promise was made in 'Letters and Syllables in Plato', from the *Philosophical Review* of 1960 (Ryle 1960), which is not in the bibliography of Runciman's book. Solution: Runciman's Preface informs us that the book was presented as a Fellowship dissertation to Trinity College, Cambridge, in 1959, and was published without revision. No doubt Ryle's promise was already keenly discussed in his friend Gwil Owen's Harvard seminars of 1958–9. It is a fine example of what Owen spoke of as 'Ryle's ... apparently inexhaustible cask of new thoughts on Plato' (Owen 1970a: 341).

[17] Keeping, with Gallop 1975: 230, the MSS τοῦτο ὅ ἔστι: 'taking ἔστι as incomplete'. Rowe and the new OCT replace Burnet's emendation τὸ 'αὐτὸ ὅ ἔστι' (which generalises the preceding αὐτὸ τὸ X formulae) by τοῦτο, τὸ 'ὅ ἔστι'. Fowler in the Loeb (1914) edition printed no more than τὸ ὅ ἔστι, with the even more minimal translation 'the seal of absolute'. In a later version (1993), Gallop made his point even clearer with the wording 'that which it is'. Rowe (1993) oscillates over the construal, but finally rejects Gallop in favour of 'what is equal', and so on.

From which it seems just to conclude as follows: the syntax of the sentences which describe philosophers as knowing the Forms does indeed resemble the syntax of (3)# more than the syntax of (3).[18]

And yet in the middle of the hustling and bustling of this debate, as far back as 1963, there had appeared a pioneering work in which every single occurrence in the Platonic corpus of a knowledge verb or knowledge noun was collected, classified, and subjected to a type of analysis more powerful than any that traditional classical scholarship could yield, and more systematic than any current in the philosophical journals of the time. I refer to Sir John Lyons' Cambridge dissertation, *Structural Semantics: An Analysis of Part of the Vocabulary of Plato*.[19] The key word in this title is 'structural'.

In the wider Anglo-Saxon world this was the period when Chomsky was beginning to take over from linguistic philosophy in the old, unsystematic Oxford style. Lyons' application of Chomskian techniques to Plato's vocabulary of knowledge should have been heralded within ancient philosophy as the moment when science vanquished superstition, and the untutored darkness of scholarly intuition was dispelled in the bright light of modern linguistics. The debate about Plato and the epistemic troika should have stopped dead in 1963, and the participants should have gone back to reread the *Phaedo* and *Republic* with fresh, de-Ryled eyes. Alas, Lyons had more effect on the || bibliographies of the debate than its content.[20] He was even cited by Lesher as scientific support for the

---

[18] A small essay could be written on the inadequate, non-propositional translations of the phrase 'αὐτὸ τὸ such-and-such' by, for example, Tredennick 1969 ('absolute'), Hackforth 1955 ('the thing itself'), Grube 1977 and in J. M. Cooper and Hutchinson 1997 ('itself'). Bluck 1955 ('that which is, all by itself') is little better. A differently telling silence is the absence of *Phaedo* 75d2 from the ten-page *index locorum* to that lively crusade against any propositional understanding of Platonic Forms: Gerson 2003. Let me simply quote, approvingly, Gallop's note *ad loc.*: 'The argument extends to all items "stamped" by the terminology for forms. That terminology originates from questions such as "what is beauty?" or "what is justice?"' (Gallop 1975). Platonic forms are objects that provide answers to those questions. The present phrase might be glossed as "that which X is", answering the question, "What is X?" So Burnet 1911 *ad* 75d2: 'the just what it is', Dixsaut 1991: 'ce que c'est', and John Cooper's revised version of Grube in J. M. Cooper 2002: 'the seal of "what it is"', not to mention from long, long ago, Schleiermacher 1817–28 (second edn): 'was wir bezeichnen, als dies selbst, was es ist'). Compare further *Rep.* 490b3: πρὶν αὐτοῦ ὃ ἔστιν ἑκάστου τῆς φύσεως ἅψασθαι – 'before getting in touch with the nature of each case of that which X itself is'.

[19] Lyons 1963. Three years later came another pioneering work in which modern linguistics cast light on ancient philosophy: Charles Kahn's 'The Greek Verb "To Be" and the Concept of Being' (Kahn 1966), to be followed by his massive study *The Verb 'Be' in Ancient Greek* (Kahn 1973).

[20] Contrast the success with which the untutored darkness of scholarly intuition was indeed dispelled when, building on modern propositional logic and the work of Jan Łukasiewicz, Benson Mates in 'Stoic Logic and the Text of Sextus Empiricus' (Mates 1949), and in his book *Stoic Logic* (Mates

contention that γιγνώσκειν/γνῶσις can be glossed as knowledge by acquaintance.[21] So my next task is to set out, as briefly and clearly as I can, in my own words rather than his, what I believe Lyons did and proved.

Platonic Greek has three prominent verbs for knowing, and three nouns for knowledge. In alphabetical order, the verbs are γιγνώσκειν, εἰδέναι, ἐπίστασθαι, and the nouns are γνῶσις, ἐπιστήμη, τέχνη. Lyons' central claim is that these six words form a *structured system*.

Everyone knows that the colour vocabulary of a language, or its kinship terminology, has to be learned as a system, whether the learning is by a native speaker or an outside investigator. So it is with the knowledge vocabulary we find in Plato's dialogues. Each of the three verbs enters into a variety of constructions (many more than three *each*), and it is only by studying the relationships, synonymies, and contrasts between them that we can understand their meaning. Similarly with the three nouns. The moral is that the act of translation cannot be achieved by a one-to-one pairing of a single Greek construction with a single English construction, let alone by a one-to-one pairing of Greek and English verbs and Greek and English nouns, irrespective of the context and construction to which they belong. The whole system is in play in each context, and only an holistic understanding will enable one to choose an appropriate English translation for some particular occurrence of one of the six words with which we are dealing.

The results of this broadly structuralist approach are many and fruitful. For me personally, when I first read the book in 1964, having been inspired as an undergraduate by hearing Lyons speak at the Cambridge B Club on 22 January 1962, they were a revelation. But for present purposes I want to concentrate on three major results, of which only the third could have been reached – and in my view jolly well should have been reached – by the intuitive methods of traditional classical scholarship.

The first result is encoded in a pair of diagrams which ought to be indelibly etched on the wax tablet of every student of Plato's dialogues:

1961), was able to make numerous compelling textual emendations (some extraordinarily simple) to ancient reports on Stoic logic. Jonathan Barnes' *magnum opus* of 2007, enigmatically entitled *Truth, etc.*, is a noble contribution to the tradition that they founded (Barnes 2009).

[21] Lesher 1969: 76–7. Lyons obliged by saying somewhat the same thing later (Lyons 1979: 116, with reference to the verb's 'most distinctive collocations'), but with a very broad notion of acquaintance that covers becoming aware that *p*, where *p* is any proposition. More on later Lyons below.

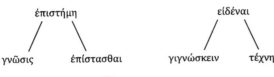

Diagram 7.1

The verb ἐπίστασθαι and the noun ἐπιστήμη are cognate with each other, but for all that *in Plato* they are semantically disparate.[22] The verb is more specialised than the noun. The noun is the most general word for knowledge in Platonic Greek. That is why the theme-question of the *Theaetetus* is τί ἐστιν ἐπιστήμη; rather than τί ἐστι τέχνη; or τί ἐστι γνῶσις; but if you look through the *Theaetetus* you will find that the verb which occurs most frequently is εἰδέναι. ἐπίστασθαι and γιγνώσκειν each have less than half as many occurrences; and the most general verb is εἰδέναι, *not* ἐπίστασθαι.

This distancing of ἐπιστήμη from ἐπίστασθαι was a major surprise. It is no exaggeration to say that it wrecks practically every attempt so far to base the epistemic troika on Plato's Greek – every attempt, that is, bar one, which for the present I am holding in reserve.

Consider Socrates' question at *Theaetetus* 209e8–210a1: τὸ γὰρ γνῶναι ἐπιστήμην που λαβεῖν ἐστιν· ἢ γάρ; – to which Theaetetus assents straightforwardly: 'Yes'. Both Runciman and Lesher cite this as a difficulty for the project of persuading Plato to distinguish between knowledge by acquaintance and knowledge that – Runciman taking it to be an insuperable difficulty, and Lesher a superable one.[23] It is a difficulty for them because they suppose that Plato would make the distinction by taking γιγνώσκειν to express knowledge by acquaintance, ἐπίστασθαι knowledge that.[24] If they had read Lyons, as Lesher thought he had, they would have known that an association in the passage quoted between the *noun* ἐπιστήμη and the verb γιγνώσκειν does not begin to cast doubt on the suggestion, thoroughly vindicated by Lyons, that there is a contrast between the two *verbs* ἐπίστασθαι and γιγνώσκειν. What it does help cast doubt on is the quite different suggestion that there is a contrast between

---

[22] Italics are mine. It will emerge that findings for Plato do not carry over in every respect to Aristotle or his Imperial commentators.
[23] Runciman 1962: 43, n. 2; Lesher 1969: 72, 78.
[24] In this supposition they are following up on a one-page intervention, Hamlyn 1957. Hamlyn's proposal was expressed in terms of 'γνῶσις and its derivatives' versus 'ἐπιστήμη and its derivatives', where his references show that 'derivatives' include the cognate verbs (for example, ἐπίστασθαι at 208a2).

the *nouns* ἐπιστήμη and γνῶσις, which scholars writing before Lyons did not distinguish from the idea of a contrast between the corresponding verbs.[25]

The second result to mention is best presented through the two diagrams. There is indeed a contrast in very many contexts between ἐπίστασθαι and γιγνώσκειν.[26] A parallel contrast holds between the nouns τέχνη and γνῶσις. With both verbs and nouns the contrast operates along the horizontal dimension of the diagrams: as ‖ ἐπίστασθαι is to γιγνώσκειν, so τέχνη *(not* ἐπιστήμη) is to γνῶσις. Along the vertical dimension there is, by and large, no contrast. In some contexts and constructions, εἰδέναι is convertible with and, according to Lyons, synonymous with ἐπίστασθαι, while in others it is convertible with and, according to Lyons, synonymous with γιγνώσκειν. Likewise ἐπιστήμη in relation to τέχνη and γνῶσις. In such contexts, εἰδέναι and ἐπιστήμη have no specific meaning of their own. They substitute for whichever more specific word is appropriate.

This leads me to the third point – the one that traditional classical scholarship should have and could have noticed. Runciman and Lesher were right to suggest a contrast between ἐπίστασθαι and γιγνώσκειν, but quite wrong to associate the former with knowledge that,[27] and the latter with knowledge by acquaintance.[28] ἐπίστασθαι in Plato very seldom governs a 'that'-clause or indirect question: Lyons counts just seven cases in the corpus where ἐπίστασθαι takes a clause in *oratio obliqua*, and I make it a few less.[29] By contrast, γιγνώσκειν with a 'that'-clause or indirect

---

[25] More recently, Waterfield 1987: 236–7 did read Lyons, but having failed to take his warning that the verbs and the nouns are not on a par in Plato, he too cites *Tht.* 209e8–210a1 to show that 'apart from minor differences in grammatical construction, the two terms [*sc.* γνῶσις and ἐπιστήμη plus their cognate verbs] are synonymous'.

[26] A nice example that Lyons' results can alert one to is *Rep.* 488b2–3, where to substitute ἐπιστάμενον for γιγνώσκοντα would wreck the point by implying that the burly shipmaster does have the systematic τέχνη which Socrates means to deny him. The man's knowing a thing or two about nautical matters is meant to be on a par with his being rather short-sighted and somewhat hard of hearing (b1–2).

[27] Runciman 1962: 34 ('knowledge of facts or possession of skills'), alleging that the verb is simultaneously confused with knowledge by acquaintance; Lesher 1969: 72, 'intellectual knowledge or knowledge that something is the case'. Both authors treat verb and noun on a par, arguing from one to the other.

[28] Runciman 1962: 35, with n. 2 and the same allegation; Lesher 1969, *loc. cit.*

[29] Lyons 1963: 205–7, with ns. 1–3. His list (207, ns. 1–3), with an asterisk marking the cases I think might need a more complicated explanation, is *Euthyd.* 296e, *Hipp. Mi.* 365e*, *Lach.* 188b, *Lys.* 205a*, *Phd.* 97b, *Tht.* 163e*, *Tim.* 76e*. *LSJ* shows other authors more generous about adding *oratio obliqua* to ἐπίστασθαι. Aristotle is the important case that will concern us later, but a glance at Sturz's *Lexicon Xenophonteum* shows Xenophon profligate with all manner of *oratio obliqua* constructions for ἐπίστασθαι (Sturz 1801), while Herodotus even allows the verb to take a clause which turns out (or, on occasion is already declared!) to be false: see Powell 1938, s.v. and Vlastos'

question is frequent: 66 cases in the corpus. Even more frequent with *oratio obliqua* clauses is εἰδέναι: 277 cases in the corpus. The question is: should we say that the *oratio obliqua* type of construction is special in that εἰδέναι here has a specific meaning of its own, though one that overlaps with γιγνώσκειν, or should we repeat the message of the diagrams and say that even with clauses of *oratio obliqua*, εἰδέναι merely substitutes for γιγνώσκειν with the same construction?

I tend towards the second option, and will later cite Alexander of Aphrodisias on my side.[30] Lyons' findings make it obvious that γιγνώσκειν is not *more* closely connected with acquaintance-knowledge than with knowledge that.[31] Besides, a large number of contexts in which γιγνώσκειν governs a noun phrase in direct object construction are contexts that philosophers would class as knowledge that, rather than knowledge by acquaintance. For example, μὴ πᾶν γύναιον καὶ παιδίον, καὶ θηρίον δέ, ἱκανὸν εἶναι ἰᾶσθαι αὑτὸ γιγνῶσκον ἑαυτῷ τὸ ὑγιεινόν (*Tht.* 171e5–7) means that not every woman, child, or beast knows what is healthy for itself, where the last three words express an indirect question to which the answer would be expressed in a that-clause: 'Juliette does not know *that Guinness is good for her*'. It does not mean that ‖ not every woman, child, and beast is acquainted with an abstract object called τὸ ὑγιεινόν.

It is true that if you want to know the Greek for 'knowledge by acquaintance', a good answer is γιγνώσκειν. But it is also true that if you want to know the Greek for 'knowledge that', a good answer is γιγνώσκειν. An equally good answer to *either* question is εἰδέναι. Neither verb, I contend, can be tied to either term of the Rylean contrast between knowledge that and knowledge by acquaintance. Both express both.

In fact, the only part of the epistemic troika that can be partially located in the diagrams is the contrast between knowledge how and knowledge that. ἐπίστασθαι plus infinitive, or plus a τέχνη-denoting noun phrase in direct object construction,[32] is often appropriately translated by English 'know how', and can be seen to contrast with γιγνώσκειν (εἰδέναι) plus a clause of *oratio obliqua*.

---

debate with Snell (Vlastos 1981: 208–9). An ironic use of ἐπίστασθαι plus *oratio obliqua* in Heraclitus, frag. 57, will be the final surprise of this essay.

[30] See p. 251ff. below.

[31] The table at Lyons 1963: 182 reveals 27 occurrences of γιγνώσκειν plus a personal noun as object, and 66 with a clause in *oratio obliqua*. This disparity will be crucial below.

[32] See Lyons 1963: 183ff.

This completes my account of the reasons why, in my opinion, the debate about Plato and the epistemic troika should have stopped dead in 1963 when Lyons' book was published. Sadly, I must now reveal something about which very few ancient philosophy specialists are aware. Lyons himself made a late entry into the debate with a pair of articles published in 1979 and 1981 – the latter carrying the title 'Structural Semantics in Retrospect'. A better title for this apostasy would have been 'Structural Semantics Abandoned', for his new proposal was to associate the epistemic troika with Plato's trio of verbs and the three corresponding nouns in such a way that εἰδέναι/ἐπιστήμη would *focally* or *prototypically* express knowledge that, ἐπίστασθαι/τέχνη knowledge how, and γιγνώσκειν/ γνῶσις knowledge by acquaintance.[33]

The argument for this hypothesis rests on certain key results of *Structural Semantics*, to wit:

(a) γιγνώσκειν is the only one of the three verbs that is employed normally and frequently with a person-referring nominal as its direct object;
(b) ἐπίστασθαι is the only one that regularly takes an infinitive; and
(c) εἰδέναι occurs far more frequently with the equivalent of an English that-clause as its object than it does in any other construction.[34]

The focal, or prototypical, meaning 'is revealed in, though not of course to be identified with, its most frequent or most characteristic, collocations. It is also the meaning which the native speaker would think of first and would find easiest to exemplify.'[35]

I should underline that the proposal is described as 'tentative' and (ambiguously) as 'definitely going beyond, if not actually contradicting, what was said in *Structural Semantics*'. Note also that in cases (a) and (b) the frequency referred to is frequency ‖ relative to that of the other two verbs, whereas in case (c) it is frequency within the occurrences of εἰδέναι. This difference will be crucial to my critique.

As sources or precedents for the idea of focal or prototypical meaning Lyons cites five linguists and the work of one philosopher: Hilary Putnam's well-known paper 'The Meaning of "Meaning"' (1975).[36]

---

[33] Note that under the new proposal the noun ἐπιστήμη still remains more general than the verb ἐπίστασθαι.
[34] The extract is quoted from Lyons 1981: 83–4, referring to the table of results given at Lyons 1963: 182. I have changed his transliterations back into Greek and inserted (a), (b), and (c) for ease of subsequent reference.
[35] Lyons 1981: 81.   [36] Putnam 1975: 215–71; Lyons 1981: 81, n. 18.

Since I am not a linguist but a philosopher writing *for* a philosopher who has also made use of Lyons' book, Putnam's is the work I shall start from, even though he does not speak of 'prototypical' or 'focal meaning', which in this context are linguists' terms of art.[37] His key term is 'stereotype'.

Putnam's example of a stereotype is that to understand the word 'tiger' you must have learned that tigers are feline, large, yellow with black stripes, that they live (typically) in the jungle, and are fierce.[38] These are not necessary and sufficient conditions for being a tiger, nor are they analytically part of the concept of a tiger. Tame tigers may well exist, even outside the pages of G. E. Moore. And if Aristotle can entertain the counterfactual possibility (as he wrongly believes it to be) of black swans, or the occasional actuality (as he also supposes) of ravens turned permanently white by a sharp frost (*APr.* II.3, 55a4–10; *HA* III.12, 519a3–6), so we may consider the (perhaps redundant) possibility of a black tiger with yellow stripes, not to mention the occasional actuality of albino ('leucistic') tigers whose genetic condition leaves them with black stripes on a white background. Putnam's claim is that white tigers would not count as possible *tigers* unless we had first learned the stereotype associated with the word 'tiger'[39] – similarly, one might add, with Aristotle's ability to envisage black swans such as those that thrive down the road from where I write. The new Lyons' putative parallel to this is the suggestion that εἰδέναι *prototypically* expresses knowledge that, ἐπίστασθαι knowledge how, and γιγνώσκειν knowledge by acquaintance.

You will not expect me to have much sympathy with this proposal, even though the new Lyons believes he has said nothing which is actually incompatible with the old Lyons, only different and additional. I ask a simple and, to my mind, crushing question: If the epistemic troika does fix the prototypical meanings of our three Greek verbs, how on earth does this help the theorist to explain, or the language learner to learn, the fact that in some Platonic contexts and constructions εἰδέναι is convertible and synonymous with ἐπίστασθαι, while in others with γιγνώσκειν? The old Lyons showed that this alternative convertibility is much the most important fact about the semantics of εἰδέναι. The new Lyons, it seems to me, has made that fact well-nigh impossible to grasp.

---

[37] Philosophers please note that the phrase 'focal meaning' here has nothing to do with G. E. L. Owen's work on Aristotle. Lyons 1981, n. 19, cites the distinguished linguist William Haas, for whose *Festschrift* he wrote Lyons 1979.

[38] Putnam 1975: 251–2.   [39] Putnam 1975: 256.

I have other quarrels to pick with the new Lyons. It seems to me that to move, as he requires, from γιγνώσκειν plus a noun phrase in direct object construction taken as expressing knowledge by acquaintance to γιγνώσκειν plus clauses of *oratio obliqua*, || involves a good deal more than a contextual adjustment of the kind necessary to accommodate albino tigers or the whiteness of chemically pure gold.[40] I would also question some aspects of the use which Lyons makes of his previous counts. Worse, there is one highly significant count which he does not mention.

The table for γιγνώσκειν at *Structural Semantics*, p. 182, shows 27 occurrences for the verb's use with a person-referring nominal as its direct object: more, certainly, than the seven such constructions listed for εἰδέναι and the solitary one for ἐπίστασθαι, but significantly fewer than the 66 cases counted where γιγνώσκειν governs an *oratio obliqua* construction. Granted, this last figure is a lot less than the 277 *oratio obliqua* constructions with εἰδέναι. The fact remains that it is easily the most numerous of the constructions admitted by the verb γιγνώσκειν in the works of Plato — more than twice as many cases as the new Lyons can cite for his choice of the verb's prototypical or focal meaning. Yet this fact is never so much as mentioned in the two articles under discussion!

I noted earlier that in cases (a) and (b) the frequency referred to is frequency relative to that of the other two verbs, whereas in case (c) it is frequency within the occurrences of εἰδέναι.[41] If (b)'s frequency were to be assessed in the same way as (c)'s, the finding would be that the focal or prototypical meaning of γιγνώσκειν is revealed by its use with an *oratio obliqua* construction, *not* its use with a person-referring nominal as direct object. Yes, the *oratio obliqua* use for γιγνώσκειν is significantly *less* frequent than the corresponding cases of εἰδέναι. But is not that quite in keeping with the great unexpected and wonderfully revealing discovery of *Structural Semantics*, that εἰδέναι has no core meaning of its own, but substitutes either for ἐπίστασθαι or for γιγνώσκειν?

My next move is to offer a more positive way ahead out of the new Lyons' den by introducing, at last, the evidence of a native speaker. Recall that according to the new Lyons, the prototypical meaning of a word is the

---

[40] Putnam's examples: Putnam 1975: 250.
[41] I should also add that 'frequency' is not a count of each token of the word counted, since Plato often has occasion to develop arguments in which the same word in the same construction is continuously repeated again and again. Lyons 1963: 181–2 cites the case of *Tht.* 192ac, which contains no less than 15 occurrences of εἰδέναι in the same (highly repetitive) environment. In the crucial table on p. 182, that is quite properly recorded as just one.

meaning which a native speaker would think of first and would find it easiest to exemplify.

The earliest extant debate which I have encountered about ancient Greek verbs of knowing took place in the sixth century of the Christian era, when the neo-Platonist commentator Simplicius presumed to disagree with the greatest Aristotelian scholar of all time about the phrase: τὸ εἰδέναι καὶ τὸ ἐπίστασθαι in the following sentence – the very first of Aristotle's *Physics*:

> ἐπειδὴ τὸ εἰδέναι καὶ τὸ ἐπίστασθαι συμβαίνει περὶ πάσας τὰς μεθόδους, ὧν εἰσὶν ἀρχαὶ ἢ αἴτια ἢ στοιχεῖα, ἐκ τοῦ ταῦτα γνωρίζειν (τότε γὰρ οἰόμεθα γιγνώσκειν ἕκαστον, ὅταν τὰ αἴτια γνωρίσωμεν τὰ πρῶτα καὶ τὰς ἀρχὰς τὰς πρώτας καὶ μέχρι τῶν στοιχείων), δῆλον ὅτι καὶ τῆς περὶ φύσεως ἐπιστήμης πειρατέον διορίσασθαι πρῶτον τὰ περὶ τὰς ἀρχάς. (184a10–16) ||
>
> When the objects of an inquiry, in any department, have principles, causes, or elements, it is through acquaintance [γνωρίζειν] with these that knowledge and understanding [τὸ εἰδέναι καὶ τὸ ἐπίστασθαι] is[42] attained. For we do not think that we know [γιγνώσκειν] a thing until we are acquainted [γνωρίσωμεν] with its primary causes or first principles, and have carried our analysis as far as its elements. Plainly, therefore, in the science [ἐπιστήμη] of nature too our first task will be to try to determine what relates to its principles. (Oxford translation by R. P. Hardie and R. K. Gaye, 1930)

We shall soon find Simplicius, like the new Lyons, determined to regiment Aristotle's vocabulary into conformity with the accepted philosophical tenets of the period in which he was writing, which then of course were of neo-Platonic rather than of Rylean or Putnamic origin. His opponent Alexander, three centuries earlier, had no such philosophical axe to grind. He was just doing his usual superb best to understand Aristotle.

But first let me pause to explain why the English version I have appended to clarify Aristotle's Greek is from the Oxford translation of 1930. This is because of the translators' charmingly unphilosophical use of the term 'acquaintance'.[43] It is perfectly good English to render ὅταν τὰ

---

[42] Note the translators' singular verb, to be recalled in n. 48 below.
[43] Likewise the very similar Loeb translation Cornford and Wicksteed 1929–34: 'In all sciences that are concerned with principles or causes or elements, it is acquaintance with these that constitutes knowledge or understanding.' Wicksteed – a Unitarian clergyman, a lover, translator, and annotator of Dante, a student of Aquinas, and a notable economist – lived from 1844 to 1927, when he died a few days after summoning Cornford – whom he had met just once, years before (though they had friends in common, very probably including Gilbert Murray) – to travel from Cambridge to his

αἴτια γνωρίσωμεν (184a13) by 'when we are acquainted with its causes', but no contemporary philosopher would count this a case of knowledge by acquaintance. τὰ αἴτια is not the same accusative as in (3), but more like 'the answer to the question' in (3)#: causes are by definition causes explanatory *of* something. What this shows is that 'acquaintance' as it occurs in modern Anglophone discussions of ancient epistemic vocabulary is a term of art. We cannot tell which cases of K + noun phrase in direct object construction express knowledge by acquaintance until the term of art has been defined and explained independently of its surface linguistic expression.

Nobody but Russell has ever done this. Lyons remarks that knowledge by acquaintance 'is manifest most characteristically in our ability to recognise and || reidentify persons and things that we have previously encountered'.[44] But in what sense, if any, is knowing causes knowing things? In what sense are causes things? 'Everything is a thing', you may say, truly enough. One may know the causes of the First World War, know French, know Pythagoras' theorem, know one's neighbour – all of them 'things'. But does Lyons seriously mean 'in the sense in which we speak of knowing persons and *everything* else'? Those who use the Russellian terminology tend to say that they do not wish 'acquaintance' to be taken in its exact technical Russellian meaning – presumably because in Russell this is tied to sense-datum theory. But then, instead of explaining what meaning 'acquaintance' *is* to have, they give an example like (3) and hope we will catch on. Hence the extraordinary lack of focus in discussions of the question of whether Plato conceives the philosopher's knowledge of the Forms as acquaintance. No one, I believe, has a clear idea what they are debating. Nor is this irrelevant to Aristotle, because for Plato, knowledge of the Forms *is* knowledge of causes: the Forms are causes of the things

---

home in Childrey, Oxfordshire, there to take over the project to which Wicksteed had devoted his final years. An older friend, named Saunders, had already agreed to help if Wicksteed did not live to complete it himself (Herford 1931, p. 176), but Cornford's part of the Preface to vol. 1 of the Loeb edition (pp. xi–xiv) makes clear that it was he who found himself suddenly landed with the huge task of finishing a work which the Loeb editors had accepted for publication in 1924. Now Wicksteed was preparing a paraphrase rather than a translation, and no serious work on the Greek text. Cornford issued the first volume in 1929 – just two years later – but the second did not appear until 1934. Its Preface begins: 'In this volume, *as in the previous one* [my italics], I am solely responsible for the Greek text.' Nowhere in successive issues of the Loeb edition is the extent of Cornford's contribution clearly explained, but the impression that theirs was a joint project is patently false. It was Cornford's taking over that produced the excellent resource which the Loeb Classical Library has kept in print for so many years. That said, it would seem uncharitable not to assign the very first sentence to Wicksteed's pen! (For more on Wicksteed, see Herford 1931.)

[44] Lyons 1981: 83.

that depend upon them. The causes and principles of which Aristotle speaks in the text before us are his alternative to the Platonic Forms.

So now to the debate between Simplicius and Alexander about Aristotle's exordium. That τὸ εἰδέναι καὶ τὸ ἐπίστασθαι is not a pleonasm, Alexander did well to insist upon, saying:

> Pleonasms have a difference of words alone and sameness of thing. For this reason any one of the words involved is equivalent in meaning to every other. But τὸ εἰδέναι καὶ τὸ ἐπίστασθαι does not mean the same as τὸ εἰδέναι by itself. For we are said to εἰδέναι both the things we grasp through perception and judgement (τὰ δι' αἰσθήσεως καὶ δόξης)[45] and the immediate premises, none of which we know εἰδέναι) through demonstration; that is to say, it is not by way of ἐπιστήμη that we know them.

Thus far Alexander spoke well. But how both terms are to be taken *here*, he did not go on to say. It looks as though he orders εἴδησις ahead of ἐπιστήμη, as being its genus, as if he [Aristotle] was speaking of γιγνώσκειν ἐπιστημονικῶς. This is like saying, 'He who says something and says it in such a way as to assert it (ὁ λέγων τι καὶ οὕτως λέγων ὡς ἀποφαίνεσθαι), either speaks truly or speaks falsely.' For speech (λόγος) is the genus of assertion, just as εἴδησις, i.e. γνῶσις, is the genus of ἐπιστήμη. And that he [Aristotle] knows that εἴδησις is spoken of also in the case of perception was shown by the opening of the *Metaphysics*: 'All men by nature desire to εἰδέναι: witness their delight in the senses.' But may it not be that in the present passage Aristotle took εἴδησις in its proper (κυρίως) sense and equated it with ἐπιστήμη? For Plato says that the mathematicians do not εἰδέναι their own starting points, obviously meaning that they do not εἰδέναι them ἐπιστημονικῶς, which implies that εἴδησις in the proper sense is ἐπιστημονικὴ εἴδησις. 'For', he says, 'where the starting point is something one does not know (οἶδε), and the intermediate steps and the conclusion are composed of things one does not know (οἶδε), how is it possible to call this εἰδέναι or ἐπιστήμη?'[46] And he [Plato] clearly says that || δόξα is different from γνῶσις when he says, 'What, then, if this person whom we say δοξάζει and does not γινώσκει should get angry with us?', and likewise he distinguishes the δοξαστόν from the γνωστόν when he says, 'We agreed before that if anything of this sort should turn up, it ought to be called δοξαστόν, not γνωστόν.'[47] It is clear that Aristotle too takes εἴδησις, which is the same as to say γνῶσις, not in its common sense, but in

---

[45] This phrase had better be a hendiadys, on pain of allowing the absurdity of knowledge gained through δόξα.
[46] A version of Plato, *Rep.* 533c3–5, preferring Torstrik's emendation τοῦτο ἢ for τούτῳ in the unsatisfactory *Commentaria in Aristotelem Graeca* text of Simplicius 13.1. Thus emended, the passage fits the standard Platonic parallel, discovered by Lyons, between the verb εἰδέναι and the noun ἐπιστήμη.
[47] This quote and its predecessor are accurate excerpts from *Rep.* 476d and 479d, respectively.

its ἐπιστημονικός sense. That is clear from the considerations he adduces: 'For', he says, 'we think we γιγνώσκειν each thing when we γνωρίζειν its first causes and first principles.' He is evidently speaking of the kind of γνῶσις which is γνῶσις from the principles, and this is γνῶσις ἐπιστημονική. And that δοξάζειν is one thing, ἐπίστασθαι another, Socrates showed in the *Theaetetus* from the fact that there is both true and false δόξα, whereas ἐπιστήμη is only true. This latter proof Alexander used as well. (Simplicius, *in Ar. Phys.* 1.12.14–13.13)

The issue in dispute between Simplicius and Alexander starts out as a simple question of linguistic meaning. Are εἰδέναι and ἐπίστασθαι synonymous in the first sentence of Aristotle's *Physics*? Simplicius agrees with Alexander that in Aristotle's usage the two verbs are not in general synonymous. But here, he thinks, they are. Simplicius, in other words, takes the intervening καί as 'namely',[48] whereas Alexander understands it, quite in accord with the Lyons schema, as a way of passing from a more generic to a more specific verb: εἰδέναι and, more particularly, ἐπίστασθαι – 'und zwar' in German.[49] The construal of that καί turns out to have momentous consequences. For if Simplicius is right about it, Aristotle's epistemology is gratifyingly (for a Platonist) in complete agreement with Plato's.

However, my interest is in the question of language. Why does Aristotle use two verbs instead of one? And what do the two verbs mean in Aristotle's usage? This is a question of much importance for a modern translator of Aristotle – especially a translator of the *Posterior Analytics*.

In the first edition (1975) of the translation of this work which Barnes contributed to the Clarendon Aristotle series, he adopted the 'tedious device' (his phrase) of tagging each of the three verbs ἐπίστασθαι, γιγνώσκειν, and εἰδέναι with its own English substitute: respectively, 'understand', 'be aware of', and 'know'.[50] This made for considerable artificiality in the translation. Tagging is not translating. All it was meant to convey to a Greekless reader was that Aristotle deployed three different Greek verbs within the territory of English talk about knowledge. There

---

[48] So too the Oxford translation of Aristotle's *Physics*, as revealed by the singular verb at the end of the first sentence: '... knowledge and understanding *is* attained' (my italics). Pellegrin 2000 *ad loc.* diagnoses hendiadys: 'le premier terme désigne le savoir en général, le second le savoir scientifique'.

[49] The noun ἐπιστήμη, by contrast, which in Lyons' scheme is the most general noun, Alexander's last sentence treats as coordinate with ἐπίστασθαι. This is true to Aristotle and a change from Plato, with which we shall reckon shortly.

[50] See Barnes 1975: xviii with pp. 264–5 of the Glossary, and p. 90 ad *APo.* 71a2, where he endorses Lyons' scheme as appropriate to Aristotle's knowledge vocabulary as well as Plato's, and proposes separate English terms to match each of the Greek verbs and their corresponding nouns.

was no claim to render the || specific *meaning* of the Greek verbs – only that there were three of them in the ancient text. Barnes might as well have written *x*, *y*, and *z* and equipped them with the appropriate suffixes: '*x*ing', '*y*ed', and '*z*'s'. Indeed, in 1980 he declared that 'understand' in his translation is 'employed as a term of art, and means precisely the same as "know"'.[51]

As time passed, Barnes repented the infelicities of his original version. In 1985 he confessed that 'my own translation of the *Posterior Analytics*, which aimed self-consciously at literal fidelity, produced English which is in many places barbarously unfaithful to Aristotle'.[52] Subsequently, the second edition of his *Posterior Analytics* (1994) allowed γιγνώσκειν as well as εἰδέναι to be Englished as 'know'. This left readers with a single contrast between 'knowing' (γιγνώσκειν, εἰδέναι) and 'understanding' (ἐπίστασθαι), which Barnes now declared to be, in his opinion, the only contrast intended by Aristotle himself.[53] I believe that the debate between Alexander and Simplicius can help us to see that this was fundamentally right. So it is with regret that I have to report that, more recently, Barnes appears to have become a complete sceptic about there being any satisfactory way to make modern sense of Aristotle's three verbs.

In his introduction to our late friend Mario Mignucci's Italian translation and commentary on the *Posterior Analytics* (2007), Barnes discusses at some length[54] Aristotle's opening account of ἐπίστασθαι, which his own first edition (1973) rendered as follows:

> We think we understand a thing (ἐπίστασθαι δὲ οἰόμεθ' ἕκαστον)... whenever we think we are aware (οἰώμεθα γιγνώσκειν) both that the explanation because of which the object is (τὴν τ' αἰτίαν ... δι' ἣν τὸ πρᾶγμά ἐστιν) is its explanation, and that it is not possible for this to be otherwise. (*APo.* 1.2, 71b9–12; Greek insertions mine)

His second edition (1994) put it this way: We think we understand something ... when we think we know of the explanation because of

---

[51] 'Socrates and the Jury' (n. 53 below), n. 22.
[52] Quoted from the 'Booknotes' section which he wrote as Editor of *Phronesis*, 30 (1985), 326–7.
[53] See his second-edition note *ad* 71a2: 'I am no longer convinced that Aristotle intended or felt any semantic differences among these elements – with the exception of *epistēmē*' (Barnes 1993). This stance was close to my own advocacy of 'understanding' for ἐπιστήμη, ἐπίστασθαι in Aristotle and 'knowledge' for his use of the remaining verbs and nouns (a) in 'Aristotle on Understanding Knowledge', Burnyeat 1981 [Chapter 6 in *EAMP* vol. II] and (b) in debate with Jonathan Barnes under the title 'Socrates and the Jury: Paradoxes in Plato's Distinction between Knowledge and True Belief', Burnyeat and Barnes 1980 [Chapter 5 in *EAMP* vol. II]. Lesher 2001 offers some useful qualifications and clarifications to my proposal – the most useful being his reference to Neil Cooper's wonderfully inclusive essay 'Understanding' (N. Cooper 1994).
[54] Barnes 2007.

which the object holds that it is its explanation, and also that it is not possible for it to be otherwise.⁵⁵ ||

As on those two occasions, he now looks for a translation which will avoid the definitional circularity that threatens if both ἐπίστασθαι and γιγνώσκειν are rendered by the English verb 'know' or Italian 'conoscere/sapere'. He claims there are only two serious candidates for ἐπίστασθαι as Aristotle defines it: 'conoscere scientificamente' ('to know scientifically'), adopted by Mignucci,⁵⁶ and 'comprendere', the Italian equivalent of the verb 'to understand', which Barnes used for ἐπίστασθαι in both editions of his translation, although only the second edition claimed to mean what his English said. He now prefers Mignucci's 'conoscere scientificamente' on the grounds that the normal use of 'comprendere che' is irrelevant to Aristotle's concerns.⁵⁷

The normal use of English 'understand that', as in 'I understand that he is ill', is equally irrelevant. But switch to 'Do you understand the fact that winters get longer the further away from the equator you live?' The phrase 'the fact that', presupposing as it does the truth of what follows, ensures that the question is not whether, but *why*, the length of winters varies with distance from the equator.⁵⁸ Which does connect with Aristotle's concerns. What is more, of the three Greek verbs for knowing, ἐπίστασθαι is the one which is standardly used to claim or ascribe mastery of a *body* of knowledge – a τέχνη, as opposed to individual items of knowledge.⁵⁹ Therefore, this seems to be the right verb for Aristotle to use when setting up the world's first model for systematic science. The 'we' of 'We think we understand a thing whenever we think we are aware . . .' is not the 'we' of ordinary life but the 'we' of Aristotle's school, who are being initiated into

---

⁵⁵ Readers may find this sentence easier to parse if they supply a comma after 'holds', as in Mignucci's version (Mignucci 2007): 'Riteniamo di conoscere scientificamente qualcosa . . . quando riteniamo di conoscere la ragione per la quale la cosa è, che essa è la ragione di quella cosa, e che ciò non può essere altrimenti.'

⁵⁶ Except in the very first chapter, before the definition is formulated in ch. 2.

⁵⁷ There is an ambiguity in the Italian text: does 'l'uso normale del secondo, intendo *comprendere che*' give the explanans or the explanandum? The first would be a flagrant falsehood, so I choose the second: we are explaining the normal use of *comprendere che*, not the normal use of *comprendere*. (Here I am indebted to Francesco Ademollo in his capacity as one of the editors of Mignucci 2007.) Compare *OED* s.v. 'understand' §3.

⁵⁸ Mignucci's rendering of τὴν τ' αἰτίαν . . . δι' ἣν τὸ πρᾶγμα ἐστιν is 'la ragione per la quale la cosa è'. Like Barnes' phrase 'the explanation because of which the object is', this unduly focuses the modern reader on objects as contrasted with states of affairs and event-like phenomena such as eclipses, which the Greek πρᾶγμα covers equally well and which in practice bulk much larger in Aristotle's text.

⁵⁹ See columns A, B, and C in the table at Lyons 1963: 182, and n. 25 above, plus LSJ s.v. ἐπίστασθαι II.

the world's first ever logic and methodology of science.⁶⁰ It is true even today that what counts as 'knowing' or 'understanding' is more stringent in a scientific context than elsewhere.⁶¹ Such is the context over which Alexander and Simplicius later wrangled.

Alexander's story is that the verb εἰδέναι, as used by Aristotle, expresses the generic concept under which can be subsumed ἐπίστασθαι on the one side and, on the other, εἰδέναι τὰ δι' αἰσθήσεως καὶ δόξης καὶ τὰς ἀμέσους προτάσεις: ‖

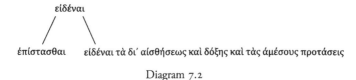

Diagram 7.2

He is thinking of *Posterior Analytics* 1.2, and of Aristotle's definition of ἐπίστασθαι as the knowledge (γιγνώσκειν) of causes achieved by demonstration. This restrictive definition of ἐπίστασθαι has the consequence that there can be no ἐπίστασθαι of the immediate first principles of demonstration, nor of contingent truths and states of affairs. Aristotle accepts the consequence. Of first principles we have νοῦς, not ἐπίστασθαι in the defined sense (*APo.* B.19). Of contingent states of affairs we have δόξα (*APo.* A.33) or αἴσθησις (A.18, A.31). But Aristotle makes it perfectly clear that just as he is not saying that we have no knowledge of first principles, so too he is not saying that we have no knowledge of contingent/sensible states of affairs. He is quite prepared to use γιγνώσκειν/γνωρίζειν of such cases.⁶² What he denies, for either of the cases on the right-hand side of Alexander's scheme, is that they count as ἐπίστασθαι.

Now, I believe that to carry over to Aristotle Lyons' scheme for the Greek verbs of knowing, all we need to do is take note of the following:

(i) ἐπίστασθαι in Aristotle, contrary to Plato's normal practice (but in accordance with at least some other Greek authors),⁶³ does often take a clause of *oratio obliqua*. When it does, it can be defined in

---

⁶⁰ Similarly, if tentatively, Barnes 1975: 97: 'The "we think" argument will then refer not to linguistic consensus but rather to the views of Aristotle and his fellows on the proper limits of scientific endeavour.'
⁶¹ For a helpful guide to the way in which greater stringency for the application of a term need not bring with it a change of meaning, see Lewis 1979, where p. 247 touches on the case of knowledge.
⁶² If proof be needed, see γιγνώσκειν at *EE* VII.4, 1239a35–b2, γνωρίζειν at *Top.* II.7, 113a31–2, *Mem.* 1, 449b13–15.
⁶³ LSJ s.v. II 2 and III.

terms of γιγνώσκειν plus a clause of *oratio obliqua*. Roughly, and using the translations I have argued for on other occasions,[64] *x* ἐπίσταται (understands) that p, iff for some *q* (better: for some *q* from a carefully defined class *C*), *x* γιγνώσκει (knows) that *p* because q.

(ii) The most important point to highlight in this definition is the contrast between ἐπίστασθαι and γιγνώσκειν along the horizontal dimension. This is what secures that the definition is non-circular. Thus far Barnes and I agree. We disagree when, as described above (p. 253), Barnes puts εἰδέναι alongside γιγνώσκειν in the horizontal contrast with ἐπίστασθαι. In Aristotle as in Plato, εἰδέναι stands in for *either* term in context: for example, at *APo*. 1.2, 71b17 it substitutes for ἐπίστασθαι, at 11.11, 94a20 for γιγνώσκειν, while at *Met*. A.2, 982b19–21 εἰδέναι elucidates ἐπίστασθαι, being itself elucidated at A.3, 983a25–6 by γνωρίζειν of a thing's primary cause.

Now look back to the *parenthetical* section of the opening passage of the *Physics* (184a12–14, at p. 249 above). There we find the standard definition differently expressed: instead of ἐπίστασθαι or εἰδέναι γιγνώσκειν is used for the definiendum, and γνωρίζειν is brought in for the definiens. I conclude that the particular words chosen matter less than the *system* of contrasts; that is – ||

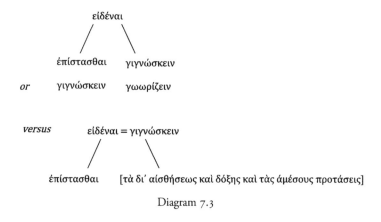

Diagram 7.3

Alexander chooses the first, expressed either way, and Simplicius the second. Let me now adjudicate.

---

[64] See references cited in n. 53.

Simplicius, in 1.13.9–10, appreciates the point that γιγνώσκειν in the *Physics* parenthesis means demonstrative knowledge (the knowledge which Barnes and I have agreed, at times, to call understanding), but he takes this to mean that ἐπίστασθαι is a species of γιγνώσκειν, and hence that εἰδέναι = γιγνώσκειν. If this was right, the *Physics* definition of γιγνώσκειν would be comparable to someone saying, 'My parent is the person who gave birth to me', using the generic 'parent' when they really mean 'mother'. The great awkwardness of this is to my mind good reason to adhere to Lyons' *system* of contrasts, resisting Simplicius' suggestion that γιγνώσκειν is as generic as εἰδέναι. I shall return to this issue after examining the nouns.

The main point to emphasise here is that ἐπιστήμη in Aristotle is not only cognate with, but genuinely coordinate with ἐπίστασθαι (*APo*. 1.2, 71b9–16: at least for οὗ ἁπλῶς ἔστιν ἐπιστήμη, 'that of which there is understanding *simpliciter*'). It is the science known or the scientific knowledge of the person who ἐπίσταται. This enables it to contrast straightforwardly with γνῶσις as ἐπίστασθαι contrasts with γιγνώσκειν (*APo*. II.19) – a contrast helped by the fact that τέχνη in Aristotle is officially restricted to productive skills; it does not normally extend, as it does at times in Plato, to theoretical sciences and mathematics[65] Piece all this together, and the effect is that ἐπιστήμη moves down to replace τέχνη, leaving a vacancy in the top slot of Lyons' original scheme:

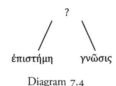

Diagram 7.4

|| It is fascinating to see the commentators (already Alexander *ap*. Simpl. *in Ar. Phys*. 1.14.13) filling the slot with the word εἴδησις, which in Aristotle

---

[65] I say 'officially' because *Met*. A.1, 981b25–7, cites *EN* VI.4, 1140a6ff., as the place where the difference between τέχνη, ἐπιστήμη, and other cognitive states is explained, and there τέχνη is indeed so confined. Yet Bonitz 1955 s.v. lists numerous places where Aristotle uses τέχνη of mathematics and other non-productive knowledge – most notably the immediately preceding sentence of *Met*. A.1! Conversely, wherever ἐπίστασθαι denotes a practical skill, ἐπιστήμη is the coordinate noun, with the result that the *Politics* can speak of δουλικαὶ ἐπιστῆμαι like housework (1.7, 1255b22–30), and *Metaphysics* A.4, 985a10–17, can compare the early physicists to untrained fighters who on occasion can get in a fine blow but not ἀπὸ ἐπιστήμης (ridiculously rendered by Ross in the 1928 Oxford translation [Ross 1928a] as 'not … on scientific principles'!). More examples where to translate 'science' would be wholly inappropriate are in Bonitz 1955 *ad* 279b51–280a4.

occurs just once, in the opening phrase of his *De Anima*: τῶν καλῶν καὶ τιμίων τὴν εἴδησιν ὑπολαμβάνοντες.[66] The effect is that verbs and nouns can now be placed in perfect correspondence:

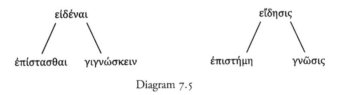

Diagram 7.5

Or, if you follow Simplicius:

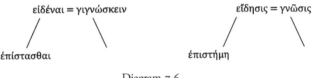

Diagram 7.6

I can now add further support to my claim that we should not follow Simplicius.

It is Simplicius (12.22–3, 12.25, 13.6) who insists that γνῶσις = εἴδησις, γιγνώσκειν = εἰδέναι. The reason why γνῶσις and γιγνώσκειν matter to Simplicius here is because they are the key words in the quotations from Plato's *Republic* at 13.3 and 5. Alexander is cited at 13.10–13 as having distinguished δόξα from ἐπίστασθαι (not necessarily by reference to the *Theaetetus*). He is not cited for having distinguished δόξα from γνῶσις. Nor is there any occurrence of γνῶσις/γιγνώσκειν in the actual quotation from Alexander. I incline to think that Alexander, whose *Physics* commentary is lost, said nothing about γνῶσις or γιγνώσκειν. The only thing that concerned him was the relation of εἰδέναι and ἐπίστασθαι in Aristotle's phrase τὸ εἰδέναι καὶ τὸ ἐπίστασθαι on page 1 of the *Physics*. Simplicius' equation of εἴδησις and γνῶσις is to be seen, therefore, as a device for bringing to bear on that Aristotelian phrase, first Plato's *Republic*, and second the parenthetical definition of γιγνώσκειν later in the *Physics* paragraph. Simplicius can then make out that Aristotle agrees with Plato that the strict or proper

---

[66] This is the first attested occurrence of the word. LSJ s.v. misleadingly starts with a quote from Nausiphanes, who was some 20 years junior to Aristotle.

sense of εἰδέναι is ἐπίστασθαι – γιγνώσκειν as elucidated in the *Republic*. If we reject this as the special pleading that it is, we are left with Alexander's conclusion that εἰδέναι is to ἐπίστασθαι as genus to species. And remember here that as a good Aristotelian, Alexander will believe that the genus has no independent content of its own: it is merely the potential which is variously differentiated in its several contrasting species. This fits the old Lyons very well – very well indeed.

Remember also that Simplicius concedes that Alexander is right about Aristotle's usage in general. It is only this passage for which he wants to plead a special Platonic understanding of Aristotelian knowledge. And even his special equation of εἰδέναι and ἐπίστασθαι for this passage is closer to the old Lyons than the new Lyons. ||

More important still, to my mind, is that this whole debate between Alexander and Simplicius is conducted without the slightest indication that the three verbs in dispute might be differentiated by their preferred constructions – the source from which the new Lyons, you will recall, wants to derive their prototypical meaning. All three verbs are expected to take the *same* constructions, be it *oratio obliqua* or the accusative noun phrases such as 'causes', 'principles', or 'elements' which Hardie and Gaye, and Wicksteed and Cornford, translate as objects of acquaintance, but which themselves require spelling out in propositional terms. What I have tried to show is that with suitable qualifications, adaptations, and adjustments, the old Lyons can help us understand what is going on in the Alexander–Simplicius debate. The new Lyons cannot.

I acknowledge, of course, that Alexander and Simplicius wrote many centuries after the texts which they are expounding. But they know these texts and their language pretty well by heart – witness the small slips that Simplicius makes when citing the *Republic*, *Theaetetus*, and *Metaphysics*. They are much closer to being insiders than we are.

I now return to the point where I concluded above that in Aristotle the particular words chosen matter less than the *system* of contrasts:

Diagram 7.7

In each case, Aristotle defines the left-hand verb (be it ἐπίστασθαι or γιγνώσκειν) by the right-hand verb (be it γιγνώσκειν or γνωρίζειν) as follows: ἐπίστασθαι/γιγνώσκειν X = γιγνώσκειν/γνωρίζειν the *cause* of X, where 'cause' may be taken as broadly as preferred, to include any or all of the standard Aristotelian causes, and X may be anything which such causes can explain; which Aristotle claims is everything – or rather, everything explicable.[67] The important point is that Aristotle's four epistemic verbs combine in different ways to express just *two* epistemic *concepts*: on the one hand, explanatory knowledge that *p* because *q*; and on the other, the plain knowledge that *p* and the plain knowledge that q, which, when truly linked by 'because', express the former – namely, the highly commendable state which is called γινώσκειν ἐπιστημονικῶς by Simplicius, 'conoscere scientificamente' by Mignucci, and 'understanding' by Barnes and myself.

It is the same story with Aristotle's treatment of the nouns. Once τέχνη is siphoned off elsewhere and ἐπιστήμη becomes coordinate with its cognate verb as diagrammed above, contrasting with γνῶσις as ἐπίστασθαι contrasts with γιγνώσκειν, there remain just two concepts for the nouns which Aristotle uses to represent the three verbs:[68] ||

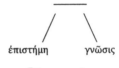

Diagram 7.8

A good way to acquire a sense of the difference between Aristotle's cognitive vocabulary and Plato's is to read through the deservedly famous chapter on weakness of will, in *Nicomachean Ethics* VII.3. Weakness of will is acting against one's knowledge of what one ought to do. *EN* VII.3 is a long chapter, yet in the descriptions of the knowledge acted against there is not one instance of γνῶσις, γιγνώσκειν or their derivatives. The field is wholly occupied by the noun ἐπιστήμη and the verbs ἐπίστασθαι and εἰδέναι. ἐπιστήμη and ἐπίστασθαι are treated as on a par, in accordance with the diagrams that I have proposed for Aristotle's vocabulary. εἰδέναι remains the general verb, as it was in Plato, substituting for ἐπίστασθαι when convenient, but εἴδησις does not return as the corresponding noun.

---

[67] On things inexplicable, see *Met.* Δ.30 and Z.9.
[68] I disregard here the solitary occurrence of εἴδησις noted above, p. 257–8.

Therefore, there is all the more reason to wonder whether the choice of the noun ἐπιστήμη in preference to γνῶσις is significant.

I propose that it is. Once you read the chapter in the light of the above diagram for the epistemic nouns in *Aristotle*, you (should) find yourself constantly reminded that the issue which Aristotle is addressing is not the issue of what is going on when someone acts contrary to a single correct moral belief (which might coexist with much wickedness), but rather the intelligibility of their doing something which goes against their whole moral outlook. In Aristotelian Greek, παρὰ τὴν ἐπιστήμην does not mean 'contrary to my normal, settled knowledge and belief on a certain issue' – for example, about what to do when offered a bribe. It means 'contrary to *everything* I know and believe is morally proper'.

But perhaps the best way to draw the sting of objections concerning the belatedness of my native speakers is to conclude by producing one final text, from a prose artist much older than Plato. A text which the old Lyons can help us understand, but the new Lyons cannot elucidate at all:

> Διδάσκαλος δὲ πλείστων Ἡσίοδος· τοῦτον ἐπίστανται πλεῖστα εἰδέναι, ὅστις ἡμέρην καὶ εὐφροσύνην οὐκ ἐγίνωσκεν· ἔστι γὰρ ἕν.

> The teacher of most is Hesiod. It is him they know as knowing the most, the man who did not know day and night: for they are one. (Heraclitus Fragment 57)

It should be obvious that Heraclitus frag. 57 is playing his three knowledge verbs off against each other.[69] Well then: ||

(1) The γινώσκειν he denies to Hesiod and the multitude who take him as their teacher is precisely *not* knowledge by acquaintance. For if there is such a thing as knowledge by acquaintance, concerning night and day everybody has it. γινώσκειν here, therefore, is not a matter of having had experience of night and day and being able to recognise

---

[69] A point appreciated by Kahn 1979: 109, but ignored on both sides of the dispute between Vlastos 1957: 208–9 and Gould 1955: 10, n. 6, concerning the value of ἐπίστασθαι here. Vlastos for once allows Gould's rendering (pp. 10–11, following Snell) in terms of 'subjective faith' – a surprise meaning of the verb indisputably attested for Heraclitus' fellow Ionian Herodotus (n. 28 above.) Barnes also, in his exhilarating two-volume opus, *The Presocratic Philosophers*, 'they are convinced' (Barnes 1979, vol. 1, p. 72). My objection is that the word-play is lost unless we translate all three verbs by our one verb 'know'. Even for Herodotus it is the exception rather than the rule that ἐπίστασθαι carries no implication of truth. I suspect that the readiness of scholars as distinguished as Kirk (Kirk 1954: 155), and Marcovich (Marcovich 1967: 223), to translate in subjective terms, without supplying any argument, may stem from the simple fact that LSJ s.v. ἐπίσταμαι quotes this very fragment to illustrate the meaning 'to be assured, feel sure that...' before continuing with a string of references to Herodotus *and no one else*.

which it is when you go out of the door of your house. This γινώσκειν is realising that night and day are a unity, or (if you prefer) grasping the unity which is their real nature. A deep, not a superficial, everyday accomplishment.

(2) εἰδέναι is surely not chosen to suggest, even in the first instance, knowledge that. Knowledge that would fit Hesiod as the author of the *Theogony* well enough, but Hesiod is equally important as the author of *Works and Days*, which teaches knowledge how as well as – indeed more than – knowledge that. In short, εἰδέναι is just the right verb for πλεῖστα: because (as appears so clearly from the old Lyons' schema) εἰδέναι is open and indeterminate: it can ascribe to Hesiod as much knowledge, of as many kinds (that, how, or whatever), as anyone could have.

(3) Finally, ἐπίστανται is clearly not knowledge how. One of the old Lyons' firmest points, and the one with which his exposition begins (so as to accustom us to the idea and methods of transformational analysis), is that ἐπίστασθαι stands in a relation of consequence to μανθάνειν. It is the knowledge you have from teaching (self-teaching – learning – included), regardless of the theoretical-practical distinction. This produces a nice Heraclitean twist to the whole saying, as follows:

(4) Men have learned (ἐπίστανται) that Hesiod knows (εἰδέναι) most – more than anyone else. From whom have they learned it? From their teacher, Hesiod himself, who never realised (οὐκ ἐγίνωσκεν)[70] that day and night are (in some crucial way) not two opposites, but one unity.[71]

---

[70] Note the imperfect tense of ἐγίνωσκεν: Hesiod's was a life-long failure.

[71] For helpful comments on intermittent drafts of this paper, I am grateful for discussion over the years in Budapest, Cornell, London, Oxford, and Paris. More recent thanks for insightful criticism are due to Pavel Gregoric and Ben Morison. Above all, I am grateful to John Lyons both for his wonderfully enlightening book and for his taking time to send me a challenging set of comments on an earlier draft of this essay, plus more recent correspondence.

PART II
Physics and optics

CHAPTER 8

ΕΙΚΩΣ ΜΥΘΟΣ

In memoriam Heda Šegvić

The account of the sensible world in Plato's *Timaeus* is presented as an εἰκὼς μῦθος. That much is common knowledge. We readers should be content with an εἰκὼς μῦθος. But what does it mean? And why is it true?

The phrase is typically translated 'a probable story', 'a likely tale', *vel sim*. I believe that for present-day readers such a translation is at best misleading, at worst an utter distortion of Plato's intent. To begin with, it is too suggestive of the cautious atmosphere of modern empiricist philosophy of science, according to which a scientific hypothesis is (to quote A. E. Taylor's Whitehead-inspired gloss on εἰκὼς μῦθος) always 'provisional', because held subject to revision as we learn more and more about the physical world.[1]

Alternatively, the standard translation encourages the thought that the reason why readers of the *Timaeus* are offered a likely story – or *only* a likely story, as it is sometimes (but illegitimately) put[2] – is that no statement about the world of becoming can be certain. Any number of scholars will tell you that the subject matter of physics precludes anything better than probability, because physics deals with the changeable realm of becoming, not the fixed realm of being. But this is not in fact – I repeat *not* – the reason we are given why we should be content with an εἰκὼς μῦθος. The reason Timaeus gives is a more subtle one that leads us far away, not only from modern empiricist ‖ philosophies of science, but also from standard understandings of the Platonic contrast between being and

---

[1] A. E. Taylor 1928: 59–61. Compare A. E. Taylor 1926: 440–1. A note in Whitehead 1929: ix suggests that the influence was mutual.

[2] So Cornford 1937: 28–9, just after translating 29c2 as follows: 'an account of what is *only* a likeness will itself be *but* likely', where the words I have italicised have no correlate in the Greek. Cornford presumably follows A. E. Taylor 1929: 'discourses concerning that which is ... but a likeness, [are] themselves but likely'. I say 'presumably' on the grounds that Cornford's translation has the merit of plundering at will from Taylor's splendidly elevated imitation of Plato's *Timaeus* style.

becoming. If the usual translations of εἰκὼς μῦθος make it hard to read what Timaeus actually says about why we should be content with an εἰκὼς μῦθος, we would do well to re-examine the question of translation *ab initio*.

In the beginning was Cicero. He was the first translator of the *Timaeus*. He rendered the two-word phrase εἰκὼς μῦθος by the single word *probabilia*. Never mind what his reasons for this might have been (he can scarcely have been unaware that he was refusing to give physics the status it had for Plato).[3] I trust you will agree that the word μῦθος should not be passed over in silence. But will you agree[4] that a translator should write 'myth', not some anodyne substitute such as 'story', 'tale', 'account'? I offer two reasons why you should accept the stronger, stranger rendering.

The first reason is that the word μῦθος has occurred several times in the dialogue, clearly in the sense 'myth', before we reach the phrase εἰκὼς μῦθος. At 22bd Critias tells of Solon recounting (μυθολογεῖν) the myth of Deucalion's flood and of the Egyptian priest responding that such floods and periodic destructions are historically real events; the priest, he reports Solon reporting, cited the story of Phaethon as a real world conflagration, the memory of which survived in the form of a myth (22c7: μύθου σχῆμα ἔχον). Critias goes on to describe the account of the ideal city and its inhabitants given by Socrates on the previous day as a πλασθέντα μῦθον in contrast to his own forthcoming account of Atlantis, which he calls an ἀληθινὸν λόγον (26ce; cf. 20d).[5] In all these cases by μῦθος is meant a narrative of things that did not in the real world of history take place as described – but also, in each case, a narrative that makes important reference to the divine. Only three Stephanus pages separate the last occurrence of μῦθος from εἰκὼς μῦθος at 29d, where there is no indication that the word μῦθος is now to be taken in a different sense.

A second, more positive reason to translate εἰκὼς μῦθος as an εἰκὼς myth is that what is to follow is nothing less than a theogony. The cosmos is a || god. The birth of the cosmos is the birth of a god. This at once raises questions about the relation of the *Timaeus*, first to Hesiod's *Theogony*, and second to the περὶ φύσεως tradition of the sixth and fifth centuries BC,

---

[3] Lévy (2003) is a valuable discussion of this topic. Even more dreary than leaving out μῦθος altogether is Calcidius' rendering of it as *explanatio*.
[4] With Brisson and Patillon 1992 but no others that I have found.
[5] To this day, seekers after the real Atlantis cite Critias' words as Plato's own opinion (e.g. Zangger 1992: 46, on 20d7–8). As for Socrates' earlier discourse, our *Republic* (which is alluded to, if not directly referred to) already uses μῦθος, ἐν μύθῳ μυθολογεῖν to characterise its narrative of the coming to be of the ideal city and the education of the Guards within it (376de, 501e).

which defined itself as a naturalistic alternative to the Hesiodic account of the origin of things. Which side of the divide will Timaeus opt for? Or will he transcend the opposition by giving us a περὶ φύσεως which is simultaneously a myth: a religious story as well as a scientifico-mathematical one?

The objection to translating 'myth' has standardly been that, as Timaeus' discourse proceeds, he uses the phrase εἰκὼς λόγος as well as, and a lot more often than, εἰκὼς μῦθος. So, it is argued, especially by Vlastos,[6] μῦθος must just mean a narrative story. It does not stand in contrast to λόγος as it did when the περὶ φύσεως tradition set itself up in opposition to Hesiod. My reply to this objection will be that the ease and frequency with which εἰκὼς λόγος can substitute for εἰκὼς μῦθος has a different explanation. It is not that μῦθος is equivalent to, and no different from λόγος, but that an εἰκὼς μῦθος is a λόγος as well as a myth. Timaeus' myth, unlike Hesiod's, is as well reasoned as any of the Presocratic cosmogonies in the περὶ φύσεως tradition. But unlike your typical Presocratic, whom Plato tends to regard as an atheistic materialist (*Laws* x), Timaeus' cosmogony will be a theogony too.

This brings me back to Cicero and his choice of the Latin word *probabilis* to render εἰκώς. Εἰκώς is not the only Greek word that Cicero translated *probabilis*. In the *De Finibus* he used *probabilis* for the Stoic εὔλογον (the 'reasonable'), while concurrently in the *Academica* using it for πίθανον (the 'convincing' or 'persuasive'); earlier in *De Inventione* 1.44–9 he had adopted the same term for the Aristotelian ἔνδοξον, which he treated (with some precedent in Aristotle) as a species of εἰκώς. That's an awful lot of different Greek concepts from different philosophical traditions to pack into the single word *probabilis*. The common denominator, which Cicero presumably had in view, is that the Greek originals all conceptualise, albeit in different and incompatible ways, something that an agent can approve (*probare*) as a basis for decision or action. This practical orientation will be vindicated below. Meanwhile, it is important to recognise that our present-day understanding of probability, especially in scientific contexts, has very little in common with *either* the Stoic εὔλογον *or* the Academic πίθανον *or* the Aristotelian ἔνδοξον *or* the Platonic-Aristotelian εἰκώς. In the centuries since Cicero, important new conceptual elements have accrued to the descendants of *probabilis* in modern languages, with the result that 'probable' || becomes more and more different from *probabilis* as Cicero understood it. So long as classical scholars wrote their commentaries and treatises in Latin, the problem

---

[6] Vlastos 1939: 380–3, echoed emphatically by Rowe 2003.

could be disguised in the respectable murk of *probabilis*. But modern languages bring modern meanings into our translations of the *Timaeus*. What was once a pretty fair rendering of εἰκώς is no longer so appropriate.

To explain why εἰκώς is a problem for translators, I want to compare the range of the Greek word with that of modern terms such as 'probable' and 'likely'. I start with the range of overlap between ancient and modern, and proceed to the area of divergence.

Εἰκώς is of course a participial form associated with the verb ἔοικα, 'to be like'.[7] This is the basis for the connection with the word εἰκών, a likeness, to which Plato draws attention at 29c2. In English, the words 'likeness' and 'likely' no longer have a palpable connection with each other that the average speaker is aware of. But other languages do still preserve the connection that English has lost sight of. 'Verisimilis' in Latin, 'verosimile' in Italian, 'vraisemblable' in French, 'wahrscheinlich' in German, правдоподобный in Russian, all mean 'like what is true'. And it was certainly a well-established meaning by Plato's time that something can be called εἰκώς if it is like what is (already known or believed to be) true. In such contexts, the translation 'likely' or indeed 'probable' fits perfectly well.

But Greek εἰκώς has a much broader range than this, a range into which 'verosimile' and правдоподобный cannot follow, nor can English 'probable' – at least as it is used today. Something is εἰκώς not only if it is like what is true, but also if it is like what ought to be, or it is like what you or the situation need and require. There are many contexts, from Homer on, in both poetry and prose, where 'likely' and 'probable' are just impossible translations for εἰκώς and one uses instead words like 'appropriate', 'fitting', 'fair', 'natural', 'reasonable'. To cite a case from Plato himself, at *Sophist* 225a the Eleatic Stranger pauses in the midst of his divisions because he needs a word to mark off a certain kind of fighting, one in which body struggles against body. He says that an εἰκὸς καὶ πρέπον ὄνομα would be the word βιαστικόν. You could not, in modern English, call βιαστικόν a 'probable' word for this kind of fighting. I say 'modern English' because as late as 1860–1, in Charles Dickens' *Great Expectations*, when Pip sees the would-be actor Mr Wopsle dressed up to play Hamlet, he comments, 'I could have wished that his curls and forehead had been more probable', meaning 'more appropriate to the role'.[8] I trust that this

---

[7] Thus, for example, at 30c5 if the cosmos is ἀτελεῖ ἐοικός – if it is like something incomplete – it cannot be beautiful (καλόν).
[8] Dickens 2003: 253.

sounds strange to your ear now. 'Probable' no longer pairs with 'appropriate' in the manner of Plato's phrase εἰκώς καὶ πρέπον.

There is a similar juxtaposition of εἰκώς and πρέποι τ' ἄν at *Timaeus* 67d1–2, compounded this time with ἐπιεικεῖ. Cornford (1952) translates, 'It is natural (εἰκώς) and fitting (πρέποι τ' ἄν) to add here a reasonable (ἐπιεικεῖ) account of the colours'. Zeyl (2000) has 'Now, at this point, it is particularly appropriate to provide a well-reasoned account of colours'.[9] The fact is, the translator of the *Timaeus* will find all the meanings, 'appropriate', 'fitting', 'natural', 'reasonable', needed at one point or another, as well as (I happily admit) the rendering 'likely' or 'probable'. Plato, being the creative craftsman he is, exploits the full range of his key word, and makes frequent use also of the related adverb εἰκότως, 'reasonably'.

The next step is to consider the context where the phrase εἰκὼς μῦθος is first introduced, in order to determine whether it situates εἰκώς in the range where it overlaps with our word 'probable' or in the range where 'probable' has to be replaced by evaluative words such as 'reasonable', 'appropriate', 'fitting', etc. I offer first a translation, then a point by point analysis of the relevant details of the 'prelude' (προοίμιον)[10] to Timaeus' discourse (29b1–d3) – a passage that would be my favourite candidate for the well-known title 'A Much Misread Passage of the *Timaeus*'.

Translation
(A) Again, these things being so, our world is necessarily the likeness of something. (B) Now in any matter it is most important to begin at the natural beginning. Accordingly [i.e. this is our beginning], we should make the following distinction concerning a likeness and its model, to wit: accounts [λόγοι] are akin to those things of which they are ἐξηγηταί. (C) On the one hand, (i) accounts exegetic of that which is permanent and stable and manifest to reason [μετὰ νοῦ καταφανοῦς: manifest if you use reason to grasp it] are themselves permanent and unchangeable – to the extent that it is possible and fitting for accounts to be irrefutable and invincible, there ought [δεῖ] to be no falling short of this. (D) On the other hand, (ii) accounts exegetic of that which is (a) made to be like that other [ἐκεῖνο = that which is permanent and stable and manifest to reason] ‖ and so is itself a likeness will themselves be εἰκότες[11] and will stand to those

---

[9] Contrast Bury 1929: 'Concerning colours, then, the following explanation will be the most probable and worthy of a judicious account.'
[10] So called by Socrates at 29d.
[11] Cf. n. 2 above on Cornford's tendentious insertions. I leave εἰκότες untranslated here because on my proposal to translate 'likeness'/'appropriate' rather than 'likeness'/'likely' English cannot match the

other [type (i)] accounts in the following proportion: as being is to becoming, so truth is to conviction [πίστις]. (E) If, therefore [οὖν draws the consequence], Socrates, in many respects concerning many things [i.e. *not* in all respects or all things], regarding the gods and the generation of the universe,[12] we find ourselves unable to furnish accounts which are entirely and in every way in agreement with each other [αὐτοὺς ἑαυτοῖς ὁμολογουμένους] and made completely precise, do not be surprised. But if we can offer accounts which are no less εἰκότες than another's,[13] we ought to be content, remembering that I the speaker and you the judges [κριταί] have human nature. Consequently, about these things [*sc*. the 'many things' just referred to] it is fitting to accept [ἀποδεχομένους] the[14] εἰκότα μῦθον and seek nothing further. (29c4–d3)

Analysis
(A) Again, these things being so, this world of ours is necessarily the likeness of something. ‖

This is the first introduction of the notion of an εἰκών. That our world is a likeness follows from the claim, proved in the immediately preceding section (28c–29a), that it was crafted on the model of that which is unchanging and comprehensible by a rational account (λόγος) and wisdom (φρόνησις).

Timaeus continues,

(B) Now in any matter it is most important to begin at the natural beginning. Accordingly [i.e. this is our beginning], we should make the following distinction concerning a likeness and its model, to wit: accounts [λόγοι] are akin to those things of which they are ἐξηγηταί.

This is usually rendered 'accounts are akin to that which they set forth' (Cornford 1937; similarly Zeyl 2000), 'akin in their character to that

---

word-play εἰκών–εἰκός. In the Greek the word-play remains, however we translate, because likeness is common to both 'like what is true' and 'like what is needful'.

[12] τὸ πᾶν here, as at 29d7–e1, is only part of what a Platonist calls τὸ πᾶν, so the whole phrase amounts to: in many respects concerning many of the things discussed by Hesiod and the Presocratics who wrote περὶ φύσεως.

[13] I take μηδενός as masculine, with Calcidius and A. E. Taylor 1929, A. E. Taylor 1928, versus Bury 1929, Cornford 1937, Lee 1965, Brisson and Patillon 1992, Zeyl 2000, Johansen 2004: 49. The same problem arises at 48d3. My preference for the minority's choice of the personal is guided (a) by the immediate sequel, emphasising that Timaeus and his listeners are but human, which connects with (b) the resultant echo of Parmenides fr. 8, 60–1 τόν σοι ἐγὼ διάκοσμον ἐοικότα πάντα φατίζω, ὡς οὐ μή ποτέ τίς σε βροτῶν γνώμη παρελάσσῃ (see below), and (c) by the dramatic entry at 55d of an ἄλλος who supports a contrary opinion to Timaeus' on the question whether κατὰ τὸν εἰκότα λόγον there is just one universe or five (discussed below).

[14] The definite article is standardly referred to the entire cosmology, as must be the case with τῷ μύθῳ at 69b1. But in the wake of περὶ τούτων it could be distributive: a μῦθος for each of the many things to be discussed, as in the plural τῶν εἰκότων μύθων at 59c6.

which they expound' (A. E. Taylor 1929), 'ayant une parenté avec les objets mêmes qu'ils expliquent' (Rivaud 1925), or 'akin to the diverse objects which they serve to explain' (Bury 1929). Then the translators proceed as if nothing extraordinary had been said.[15] I have left the word ἐξηγηταί untranslated, to flag it as a term in need of elucidation. Not only is it a striking and solemn word in itself, but everywhere else it refers to a *person*: most commonly, the exegete who expounds an oracle, explains a dream, tells you the meaning of a ritual ceremony,[16] or advises on problems of expiation (it was to a board of ἐξηγηταί at Athens that Euthyphro's father sent to inquire what he should do with the murderous servant he had left tied up in a ditch: *Euthphr.* 4c, 9a). In later Greek ἐξηγητής also refers to the guide who takes you round a sanctuary or temple (Pausanias v.15.10, *SIG* 1021.20); it would not be inappropriate to think of Timaeus as our guide to the beautiful design of the cosmos we inhabit.

Thus the accounts (λόγοι) we are talking about are not any old statements, arguments, or discourses about the physical world. They are very special accounts personified as the exegetes who expound or explain the unobvious significance of an object like a dream, ritual, or oracle which does not bear its meaning on its surface, because it comes from, or has some important connection with, the divine. The appropriate English translation is 'exegete', as we would speak of those who engage in exegesis of the Bible. It is a word that || should jump off the page to surprise us, showing us how far away we are from the cautious atmosphere of modern empiricist philosophy of science – but also how far from the atmosphere engendered by the metaphysical downgrading of the sensible world in the central Books of the *Republic*. The *Republic* did indeed bid us become spectators of all time and all being (486a), but it said little or nothing to imply that we should become connoisseurs of the visible realm in the detailed way Timaeus will teach us to be. A good way to capture the tone of our passage is to quote Epictetus (1.6.17–22), who says that a human is born to be, not only a spectator, but also an exegete, of God and his works (ἔργα).

---

[15] Even worse is Ammonius *in de Int.* 154.18–20, who reports Plato as saying no more than that '*p*' is true if and only if *p*.

[16] At *Rep.* 427c Apollo himself is described as ἐξηγητής for all mankind of what their rituals should be, but readers would know that the utterances of the Pythia through whom he spoke required ἐξηγεταί to render their meaning.

Back to the text:

> (C) On the one hand, (i) accounts exegetic of that which is permanent and stable and manifest to reason [μετὰ νοῦ καταφανοῦς: manifest if you use reason to grasp it] are themselves permanent and unchangeable: to the extent that it is possible and fitting for accounts to be irrefutable and invincible, there ought [δεῖ] to be no falling short of this.

Note the 'ought'. Stability and irrefutability are not automatic consequences of the accounts having a stable unchanging subject matter. Rather, they are standards the accounts are expected to live up to. The point is not that you cannot go wrong when expounding a stable unchanging subject matter, e.g. that you cannot make mistakes in mathematics (like the slave in the *Meno*) or when talking about Forms (like Socrates in the *Parmenides*). Of course you can. But you ought not to. If you do, you are falling short of the standards required for successful exegesis *of such things*.

If this is correct, we should expect a parallel message in the other half of the contrast between two types of account. Being εἰκώς will not be an automatic consequence of undertaking the exegesis of a likeness, still less a depressing consequence of speaking about the physical world at all. Rather, it will be an *aspiration* that Timaeus' discourse will try to live up to, a standard to judge it by.[17] And it will be a difficult aspiration: that is why he prays for divine help to get there, not only at 27c before the phrase εἰκώς μῦθος has been mentioned, but later in the last sentence of 48d, at the start of Part II:

> Let us therefore at the outset of this discourse call upon the god to be our saviour this time, too, to give us safe passage through[18] a strange and unfamiliar narration || (διήγησις), and lead us to a view of what is likely/appropriate (πρὸς τὸ τῶν εἰκότων δόγμα).[19] (tr. after Zeyl 2000)

---

[17] This is confirmed by the phrase τὴν τῶν εἰκότων μύθων μεταδιώκοντα ἰδέαν at 59c6–7, discussed below n. 32.

[18] So A. E. Taylor 1929 and others *versus* Rivaud 1925: 'pour qu'il nous sauve des considérations absurdes et incohérentes'.

[19] Here I transcribe, without going so far as to endorse, the interesting note *ad loc.* in A. E. Taylor 1928: 'The port to which a safe passage is entreated is τὸ τῶν εἰκότων δόγμα. His hearers will feel themselves safe in "home waters" when the theory has got so far as to bring in the "four roots" (this is plainly the particular δόγμα he has in mind), and to explain other things as compounds of them. The stormy sea which the vessel must cross before it makes these "home waters" is the geometrical construction of the "roots", or rather the account of space which is preliminary to that construction. It is this which Timaeus foresees the others will find it hard to follow.'

To confirm that εἰκώς is a standard to live up to, let me point you to a passage of the *Timaeus* which fails to live up to it. This is the account of the traditional gods at 40de:

> As for the other divinities (δαίμονες), it is too high a task for us to declare and know their generation; we must trust those who have declared it in former times: being, as they said, descendants of gods, they must, no doubt, have had certain knowledge of their own ancestors. We cannot, then, mistrust the children of gods, though they speak without probable or necessary proofs (καίπερ ἄνευ τε εἰκότων καὶ ἀναγκαίων ἀποδείξεων λέγουσιν); when they profess to report their family history, we must follow established usage and accept what they say. Let us, then, take on their word this account of the generation of these gods. As children of Earth and Heaven were born Oceanus and Tethys ... (tr. after Cornford 1952)

It sounds pretty ironic to me.[20] But the irony, if such it be, presupposes that a statement being about the temporal realm does not *eo ipso* make it an εἰκὼς λόγος. Please notice also, while you have your eye on the passage, that εἰκώς and ἀναγκαῖος appear here as adjectives characterising two kinds of proof (ἀποδείξεις) or argument. The immediate point is that neither type of argument is characteristic of your traditional theogonic narrative.[21] The next lesson is that εἰκώς argumentation is to be a distinguishing feature of Plato's theogony.

We turn, then, to the other half of Timaeus' methodological contrast, the half that deals with type (ii) accounts. Please note that the subject of the sentence is not any old statement || about a likeness, still less any old statement about the sensible world, but accounts exegetic of a certain type of likeness, namely, one fashioned after an eternal unchanging model. These accounts will be akin to their subject matter in the sense of being εἰκότες accounts of that subject matter:

> (D) On the other hand, (ii) accounts exegetic of that which is (a) made to be like that other [ἐκεῖνο = that which is permanent and stable and manifest to reason] and so is itself a likeness will themselves be εἰκότες and will stand to those other [type (i)] accounts in the following proportion: as being is to becoming, so is truth to conviction [πίστις].

The verb is indicative, as it was in the previous sentence (ὄντας), where the 'ought'-sentence spelling out that unchangeability is a standard to live up to shows that the phrase 'accounts exegetic of ...' in both cases means

---

[20] As also to A. E. Taylor 1928 *ad loc.*; a mollified version of the same in Cornford 1937.
[21] I follow Betegh 2004: 146–9, in doubting that Plato has any particular known theogony in mind.

accounts which *succeed* in providing an exegesis of their subject matter. A successful explanation of type (i) will be unchangeable, a successful explanation of type (ii) will be εἰκώς – whatever that means, which is the mystery we are trying to unravel.

The next problem is the proportion. Successful type (i) accounts will stand to successful type (ii) accounts in the proportion: as being is to becoming, so is ἀλήθεια to πίστις. The proportion makes everyone think of the *Republic*, rightly I am sure. Yet you will not find quite this proportion, 'as being is to becoming, so is ἀλήθεια to πίστις', in any of the places where proportions are set out in the *Republic* (510a, 511e, 534a). The closest is *Republic* 534a, which does say, among other things, that being is to becoming as ἐπιστήμη (not ἀλήθεια) is to πίστις (and διάνοια to εἰκασία). Now in the *Republic* the various proportions illustrate degrees of ἀλήθεια and σαφήνεια, where degrees of ἀλήθεια characterise the objects of mind and degrees of σαφήνεια the corresponding mental state (510a, 511e). In the *Timaeus*, ἀλήθεια is itself a term in the proportion. It stands where ἐπιστήμη stood in *Republic* 534a, on the side of mind rather than the objects of mind. It therefore has to refer to a cognitive state rather than a cognised object.[22] The outcome should be: ||

> As being is to becoming, so is ἀλήθεια to πίστις *and* so are (successful) type (i) accounts to (successful) type (ii) accounts.

Here it will make a difference whether we think of accounts (λόγοι) as individual statements or as complexes of statements standing to each other in some logical relation. If we think of accounts as individual statements, then the reason why type (i) accounts ought to be stable, irrefutable, and incontrovertible is that they aim to express individual necessary truths about Forms or mathematical objects. If we think, rather, of the sorts of explanatory accounts we encounter in the sequel, reasoned *complexes* of statements dealing, for example, with the uniqueness of the cosmos (an example we will look at shortly), then the analogue for type (i) accounts will be mathematical *proofs*. Recall the comparison between necessary and εἰκότες ἀποδείξεις at 40e. Type (i) accounts ought to be stable, irrefutable,

---

[22] Here I am indebted to Szaif 1996, esp. 61–7, a discussion which is both incisive and decisive. He aptly refers to the Stoic distinction between ἡ ἀλήθεια and τὸ ἀληθές, reported at S.E. *PH* II.80–3, *M* VII.38–44, the former being systematic knowledge of the latter. It is well known that the Stoics were keen students of the *Timaeus*. This solution leaves room for statements and beliefs about the realm of becoming to count not only as true in the ordinary sense (30b, 37b, 51b, 51de, 53e, 56b, 72d), but even certain as well (37b); cf. Johansen 2004: 50.

and incontrovertible, because their subject matter is such that you can aim to establish results as definitively as Pythagoras' theorem, by rigorously proving it *must* be so.

But a μῦθος could not possibly be a single statement. It must refer to a whole complex of statements. If εἰκώς is to apply to a μῦθος, it must express a property appropriate to complexes of statements. Hence I propose that the two types of λόγοι are explanatory accounts, each token of which consists of a *number* of statements standing to each other in some logical relation. I further propose that the contrast Timaeus' proportion illustrates is a contrast in degrees of argumentative rigour: precisely the contrast we will later meet at 40de as the contrast between necessary and εἰκότες ἀποδείξεις in discourse about the birth of gods. He is both echoing and subverting Parmenides' distinction between 'the unshaken heart of well-rounded ἀλήθεια', on the one hand, and on the other, 'the opinions of mortals, in which there is no true πίστις' (fr. 1, 29–30). Like Parmenides, Timaeus contrasts the rigorous reasoning of the way of truth with a διάκοσμον ἐοικότα (fr. 8, 60), an appropriately ordered account of the sensible world, which he – again like Parmenides (fr. 8, 60–1) – hopes will surpass any given by other mortal minds.[23] But his account aims to be appropriately argued, not just appropriately ordered. Instead of denying all probative force to λόγοι about the visible cosmos, he makes them analogous to πίστις: πίστις which aspires to be εἰκώς in its own right, as πίστις. And here we should remember that by Plato's day πίστις was in use as the orator's word for the kind of 'proof' or 'argument' one hears in court or assembly. Not ‖ that I myself wish to characterise Timaeus' reasoning as rhetorical,[24] for in the proportion πίστις, like ἀλήθεια, is a cognitive state, not the εἰκότες λόγοι that give rise to it. But I do want to celebrate Plato's insight that reasoning which lacks the rigour of mathematical proof or Parmenidean logic may nonetheless have standards of its own by which it can be judged to succeed or fail.

Let us then turn to the final section of the Prelude, where Timaeus describes the lesser rigour of type (ii) λόγοι:

> (E) If, therefore [οὖν draws the consequence], Socrates, in many respects concerning many things [i.e. *not* in all respects or all things], regarding the gods and the generation of the universe, we find ourselves unable to furnish accounts which are entirely and in every way in agreement with each other [αὐτοὺς ἑαυτοῖς ὁμολογουμένους] and made completely precise, do not be surprised. But if we can offer accounts which are no less εἰκότες than

---

[23] Cf. n. 13 above. [24] A view entertained by Johansen 2004, ch. 3, 52 with n. 5.

another's, we ought to be content, remembering that I the speaker and you the judges [κριταί] have human nature. Consequently, about these things [*sc.* the 'many things' just referred to] it is fitting to accept [ἀποδεχομένους] the εἰκότα μῦθον and seek nothing further.

Socrates agrees that that is how the discourse should be received and settles back to listen and learn,[25] not speaking again until the *Critias*.

(1) My first comment concerns the verb ἀποδέχομαι, 'to receive'. It is helpful to compare a passage in Aristotle, *De Partibus Animalium* 1.1 639a1–16, which describes what it is to be educated (πεπαιδευμένος) in a subject, as opposed to an expert in it. It is to be able to judge (κρῖναι), not whether what the speaker says is true, but whether they are using the appropriate methods of inquiry and giving the right *sorts* of explanation. Aristotle's word for what the listeners (readers) have to do is ἀποδέχεσθαι, 'to receive it', exactly as in Timaeus' injunction to his 'judges'. The word recurs in a similarly 'preludic' passage of Aristotle's *Nicomachean Ethics* 1.3, 1094b11–1095a13, ending with the phrase πεφροιμιάσθω ταῦτα and instructing us how to 'receive' his ethical discussions.[26] The same verb is used at the beginning of *Republic* II when ‖ Glaucon and Adeimantus refuse to accept Socrates' refutation of Thrasymachus (357a, 368b). The rest of the *Republic* vindicates their claim that the arguments of Book I were not of the right sort to produce genuine conviction about the superiority of justice over injustice.[27]

These parallels for the use of the verb ἀποδέχεσθαι confirm, I submit, that to be εἰκώς is an aspiration for Timaeus' μῦθος to live up to. It is not a foregone conclusion that his μῦθος will meet with success in the judgement of his audience – which, by the way, is not any old audience, but a group of people highly competent in two areas that will turn out to be relevant to world building: mathematics and politics (of that, more later).

Immediately after the passage quoted, Socrates in reply, in his last speech before the main discourse, agrees that this is how Timaeus' discourse *should* be accepted, and adds that the audience has already found

---

[25] That 'learn' is the correct translation of μάθοιτε at 27d2, following Bury 1929, rather than 'understand' or 'follow' as preferred by Rivaud 1925, A. E. Taylor 1929, Cornford 1937, and Brisson and Patillon 1992, is clinched to my mind by Socrates' desire to learn (μαθητὴς γενέσθαι, μαθεῖν) teleological physics at *Phaedo* 99c. On the relation between the *Phaedo* and the *Timaeus*, see the now classic article Sedley 1989.

[26] Cf. also *Met.* A.3, 995a 12–16.

[27] A rather different instance of Glaucon exercising his judgement over what to ἀποδέχεσθαι is *Rep.* 532d2–7. Again, the listeners' unanimous refusal to ἀποδέχεσθαι (450a10) Socrates' proposal for 'women and children in common' is what launches the 'three waves' with which Socrates battles in the central Books.

the prelude exceedingly accept*able* (θαυμασίως ἀπεδεξάμεθα σου). The audience's role is crucial, and so is the fact that Timaeus hopes to offer accounts that are no less εἰκότες than anyone else's; 48d3 hopes they will be *more* so.

(2) My second comment is on the plural λόγοι at 29c6 (which I would set beside the plural εἰκότων μύθων at 59c6). The λόγοι we meet in the sequel are a series of well-marked units, as displayed by the paragraphing in Burnet's Oxford Classical Text. Each unit is a λόγος in the sense of a complex of statements standing to each other in some logical relation and dealing with a particular explanandum.[28] If these units are the type (ii) accounts which aim to be εἰκότες, they are the λόγοι about which we are warned not to expect them to agree with each other in absolutely every respect. One such account is at variance with another (ἑαυτοῖς here = ἀλλήλοις). I shall later suggest one of the ways that might happen. I trust that everyone will agree that this interpretation is preferable to one that understands Timaeus to mean that a given account may be internally inconsistent, at variance with itself.[29] That would give it zero probability at once.

After these two comments, I turn to the question why the audience must agree to judge type (ii) accounts by the standard of how εἰκότες they are, and why they ‖ must be tolerant if one such account is at variance in some way with another. It is, as our passage says, because of the subject matter for which Timaeus will offer an exegesis. That subject matter is specified at 29c1–2, not as the realm of γένεσις *tout court*, nor even (as Proclus well noticed: *in Tim.* 343.18 ff.) as a likeness *simpliciter*, but rather as a likeness of that which is permanent and stable and manifest to reason. A likeness of an eternal rational order. I conclude that the exegesis Timaeus will offer is precisely an exegesis, explanation, exposition, or revelation of the rationality embodied by the Maker in the cosmos he produced. Timaeus will attempt as best he can to disclose the reasonableness of the cosmos in all its aspects, even – or perhaps especially – when it comes to the Divine Craftsman's dealings with the realm of necessity (48d, 53d), and accounts that expound what is reasonable should themselves be reasonable, just as accounts that expound what is unchangeable should themselves be unchangeable. Hence I suggest that the best translation for εἰκότα when we *first* read the Prelude is 'reasonable' 'rational', which for the phrase εἰκὼς μῦθος yields the strikingly oxymoronic translation 'a

---

[28] Cf. Rivaud 1925: 6: 'ces brefs tableaux dont se compose le *Timée*'.
[29] Szaif 1996: 296, with n. 114.

rational/reasonable myth' confirming that Plato's Περὶ φύσεως will indeed overcome the traditional opposition between μῦθος and λόγος.

That, as I said, is my translation for our first reading. But the very next paragraph of Timaeus' discourse will enable me to go back to the Prelude for a second reading and translate εἰκὼς μῦθος as 'a probable myth'. Because what we learn in the next paragraph is that the most reasonable account of the cosmos, the one that explains how reasonable its construction really is, is simultaneously and thereby the most probable account. To introduce this idea, let me invite you to consider the question: What would it be to disclose the reasonableness of the cosmos?

Consider some of the ways in which we disclose the reasonableness and appropriateness of an architect's or a carpenter's creation. The table legs are made thus and so because that is a good way to combine stability with grace. The ceilings are raised high to give people using the building a sense of space and freedom, which is an excellent thing in a building if you can afford it. The 'because' or 'to give this result' in such sentences refers the good features of the table or the building to the choices made by the craftsmen and the teleological reasons they had for making them that way. 'They are made thus and so for this reason' implies 'They were made for this reason by the maker'. But the *Divine* Craftsman does not just have teleological reasons for his choices. His overall goal simply is to impose reason on necessity, to introduce rational order into the disorderly chaos. In his case, the product he aims for is precisely that, rational order. For us, therefore, to become connoisseurs of the cosmos is to appreciate the rationality of its order. And to do that is to come to appreciate something of || the reasons for which it was created as it was. To the extent that Timaeus succeeds in disclosing the reasons the Divine Intellect has for making the cosmos thus and so, to that extent he will be retracing the reasoning that lies behind the act of creation. As with the carpenter, the exegesis 'They are made thus and so for such-and-such a reason' implies 'They were made so for that reason'.[30] Creation in the *Timaeus* is not of course creation *ex nihilo*, but, as in any craft, it is bringing the materials confronting the Divine Craftsman into good 'rational' order. The materials resist, and the maker must adjust his plans to them. He does not have a totally free choice. But he does have to make choices nonetheless. He has

---

[30] Like Plato, I use the past tense here solely for ease of exposition and to sustain the analogy with a human craftsman. The notorious γέγονε of 28b7 turns up at *Prm.* 141e5 both in a list of verbs of past time and in a list of verbs of present time. For the latter use in Timaeus' practice, see 68b6 with c3.

to work out what is best and most appropriate among the alternatives the materials allow. And at each stage he will be constrained by the results of his previous choices, which will gradually eliminate some of the alternatives that would have been open before. When you have laid the foundations of a house, you have completely determined its shape and partially determined how high it can be.

What I should like to emphasise is that this reasoning, like any craftsman's reasoning, will be *practical* reasoning rather than theoretical. The Divine Craftsman is not trying to disclose the truth, but to *make* true the best order he can. The same holds for the Lesser Gods when they take over for the messy job of constructing our mortal selves. Correspondingly, Timaeus is not trying to disclose what is true about the physical world so much as to disclose why this is the best of all possible worlds that the materials allow the Maker(s) to make: just what Socrates wished for in the *Phaedo* (99c).

By way of illustration, consider the compromise described in the account of the human head at 75bc:

> ... the substance which of necessity is born with us and grows with us in no wise permits thickness of bone and abundance of flesh to be accompanied by quick sensibility. If the two would combine, they would be found most of all in the structure of the head; with a strong, fleshy and sinewy head on their shoulders, mankind would have enjoyed twice and much more than twice the present term of life, better health and greater freedom from pain. As it was, the Makers (δημιουργοῖς)[31] of our race considered whether they were to produce a more ‖ long-lived and worse creature or a more short-lived and better, and agreed with one accord that on every ground and for every creature briefer and better life is to be preferred before longer and sorrier. Accordingly, for all these reasons the head that was joined to the body in every man was more sensitive and more intelligent, but much weaker (εὐαισθητοτέρα μὲν καὶ φρονιμωτέρα, πολὺ δὲ ἀσθενεστέρα). (tr. after Taylor 1929)

We should already have inferred that the human head is imperfect. We were told at 44d that it was fashioned after the shape of the created cosmos, which implies, by the principle laid down at 28b, that it is not beautiful. Although at 44d Timaeus describes both the cosmos and the head as spherical, we later learn that they are only imperfectly so, since the cosmos is in fact a dodekahedron (55c; cf. *Phd.* 110b). And when we move on to

---

[31] The plural does not alter the logical properties of demiurgic reasoning. The Lesser Gods operate under orders from the Demiurge and imitate his style of craftsmanship (69c).

75bc we discover that, because of the constraints imposed by the materials now available to work with, a choice has to be made between two conflicting values: long life and intelligence. These are conflicting in the sense that they cannot both be realised together. Intelligence is judged the better, so we humans end up with a life span shorter than it could have been.

This is but one example of many that show how Timaeus' task is to give us a series of good practical reasons why the cosmos has this feature or that. The way he does it is to exhibit specimens of practical reasoning which justify the divine choices. These reasonings will disclose how reasonable the chosen feature is. Our task as learners is to judge how *reasonable* Timaeus has made them appear. That is why the standard aimed at is to be εἰκώς in the sense of reasonable or appropriate: as like what reason says *ought* to be as the materials allow. That is why the audience selected to judge the acceptability of Timaeus' account is an audience, not merely of people who know enough mathematics, but of people who are also experienced in political matters (20ab; more on this below). That is why to spend time doing physics in this way, with the aim of framing reasonable myths[32] to give oneself a relaxing break from discussions about eternal things, || is to add to one's life a μέτριον... παιδιὰν καὶ φρόνιμον, a modest and reasonable pastime (59cd). For remember: Plato holds that you become like what you study. Physics too is ὁμοίωσις θεῷ, becoming like unto god.

This brings me, finally, to the point about argumentative rigour. Practical reasoning is seldom, if ever, deductively valid. Aristotle's example, '"I should make something good; a house is something good"; at once he makes a house' (*De Motu Animalium* 7, 701a16–17) – an example notorious for its deductive invalidity – will serve well as a small-scale example of Demiurgic reasoning. Indeed, substitute 'cosmos' for 'house' and you have

---

[32] Note the plural τὴν τῶν εἰκότων μύθων μεταδιώκοντα ἰδέαν. Although this is the third and last occurrence in the dialogue of the collocation εἰκώς + μῦθος, with the latter term replaced at once by λόγος (59c8–9), 59d2–3 announces that the pursuit of εἰκότα will continue with abandon. Already at 57d we were invited to marvel at the variety (ποικιλία) of elemental possibilities that result from the Demiurge's mathematical craftsmanship: what was there called εἰκότι λόγῳ is here spoken of first in terms of εἰκότων μύθων (but ones that enable us to διαλογίσασθαι the phenomena), then called λόγος again. It seems clear that Plato is deliberately running μῦθος and λόγος in tandem, giving both a strongly mathematical slant. Another mathematical myth in the offing (68d2), but beyond human grasp, would tell of the proportions through which the Maker contrives the production of different colours (67c–68d). The mathematical proportions through which the Maker brings order to the realm of Necessity are unambiguously part of the μῦθος which Timaeus undertakes to complete at 69bc.

more or less the reasoning with which the Divine Craftsman starts the ball rolling at 29d–30c:

> Let us then state for what cause becoming and this universe were framed by him who framed them. He was good, and none that is good is ever grudging.[33] Being without grudging, then, he desired all things to become as like as might be to himself. That this is the true sovereign source of becoming and of the cosmos, one is most surely right to accept (ἀποδεχόμενος ὀρθότατα ἀποδέχοιτ' ἄν) from men of wisdom (ἀνδρῶν φρονίμων). God's desire was that all things should be good, and nothing, so far as might be, shabby (φλαῦρον). So he took in hand all that was visible – he found it not at rest, but in discordant and disorderly motion – and brought it from disorder to order, since he judged this in every way better than that. Now for him that is most good it neither was nor is permissible to do anything save what is most fair (τὸ κάλλιστον). Taking thought, therefore, he found that, among things that are by nature visible, no product (ἔργον) that is without understanding (νοῦς) will ever be better (κάλλιον) than one that has understanding, when each is taken as a whole, and further that understanding cannot accrue to anything apart from soul. Guided by this reasoning, he framed understanding within soul and soul within body, and so made the fabric of the universe, in order that the product of his fashioning might be in its nature as beautiful and excellent (κάλλιστον ... ἄριστόν τε) as possible.
>
> This, then, is how we should say, according to the appropriate/likely account (κατὰ λόγον τὸν εἰκότα), that this our world – a creature with life, soul and understanding – verily (τῇ ἀληθείᾳ) came to be through the providence of God. (29d–30c; tr. after Taylor and Cornford) ||

The conclusion is affirmed as an unqualified truth. This cosmos is in truth a living creature with soul and understanding. It is so in truth, but not because it follows from the premises from which the Craftsman reasons:

(1) $(x)(y)$ (x has understanding & y has not) $\rightarrow$ (x as a whole is finer than y as a whole).
(2) (x) (x has understanding) $\rightarrow$ (x has soul).

Nothing follows from (1) and (2) about the cosmos, because they do not so much as mention the cosmos. The conclusion

(3) This cosmos is a living creature with soul and understanding

---

[33] A. E. Taylor 1928: 78, is brilliant on φθόνος as the wish to keep all good to oneself. Jowett 1875, Cornford 1937, Brisson and Patillon 1992, and Zeyl 2000 translate 'jealousy', Rivaud 1925, Bury 1929, and Lee 1965 'envy', both of which require another person as their target, who *ex hypothesi* does not yet exist.

is a conclusion the Craftsman *made* true, *in order that* (30b5: ὅπως) the cosmos would be as good and beautiful as possible. What Timaeus gives us in this paragraph is neither a deduction by him, nor a deduction by the Craftsman, but a description of the Craftsman's *practical reasoning*. Reasoning which reveals to us the reasonableness of his creation, both the process and the product. It is the reasonableness of Timaeus' exegesis that we have to judge. If we accept his teaching, we are learning to be connoisseurs of the cosmos, learning to appreciate that the realm of becoming in which we live is constituted and ordered as it is by the practice of divine reason.

For example, the value principle (1) is a strengthened version of the premise which at 75bc gives us a wiser but weaker head than we could have had. The general idea is that quality trumps quantity. Less of the better feature is preferable to more of the worse. Two examples from Aristotle are his claim that a little knowledge of the divine and eternal heaven yields more pleasure than lots of knowledge of the animals close to hand (*PA* 1.5, 644b31–645a4), and his proclamation that, while our reasoning faculty is small in bulk, it surpasses all else in power and worth, so that we should so far as possible identify our lives with its (*EN* x.7, 1177b34–1178a7).[34] Timaeus' claim here is that the cosmos itself is founded on the principle that understanding trumps absolutely, no matter what else is true of a thing.

The next paragraph of text, i.e. the next of the λόγοι that together make up the larger μῦθος, is 30c2–31b3, where Timaeus reveals that the cosmos is unique (εἷς ὅδε μονογενής, echoing Parmenides, fr. 8, 4), the only one of its kind. According to a well-known article by David Keyt, 'The Mad Craftsman of the *Timaeus*',[35] this claim is based on the following deductive argument: ||

> (1) The cosmos was made according to its model.
> (2) Its model is unique.
> *Ergo* (3) the cosmos is unique.

To which Keyt quite properly objects that every Form is unique, so if the argument form is valid, there should be only one instance of each kind of thing that is modelled after an eternal Form. That is patently false. Ergo, the argument form is not valid.

---

[34] These examples may be set beside Aristotle's empirical critique at *PA* II.12 656a13–24 of Timaeus' account of our head (discussed by Gregorić 2005 in this issue [of *Rhizai*]).
[35] Keyt 1971, endorsed by Vlastos 1975: 29, n. 8.

But was (3) *meant* to follow from its premises in deductive mode? There is a deductive argument in the paragraph, viz. the proof at 31a4–8 that the model Divine Creature is necessarily unique, for it is by definition inclusive of all kinds of Living Creature. But the next sentence begins ἵνα οὖν, 'to the end that . . .', not simply οὖν. Timaeus does not say, '*Therefore, of necessity*, the cosmos is unique' (or, 'had to be unique, on pain of not being like its model'). He says, '*In order therefore* to make it like its model in respect of uniqueness (κατὰ τὴν μόνωσιν), he made just one cosmos, not two or an infinite number of them'. The question we have to ask as judges of Timaeus' cosmic discourse is not 'Does that follow?', but 'Was that a reasonable choice, was it for the best?'.

And in this case we know there was a choice. It is not just that the alternatives 'two' and 'infinity' are mentioned here, but later on, at 55cd, Timaeus says one might reasonably (ἐμμελῶς, εἰκότως) puzzle whether to say there is one cosmos or five – in context, this is inspired by the fact that we have just been through the five perfect solids, one of which (the dodecahedron) was chosen for the shape of the whole cosmos. Why not, then, four more cosmoi, a cube, a pyramid, an octohedron and an icosahedron, one for each of the five ways of being a perfect solid? Timaeus reaffirms his earlier claim that the cosmos is unique, but allows that someone might think differently, on the basis of other considerations (ἄλλα πῇ βλέψας ἕτερα δοξάσει) – other, that is, than the one consideration which Timaeus took to have guided the Divine Craftsman in the passage under discussion. For example, someone might give greater weight to the consideration that there are precisely five ways of being a perfect solid.

This would be nonsense if Timaeus took himself to have given earlier what A. E. Taylor calls 'conclusive proof that there is only one οὐρανός'.[36] But in the sphere of practical reasoning it is a familiar fact that choices are made between alternatives each of which may be supported by considerations other than the considerations that finally prove decisive. Different values yield different results || (as we noted in the case of the human head). I propose this as one reason at least why we were warned not to expect our λόγοι to agree with each other in every respect. To go back to Aristotle, even though a house is a good, a cloak is something good too, so why not make a cloak instead of a house? Or a cloak as well as a house (refugees may well need both)? What Timaeus is reaffirming, when he dismisses the

---

[36] A. E. Taylor 1928: 379.

case for five cosmoi, is that uniqueness was the best *practical* choice made for the best of reasons.

We are now rid of what Vlastos called 'those preposterous inferences, legitimised by Platonic teleology, which decide what is, or is not, the case, by deduction from what would be good and beautiful, enchanting or inspiring, if it were the case'.[37]

But how can even the most practically wise (φρόνιμος) be certain of what the divine reasoning was/is? It is one thing to judge that the reasoning Timaeus puts before us is reasonable, another to judge that it was/is the Divine Craftsman's own reasoning.[38] None of us can be certain of the Maker's reasons, any more than we can in the connoisseurship of ordinary human artistic production. At the beginning of the *Critias* Timaeus invites correction if any detail of his account was said παρὰ μέλος, inappropriately, out of key, discordantly. He is not claiming infallibility on what is reasonable. This brings me back to the permissibility, after all, of translating εἰκώς as 'probable' or 'likely' – at a second reading.

Consider the phrase κατὰ λόγον τὸν εἰκότα at 30b7, in the passage discussed above, p. 281. Making the world an intelligent animal was indeed the most reasonable thing to do, given (1) and (2). But it is also, I now happily admit, the thing the Divine Craftsman most probably would do, given that he is good and wants to make everything as like himself as possible. We can translate 'likely' or 'probable' here, *provided* we realise that it is probable/likely relative to something other than truths we already know about the world – at the start, which is where we are now, there are virtually no truths to know. All we have to go on at this stage is the hypothesis, treated as a fixed starting point which it would be blasphemous to deny (29a), that the world is the product of a supremely good designer. To find out what is probable relative to *that* starting point just is to make our best estimate of what is most appropriate or reasonable. For our one certainty is that God does what is best in the circumstances. The probable and the reasonable coincide, because the || route to probability is through practical, not theoretical reason. You find out what is probable, not by inductive procedures such as Mill's Methods, but by deliberation and practical reasoning, a skill that ordinarily finds its largest scale expression in political life.

Consider now 90e: κατὰ τὸν εἰκότα λόγον cowardly males whose first life was lived unjustly were/are reborn as females. Is this the appropriate outcome of their behaviour or the probable one? Evidently, in a

---

[37] Vlastos 1975: 62.   [38] Recall n. 30 above.

providential universe it is both.[39] Either translation will do, because both meanings are in play throughout.

We can now see why it is relevant that Timaeus and his audience are not only competent in the mathematics needed to follow his discourse (53c), but are also well versed in politics (20ab). Socrates is introduced from the start as the person who spoke yesterday περὶ πολιτείας, at the request of the others. He constructed in his discourse the ideal social order, in a way that was thoroughly approved of by all the present company (17c). Any Greek reader would recognise the parallel between constructing the cosmos and constructing the social order, since one of the meanings of the word κόσμος is 'constitution' or 'political order', as when Thucydides uses μεταστῆναι τὸν κόσμον for changing the constitution (IV.76.2) or μένειν ἐν τῷ ὀλιγαρχικῷ κόσμῳ for not changing it (VIII.72.2).

To sum up by combining my first and my second readings. In Timaeus' physics, the more appropriate or reasonable the account of some phenomenon, the greater the probability of its being true, precisely because the one unchallengeable proposition about the cosmos that we must hold true, on pain of impiety, is that the Maker made it the best possible the materials allow. A far cry from the empiricist philosophies of science which so many scholars have projected anachronistically back into the *Timaeus*, where what is probable is our best extrapolation, from what we already know of the cosmos, to what is true of it in some part or aspect hitherto unexplored.

Remember that Timaeus is trying to engage us in the almost ungraspable thought experiment of imagining what it would be like to craft *everything*. A potter or architect does not and cannot craft their product by rigorous reasoning. The Divine Craftsman is in the same situation but on a vastly larger scale. That, I submit, is why Plato tells us to read the *Timaeus* as an εἰκὼς μῦθος. Practical wisdom cannot aspire to the same standards of rigour as theoretical wisdom can, so if we are learning to be connoisseurs of a product of practical wisdom, ‖ we should not ask for our teacher to be more than an εὔλογος ἐξηγητής, a reasonable exegete of the reasonable order of things.[40]

---

[39] Compare the parallel passage *Phaedo* 82a1–c9.
[40] This essay began life for the 1993 May Week Seminar in Cambridge. I am grateful for discussion on that occasion and at subsequent airings of various versions at Brandeis, Chicago, Cornell, Dubrovnik, Florence, Harvard, Notre Dame, Oxford, Philadelphia, Princeton, Stanford, and the University of Georgia at Athens. Especially valuable criticism has come from Michael Frede, both inside and outside his 2001 Oxford *Timaeus* seminar. Finally, I should acknowledge inspiration received from the last Platonist to hold the correct dualist interpretation of the *Timaeus*, Numenius of Apamea: in his account of the descent of the soul from the highest heaven, he maintained that practical reason is acquired at a later stage than theoretical, calculative reason (Macrob. *Somn. Scip.* 1.12.14 = testimonium 47 Leemans, p. 109).

CHAPTER 9

Aristotle on the foundations of sublunary physics

1 GENERALITY

The first book of Aristotle's *De Generatione et Corruptione* is hardly a work for beginners.[*] The second book is a straightforward exposition of his theory of the four elements and their transformations, together with an account of why coming to be and passing away never fail. But 'straightforward' is the last adjective one would apply to the knotty, abstract, dialectical argumentation of book 1. Our difficulties begin at the very first sentence, which announces a programme that goes far beyond earth, air, fire, and water.

We are to study (i) the causes and definitions[1] of the coming to be and passing away of things which come to be and pass away by nature – *all* of them *alike* (1.1, 314a2, ὁμοίως κατὰ πάντων). We are also to learn (ii) what growth and alteration are, and (iii) whether alteration differs from coming to be *simpliciter*. Now coming to be and passing away, alteration, and growth are very general concepts, with a wide range of application. We might expect examples from all over the world of nature. But when we read on, already in book 1 we find an overwhelming concentration on the four elements and mixtures of them. Where are the plants and animals that would verify Aristotle's claim to be explaining the coming to be and passing away of *all* sublunary natural bodies *alike*? Even in chapter 5, a remarkably abstract discussion of growth, the examples cited are animal *parts* (flesh and bone, leg and hand) rather than whole creatures and Aristotle makes no mention of a doctrine he states elsewhere (*DA* II.4, 415b23–8, 416b9–11), that growth involves soul because only living things can take in nourishment and grow; he merely speaks, quite

---

[*] This chapter was first delivered at the Symposium Aristotelicum, held at Deurne in 1999.
[1] Since Aristotle requires a scientific definition to specify the cause(s) of the phenomenon defined, 'causes' and 'definitions' are not separate objects of enquiry.

indeterminately, of an internal principle of growth (*GC* I.5, 321b6–7, 322a12). ||

Joachim's response to this puzzle is to say that a close look at the contents of the treatise reveals that Aristotle is *primarily* concerned with the coming to be and passing away of mixtures of the elemental bodies. His references to the coming to be and passing away of living things are 'quite general and vague'. But since living things are constituted out of elemental mixtures, their birth and death involves the birth and death of the mixed stuffs from which they are composed; *to this limited extent*, Aristotle's treatment of the questions he discusses will apply to plants and animals as well.[2]

When I think back to the generation that produced *The Oxford Translation of Aristotle into English*, my respect for Joachim (1868–1938), both as an Aristotelian scholar and as a philosopher in his own right (he became Wykeham Professor of Logic), is second only to my respect for Sir David Ross (1877–1971), who was also a philosopher in his own right as well as a great scholar.[3] But Joachim's restrictive judgement on the treatise he so splendidly edited will not do. For it implies that *GC*'s theory of coming to be and passing away is not (meant to be) true of plants and animals, only of their homoeomerous parts. And this plainly contradicts not only the first sentence of 1.1 but also the first sentence of 1.2:

> We must deal *in general* (ὅλως) *both* with unqualified coming to be and passing away – Do they exist or not, and how do they take place? – and with the other kinds of change, such as growth and alteration. (315a26–8)[4]

Joachim goes so far as to say that *in the last resort* every genesis of a composite natural body is the coming to be of one or more new homoeomerous parts, each of which is a chemical compound whose constituents are earth, air, fire, and water.[5] If that reductive account were true, Aristotle would have no need of substantial forms.

---

[2] Joachim 1922: xxxvi–xxxvii and note *ad* 314a2.
[3] In the English-speaking world Ross is still read for his work on ethics: *The Right and the Good* (1930), *The Foundations of Ethics* (1939). Joachim is now undeservedly neglected. Anyone interested in the origins of the school of 'Oxford philosophy' will find in Joachim's *The Nature of Truth* (1906) and *Logical Studies* (1948) significant anticipations of J. L. Austin.
[4] My translations are from E. S. Forster's Loeb edition (Forster and Furley 1955), with modifications. On the particle pair τε δή I follow (against the majority of translators) Denniston 1934: 259–60: τε means 'both' and δή emphasises either ὅλως or τε (Migliori 1976 alone allows the chapter to begin without a connective). Note the echo of Pl. *Phd.* 95e: ὅλως γὰρ δεῖ περὶ γενέσεως καὶ φθορᾶς τὴν αἰτίαν διαπραγματεύσασθαι.
[5] Note *ad* 322b1–26.

The corrective I propose is to look into the way Aristotle's other writings refer to the treatise before us. These cross-references tell us something of how he conceived what he was doing in *GC* I. ||

(1) *De Sensu* 3.440a31–b4 and 13 cites *GC* 1.10 as his theory of mixture *in general* (ἐν τοῖς περὶ μίξεως εἴρηται καθόλου περὶ πάντων). That was where he gave his account of the difference between the juxtaposition of minute amounts of different ingredients and a genuine mixture of them, where the result is not just phenomenally, but physically, different from any of its components. The type of example at issue in *GC* 1.10 was the mixture of wine and water, as served at every Greek symposium. The examples in *De Sensu* are colour mixtures such as orange, which is a mixture of red and yellow.[6] But Aristotle is not speaking just of what happens when a painter mixes yellow pigment with red, nor even about laying yellow paint over red to produce (from a suitable distance) the appearance of orange. This last he mentions, but only to get clear about the *phenomenal* orange that is permanently visible, however close you get, on the surface of a piece of fruit. He was not to know that a decisive step for mankind was the co-evolution of sensitivity to orange in certain primates and the orange colour of the fruit of a particular species of tropical tree, as a result of which those primates scattered the seeds of that tree and humans have a more varied colour vision than most colour-seeing animals. But from a modern point of view it is still an extraordinary thing for Aristotle to be saying: If you want to understand how the orange colour of those fruits is a mixture of red and yellow, go read my account of what happens when wine is mixed with water.

Now in *GC* 1.7, on action and passion, we find this:

> Body is by nature adapted so as to be affected by body, flavour by flavour, *colour by colour*, and in general that which is of the same kind by something else of the same kind. (323b33–324a1; emphasis added)

Reciprocal action and passion are a crucial factor in Aristotle's account of mixture in *GC* 1.10. The examples there are all of *bodies* interacting with bodies. There is no hint that the theory extends to certain sensible *qualities* as well, which get mixed when the bodies they qualify are mixed (*Sens.* 3. 440b13–14).[7] That hint came earlier, in *GC* 1.7, which is Aristotle's

---

[6] I switch to a modern example, because of the difficulty of matching Greek colour terms to ours. Aristotle's theory is that white or light (λευκόν) mixes with black or dark (μέλαν) to produce the intermediate colours; for elucidation and discussion see Sorabji 1972.

[7] The word 'mixture' is not used idly of the qualities as well as the bodies, because the mixed colours are a *ratio* (rational or irrational) of light and dark. This presupposes a unit and goes beyond standard

account of action and passion as such. It anticipates his application of the general theory of mixture to the limiting case, so to speak, of colour. ||

(2) *De Anima* II.5, 417a1–2 refers to *GC* I.7 as the *general* discussion of action and passion (ἐν τοῖς καθόλου λόγοις περὶ τοῦ ποιεῖν καὶ πάσχειν). Perception is another limiting case, to be subsumed under *GC*'s general theory of alteration, according to which alteration occurs when an agent *A* assimilates a patient *P* to itself: *P* takes on the quality (form) that *A* already has. For example, a fire heats the air nearby. Likewise, in perception an agent *A* makes a perceiver *P* take on the sensible form that *A* already has. But in *De Anima* II.5, unlike *De Sensu*, Aristotle does not merely apply what he said in *GC* to a new and surprising case. He refines what he said in *GC* by introducing the distinction between first and second potentiality. This makes an important difference to our understanding of *P*'s taking on the quality (form) of *A*, as that notion is used first in the theory of perception and later in the theory of intellect.[8]

Now in *GC* I.8, against the atomists' theory of pores, we read this:

> Some people hold that each patient is acted upon when the last agent – the agent in the strictest sense – enters in through certain pores, and they say that it is also in this way that we see and hear and employ our other senses. (324b25–9)

Just as Aristotle's theory of perception is adapted from his general account of alteration, so his refutation of a wrong theory of action and passion brings down with it the corresponding account of perception. He recurs to the topic of perception near the end of the chapter (326b10ff.), so the link between the general account of action and passion and the specific account of perception remains in his mind.

Not only that, but one of the *arguments* in *De Anima* II.5 is a special case of an argument couched in general terms at *GC* I.7, 323b21–4: if like acts on like, everything will constantly act on itself and nothing will be unchanging or indestructible. Move on to *De Anima* II.5 and we find the like-like principle of causation invoked at 416b35 to produce a puzzle about why the senses do not constantly cause themselves to perceive themselves (417a2–6), from which Aristotle can infer that the senses are potentialities rather than actualities – they need an external cause to set them going (417a6–13).

interactions like that between hot water and cold, which results in a mixture with intermediate temperature. Flavours are similarly a ratio of sweet and bitter (*Sens.* 4.442a12–29).
[8] For a detailed account of the refinement and its bearing on current controversies about Aristotle's theory of perception, see Burnyeat 2002 [Chapter 5 in this volume].

The opposite principle of causation, that unlike acts on unlike, also has a role in *De Anima*. At *De Anima* 1.5, 410a23–6 it makes trouble for the traditional idea that like perceives like and knows like by virtue of being like it. As in *GC* 1.7, so in *De Anima*, neither principle of causation will do as it stands, but each captures one part of a larger truth. What happens in *GC* 1.7 is a dialectical confrontation between the two inadequate || principles of causation. The outcome is that the assimilation thesis is established in the most general form possible. For an agent *A* to affect a patient *P*, *A* must *assimilate P* to itself, as when fire makes a cold thing hot or warmer than it was before. *A* and *P* start off characterised by contrary predicates from the same range; they are thus generically alike, specifically unlike. When they meet, *A* is bound to act on *P*, and *P* is bound to be acted upon by *A*, just because they are contrary to each other; that is the nature of contrariety. So *A* and *P* end up with the same or closer predicates of the range. What happens in *De Anima* II.5 is the application of that general thesis to the special case of perception: for *P* to perceive *A*, *P* and *A* must be unlike to begin with, so that *A* can affect *P* (because of the unlikeness between them) and make *P* like itself. The perceiving is an assimilation (on a refined understanding of that term) in which *P becomes* like *A*.

Here, then, is a second example where Aristotle refers to *GC* I for patterns of explanation which can be applied, with suitable adaptations and refinements, to phenomena in psychology. This gives a nice strong sense in which Aristotelian psychology is part of physics, as of course *De Anima* says it is (I.I, 402a4–7). If we have not studied *GC* I carefully, we will not understand colours and we will not understand perceptual or intellectual cognition. Nor will we understand the account of growth and nutrition in *De Anima* II.4, where the dialectic of *GC* 1.7 is silently presupposed (416a29–b9).[9]

(3) My third example is *Metaphysics* H.I, 1042b7–8. After a brief discussion of the role of substantial being as subject to the four categorially different types of change, Aristotle refers to the physical works (ἐν τοῖς φυσικοῖς εἴρηται) for an account of the difference between unqualified coming to be (τοῦ ἁπλῶς γίγνεσθαι) and coming to be *F*, where *F* is some predicate in the category of quantity, quality, or place. The first question to consider is which physical work is the most appropriate target for the reference.[10]

---

[9] Growth is another topic where the atomists invoke pores: *GC* 1.8, 325b4–5.
[10] Bonitz 1955 102b9–13 shows that the title τὰ φυσικά can refer to physical works other than the *Physics*.

Bonitz answered: *Physics* v.1, 224b35ff., and possibly also *GC* 1.3.[11] But the *Physics* passage is unsuitable. It operates at a more abstract level than Aristotle's standard classifications of the four types of change, and uses the word 'subject' (ὑποκείμενον) to cover the positive terminus in *any* change, including the white which is the terminus of alteration. ∥ More important, it nowhere mentions matter, which is the *raison d'être* of the H.1 argument that prompts the cross-reference: an argument to show that, as just stated (1042a27–8), the matter of a substantial being is itself substantial being, in the sense that, while it is not actually a so-and-so (τόδε τι), it is potentially one. We ought to be able to do better.

Accordingly Ross, while retaining the reference to *Physics* v.1 (from piety towards Bonitz?), adds *GC* 1.2, 317a17–31.[12] This is no doubt inspired by the introduction at 317a21–2 of the idea that substantial change is changing from this to that *as a whole*. But that is merely the lead-in to *GC* 1.3–4, and it is especially in 1.4 that we find a match for the two subjects (ὑποκείμενα) of H.1, 1042b2–3. Not only is it especially in *GC* 1.4 that we get this, but we do not find more than one such subject in two other central passages we might think to go to: *Physics* 1.7–8 and III.1–3. They stay with the less sophisticated triadic model of matter, form, and privation. Further, it is in *GC* 1.4 that the difference between substantial and non-substantial change is fully analysed.[13] So I propose that the cross-reference is to *GC* 1.2–4 as a continuous, unitary discussion.

My next point is that H.1 is not talking about the elemental transformations discussed in *GC* 1.2–4, but about the coming to be of metaphysically uncontroversial substantial beings like plants and animals: the sort of item which, once it has come to be, can change from healthy to sick (1042a36–7). From the perspective of first philosophy, earth, air, fire and water are mere potentialities, not proper substantial beings (Z.16, 1040b7–10). Yet Aristotle still sees his *GC* account of elemental transformations as a general schema which, with suitable additions and refinements, will account for substantial change up to the highest level of the sensible world.

---

[11] Bonitz 1955 101a21–3. Eleven years earlier, in his *Metaphysics* commentary *ad loc.*, he had added not *GC* 1.3 but the impossible 1.7. Presumably a misprint. But, sadly, the misprint lives on in the apparatus criticus of Jaeger's OCT edition (1957) of the *Metaphysics*.

[12] Ross 1936, *ad loc.*

[13] εἴρηται in cross-references often connotes more than a mere mention: e.g. *Metaph.* Z.11, 1037a21–2 has the whole of Z.4–5 in view.

Now in *GC* 1.4 we read this:

> But when the thing changes as a whole, with no perceptible subject retaining its identity – for example, when *the seed as a whole is converted into blood*, or water into air, or air as a whole into water – such a process is the coming to be of a new thing and destruction of the old. (319b14–18; emphasis added)

As with the two previous examples, a careful look finds Aristotle in *GC* I unobtrusively anticipating other contexts than the immediate one for the application of his results. The first sentence of *GC* I was no slip of the pen. ||

2 FOUNDATIONS

My suggestion, then, is that *GC* I really does have a lot more in view than the elements which are its immediate concern, and more than the homoeomerous mixtures at which Joachim drew the line. This is confirmed by a pivotal passage in *Meteorologica*, 1.1:

> (1) We have earlier (πρότερον) dealt with the first causes of nature [in *Physics*] and with all natural motion [in *Physics*, esp. books V–VIII]; (2) we have dealt also with the ordered movements of the stars in the heavens [in *Cael.* I–II], (3) and with the number, kinds and mutual transformations of the bodily elements, and with *becoming and perishing in general* (καὶ περὶ γενέσεως καὶ φθορᾶς τῆς κοινῆς) [in *Cael.* III–IV and *GC*]. (4) It remains to consider a subdivision of the present inquiry (λοιπὸν δ' ἐστὶ μέρος τῆς μεθόδου ταύτης ἔτι θεωρητέον) which all our predecessors have called meteorology. Its province is everything which happens naturally, but with a regularity less than that of the primary bodily element [*sc.* aether, the fifth element], and which takes place in the region which borders most nearly on the movements of the stars ... (5) After we have dealt with all these subjects, let us then see (διελθόντες δὲ περὶ τούτων, θεωρήσωμεν) if we can give some account, on the lines we have laid down (κατὰ τὸν ὑφηγημένον τρόπον), of animals [in the zoological works, including *De Anima*] and plants [in the lost *De Plantis*], both in general and in particular; for when we have done this we may perhaps claim that the whole investigation which we set before ourselves at the outset has been completed (τούτων ῥηθέντων τέλος ἂν εἴη γεγονὸς τῆς ἐξ ἀρχῆς ἡμῖν προαιρέσεως πάσης). (338a20–b22; 339a5–9; emphasis added)[14]

---

[14] Trans. Lee 1952, modified. The numeration is his too, as is the accompanying annotation, with which I entirely agree.

This is a large-scale map of Aristotle's natural philosophy,[15] beginning with the *Physics*, going on to *De Caelo* and *De Generatione et Corruptione*, pausing here for the *Meteorologica*, looking forward to *De Anima* and the biological works. Aristotelian physics is depicted as a systematic whole (one προαίρεσις) in which each treatise has its part to play.[16] The role of *GC*, we learn once again, is *both* to consider the elements and their mutual transformations *and* to study becoming and perishing *in general*. This is no mere conjunction of goals. For what we found earlier was Aristotle anticipating that he would adapt *GC* I's general schemata of explanation for use in the quite different context of scientific psychology. Getting to grips with the elements will equip us to study other, more complex, things. To adapt a famous phrase from the far end of the || Aristotelian cosmos, below the moon the elements are 'universal because first' (*Metaph*. E.1, 1026a30–1). They are not merely involved, ontologically, in all sublunary changes. The structure of their changes is the epistemological starting point from which to understand becoming and perishing *in general*.

A word to press into service here is 'foundational'. It was a word heard more than once during the Symposium at Deurne, as people tried to capture the peculiar character of *GC* I. No doubt Aristotle would tell us that 'foundational' is said in many ways. But all of them seem appropriate to *GC* I. I shall consider three.

(a) *Physical foundations*. One way in which *GC* as a whole is foundational is that it deals with the lowest, most basic, level of the cosmos. It is the physics of the bottom in a world that is not to be viewed and explained – certainly not fully explained – from the bottom up, as happens on the atomists' approach so severely criticised in *GC* I.2 and 7. Moreover, this physics, in contrast to the physics of Leucippus and Democritus, is to be qualitative through and through. The atomists' key device for explaining change, the combining (σύγκρισις) and dissolution (διάκρισις) of material constituents, is dethroned to the status of a mere facilitator (I.2, 317a20–30), and this despite the unusually high praise accorded to Leucippus and Democritus in contrast to Empedocles, who also appeals to processes of combination and dissolution. Empedocles contradicts both the observed facts and himself (I.1; cf. II.6). Only the atomists have a theory of sufficient power and generality to give a genuinely physical

---

[15] A charmingly conclusive vindication of its authenticity is Capelle 1912. Compare *Sens*. 1.436a1–17, a small-scale map of the treatises we know as the *Parva Naturalia*; these are expressly introduced as a sequel to *De Anima*.
[16] λοιπὸν δ' ἐστὶ μέρος τῆς μεθόδου ταύτης may also imply a major grouping of treatises into a μέθοδος comprising *Ph.*, *Cael.*, *GC*, *Mete.*, and another μέθοδος concerned with living things.

explanation of all forms of change (1.2, 315a34–b15, 316a5–14; 1.8, 324b35–325a2). Yet their theory is completely wrong.

We need not be surprised to find Aristotle praising an approach so diametrically opposed to his own. His studies in rhetoric would tell him that the more you build up your main competitors against *their* rivals, the more wonderful it is when you win the prize. Orators preparing a speech in someone's praise may be well advised to compare him with illustrious personages: 'that will strengthen your case; it is a noble thing to surpass men who are themselves great' (*Rh.* 1.9, 1368a21–2; trans. Rhys Roberts 1924). I do not mean that Aristotle's praise is insincere.[17] It is still true today that a good philosopher is one who tackles the opposition in its strongest, most systematic form. The comprehensive scope of the atomists' theory is the very thing that helps us to see why it is so wrong.

As the physics of the bottom, *GC* is twin to *De Caelo*. Not only because *De Caelo* has much to say about the four sublunary elements, but also because *De Caelo* I starts from the very top of the cosmos. Certainly, || *De Caelo* III–IV deal at length with the natural motions of the four elements and with the contrariety light–heavy, while *De Caelo* III.7–8 refute Democritus' and Plato's explanations of how the elements are generated from each other. But the treatise as we now have it leaves us looking forward (III.8, 307b19–24) to Aristotle's own positive account of elemental transformation in *GC* II, where the important contrarieties are hot–cold and wet–dry. Only when this is complete can our understanding of the sublunary elements match the detailed explanation of the properties of aether in *De Caelo* I–II. Accordingly, we might think of *De Caelo* I and *GC* I as a pincer movement, one starting from the very top and moving down to the elements, the other starting from the very bottom and moving up to homoeomerous mixtures. The two work together to fix the large-scale contours of the Aristotelian cosmology, thereby establishing the habitat for the living things to which Aristotle will devote his most scrupulous attention. (Recall the order of topics in Plato's *Timaeus*, where the demiurge first constructs the heavens, then the four elements, and finally has the lesser gods see to the creation of living things.) This pincer movement may help explain why the first books of both treatises are methodologically unique.

Where knowledge of the stars is concerned 'we have very little to start from, and we are situated at a great distance from the phenomena we are

---

[17] There are other places, e.g. *GA* II.8, 747a25–7, and IV.1, 764a1–23, where Aristotle gives better marks to Democritus than to Empedocles.

trying to investigate' (*Cael.* II.12, 292a15–17, trans. Guthrie. Cf. *PA* 1.5). This means that we cannot find out about the stars by the usual Aristotelian procedures. Humanity may have had numerous sightings of them over the years, but these data are nowhere near as elaborate and varied as those that Aristotle was able to gather on animals and political constitutions, rhetorical speeches and drama. For the stars we lack even an equivalent to the everyday familiarity we have with animals and their behaviour, or with the interactions of solids and liquids, air and fire. There is no reason to think that the reputable opinions on the subject of the heavens are likely to contain, between them, most of the truth we are seeking. Hence, although it is good to cite the ancient belief that the stars are divine (*Cael.* I.3, 270b5–9; II.1, 284a2–6), dialectic will be of limited use. In this predicament, Aristotle turns to the method of hypothesis.

Take a series of hypotheses, most crucially the hypothesis of natural places and natural motions, and deduce their consequences as rigorously as you can. *De Caelo* I contains an unusually high number of occurrences of words like ἀνάγκη which express the *necessity* of valid deductive argument. But then remember that these conclusions, even if validly deduced, depend on the initial hypotheses, about whose truth it is difficult to be certain. *De Caelo* I contains an unusually high number of occurrences of words like εἰκότως and εὔλογον which express epistemic modesty: this or that is a *reasonable* thing to believe. Understandably, for ‖ if it is difficult to be certain of the hypotheses, the conclusions deduced from them cannot be certain either. Such a combination of rigorous necessity and epistemic modesty is without parallel in the corpus.

GC I is methodologically unique too, but in a different way and for different reasons. Its subject matter is not so far from human experience. Instead of the physics of the superlunary realm, we are now to examine and define some of the fundamental concepts of sublunary physics: coming to be *simpliciter*, alteration, growth, and mixture. None of these applies to the heavens (for the proofs see *Cael.* I.3); all of them are exemplified in everyday experience; so dialectical sifting of the reputable opinions is a viable tool to get started with. And dialectic, relentless dialectic, is what we are given. Little more. This is what makes the argumentation so knotty and abstract. The puzzle is that the concepts under discussion are ones we are already supposed to be familiar with from our reading of the *Physics*,[18] which (as will be seen) is constantly referred to as 'earlier' (πρότερον). It is

---

[18] Not to mention *Cat.* 14.

as if we have to retrace our steps and problematise concepts we thought we had learned.

But it is important to appreciate that Aristotle's aim is not just to problematise, and then to clarify, these concepts. They are to be *shaped* for the specifically Aristotelian theoretical use to which they will be put throughout the physical works, up to *De Anima* and beyond.

Take first a relatively trivial illustration. *GC* I.10, 328a2–3 acknowledges that ordinary language speaks of a 'mixture' of barley and wheat, when grains of each are thoroughly mixed, side by side. But that is of no help in understanding what happens when wine is mixed with water, let alone when all four elements are mixed with each other, as they are in every single body we meet in the sublunary world (*GC* II.8, 334b31–335a23). Aristotle's solution is to distinguish 'composition' (σύνθεσις) from 'mixture' (κρᾶσις or μίξις), reserving the latter for the case where every part, however small, exhibits the same ratio between its constituent elements as does the whole (328a5–18).

A more significant illustration is I.6's narrow definition of contact in terms of reciprocal or non-reciprocal influence. To understand action and passion, and a fortiori to understand mixture, which involves reciprocal action and passion, the Aristotelian physicist requires a properly physical notion of contact. This has to be narrower in scope than the general definition of contact given in *Physics* v.2, according to which there is contact whenever two distinct magnitudes have their extremities together. That suffices for mathematics (*GC* I.6, 323a1–3), but the student of physics (323a34: ἐν τοῖς φυσικοῖς) must reckon with the causal consequences of contact. One common consequence is the imparting of motion: a travelling body pushes, or rebounds from, a body at rest.[19] Another is alteration or change of quality – think of the myriad consequences of contact, direct or indirect, with fire.[20] Contact is also the trigger for formative processes in biology (*GA* II.1, 734a3–4; II.4, 740b21–4).

In many of these cases, moreover, the two things in contact affect each other: the pushing body loses some of its momentum, the fire some of its heat. But there is also the non-reciprocal case where someone behaves hurtfully towards me: he touches me, as Aristotle puts it, without my touching him in any sense at all (323a32–3). The example might well

---

[19] Another case to mention is contact imparting (unnatural) stability, as when the columns of a temple uphold the pediment.
[20] Indirect contact is acknowledged at *GC* I.9, 327a3–6. For the multiple effects of heat see *PA* II.2, 648b11–649b8.

make one think of the prime mover moving things as an object of love, even though the prime mover has no extremities to coincide with the extremities of something else. So Joachim prefers, no doubt rightly, to suppose that Aristotle has in view contact between the first heaven and what lies below it, which does not react on its mover.[21] Another case of contact without interaction is food: the food is affected by the feeder, but not vice versa (*DA* II.4, 416a34–b1). It is also worth returning to the case of perception (pain is an exercise of the power of perception towards what is bad, because it is bad: *DA* III.7, 431a10–11). Perception requires indirect contact with a perceiver through a medium (*Ph.* VII.2, 244b2–245a11; *DA* III.13, 435a18–19), but neither the perceiver nor the medium affects the object perceived (otherwise perception would always mislead). Here again, as with nutrition, *GC* I anticipates conceptual needs that will arise in more distant, more complicated areas of natural philosophy.

But the place where the idea of reciprocal interaction comes most strikingly into prominence is Aristotle's biology. To explain inherited family resemblances he appeals to the simple cases he discussed in *GC* I, optimistically supposing that they will illuminate the interaction between male and female movements as they form an embryo. This is the most interesting, most difficult case of coming to be *simpliciter*.

The key idea is that of a movement's slackening (λύεσθαι) into a nearly connected one; for example, a movement of the semen from the biological father slackens into that of his grandfather or some more remote male ancestor. The actual sex of the offspring depends on whether the male movements prevail over the female or vice versa, but in the course of their struggle one or more of the two sets of movements may slacken. This helps to explain the production of male offspring who resemble their mother or their grandfather more than their father, and of females who resemble their father or grandmother. It is a complicated process – about that, Aristotle is surely right.[22] But if we ask why the movements are liable to slacken, he replies by referring us back to *GC* I.6–7:

> The agent is itself acted upon by that on which it acts; thus that which cuts is blunted by that which is cut by it, that which heats is cooled by that which is heated by it, and in general (ὅλως) the moving cause (except in the

---

[21] Note *ad* 322b32–323a34. Philoponus (*in GC* 138.26–139.2) feels free to list a variety of unreciprocated movers: a picture, one's beloved, any object of desire, an insult, plus the heavenly movers of the sublunary world.
[22] For a strenuous attempt to sort out the complications, see J. M. Cooper 1988.

case of the first cause of all) does itself receive some motion in return; e.g. what pushes is itself in a way pushed again and what presses on something is pressed in return. Sometimes it is altogether more acted upon than acting, so that what is heating or cooling something else is itself cooled or heated, sometimes having produced no effect, sometimes less than it has itself received. This question has been treated in our discussion of action and reaction [*GC* 1.6–7], where it is laid down in what classes of things action and reaction exist. (*GA* IV.3, 768b16–25; trans. Platt, with modifications)

The slackening is a special case of *GC* 1's reciprocal action and passion. A reader may be forgiven for finding Aristotle's examples unhelpful, to say the least, when it comes to understanding the interaction between the movements of complexly concocted biological stuffs such as male semen and the corresponding female catamenia. How many refinements and adaptations are required to reach the level of this *very* special case?[23] But the stronger our worries, the more they underwrite the importance of *GC* 1. Clearly, children do sometimes resemble a parent of the opposite sex or one of their grandparents. But how to explain this on a model according to which the male parent provides the form, the female the matter? *GC* 1 has to contain the key to the solution of a problem which Aristotle's empirical honesty will force him to confront.

There can be no doubt, I take it, that the *GC*-type examples are seriously meant to help. Aristotle is deeply committed to the idea that the sublunary cosmos is a unity. At all levels the same or analogous causes are at work, as he insists in *Metaphysics* Λ.1–5. We can expect the lower and the higher to proceed in much the same way, however much the details vary. *GC* 1 is truly foundational.[24] ||

(b) Conceptual foundations. In remarking earlier that *GC* 1 examines and defines some of the fundamental concepts of sublunary physics, I strayed into a second sense in which the first book of our treatise is foundational. To explain its significance, I need to take up a point already mentioned, that *GC* is written for an audience who already know the *Physics*. It is as if

---

[23] See J. M. Cooper 1988: 31–3 (from whom I take the phrase 'special case'). He is more sanguine than I am that the difficulties he acknowledges can be resolved.

[24] Readers familiar with the first book of the Hippocratic treatise *De Victu* may like to explore the points of similarity and difference. *De Victu* 1 is bafflingly abstract because it seeks a level of description that will bring out the kinship of microcosm (human nature, human activities) and macrocosm. The same kinds of process are to be found at all levels. The author's predecessors (Heraclitus, Empedocles, Anaxagoras, and others) are a constant presence – but as inspiring allies, not as opponents to think against. For the work is rhetorical rather than dialectical. Nonetheless, there is a clear sense in which the book is meant to be foundational with respect to the detailed medical matter of *Vict.* II–IV. *De Victu* is a work that Aristotle may well have read, since *PA* I.1, 640b11–15 is reminiscent of the Hippocratic's account of stomach and nostrils in 1.9.

we are to retrace our steps and problematise concepts we thought we had learned.

Among the numerous references from *GC* to the *Physics*, there are six clear cases where *GC* refers to the *Physics* as prior:

(i) *GC* I.3, 318a3–4: 'We dealt with the other [*sc.* efficient] cause earlier (εἴρηται πρότερον) in our discussion of motion'. This reminds us of *Physics* VIII.5–10, esp. 258b10–11.

(ii) *GC* I.6, 323a3–4: 'If, therefore, as was previously defined (ὥσπερ διωρίσθη πρότερον), for things to be in contact they must have their extremities together'. This, already discussed, refers to the definition of contact at *Physics* V.2, 226b23.

(iii) *GC* II.9, 336a13: 'We have previously explained our own view of causes in general (ἡμῖν δὲ καθόλου πρότερον εἴρηται περὶ τῶν αἰτίων)'. This sends us to Aristotle's extended discussion of the four causes in *Physics* II.3–9.

(iv) *GC* II.10, 336a18–20: 'At the same time it is evident that we were right to say earlier (τὰ πρότερον καλῶς εἴρηται) that the primary kind of change is motion, not coming to be'. This refers to *Physics* VIII.7, 260a26–261a26.

(v) *GC* II.10, 337a18: 'If there is to be movement, there must be a mover, as has been explained earlier elsewhere (ὥσπερ εἴρηται πρότερον ἐν ἑτέροις), and if the movement is to go on always, the mover must go on always'. Aristotle's enumeration of the requirements for ceaseless change in the sublunary world is grounded on the arguments of *Physics* VIII.4–6.

(vi) *GC* II.10, 337a24–5: 'Time, then, is a way of numbering some continuous movement, and therefore cyclical movement, as was determined in our discussions at the beginning (καθάπερ ἐν τοῖς ἐν ἀρχῇ λόγοις διωρίσθη)'. This refers to the proof in *Physics* VIII.9 that only cyclical movement is continuous; for time's relation to continuous movement see *Physics* IV.14, 223a29–b1.[25] ||

Conversely, the *Physics* contains three references which can be taken, with more or less plausibility, to look forward to *GC* as 'later' (ὕστερον): I.9,

---

[25] There is textual uncertainty about (vii) *GC* I.5, 320b28: 'That a separate void is impossible has been explained earlier elsewhere (εἴρηται ἐν ἑτέροις πρότερον)', i.e. in *Ph.* IV.6–9. A number of other references to the *Physics* use a past tense without adding the qualification 'earlier': *GC* I.2, 316b17–18 refers thus to *Ph.* VI.1, 231a21ff.; *GC* I.3, 317b13–14 to *Ph.* I.6–9; *GC* II.10, 336a15 and 11, 338a18 to *Ph.* VIII.7–9.

192b1–2; II.1, 193b20–1; IV.5, 213a4–5.[26] The question is: What does Aristotle mean in such contexts by 'earlier' and 'later'?[27]

Consider the word 'earlier' (πρότερον) in the first sentence of *Meteorologica* I.1, quoted at the start of Section 2 above, and the various temporal phrases that follow. If they have a chronological meaning, they ask us to believe that Aristotle has by now finished the *Physics*, *De Caelo*, and *De Generatione et Corruptione*, but has not yet written a word on biology. A most unlikely story.[28] Much better to take the temporal phrases as indicators of the order in which the treatises should be read: the order of argument and exposition. The *Physics* introduces the basic principles of Aristotelian physics, which are then applied in departmental studies of increasingly complex phenomena, climaxing in what *De Anima* I.1, 402a1–7 calls the most important and valuable part of physics, the study of soul. Only then will we be equipped to tackle biology.

It is undeniable that Aristotle *sometimes* uses temporal phrases like 'earlier' and 'later' to indicate the order of exposition. A case in point is the continuation of example (i) above:

> One signification of 'cause' is that from which we say movement originates, and another is the matter. It is the latter with which we have to deal here. For we dealt with the other cause *earlier* (εἴρηται πρότερον) in our discussion of motion [*Physics* VIII.5–10, esp. 258b10ff.], when we said there is something that remains immovable through all time and something else which is always in motion. Treatment of the first of these, the immovable original source, is the task of the other and *prior* philosophy (τῆς ἑτέρας καὶ προτέρας ... φιλοσοφίας), while regarding that which moves all other things by its own continuous motion, we shall have to explain *later* (ὕστερον) [*GC* II.10] which of the particular causes does that. *At present* (νῦν) let us speak of the cause which is placed in the class of matter, owing to which passing-away and coming-to-be never fail to occur in nature. For perhaps, if we succeed in clearing up this question, it will *simultaneously* (ἅμα) become clear what we ought to say about the thing that perplexed us *just now* (νῦν) [*GC* I.3, 317b18–33], namely, the problem of unqualified coming-to-be and passing-away. (*GC* I.3, 318a1–12) ||

Of the temporal words and phrases I have italicised, the last four plainly refer to the sequence of argument within the treatise *De Generatione*

---

[26] *Cael.* also refers several times to the *Physics* as prior (Bonitz 1955 98a43–b8), and is itself called prior at *GC* I.8, 325b34. *Meteorologica* confirms the ordering it sets out in I.1 by referring to both *Cael.* and *GC* as prior: 1.2, 339b16 and 36–7, 1.3, 340b17–19, III.1, 371b1.

[27] What follows may be read as a particular case study for a thesis about Aristotelian cross-referencing which I argue for at length in ch. 5 of Burnyeat 2001b.

[28] So says also Pellegrin 2000: 25: 'Position bien naïve'. His treatment of the *Meteorologica* passage is in complete accord with mine.

et Corruptione. They tell us nothing about the chronological order in which Aristotle composed the different portions of that work. It is equally clear that the phrase 'the other and prior (προτέρας) philosophy' has nothing to do with chronology. 'Prior' means 'earlier in the order of understanding', because the reference is to first philosophy as prior to physics. My suggestion is that when the same word πρότερος occurs (in adverbial form) in the back-reference to *Physics* VIII it is best taken to refer to priority in the order of learning, which for Aristotle is the converse of the order of completed understanding. The last four temporal adverbs signpost (part of) the sequence of argument within the treatise. The initial πρότερον does the same on a larger scale, announcing that Aristotle is presupposing the results of arguments developed elsewhere for the existence of the prime mover and the first heaven. Even if he did compose *Physics* VIII before he began *De Generatione et Corruptione*, that biographical fact is not the message here. The message is logical, not chronological. In the sequence of argument and exposition *Physics* VIII comes earlier.

This way of reading Aristotelian cross-references allows for the possibility that, given two treatises *A* and *B*, each may refer to the other as prior. On one topic *A*, on another *B* comes first in the order of argument and exposition. For example, *De Caelo* II.2, 284b13–14 refers in the perfect tense to *De Incessu Animalium* 4–5. On the non-chronological interpretation I favour, this means that, while in general the biological treatises presuppose the cosmic setting provided by the *Physics*, *De Caelo*, *GC*, and *Meteorologica*, on the particular issue of right and left, above and below, front and back, *De Caelo* presupposes *De Incessu Animalium*. As *De Caelo* explains, these distinctions are proper (οἰκεῖα) to the nature of animals, so it is a good idea to get a clear understanding of how they apply to the animals we are familiar with before venturing to ascribe a right and a left or a top and a bottom to the heaven itself.

I believe that Aristotle was a systematic philosopher in the sense that he held strong views about the appropriate order of learning and study. Just as *De Sensu* 3, *De Anima* II.5, and *Metaphysics* H.1 presuppose that you have mastered *GC* I, and just as *De Caelo* II.2 presupposes acquaintance with *De Incessu Animalium* 4–5, so *GC* as a whole presupposes familiarity with the *Physics*. Never mind in what order the several treatises were composed. Perhaps they were all composed concurrently, gradually, over a considerable period of time, with constant adjustments to fit each to the others and to the evolving overall plan. There is a sense, indeed, in which that has to be true. None of the treatises we have was published, so they could always be added to or revised. There is || abundant evidence that they often were added to and revised. In a certain sense, then, all of them are contemporaneous with each other. Of none of them can we say that it went out into the world before that other for the simple reason that, unlike Plato's dialogues and Aristotle's 'exoteric' works, none of them was sent out into the world by the author.

But that does not mean it would make sense to *read* them in any arbitrary order. Imagine starting the first-year Aristotle course with *GC* I. The students would be utterly baffled. Familiarity with the *Physics* is not a sufficient condition for understanding *GC* I, but it surely is a necessary condition. If we did not know the theory of categories, and did not know the categorial analysis of change in *Physics* III.1–3 or V.2–3, and much else besides, we would be at a loss to know what was at stake as we laboured through the abstract, dialectical argumentation of *GC* I. Aristotle's cross-referencing the *Physics* as prior merely confirms an obvious truth: *GC* I is for people who are already fairly familiar both with the Aristotelian cosmology, from the elementary bodies to the prime mover, and with the fundamental concepts that serve to explain it: coming into being *simpliciter*, alteration, growth, mixture, natural and enforced locomotion.

This is pedagogically sound. You need a strong grasp of a discipline before it makes sense to tackle questions about its conceptual foundations. A course on the foundations of mathematics would mean little or nothing to students who were not already well trained in mathematics itself. Mathematics is an abstract discipline, but meta-mathematics is more abstract still. Gödel's famous incompleteness proof, to the effect that any system of Peano arithmetic will contain a theorem which is true but unprovable in its system, moves at a level stratospherically high above the familiar whole-number arithmetic he is discussing. Or take the more accessible example of Frege's *Die Grundlagen der Arithmetik* (Frege 1950). He offers a long mordant critique of his predecessors' conception of what numbers are, from Euclid to modern times with remarkably little acknowledgement of the fact that many of these people (e.g. Descartes and Newton) were themselves outstanding mathematicians. For his foundational purposes, that is not to the point. Then he propounds an account of number in terms of the extension of concepts which many readers find difficult to relate to the numbers they learned to deal with at school. That too is not to the point. Coming closer to Aristotle's concern, J. H. Woodger is happy to confess that in his avowedly foundational *Biological Principles* (1929) the proportion of 'biology' to 'philosophy' is very small.[29] Likewise, it would be irrelevant to complain || that Aristotle's foundational treatise makes familiar concepts seem harder to understand than they were

---

[29] Woodger 1967: 6.

before. In his view, as in Woodger's, dialectical debate with one's predecessors, with an emphasis on explicit definition, is the route to real insight. Those concepts are crucial to biology.

Yet there is one noteworthy feature of *GC* I which seems designed to make it more friendly to readers than it would otherwise be. This is the unusual number of striking concrete images that Aristotle introduces to get his point across. Some of his images are opaque to a modern reader, but only because we lack the relevant background information, not for philosophical reasons. Let me collect them up. In 1.2, the sawdust; in 1.5, the beaten metal, water-measuring, and the αὐλοι (however the word should be accented and whatever it refers to); the hurtful person of 1.7; the lunatic and the Eleatic in 1.8; 1.9's veins of metal; the eyes of Lynceus in 1.10; perhaps also, in the same chapter, the metals which stutter at one another (ψελλίζεται πρὸς ἄλληλα), reluctant to make a proper alloy. My favourite is the beaten metal of 1.5, which I find a really neat way to make the point that growth involves change of place in a different way from locomotion. I know of no study of Aristotelian imagery. I propose it as a topic worth investigating.

(c) Teleological foundations. It is Aristotelian doctrine that, in general, the earlier stages of development are for the sake of the later (*PA* II.1, 646a35–b10). Try applying this to the series of works which develop his natural philosophy, in the order indicated by *Meteorologica* 1.1. The implication would be that *De Caelo*, *GC*, and *Meteorologica* are for the sake of the biological works that come later in the order of exposition. Nowadays, astrophysics, chemistry, or meteorology may be studied for their own sake, because their subject matter is interesting and worthwhile in its own right, regardless of how it relates to other disciplines. That is not, it seems, how Aristotle would teach them. The order he insists on is directed towards a definite goal, the understanding of life and living things. That, according to *Meteorologica* 1.1, is the τέλος of the entire προαίρεσις.

The rationale for this order might be simply pedagogical: start with easier, less complex things and proceed to the life sciences, where mixtures abound and the four elements still have a key role to play. But it is more likely to reflect a cosmic scale of values which grades living things as *better* than non-living (*GA* II.1, 731b28–30) and knowledge of better things as a finer, more valuable kind of knowledge (*DA* I.1, 402a1–4). As we work through the treatises on natural philosophy we approach the best kind of knowledge the sublunary world has to offer.

It is tempting to take this thought a stage further and wonder whether Aristotle might not believe that his chosen order of study is || an appropriate response to an orderly universe, in which the elements and mixtures at the lower levels exist for the sake of plants and animals. The eternity of the species cannot be maintained without a constant supply of materials to constitute the homoeomerous and anhomoeomerous parts of living bodies. That constant supply is guaranteed by the eternal cycle of elemental transformation, which ensures the continued presence in our neighbourhood of a quantity of each of the four elements; they do not all separate into their natural places, which would put a stop to life as we know it. In the sublunary world two types of cycle are said to imitate the divine, eternally circling heavens. One is the eternal cycle of elemental transformation (*GC* II.10, 336b25–337a15, *Metaph.* Θ.8, 1050b28–30), the other the eternally continuing life cycles of the biological species (*DA* II.4, 415a26–b7, *GA* II.1, 731b24–732a11), and the former is necessary for the latter. Since it is axiomatic for Aristotle that 'being is better than not being' (*GC* II.10, 336b28–9, *GA* II.1, 731b30), it is tempting to infer that the cycle of elemental transformation, as the necessary prerequisite for a good overall cosmic state of affairs, is for the sake of that most excellent of results, the eternity of the species.

Sober readers may find the temptation resistible. I have no clear text to make them succumb. But remember: Aristotle does believe that everything in the cosmos is ordered towards the good of the whole (*Metaph.* Λ.10, 1075a11–25).

3 Conclusion

I have described three ways in which *GC* I is foundational: a physical way, a conceptual one, and a third having to do with teleological ordering. It seems appropriate that as Aristotle prepares to build up his cosmos from the bottom he should at the same time turn back to analyse and, as it were, rebuild some of the basic concepts of his physical theory. Those two constructions, the physical and the conceptual, run parallel, because both the four elements themselves and concepts such as unqualified coming to be and passing away, alteration, growth, and mixture will be needed, with appropriate adaptations and refinements, over the whole range of natural philosophy. Especially in biology. That is what it is all for.

So I end on the note with which every introduction should end: Read on. Read on to *De Anima* and beyond.[30]

---

[30] I should like to thank the members of the Symposium at Deurne for their vigorous criticisms, and Michael Frede, Jaap Mansfeld, and David Wiggins for invaluable help.

CHAPTER 10

Archytas and optics

The starting point for this paper is an absence. My conclusion is that the absence is a significant chapter in the early history of mathematical optics in ancient Greece.

1. The mathematical curriculum outlined in Plato's *Republic* comprises arithmetic, plane and solid geometry, astronomy, harmonics. There is not a word about optics. This absence would be of no significance if mathematical optics did not exist at the time Plato wrote *Republic* VII. It certainly did exist soon afterwards, when Aristotle wrote the *Posterior Analytics* and classified optics as a science subordinate to geometry in the same way as harmonics is subordinate to arithmetic, mechanics to stereometry (1.7, 75b14–7; 13, 78b35–9). Mathematical harmonics is an important item in Plato's curriculum, singled out for special mention as useful for the understanding of Beauty and the Good (531c). But it is not only harmonics that has this function. The educative purpose of the entire curriculum is to prepare future rulers for the understanding of ultimate values on which ethics and politics in the ideal city depend. If Plato knew about optics when he wrote *Republic* VII and enthused about harmonics, he must have decided that optics would not advance his educational goals. Optics might even be positively harmful. It is not difficult to see why.

The mathematical programme is designed to lead the mind upwards and away from sensible things. It starts with arithmetic and plane geometry, to get the student used to abstraction, to focusing on numbers and figures which can only be grasped in thought, || not by the senses. It proceeds via solid geometry to a surprisingly abstract treatment of astronomy and harmonics, in which visual and acoustic observation are dismissed in favour of purely mathematical 'problems' (530b, 531c). Optics would bring the student back to the sensible realm, which throughout the *Republic* is typified by the visible. τὰ ὁρώμενα, visible things, are the metonym for all that the philosophers must use mathematics to struggle free from. The study of optics would undo the good work by focusing the mind on ὁρώμενα, or rather – and worse – on the *appearances* of visible things.

Thus far my thesis is conditional: *If* mathematical optics existed at the time Plato wrote the *Republic*, its absence from the curriculum is likely to have the significance just sketched. My next task is to find grounds for affirming the antecedent of this conditional.

I begin with Aristotle. He is certainly familiar with mathematical optics, which he mentions in a number of places. He wrote an ὀπτικόν of his own (D.L. v.26), and was praised for his presentation of the subject by no less an authority than Hero of Alexandria (*Cat.* 318.6–7 Nix and Schmidt). Most tellingly, when debating philosophy of mathematics with the Platonists in *Metaphysics* M–N, he takes it for granted that one of the mathematical objects whose ontological status is in dispute is the ὄψις, the line of sight which is the central concept of Greek optics. The clear implication is that optics was practiced, or at least discussed, in the Academy where the Platonists held sway. This is confirmed by the Suda's recording that Philip of Opus wrote two books on optics, two on catoptrics,[1] and by Philodemus' testimony (*Ind. Acad.* col. Y, 15–17) to advances in optics and mechanics made in the Academy during Plato's lifetime.

To discover what sort of optics Aristotle is familiar with, we may look to his account of how its subject matter differs from that of ordinary geometry:

> While geometry investigates physical lines but not *qua* physical, optics investigates mathematical lines, but *qua* physical, not *qua* mathematical. (*Ph.* II.2, 94a9–12; tr. Hardie and Gaye)

Geometry starts from the contours and shapes of physical bodies and treats them *as if* they existed independently of the bodies whose contours and shapes they are. These abstract*ed* (rather than abstract) lines and shapes have all and only the properties which are contained in or demonstrable from their definitions. That is what it means to say that geometry investigates physical lines but not *qua* physical. Optics then adds to these geometrical items certain physical properties relevant to the understanding of visual appearances, first and foremost motion. Many of the optician's lines are rays travelling outwards from the eye. Some opticians add more such properties than others. Ptolemy does, while Euclid does not, ascribe strength and weakness to the rays according to their distance from the axis

---

[1] Sv. φιλόσοφος; the entry can only be about Philip, whose name has dropped out.

of the visual cone. Euclid does not, while other opticians || do, use ray-length as a distance cue. But regardless of these additional features, the lines do not cease to be mathematical lines, abstracted items which have no more properties (mathematical or physical) than are contained in or demonstrable from their initial specification. You cannot legitimately infer that if the rays move, or have degrees of strength, they are corporeal[2] and therefore have standard properties of physical bodies such as weight and thickness. That is what it means to say that optics investigates mathematical lines, but *qua* physical, not *qua* mathematical.[3]

Thus understood, Aristotle's account seems to me a most helpful guide to the surviving corpus of ancient mathematical optics. I infer that optics in his day looked much like the optics we know from the Hellenistic period and later. The subject must have already reached some degree of sophistication to call for Aristotle's carefully layered analysis.

Granted, this evidence does not reach all the way back to the time when Plato was writing the *Republic*; it is consistent with optics and mechanics having come to the Academy's attention a bit later. However, it is clear from the text of the *Republic* itself that *some* mathematical disciplines of the time are deliberately excluded from the curriculum. One exclusion is calendaric astronomy as practiced by Meton and Euctemon in the late fifth century, which attempts to find in the observed phenomena whole-number ratios (συμμετρίαι) that will account for the relation of night to day, of these to the month, and of the month to the year (530ab). Another example is Pythagorean harmonics, which is described as a mathematical analysis of the scales used in actual music:

> They seek the numbers in these heard concords (συμφωνίαι) and do not ascend to problems to consider which numbers are concordant, which are not, and why each are so. (531c)

This is not the occasion to ponder what Plato can have had in view when making Socrates propose an astronomy of the invisible and a harmonics of the inaudible.[4] What matters is that Socrates deliberately excludes existing mathematical disciplines that would focus the mind on sensible things. And in the course of doing so he quotes a remark from, as he puts it, 'the Pythagoreans' to the effect that astronomy and harmonics are 'sister sciences' (530d: ἀδελφαὶ ἐπιστῆμαι). We can identify the author of that

---

[2] As Alexander infers to start a polemic against all forms of ray theory at *In Sens.* 28.16ff.
[3] On Aristotle's *qua* operator, see the now classic elucidation in Lear 1982.
[4] Suggestions in Burnyeat 2000b: 47–63 [now Chapter 1 in *EAMP* vol. III].

saying. It was a Pythagorean closer in age to Plato than to Socrates: the philosopher, statesman, general, and mathematician of genius, Archytas of Tarentum, whose frag. 1 claims that geometry and arithmetic, astronomy and harmonics are all sisters.[5] ||

Here is the passage where Socrates quotes from Archytas:

> 'It is probable,' I said, 'that as the eyes are framed for astronomy, so the ears are framed for harmonic motion, and that these two sciences are sisters of one another, as the Pythagoreans say – and we agree, Glaucon, do we not?'
>
> 'We do,' he said. (530d)

Socrates has already taken astronomy up to the same abstract level as geometry. He will now preserve the 'sisterhood' of astronomy and harmonics by redirecting the latter to the same abstract level as arithmetic. In other words, he agrees with Archytas' coupling of astronomy and harmonics alongside geometry and arithmetic, but condemns his empirical approach in harmonics, which seeks numbers in the observed phenomena instead of purely mathematical 'problems'. Socrates continues:

> 'Then,' I said, 'since the task is so great, shall we not inquire of them [the Pythagoreans] how they speak of these [sciences] and whether they have any other [science] to add?[6] And in all this we will be on the watch for what concerns us.'
>
> 'What is that?'
>
> 'To prevent our fosterlings trying to learn anything incomplete (ἀτελές), anything that does not come out at the destination which, as we were saying just now about astronomy, ought to be the goal of it all.' (530e)

As I read this, Socrates hints at other branches of Pythagorean mathematics he would wish to exclude. He does not name any, but it is worth recalling that Archytas was the founder of a discipline in which Archimedes was later to excel, mathematical mechanics.[7] Socrates would surely not want that on his curriculum. If, as I hope to show, Archytas was also interested in mathematical optics, this too will join the black-list of mathematical studies excluded from the *Republic*'s curriculum.

---

[5] For defence of the authenticity of fragment 1 against Burkert's suspicion (1972: 379–80, n. 46) that it was manufactured to fit Plato's quotation, see Huffman 1985.

[6] Both περὶ αὐτῶν and πρὸς τούτοις (idiomatically switching to neuter) refer to the two sister sciences.

[7] D.L. VIII.83 with Kühn's widely (but not universally) accepted emendation μαθηματικαῖς for μηχανικαῖς; cf. also DK47 A10a. My belief in Diogenes' plain and credible testimony, backed by Vitruvius VII *Praef.* 14 (= DK47 B7), has not been shaken by Huffman's doubts (Huffman 2005).

2. My journey back to Archytas starts from a passage of Iamblichus (*Comm. Math.* 25, p. 78.8–18) which Walter Burkert has identified as part of a hitherto unrecognised fragment of Aristotle. In Burkert's presentation, the reference to optics is square-bracketed as Iamblichus' addition, thus:

> οἱ δὲ Πυθαγόρειοι διατρίψαντες ἐν τοῖς μαθήμασι καὶ τό τε ἀκριβὲς τῶν λόγων ἀγαπήσαντες, ὅτι μόνα εἶχεν ἀποδείξεις ὧν μετεχειρίζοντο ἄνθρωποι, καὶ ὁμολογούμενα ὁρῶντες [ἔνισον] τὰ περὶ τὴν ἁρμονίαν ὅτι δι' ἀριθμῶν [καὶ τὰ περὶ τὴν ὄψιν τὴν ἁρμονίαν ὅτι δι' ἀριθμῶν καὶ τὰ περὶ τὴν ὄψιν μαθήματα διὰ <δια>γραμμάτων], ὅλως αἴτια τῶν ὄντων ταῦτα ᾠήθησαν εἶναι καὶ τὰς τούτων ἀρχάς· ὥστε τῷ βουλομένῳ θεωρεῖν τὰ ὄντα πῶς ἔχει, εἰς ταῦτα βλεπτέον εἶναι, τοὺς ἀριθμοὺς [καὶ τὰ γεωμετρούμενα εἴδη τῶν ὄντων] καὶ λόγους, διὰ τὸ δηλοῦσθαι πάντα διὰ τούτων. ‖

> The Pythagoreans, having devoted themselves to mathematics, and admiring the accuracy of its reasonings, because it alone among human activities knows of proofs, and seeing [equally] the facts about harmony, that they happen on account of numbers, generally admitted [and (seeing) the mathematics of optics depending on <dia>grams], they deemed these (facts of mathematics) and their principles to be, generally, causative of existing things, so that whoever wishes to comprehend the true nature of existing things should turn their attention to these, that is to numbers [and the geometrical entities among existing things] and proportions, because it is by them that everything is made clear. (Burkert 1972: 50, n. 112, and 447–8)

To vindicate the antecedent of my conditional, I shall need to remove all Burkert's square brackets and rewrite his translation.[8]

But first, the marks of Aristotle's pen. Burkert notes (a) the parallels of language with Aristotle's account of Pythagoreanism in *Metaphysics* A.5, and (b) the sandwiching of the passage between two other extracts from Aristotle. I would emphasise (c) that the passage follows the same historiographic pattern as A.5: the Pythagoreans occupied themselves with mathematics and, as a result, they took the principles of mathematics to be the principles of everything.

At the same time there are striking differences from A.5. According to A.5, it was the likenesses (ὁμοιώματα) between numbers and things (985b27–8) that inspired the generalisation from the principles of mathematics to the principles of all things. The fragment, by contrast, locates the inspiration in the precision of mathematical *proof*. In A.5 proof is never mentioned; on the contrary, Aristotle disparages Pythagorean thought as a

---

[8] Strictly, his translator's translation: in the original German edition only the Greek is given. But the translation is published with Burkert's approval.

mish-mash of numerological fantasies (esp. 986a6–8). And whereas A.5 makes number the key to the cosmos – Pythagoreans explain everything by numbers – the fragment invokes the forms studied by geometry and ratios (τὰ γεωμετρούμενα εἴδη τῶν ὄντων καὶ λόγους) as well as numbers. Numbers may be primary, but geometry has cosmic significance too.

What are we to make of this combination of similarity and difference between our passage and *Metaphysics* A.5? The contrast between Iamblichus' proofs and A.5's likenesses would be striking enough on its own, even if one accepted the brackets by which Burkert athetises the reference to geometry as well as the clause about optics. If A.5 is Aristotle's canonical picture of the Pythagoreans, there seem to be two views one could take of the Iamblichus excerpt. *Either* it is a non-canonical picture of those same Pythagoreans – most likely, of Philolaus, who since Burkert has been widely (though not universally) accepted as the main source for A.5 – *or* it is a picture of some non-canonical Pythagoreans.

I propose to argue for the second alternative. I am persuaded by Burkert that our passage is indeed from Aristotle, but my argument will not depend on || the attribution. What matters is that Iamblichus presents (from some source or other) a picture of a Pythagorean philosophy which emphasises proof and is different from the Pythagoreanism of A.5, where likeness is the key because Aristotle is looking for the antecedents of Plato's theory that sensible things are to be explained as likenesses of the Forms and, ultimately, Form numbers (*Met.* A.6).

3. The first step in the argument is to defend the references to optics and geometry against Burkert's excisions. In Festa's Teubner text of Iamblichus the only excision is the word ὅτι before δι' ἀριθμῶν in line 4. But Burkert's concern is to restore the text of Aristotle. To this end he retains ὅτι and excises both the mention of optics in line 4 and the phrase about geometrical objects in line 7. What remains is all about number, harmony, proportion, so that the fragment's picture of Pythagoreanism is assimilated to the familiar account in A.5.[9] Burkert says nothing about the excerpt's emphasis on mathematical proof. The main reason for his drastic surgery is precisely that geometry plays no role in the canonical picture given by Aristotle and confirmed by Aristoxenus (frag. 23 Wehrli). He suggests that Iamblichus added the references to optics and geometry 'to emphasize the many-sidedness of Pythagorean μαθήματα'.

---

[9] Burkert's excisions and interpretation are followed by Huffman 1993: 70, n. 18, 114.

My first puzzle is why, if that was Iamblichus' motivation, he should start by adducing a minor branch of mathematics such as optics, instead of geometry itself. Second, Burkert's translation of the remark about harmonics in lines 3–4, which he admits as Aristotelian, barely makes sense. Consequently, if ὅτι means 'that', I would prefer to follow Festa in deleting it. But of course, ὅτι need not mean 'that'. It can also mean 'because' (as at line 2), and so translated it yields much better sense, as follows: 'seeing that the facts about harmony are generally admitted *because* they are through numbers', *scilicet* 'because they are established or proved through numbers'.

Just this is what the fragment is reporting. The Pythagoreans were impressed by mathematics because only in mathematics does one find proofs (ἀποδείξεις, line 2). It is proofs – in the case of harmonics, proofs by means of number theory – that bring it about that discoveries about harmony win widespread acceptance.[10] So likewise, I suggest the sentence continues, mathematical theories about vision win widespread acceptance because they are established through διαγράμματα. (Understand ὅτι from ὅτι δι' ἀριθμῶν or suppose that a second ὅτι διά dropped out in line 4 because the scribe's eye jumped ahead to διαγράμματα).[11] And διαγράμματα here naturally does not mean diagrams as such, but rather proofs conducted with a diagram in the manner we can ‖ see exemplified on any page of Euclid, including the *Optics*.[12] To translate once more in the light of the interpretation now on offer:

> The Pythagoreans devoted themselves to mathematics. They both admired the accuracy of its reasonings, because it alone among human activities contains proofs, and they saw that general agreement is given in equal measure to theorems concerning attunement, because they are <established> through numbers, and to the mathematical studies that deal with vision, because they are <established> through diagrams. This led them to think that these things[13] and their principles are quite generally the causes of existing things. Consequently, these are what anyone who wishes to comprehend the true nature of existing things should turn their attention to – the numbers and geometrical forms of existing things and ratios – because it is by them that everything is made clear.

---

[10] I would compare ὁμολογούμενα with Plato, *Rep.* 510d ὁμολογουμένως, 533c ὁμολογία. Huffman 2005 compares Archytas frag. 3 where proportion brings about political concord.

[11] In which case Vitelli's angled brackets really belong around the first διά. The alternative of reading simply διὰ γραμμῶν, which in later mathematical authors may contrast with δι' ἀριθμῶν (Heath 1981 [1921], Vol. II 257–8; Netz 1999: 36), finds no parallel in extant Aristotle.

[12] In Plato's *Hippias Minor* 366c–367e διαγράμματα stand to geometry as calculations (λογισμοί) to λογιστική; they are the whole of what the geometer busies himself with. The same word at *Cratylus* 436c8–d8 only makes sense if translated 'proofs'.

[13] It is unclear whether ταῦτα are the numbers and diagrams or the results obtained through them.

If this is a reasonable translation, we can see why the passage should mention optics and not geometry in general. It is *applied* number theory, as in harmonics, and *applied* geometry, as in optics, from which this Pythagorean train of thought begins. Because the power of mathematical proof can be brought to bear on the objects of hearing and vision, achieving in these areas results that are ὁμολογούμενα, generally admitted, for this reason – and here comes the characteristically Pythagorean generalisation signalled by ὅλως in line 5 – it is mathematics that will give us an understanding of the world in general.

I submit that the sense and sequence of thought now won from the first five lines of our passage is so far superior to that in Burkert's translation that we have sufficient reason to strike out his first two sets of square brackets. Anyone worried by the word ἔνισον (a ἅπαξ λεγόνμενον) can easily emend to ἐπ' ἴσον (Vitelli – a good Aristotelian phrase) or ἐξ ἴσου (Burkert) or ἐν ἴσῳ (a nice parallel at Thuc. IV.65), according to taste.[14] I shall move on to the third segment Burkert would excise, the mention of the forms studied by geometry: καὶ τὰ γεωμετρούμενα εἴδη τῶν ὄντων (lines 7–8).

Burkert says that τὰ γεωμετρούμενα is a school term from late antiquity, citing Plutarch and others. I reply that the verb γεωμετρεῖν had been available since the fifth century BC as a transitive verb meaning 'to measure, to survey land'. In two quite evocative contexts (Aristophanes, *Birds* 995; Plato, *Theaetetus* 173e) it carries a strong suggestion of applied geometry, not just pacing out the length of a field. Now a transitive verb || can be put into the passive by any native speaker. It is true that in extant Aristotle γεωμετρεῖν occurs only in its intransitive use 'to practise geometry'. But that is no reason to deny that he has the transitive use available in his lexicon. In which case, the passive is there as well.[15]

That leaves εἴδη. Even extant Aristotle uses this word in connection with geometry and mathematics generally: τὰ μαθήματα περὶ εἴδη ἐστίν

---

[14] There remains Burkert's complaint about the absence of an article before λόγους. Easy as it would be to supply <τούς>, Huffman 2005 has a better answer. ἀριθμούς and εἴδη both go with the dependent genitive τῶν ὄντων: they are the numbers and the forms *of* existing things. To talk of the ratios or proportions *of existing things* would make little sense, since ratios and proportions are relations between numbers or between geometrical magnitudes. Hence καὶ λόγους is sensibly placed, without an article, after τῶν ὄντων, whose numbers and forms enter into ratios and proportions with one another.

[15] A good example to shake up preconceptions about the passive is the astonishing ἀστρονομεῖται at Pl. *Rep.* 530c. Giuseppe Cambiano kindly pointed me to D.L. VIII.88, where Hermippus (third century BC) is cited for the information that Eudoxus wrote both ἀστρολογούμενα and γεωμετρούμενα. This is quite likely to reflect Hermippus' own wording, long before Plutarch.

(*APo.* 1.13, 79a7–8). It is a difficult passage, on which the commentators are not much help, but I am quite sure that Aristotle is not here claiming that mathematics is about Platonic Forms. He is making some sort of contrast between substance and attribute. The εἴδη studied by geometry and other branches of mathematics are attributes or aspects of substantial beings, although they are treated in abstraction from the subjects they belong to. Alternatively, εἴδη might refer to the diagrams used by the mathematicians – compare κέχρηται τοῖς εἴδεσιν (79a7) with τοῖς ὁρωμένοις εἴδεσιν προσχρῶνται at Plato *Rep.* 510d5 – the point being that these diagrams represent attributes abstracted from substantial beings. At the worst, the passage shows we can defend the word, even if we do not fully understand it.

This completes my restoration of a picture of a non-canonical Pythagorean philosophy which emphasises mathematical proof. If the picture was not drawn by Aristotle, as it probably was, it still conforms to the same historiographic pattern as his canonical picture in *Metaphysics* A.5, which is probably based on Philolaus. The next step is to propose Archytas as the original of the non-canonical portrait reproduced by Iamblichus.

4. Aristotle wrote a three-volume work *On the Philosophy of Archytas*, and we hear also of a book of extracts he made 'from the *Timaeus* and the works of Archytas' (D.L. v.25). Compared with his two books dealing with the Pythagoreans in general, this is a sign of serious interest and, perhaps, respect. Aristotle would not share Plato's dismissive attitude to applied mathematics, so if Archytas' achievement in optics was as notable as we know it was in harmonics, he would touch his cap to a Pythagorean so different from those he scorns in *Metaphysics* A.5.

This brings me to Archytas frag. 4, which emphasises proof:

> With respect to wisdom, arithmetic (λογιστικά) seems to be much superior to the other disciplines and to deal with what it wishes more clearly even than geometry.[16] And again, in cases where geometry is deficient, arithmetic completes proofs (ἀποδείξιας), and || likewise, if, on the one hand, the subject is forms (εἰδέων), [it completes] the treatment of forms ...[17]

Burkert impugns the fragment for Platonic language and mathematical nonsense (1972: 200–21, n. 14). The first objection – to 'the tell-tale

---

[16] I follow Huffman 2005 in the view that there was no need for DK to mark a lacuna between this sentence and the next.

[17] The sense of lines 10–11 is doubtful, and translation a gamble, because the fragment breaks off in mid-sentence with no response to μέν.

εἰδέων πραγματεία'– is easily met. In Plato's *Republic* geometers are said to talk about visible forms (510d: ὁρωμένοις εἴδεσι) in order to think about the invisible forms they resemble. Even the invisible forms cannot be Platonic Forms, because the Platonic Form of, e.g., Square is necessarily unique, while Pythagoras' theorem states a relation between three distinct squares.[18] Archytas does not make the characteristically Platonic distinction between the visible and the invisible, but the fragment can hardly be faulted for saying, like Aristotle in the passage just cited, that mathematics, or some mathematics, deals with forms. It is common sense that geometry, for example, is about the shapes of things. Granted, Archytas seems here to contrast geometry with the treatment of forms. But good as it would be to know what he might mean by εἴδη,[19] to defend the fragment it is enough to insist that the word need not stink of Platonism. The more serious issue is whether the assertion that arithmetic helps where geometry fails is 'nonsense mathematically'.

There is surely no need to agree with Burkert that frag. 4 advances the deeply incompetent idea that incommensurables can be determined arithmetically. One alternative, suggested by Wilbur Knorr, is that the very notion of incommensurability involves arithmetic, for it is the notion of two magnitudes which fail to have to one another the ratio of an integer to an integer (Knorr 1975: 310–11). (But the same might be said of many geometrical notions, e.g. doubling the cube.) Another suggestion, due to Ian Mueller, is that the fragment is only saying that arithmetic yields true results where geometry yields false ones, since 'the Pythagoreans used the numerical relations of musical intervals to argue that, e.g., there was no such thing as a half tone (the tone being represented by 9:8 and there being no numbers *n*, *m*, *k*, such that *n*:*m* :: 9:8 and *n*:*k* :: *k*:*m*), whereas the representation of the intervals as straight lines would imply the existence of a half tone' (Mueller 1991: 90, n. 12). Both these proposals are mathematically competent, but neither to my mind does justice to the fragment's emphasis on proof. Can we think of a case where arithmetic completes a proof that geometry cannot complete?

Well, the classic (so-called Pythagorean) proof of the incommensurability of the side and diagonal of a square proceeds by arguing that if the side and diagonal were ‖ commensurable, the same number would be both odd

---

[18] More on this point in Burnyeat 2000b: 35–42 [Chapter 1 in *EAMP* vol. III, pp. 33–40].

[19] Cambiano offers an admittedly speculative but interesting hypothesis based on Archytas' report (DK 45.2–3) of the commendably thorough Eurytus, pupil of Philolaus (Cambiano 1998: 316–22). Eurytus' pebbles were set out in an attempt to arrive at some sort of numerical specification of different εἴδη (= kinds, as in Philolaus frag. 5) of animal or plant.

and even, which is impossible. A principle of arithmetic is called in to complete the proof of a result in geometry. Now historians think that this proof is old, and possibly even Pythagorean, because it contains a special step for unity (μόνας). This is required if the proof is to satisfy someone who holds that one is both odd and even. A strange idea, no doubt, but it is found in Philolaus frag. 5 and reported for Archytas (DK 47 A21). Thus for Archytas the incommensurability proof would not work unless it ruled out the single case where the same number not only can be, but is, both odd and even. Add that extra step, as we find it in Euclid *Elements* x, Appendix 27, and the proof becomes compelling. It is a proof that makes good use of antique number theory.

Objection: this does not establish incommensurability as a case where geometry cannot manage on its own, because another way of proving the same result is by the wholly geometrical method of mutual subtraction (ἀνθυφαίρεως). *Elements* x.2 shows that, quite generally, if no common measure of two magnitudes will ever be found by mutual subtraction, the magnitudes are incommensurable. Reply: if that *general* proof was not yet available (because Theaetetus and Eudoxus had not yet laid the basis for the study of irrationals in *Elements* x), one might reasonably respond to a particular case of mutual subtraction by saying, "I can see that the process *will* never end, but I cannot see that it is *impossible* for it to end." Aristotle at *Metaphysics* Θ.4, 1047b5–6, envisages an opponent saying, 'It is not impossible for the diagonal to be measured – it just never will be measured'. His reply is that something which is possible, but will never come about, can be supposed true without any impossibility resulting, whereas the hypothesis that the diagonal has been measured does result in an impossibility – and here he is bound to be thinking of the impossibility of the same number being both odd and even (cf. *APr.* 1.23, 41a25–30). If proof by mutual subtraction is what Aristotle means to contrast with the familiar *reductio*,[20] the supposition that Archytas frag. 4 reflects similar thinking would lend it a controversial edge.

You may think I am on the verge of suggesting that Archytas might himself be the author of the *reductio* proof and writes frag. 4 to boost its superiority to proof by mutual subtraction. No verifiable historical fact stands in the way, but I shall be more modest. Frag. 4 is genuine. Hence Archytas is the first Pythagorean we know of to emphasise the importance of mathematical proof. Indeed, he is the only Pythagorean we know of to

---

[20] Here I am indebted to David Sedley's presentation on Θ.4 at a Cambridge seminar in 1995 (cf. also Knorr 1975: 34).

speak about mathematical proof. He has every right to do so, since he is by far and away the most skilled Pythagorean practitioner of proof; his duplication of the cube (DK 47 A14) is a stunning example of sophisticated Greek mathematics.[21] Archytas is eminently suited to be the original of Iamblichus' non-canonical portrait. ‖

5. We are now ready for optics. What the word διαγράμματα in the Iamblichus passage leads us to expect is real mathematical proofs with diagrams, such as we find in Euclid's *Optics* and *Catoptrics*. If we can confirm this, Archytas will emerge as very probably the founder of the discipline of mathematical optics as well as mechanics. Let me admit at once that the central concept of the ὄψις, the straight line of sight that travels outwards from the eye even as far as the Sun, is first attested for the fifth-century mathematician Hippocrates of Chios. It is to be found in Aristotle's report of his theory that the tails of comets are to be explained as phenomena of reflection (*Meteor.* 1.6, 342b35–343a20; DK 42.5–6). But Aristotle's report does not indicate a particularly mathematical treatment of the issue, still less a general mathematical study of reflection. We know that Archytas was indebted to Hippocrates for his proof that the problem of duplicating a cube could be reduced to that of finding two mean proportionals. It would be entirely in keeping with our evidence for relations between these two mathematicians for Archytas to have borrowed a concept from Hippocrates and put it to constructive further use. In frag. 1 Archytas himself looks back at his predecessors and remarks on their outstanding achievements in astronomy, geometry, arithmetic, and harmonics. No mention of stereometry, mechanics, or optics: a silence which may suggest that before Archytas these disciplines did not exist or did not achieve results of significance.[22]

So on to the evidence for Archytas' interest in optics, more particularly catoptrics. Our source is the *Apologia* of Apuleius, written in the middle of the second century AD. In chapter 15 Apuleius enumerates four accounts of why we see ourselves in a mirror:[23]

> Quid, quod nec ob haec debet tantummodo philosophus speculum invisere? Nam saepe oportet non modo similitudinem suam, verum etiam ipsius

---

[21] Cf. also the *reductio* proof preserved by Boethius in DK 47 A19, that a superparticular ratio cannot be divided into equal parts by insertion of a mean proportional.

[22] Aristotle twice implies that a proper understanding of the phenomena of reflection is relatively recent (*Meteor.* II.9, 370a16–21; *Sens.* 2, 438a5–10).

[23] The excerpt in DK 47 A25 stops mid-sentence with Archytas, omitting the Stoics.

similitudinis rationem considerare: num, ut ait Epicurus, (1) profectae a nobis imagines velut quaedam exuviae iugi fluore a corporibus manantes, cum leve aliquid et solidum offenderunt, illisae reflectantur et retro expressae contraversim respondeant an, ut alii philosophi disputant, (2) radii nostri seu (i) mediis oculis proliquati et lumini extrario mixti atque ita uniti, ut Plato arbitratur, seu (ii) tantum oculis profecti sine ullo foris amminiculo, ut Archytas putat, seu (iii) intentu aëris coacti, ut Stoici rentur, cum alicui corpori inciderunt spisso et splendido et levi, paribus angulis quibus inciderant resultent ad faciem suam reduces atque ita, quod extra tangant ac visant, id intra speculum imaginentur.

What about the point that these are not the only reasons for a philosopher to look into a mirror? Often enough he is bound to contemplate, not only his own likeness, but also the explanation of that likeness.[24] Is Epicurus right when he asserts that (1) images || proceed forth from us – as it were a kind of slough that continually streams from our bodies – which, when they strike anything smooth and solid, are reflected by the shock and reversed in such wise as to give back an image turned to face its original? Or should we accept the view maintained by other philosophers that (2) our own rays – either (i) rays filtered forth from the centre of the eyes to mix and thereby unite with the light outside, as Plato holds, or (ii) rays advancing only from our eyes without any external support (*sine ullo foris amminiculo*), as Archytas thinks, or (iii) rays constituted by the tension of the air, as the Stoics suppose – when they strike a dense and shiny and smooth body, rebound back to the face they came from at an angle equal to the angle of incidence, thereby making an image within the mirror of the thing they approach and touch without? (tr. after Butler)

Three of these theories are familiar from elsewhere, but nowhere in other doxographical sources is Archytas credited by name with an account of vision or reflection.[25] The four theories come in two groups, distinguished by the direction in which vision in general is supposed to work. The view of Epicurus, that something travels from the object seen to the perceiving subject, stands opposed to three versions of the idea that visual rays (*radii* = Greek ὄψεις or ἀκτῖνες) go out from the eye to the object perceived. But 'going out' is importantly ambiguous. Spatial travelling is appropriate to the theories of Plato and Archytas, but not to the Stoics. Their theory involves directionality (from eye to object), but not travel. The rays are lines of tension that form a cone in the air between eye and object, and

---

[24] My rendering of *oportet* emphasises that a philosopher is just the person you can expect to go looking for an explanation. The τόπος 'philosophy begins from wonder' is first found at Plato, *Theaetetus* 155d, where the example is another phenomenon of reflection: the rainbow.

[25] No mention of Archytas in a very similar report of Stoic, Epicurean, and Platonic theories of vision by Apuleius' contemporary Aulus Gellius v.16.

seeing is compared with feeling something at a distance through a stick.[26] It is Plato and Archytas who require the rays to travel from eye to object. What we need to understand is the difference between their rival theories of the outwardly travelling ray. Apuleius marks the difference by saying that Archytas' rays travel *sine ullo foris amminiculo*, without any external support. What does this mean?

Amminiculum denotes something to lean on for support. The word is used of the prop for a vine and other supporting devices. That made me think it should be the Latin equivalent of the Greek ἐπέρεισμα. Subsequently I found the related noun ἐπέρεισις used by Alexander of Aphrodisias (perhaps quoting Chrysippus) to indicate what light would have if (contrary to Aristotle's philosophy) it was a body (*De Anima* 132.30 = *SVF* II 432). It would have some bodily support. I conclude that Archytas' rays travel without requiring any external vehicle.

By contrast, Plato's *Timaeus* is emphatic that vision is a body. It is a body (45b: σῶμα) of fire, streaming out from within the eye, which coalesces with the fire of daylight outside to form a single body (45c: ἓν σῶμα) as it comes up against the object seen. The ‖ internal fire's need for external support is shown by what happens at night: the visual rays are extinguished when they emerge into the dark air. Apuleius reports Plato's view quite correctly in the words *mediis oculis proliquati et lumini extravio mixti atque ita uniti*. He thereby casts the external body of fiery light as the support (*amminiculum*) that Archytas' theory does without. Archytas' rays, travelling unsupported to the object seen, behave just like the ὄψεις in Euclid.[27]

In principle, this would be compatible with their being rays of fire, or some other bodily substance, coming out from within the eye, just so long as they do not require any *external* bodily support such as Plato insists upon.[28] But Apuleius' contrast between *mediis oculis proliquati* ('filtered forth from the centre of the eyes') and *tantum oculis profecti* ('advancing

---

[26] The sources assembled in *SVF* II.863–71 are not unequivocally against travel, but Ingenkamp agrees that the stick comparison is decisive (Ingenkamp 1971). Hence in Apuleius we can and should read *facti* with the MSS and Butler 1909 and Hunink 1997, not the emendation *coacti* adopted from Purser 1907: 366–7, by Butler and Owen 1914 and Vallette's Budé (1924), still less the more bizarre emendations mentioned in the Butler–Owen apparatus. The modest 'perhaps' which Purser attached to his proposal has not been repeated.

[27] Compare Epicurus *Ep. Hdt.* 49, who distinguishes two versions of the outwardly travelling story he rejects: οὐδὲ διὰ τῶν ἀκτίνων ἢ ὡνδήποτε ῥευμάτων. The ῥεύματα presumably allude to the 'stream of sight' at *Timaeus* 45c3, while ἀκτῖνες is a standard term for the rays postulated in mathematical optics.

[28] Thus O'Brien: 'Archytas is specifically distinguished from Plato as having held a theory of vision by outward-flowing fire alone' (O'Brien 1970: 157).

only from our eyes') suggests that Archytas' rays start *at* the eyes, not behind and inside them. Bodily substance would require the latter. The former fits the practice of Euclidean diagrams, which show the eye as a point from which the rays fan out. If Archytas was responsible for the optical διαγράμματα reported in the Iamblichus passage, he would most likely do the same. For all that matters for the mathematics is that a ray can be diagrammed as a geometrically straight line from eye to object.

The next paragraph of the *Timaeus* begins, 'It is not difficult to see (κατιδεῖν οὐδὲν ἔτι χαλεπόν) how mirror images are formed' (46a). Note the ironical word-play: understanding reflection is as easy as looking into a mirror, which anyone can do. Just so, reflections in a mirror are easy to understand because they are produced by necessity (46b: ἐξ ἀνάγκης). Timaeus then explains how the mixture of inner and outer fire constituting the visual ray gives rise to left–right reversal and other phenomena of reflection standard in books on catoptrics. This account is entirely mechanical, without a trace of mathematics. There are those who infer that at the time Plato wrote the *Timaeus* mathematical optics did not yet exist; it started later with Philip of Opus (Lasserre 1987: 647–8; G. Simon 1988: 22, 46). But if we believe Apuleius, it would seem that catoptrics already existed. Archytas had some interest in it. He may even have formulated the principle that the angle of reflection is equal to the angle of incidence (*paribus angulis quibus inciderant resultent*), which Apuleius implies was common ground to all the ray-theorists mentioned. Hence, if we believe Apuleius, we should infer that Plato, when writing the *Timaeus*, deliberately declined to mention the possibility of a mathematical account of reflection. It is by polemical design that he chose the rather surprising example of reflection to lead into the dialogue's first statement of the key distinction between reason and necessity, αἴτια and συναίτια. The polemic is a polemic || against the idea of a mathematics of visual appearances. Hence the scornful word-play about how easy it is to understand mirror images.

This goes well beyond the *Republic*'s exclusion of various branches of mathematics from a curriculum designed to turn the minds of future rulers towards the intelligible realm. The *Republic* acknowledged that mathematics, when applied to the sensible world, has certain useful 'by-products' (πάρεργα), as when a general uses arithmetic in marshalling his troops or geometry when laying out a camp site. These worldly benefits were faintly praised as 'not small' (527c), but dismissed as irrelevant to knowledge of the Good.²⁹ In the *Timaeus* we learn that the teleological cause of our having eyes at all is to observe the heavens and thereby acquire the notion of number and time, thus to be launched into philosophy in its broadest sense, including physics (47ac). In effect, we are told that the proper use of mathematics is what human nature is for. The implication, if we believe Apuleius, is that a mathematics of mirror images is a misuse of one of our most important endowments.³⁰

The point is rammed home by a quotation from the end of Euripides' *Phoenissae* (1762), which Timaeus applies to the lesser benefits of eyesight: let these be 'mourned in vain' by a non-philosopher who has gone blind (47b4–5). As usual in Plato, the original context of the quotation is pertinent to the context of reuse. The speaker is the self-blinded Oedipus, the man who sought knowledge it would have been better for him not to know. His next and final line is, 'Being mortal, I must bear the necessities (ἀνάγκας) sent by the gods'.

6. But is Apuleius to be believed? Where would the novelist famous for the tale of Lucius and the Golden Ass obtain recherché information on Archytas, information which is not found anywhere else? Apuleius is, of course, much more than a novelist. He is a Platonist philosopher, translator of the *Phaedo*, author of *De dogmate Platonis* and other philosophical works. He is learned in many fields, including mathematics: he wrote a work on astronomy (attested by John Lydus), a translation of Nicomachus' *Arithmetica*, and a treatise *De Musica* (both attested by Cassiodorus). The translation of Nicomachus served the Romans as their main source of information about Greek mathematics. As for the source of Apuleius' account of Archytas, read on to the next chapter of the *Apology*, where he lists a selection of the matters treated in a massive work (*volumine ingenti*) on catoptrics by Archimedes: the effect of plane, convex and concave mirrors on the apparent size of an image in comparison with its original; left–right reversal; apparent motion of the image in response to forward and backward motion of the original; the burning glass; rainbows, parhelia and other such phenomena. Archimedes, a contemporary of the Stoic Chrysippus, is the obvious source for Apuleius to have used – and Archimedes would have had special reason to study the writings of Archytas, the founder of mathematical mechanics. ||

---

²⁹ The several passages need to be read together, as a sequence (Burnyeat 2000b: 9–13; [Chapter 1 in *EAMP* vol. III, pp. 11–15]).
³⁰ Compare 68bd on the vanity, even impiety, of attempting to declare the proportions in which the different colours are mixed, *even if one knows what they are*.

Admittedly, Archimedes' authorship of a *Catoptrics* has been impugned by Knorr, who argues that Apuleius was the unwitting victim of a mistake of identity (Knorr 1985). The treatise he is referring to is in fact the *Catoptrics* which has come down to us in the corpus of Euclid. The celebrated name of Archimedes had somehow become attached to the work, with the result that not only Apuleius, but also later authors such as Theon, Olympiodorus, and the scholiast on Euclid *Cat.* 1, cite it as the *Catoptrics* of Archimedes.[31] But the major extant writers on optics never mention Archimedes as one of their predecessors. There is no mention of him in (what remains of) Ptolemy's *Optics*, in Hero's *Catoptrics*, or, most tellingly (if we disregard the problems of transmission via the Arabic), in Diocles' *On Burning Mirrors*, who expressly distinguishes four predecessors, among whom Archimedes is not included (Knorr 1985, n. 18).[32]

I am not persuaded. It looks to me as though Knorr makes quite a good case for rejecting the long-standard view that the *Catoptrics* ascribed to Euclid is a late compilation, by Theon or someone else, out of Ptolemy, Hero, and others. So let us date the Euclidean work early rather than late: BC rather than AD, indeed earlier than Diocles, who appears expressly to reject a key part of the Euclidean treatment of burning mirrors (Knorr 1985: 80, Knorr 1994: 19).[33] That makes it *possible* that the Euclidean work is the one cited by Theon, Olympiodorus, and the Euclid scholium as Archimedes' *Catoptrics*. But it does not yet make it *likely*.

To make the case for likelihood, Knorr emphasises the overlap between the problems listed by Apuleius and the problems actually dealt with by Euclid. Our Euclidean *Catoptrics* does not in fact deal with the rainbow or other meteorological phenomena, so overlap is all it is, not a perfect match. Knorr has to postulate that the *Catoptrics* Apuleius consulted did have a meteorological section (prepared for by the otherwise unused Euclidean postulate 6, on refracted rays), but it was cut out by a later editor.

In fact, the problems are a fairly standard list which would be likely to turn up in any work on phenomena of reflection, physical or mathematical. The *Timaeus'* discussion of left–right reversal in differently shaped mirrors may be compared with Lucretius, for example, whose long account of visual illusions (Lucretius IV.269–323) covers both left–right reversal

---

[31] The testimonia are collected in Heiberg's edition of Archimedes, Heiberg 1972: 549–51.
[32] But note that Diocles does not include Euclid either. On mathematicians' references to their predecessors, see now Mansfeld 1998.
[33] Knorr's case for attributing the work to the well-known Euclid himself, which becomes stronger in Knorr 1994, only makes it harder to imagine its being mistaken for Archimedes. Simon proposes that the work is from Euclid's time *or earlier* (G. Simon 1994).

and the depth of mirror images. Knorr himself acknowledges overlap between Hero's *Catoptrics* and the Euclidean one. But my main objection is that the Euclidean *Catoptrics* occupies no more than 28 pages of the (rather small) Teubner text – considerably less than Knorr's 76-page article on the subject. Even with a section on ‖ meteorological phenomena added back in, Apuleius could hardly have described that as a massive volume.[34]

Another of Knorr's arguments actually tells against the idea that Apuleius has been reading Euclid. Among the problems listed in chapter 16 is this: Why in plane mirrors does the image appear practically (*ferme*) equal to its original? That, says Knorr, 'can hardly have appeared in a technical work by Archimedes' (Knorr 1985, n. 13). But nor is it what we read in the Euclidean *Catoptrics* 19, which does not qualify its proof that image and original appear equal. Certainly, the adverb has no place in a mathematical proof. But given the imperfectly even surface of ancient mirrors, Archimedes could well use it to make a more discursive point about applying the mathematics to physical reality (so Butler and Owen [1914] 1983). (Seneca *NQ* 1.4.1 offers a suitable context: an explanation of the rainbow as a cloud's distorted mirroring of the sun.) Again, it was not in Euclid that Apuleius found the four theories of vision.

As for the question why Archimedes should mention Archytas alongside the more familiar ray theories of Plato and the Stoics, the most economical answer (besides any reason of South Italian patriotism) is signalled at the end of my excerpt from Apuleius: the differences between the three theories do not stop them agreeing on the fundamental mathematical principle that the angle of reflection equals the angle of incidence. For that is what explains why it is your own face you see when you look into a mirror. The principle may well have received its first formulation from Archytas.[35]

If this was Archimedes' attitude, it finds an interesting parallel in Geminus *ap.* Damianus 24.7–15. Schöne, who declares that mathematical optics does not concern itself with deciding between rival theories of how vision is effected (rays from the eye vs. images from the object seen or

---

[34] Although Knorr quotes the phrase (1985: 32) and construes Theon as referring to two or more books of Archimedes' *Catoptrics* (1985: 36, n. 27), nowhere does he face up to the problem of size. Knorr suggests that the lost meteorological part was the second of an edition in two papyrus rolls (Knorr 1994: 6), but by ancient standards that is not massive: Ptolemy's *Optics* (from the same century as Apuleius) was in five volumes. A further puzzle is the total absence of colour from the Euclidean treatise: that would surely be needed for discussion of rainbows in the alleged second roll.

[35] Cf. Knorr 1994: 22, inferring from Apuleius that 'Archytas ... conceptualized optical phenomena via geometric rays and knew the equal angles property of reflected rays'.

tension in the air between), just so long as the basic principles of optics are 'saved' (σῴζεται). Provided vision can be represented as a straight line and apparent size diagrammed by the angle at the eye, the mathematics goes ahead. Similarly, Archimedes would be saying that his catoptrical investigations will be compatible with any theory of vision that preserves the equality of the angles of incidence and reflection.[36]

To sum up, I propose we have good reason to believe Apuleius. Archimedes did write on catoptrics, citing Archytas as a mathematically oriented predecessor to set against the heavily physical accounts of Plato and the Stoics. Consequently, it will be to Archytas that the following doxographical notice alludes: ||

> The followers of Pythagoras and the mathematicians[37] [hold that mirror images are formed] by reflection of the visual ray (κατ' ἀνάκλασιν τῆς ὄψεως). The ray travels stretching out towards the mirror, but, on being struck by the dense smooth surface it encounters, it turns back upon itself like an arm that is stretched out and bent back towards the shoulder.[38]
> (*Dox Gr.* 405.15–23 = Stobaeus *Ecl.* 1.52)

Philip of Opus was no doubt inspired by Archytas' example. Now to do mathematical catoptrics, one needs to represent the visual ray (ὄψις) as a geometrically straight line. This concept had been available since Hippocrates of Chios in the fifth century and, for the reasons given, I believe Apuleius when he says that Archytas made use of it. It is this use of a geometrical concept that Plato did not like. That is why in the *Timaeus* he insists on the bodily nature of vision and reduces the explanation of reflection to the realm of Necessity. As in the *Republic*, so in the *Timaeus* his attitude to Archytas is polemical. Equally, to return to my original question, that is why optics has no place in the curriculum of the *Republic*. An optics of 'problems', without reference to the visual realm, would be nothing but some rather trivial geometry.

Finally, a last glance at Iamblichus. I hope that by now this testimony seems worthy of credence as a portrait of a non-canonical Pythagorean who devised proofs to solve problems in catoptrics. But notice that the passage speaks of τὰ περὶ τὴν ὄψιν μαθήματα in the plural. If one of the studies that deal with vision is catoptrics, the other must be optics in the more

---

[36] Including the Epicurean theory: Lucr. IV.323.
[37] Either (a) Pythagoreans and non-Pythagorean mathematicians like Hippocrates, or (b) Pythagoreans and, more specifically, those of them who are μαθηματικοί rather than ἀκουσματικοί.
[38] Cf. Archytas' use of his arm to dispute the idea of a finite universe (DK 47 A24).

exact sense of the theory of visual appearances such as we find in Euclid's *Optics*. Recall that Philip of Opus worked in optics as well as catoptrics. It so happens that South Italy during the fourth century BC was where the art of perspective painting for the theatre underwent rapid development. Just the time and the place for someone to found a mathematical theory of perspective.[39] The most famous illustration of theatrical perspective is the Würzburg vase, painted in Tarentum around 360–350 BC.[40] Archytas was living and writing in Tarentum, South Italy, during the first half of the fourth century BC. I nominate him as that someone.[41] ||

---

[39] Many scholars have supposed, on the strength of Vitruvius VII *Praef.* 10–12, that the art of perspective was invented by the painter Agatharchus in the fifth century BC, who wrote a book about it, which stimulated Anaxagoras and Democritus to write about perspective too. None of this is true, according to my analysis of the evidence in '"All the World's a Stage-Painting": Scenery, Optics, and Greek Epistemology' (Burnyeat 2017: [Chapter 11 in this volume]). To summarise the conclusions relevant here: (a) What Vitruvius says Agatharchus was the first to do is write a book on a technical architectural theme, viz. making the stage building (σκήνη). (b) In this book he evidently said something about the use of recession to imply depth when the σκήνη is painted to represent a temple or other building. (c) Anaxagoras and Democritus responded to this in writing, but we should not assume they theorised about perspective as such. In fact, I believe they merely cited pictorial recession as an image or model for the general epistemological principle 'Appearances are a sight of things unseen' (ὄψις τῶν ἀδήλων τὰ φαινόμενα). In any case, Vitruvius says nothing whatever about any of these writers taking a *mathematical* approach to their subject.

[40] E. Simon 1982: 23 and plate 10, is just one of many reproductions.

[41] This paper began life at a term-long seminar on Archytas, held in Cambridge in 1995. I am grateful for the discussion on that occasion and at subsequent meetings in Liège (The World Congress of History and Philosophy of Science), Lille, and Pittsburgh. Helpful individual comments came from Jonathan Barnes, David Fowler, Carl Huffman (who kindly showed me drafts of his forthcoming edition [Huffman 2005]), Ian Mueller, Reviel Netz, David Sedley, and Gérard Simon.

CHAPTER 11

'All the world's a stage-painting': scenery, optics, and Greek epistemology

Anaxarchus of Abdera is not your most famous Greek philosopher, and I have no wish to argue that he deserves better.[*] He was known as the Happiness Man (*ho eudaimonikos*), either from his equable temperament or, according to other sources, because he led something called the Happiness School (*hoi eudaimonikoi*),[1] and he || features prominently in the biography of Alexander the Great, at whose kingly presence he aims a number of caustic remarks. But all that is forgiven, I hope, in return for the

---

[*] [Note from the editor introducing the article's publication in *Oxford Studies in Ancient Philosophy*, 2016; subsequent editorial notes in brackets are also from that publication.] The following is the text of an unpublished lecture: Professor Burnyeat gave this paper frequently in the late 1980s and the 1990s. Like many of his unpublished papers, he requested that it not be circulated without his express permission, and so as a result relatively few people had access to it, sometimes through *samizdat* copies. But as it continues to be regarded highly and cited regularly, I felt it was valuable to make it available to a wider audience. I am grateful to Professor Burnyeat, who has kindly given his permission to publish it in this form, to Professors Sedley and Hobbs for their advice, and to my assistant David Morphew for his meticulous work in tracking down the references.
  Professor Burnyeat has not revised the typescript further for publication here and has not been involved in its editing. The manuscript is very polished, however, and appears to have reached a stable form by the late 1990s: the only variations we found in two typescripts were that a small number of handwritten marginalia in one had been incorporated into the text of the other, along with the deletion of two paragraphs (which I have retained, but placed in double brackets). Only a few footnotes were left blank or with promissory notes. Otherwise I have kept the paper as it was, including many of the hallmarks of oral delivery, limiting myself to filling in the citations and references, sometimes with a more recent edition, all without comment. Any supplement editorially added (for the *Oxford Studies in Ancient Philosophy* publication in 2016) has been placed in square brackets, beginning with the abbreviation 'OSAP'.
  Had Professor Burnyeat revised the lecture for publication, he would almost certainly have provided translations of his own. I have instead provided the texts as they occur on his handout, which, in keeping with his usual practice, was mostly composed from xeroxes, cut and pasted from bilingual editions such as the Loeb Classical Library, with his own annotations or modifications (which we have included, using italics, bold print, and underlining). Where he did not provide a translation, I have simply supplied the Loeb translation, when available, in keeping with his practice in the rest of the lecture, or another recent translation, with the translator's name always preceded by an asterisk.
[1] The first according to D.L. IX.60, but references to the second in LSJ s.v. εὐδαιμονικός (D.L. I.17; Clearchus 14 [fr. 60 Wehrli]=] = Athen. XII.548b). [See also S.E. *M* VII.48.]

splendid saying which I have borrowed for my title 'All the world's a stage-painting'.

I have of course reconstructed the saying from the paraphrase in Text 1, which comes from a history of theories of knowledge compiled in the first century BC, probably by the sceptic philosopher Aenesidemus,, and later used by Sextus Empiricus.

T1   οὐκ ὀλίγοι δὲ ἦσαν, ὡς προεῖπον, οἱ καὶ τοὺς περὶ Μητρόδωρον καὶ Ἀνάξαρχον ἔτι δὲ Μόνιμον φήσαντες ἀνῃρηκέναι τὸ κριτήριον, ἀλλὰ Μητρόδωρον μὲν ὅτι εἶπεν "οὐδὲν ἴσμεν, οὐδ' αὐτὸ τοῦτο ἴσμεν ὅτι οὐδὲν ἴσμεν," Ἀνάξαρχον δὲ καὶ Μόνιμον ὅτι <u>σκηνογραφίᾳ</u> ἀπείκασαν τὰ ὄντα, τοῖς τε κατὰ ὕπνους ἢ μανίαν προσπίπτουσι ταῦτα ὡμοιῶσθαι ὑπέλαβον.

As I said above, there have been not a few who have asserted that Metrodorus and Anaxarchus, and also Monimus, abolished the criterion – Metrodorus because he said 'We know nothing, nor do we even know the very fact that we know nothing'; and *Anaxarchus and Monimus because they likened existing things to a <u>scene-painting</u> and supposed them to resemble the impressions experienced in sleep or madness.* (Sextus Empiricus *M.* VII.87–8, trans. Bury 1933–49, emphasis added)

In the first sentence of the excerpt before you, Sextus is the 'I' of *hōs proeipon*, Aenesidemus the *ouk oligoi* from whom Sextus's information comes. But if Sextus' paraphrase lacks the Shakespearean splendour which I am imagining the original to have had, nonetheless his report gives us valuable information about the philosophical context in which the saying made its mark. For the passage mentions two other philosophers beside Anaxarchus, Metrodorus and Monimus. Let me introduce them, two minor characters in what will, I fear, be quite a large cast of players.

Metrodorus is the best known of several fourth-century followers of Democritus who pushed to extremes the sceptical tendencies in the epistemology of fifth-century Atomism; when Epicurus at the end of the fourth century set himself to give Atomism a more secure epistemological foundation, Metrodorus was a target of particular concern.[2] Monimus is a Cynic, a follower of Diogenes in his barrel, and he is one of a number of Cynics who seem to have used || Democritean sayings more for their moral than for their epistemological value;[3] Text 2 suggests that in his

---

[2] For citations and discussion see Burnyeat 1978: 204, and n. 25 [Chapter 3 in *EAMP* vol. I]; Sedley 1983: 33.
[3] See Z. Stewart 1958: 180–8; Demetrius *ap.* Seneca ('truth in the depths', *De Beneficiis* 7.1.5). [Demetrius is the Cynic speaker in Seneca's *De Beneficiis* VII.1.5, who is presenting Democritean material. For discussion of this passage, see Stewart 1958: 181.]

mouth 'All the world's a stage-painting' would have meant 'All is vanity' in the spirit of Ecclesiastes, rather than 'It's all a big illusion' in the spirit of Descartes' *First Meditation*.

T2   Ξενιάδης μὲν οὖν ὁ Κορίνθιος, ὡς ἀνώτερον ὑπεδείκνυμεν, μηθὲν εἶναί φησιν ἀληθές· τάχα δὲ καὶ Μόνιμος ὁ κύων, τῦφον εἰπὼν τὰ πάντα, ὅπερ οἴησίς ἐστι τῶν οὐκ ὄντων ὡς ὄντων.

Thus Xeniades the Corinthian, as we indicated above, declares that nothing is true; and so also, perhaps, Monimus the Cynic when he said that 'All things are vanity' (that is to say, a vain fancy that non-existents are existent). (Sextus Empiricus *M.* VIII.5, trans. Bury)

In between comes Anaxarchus, a vigorous moraliser too, but also an Atomist; this is presupposed by the anecdote in which he discourses to Alexander about the innumerable worlds postulated by Democritus' cosmology and Alexander bursts into tears because he is not yet master of one world:

T3   Ἀλέξανδρος Ἀναξάρχου περὶ κόσμων ἀπειρίας ἀκούων ἐδάκρυε, καὶ τῶν φίλων ἐρωτώντων ὅ τι πέπονθεν, 'οὐκ ἄξιον' ἔφη 'δακρύειν, εἰ κόσμων ὄντων ἀπείρων ἑνὸς οὐδέπω κύριοι γεγόναμεν;'

Alexander wept when he heard Anaxarchus discourse about an infinite number of worlds, and when his friends inquired what ailed him, 'Is it not worthy of tears,' he said, 'that, when the number of worlds is infinite, we have not yet become lords of a single one?' (Plutarch *De Tranquillitate Animi* 466d = Anaxarchus 72 A 11 DK; trans. Helmbold)

iam Alexandri pectus insatiabile laudis, qui Anaxarcho comiti suo ex auctoritate Democriti praeceptoris innumerabiles mundos esse referenti 'heu me' inquit 'me miserum quod ne uno quidem adhuc potitus sum'.

Alexander's appetite for fame was insatiable. He said to his companion Anaxarchus, who was retailing on the authority of his teacher || Democritus the existence of innumerable worlds: 'Alas for me, I have not yet made myself master of one!' (Valerius Maximus VII.14 ext. 2 = Anaxarchus 72 A11 DK, trans. Shackleton Bailey)

Having sketched a context for Anaxarchus' saying 'All the world's a stage-painting', I can now ask the question which this lecture will try to answer. Why, if you are a fourth-century Atomist looking for a memorable way to express, whether for epistemological or for moralistic purposes, the sceptical outlook that Metrodorus has made fashionable – why do you choose the image of scene painting?

This is, after all, one of the earliest extant occurrences of the word *skēnographia*. The only other certainly fourth-century occurrence[4] is that famously truncated sentence of Aristotle's *Poetics* (Text 4) about Sophocles introducing the third actor and *skēnographia*:

T4 καὶ τό τε τῶν ὑποκριτῶν πλῆθος ἐξ ἑνὸς εἰς δύο πρῶτος Αἰσχύλος ἤγαγε καὶ τὰ τοῦ χοροῦ ἠλάττωσε καὶ τὸν λόγον πρωταγωνιστὴν παρεσκεύασεν, τρεῖς δὲ καὶ σκηνογραφίαν Σοφοκλῆς.

> Aeschylus first introduced a second actor; he diminished the importance of the Chorus, and assigned the leading part to the dialogue. Sophocles <raised the number of actors to> three, and <added> scene-painting. (Aristotle *Poet.* 1449a15–19, trans. Butcher 1907, brackets added)

So, innocent souls who believe Aristotle incapable of writing such a sentence – quite a number of scholars wish to regard it as an interpolation – must look to Anaxarchus as the first known user of the term.[5] Thus scene painting is not such a common topic of discussion that there is no need to ask why it should turn up on the lips of a fourth-century Abderite Atomist who trails around the world in the court of a conquering king.

However, these fourth-century Atomists are not, so far as one can tell, particularly original. Their material derives from Democritus, even if they sharpen the scepticism and put a harder, more Cynic edge on the morals. More likely than not, Anaxarchus is developing a thought that was already formulated by the fifth-century Atomist Democritus.

This brings me to a well-known passage in Vitruvius, which has received a great deal of discussion from historians of the tragic stage, and even more from historians of ancient painting, but very little discussion, I regret to say, from historians of ancient philosophy, even though (in the second paragraph) it mentions both Democritus and Anaxagoras – in that order, which is the reverse of the chronological order, for we have Democritus's own word for it that he was younger than Anaxagoras by some forty years.[6] At present the order of names will seem a rather small and insignificant detail, but then this passage of Vitruvius, vital as it is for the early history of

---

[4] Timaeus, *FGrH* 566F7 (= Polybius XII.28a.1) is 350–250 BC.
[5] A. L. Brown 1984: 1–8; Taplin 1977: 457–8, n. 4. Answer A. L. Brown and G. F. Else (A. L. Brown 1984: 1–2, 5–6; Else 1957: 164–79; Else 1939 on ὀψέ by reference to the *life* of tragedy and Plato, *Laws* on ὀψέ ποτε (*Laws* VII.819d5–9), i.e. late in its own development, not lately relative to the time of Aristotle's writing. Correct A. L. Brown (*op. cit.*, 8 & n. 31) on whether in this instance S.E. is a 'late source'. [The last promissory note appears to have gone unfulfilled.]
[6] KRS 549 = D.L. IX.34.

the tragic stage, has never been approached from the direction I am coming from, with a view to answering a question about Anaxarchus.

T5 (10) ego vero, Caesar, neque alienis indicibus mutatis interposito nomine meo id profero corpus neque ullius cogitata vituperans institui ex eo me adprobare, sed omnibus scriptioribus infinitas ago gratias, quod egregiis ingeniorum sollertiis ex aevo conlatis abundantes alius alio genere copias praeparaverunt, unde nos uti fontibus haurientes aquam et ad propria proposita traducentes facundiores et expeditiores habemus ad scribendum facultates talibusque confidentes auctoribus audemus, institutiones novas comparare. (11) Igitur tales ingressus eorum quia ad propositi mei rationes animadverti praeparatos, inde sumendo progredi coepi. Namque primum Agatharchus Athenis Aeschylo docente tragoediam scaenam[7] fecit, et de ea commentarium reliquit. Ex eo moniti Democritus et Anaxagoras de eadem re scripserunt,

> quemadmodum oporteat, ad aciem oculorum radiorumque extentionem certo loco centro constituto, lineas[8] ratione naturali respondere,

uti de incerta re certae[9] imagines aedificiorum in scaenarum || picturis redderent speciem et, quae in directis planisque frontibus sint figurata, alia abscedentia, alia prominentia esse videantur. (12) Postea Silenus de symmetriis doricorum edidit volumen; de aede ionica Iunionis, quae est Sami dorica, Theodorus;[10] ionice Ephesi quae est Dianae, Chersiphron et Metagenes ...

(10) But for my part, Caesar, I am not bringing forward the present treatise after changing the titles of other men's books and inserting my own name, nor has it been my plan to win approbation by finding fault with the ideas of another. On the contrary, I express unlimited thanks to all the authors that have in the past, by compiling from antiquity remarkable instances of the skill shown by genius, provided us with abundant materials of different kinds. Drawing from them as it were water from springs, and converting them to our own purposes, we find our powers of writing rendered more fluent and easy, and, relying upon such authorities, we venture to produce new systems of instruction. (11) Hence, as I saw that such beginnings on

---

[7] *ad scaenam e₂*, Granger 1931–4. [8] *adlineas* codd.: corr. Schneider 1807–8: *ad lineas* Granger
[9] *incerta re- certae* H: *dein certarem certae* c: *incerta re incertae* h: *incerta re certae alii*: *de certa re certae* Krohn 1912. Granger (1931–4) notes that the flourish attached to *re* in H (the oldest and primary MS, from which he contends, against both previous and subsequent editors, that all others derive) is like the symbol for *m* (cf. c's *certarem*) and suggests that this *m* is the scribe's misreading of *in*. He prints *incertae*, basically because he believes it to be required by Democritean doctrine. The alternative is to suppose that c and h exhibit progressive corruption of the original *certae*. Professor Michael Reeve has looked at H for me and reports as follows: 'The passage reads in all clarity (spacing excepted) *uti de incerta re certe imagines*. The squiggle or flourish after *re* is pure imagination: the centre of *e* protrudes with a modest flourish, but so it does in many other places on the same page.'
[10] *de aede ionica Iunonis quae est Sami Rhoecus et Theodorus* conj. Granger, on grounds of truth.

their part formed an introduction suited to the nature of my own purpose, I set out to draw from them, and to go somewhat further. In the first place Agatharchus, in Athens, when Aeschylus was bringing out a tragedy, painted a scene,[11] and left a commentary about it. This led Democritus and Anaxagoras to write on the same subject:

> showing how, given a centre in a definite place, the lines should naturally correspond with due regard to the point of sight and the divergence of the visual rays,[12]

so that by this deception a faithful representation of the appearance of buildings might be given in painted scenery,[13] and so that, though || all is drawn on a vertical flat façade, some parts may seem to be withdrawing into the background, and others to be standing out in front. (12) Afterwards Silenus published a book on the proportions of Doric structures; Theodorus, on the Doric temple of Juno which is in Samos; Chersiphron and Metagenes, on the Ionic temple at Ephesus which is Diana's ... (Vitruvius VII, *praef.* 10–12, trans. Morgan 1960)

This paper is therefore going to be a plea for the unity of the Classics. We have become so divided into specialisms that we seldom share our knowledge or consider whether our specialised perspectives are complementary rather than conflicting. Perhaps a historian of philosophy can help with the problems that have exercised other branches of the Classics in connection with this vexed passage of Vitruvius. I am sure that the attempt should be made, even though it will mean that I must ask you to forgive my talking with a shameless abandon about lots of things whose larger frameworks I know nothing about. For I hope also to show that, in return, the history of ancient philosophy has much to gain from considering the history of the tragic stage and the development of painting.

Let us then begin the approach to Vitruvius. Anaxarchus, as I said, points us to Democritus, whose name precedes that of the older philosopher Anaxagoras. But it is immediately obvious that Democritus' place in Vitruvius' story can only be understood by reference to the previous

---

[11] 'eine perspektivische Bühnendekoration gemalt', Frank 1923: 234; 'painted a perspective stage set', (paraphrase, E. Simon 1982: 22); 'was in control of the stage', Granger 1931–4: 'set the stage', J. White 1956: 46.

[12] 'how it is necessary that, a fixed centre being established, the lines correspond by natural law to the sight of the eyes and the extension of the rays', J. White 1956.

[13] 'so that from an uncertain object certain images may render the appearance of buildings in the paintings of the stages', J. White 1956; 'such that *from* an uncertain object, *uncertain* images may give the appearance of buildings in the scenery of the stage', Granger 1931–4; 'so that ... *clear* pictures can reproduce the appearance of buildings in stage-scenery', E. Simon 1982: 'damit *von* der undeutlichen Sache *deutliche* Bilder den Anblick von Gebäuden bei den Bühnenmalereien wiedergeben', Fensterbusch 1964: 'so dass *über* eine ungenaue Sache *genaue* Abbilder die Gestalt der Gebäude auf der Bühnendekoration wiedergeben' Frank 1923: 235. [Emphasis added]

sentence about Agatharchus, whom we know from other sources to have enjoyed a certain fame as a painter in fifth-century Athens. We must therefore start with the sentence about Agatharchus.

It is remarkable how often this sentence is reported, sometimes even *translated*, by reputable scholars as saying that Agatharchus invented perspective[14] or that he was the first to do scene painting.[15] We shall be talking in a minute about the word *primum*. For the || moment let us take *scaenam fecit* by itself and, being warned by the variant translations recorded in nn. 11–13, let us not take it for granted that this means, as Morgan's translation has it, that Agatharchus painted, or made, the scenery or the scenic background for a play of Aeschylus. It is not that the words *could* not mean this in Vitruvius' Latin. They certainly could (cf. VII.5.5). But it will become increasingly likely as we proceed that in this context the words represent the Greek *skēnēn epoiēse* in a Greek source, and *skēnēn epoiēse* means that Agatharchus made the stage-building for a play of Aeschylus. Granger's alternative text *ad scaenam fecit*[16] means that Agatharchus busied himself with the stage-building. But we shall find reason later to think that Granger's textual judgement is not to be trusted. And if we adopt as the safest, because minimal, translation, 'he made the stage', then two results follow, both of which will be confirmed shortly.

The first result is that it is wrong to think, as many scholars have done, that Vitruvius' report is at odds with the statement in Aristotle's *Poetics* (Text 4) that scene painting began with Sophocles rather than with a play of Aeschylus.[17] So far, given our translation, Vitruvius has said nothing about scene painting. (We will see in a moment that even on the Morgan translation there is no inconsistency with Aristotle.) The second result, more germane to my question about Anaxarchus, is that whatever Agatharchus did to interest Democritus and Anaxagoras, it was not that he produced a striking *tour de force* of perspective for a tragic festival which they saw or heard about.

Vitruvius makes it perfectly clear what, according to him, interested the two philosophers. It was the written word, not the painted scenery. *Ex eo moniti*, he says, where *eo* is the *commentarium*, *hypomnema* or treatise which Agatharchus wrote *de ea*, where *ea* on || the safe minimal translation of *scaenam fecit* is the stage-building he made or busied himself with.

---

[14] Pollitt 1974: 240–7.
[15] [This note was left blank by the author, to be completed at a later date. The relevant claim can, however, be found in the following works: Gardner 1899: 253; Webster 1939: 74; Robertson 1959: 164; Baldry 1971: 46–7; Melchinger 1974: 162–3.]
[16] Petronius 62.4 (*homo meus coepit ad stelas facere*) – OLD says 'perhaps' under 27b.
[17] Inconsistent: Gogos 1983: 71; Lefkowitz 1984: 152–3. Not inconsistent: Webster 1956: 13–14; E. Simon 1982: 22 n. 84; Pollitt 1974: 245.

Agatharchus, according to this testimony, wrote something about making or organising the stage-building, not a book specifically devoted to scene painting, still less a treatise on perspective. No doubt he included some remarks about scene painting (recently introduced by Sophocles, who first won the tragedy prize in 468). Agatharchus was after all a painter. Perhaps he even made some remarks about perspectival effects in painted scenery, for the remainder of our Vitruvius text leaves us in no doubt that it *was* something said about scene painting that interested Democritus and Anaxagoras. But the point I wish to emphasise for the moment is that it is to something *said*, and said in writing, that we must look for the beginning of the story that leads to Anaxarchus saying 'All the world's a stage-painting', not to something done with brush and paint.

This is confirmed by the fact that what Vitruvius wishes to tell us is that Agatharchus was the first to *write* on any architectural matter, the matter in his case being stage construction. The weight of *primum* does not fall on (*ad*) *scaenam fecit* but on *commentarium reliquit*. *Primum* contrasts with *postea* at the beginning of the next paragraph. Agatharchus wrote first, then came Silenus's book on the proportions of Doric structures. Hence *scaenam fecit* describes what Agatharchus was the first to write about, not what he was the first to do. This confirms that there is no conflict between Vitruvius and the statement in the *Poetics* that Sophocles was the first to introduce scene painting. There is no conflict even if *scaenam fecit* means that he made or painted the scenery, for Vitruvius is not saying that he was the first to do so. He is saying that he was the first to write about it or, if you like, the first to combine doing it and writing about it. The entire context in Vitruvius is concerned not with the history of architectural achievements, still less with the history of painting, but with the history of architectural *writings*.

At this point it is only prudent for me to remind myself that prose writings from the early fifth century do not come at two a drachma. The evidence for their existence is often suspect. What reason have I to think that Vitruvius is to be believed when he writes in the twenties or thirties of the first century BC about Agatharchus writing in the fifth century BC?[18] ||

Vitruvius certainly does not claim to have seen this work of Agatharchus' himself. What he says, in the first paragraph, is that he is immensely grateful to earlier writers who collected from still earlier ages

---

[18] *RE*, s.v. 'Vitruvius': wrote in the thirties, published in the twenties, on account of *De architectura* 1.1. [OSAP: The dedication to Augustus that opens *De Architectura* 1.1 makes reference to his victory at Actium (31 BC) and ascendency to imperial rule, and his holding off from publication until later.]

(*ex aevo conlatis*) the 'stores' (*copias*) from which he can draw off material for his own use. Like Sextus in the text we began from [Text 1], he is relying on an earlier compilation, and his value as a source is dependent on the value of the compilation he is using. We know quite a lot about the value of the compilation Sextus uses, for on a number of occasions he preserves a mention by Aenesidemus (assuming *he* was the author of the compilation) of the particular first century BC authority he is drawing on for his account of a given philosopher. Vitruvius is not quite so helpful, but he tells in Text 6, in connection with writers on symmetry, that he has had access to both Greek and Latin compilations.

T6 *quorum ex commentariis, quae utilia esse his rebus animadverti, [collecta in unum coegi corpus, et ideo maxime, quod animadverti] in ea re ab Graecis volumina plura edita, ab nostris oppido quam pauca. Fufidius enim mirum de his rebus primus instituit edere volumen, item Terentius Varro de novem disciplinis unum de architectura, P. Septimius duo.*

As to the useful contributions to our subject which I found in their commentaries, many volumes have been published by the Greeks, exceedingly few by our own writers. For Fufidius curiously enough was the first to publish a volume on these topics. Further, Varro included one volume in his work *On the Nine Disciplines*; Publius Septimius wrote two volumes. (Vitruvius VII, *praef.* 14, trans. Granger)

He has clearly *read* about Agatharchus' writing,[19] and it would be unfair to dismiss his testimony, as some scholars do, without investigating the possibility that his source had access through the Hellenistic libraries to information which is lost to us. Quite apart from the further writings on architectural themes which Vitruvius lists (last paragraph of passage), we can point to early prose writings about other technical subjects, music, for example, on which the first written treatise, by Lasus of Hermione, quite certainly goes || back to the sixth century BC.[20] The technical treatise on how to do something is one of the earliest prose genres, and some fifth-century examples of the genre – Polyclitus' *Canon*, for instance, and Damon on music – won attention from intellectuals generally.

[[This is where a historian of philosophy can perhaps offer some help.[21] For Democritus and Anaxagoras were not the only ancient philosophers to

---

[19] *Contra* Lefkowitz's 'wishful memory' (1984: 153).
[20] *Suda* s.v. 'Λᾶσος'; Burkert 1972: 372, n. 12, and 378.
[21] [This and the following paragraph were crossed out in the copy of the manuscript used by OSAP for the 2016 publication, and absent from another copy of the manuscript found in MFB's files, but appear integral to the argument of the paper and may have been so marked in preparation for delivery on a specific occasion.]

be interested in Agatharchus. The evidence of these other philosophers is seldom even mentioned, and it has certainly never been analysed, by historians of the tragic stage or of ancient painting. But it does, I shall argue, preserve a faint but valuable trace not only of the actual existence of Agatharchus' treatise, but also of something he wrote. It will take quite a lengthy digression to analyse this evidence before I can return to Vitruvius, Democritus and Anaxagoras. But I believe that the analysis is worth undertaking both for its intrinsic interest and because it illustrates another, equally important aspect of the unity of the Classics: unity through time. All too many scholarly footnotes use the phrase 'a late source' dismissively, as if to be a late source was some kind of sin, or a rather ugly disease. The truth, of course, as we all in our heart of hearts know perfectly well, is that late sources are a manifestation of the extraordinary *continuity* of interest and discussion, in every department of knowledge, which characterised the ancient world from the sixth century BC or before to the sixth century AD. As such, a late source is something to be understood, not something to be spurned, and understanding it involves trying to appreciate the way one period of antiquity regarded another. Let us therefore plunge into the sixth century AD.

In the sixth century AD the neo-Platonist philosopher Olympiodorus wrote a commentary on Plato's *Phaedo*. Not all of what has come down to us in the MS under that title is by Olympiodorus, however. The part that will interest us is probably due to a somewhat earlier neo-Platonist, Damascius.[22] In various sections of this Damascius portion are to be found what purport to be excerpts from Plutarch. In one of these sections, under the heading || 'Further proofs from Plutarch of Chaeronea', we find Text 7, which mentions Agatharchus. And it so happens that the context in which Agatharchus is mentioned is one that we know quite a lot about, because it was set up by Strato of Lampsacus.]]

Strato was a pupil of Theophrastus, then until *circa* 285 BC tutor to the future king of Egypt Ptolemy Philadelphus, subsequently Head of the Peripatetic school at Athens. He wrote among other things a rather cogently argued critique of Plato's *Phaedo*. A number of his objections are preserved in the portion of the Olympiodorus commentary which is probably due to Damascius. Text 7 contains one of them, an objection to the Platonic theory of recollection. Text 7 also contains a reply to Strato's objection, and it is the first part of the reply that brings in Agatharchus.

---

[22] *RE*, s.v. 'Olympiodorus'.

T7 ὅτι Στράτων ἠπόρει, εἰ ἔστιν ἀνάμνησις, πῶς ἄνευ ἀποδείξεων οὐ γιγνόμεθα ἐπιστήμονες· πῶς δ' οὐδεὶς αὐλητὴς ἢ κιθαριστὴς γέγονεν ἄνευ μελέτης. ἢ μάλιστα μὲν γεγόνασί τινες αὐτοδίδακτοι· Ἡράκλειτος, ὁ Αἰγύπτιος γεωργός, Φήμιος ὁ Ὁμήρου, Ἀγάθαρχος ὁ γραφεύς. εἶτα καὶ αἱ ψυχαὶ πολλῷ τῷ κάρῳ κατεχόμεναι τῆς γενέσεως πολλῆς πρὸς ἀνάμνησιν δέονται τῆς μοχλείας· διὸ καὶ τῶν αἰσθητῶν χρῄζουσιν.

That Strato raised this difficulty: if 'remembering' is a fact, how is it that we do not become possessed of knowledge without demonstrative proof? And how is it that no-one has become a flute-player or a harp-player without practice? Or have there in fact been some self-taught men – Heraclitus, the Egyptian farmer, Homer's Phemius, the painter Agatharchus? Then souls are overcome by much drowsiness at birth and need much therapeutic exercise if they are to recollect. And this is why they require sense-objects. ([Olympiodorus], *in Plat. Phaed.* 158.6–12 Norvin = Plutarch frag. 216g Sandbach; ὅτι ... μελέτης = Strato frag. 126 Wehrli; frag. 14c Gottschalk, trans. Sandbach)

Strato's objection is that it takes an awful lot of hard work to get knowledge: for theoretical knowledge you have to master proofs, for practical skills like flute playing you need to practise, and this (it is implied) is something that the theory of recollection cannot account for. The reply is that young souls are drowsy and need much therapeutic exercise, i.e. the theory of recollection positively predicts the hard work that bothers Strato, so the objection fails. The other part of the reply (placed first) is a suggestion that there have in fact been some self-taught men, *autodidaktoi*, viz Heraclitus, the Egyptian farmer, Homer's Phemius, the painter Agatharchus. Who, we may ask, composed this list of four people who ‖ provide, as it were, empirical proof of the Platonic theory of recollection? When was the list composed? And what did Agatharchus do to merit inclusion in the gang of four?

We can, I think, exclude the possibility that the list derives directly from Damascius. This theory, which is put forward by Gottschalk in his book on Strato, seems to be ruled out by item (e) in Text 8:[23]

T8 ἐπιχειρημάτων διαφόρων συναγωγὴ δεικνύντων ἀναμνήσεις εἶναι τὰς μαθήσεις ἐκ τῶν τοῦ Χαιρωνέως Πλουτάρχου·

(a) εἰ ἀφ' ἑτέρου ἕτερον ἐννοοῦμεν. οὐκ ἂν εἰ μὴ προέγνωστο. τὸ ἐπιχείρημα Πλατωνικόν.
(b) εἰ προστίθεμεν τὸ ἐλλεῖπον τοῖς αἰσθητοῖς· καὶ αὐτὸ Πλατωνικόν.

---

[23] Gottschalk 1965: 164.

(c) εἰ παῖδες εὐμαθέστεροι, ὡς ἐγγίους τῆς προβιοτῆς, ἐν ᾗ ἡ μνήμη ἐσῴζετο. ἐπιπόλαιος ὁ λόγος.
(d) εἰ ἄλλοι πρὸς ἄλλο μάθημα ἐπιτηδειότεροι.
(e) εἰ πολλοὶ αὐτοδίδακτοι ὅλων τεχνῶν.

A collection of various arguments to show that acts of learning are acts of remembering, from Plutarch of Chaeronea:

(a) Whether we think of one thing from another. We should not unless it had been known previously. The argument is Platonic.

(b) Whether we mentally add to percepts that by which they are deficient. This too is Platonic.

(c) Whether children are quicker to learn, as being nearer to the previous existence, in which memory was retained. The argument is an obvious one.

(d) Whether men differ in their capacity for different kinds of learning.

(e) Whether many men have taught themselves complete skills. ([Olympiodorus], *in Plat. Phaed.* 212. 1–11 Norvin = Plut. frag. 217 Sandbach, trans. Sandbach)

This is Plutarch frag. 217 (our previous excerpt was frag. 216), and frag. 217 is a *separate* set of Plutarch excerpts in the commentary; item (e) in frag. 217 indicates that the commentator found *autodidaktoi* cited already in the source he calls Plutarch. (This parallel is indeed what persuades Sandbach, as editor of the Plutarch fragments, to extend frag. 216 as far as (g) = our Text 7. Wyttenbach extends the fragment much further, for || the commentary gives no indication of where the excerpts of fragment 216 come to a stop;[24] the asterisk of hesitation in Sandbach's text signals that he was somewhat reluctant to go even as far as (g), but that he was impelled to do so – rightly, I am sure – by the parallel with 217 (e).) So I shall take it that Damascius is not the original author of our list.

To make further progress than this elimination of just one suspect, we need to examine the list itself and try to see the relevance of these four names to the philosophical point in dispute between Strato and his Platonist opponents. Recall that the theory of recollection, as stated in the *Phaedo*, is that we have latent within ourselves knowledge and *orthos logos*:

T9 ἑνὶ μὲν λόγῳ, ἔφη ὁ Κέβης, καλλίστῳ, ὅτι ἐρωτώμενοι οἱ ἄνθρωποι, ἐάν τις καλῶς ἐρωτᾷ, αὐτοὶ λέγουσιν πάντα ᾗ ἔχει· καίτοι εἰ μὴ ἐτύγχανεν αὐτοῖς ἐπιστήμη ἐνοῦσα καὶ <u>ὀρθὸς λόγος</u>, οὐκ ἂν οἷοί τ' ἦσαν τοῦτο ποιῆσαι.

---

[24] Sandbach 1969; Wyttenbach 1795–1830, vol. v 2, pp. 738–9.

'I can give you one excellent reason,' said Cebes. 'When people are asked something, if the question is well put, they themselves explain everything – and yet if they hadn't got knowledge and a *right account* of the matter stored away inside them, they couldn't do that.' (Plato, *Phaedo* 73a, trans. Bluck 1955, emphasis added)

Logos comes in here because, for Plato, to be able to give the correct account of something is the proof and the expression of knowledge, but we should bear in mind that the term *logos* can also cover speech and discourse of any kind. Such being Plato's theory, how could our four names be thought to exemplify it?

It would be quite irrelevant to the philosophical point at issue to offer in support of Plato a list of *inventors* of the *prōtos heuretēs* type. Necessity can be the mother of invention, and was often said to be, meaning that men are driven to invent things by exposure to the uncomfortable world we live in. This counted as a point for empiricism, for the idea that knowledge comes from our interaction with the empirical world, whereas Plato held that we have knowledge already present within the soul, prior to and independently of our dealings with the empirical world. Besides, Phemius, the bard in Homer's *Odyssey* is not the inventor of song.

T10   αὐτοδίδακτος δ' εἰμί, θεὸς δέ μοι ἐν φρεσὶν οἴμας ||
παντοίας ἐνέφυσεν· ἔοικα δέ τοι παραείδειν
ὥς τε θεῷ· τῷ μή με λιλαίεο δειροτομῆσαι.

Self-taught am I, and the god has planted in my heart
all manner of lays, and worthy am I to sing to thee
as to a god; wherefore be not eager to cut my throat.
(Homer *Odyssey* 22. 347–9, trans. Murray)

Phemius explains himself, in Text 10, the sense in which he is *autodidaktos*: the paths of song are divinely implanted within him and derive from his own *phrenes*. Not a bad model for the Platonic theory of recollection if you allow poetic discourse to count as *logos*.

Similarly, Heraclitus would be horrified to be called the inventor of the *logos* which is the central theme of his philosophy. Heraclitus's inclusion in the list is to be explained by Text 11, a Hellenistic interpretation of the well-known fragment (22 B 101 DK = Plut. *adv. Colot.* 1118c) in which he says *edizēsamēn emeōuton*, 'I inquired of myself':

T11 ἤκουσέ τ' οὐδενός, ἀλλ' αὐτὸν ἔφη διζήσασθαι καὶ μαθεῖν πάντα παρ' ἑαυτοῦ.

He was nobody's pupil, but he declared that he 'inquired of himself', and learned everything from himself. (D.L. ix.5, trans. Hicks)

When this is understood as meaning that he learnt the *logos* from himself, without becoming the pupil of any teacher, Heraclitus becomes a perfect example of someone who finds *orthos logos* within his own soul.

It should now be clear where this investigation is tending. With both Phemius and Heraclitus the list maker has got his examples from written texts and the basis for his interpretation is something said within the texts themselves. If the Egyptian farmer resembles Phemius and Heraclitus in the philosophically relevant respect, namely, he illustrates the *logos* within, and if the basis for including him on the list is something said in writing, there will be a strong case for viewing Agatharchus in the same light. So, who is the Egyptian farmer?

Norvin, the editor of Olympiodorus, followed by Sandbach in the Teubner Plutarch, cites a passage of Dionysius Periegetes (Text 12) according to which the Egyptians (plural) invented agriculture as well as astronomy. ‖

T12 κεῖθεν δ' ἐς βορέην τετανυσμένος ἄλλυδις ἄλλος,
ἑπτὰ διὰ στομάτων εἰλιγμένος εἰς ἅλα πίπτει,
ὕδασι πιαίνων λιπαρὸν πέδον Αἰγύπτοιο.
Οὐ γάρ τις ποταμῶν ἐναλίγκιος ἔπλετο Νείλῳ,
οὔτ' ἰλὺν βαλέειν, οὔτε χθονὸς ὄλβον ἀέξειν·
ὅς ῥά τε καὶ Λιβύην ἀποτέμνεται Ἀσίδος αἴης,
ἐς λίβα μὲν Λιβύην, ἐς δ' αὐγὰς Ἀσίδα γαῖαν.
Τῷ πάρα ναιετάουσιν ἀριπρεπέων γένος ἀνδρῶν,
οἳ πρῶτοι βιότοιο διεστήσαντο κελεύθους,
**πρῶτοι δ' ἱμερόεντος ἐπειρήθησαν ἀρότρου
καὶ σπόρον ἰθυτάτης ὑπὲρ αὔλακος ἁπλώσαντο,**
πρῶτοι δὲ γραμμῇσι πόλον διεμετρήσαντο,
θυμῷ φρασσάμενοι λοξὸν δρόμον ἠελίοιο.

*inde ad boream prolapsus varius varias in partes
septem per ostia distractus in mare devolvitur,
opimum Ægypti solum aquis pinguefaciens.
Non enim fluviorum quisquam cum Nilo comparandus,
ad limum immittendum terraeque fertilitatem augendam,
qui et Libyam dirimit a regione Asiatica,
Ita ut in libem sit Libya, in ortum vero Asia.
Hunc insignium virorum gens accolit,*

> *qui primi vitae distinxerunt ordines,*
> **primique jucundum experti sunt aratrum,**
> **ac sementem per directum sulcum disperserunt,**
> *Iidemque primi lineis coelum sunt emensi,*
> *Quum mente obliquum solis cusum percepissent.*
>
> From then, stretched sprawlingly towards the north,
> Through seven mouths flexed, it falls into the sea,
> Making Egypt's rich plain pregnant with its waters.
> No river can be likened to the Nile
> For laying mud, for bringing forth earth's tilth.
> It sunders Libya from the Asian land,
> Libya westwards, Asia to the east.
> A race of famous men live thereabouts,
> Who first contrived the proper means to live,
> *Were first to make trial of the lovely plough,*
> *And over the straight furrow broadcast seed,*
> And demarcated first the pole with lines,
> Having discovered the sun's slanted course.
> (Dionysius Periegetes, *Orbis descriptio* 225–37
> Müller, *trans. Lightfoot 2014) ||

They suggest that the Egyptian farmer is supposed to be the inventor of agriculture.

This won't do, and not just because the singular is essential to the philosophical argument. We have already seen that our list is not a list of inventors and would not be relevant to Plato if it was. The Egyptian farmer ought to be someone who produces some sort of *logos* from within himself.

Let me then tell you the Tale of the Eloquent Peasant.

There was once a man called Khunanup, who was a peasant[25] of the Wadi Natroun – i.e. the Valley of Salt, an oasis in the desert due south of Alexandria and north-west of Cairo. Now this peasant went down to Egypt, as the story puts it, with his donkeys laden with the goodly products of the Wadi Natroun, intending to trade his products for provisions. When he had reached the Nile and was journeying along it, he was seen by a man called Djehutinakhte, who thought it would be a good idea to grab the donkeys. Having conceived this dastardly plan, Djehutinakhte spread a cloth all the way across the narrow riverside path along which Khunanup was coming. On the one side, then, the river Nile, on the other, a field of barley belonging to Djehutinakhte. The peasant had no choice, if he was to avoid the cloth, but to take his donkeys up along the

---

[25] Doubted by G. Lefebvre, 'Le conte de l'Oasien (le Paysan)', in Lefebvre 1949: 41–69, at 41.

bank of the field. At once Djehutinakhte accused him of trampling his crops, an altercation broke out, and while the two men were arguing one of the donkeys ate a wisp of barley. 'Aha', said Djehutinakhte, 'I shall confiscate your donkey for eating my barley', and he did.

For the next ten days the peasant pleads with Djehutinakhte, but in vain. So he goes to the High Steward Rensi, to appeal to him. Now when Rensi hears the peasant's appeal he goes to the King to tell him of the quite extraordinary eloquence this uneducated peasant has displayed. 'Then keep him talking,' replies the King, 'and have someone write it all down for me.' Nine times the peasant comes before the High Steward and makes his appeal: nine different speeches, each of amazing Gorgianic grandiloquence. Nine times his words are written down for the King's delight – and the peasant is sent away without an answer. Finally, when the King has a papyrus roll full of marvellous speeches, Rensi is permitted to give || judgement: Djehutinakhte's house and goods are confiscated and given to the peasant Khunanup. End of story.[26]

The Tale of the Eloquent Peasant was popular in Egypt during the Middle Kingdom, which lasted from 2040 to the middle of the seventeenth century BC. The surviving MSS are XII–XIIIth Dynasty, i.e. from a period from between about 1991 and 1633 BC. The only other Egyptian trace of the story is an inaccurate quotation on a Ramesside ostracon about five hundred years later,[27] which still leaves a gap of some eight hundred years until we reach Strato or twelve hundred years to Plutarch, who was born around 46 AD. For an Egyptian story these Greek philosophers are a very late source indeed. But Egyptian stories were translated into Greek, and in one case 'the Legend of Tefnut' we have the text in both languages. And I trust you will agree with me that Khunanup is a splendid example of a man whose rhetorical *logoi* come from within in a manner perfectly designed to illustrate the Platonic theory of recollection as that theory is understood in the debate between Strato and his opponent. In fact, the example is so splendid, the parallel with Phemius and Heraclitus is so close, that there can, I submit, be no doubt that we have now identified the person who is referred as the Egyptian farmer in a collection of truncated excerpts from Plutarch which has come down to us in what purports to be a commentary on Plato's *Phaedo* written by Olympiodorus in the sixth century AD, over a millennium and a half later than the last known trace of the Tale itself. Moreover, like Phemius and Heraclitus, the Egyptian farmer earns his place in the gang of four in virtue of a written text and

---

[26] Discussions in Lefebvre 1949: 41–69.   [27] Gardiner 1923: 25.

what is said in that text. The only remaining question is, which Greek got to know, or to know about, that text, and when?

The obvious candidate is Plutarch himself. He spent time in Egypt,[28] and his work on *Isis and Osiris* shows him to have been an Egyptologist of sorts, and he was, of course, a Platonist who is independently known to have worked seriously at defending the theory of recollection. But Strato too spent time in Alexandria, in his tutoring days, and we cannot exclude the possibility that Text 7 derives entirely from Strato, weighing up the arguments *for* the theory of || recollection as well as the arguments against, this being the proper Peripatetic way to approach a philosophical problem. And there are any number of other possibilities. But even if we have to suspend judgement on the ultimate origin of our list, it is enough for my purposes that we can at least be confident that the first three names are, all of them, examples of the *logos* within. We can see, moreover, that each example illustrates a distinct genre of *logos*: Phemius represents poetry, Heraclitus philosophy, Khunanup rhetoric. It becomes overwhelmingly tempting to extrapolate to Agatharchus as follows:

(1) He represents technical *logoi* of the genre from which Vitruvius lists so many specimens.
(2) Agatharchus' *logos* or *hypomnēma* on stage construction could be read, or more probably read about, in the libraries of the Hellenistic period.
(3) The list maker's evidence for considering Agatharchus to be self-taught in the peculiar sense signified by a Platonist's use of the term *autodidaktos* was of the same type as his evidence in the other three cases, namely, something said in the text in question. So the next question is whether we can conjecture what that written something was that the listmaker took as evidence for Agatharchus being *autodidaktos*.

I suggest that it was the opening words of Agatharchus' treatise. Hecataeus of Miletus began a very early genealogical treatise with the sentence 'I write these things, as they seem to me to be true; for the *logoi* of the Greeks, in my view, are both many and absurd.'[29] Heraclitus a little later starts his *logos* by telling his readers that they haven't a hope of understanding it. Several Hippocratic treatises open with a similarly aggressive bid for the reader's attention. Suppose, then, that Agatharchus started by proclaiming

---

[28] Plut. *Mor.* 678c: on 'my return from Alexandria' (trans. Clement-Hoffleit).
[29] [OSAP: Hecataeus *FGrH* 1 F1a = Demetrius *De Elocutione* 12.]

his originality as a writer in some such terms as this: I am the first to write on these matters, I have had neither teacher nor predecessor in writing about the things I am going to tell you about. Hellenistic compilations love to quote the opening words of earlier books – the quotation from Metrodorus in Text 1 is a case in point, for we know from other citations that these were his opening words – and if Agatharchus did trumpet his originality as an author in the manner I have suggested, we have the perfect explanation for Vitruvius thinking || he knows that Agatharchus was the first to write on an architectural theme. He knows this because the compiler he is following took Agatharchus' own word for it.

The situation is actually a little more complicated than this, and complicated in a way that tends to confirm my hypothesis. Agatharchus could well have claimed, and been recorded by some compiler as claiming, to be the first to write about *the stage-building*. For if Agatharchus wrote within the lifetime of Aeschylus, the *skēnē* or stage-building had not long been in existence for anyone to write about. But if Agatharchus presented himself in the way Vitruvius presents him, as the first to write on any *architectural* matter at all, his claim is in conflict with the testimony of Vitruvius himself in the next paragraph of our passage. About Silenus we know nothing but what is recorded here, but the temples and authors next mentioned can be dated independently of Vitruvius to the *sixth* century BC. I very much doubt one can get around this conflict by giving *primum... postea* a non-temporal classificatory sense, for a few pages later, in Text 13, when the temple at Ephesus is mentioned again, the coupling of *primum* and *postea* is clearly temporal, as indeed it is taken to be by all translators of our main passage.

> **T13** *primum*que aedes Ephesi Dianae ionico genere ab Chersiphrone Gnosio et filio eius Metagene est instituta, quam *postea* Demetrius, ipsius Dianae servos, et Paeonius Ephesius dicuntur perfecisse.
>
> *First of all* the temple of Diana at Ephesus was planned in the Ionic style by Chersiphron of Cnossus and his son Metagenes; *afterwards* Demetrius, a temple warden of Diana, and Paeonius of Ephesus are said to have completed it. (Vitruvius VII, *praef.* 16, trans. Granger)

Consequently, we must look for an explanation which accepts that Vitruvius has made a mistake. I propose that the most likely explanation is this, that Vitruvius or his compiler was hazy about the chronology of archaic Greek temples and overlooked the restricted scope of Agatharchus' original claim when incorporating it into the wider context of a history of writings on architecture generally. Anyone who deals regularly with ancient doxography will know similar cases. Viewed in this light, Vitruvius' inadvertent slip strongly suggests that Agatharchus was recorded as claiming originality as an author.

It is even possible that Agatharchus expressed his claim to || originality with the word *autodidaktos* itself. The word is not common. Its only extant occurrence in early literature outside the *Odyssey* (Text 10) is in the *Agamemnon* of Aeschylus: Text 14.

T14   τὸν δ' ἄνευ λύρας ὅμως ὑμνῳδεῖ
         θρῆνον Ἐρινύος αὐτοδίδακτος ἔσωθεν
         θυμός,

The *thumos* sings, without a lyre,
from within, self-taught,
the song of Erinys
(Aeschylus *Agamemnon* 990–3, trans. Burnyeat)

I hesitate to build one conjecture on another, but after all that Oliver Taplin[30] has done to make good Wilamowitz's theory that the *Oresteia* of 458 BC is where Aeschylus first makes use of the recently introduced stage-building, and first exploits the dramatic resonance of the idea of the house which the *skēnē* represents, it would certainly seem to be a most appropriate occasion for the stage-designer to write a book about – a book telling of his own contribution to that memorable occasion and perhaps – I say again, perhaps – borrowing from his playwright the poetic word *autodidaktos*, with its associations of divine inspiration, in order to proclaim that technical literature too, not just poetry, can be divinely inspired.[31] For we can be sure that if all of that did happen, Agatharchus would have virtually written his own certificate of worthiness to be included, along with Phemius, Heraclitus and the Egyptian farmer, in the list we have been examining. All it would take for him to be put on the list is that the Hellenistic compilers should preserve his opening words as they preserved the opening words of countless other authors.

I cannot, of course, prove that the *Oresteia* is the *tragoedia* of Aeschylus to which Vitruvius refers, as those scholars who trust Vitruvius have

---

[30] Taplin 1977, 'Appendix C: The Skene in Aeschylus', 452–9.
[31] Taplin: Aeschylus' use is itself a recall of Homer and his odd word. [OSAP: We were unable to locate a reference for this claim. When consulted, Professor Taplin assured us that he has never made such a claim in print, but thought it possible that he might have discussed the issue with Professor Burnyeat on some occasion.]

regularly assumed, but the main rival theory is Rumpf's influential suggestion – adopted by Webster and Taplin among historians of the stage[32] and by Robertson and Pollitt among historians of art[33] – that the phrase *Aeschylo docente* does not mean what the words plainly say, but refers to a revival of an Aeschylean drama around 430, well after Aeschylus' death in 456/5.[34] This late dating is motivated in part by the thought that 458 would be too early for Agatharchus to invent a sophisticated system of perspective. But we have already seen that it is not in fact as the inventor of perspectives but as a writer that Agatharchus comes into Vitruvius' story. And it is important to realise that Rumpf's *only* evidence for postponing Agatharchus' activity until around 430 is Text 15,[35] a story originating with some fourth-century orators – who tell it all too plainly *as a story* – in which Alcibiades locks Agatharchus in his house to make sure he finishes the painting, or alternatively – and this is the version Rumpf relies on – he locks him up because he has found the painter making love to his mistress.

T15 εἶρξεν Ἀγάθαρχον τὸν γραφέα· καὶ γὰρ ταῦτα λέγουσιν. λαβών γέ τι πλημμελοῦνθ᾽, ὥς φασιν, ὅπερ οὐδ᾽ ὀνειδίζειν ἄξιον.

Another *story* is that he imprisoned the painter Agatharchus. Yes, but he had caught him in an act of trespass, or so we are told; so that it is unfair to blame him for that. (Demosthenes 21, *Against Meidias*, 147, trans. Vince 1935, emphasis added)

εἶρξεν Ἀγάθαρχον] ζωγράφος οὗτος ὢν ἐφωράθη συνὼν τῇ παλλακίδι τοῦ Ἀλκιβιάδου, ὃν λαβὼν καθεῖρξε, καὶ κατὰ τοῦτο ἥμαρτε μὴ παραδοὺς τοῖς νόμοις, ἀπεσιώπησε δὲ τὸ ἁμάρτημα ὡς μικρόν, ἵνα μεῖζόν τι ὑποπτεύσωσιν οἱ δικάζοντες. τὸ ἀμφισβητούμενον οὖν ὡς ὁμολογούμενον ἔθηκεν. ἔχει γὰρ αὐτῷ συναγωνιζομένην τὴν κατάγνωσιν τοῦ δήμου. τινὲς δὲ τὸ 'εἶρξεν' οἷον ἐξέωσε τοῦ θεάτρου ὡς ἀσελγῆ. διὸ καὶ εἶπεν 'ὅπερ οὐδὲ ὀνειδίζειν ἄξιον'.

'He locked up Agatharchus.' This painter was caught having sex with the concubine of Alcibiades, who seized and confined him, thereby doing wrong by not turning him over to the law. [Alcibiades] concealed how minor the wrong was, so that the jurors would suspect something greater. He thus stipulated something that was in dispute as though it were agreed upon, since he had on his side the censure of the people. Some take 'locked up' to mean something like 'he threw him out of the theatre on the grounds

---

[32] Webster 1956: 13–14; Taplin 1977, 457–8 n. 4; see also *op. cit.* 107 and *438 n. 2*.
[33] Robertson 1975: 1.414–15; Pollitt 1974: 244–5.
[34] Rumpf 1947: 13; *Marmor Parium* 59; Schol. *ad Ar. Ach.* 10 C.   [35] Rumpf 1947: 13.

that he was || behaving outrageously', for which reason [Demosthenes] adds 'which is not even worth criticizing'. (Scholium to the above, 21.506 Dilts, trans. Caston)

ὃς εἰς τοσοῦτον ἐλήλυθε τόλμης, ὥστε πείσας Ἀγάθαρχον τὸν γραφέα συνεισελθεῖν [οἴκαδε] τὴν οἰκίαν ἐπηνάγκασε γράφειν, δεομένου δὲ καὶ προφάσεις ἀληθεῖς λέγοντος, ὡς οὐκ ἂν δύναιτο ταῦτα πράττειν ἤδη διὰ τὸ συγγραφὰς ἔχειν παρ' ἑτέρων, προεῖπεν αὐτῷ δήσειν, εἰ μὴ πάνυ ταχέως γράφοι. ὅπερ ἐποίησε· καὶ οὐ πρότερον ἀπηλλάγη, πρὶν ἀποδρὰς ᾤχετο τετάρτῳ μηνί, τοὺς φύλακας λαθών, ὥσπερ παρὰ βασιλέως.

Why, there are no limits to his impudence. He persuaded Agatharchus, the artist, to accompany him home, and then forced him to paint; and when Agatharchus appealed to him, stating with perfect truth that he could not oblige him at the moment because he had other engagements, Alcibiades threatened him with imprisonment, unless he started painting straight away. And he carried out his threat. Agatharchus only made his escape three months later, by slipping past his guards and running away as he might have done from the king of Persia. ([Andocides] *Against Alcibiades* 4.17, trans. Maidment)[36]

If we take this anecdote seriously – and I suggest that we are in fact dealing merely with the echo of a comic plot – Agatharchus must be alive and well in the decade after 430, when Alcibiades emerges into the limelight. Fine, but this does not even begin to show that Agatharchus could not have worked for Aeschylus in 458 – at the age of thirty, say – unless you believe that a man of, say, sixty plus would not be capable of the part assigned to him in the story. I trust that you will agree that Rumpf's argument does not stand up.

Besides Anaxagoras probably died in 428/7, far away in Lampsacus, after residing there long enough to inspire the Lampsacenes to pay him extensive honours at his death. Anaxagoras' response to Agatharchus's book, once we take that seriously, favours an earlier rather than a later date for Agatharchus's writing.

Let us then turn to Anaxagoras. What could Agatharchus have said that might interest him? It was not the opening words of his book, Vitruvius implies [in Text 5], but something about which Democritus and Anaxagoras also wrote (*de eadem re scripserunt*). Vitruvius proceeds to identify the topic on which all three writers had something to say, in a long complex sentence which needs to be || divided into two parts. The part

---

[36] Cf. also Plut. *Alc.* 4. [OSAP: The precise interpretation of the events behind these reports are much disputed. For a brief survey of the issues, see MacDowell 1990: 362–3.]

which I have indented is the explanation of the phenomenon described from *uti* ('so that') onwards.

> Namque primum Agatharchus Athenis Aeschylo docente tragoediam scaenam fecit, et de ea commentarium reliquit. Ex eo moniti Democritus et Anaxagoras de eadem re scripserunt,
>
>> quemadmodum oporteat, ad aciem oculorum radiorumque extentionem certo loco centro constituto, lineas ratione naturali respondere,
>
> uti ...
>
> In the first place Agatharchus, in Athens, when Aeschylus was bringing out a tragedy, painted a scene, and left a commentary about it. This led Democritus and Anaxagoras to write on the same subject,
>
>> showing how, given a centre in a definite place, the lines should naturally correspond with due regard to the point of sight and the divergence of the visual rays,
>
> so that ... (Vitruvius VII, *praef.* 11, trans. Morgan)

The indented explanation is extraordinarily sophisticated. Thanks to John White's careful analysis,[37] we are now able to regard it as one of just two ancient texts – the other being Text 16, again from Vitruvius – to formulate explicitly, even if somewhat clumsily, the idea of centralised system of pictorial perspective complete with a vanishing point:

T16 item scaenographia est frontis et laterum abscedentium adumbratio ad circinique centrum omnium linearum responsus.

> In like manner, scenography is the sketching of the front and of the retreating sides and the correspondence of all the lines to the point of the compasses. (Vitruvius 1.2.2, trans. White)

As such, it may have been known to Alberti and may have played its part in the Renaissance rediscovery of perspective. But by the same token no-one doubts – no-one sensible at least[38] – that no such idea could have been formulated in a fifth-century treatise, by Agatharchus or by Anaxagoras. It is well in advance of Euclid's *Optics* of around 300 BC. It must have been inserted into the doxographical tradition sometime between 300 and the compilation Vitruvius is using, with the result that the fifth-century writers' observations are served up, in a manner which will again be

---

[37] J. White 1956: 43–69.   [38] Unsensible: Gogos 1983: 71–86, esp. 84–5.

56–58] *Scenery, optics, and Greek epistemology* 347

familiar to those who have worked regularly with doxography, in the illuminating light of the most modern explanation. ||

Accordingly, to discover what Anaxagoras or Democritus learnt from Agatharchus, we must turn to the second half of the sentence, the bit after the indentation [in Text 5], beginning with *uti* or 'so that'.

> uti de incerta re certae imagines aedificiorum in scaenarum picturis redderent speciem et, quae in directis planisque frontibus sint figurata, alia abscedentia, alia prominentia esse videantur.
>
> so that by this deception a faithful representation of the appearance of buildings might be given in painted scenery, and so that, though all is drawn on a vertical flat façade, some parts may seem to be withdrawing into the background, and others to be standing out in front. (Vitruvius VII, *praef.* 11, trans. Morgan)

At once we meet a problem of translation again, compounded by a problem about the text: should we read *certae* or *incertae imagines*? I propose that we tackle the translation problem first, for the moment just leaving the adjective *(in)certae* out of the reckoning.

That there is a problem of translation is evident from Morgan's absurd rendering of the Latin *de incerta re* as 'by this deception'.[39] Notice also the dots of despair in Erika Simon's version quoted in my English apparatus (n. 13). But the rival translations in the apparatus have a dangling 'from an uncertain object' which is equally puzzling. For example, White translates 'so that from an uncertain object certain images may render the appearance of buildings' (n. 13). *What* uncertain object do the images come from? Surely they don't come *from* anywhere; they are just there, painted on the wall of the stage-building.

The difficulty arises, I suggest, from the assumption that *de* means 'from'. Given this assumption, *de incerta re* must depend upon *imagines* and then *aedificiorum* is left to depend on *speciem*. But if *de* could mean 'concerning' or 'about', as it did just a bit earlier in the phrase *de eadem re*, and as Erich Frank alone is prepared to take it, then *aedificiorum* could be detached from *speciem* and made to depend on *imagines*, which is after all the word it is adjacent to. We would then have this: 'concerning an unclear object, the images of buildings in stage paintings give || a view'. *De incerta*

---

[39] Cf. the elaborately odd interpretation in Pollitt 1974: 241–2, close to Schneider Schneider 1807–8 *ad loc.* [OSAP: Pollitt writes, 'I take the meaning of the phrase to be that an assemblage of drawn lines, which, when viewed without regard to its illusionistic quality, has no meaning or significance in itself (*incerta res*), becomes, when understood illusionistically, a definite thing, *certa res*, for example, a building' (Pollitt 1974: 242).]

re would then have an introductory function, and would be connected in sense, though not in grammar, with *speciem* instead of *imagines*.

Before asking you to accept this translation, I want to ask you to try putting it into Greek. Alberti remarked that Vitruvius is 'Greek to the Romans and Roman to the Greek',[40] and we saw in Text 6 that Vitruvius is using Greek compilations as well as Latin ones; in any case the Latin doxographers will themselves have been borrowing from Greek predecessors. So what would our sentence have looked like in Greek?

Well, in Cicero's philosophical writings, he commonly uses *incertus* where we know his Greek source would have had *adēlos*, non-evident. There's a good example in Text 17:

T17   interdum enim cum adhibemus ad eos orationem eius modi, si ea quae disputentur vera sint, tum omnia fore *incerta*, respondent: 'Quid ergo istud ad nos? num nostra culpa est? naturam accusa, quae in profundo veritatem, ut ait Democritus, penitus abstruserit.' Alii autem elegantius, qui etiam queruntur quod eos insimule-mus omnia *incerta* dicere, quantumque intersit inter *incertum* et id quod percipi non possit docere conantur eaque distinguere. Cum his igitur agamus qui haec distinguunt, illos qui omnia sic *incerta* dicunt ut stellarum numerus par an impar sit quasi desperatos aliquos relinquamus.

For sometimes when we address them in this sort of language, 'If your contentions are true, then everything will be *uncertain*', they reply, 'Well, what has that to do with us? surely it is not our fault; blame nature for having hidden truth quite away, in an abyss, as Democritus says.' But others make a more elaborate answer, and actually complain because we charge them with saying that everything is *uncertain*, and they try to explain the difference between what is *uncertain* and what cannot be grasped, and to distinguish between them. Let us therefore deal with those who make this distinction, and leave on one side as a hopeless sort of persons the others who say that all things are as *uncertain* as whether the number of the stars is odd or even. (Cicero *Academica* II.32, trans Rackham 1951, emphasis added)

– and *species* is the Latin for *opsis*. With two such clues it is hardly necessary to add Text 18 to show that *imago* can render *phantasia*, one of several Greek nouns connected with the verb *phainesthai*. ||

T18   quare capiendae sunt illae, de quibus dixi, rerum *imagines*, quas vocari φαντασίας indicavimus.

Consequently those *vivid conceptions* of which I spoke and which, as I remarked, are called φαντασίαι. (Quintilian x.7.15, trans. Butler 1920, emphasis added)

---

[40] Dyer 1891: 364.

quas φαντασίας Graeci vocant, nos sane visiones appellemus, per quas imagines rerum absentium ita repraesentantur animo, ut eas cernere oculis ac praesentes habere videamur. has quisquis bene conceperit, is erit in adfectibus potentissimus. Hunc quidam dicunt εὐφαντασίωτον, qui sibi res, voces, actus secundum verum optime finget; quod quidem nobis volentibus facile continget.

There are certain experiences which the Greeks call φαντασίαι, and the Romans *visions*, whereby things absent are presented to our imagination with such extreme vividness that they seem actually to be before our very eyes. It is the man who is really sensitive to such impressions who will have the greatest power over the emotions. Some writers describe the possessor of this power of vivid imagination, whereby things, words and actions are presented in the most realistic manner, by the Greek word εὐφαντασίωτος; and it is a power which all may readily acquire if they will. (Quintilian VI.2.29–30, trans. Butler)

Hidden for all to see in Vitruvius' Latin is a close relative of that famous dictum of Anaxagoras, *opsis tōn adēlōn ta phainomena*, appearances are a sight of things unseen (DK 59 B 21a).

Now look at Text 19, paragraph 140, but for which we would never have known that Anaxagoras said that famous thing. (And by the way, the angled brackets in the Greek text are misleading: the words *opsis tōn adēlōn ta phainomena* are not an insertion conjectured by the editor, but an omission in MSS other than N.)

T19 καὶ δὴ ἐν μὲν τούτοις πᾶσαν σχεδὸν κινεῖ κατάληψιν, εἰ καὶ μόνων ἐξαιρέτως καθάπτεται τῶν αἰσθήσεων· (138) ἐν δὲ τοῖς κανόσι δύο φησὶν εἶναι γνώσεις, τὴν μὲν διὰ τῶν αἰσθήσεων τὴν δὲ διὰ τῆς διανοίας, ὧν τὴν μὲν διὰ τῆς διανοίας γνησίην καλεῖ, προσμαρτυρῶν αὐτῇ τὸ πιστὸν εἰς ἀληθείας κρίσιν, τὴν δὲ διὰ τῶν αἰσθήσεων σκοτίην ὀνομάζει, ἀφαιρούμενος αὐτῆς τὸ πρὸς διάγνωσιν τοῦ ἀληθοῦς ἀπλανές. (139) λέγει δὲ κατὰ λέξιν 'γνώμης δὲ δύο εἰσὶν ἰδέαι, ἡ μὲν γνησίη ἡ δὲ σκοτίη· καὶ σκοτίης μὲν τάδε σύμπαντα, || ὄψις ἀκοὴ ὀδμὴ γεῦσις ψαῦσις, ἡ δὲ γνησίη, ἀποκεκριμένη δὲ ταύτης.' εἶτα προκρίνων τῆς σκοτίης τὴν γνησίην ἐπιφέρει λέγων 'ὅταν ἡ σκοτίη μηκέτι δύναται μήτε ὁρῆν ἐπ' ἔλαττον μήτε ἀκούειν μήτε ὀδμᾶσθαι μήτε γεύεσθαι μήτε ἐν τῇ ψαύσει αἰσθάνεσθαι, ἀλλ' ἐπὶ λεπτότερον.'[41] οὐκοῦν καὶ κατὰ τοῦτον ὁ λόγος ἐστὶ κριτήριον, ὃν γνησίην γνώμην καλεῖ. (140) Διότιμος δὲ τρία κατ' αὐτὸν ἔλεγεν εἶναι κριτήρια, τῆς μὲν τῶν ἀδήλων καταλήψεως τὰ φαινόμενα, <ὄψις γὰρ τῶν ἀδήλων τὰ φαινόμενα,>[42] ὥς φησιν Ἀναξαγόρας, ὃν ἐπὶ τούτῳ

---

[41] Mutschmann (after Diels) marks a lacuna after λεπτότερον. Otherwise we might read ἄλλο τι <ληπτέον> λεπτ., 'some other finer (more delicate) <instrument> must be adopted.'
[42] <ὄψις ... φαινόμενα> add. *N*: om. cet., Bekk.

Δημόκριτος ἐπαινεῖ, ζητήσεως δὲ τὴν ἔννοιαν (περὶ παντὸς γάρ, ὦ παῖ, μία ἀρχὴ τὸ εἰδέναι περὶ ὅτου ἔστιν ἡ ζήτησις), αἱρέσεως δὲ καὶ φυγῆς τὰ πάθη· …

> Now in these passages he almost rejects apprehension altogether, although it is the senses only that he specially attacks. (138) But in his 'Canons' he says that there are two kinds of knowledge, one by means of the senses, the other by means of the intelligence; and of these he calls that by means of the intelligence 'genuine,' ascribing to it trustworthiness in the judgement of truth, but that by means of the senses he terms 'bastard,' denying it inerrancy in the distinguishing of what is true. (139) He expressly declares – 'Of knowledge there are two forms, the genuine and the bastard; and to the bastard belong all these – sight, hearing, smell, taste, touch; but the other form is *distinct from* this and genuine.' Then, while thus preferring the genuine to the bastard, he proceeds: 'Whenever the bastard kind is unable any longer to see what has become too small, or to hear or smell or taste or perceive it by touch, <one must have recourse to> another and finer <instrument>.' Thus, according to this man also, reason is the criterion, and he calls it 'genuine knowledge.' (140) But Diotimus used to say that according to Democritus there are three criteria – namely, the criterion of the apprehension of things non-evident, which is the things apparent; for, *as Anaxagoras says (and Democritus commends him for it), the things apparent are the vision of the things non-evident*; and the criterion of investigation, which is the conception – 'for in every case, my child, the one starting-point is to know what the subject of investigation is' [cf. Plato, *Phaedrus* 237b]; and the criterion of choice and aversion, which is the affections… (Sextus Empiricus. *M.* VII.137–40, trans. Bury, emphasis added)

The anti-chronological order of the names in Vitruvius, first Democritus and then Anaxagoras, becomes understandable when we learn that Democritus commended Anaxagoras for the famous dictum. We learn this on the word of one Diotimus, who is independently attested in Text 20 as an expositor of Democritus. ||

T20 ἔτι πρὸς τούτοις [*sc.* Democritus, Hecataeus, Apollodorus, Nausiphanes] Διότιμος τὴν παντέλειαν τῶν ἀγαθῶν ἣν εὐεστὼ προσαγορεύεσθαι [68 B 4. 140], τέλος ἀπέφηνεν.

> In addition, Diotimus declared the goal to be a full complement of the things that are good, which he called well-being (Diotimus 76 A2 DK = Clem. *Strom.* 2.130 Diels, trans. Ferguson 1991)

The chances are that Diotimus got this information by studying the works of Democritus himself: hence the order of names. We do not know Diotimus' date, but he uses the language of Hellenistic philosophy and quotes Plato's *Phaedrus*. He writes about Democritus more as a historian than as a follower – he may in fact be identical with a second-century BC Stoic Diotimus – and he comes into Aenesidemus' history as the author of an empiricist interpretation of Democritus which diverges from the more rationalistic interpretation of the preceding paragraphs 138–9, which give the view of Aenesidemus' main authority for Democritus, who can, I believe, be shown to be Posidonius. But if the best we can do for Diotimus is to say that he is a Hellenistic scholar writing before Posidonius, that is enough to show that there is information in the Hellenistic libraries about Democritus responding to Anaxagoras on the issue that concerns us, information which is hard to explain except on the supposition that it comes ultimately from Democritus himself. The important thing is not to trace routes between Vitruvius and Democritus, but to satisfy ourselves that one or more routes are available. For I hope it is now looking very plausible indeed that what Agatharchus said to interest Anaxagoras and Democritus was closely connected with the philosophical dictum 'Appearances are a sight of things unseen'.

The most economical hypothesis is simply this. Agatharchus' treatise included, among all the other topics to do with stage construction, a section on scene painting. (We may even be tempted to wonder if it wasn't this section that told Aristotle that scene painting had recently been introduced by Sophocles; at any rate the possibility cannot now be excluded.) In this section, be it long or short, one thing Agatharchus could have said was – well, more or less what we find in Vitruvius: concerning what is not evident to the audience, you can give them a view, i.e. let them as it were 'see' it, by painting images of buildings on the stage wall, and doing it || in such a way that although all is drawn on a vertical flat façade, some parts seem to be receding into the background and others to be standing out in front. Painted scenery gives the audience a sight of the unseen.

That would be an exciting and relevant contribution, from the technician's point of view, to all the play with the seen and the unseen that goes on in the *Oresteia* and subsequent tragedies. Yet it does not presuppose more than the simplest and most primitive indications of recession in the painting itself. Four columns under a roof, with the inner columns smaller than the outer ones, would be quite enough to give rise to the *written boast* which is what, as we have seen, inspired Anaxagoras. As for the actual scene painting that Agatharchus is boasting about, we should not look ahead, as the indented explanation inserted by Vitruvius' compiler tells us to do, but back – back to the lost mural paintings of the early fifth century. These can only be studied through descriptions in Pausanias and the distorting mirror of vase-paintings, but the evidence leads art historians like John Barron to talk of 'multi-level compositions',[43] and Martin Robertson of the beginning of the idea of pictorial space, of the picture as 'a window opening on a feigned world'.[44] In so speaking they are referring to murals by Polygnotus and Mikon painted in the 470s – well before the *Oresteia* in 458. Agatharchus, then, was not the first Greek painter to start exploring the third dimension; but he could well, compatibly with the art-historical evidence, be the first to boast in writing about its application to the stage.

We can now solve the textual problem which we left aside earlier. Granger, as you see from the textual notes to Text 5 (n. 9), reads *incertae* on the grounds that it is required by Democritean doctrines. But even supposing he interprets Democritus's views about images correctly, it is not Democritus' view that matters here but Agatharchus'. Agatharchus would certainly want his painted columns to stand out bright and clear for the audience to see. That, then, is how he would describe them in the book. Alternatively, by Hellenistic times *opsis tōn adēlōn ta phainomena* has become a common tag which is quoted all over the place, and Hellenistic *phainomena* are invariably *enargē* or *dēla*, clear (see Text 21), never *adēla*. ||

T21 ἔτι τῶν ὄντων τὰ μέν ἐστι πρόδηλα τὰ δὲ ἄδηλα, ὡς αὐτοί φασιν, καὶ σημαίνοντα μὲν τὰ φαινόμενα, σημαινόμενα δὲ ὑπὸ τῶν φαινομένων τὰ ἄδηλα· ὄψις γὰρ κατ' αὐτοὺς τῶν ἀδήλων τὰ φαινόμενα.

Further, some existing things are '*pre-evident*', as they say, others non-evident; and the *apparent things* are significant, but the non-evident signified by the apparent; for according to them 'the things apparent are the vision of the non-evident'. (Sextus Empiricus *PH* 1.138, trans. Bury, emphasis added)

Thus whether the adjective stems from Agatharchus or the Hellenistic compiler, *certae* is the reading we want. Granger's mistaken choice, which he actually uses as evidence for his reconstruction of the history of the Vitruvius MSS, is just one of the eccentricities which mar his widely used edition of an important author.

I have laboured long – I hope not too wearisomely – to establish, with varying degrees of probability, the existence, the date, the gist of the opening words and the gist of one other fragment, of a written work on stage construction by Agatharchus. The historian can seldom supply proof beyond reasonable doubt. All I have aimed for is to win on the balance of a set of interconnected probabilities. If I have succeeded, the gain for the

---

[43] Barron 1972: 25, 28, 31–44. [44] Robertson 1959: 122.

history of philosophy is considerable. We have a new and richer context for Anaxagoras' famous dictum 'Appearances are a sight of things unseen'. A context which involves reference to the powers of scene painting.

I think we can see at once why Agatharchus' remark about scene painting would have caught the attention of Anaxagoras. The central postulate of Anaxagorean physics is that there is no break between the macroscopic world of ordinary observation and the microscopic world which explains it. Sensible qualities like colour do not cease to exist below the threshold of perception: they continue all the way down in the sense that any portion of matter, however small, has colour, even if our eyes are too weak to see it:

T22 ἔνθεν ὁ μὲν φυσικώτατος Ἀναξαγόρας ὡς ἀσθενεῖς διαβάλλων τὰς αἰσθήσεις 'ὑπὸ ἀφαυρότητος αὐτῶν' φησὶν 'οὐ δυνατοί ἐσμεν κρίνειν τἀληθές.' τίθησί τε πίστιν αὐτῶν τῆς ἀπιστίας τὴν παρὰ μικρὸν τῶν χρωμάτων ἐξαλλαγήν· εἰ γὰρ δύο λάβοιμεν χρώματα, μέλαν καὶ λευκόν, εἶτα ἐκ θατέρου εἰς θάτερον κατὰ σταγόνα παρεκχέοιμεν, οὐ δυνήσεται ἡ ὄψις διακρίνειν τὰς παρὰ μικρὸν μεταβολάς, καίπερ πρὸς τὴν φύσιν ὑποκειμένας.

> Hence the greatest of the Physicists, Anaxagoras, in disparaging the senses on the ground of their weakness, says, 'Owing to their ‖ infirmity we are unable to judge what is true.' And as an assurance of their lack of sureness he alleges the gradual change in colours: for if we were to take two colours, black and white, and pour some of the one into the other drop by drop, our sense of sight will be unable to distinguish the gradual alterations although they subsist as actual facts. (Sextus Empiricus *M.* VII.90, trans. Bury)

Anaxagoras goes further still and maintains the puzzling thesis that any portion of matter, however small, contains *every* colour and every other quality as well. What we perceive, in those portions of matter which are large enough for us to perceive them, is the colours and qualities which predominate and which, because they predominate, are the qualities most evident to us:

T23 ἕτερον δὲ οὐδέν ἐστιν ὅμοιον οὐδενί, ἀλλ' ὅτων πλεῖστα ἔνι, ταῦτα ἐνδηλότατα ἓν ἕκαστόν ἐστι καὶ ἦν.

> nothing else is like anything else, but each single body is and was most plainly those things of which it contains most. (Anaxagoras 59 B 12 DK = Simpl. *In Phys.* 157. 3–4 Diels, trans. KRS 476)

To use a theatrical metaphor inspired by Lucretius' account of Anaxagoras in Text 24 (the last line), the qualities we perceive in things are those that are 'out front'.

T24 linquitur hic quaedam latitandi copia tenuis,
id quod Anaxagoras sibi sumit, ut omnibus omnis
res putet inmixtas rebus latitare, sed illud
apparere unum cuius sint plurima mixta
et magis in promptu primaque *in fronte locata*.

Herein there is left a slight chance of hiding from justice,
which Anaxagoras grasps for himself, to hold that all things
are mingled, though in hiding, in all things, but that that one
thing comes out clear, whereof there are most parts mingled in,
stationed more ready to view and *in the forefront*.
(Lucretius *De Rerum Natura* 1.876–80, trans. Bailey 1921, emphasis added)

Thus for Anaxagoras the world as we observe it is very like a scene painting such as Agatharchus describes. We cannot actually see all the parts as they recede into the microscopic background, but a simple experiment with a black and a white paint pot (as in Text 22) will show that the recession we do see implies further recessions that we don't see. Concerning what is not evident, the bits of paint ‖ you do see give you a view, as Agatharchus said, *provided* – and this is the point that will, I hope, convince the art historians – provided the perspectival effect alluded to is rather primitive. The marvellous perspectival achievements from Vitruvius' own day in the House of Augustus (see Figure 11.2) or even Boscoreale, would be much less suitable illustrations for the philosopher's message. For the Roman paintings leave too little to the visual imagination. We see, in fact, and see with perfect clarity, all there is to be seen from where we stand in relation to the house represented in the painting. We are not challenged to complete the picture in our mind's eye, for visually speaking it is already complete.

I am suggesting, then, that the first philosopher to compare the ‖ observed world to a scene painting was in fact Anaxagoras. And indeed what better model could he have found for his peculiar physics than the front of the *skēnē* or stage-building, that great centre of Athenian attention inside which the actors, unseen, changed their clothes and masks before coming out front to create a world in which who you are depends on which mask and costume is the predominating factor in your appearance? The front of the *skēnē* is just a wooden wall. But it is a wall rich in implications for a physicist to ponder.

Let us now imagine Democritus pondering this model, as he found it in Anaxagoras' book. For if scene painting was to Anaxagoras just a model for his physics, it becomes quite unnecessary to postulate, as some optimistic scholars have done, a treatise by Anaxagoras on perspective over and above the work *On Nature* which could be bought in the market place at Athens

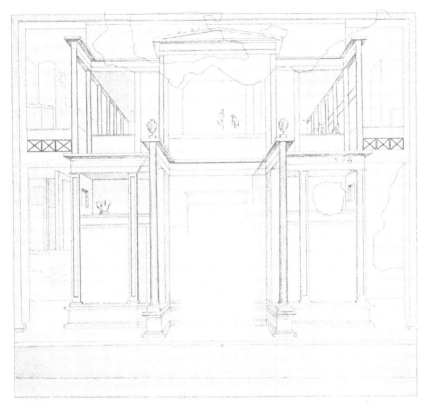

Figure 11.1 House of Augustus, Room of the Perspectival Wall Paintings (Room 11). Drawing by L. Pannuti, from Gianfilippo Carettoni, 'La decorazione pittorica della Casa di Augusto sul Palatino', *Mitteilungen des Deutschen archäologischen Instituts, Römische Abteilung* 90/2 (1983), 373–419, fig. 4 (pp. 386–7).

for a drachma.[45] Not only is it unnecessary, but it is contrary to the explicit statement of D.L. 1.16 numbering Anaxagoras among those philosophers who left just one book. More interesting is a tradition that Anaxagoras was the first to publish a book with diagrams.[46] But to return to Democritus. The great disagreement between Democritus and Anaxagoras concerns precisely the question whether the microscopic world is continuous with the macroscopic. Democritus says it is not. The atoms have no colour.

[45] Burnet 1924 *ad Plat. Ap.* 26d10.
[46] D.L. II.11 (see Hicks' note b, *ad loc.*); Plut. *Nic.* 23; Clem. *Strom.* 1.78 Diels.

As you cut smaller, nearly all the sensible qualities of ordinary observation disappear, until you are left just with atoms and void, whose properties must be determined by reason, not by extrapolating from information provided by the senses.

This rationalist, anti-empirical epistemology may surprise the modern reader, who is used to the idea that good scientific theories – and we all think of Atomism as one of the very best theories that antiquity produced – good scientific theories gain their support, even if indirectly, from the evidence of observation. But there is plenty of evidence that Democritean Atomism was based on *a priori* reasoning, not on observation, and the quotations in paragraphs 138–9 of Text 19 are clear evidence that his epistemology had a thoroughly rationalist character. This means that Diotimus' empiricist interpretation of what Democritus meant by || *opsis tōn adēlōn ta phainomena* must be wrong. (Incidentally, this is not the first time in the compilation Sextus is using that a rival interpretation is introduced – as we introduce the views of other scholars – precisely in order to show that it is wrong.)[47] Contrary to Diotimus' interpretation, Democritus does not think that appearances give us a sight or grasp (*katalēpsis*) of things unseen. So how could Democritus have commended Anaxagoras for his dictum?

Well, the word *opsis* has a passive sense as well as an active one. Suppose Democritus said, with a touch of irony, Yes, appearances are the *opsis* of things unseen – the *phainomena* are just the façade, the visible show put on by atoms and the void – using *opsis* in the passive and potentially pejorative sense it bears in Aristotle's *Poetics*. His point would be that only reason can discover what happens behind the façade in the microscopic world. Given a scene painting such as Agatharchus boasted about, you have to complete the picture with your mind, your reason; the senses don't lead you on, there is no such thing as seeing the four columns as implying more of the same sort. Look at Democritus's own words in paragraph 139 of Text 19:

> γνώμης δὲ δύο εἰσὶν ἰδέαι, ἡ μὲν γνησίη ἡ δὲ σκοτίη· καὶ σκοτίης μὲν τάδε σύμπαντα, ὄψις ἀκοὴ ὀδμὴ γεῦσις ψαῦσις, ἡ δὲ γνησίη, ἀποκεκριμένη δὲ ταύτης.
>
> There are two kinds of *gnōmē* (which means judgement or cognitive capacity rather than *knowledge*), the genuine kind and the bastard. And to

---

[47] The paragraphs on Empedocles. [OSAP: Professor Burnyeat presumably intended to fill this note out further, but in any case the passages he has in mind from Sextus seem to be *M*. VII.115 and 122.]

the bastard belong all these: sight, hearing, smell, taste, touch; while the other kind is genuine and cut off from these.⁴⁸

He goes on,

ὅταν ἡ σκοτίη μηκέτι δύναται μήτε ὁρῆν ἐπ' ἔλαττον μήτε ἀκούειν μήτε ὀδμᾶσθαι μήτε γεύεσθαι μήτε ἐν τῇ ψαύσει αἰσθάνεσθαι, ἀλλ' ἐπὶ λεπτότερον ...

When the bastard kind is unable any longer to see smaller or hear or smell or taste or perceive by touch, but for finer ...

and there the Greek text stops, but as you see from the English translation, every reader's mind easily completes the thought by postulating some unseen letters to complete and explain the whole || of which the visible letters are just the bit that shows. (Please don't misunderstand me. I am not seriously suggesting that the sentence is written to exemplify its own message, so that we need postulate no lacuna after *all' epi leptoteron*. Any sober classical scholar will prefer to say there is an omission in the MSS just like the omission of *opsis tōn adēlōn ta phainomena* in all MSS but N lower down in Text 19.) The point I wish to emphasise is that Democritus' view that reason is cut off from the senses is the epistemological correlate to his view that the macroscopic is discontinuous with the microscopic. Hence his saying, in Text 26, from the previous page of Sextus' history,

T25 ἐν δὲ τῷ περὶ Ἰδεῶν 'γιγνώσκειν τε χρή' φησὶν 'ἄνθρωπον τῷδε τῷ κανόνι ὅτι ἐτεῆς ἀπήλλακται.'

And in his book *Concerning Forms* he says, 'Man must get knowledge by this rule, that he is cut off from truth/reality'. (Sextus Empiricus *M.* VII.137, trans. Bury, with modifications)

What cuts man off from the truth is precisely the scene painting, the façade between us and the real world of atoms and void.

One final step will take us back, at last, to Anaxarchus. If Democritus' attitude to the *skēnographia* comparison was as I have reconstructed it, the difference between 'All the world's a stage-painting' as approved by Democritus and the sceptical slant it acquires on the lips of Anaxarchus is the difference between an original thinker who believes that reason has the power to penetrate behind the scenes and a follower who has lost that faith, who, unlike Alexander, is Cynically certain that you can't conquer

---

⁴⁸ [OSAP: Burnyeat has slightly altered the translation printed earlier in Text 19: instead of Bury's 'distinct from' for the word ἀποκεκριμένη emphasised there, he uses 'cut off from', a phrase that recurs below.]

the secrets of the world you live in. This difference between Democritus and Anaxarchus is easily explained. Between the two comes the generalised sceptical doubt of Metrodorus (Text 1), who introduced an Atomist cosmology with opening words that were carefully preserved by the Hellenistic compilers: 'We know nothing, not even this very thing, that we know nothing'.

I have now answered the question I began with. Anaxarchus chose the model of scene painting to express his scepticism because *skēnographia* was already the name and the image of the epistemological problem in the debate between Democritus and Anaxagoras. It remains only to explain why I have so far said virtually nothing about optics.

The reason is that I believe that, where Anaxagoras and || Democritus are concerned, there is nothing to say. Many scholars have credited them with writing treatises on perspective. Eva Keuls, in her book *Plato and Greek Painting*, goes as far as to make Democritus' theory of perspective a major influence on the Sicyonian school of painters.[49] In this lecture I have tried to show that a careful reading of Vitruvius removes the basis for thinking that either Democritus or Anaxagoras had a mathematician's interest in *skēnographia*. For them, *skēnographia* was a topic in general epistemology. It is only later that *skēnographia* becomes a recognised branch of mathematical optics. And before that can happen, mathematical optics must itself come into existence.

It would take another paper, with more analysis of so-called 'late sources' and more balancing of probabilities, to show that mathematical optics does not develop in Athens or Abdera, but in South Italy – the area of the Würzburg vase reproduced in Figure 11.2 (mid-fourth century BC) and other illustrations in Trendall and Webster which show, from vases, the advances made by the art of scene || painting in the Greek cities of fourth-century Italy.[50] It is also in fourth-century Italy, when the Pythagoreans begin at last to do some real mathematics under the leadership of Archytas, that mathematical optics is first attested, and from there it reaches the Academy at Athens. But while Aristotle refers frequently to mathematical optics, it seems to have had no effect on his theory of vision. It is only with the Hellenistic philosophers that optics begins to leave its trace on general epistemology. Text 26 shows Chrysippus incorporating the Euclidean concept of the visual cone into his account of sight.

---

[49] Keuls 1978: 140–50, esp. 140–1 and 147–50.   [50] Trendall and Webster 1971.

Figure 11.2 Reconstruction of the Würzburg skēnographia. From Apulian calyx krater fragments in several colours, *circa* 350 BC, Martin von Wagner Museum der Universität Würzburg, inv. H4696+H 4701. Drawing by Brinna Otto, Universität Innsbruck, from E. Simon and B. Otto, 'Eine neue Rekonstruktion der Würzburger Skenographie', *Archäologischer Anzeiger* 88/1 (1973), 121–31, fig. 3 (p. 125). Reproduced by kind permission of Professor Otto.

T26 ὁρᾶν δὲ τοῦ μεταξὺ τῆς ὁράσεως καὶ τοῦ ὑποκειμένου φωτὸς ἐντεινομένου κωνοειδῶς, καθά φησι Χρύσιππος ἐν δευτέρῳ τῶν Φυσικῶν καὶ Ἀπολλόδωρος. γίνεσθαι μέντοι τὸ κωνοειδὲς τοῦ ἀέρος πρὸς τῇ ὄψει, τὴν δὲ βάσιν πρὸς τῷ ὁρωμένῳ· ὡς διὰ βακτηρίας οὖν τοῦ ταθέντος ἀέρος τὸ βλεπόμενον ἀναγγέλλεσθαι.

> They hold that we see when the light between the visual organ and the object stretches in the form of a cone: so Chrysippus in the second book of his *Physics* and Apollodorus. The *apex of the cone* in the air is at the eye, the base at the object seen. Thus the thing seen is reported to us by the medium of the air stretching out towards it, as if by a stick. (Diogenes Laertius VII.157, trans. Hicks)

But interestingly enough Epicurus is the one who makes most use of the newly developed mathematical understanding of visual perspective – just because, I would suggest, in the Atomist tradition, *skēnographia* had been, as I said, the name and the image of the problem.

Epicurus' task was to refute the scepticism of Metrodorus and establish Atomism on a secure epistemological foundation in the evidence of the senses. To do this he must explain standard examples of perceptual illusion, such as the square tower which appears round at a distance. It turns out that mathematical optics is the tool that enables him to succeed. All he needs to add is his famous theory of *eidōla* (*simulacra* in Lucretius) so as to provide a suitable physical embodiment for the diagrams with which the mathematician works out his theorems. To many people this will seem a strong and surprising claim. Lucretius' account, in Book IV of *De Rerum Natura*, of the way we see things through the very thin || *simulacra* or films that bodies are constantly giving off, strikes most readers as one of the more curious and unpromising products of ancient speculation. But that reaction, I believe, is at least partly due to our neglect of a third dimension of the unity of the Classics, the unity of art and science in the ancient world. Obviously, I cannot expand on this theme now. But I can offer one little titbit to advertise its importance.

Anyone who comes to Lucretius Book IV after reading the surviving ancient literature on mathematical optics will find it obvious that in the

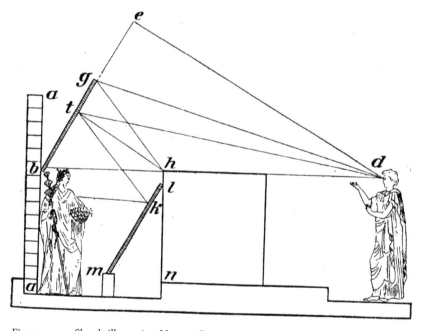

Figure 11.3 Sketch illustrating Heron, *Catoptrica*, prop. 18. From *Heronis Alexandrini opera quae supersunt omnia*, ed. L. Nix and W. Schmidt, ii/1. *Catoptrica* (Leipzig, 1900), fig. 91a (p. 358).

Figure 11.4 Sketch illustrating Heron, *Catoptrica*, prop. 18. From *Heronis Alexandrini opera quae supersunt omnia*, ed. L. Nix and W. Schmidt, ii/1. *Catoptrica* (Leipzig, 1900), fig. 91b (p. 361).

last line of Text 27 *in aedibus* should be translated 'in the temple', not 'in the house'.

T27 fit quoque de speculo in speculum ut tradatur imago,
quinque etiam <aut> sex ut fieri simulacra süerint.
nam quaecumque retro parte interiore latebunt,
inde tamen, quamvis torte penitusque remota,
omnia per flexos aditus educta licebit
pluribus haec speculis videantur in *aedibus* esse.

It comes to pass too that the image is handed on from mirror to mirror, so that even five or six idols are wont to be made. For even when things are hidden far back in an inner part of the room, yet, however far distant from the sight along a twisting path, it may be that they will all be brought out thence by winding passages, and, thanks to the several mirrors, be seen to be *in the house*. (Lucretius *De Rerum Natura* IV.302–8, trans. Bailey, emphasis added)

Lucretius is not describing a phenomenon you might come across anywhere as you stroll through the streets of Rome. In good Epicurean style, he is debunking, by giving a rational explanation of, a piece of temple magic, the mathematics of which is beautifully set out in the *Catoptrics* of Heron of Alexandria (*Catoptr.* 18). One diagram shows what you see as you approach the temple, the other shows how the trick is effected. It is in a parallel way, I believe, that the general Epicurean theory of vision sets out, with the aid of Euclidean optics, to debunk, by giving a rational explanation of, the perceptual illusions which foment scepticism. Eventually, *skēnographia* ceases to be the name of the problem and becomes the name of the solution.

But to show all that in enough detail to be convincing would, as I said, require another paper. For this occasion I shall be content if the philosophical perspectives I have offered on one passage of Vitruvius contribute to a better understanding and appreciation, || in Classical circles generally, of a technical author who not only changed the face of Europe, but who also expressed his own vision of the unity of the Classics when he wrote that an architect needs to be philosopher as well, otherwise he won't know how to get the air bubbles out of his pipework (1.7).

Bibliography

Ackrill, J. L. (1963) *Aristotle's Categories and De Interpretatione*, Oxford
  (1965) 'Aristotle's distinction between *Energeia* and *Kinesis*', in R. Bambrough, ed., *New Essays on Plato and Aristotle* (London) 121–41
  (1997) *Essays on Plato and Aristotle*, Oxford
Adam, J. (1963) *The Republic of Plato*, ed. D. A. Rees, 2 vols., 2nd edn, Cambridge
Alexandru, S. (1999) 'A new manuscript of Pseudo-Philoponus' commentary on Aristotle's *Metaphysics* containing a hitherto unknown ascription of the work', *Phronesis* 44: 347–52
  (2000) 'Traces of ancient *reclamantes* surviving in further manuscripts of Aristotle's *Metaphysics*', *Zeitschrift für Papyrologie und Epigraphik* 131: 13–14
Allen, R. E. (1965) (ed.) *Studies in Plato's Metaphysics*, London–New York
Anton, J. P. and Preus, A. (1992) (eds.) *Aristotle's Ontology*, Albany
Aquinas, T. (1961) *Summa Theologica, Prima Pars, Dominican Edition*, 3rd edn, Madrid
Armstrong, A. H. (1967) *Plotinus. Vol. III, Enneads III. 1–9*, eds. P. Henry and H.-R. Schwyzer, Cambridge, MA–London
  (1988) *Plotinus. Vol. VI, Enneads VI. 1–5*, Cambridge, MA–London
Arrighetti, G. (1973) *Opere, Epicuro*, 2nd edn, Turin
Aubenque, P. (1962) *Le Problème de l'être chez Aristote: essai sur la problématique aristotélicienne*, Paris
Aubry, G. (2006) *Dieu sans la puissance: Dunamis et Energeia chez Aristote et chez Plotin*, Paris
Ayer, A. J. (1956) *The Problem of Knowledge*, London
Bailey, C. (1921) *Lucretius: On the Nature of Things*, Oxford
  (1926) *Epicurus: The Extant Remains, with Short Critical Apparatus, Translation, and Notes*, Oxford
Baldry, H. C. (1971) *The Greek Tragic Theatre*, London
Baltes, M. (1997) 'Is the Idea of the Good in Plato's Republic beyond Being?', in M. Joyal, ed., *Studies in Plato and the Platonic Tradition: Essays Presented to John Whittaker* (Aldershot) 3–23
  (1999) *Dianoēmata: kleine Schriften zu Platon und zum Platonismus*, eds. A. Hüffmeier, M.-L. Lakmann and M. Vorwerk, Stuttgart
Barbotin, E. and Jannone, A. (1966) *Aristote: De l'âme*, Paris

Barnes, J. (1975) *Aristotle's Posterior Analytics*, Oxford
  (1979) *The Presocratic Philosophers*, 2 vols., London
  (1993) *Aristotle: Posterior Analytics*, 2nd edn, Oxford
  (2007) 'Introduzione: Conoscenza dimostrativa', in M. Mignucci, ed., *Aristotele: Analitici secondi: Organon* IV (Rome) vii–xxx
  (2009) *Truth, Etc.: Six Lectures on Ancient Logic*, Oxford
  (1984) (ed.) *The Complete Works of Aristotle: The Revised Oxford Translation*, Princeton
Barnes, J., Schofield, M. and Sorabji, R. (1977) (eds.) *Articles on Aristotle. 2, Ethics and Politics*, London
Barrett, W. S. (1992) *Euripides: Hippolytos*, Oxford
Barron, J. P. (1972) 'New light on old walls: the murals of the Theseion', *Journal of Hellenic Studies* 92: 20–45
Bauer, G. (1970) 'The English "perfect" reconsidered', *Journal of Linguistics* 6: 189–98
Bechtle, G. (2000) 'The question of being and the dating of the Anonymous Parmenides Commentary', *Ancient Philosophy* 20: 393–414
Bekker, I. (1831) *Aristoteles graece ex recensione Immanuelis Bekkeri, edidit Academia Regia Borussica*, 2 vols., Berlin
Bernadinello, S. (1970) *Eliminatio codicum della Metafisica di Aristotele*, Padua
Bessarion, J. and Argyropylus, B. (1515) *Contenta. Continetur hic Aristotelis castigatissime recognitum Opus metaphysicum a Bessarione Latinate foeliciter donateum, XIIII libris distinctum: cum adj. in XII primos Argyropylus Byzantii interpretamento ...: Theophrasto Metaphysicorum liber I: item Metaphysica introductio: quator dialogorum libris elucidara*, eds. J. Faber and H. Estienne, Paris
Betegh, G. (2004) *The Derveni Papyrus: Cosmology, Theology and Interpretation*, Cambridge
Blass, F. (1875) 'Aristotelisches', *Rheinisches Museum für Philologie* 30: 481–505
Block, I. (1961) 'Truth and error in Aristotle's theory of sense perception', *Philosophical Quarterly* 11: 1–9
Block, N. (1980) (ed.) *Readings in Philosophy of Psychology*, Vol. 1, Cambridge, MA
Bloom, A. D. (1968) *The Republic of Plato*, New York
Bluck, R. S. (1955) *Plato: Phaedo*, London
  (1961) *Plato: Meno*, Cambridge
Bodéüs, R. (2001) *Aristote Catégories*, Paris
Bonitz, H. (1847) *Alexander: Commentarius in libros metaphysicos Aristotelis*, Berlin
  (1848) *Aristotelis Metaphysica*, Bonn
  (1886) *Platonische Studien*, 3rd edn, Berlin
  (1955) *Index Aristotelicus*, eds. J. Bona Meyer and B. A. Langkavel, 2nd edn, Graz
Borges, J. L. (1999) *Selected Non-fictions*, ed. E. Weinberger, trans. E. Allen, S. J. Levine and E. Weinberger, New York–London
Bostock, D. (1988) 'Pleasure and activity in Aristotle's ethics', *Phronesis* 33: 251–72

Boys-Stones, G. R. (2001) *Post-Hellenistic Philosophy: A Study of Its Development from the Stoics to Origen*, Oxford
Brague, R. (1988) *Aristote et la question du monde: essai sur le contexte cosmologique et anthropologique de l'ontologie*, Paris
Brandis, C. A. (1823) *Aristotelis et Theophrasti Metaphysica ad veterum codicum manuscriptorum fidem recensita indicibusque instructa in usum scholarum edidit Christianus Augustus Brandis*, Berlin
  (1836) *Scholia in Aristotelem*, Berlin
Bréhier, É. (1924–36) *Plotin: Ennéades*, eds. É. Bréhier and Porphyry, Paris
Brentano, F. (1977) *The Psychology of Aristotle: In Particular His Doctrine of the Active Intellect: With an Appendix Concerning the Activity of Aristotle's God*, ed. and trans. R. George, Berkeley
Brickhouse, T. C. and Smith, N. D. (1994) *Plato's Socrates*, New York–Oxford
  (2002) (eds.) *The Trial and Execution of Socrates: Sources and Controversies*, New York–Oxford
Brinton, L. J. (1988) *The Development of English Aspectual Systems – Aspectualizers and Post-Verbal Particles*, Cambridge
Brisson, L. (1997) *Platon: Apologie de Socrate, Criton*, Paris
Brisson, L. and Patillon, M. (1992) *Platon: Timée-Critias*, Paris
Broackes, J. (1999) 'Aristotle, objectivity, and perception', *Oxford Studies in Ancient Philosophy* 17: 57–113
Broadie, S. (1992) 'Aristotle and perceptual realism', *Southern Journal of Philosophy*, 31: 137–59
Brown, A. L. (1984) 'Three and scene-painting Sophocles', *Proceedings of the Cambridge Philological Society* 30: 1–17
Brown, L. (1986) 'Being in the Sophist: a syntactical enquiry', *Oxford Studies in Ancient Philosophy* 4: 49–70
  (1994) 'The verb "to be" in Greek philosophy: some remarks', in S. Everson, ed., *Companions to Ancient Thought 3: Language* (Cambridge) 212–36
Browning, R. (1962) 'An unpublished funeral oration on Anna Comnena', *Proceedings of the Cambridge Philological Society* 8: 1–12
Brunschwig, J. (1967) *Aristote: Topiques, Vol I*, Paris
  (1985) 'Le Problème de la self-participation chez Platon', in A. Cazenave and J.-F. Lyotard, eds., *L'Art des Confins* (Paris) 121–35
  (1994) *Papers in Hellenistic Philosophy*, trans. J. Lloyd, Cambridge
Burkert, W. (1962/72) *Lore and Science in Ancient Pythagoreanism*, trans. E. L. Minar, Cambridge, MA
Burnet, J. (1911) *Plato's Phaedo*, Oxford
  (1924) *Plato: Euthyphro, Apology of Socrates and Crito*, Oxford
Burnyeat, M. F. (1971) 'Virtues in action', in G. Vlastos, ed., *The Philosophy of Socrates: A Collection of Critical Essays* (Garden City) 209–34 = *EAMP* vol. II, chapter 10
  (1976a) 'Protagoras and self-refutation in later Greek philosophy', *Philosophical Review* 85: 44–69 = *EAMP* vol. I, chapter 1

(1976b) 'Plato on the grammar of perceiving', *Classical Quarterly* 26: 29–51 = *EAMP* vol. II, chapter 4

(1978) 'The upside-down back-to-front sceptic of Lucretius IV 472', *Philologus* 122: 197–206 = *EAMP* vol. I, chapter 3

(1981) 'Aristotle on understanding knowledge', in E. Berti, ed., *Aristotle on Science: The Posterior Analytics. Proceedings of the Eighth Symposium Aristotelicum Held in Padua from September 7 to 15, 1978* (Padua) 97–139 = *EAMP* vol. II, chapter 6

(1984a) 'The Sceptic in his place and time', in R. Rorty, J. B. Schneewind and Q. Skinner, eds., *Philosophy in History: Essays on the Historiography of Philosophy* (Cambridge) 225–54 = *EAMP* vol. I, chapter 12

(1984b) *Notes on Books Eta and Theta of Aristotle's Metaphysics: Being the Record by Myles Burnyeat and Others of a Seminar Held in London, 1979–1982*, Oxford

(1989) 'The practicability of Plato's ideally just city', in K. Boudouris, ed., *On Justice. Plato's and Aristotle's Conception of Justice in Relation to Modern and Contemporary Theories of Justice* (Athens) 95–104

(1990) *The Theaetetus of Plato, with Translation by M. J. Levett*, Indianapolis

(1992a) 'Utopia and fantasy: the practicability of Plato's ideal city', in J. Hopkins and A. Savile, eds., *Psychoanalysis, Mind and Art: Perspectives on Richard Wollheim* (Oxford) 175–87

(1992b) 'Is an Aristotelian philosophy of mind still credible? A draft', in M. C. Nussbaum and A. O. Rorty, eds., *Essays on Aristotle's De Anima* (Oxford) 15–26

(1994) 'Enthymeme: Aristotle on the logic of persuasion', in D. J. Furley and A. Nehamas, eds., *Aristotle's Rhetoric: Philosophical Essays* (Princeton) 3–55 = *EAMP* vol. I, chapter 7

(1995) 'How much happens when Aristotle sees red and hears middle C? Remarks on *De Anima* 2.7–8', in M. C. Nussbaum and A. O. Rorty, eds., *Essays on Aristotle's De anima*, paperback edn, (Oxford) 422–34

(1997a) 'The Sceptic in his place and time', in M. F. Burnyeat and M. Frede, eds., *The Original Sceptics: A Controversy* (Indianapolis) 92–126 (= Burnyeat 1984a)

(1997b) 'The impiety of Socrates', *Ancient Philosophy* 17: 1–12 = *EAMP* vol. II, chapter 11

(2000a) 'Utopia and fantasy: the practicability of Plato's ideally just city', in G. Fine, ed., *Plato* (Oxford) 779–90 (= Burnyeat 1992a)

(2000b) 'Plato on why mathematics is good for the soul', in T. J. Smiley, ed., *Mathematics and Necessity* (London) 1–81 = *EAMP* vol. III, chapter 1

(2001a) 'Aquinas on "spiritual change" in perception', in D. Perler, ed., *Ancient and Medieval Theories of Intentionality* (Leiden) 129–53 = *EAMP* vol. IV, chapter 6

(2001b) *A Map of Metaphysics Zeta*, Pittsburgh

(2002) 'De Anima II 5', *Phronesis* 47: 28–90. = *EAMP* vol. IV, chapter 5

(2004a) 'Ryle, Gilbert (1900–76)', in R. B. Todd, ed., *The Dictionary of British Classicists*, *3* (Bristol) 846–9

(2004b) 'Introduction: Aristotle on the foundations of sublunary physics', in J. Mansfeld and F. de Hass, eds., *Aristotle: On Generation and Corruption, Book 1* (Oxford) 7–24 = *EAMP* vol. IV, chapter 9

(2005a) 'On the source of Burnet's construal of *Apology* 30b2–4: a correction', *Journal of Hellenic Studies* 125: 139–42 = *EAMP* vol. IV, chapter 1b

(2005b) 'Апология» 30b 2–4: Сократ, деньги и синтаксис глагола γίγνεσθαι (в защиту перевода Бернета)', trans. I. Levinskaya, *АКАΔНМЕIA Материалы И Исследования По Истории Платонизма*, 6: 105–37 (Russian translation of an earlier version of Ch. 1a; online at http://platoakademeia.ru/index.php/ru/academeia/item list/category/7-academeia_6)

(2008a) '*Kinēsis* vs. *energeia*: a much-read passage in (but not of) Aristotle's Metaphysics', *Oxford Studies in Ancient Philosophy* 34: 219–92 = *EAMP* vol. IV, chapter 4

(2008b) *Aristotle's Divine Intellect*, Milwaukee

(2013) 'Dramatic aspects of Plato's *Protagoras*', *Classical Quarterly* 63: 419–22

(2017) '"All the world's a stage-painting": scenery, optics, and Greek epistemology', *Oxford Studies in Ancient Philosophy* 52: 33–75 = *EAMP* vol. IV, chapter 11

Burnyeat, M. F. and Barnes, J. (1980) 'Socrates and the jury: paradoxes in Plato's distinction between knowledge and true belief', *Aristotelian Society Supplementary Volume* 54: 173–206. = *EAMP* vol. II, chapter 5

Bury, R. G. (1929) *Plato: Timaeus, Critias, Cleitophon, Menexenus, Epistles*, Cambridge, MA–London

(1933–49) *Sextus Empiricus*, 3 vols., Cambridge, MA–London

Butcher, S. H. (1907) *Aristotle's Theory of Poetry and Fine Art: With a Critical Text and Translation of The Poetics*, 4th edn, London

Butler, H. E. (1909) *The Apologia and Florida of Apuleius of Madaura*, Oxford

(1920) *Quintilian: Institutio Oratoria*, 4 vols., Cambridge, MA–London

Butler, H. E. and Owen, A. S. (1914) *Apulei Apologia: sive Pro se de magia liber*, Oxford

Cambiano, G. (1998) 'Archimede meccanico e la meccanica di Archita', *Elenchos* 19: 289–324

Canto-Sperber, M. (1989) *Platon: Euthydème*, Paris

Capelle, W. (1912) 'Das Proömium der Meteorologie', *Hermes* 47: 514–35

Carteron, H. (1926–31) *Aristote: Physique*, Paris

Caston, V. (1996) 'Why Aristotle needs imagination', *Phronesis* 41: 20–55

Chantraine, P. (1927) *Histoire du parfait grec*, Paris

Charles, D. (2000) *Aristotle on Meaning and Essence*, Oxford

Cherniss, H. (1944) *Aristotle's Criticism of Plato and the Academy. Vol. 1*, Baltimore

Chiaradonna, R. (2002) *Sostanza, Movimento, Analogia: Plotino critico di Aristotele*, Naples

Christ, W. von (1886/1895) *Aristotelis Metaphysica*, Leipzig
Cobb, R. A. (1973) 'The present progressive: periphrasis and the *Metaphysics* of Aristotle', *Phronesis* 18: 80–90
Code, A. and Moravcsik, J. M. E. (1992) 'Explaining various forms of living', in M. C. Nussbaum and A. O. Rorty, eds., *Essays on Aristotle's De Anima* (Oxford) 129–45
Cohen, S. M. (1982) 'St Thomas Aquinas on the immaterial reception of sensible forms', *Philosophical Review* 91: 193–209
Collingwood, R. G. (1939/1970) *An Autobiography*, Oxford
Comrie, B. (1976) *Aspect: An Introduction to the Study of Verbal Aspect and Related Problems*, Cambridge
Cooper, J. M. (1985) 'Aristotle on the goods of fortune', *Philosophical Review* 94: 173–96
  (1988) 'Metaphysics in Aristotle's embryology', *Proceedings of the Cambridge Philological Society* 34: 14–41
  (1999) *Reason and Emotion: Essays on Ancient Moral Psychology and Ethical Theory*, Princeton
Cooper, J. M. (2002) (ed.) *Plato: Five Dialogues*, trans. G. M. A. Grube, 2nd rev. edn, Indianapolis
Cooper, J. M. and Hutchinson, D. S. (1997) (eds.) *Plato: Complete Works*, Indianapolis
Cooper, N. (1994) 'Understanding', *Aristotelian Society Supplementary Volume* 68: 1–26
Cornford, F. M. (1932) *Before and After Socrates*, ed. R. Gerhard, Cambridge
  (1935) *Plato's Theory of Knowledge: The Theaetetus and the Sophist of Plato*, London
  (1937) *Plato's Cosmology: The Timaeus of Plato*, London
  (1941) *The Republic of Plato*, Oxford
Cornford, F. M. and Wicksteed, P. H. (1929–34) *Aristotle: The Physics*, Cambridge, MA
Craig, E. (1990) *Knowledge and the State of Nature: An Essay in Conceptual Synthesis*, Oxford
  (1998) (ed.) *Routledge Encyclopedia of Philosophy*, London–New York
Croese, I. (1998) 'Simplicius on continuous and instantaneous change: Neoplatonic elements in Simplicius' interpretation of Aristotelian physics', PhD thesis (Zeno Institute for Philosophy)
Crombie, I. M. (1967) 'Review: Renford Bambrough (ed.) *New Essays on Plato and Aristotle*', *Classical Review* 17: 30–3
De Corte, M. (1932) 'Notes critiques sur le "De Anima" d'Aristote', *Revue des Études Grecques* 210: 163–94
De Groot, J. C. (1983) 'Philoponus on *De Anima* II.5, *Physics* III.3, and the propagation of light', *Phronesis* 28: 177–96
Decleva Caizzi, F. (1996) *Platone: Eutidemo*, Milan
Denniston, J. D. (1934) *The Greek Particles*, Oxford
  (1952) *Greek Prose Style*, Oxford

(1954) *The Greek Particles*, ed. K. J. Dover, 2nd edn, Oxford
Denyer, N. (1991) *Language, Thought and Falsehood in Ancient Greek Philosophy*, London
Des Places, E. (1973) (ed.) *Numenius: Fragments*, Paris
Devine, A. M. and Stephens, L. D. (2000) *Discontinuous Syntax: Hyperbaton in Greek*, New York–Oxford
Dickens, C. (1861/2003) *Great Expectations*, eds. C. Mitchell and D. Trotter, London
Dillon, J. (1977) *The Middle Platonists: A Study of Platonism, 80 BC to AD 220*, London
Dixsaut, M. (1991) *Platon: Phédon*, Paris
Dodds, E. R. (1959) *Gorgias: A Revised Text*, Oxford
  (1960) 'Numenius and Ammonius', in E. R. Dodds and others, *Les Sources de Plotin: Dix exposés et discussions* (Geneva) 1–32
Dorion, L.-A. (1995) *Aristote: Les Réfutations sophistiques*, Paris
Dörrie, H. (1955) 'ὑπόστασις: Wort und Bedeutungsgeschichte', *Nachrichten der Akademie der Wissenschaften zu Göttingen, Philologisch-Historische Klasse* 1: 35–92
Dufour, M. (2001) 'La Distinction ενεργεια-κινησις en *Métaph.* θ 6: deux manières d'être dans le temps', *Revue de Philosophie Ancienne* 19: 3–43
Duhoux, Y. (1992) *Le Verbe grec ancien: éléments de morphologie et de syntaxe historiques*, Louvain-la-Neuve
Düring, I. (1961) *Aristotle's Protrepticus: An Attempt at Reconstruction*, Göteborg
Dyer, L. (1891) 'Vitruvius' account of the Greek stage', *Journal of Hellenic Studies* 12: 356–65
Ebbesen, S. (1981) *Commentators and Commentaries on Aristotle's Sophistici Elenchi: A Study of Post-Aristotelian Ancient and Medieval Writings on Fallacies*, Leiden
  (1990) 'Philoponus, "Alexander" and the origins of medieval logic', in R. Sorabji, ed., *Aristotle Transformed: The Ancient Commentators and Their Influence* (London) 445–61
Edwards, M. J. (1989) 'Numenius, Fr. 13 (Des Places): A note on interpretation', *Mnemosyne* 42: 478–82
  (1990a) 'Atticising Moses? Numenius, the Fathers and the Jews', *Vigiliae Christianae* 44: 64–75
  (1990b) 'Porphyry and the intelligible triad', *Journal of Hellenic Studies* 110: 14–25
Else, G. F. (1939) 'Aristotle and satyr-play. 1', *Transactions and Proceedings of the American Philological Association* 70: 139–57
  (1957) *Aristotle's Poetics: The Argument*, Cambridge, MA
Emilsson, E. K. (2007) *Plotinus on Intellect*, Oxford
Erasmus, D. (1550) *Aristotelous hapanta = Aristotelis summi semper philosophi, et in quem unum uim suam uniuersam contulisse natura rerum uidetur, opera quæcunq[ue] hactenus extiterunt omnia: quæ quidem ut antea integris aliquot libris supra priores æditiones omnes à nobis aucta prodieru[n]t, ita nunc quoq*

[ue] lucis & memoriæ causa, in capita diligenter distincta in lucem emittimus. Præterea quam diligentiam, ut omnibus æditionibus reliquis, omnia hæc exirent a nostra officina emendatiora, adhibuerimus, quoniam uno uerbo dici non potest, ex sequenti pagina plenius cognoscere licebit, ed. M. Isengrin, Basel

Everson, S. (1997) *Aristotle on Perception*, Oxford

Fensterbusch, C. (1964) *Vitruvius: Zehn Bücher über Architektur*, Darmstadt

Ferguson, J. (1991) *Clement of Alexandria: Stromateis, Books One to Three*, Washington, DC

Ferrari, G. R. F. and Griffith, T. (2000) *Plato: The Republic*, Cambridge

Fonseca, P. da (1613) *Commentariorvm Petri Fonsecæ Lvsitani, doctoris theologi Societatis Iesv, in libros Metaphysicorum Aristotelis Stagiritæ*, 4 vols., Cologne

Förster, A. (1912) *Aristotelis De anima libri III*, Budapest

Forster, E. S. and Furley, D. J. (1955) *Aristotle: On Sophistical Refutations, On Coming-to-be and Passing-away, On the Cosmos*, Cambridge, MA–London

Foster, K. and Humphries, S. (1951) *Aristotle's De Anima, in the Version of William of Moerbeke and the Commentary of St. Thomas Aquinas*, London

Frank, E. (1923) *Plato und die sogennanten Pythagoreer: ein Kapitel aus der Geschichte des griechischen Geistes*, Halle

Frede, M. (1987) 'Numenius', *Aufstieg und Niedergang der römischen Welt* 36: 1034–75

(1988) 'Being and becoming in Plato', in J. Annas and R. H. Grimm, eds., *Oxford Studies in Ancient Philosophy, Supplementary Volume* (Oxford) 37–52

(1989) 'Chaeremon der Stoiker', *Aufstieg und Niedergang der römischen Welt* 36: 2067–103

(1992) 'On Aristotle's conception of soul', in M. C. Nussbaum and A. O. Rorty, eds., *Essays on Aristotle's De Anima* (Oxford) 93–107

(1993) 'The Stoic doctrine of the tenses of the verb', in K. Döring and T. Ebert, eds., *Dialektiker und Stoiker: Zur Logik der Stoa und ihrer Vorläufer* (Stuttgart) 141–54

(1994) 'Celsus philosophus Platonicus', *Aufstieg und Niedergang der römischen Welt* 36: 5183–213

(2001) 'Aristotle's notion of potentiality in *Metaphysics* Θ', in T. Scaltsas, D. Charles and M. L. Gill, eds., *Unity, Identity, and Explanation in Aristotle's Metaphysics* (Oxford) 173–93

Frede, M. and Patzig, G. (1988) *Aristoteles 'Metaphysik Z': Text, Übersetzung und Kommentar*, Munich

Frege, G. (1884/1950) *The Foundations of Arithmetic: A Logico-Mathematical Enquiry into the Concept of Number*, trans. J. L. Austin, Oxford

(1953) *The Foundations of Arithmetic: A Logico-Mathematical Enquiry into the Concept of Number*, trans. J. L. Austin, 2nd rev. edn, Oxford

Fritz, K. von (1938) *Philosophie und sprachlicher Ausdruck bei Demokrit, Plato und Aristoteles*, New York

Furley, D. (1989) *Cosmic Problems: Essays on Greek and Roman Philosophy of Nature*, Cambridge

Furth, M. (1985) *Aristotle Metaphysics Books* VII–X: *zeta, eta, theta, iota*, Indianapolis
Gager, J. G. (1972) *Moses in Greco-Roman Paganism*, Nashville
Gaiser, K. (1959) *Protreptik und Pärenese bei Platon: Untersuchungen zur Form des Platonischen Dialogs*, Stuttgart
Gallop, D. (1975) *Plato: Phaedo*, Oxford
  (1993) *Plato: Phaedo* (Oxford World's Classics) Oxford
Gardiner, A. H. (1923) 'The eloquent peasant', *Journal of Egyptian Archaeology* 9: 5–25
Gardner, P. (1899) 'The scenery of the Greek stage', *Journal of Hellenic Studies* 19: 252–64
Gercke, A. (1892) 'Aristoteleum', *Wiener Studien* 14: 146–8
Gerson, L. P. (2003) *Knowing Persons: A Study in Plato*, Oxford
Gifford, E. H. (1903) *Eusebius: Evangelicae Praeparationis, Libri* XV, 4 vols., Oxford
  (1905) *The Euthydemus of Plato, with Revised Text, Introduction, Notes and Indices*, Oxford
Gill, M. L. (1980) 'Aristotle's theory of causal action in *Physics* III 3', *Phronesis* 25: 129–47
  (1989) *Aristotle on Substance: The Paradox of Unity*, Princeton
Gilson, É. (1948) *L'Être et l'essence*, Paris
Glucker, J. (1994) 'The origin of ὑπάρχω and ὕπαρξις as philosophical terms', in F. Romano and D. P. Taormina, eds., *Hyparxis e hypostasis nel Neoplatonismo* (Florence) 1–23
Gogos, S. (1983) 'Bühnenarchitektur und antike Bühnenmalerei – zwei Rekonstruktionsversuche nach griechischen Vasen', *Jahreshefte des Österreichischen archäologischen Instituts in Wien* 54: 59–86
Gohlke, P. (1961) *Die Lehrschriften: Vol. 5, Metaphysik*, 2nd edn, Paderborn
Goldschmidt, V. (1982) *Temps physique et temps tragique chez Aristote: commentaire sur le Quatrième livre de la Physique (10–14) et sur la Poètique*, Paris
Goodwin, W. W. (1897) *Syntax of the Moods and Tenses of the Greek Verb*, revised edn, London
Gosling, J. C. B. (1968) 'Δόξα and δύναμις in Plato's *Republic*', *Phronesis* 13: 119–30
Gosling, J. C. B. and Taylor, C. C. W. (1982) *The Greeks on Pleasure*, Oxford
Gottschalk, H. B. (1965) *Strato of Lampsacus: Some Texts*, Leeds
Gould, J. (1955) *The Development of Plato's Ethics*, Cambridge
Goulet, R. (2003) (ed.) *Dictionnaire des philosophes antiques. Supplément*, Paris
Graham, D. W. (1980) 'States and performances: Aristotle's test', *Philosophical Quarterly* 30: 117–30
Granger, F. (1931–34) *Vitruvius: On Architecture*, Cambridge, MA–London
Gregorić, P. (2005) 'Plato's and Aristotle's explanation of human posture', *Rhizai* 2: 183–96
Grote, G. (1888) *A History of Greece: From the Earliest Period to the Close of the Generation Contemporary with Alexander the Great*, 10 vols., new edn, London

Grube, G. M. A. (1974) *Plato: The Republic*, Indianapolis
  (1975) *Plato: The Trial and Death of Socrates*, Indianapolis
  (1977) *Plato's Phaedo*, Indianapolis
Hackforth, R. (1955) *Plato: Phaedo*, Cambridge
Hadot, P. (1968) *Porphyre et Victorinus*, Paris
  (1996a) 'La Conception plotinienne de l'identité entre l'intellect et son objet: Plotin et le *De Anima* de l'Aristote', in G. Romeyer-Dherbey and C. Viano, eds., *Corps et âme: sur le De anima d'Aristote* (Paris) 367–76
  (1996b) '"Porphyre et Victorinus". Questions et hypothéses', *Res Orientales* 9: 117–25
Haldane, J. J. (1983) 'Aquinas on sense-perception', *Philosophical Review* 92: 233–9
Halliwell, S. (1993) *Plato: Republic 5*, Warminster
Hamblin, C. L. (1970) *Fallacies*, London
Hamlyn, D. W. (1957) 'Forms and knowledge in Plato's *Theaetetus*: a reply to Mr. Bluck', *Mind* 66: 547–47
  (1961) *Sensation and Perception: A History of the Philosophy of Perception*, New York, NY–London
  (1968) *Aristotle's De Anima: Books II and III, with Certain Passages from Book I*, Oxford
  (1970) *The Theory of Knowledge*, Basingstoke
Harlfinger, D. (1979) 'Zur Überlieferungsgeschichte der Metaphysik', in P. Aubenque, ed., *Études sur la Métaphysique d'Aristote: actes du VIe symposium Aristotelicum* (Paris) 7–36
Hartman, E. (1977) *Substance, Body, and Soul: Aristotelian Investigations*, Princeton
Hawtrey, R. S. W. (1981) *Commentary on Plato's Euthydemus*, Philadelphia
Hayduck, M. (1877) *Emendationes Aristoteleae*, Meldorf
Heath, T. L. (1921/1981) *A History of Greek Mathematics*, 2 vols., New York
Hecquet-Devienne, M. (2000) 'Les Mains du "Parisinus graecus" 1853: une nouvelle collation des quatre premiers livres de la Métaphysique d'Aristote (folios 225v–247v)', *Scrittura e Civiltà* 24: 103–71
Heiberg, J. L. (1880–1/1972) *Archimedis opera omnia: Volumen II*, Berlin
Henry, P. and Schwyzer, H.-R. (1951–73) *Plotini Opera*, 3 vols., Paris–Brussels
  (1951) (eds.) *Plotini Opera Tomus I: Porphyrii vita Plotini, Enneades I–III*, Paris
  (1964) (eds.) *Plotini Opera. Tomus I, Porphyrii vita Plotini Enneades II–III*, Oxford
Herford, C. H. (1931) *Philip Henry Wicksteed, His Life and Work*, London-Toronto
Hett, W. S. (1935) *Aristotle On the Soul, Parva Naturalia, On Breath*, Cambridge, MA
Hicks, R. D. (1907) *Aristotle: De Anima*, Cambridge
Hildebrandt, K. (1936) (ed.) *Platons vaterländische Reden: Apologie, Kriton, Menexenos*, Leipzig

Hintikka, J. (1967) 'Time, truth, and knowledge in ancient Greek philosophy', *American Philosophical Quarterly* 4: 1–14
Hope, R. (1952) *Aristotle's Metaphysics: Newly Translated as a Postscript to Natural Science*, New York
Huby, P. (1999) *Theophrastus of Eresus: Sources for His Life, Writings, Thought, and Influence. Commentary. 4, Psychology: Texts 265–327*, Leiden
Huffman, C. A. (1985) 'The authenticity of Archytas fr. 1', *Classical Quarterly* 35: 344–8
  (1993) *Philolaus of Croton: Pythagorean and Presocratic: A Commentary on the Fragments and Testimonia with Interpretive Essays*, Cambridge
  (2005) *Archytas of Tarentum: Pythagorean, Philosopher and Mathematician King*, Cambridge
Hunink, V. (1997) *Apuleius of Madauros: Pro se de magia (Apologia)*, Amsterdam
Hussey, E. (1983) *Aristotle's Physics: Books III and IV*, Oxford
Hutchinson, D. S. (1987) 'Restoring the order of Aristotle's *De Anima*', *Classical Quarterly* 37: 373–81
Ingenkamp, H. G. (1971) 'Zur stoischen Lehre vom Sehen', *Rheinisches Museum für Philologie* 114: 240–6
Irwin, T. (1988) *Aristotle's First Principles*, Oxford
Irwin, T. and Fine, G. (1996) *Aristotle: Introductory Readings*, Indianapolis
Jackson, R. (1990) 'Socrates' Iolaos: myth and eristic in Plato's *Euthydemus*', *Classical Quarterly* 40: 378–95
Jacobson, H. (1982) (ed.) *The Exagoge of Ezekiel*, Cambridge
Jaeger, W. (1957) *Aristotelis Metaphysica*, Oxford
Janáček, K. (1948) *Prolegomena to Sextus Empiricus*, Nakladem Palackeho
Jansen, L. (2002) *Tun und Können: ein systematischer Kommentar zu Aristoteles' Theorie der Vermögen im neunten Buch der "Metaphysik"*, Frankfurt
Joachim, H. H. (1906) *The Nature of Truth: An Essay*, Oxford
  (1922) *Aristotle: On Coming-to-Be and Passing-Away (De Generatione et Corruptione)*, Oxford
  (1948) *Logical Studies*, Oxford
Johansen, T. K. (1998) *Aristotle on the Sense-organs*, Cambridge
  (2004) *Plato's Natural Philosophy: A Study of the Timaeus-Critias*, Cambridge
Jowett, B. (1875) *The Dialogues of Plato*, 5 vols., 2nd edn, Oxford
Kahn, C. H. (1966) 'The Greek verb "to be" and the concept of being', *Foundations of Language* 2: 245–65
  (1973) *The Verb "Be" in Ancient Greek*, Dordrecht
  (1976) 'Why existence does not emerge as a distinct concept in Greek philosophy', *Archiv für Geschichte der Philosophie* 58: 323–34
  (1979) *The Art and Thought of Heraclitus: An Edition of the Fragments with Translation and Commentary*, Cambridge
  (1981) 'Some philosophical uses of "to be" in Plato', *Phronesis* 26: 105–34
  (1985) 'On the intended interpretation of Aristotle's *Metaphysics*', in J. Wiesner, ed., *Aristoteles: Werk und Wirkung, i. Aristoteles und seine Schule* (Berlin–New York) 311–38

Kalligas, P. (2001) 'Traces of Longinus' library in Eusebius' *Praeparatio Evangelica*', *Classical Quarterly* 51: 584–98
Kenny, A. (1963) *Action, Emotion and Will*, London
Keulen, H. (1971) *Untersuchungen zu Platons Euthydem*, Wiesbaden
Keuls, E. C. (1978) *Plato and Greek Painting*, Leiden
Keyser, P. T. (1992) 'Stylometric method and the chronology of Plato's works': review of Leonard Brandwood, Chronology of Plato's Dialogues (Cambridge 1990)', *Bryn Mawr Classical Review* 3: 58–74
Keyt, D. (1971) 'The mad craftsman of the *Timaeus*', *Philosophical Review* 80: 230–5
Kirchmann, J. H. von (1871) *Die Metaphysik des Aristoteles*, Berlin
Kirk, G. S. (1954) *Heraclitus: The Cosmic Fragments*, Cambridge
Kneale, W. and Moore, G. E. (1936) 'Symposium: is existence a predicate?', *Aristotelian Society Supplementary Volume* 15: 154–88
Knorr, W. (1975) *The Evolution of the Euclidean Elements: A Study of the Theory of Incommensurable Magnitudes and Its Significance for Early Greek Geometry*, Dordrecht
  (1985) 'Archimedes and the Pseudo-Euclidean *Catoptrics*: early stages in the geometric theory of mirrors', *Archives Internationales d'Histoire des Sciences*, 35: 28–103
  (1994) 'Pseudo-Euclidean reflections in ancient optics: a re-examination of textual issues pertaining to the Euclidean *Optica* and *Catoptrica*', *Physis* 31: 1–45
Kosman, L. A. (1969) 'Aristotle's definition of motion', *Phronesis* 14: 40–62
  (1984) 'Substance, being, and *energeia*', *Oxford Studies in Ancient Philosophy* 2: 121–49
Krohn, F. (1912) *Vitruvii De architectura libri decem*, Leipzig
Lasserre, F. (1987) *De Léodamas de Thasos à Philippe d'Oponte: témoignages et fragments*, Naples
Lasson, A. (1907) *Aristoteles Metaphysik*, Jena
Lear, J. (1982) 'Aristotle's philosophy of mathematics', *Philosophical Review* 91: 161–92
Lee, H. D. P. (1952) *Aristotle: Meteorologica*, Cambridge, MA–London
  (1955) *Plato: The Republic*, Harmondsworth
  (1965) *Plato: Timaeus*, Harmondsworth
Lefebvre, G. (1949) *Romans et contes égyptiens de l'époque pharaonique*, Paris
Lefkowitz, M. R. (1984) 'Aristophanes and other historians of the fifth-century theater', *Hermes* 112: 143–53
Lehrer, K. (1974) *Knowledge*, Oxford
Lesher, J. H. (1969) 'ΓΝΩΣΙΣ and ΕΠΙΣΤΗΜΗ in Socrates' dream in the *Theaetetus*', *Journal of Hellenic Studies* 89: 72–8
  (2001) 'On Aristotelian ἐπιστήμη as "understanding"', *Ancient Philosophy* 21: 45–55
Levy, C. (2003) 'Cicero and the *Timaeus*', in G. Reydams-Schils, ed., *Plato's Timaeus as Cultural Icon* (Notre Dame) 95–110

Lewis, D. (1979) 'Scorekeeping in a language game', *Journal of Philosophical Logic* 8: 339–59
Lightfoot, J. L. (2014) *Dionysius Periegetes: Description of the Known World*, Oxford
Lindsay, A. D. (1935) *Plato's Republic*, London
Linguiti, A. (1995) 'Anon. In Plat. Parm.', *Corpus dei papiri filosofici greci e latini: Parte III Commentari, Corpus dei papiri filosofici greci e latini (CPF): testi e lessico nei papiri di cultura greca e latina*, Florence
  (2000) *La Felicità e il Tempo: Plotino, Enneadi, I4–I5, con testo greco*, Milan
Liske, M.-T. (1991) 'Kinesis und Energeia bei Aristoteles', *Phronesis* 36: 161–78
Livingstone, R. W. (1938) (ed.) *Portrait of Socrates: Being the Apology, Crito, and Phaedo of Plato in an English Translation*, trans. B. Jowett, Oxford
Lloyd, G. (1990) *Demystifying Mentalities*, Cambridge
Lohr, C. H. (1991) *Pseudo-Johannis Philoponi Expositiones in omnes XIV Aristotelis libros metaphysicos / übersetzt von Franciscus Patritius, Neudruck der ersten Ausgabe Ferrara 1583*, Stuttgart–Bad Cannstatt
Luna, C. (2001) *Trois études sur la tradition des commentaires anciens à la métaphysique d'Aristote*, Leiden
  (2005) 'Observations sur le texte des livres M–N de la *Métaphysique* d'Aristote', *Documenti e studi sulla tradizione filosofica medievale* 16: 553–93
Lyons, J. (1963) *Structural Semantics: An Analysis of Part of the Vocabulary of Plato*, Oxford
  (1979) 'Knowledge and truth: a localistic approach', in D. J. Allerton, E. Carney and D. Holdcraft, eds., *Function and Context in Linguistic Analysis: A Festschrift for William Haas* (Cambridge) 111–41
  (1981) '*Structural Semantics* in retrospect', in T. E. Hope et al., eds., *Language, Meaning, and Style: Essays in Memory of Stephen Ullmann* (Leeds) 73–90
MacDowell, D. M. (1990) *Demosthenes: Against Meidias, Oration 21*, Oxford
Mackenna, S. (1956) *Plotinus: The Enneads*, 2nd edn, London
Magee, J. (2000) 'Sense organs and the activity of sensation in Aristotle', *Phronesis* 45: 306–30
Makin, S. (2006) *Aristotle: Metaphysics Book Θ*, Oxford
Mamo, P. S. (1970) 'Energia and kinesis in Metaphysics Θ.6', *Apeiron* 4: 24–34
Mansfeld, J. (1997), 'Notes on the Didaskalicus', in M. Joyal, ed., *Studies in Plato and the Platonic Tradition: Essays Presented to John Whittaker* (Aldershot) 248–54
  (1998) *Prolegomena Mathematica: From Apollonius of Perga to Late Neoplatonism: With an Appendix on Pappus and the History of Platonism*, Leiden
Marcovich, M. (1967) *Heraclitus: Greek Text with a Short Commentary*, Mérida
Mates, B. (1949) 'Stoic logic and the text of Sextus Empiricus', *American Journal of Philology* 70: 290–8
  (1961) *Stoic Logic*, Berkeley
  (1979) 'Identity and predication in Plato', *Phronesis* 24: 211–29

McDowell, J. (1969) 'Identity mistakes: Plato and the Logical Atomists', *Proceedings of the Aristotelian Society* 70: 181–95
  (1973) *Plato: Theaetetus, Translated with Notes*, Oxford
Meillet, A. (1924) 'Le Sens de γενήσομαι à propos de Parménide 141', *Revue de Philologie, de Littérature et d'Histoire Anciennes*, 43–9
Melchinger, S. (1974) *Das Theater der Tragödie: Aischylos, Sophokles, Euripides auf der Bühne ihrer Zeit*, Munich
Menn, S. (1994) 'The origins of Aristotle's concept of ἐνέργεια: ἐνέργεια and δύναμις', *Ancient Philosophy* 14: 73–114
Mercken, H. P. F. (1973) *The Greek Commentaries on the Nicomachean Ethics of Aristotle: In the Latin Translation of Robert Grosseteste, Bishop of Lincoln, Vol. 1*, Leiden
Migliori, M. (1976) *Aristotele: La Generazione e la corruzione*, Naples
Mignucci, M. (2007) *Aristotele: Analitici secondi: Organon IV*, Rome
Mihevc, E. (1959) 'La Disparition du parfait dans le grec de la basse époque', *Razaprave Slovenska akademija znanosti in umetnosti, razred za filološke in literarne vede* 5: 93–154
Mioni, E. (1968) 'Bessarione bibliofilo e filologo', *Rivista di studi bizantini e neoellenici* 5: 61–83
Momigliano, A. (1978) *Alien Wisdom: The Limits of Hellenization*, Cambridge
Moore, G. E. (1959) *Philosophical Papers*, London
Moraux, P. (1951) *Les Listes anciennes des ouvrages d'Aristote*, Louvain
Morgan, M. H. (1914/1960) *Vitruvius: The Ten Books on Architecture*, New York
Morison, B. and Ierodiakonou, K. (2011), eds., *Episteme, Etc.: Essays in Honour of Jonathan Barnes*, Oxford
Mourelatos, A. (1978) 'Events, processes, and states', *Linguistic Philosophy* 2: 415–34
Mueller, I. (1991) 'Mathematics and education: some notes on the Platonic program', *Apeiron* 24: 85–104
Muirhead, J. H. (1925) (ed.) *Contemporary British Philosophy: Personal Statements (Second Series)*, London
Narcy, M. (1984) *Le Philosophe et son double: un commentaire de l'Euthydème de Platon*, Paris
Natali, C. (1991) 'Movimenti ed attività: l'interpretazione di Aristotele, *Metaph.* Θ', *Elenchos* 12: 67–90
  (1999) 'La critica di Plotino ai concetti di attualità e movimento in Aristotele', in C. Natali and S. Maso, eds., *Antiaristotelismo* (Amsterdam) 211–29
  (2004) *L'Action efficace: études sur la philosophie de l'action d'Aristote*, Louvain-la-Neuve
Netz, R. (1999) *The Shaping of Deduction in Greek Mathematics: A Study in Cognitive History*, Cambridge
Newman, W. L. (1887) *The Politics of Aristotle*, 4 vols., Oxford
Nozick, R. (2003) *Philosophical Explanations*, Cambridge, MA
Nussbaum, M. C. (1976) 'The text of Aristotle's *De motu animalium*', *Harvard Studies in Classical Philology* 80: 111–59

(1978) *Aristotle's De Motu Animalium: Text with Translation, Commentary, and Interpretive Essays*, Princeton
Nussbaum, M. C. and Putnam, H. (1992) 'Changing Aristotle's mind', in M. C. Nussbaum and A. O. Rorty, eds., *Essays on Aristotle's De Anima* (Oxford) 27–56
Nussbaum, M. C. and Rorty, A. O. (1992) *Essays on Aristotle's De Anima*, Oxford
O'Brien, D. (1970) 'The effect of a simile: Empedocles' theories of seeing and breathing', *Journal of Hellenic Studies* 90: 140–79
Owen, G. E. L. (1966) 'Plato and Parmenides on the timeless present', *The Monist* 50: 317–40
  (1970a) 'Notes on Ryle's Plato', in O. P. Wood and G. Pitcher, eds., *Ryle: A Collection of Critical Essays* (New York) 341–72
  (1970b) 'Plato on not-being', in G. Vlastos, ed., *Plato: A Collection of Critical Essays. Vol. 1: Metaphysics and Epistemology* (Garden City) 223–67
  (1971–2) 'Aristotelian pleasures', *Proceedings of the Aristotelian Society* 72: 135–52
  (1986) *Logic, Science, and Dialectic: Collected Papers in Greek Philosophy*, ed. M. C. Nussbaum, London
Pappa, E. (2002) *George Pachymeres: Philosophia. Buch 10, Kommentar zur Metaphysik des Aristoteles*, Athens
Pasnau, R. (1997) *Theories of Cognition in the Later Middle Ages*, Cambridge
  (1999) *Thomas Aquinas: A Commentary on Aristotle's De Anima*, New Haven
Patzer, A. (1986) *Der Sophist Hippias als Philosophiehistoriker*, Freiburg
Pears, D. F. (1972) *What Is Knowledge?*, London
Pellegrin, P. (2000) *Aristote: Physique*, Paris
  (2005) *Aristote: Seconds analytiques*, Paris
Penner, T. (1970) 'Verbs and the identity of actions: a philosophical exercise in the interpretation of Aristotle', in O. P. Wood and G. Pitcher, eds., *Ryle: A Collection of Critical Essays, Introduction by Gilbert Ryle* (New York) 393–460
Pinès, S. (1971) 'Les Textes arabes dits plotiniens et le courant "porphyrien" dans le néoplatonisme grec', in P. Hadot and P. M. Schuhl, eds., *Le Néoplatonisme* (Paris) 303–13
Pirotta, A. M. (1934) (ed.) *Aquinas: In Decem Libros Ethicorum Aristotelis ad Nicomachum*, Turin
  (1959) *Aquinas: In Aristotelis Librum de Anima Commentarium*, Turin–Rome
Polansky, R. (1983) '*Energeia* in Aristotle's *Metaphysics* ix', *Ancient Philosophy* 3: 160–70
Pollitt, J. J. (1974) *The Ancient View of Greek Art: Criticism, History and Terminology*, New Haven
Poste, E. (1866) *Aristotle on Fallacies, or the Sophistici Elenchi*, London
Potts, T. C. (1965) 'States, activities and performances', *Proceedings of the Aristotelian Society, Supplementary Volume* 39: 65–84
Powell, J. E. (1938) *A Lexicon to Herodotus*, Cambridge
Purser, L. C. (1907) 'Notes on Apuleius', *Hermathena* 14: 360–412

Putnam, H. (1975) *Philosophical Papers. Vol. 2. Mind, Language and Reality*, Cambridge
Rackham, H. (1934) *Aristotle: The Nicomachean Ethics*, 2nd edn, Cambridge, MA–London
 (1951) *Cicero: De Natura Deorum, Academica*, revised edn, Cambridge, MA–London
Reeve, C. D. C. (1989) *Socrates in the Apology: An Essay on Plato's Apology of Socrates*, Indianapolis
Reeve, C. D. C. and Grube, G. M. A. (1992) *Plato: Republic*, Indianapolis
Reynolds, L. D. and Wilson, N. G. (2000) *Scribes and Scholars: A Guide to the Transmission of Greek and Latin Literature*, 3rd edn, Oxford
Rhodes, P. J. (1981) *A Commentary on the Aristotelian Athenaion Politeia*, Oxford
Rhys Roberts, W. (1924) *Aristotle: Rhetorica, De Rhetorica ad Alexandrum, De Poetica*, Oxford
Riddell, J. (1877) *The Apology of Plato: With a Revised Text and English Notes, and a Digest of Platonic Idioms*, Oxford
Rijksbaron, A. (1989) *Aristotle, Verb Meaning and Functional Grammar: Towards a New Typology of States of Affairs, with an Appendix on Aristotle's Distinction Between kinesis and energeia*, Amsterdam
Rist, J. M. (1984) 'The theory and practice of Plato's *Cratylus*', in D. E. Gerber, ed., *Greek Poetry and Philosophy: Studies in Honour of Leonard Woodbury* (Chico) 207–18
 (1996) *Man, Soul, and Body: Essays in Ancient Thought from Plato to Dionysius*, Aldershot
Rivaud, A. (1925) *Platon: Œuvres complètes Vol 10: Timée, Critias*, Paris
Robb, J. H. (1968) (ed.) *Aquinas: Quaestiones De Anima*, Toronto
Robertson, M. (1959) *Greek Painting*, Geneva
 (1975) *A History of Greek Art*, 2 vols., London
Robin, L. (1955) *Platon: Œuvres complètes*, Paris
Robinson, R. (1942) 'Plato's consciousness of fallacy', *Mind* 51: 97–114
 (1969) *Essays in Greek Philosophy*, Oxford
Rodier, G. (1900) *Aristote: Traité de l'âme*, Paris
Romano, F. and Taormina, D. P. (1994) (eds.) *Hyparxis e hypostasis nel Neoplatonismo*, Florence
Ross, W. D. (1908) *The Works of Aristotle. Vol. 8, Metaphysica*, eds. W. D. Ross and J. A. Smith, Oxford
 (1924) *Aristotle's Metaphysics*, 2 vols., Oxford
 (1928a) *The Works of Aristotle Translated into English. Vol. 8, Metaphysica*, 2nd edn, Oxford
 (1930) *The Right and the Good*, Oxford
 (1936) *Aristotle's Physics*, Oxford
 (1939) *Foundations of Ethics: Gifford Lectures, 1935–1936*, Oxford
 (1949) *Aristotle*, London
 (1956) *Aristotelis De Anima*, Oxford
 (1961) *Aristotle De Anima*, Oxford

(1928b) (ed.) *The Works of Aristotle Translated into English under the Editorship of W. D. Ross. Volume 1*, Oxford
Rowe, C. J. (1986) *Plato: Phaedrus*, Warminster
  (1993) *Plato: Phaedo*, Cambridge
  (2003) 'The status of the "myth" in Plato's *Timaeus*', in C. Natali and S. Maso, eds., *Plato Physicus: Cosmologia e antropologia nel Timeo* (Amsterdam) 21–31
Rumfitt, I. (2003) 'Savoir faire', *Journal of Philosophy* 100: 158–66
Rumpf, A. (1947) 'Classical and post-classical Greek painting', *Journal of Hellenic Studies* 67: 10–21
Runciman, W. G. (1962) *Plato's Later Epistemology*, Cambridge
Russo, A. (1992) *Aristote, Opere, Volume sesto [VI], Metafisica*, Bari
Ryle, G. (1937) 'Taking sides in philosophy', *Philosophy* 12: 317–32
  (1939) 'Plato's *Parmenides*', *Mind* 48: 129–51, 302–25
  (1945) 'Knowing how and knowing that: the presidential address', *Proceedings of the Aristotelian Society* 46: 1–16
  (1954) *Dilemmas*, Cambridge
  (1960) 'Letters and syllables in Plato', *Philosophical Review* 69: 431–51
  (1971a) *Collected Papers. Vol. 2, Collected Essays 1929–1968*, London
  (1971b) *Collected Papers. Vol. 1, Critical Essays*, London
  (1990) 'Logical atomism in Plato's *Theaetetus*', *Phronesis* 35: 21–46
Sandbach, F. H. (1969) *Plutarch: Moralia Volume XV, Text with English Translation*, Cambridge, MA–London
Scheffler, I. (1965) *Conditions of Knowledge: An Introduction to Epistemology and Education*, Chicago
Schleiermacher, F. (1817–28) *Platons Werke*, ed. F. Schleiermacher, Berlin
Schneewind, J. B. (1998) *The Invention of Autonomy: A History of Modern Moral Philosophy*, Cambridge
Schneider, J. G. (1807–8) *Marci Vitruvii Pollionis De architectura libri decem*, ed. P. Fraser, Leipzig
Schofield, M. (1988) 'The retrenchable present', in J. Barnes and M. Mignucci, eds., *Matter and Metaphysics (Proceedings of the Fourth Symposium Hellenisticum)* (Naples) 329–74
Schwegler, A. (1847) *Die Metaphysik des Aristoteles: Grundtext, Übersetzung und Commentar*, Tübingen
Sedley, D. N. (1983) 'Epicurus' refutation of determinism', in M. Gigante, ed., *ΣΥΖΗΤΗΣΙΣ: Studi sull'epicureismo greco e latino offerto a Marcello Gigante*, Vol. 1 (Naples) 11–51
  (1989) 'Teleology and myth in the *Phaedo*', *Proceedings of the Boston Area Colloquium in Ancient Philosophy* 5: 359–83
  (2005) 'Stoic metaphysics at Rome', in R. Salles, ed., *Metaphysics, Soul, and Ethics in Ancient Thought: Themes from the Work of Richard Sorabji* (Oxford) 117–42
Shackleton Bailey, D. R. (2000) *Valerius Maximus: Memorable Doings and Sayings*, Cambridge, MA–London

Shorey, P. (1937) *Plato Republic 1: Books I–V*, revised edn, Cambridge, MA–London
Sicherl, M. (1976) 'Handschriftliche Vorlagen der editio princeps des Aristoteles', *Akademie der Wissenschaften und der Literatur, Mainz, Abhandlungen der Geistes- und Sozialwissenschaftlichen Klasse*, 8: 1–90
Simon, E. (1972/1982) *The Ancient Theatre*, trans. C. E. Vafopoulou-Richardson, London
Simon, E. and B. Otto (1973) 'Eine neue Rekonstruktion der Würzburger Skenographie', *Archäologischer Anzeiger* 88: 121–31
Simon, G. (1988) *Le Regard, l'être et l'apparence dans l'optique de l'antiquité*, Paris
 (1994) 'Aux origines de la théorie des miroirs. Sur l'authenticité de la Catoptrique d'Euclide', *Révue d'histoire des sciences* 47: 259–72
Siwek, P. (1965) *Aristotelis Tractatus De Anima: Graece et Latine*, Rome
Skemp, J. B. (1979) 'The activity of immobility', in P. Aubenque, ed., *Études sur la Métaphysique d'Aristote: actes du VIe symposium Aristotelicum* (Paris) 229–45
Smeets, A. (1952) *Act en potentie in de Metaphysica van Aristeles: historisch-philologisch onderzoek van boek IX en boek V der Metaphysica*, Leuven
Smith, J. A. (1917) 'General relative clauses in Greek', *Classical Review* 31: 69–71
 (1920) 'Aristotelica', *Classical Quarterly* 14: 16–22
 (1931) *De Anima*, in W. D. Ross, ed., *The Works of Aristotle Translated into English*. Vol. 3 (Oxford)
Snell, B. (1924) *Die Ausdrücke für den Begriff des Wissens in der vorplatonischen Philosophie: (sophia, gnōmē, sinesis, historia, mathēma, epistēmē)*, Berlin
 (1948/1953) *The Discovery of the Mind: The Greek Origins of European Thought*, trans. T. G. Rosenmeyer, Oxford
Snowdon, P. (2004) 'Knowing how and knowing that: a distinction reconsidered', *Proceedings of the Aristotelian Society* 104: 1–29
Sorabji, R. (1972) 'Aristotle, mathematics, and colour', *Classical Quarterly* 22: 293–308
 (1974) 'Body and soul in Aristotle', *Philosophy* 49: 63–89
 (1979) 'Body and soul in Aristotle', in J. Barnes, M. Schofield and R. Sorabji, eds., *Articles on Aristotle. 4, Psychology and Aesthetics* (London) 42–64
 (1983) *Time, Creation, and the Continuum: Theories in Antiquity and the Early Middle Ages*, London
 (1991) 'From Aristotle to Brentano: the development of the concept of intentionality', in H. Blumenthal and H. Robinson, eds., *Aristotle and the Later Tradition, Oxford Studies in Ancient Philosophy, Supplementary Volume* (Oxford) 227–59
 (1992) 'Intentionality and physiological processes: Aristotle's theory of sense-perception', in M. C. Nussbaum and A. O. Rorty, eds., *Essays on Aristotle's De anima* (Oxford) 195–225
 (2001) 'Aristotle on sensory processes and intentionality: A reply to Myles Burnyeat', in D. Perler, ed., *Ancient and Medieval Theories of Intentionality* (Leiden) 49–61

(1990) (ed.) *Aristotle Transformed: The Ancient Commentators and Their Influence*, London
Spens, H. (1763) *The Republic of Plato. In Ten Books. With a Preliminary Discourse Concerning the Philosophy of the Ancients by the Translator*, Glasgow
Spiazzi, R. M (1949) (ed.) *In Aristotelis Libros de Sensu et Sensato, de Memoria et Reminiscentia*, 3rd edn, Turin–Rome
Sprague, R. K. (1965) *Plato: Euthydemus*, Indianapolis
Stanley, J. and Williamson, T. (2001) 'Knowing how', *Journal of Philosophy* 98: 411–44
Sterling, R. W. and Scott, W. C. (1985) *Plato: The Republic*, New York–London
Stern, M. (1980) *Greek and Latin Authors on Jews and Judaism. Vol. 2. From Tacitus to Simplicius*, Jerusalem
Stewart, M. A. and Sprague, R. K. (1977) 'Plato's sophistry', *Proceedings of the Aristotelian Society, Supplementary Volume* 51: 21–61
Stewart, Z. (1958) 'Democritus and the Cynics', *Harvard Studies in Classical Philology* 63: 179–91
Stokes, M. C. (1996) 'Review of Plato's *Apology of Socrates*, a literary and philosophical study with a running commentary', *Archiv für Geschichte der Philosophie* 78: 192–8
(1997) *Plato: Apology of Socrates*, Warminster
Strycker, E. de (1994) *Plato's Apology of Socrates: A Literary and Philosophical Study with a Running Commentary*, ed. S. R. Slings, Leiden
Stump, E. and Kretzman, N. (1981) 'Eternity', *Journal of Philosophy* 78: 429–58
Sturz, F. W. (1801) *Lexicon Xenophonteum*, eds. C. A. Thieme, C. Mayo and W. Wyse, Leipzig
Szaif, J. (1996) *Platons Begriff der Wahrheit*, Freiburg
Taplin, O. (1977) *The Stagecraft of Aeschylus: The Dramatic Use of Exits and Entrances in Greek Tragedy*, Oxford
Tardieu, M. (1996) 'Recherches sur la formation de l'Apocalypse de Zostrien et les sources de Marius Victorinus', *Res Orientales* 9: 9–114
Taylor, A. E. (1926) *Plato: The Man and His Work*, London
(1928) *A Commentary on Plato's Timaeus*, Oxford
(1929) *Plato: Timaeus and Critias*, London
Taylor SJ, J. H. (1973) 'Virtue and wealth according to Socrates (Apol. 30b)', *Classical Bulletin* 49: 49–52
Taylor, T. (1801) *The Metaphysics of Aristotle: Translated from the Greek with Copious Notes, in which the Pythagoric and Platonic Dogmas Respecting Numbers and Ideas are Unfolded to Which is Added, a Dissertation on Nullities and Diverging Series*, London
Tedeschi, P. J. and Zaenen, A. E. (1981) *Tense and Aspect*, New York
Tellkamp, J. A. (1999) *Sinne, Gegenstände und Sensibilia: zur Wahrnehmungslehre des Thomas von Aquin*, Leiden
Theiler, W. (1959) *Aristoteles Über die Seele*, Berlin
Torstrik, A. (1862) *Aristotelis De Anima Libri III*, Berlin

Tredennick, H. (1933) *Aristotle: The Metaphysics*, Cambridge, MA
  (1969) *Plato: The Last Days of Socrates: Euthyphro, The Apology, Crito, Phaedo*, London
Trendall, A. D. and Webster, T. B. L. (1971) *Illustrations of Greek Drama*, London
Tricot, J. (1959) *Aristote De l'âme = Peri psychēs = De anima*, new edn, Paris
  (1964) *Aristote: La Métaphysique*, new edn, Paris
Vallette, P. (1924) *Apulée: Apologie, Florides*, Paris
Vince, J. H. (1935) *Demosthenes. Against Meidias, Androtion, Aristocrates, Timocrates, Aristogeiton*, Cambridge, MA–London
Vlastos, G. (1939) 'The disorderly motion in the *Timaios*', *Classical Quarterly* 33: 71–83
  (1957) 'Socratic knowledge and Platonic "pessimism"', *Philosophical Review* 66: 226–38
  (1975) *Plato's Universe*, Oxford
  (1981) *Platonic Studies*, Princeton
  (1991) *Socrates, Ironist and Moral Philosopher*, Cambridge
Vries, G. J. de (1969) *A Commentary on the Phaedrus of Plato*, Amsterdam
Vuillemin-Diem, G. (1976) *Aristoteles Metaphysica lib. I–X, XII–XIV: translatio anonyma sive 'media'*, Leiden
  (1995) *Aristoteles Metaphysica Lib. I–XIV: recensio et translatio Guillelmi de Moerbeka*, Leiden
Wagner, M. F. (1996) 'Plotinus on the nature of physical reality', in L. P. Gerson, ed., *The Cambridge Companion to Plotinus* (Cambridge) 130–70
Wallace, E. (1882) *Aristotle's Psychology: In Greek and English*, ed. H. Jackson, Cambridge
Wardy, R. (1990) *The Chain of Change: A Study of Aristotle's Physics VII*, Cambridge
Wartelle, A. (1963) *Inventaire des manuscrits grecs d'Aristote: et de ses commentateurs: contribution à l'histoire du texte d'Aristote*, Paris
Waterfield, R. (1987) *Plato: Theaetetus*, Harmondsworth
  (1993) *Plato: Republic*, Oxford
Waterlow, S. (1988) *Nature, Change, and Agency in Aristotle's Physics: A Philosophical Study*, Oxford
Webb, P. (1982) 'Bodily structure and psychic faculties in Aristotle's theory of perception', *Hermes* 110: 25–50
Webster, T. B. L. (1939) *Greek Art and Literature, 530–400 BC*, Oxford
  (1956) *Greek Theatre Production*, London
Weidemann, H. (1994) *Aristoteles: Hermeneutik = Peri Hermeneias*, Berlin
Welsch, W. (1987) *Aisthesis: Grundzüge und Perspektiven der Aristotelischen Sinneslehre*, Stuttgart
Whitaker, C. W. A. (1996) *Aristotle's De Interpretatione: Contradiction and Dialectic*, Oxford
White, J. (1956) *Perspective in Ancient Drawing and Painting*, London

White, M. J. (1980) 'Aristotle's concept of θεωρία and the ἐνέργεια-κίνησις distinction', *Journal of the History of Philosophy* 18: 253–63
Whitehead, A. N. (1929) *Process and Reality: An Essay in Cosmology*, Cambridge
Whittaker, J. (1967) 'Moses Atticising', *Phoenix* 21: 196–201
  (1978) 'Numenius and Alcinous on the first principle', *Phoenix* 32: 144–54
Wiggins, D. (1971) 'On sentence-sense, word-sense and difference of word-sense. Towards a philosophical theory of dictionaries', in D. D. Steinberg and L. A. Jakobovits, eds., *Semantics: An Interdisciplinary Reader in Philosophy, Linguistics and Psychology* (Cambridge) 14–34
  (1972) 'Sentence meaning, negation, and Plato's problem of non-being', in G. Vlastos, ed., *Plato: A Collection of Critical Essays 2, Ethics, Politics, and Philosophy of Art and Religion* (Garden City) 268–303
Williams, C. J. F. (1982) *Aristotle's De Generatione et Corruptione*, Oxford
Williamson, H. (1908) *Plato's Apology of Socrates*, London
Woodger, J. H. (1929/1967) *Biological Principles: A Critical Study*, London–New York
Woods, M. J. (1982) *Aristotle's Eudemian Ethics, Books I, II, and VIII*, Oxford
Wyttenbach, D. A. (1795–1830) *Ploutarchou tou chairōneōs ta ēthika = Plutarchi chæronensis moralia, id est opera, exceptis vitis, reliqua*, 8 vols., Oxford
Zangger, E. (1992) *The Flood from Heaven: Deciphering the Atlantis Legend*, London
Zeyl, D. J. (2000) *Plato: Timaeus*, Indianapolis

Index locorum

Aenesidemus, 326
Aeschylus
  Agamemnon
    990–3, 343
Aetius
  Dox. Gr.
    304.24, 77
Agatharchus, 331, 351
Alcinous
  Didaskalikos
    159.38–42, 59
  Handbook of Platonism
    164.8, 77
    164.33–4, 77
Alexander of Aphrodisias
  De Anima
    132.30, 318
  On the Prior Analytics
    4.9–11, 34
  On the Topics
    52.25–53.10, 25
    301.19, 23
  Quaestiones
    III.3, 83.27–30, 207
Anaxagoras, 328, 353–4
  Fragment 12 DK, 353
  Fragment 21a, 349
Anaxarchus of Abdera, 325–6, 330, 357
  A11 DK, 327
[Andocides]
  Against Alcibiades 17, 345
Anonymous
  On Plato's Parmenides
    XII.23–35, 76
Apuleius
  Apologia
    15, 316
Aquinas, Thomas, 108
  In Aristotelis Libros de Sensu et Sensato, de Memoria et Reminiscentia
    48–52, 229

In Aristotelis Librum de Anima Commentarium
  200, 228
  417, 215
  418, 216, 223, 225
  420, 221
  493–495, 221
  551–553, 223
  553, 223
  563, 232
  589–90, 217
Summa Theologiae
  Ia, q. 13, a. 11, 81
  Ia, q. 75, a. 3, 226
  Ia, q. 78, a. 1, 228
  Ia, q. 78, a. 3, 219–20
Archimedes
  Catoptrics, 321
Archytas, 358
  Fragment 1, 316
  Fragment 4, 313, 315
  Testimony A21, 315
Argyropoulos, Ioannis
  Metaphysics, 108
Aristophanes
  Birds 995, 312
Aristotle
  Categories
    8
      11a15–19, 161
  De Anima
    I.1
      402a1, 258
      402a1–4, 303
      402a1–7, 300
      402a1–11, 162
      402a4–7, 290
      402a7–8, 232
      403a25–b12, 213
    I.2
      403b20–8, 159

404a27–b6, 184
404b9, 224
405b15, 161
404b317–18, 161
I.3
　406a12–13, 161
　407a2–3, 184
　407a23–5, 125
I.5
　409b24–25, 224
　409b26–8, 161
　410a23–6, 163, 290
　410a25 162
　410a25–6, 160, 200
　411a24–6, 184
II.1
　412a22–8, 175
　412a27, 175
　412b5, 175
　412b15–17, 175
　412b25–6, 175
II.2
　413b1–4, 159
　414a19–20, 184
II.4
　415a18–22, 115
　415a26–b7, 304
　415b23–8, 286
　415b28–416a3, 184
　416a29–b9, 290
　416a34–b1, 297
　416b1–3, 180, 184
　416b8–9, 184
　416b9–11, 286
II.5, 94, 155–210, 225, 230
　416b32–3, 159
　416b33–4, 200
　416b33–5, 160
　416b35, 289
　417a1–2, 289
　417a2–6, 165, 289
　417a6–9, 167
　417a6–13, 289
　417a14–17, 171
　417a16, 140
　417a16–17, 130, 167
　417a17–18, 169
　417a18–20, 166
　417a21, 140
　417a21–2, 172
　417a22–8, 143, 172
　417a22–b16, 183
　417a27, 187
　417a30–b2, 206
　417a30–b7, 158
417a31–2, 155
417a32, 188
417b1–7, 185
417b2–3, 155
417b3–4, 156
417b5–7, 185, 210–11
417b6–14, 191
417b6–7, 140
417b8–9, 183
417b12–15, 185
417b13–15, 140
417b16, 187
417b19–26, 182
417b19–28, 181
417b28–418a3, 143
417b29–418a1, 176, 193
418a1–3, 155, 196
418a2–3, 194–5
418a3–6, 169
II.6
　418a14–16, 170
II.8
　420a9–11, 157
II.10
　424a7–10, 157
II.11
　423b29, 164
II.12
　424a17–24, 202, 222
　424b14–18, 232
III.2
　425b2–3, 198
　425b26–426a26, 199
III.3
　427a17–19, 184
　427a21–2, 184
　428b10, 198
III.4, 231
　429a13–18, 143
　429a14–15, 194
　429b24–6, 194
　429b29, 194
III.7
　431a4–7, 192
　431a6–7, 130, 169
　431a10–11, 297
III.13
　435a18–19, 297
De Caelo
I.3
　270b5–9, 295
I.7
　274b15–16, 29
I.9
　279a22–8, 89

Aristotle (cont.)
  II.2
    284b13–14, 301
  II.12
    292a15–17, 294
    292a22–b25, 115
    292b1–2, 115
  III.8
    307b19–24, 294
  De Generatione Animalium
  I.23
    731a25, 115
  II.1
    731b, 304
    731b24–732a11, 304
    731b28–30, 303
    734a3–4, 296
    735a11–17, 187
  IV.3
    768b16–25, 297
  V.1
    778b33–4, 189
  V.8
    789a4–6, 126
  De Generatione et Corruptione
  I.1
    314a2, 286
  I.2
    315a26–8, 287
    315a34–b15, 294
    316a5–14, 294
    317a17–31, 291
    317a20–30, 293
  I.2–5, 29
  I.3
    318a1–12, 300
    318a3–4, 299
  I.4
    319b14–8, 292
  I.5
    321b6–7, 287
  I.6
    323a1–3, 296
    323a16–20, 164
    323a32–3, 296
    323a3–4, 296
    323a34, 299
  I.6–7, 218
  I.7, 166, 224, 230–1
    323b1–15, 163, 165
    323b18–29, 165
    323b21–4, 289
    323b29–324a14, 165
    323b33–324a1, 288
    324a5–14, 155
    324a10–11, 164
  I.8, 233
    324b25–9, 289
    324b35–325a2, 294
    328a5–18, 296
  I.10, 288
    328a2–3, 296
  II.8
    334b31–335a23, 296
  II.9
    336a13, 299
  II.10
    336a18–20, 299
    336b25–337a15, 304
    337a18, 299
    337a24–5, 299
  De Interpretatione
    3.16b19–25, 23
    10.19b12–15, 27
    10.19b19–22, 28
    11.21a25–33, 23
  De Motu Animalium
    7.701a16–17, 280
    7.701b13–18, 203
    7.701b17–18, 202
    7.701b18–23, 203
    7.701b26–8, 203
  De Partibus Animalium
  I.1
    639a1–16, 276
    641a32–b12, 194
  I.5
    644b31–645a4, 282
    645b14–35, 115
  II.1
    646a35–b10, 303
  De Sensu
    1.436a4, 115
    1.436a5, 171
    2.438a5–12, 229
    3.440a31–b4, 288
    3.440b13–14, 288
    6.446b2–6, 129, 191
    6.446b3–4, 196
  Eudemian Ethics
  II.1
    1219a16, 191
  VII
    1248b26–34, 14
  VII.12
    1244b29–30, 127
  VIII.3
    1249a17–21, 141
  Historia Animalium

III.12
  519a3–6, 247
VIII.1
  589a3, 115
VIII.10
  596b20–21, 115

Metaphysics
A.2
  982b19–21, 256
A.5
  985b27–8, 309
  986a6–8, 310
B.1
  996a4–7, 78
B.3
  998b17–21, 78
Γ.5
  1009b12–15, 184
  1010b3, 199
Δ.2
  1013a35–b1, 123
Δ.7, 28
  1017a35–b2, 209
  1017a35–b9, 173
Δ.29
  1024b26–34, 54
E.1
  1026a30–1, 293
E.2
  1026a33–b2, 28
  1026b1–2, 209
Z.1
  1028a30–1, 22, 29
  1028a32–3, 100
  1028b2–4, 86
Z.7
  1032a13–14, 30
  1032a18, 32
Z.13
  1038b28, 100
Z.16
  1040b7–10, 291
H.1
  1042a27–8, 291
  1042b2–3, 291
  1042b7–8, 290
  1045a32–4, 28
Θ.1
  1045b27–1046a4, 94
  1045b33–4, 209
  1045b35–1046a13, 96
Θ.3
  1047a30–2, 97
  1047a32–5, 23
Θ.4
  1047b5–6, 315
Θ.6
  1048a25–30, 94
  1048a26–7, 99
  1048a34–5, 209
  1048b6–9, 94
  1048b8, 114
  1048b8–9, 113, 131
  1048b9–17, 100
  1048b18–35, 93–152, 168
  1048b23, 95
  1048b23–5, 116
  1048b23–34, 191
  1048b24–5, 191
  1048b25–7, 120
  1048b29, 191
  1048b29–31, 95
  1048b33–4, 95, 117
  1048b35–6, 99
Θ.8
  1049b29–1050a2, 177
  1049b29–1050a3, 138
  1050a23–5, 191
  1050a23–b2, 96, 113, 191
  1050b1–2, 116
  1050b28–30, 304
Λ.1
  1069a26–8, 44
Λ.5
  1071a3–5, 209
Λ.6
  1071b19–20, 114
Λ.7
  1072b16, 114
  1072b26–8, 114
Λ.8
  1074a38–b14, 124
Λ.9
  1074a18–21, 114
Λ.10
  1075b28–30, 304

Meteorologica
I.1
  338a20–b22, 292
  339a5–9, 292
I.6
  342b35–343a20, 316

Nicomachean Ethics
I.1
  1094a16–17, 132
I.3
  1094b11–1095a13, 276

Aristotle (cont.)
  I.8
    1099a31–b8, 14
  III.5
    1114b2, 44
  VI.2
    1139a35–b4, 115
  VI.5
    1140b6–7, 115
  VI.13
    1144b24–30, 43
  VII.3, 260
  VII.12
    1153a7–12, 135, 139
    1153a7–17, 134
    1153a15–17, 132, 135
    1153a22–3, 135
    1154a13–15, 135
  VII.14
    1154b20, 115
    1154b26–8, 139
  IX.11
    1171a35–b1, 126
  X, 94
  X.2, 109
  X.3, 136
    1173a29–31, 134
    1173a32–b4, 136
    1173b4–7, 136
    1173b19, 136
    1174b47, 132
  X.4
    1174a13–b14, 191
    1174a14–b14, 136
    1174a19–21, 126
    1174a32, 126
    1174b10, 136
    1174b12–13, 196
    1174b13, 136
    1174b14–17, 137
  X.5
    1175a25–6, 133
    1175a30–35, 138
    1175b36–1176a1, 215
  X.6
    1176a35–b7, 140
  X.7
    1177b34–1178a7, 282
On the Philosophy of Archytas, 313
Physics
  I.1
    184a10–16, 249
    184a12–14, 256
  I.3
    186a15–16, 150

  I.7
    190a31–b1, 32
  I.9
    192b1–2, 299
  II.1
    192b21–2, 194
    193b20–1, 300
  II.2
    94a9–12, 306
  II.5
    197b5, 116
  III.1
    200b33–201a3, 180
    201a10–12, 176
    201a11–12, 167, 189
  III.1–3, 231
  III.2
    201b31–2, 148
    201b31–3, 130
    201b32–3, 169
    201b33–5, 168
    202a9–13, 169
  III.5
    205a6, 208
  III.6
    206a21–5, 101
    207a25–6, 100
    258b10–11, 299
  IV.5
    213a4–5, 299
  IV.14
    223a29–b1, 299
  V.1
    224a35, 197
    224b10, 136
    224b35, 291
    224b7–10, 208
  V.2
    226b1–8, 155
  VI.5
    235b6, 208
  VII.2
    244b2–245a11, 297
  VII.3
    247b9–8a9, 187
  VIII.1
    251a8–10, 136
  VIII.4
    255a30–31, 173
  VIII.5
    257b8–9, 168
Poetics
  1449a15–19, 328

1457b11–13, 89
Politics
  VII.1
    1323a21–3, 15
    1323a37–8, 15
    1323a40–1, 15
    1323b36–40, 15
    1323b40–1324a2, 15
  VIII.3
    1338a1–3, 127
Posterior Analytics
  I.2, 255
    71b9–12, 253
    71b9–16, 257
    71b17, 256
  I.7
    75b14–7, 305
  I.13
    78b35–9, 305
    79a7–8, 313
  I.18, 255
  I.31, 255
  I.33, 255
  II.1
    89b31–5, 27
  II.11
    94a20, 256
  II.19, 255, 257
Prior Analytics
  I.36
    48b2–4, 33
  II.3
    55a4–10, 247
Protrepticus, 15
Rhetoric
  I.5
    1360a4–28, 14
  I.9
    1368a21–2, 294
Sophistical Refutations
  4.165b23–24, 59
  5.167a1–2, 23
  16.175a14–16, 46
  22.178a9–28, 128, 191
  24.183b34–184a4, 61
Topics
  I.11
    104b20–21, 54
  VI.8
    146b13–16, 127
[Aristotle]
  Rhet. ad Alex.
    23.1434b18–19, 127

Aristoxenus
  Fragment 23 Wehrli, 310
Athenaeus
  512a, 142
Augustine of Hippo
  Confessions
    XI.13, 81
Ayer, A. J.
  The Problem of Knowledge, 236

Barnes, Jonathan
  'Socrates and the Jury', 253
Boethius
  Consolation of Philosophy
    V.5, 82
    V.6, 90
Bonitz, Hermann
  Aristotelis Metaphysica, 112

Chrysippus, 318, 358
Cicero
  Academica
    II.32, 348
  De Finibus, 267
  De Inventione
    I.44–49, 267

Democritus, 326, 354, 358
Demosthenes
  Against Meidias
    147, 344
Dickens, Charles
  Great Expectations, 268
Diocles
  On Burning Mirrors, 321
Diogenes of Sinope, 326
Diogenes Laertius
  Lives of the Philosophers
  I
    16, 355
  IV
    4, 142
    12, 142
  V
    25, 313
    26, 306
    44, 142
    46, 142
    59, 142
  VII
    157, 359
  IX
    5, 338

Dionysius of Halicarnassus
  Demosthenes
    5, 70
Dionysius Periegetes
  Orbis descriptio
    225–37, 338
Diotimus
  Testimony A2 DK, 350
Dissoi Logoi (DK 90)
  5.5, 20

Empedocles
  Fragment 109
    1, 118
Epictetus
  Discourses
    1.6.17–22, 271
    1.12.1, 22
Epicurus, 359
  Kyriai Doxai
    22, 33
Euclid
  Elements
    x
      2, 315
      Appendix 27, 315
  Optics, 346
[Euclid]
  Catoptrics
    19, 322
Eudemus of Rhodes
  Fragment 27 Wehrli, 27
Euripides
  Phoenissae
    1762, 320
Eusebius of Caesarea
  Preparation for the Gospel
    XI.8.1, 68

Frede, Michael
  'Aristotle's notion of potentiality in Metaphysics Θ', 94
Frege, Gottlob
  The Foundations of Arithmetic, 302

Galen
  Introduction to Logic
    2, p.5.1–3 Kalbfleisch, 24
    2, p.5.3–22 Kalbfleisch, 24
    3, p.7.19–22 Kalbfleisch, 33
    14, p.32.6–11 Kalbfleisch, 25
Geminus
  ap. Damianus 24.7–15, 322

Gilson, Étienne
  L'Être et l'essence, 35
Gould, John
  The Development of Plato's Ethics, 236
Grote, George
  History of Greece
    VII, 60

Hamlyn, D. W.
  The Theory of Knowledge, 236
Hecataeus of Miletus
  Fragment 1a, 341
Heraclitus
  Fragment 57, 261
  Fragment 101, 337
Heron of Alexandria
  Catoptrica, 321
    18, 362
    318.6–7, 306
Hippias (DK 86)
  Fragment B6, 70
Hippocrates of Chios
  42.5–6, 316
Hobbes, Thomas
  Leviathan
    Chapter 46, 81
Homer
  Iliad
    II.272, 89
  Odyssey
    XIII.102–3, 19
    XXII.347–9, 337

Iamblichus
  De communi mathematica scientia
    25, 309

Lehrer, Keith
  Knowledge, 236
Lloyd, Geoffrey
  Demystifying Mentalities, 78
Lucretius
  De Rerum Natura
    1.876–80, 354
    IV.269–323, 321
    IV.302–8, 361
Lyons, John
  'Structural Semantics in retrospect', 246
  Structural Semantics: An Analysis of Part of the Vocabulary of Plato, 241

Melissus
  Fragment 2, 80

Metrodorus, 326, 358
Michael of Ephesus
  On the Nicomachean Ethics
    543.22 Heylbut, 144
Monimus, 326

New Testament
  Matthew
    6:33, 5
    19:23, 6
  Timothy
    3:8, 73
Numenius of Apamea
  Fragment 1a, 68
  Fragment 1b, 68
  Fragment 1c, 70
  Fragment 2
    5, 78
    23, 78
  Fragment 3, 79
    1, 78
  Fragment 4a
    7–9, 78
    25–32, 79
  Fragment 5
    1–20, 79
  Fragment 6, 84
    5–6, 88
    7, 86
    7–12, 87
  Fragment 8
    13, 67
  Fragment 9, 69, 73–4
  Fragment 10a, 70
  Fragment 12
    7–14, 87
  Fragment 13, 73, 75
  Fragment 16
    8–10, 76
    15–16, 76
  Fragment 17, 74, 87
  Fragment 19, 76
  Fragment 20, 76
  Fragment 24
    18–20, 71
    57–62, 72
    66–70, 72
    73–4, 72
  Fragment 52
    15–24, 72
    3–4, 72
  On the Good, 68
    1, 78
    VI, 74
Nussbaum, Martha and Putnam, Hilary
  'Changing Aristotle's mind', 201

Old Testament
  Deuteronomy
    32:39, 26
  Exodus
    3:14, 67, 73
    20:3, 75
[Olympiodorus]
  On Plato's Phaedo
    158.6–12 Norvin, 335
    212.1–11, 335
  On Aristotle's Physics
    12.22–3, 258
    12.25, 258
    13.6, 258
    13.9–10, 257
Origen
  Contra Celsum, 71
    VI 64.14–28, 78
Owen, G.E.L.
  'Plato and Parmenides on the timeless present', 83
  'Plato on not-being', 53

Parmenides
  Fragment 1
    29–30, 275
  Fragment 8
    4, 282
    5–6, 81
    60–61, 275
Pausanias
  V.15.10, 271
Pears, David
  What Is Knowledge?, 236
Philo Judaeus
  Quod Deus
    32–3, 74
Philodemus
  Index Academicorum
    col. Y, 15–17, 306
Philolaus
  Fragment 5, 315
Philoponus
  De Aeternitate Mundi
    69.4, 207
    69.22–70.1, 207
    71.17–20, 207
    IV.4, 114

Philoponus (cont.)
  On Aristotle's De Anima
    300.8–30, 207
Pindar
  Pythian Odes
    4.205, 25
Plato
  Apology
    30b2–4, 5–22, 38, 41–5
    31d–32c, 39
    41d, 9
  Cratylus
    421ab, 88
    429cd, 46
  Crito
    48c, 9
  Euthydemus
    271a, 66
    272bd, 61
    272d, 65
    273a2, 61
    274b2–6, 61
    274b3, 61
    274c4–d1, 61
    274c7–d1, 61
    278a, 59
    279a, 9
    279c–280b, 65
    279d6–8, 65
    280b–281e, 5, 12
    281de, 65
    282ab, 62
    283a–288a, 46–66
    283cd, 62–4
    283e, 56
    284a1–4, 56
    284a5–6, 56
    284b, 56–7
    284b8–c1, 57
    284c1–6, 58
    284c7–8, 59
    284d1, 60
    284e4–5, 60
    285cd, 63
    285e–286a, 55
    286ab, 55
    287a, 58
    287e–288a, 46
    295b–296d, 59
    304bc, 61
    306e–307c, 66
    307a, 9
  Euthyphro
    4c, 271
    9a, 271
  Gorgias
    452c, 9
    467e, 9
    470e, 5
    507c–508b, 5
    522ce, 5
    527cd, 5
  Ion
    530a8, 120
  Laws
    I
      631bc, 10, 13
    III
      697bc, 13
    V
      742e–743c, 13
    VII
      798d1–2, 40
    IX
      870ab, 13
    X
      887b7–8, 22
      901c8–d2, 22
  Lysis
    220a, 9
  Meno
    78e, 9
    87e–89a, 5, 12
  Parmenides
    162d5–8, 62
  Phaedo
    59b, 64
    64a, 64
    73a, 336
    75cd, 240
    99c, 279
    102bd, 50
    115c, 61
  Phaedrus, 350
    245d1–3, 37
    279c, 6
  Philebus
    54b, 134
    54cd, 134
    54e, 134
  Protagoras
    313a, 5
    316b3–4, 119
    316c3–4, 120
    323d6–7, 16
    353c–354b, 9
    361e6, 120
  Republic
    I
      331ab, 16

Index locorum

331b, 11
II
  357a, 276
  357cd, 9
  360e–362c, 10
  362ac, 11
  362bc, 11
  363a, 11, 126
  368b, 276
  373d–374a, 12
  373e6–7, 16
III
  416e–417a, 6
IV
  434c, 12
  439d, 12
  441a, 12
V
  476d, 21
  476d8–e2, 36
  477a6, 56
  478b, 46
  479d4–5, 21
VI
  484b3–6, 36
  485a10–b3, 36
  486a, 271
  506d, 85
  509b, 75
  509c1–2, 78, 85
  510a, 274
  510d, 314
  510d5, 313
  511e, 274
  532c5–6, 78
VII
  518c, 91
  518c9, 78
  521a, 6
  526e3–4, 78
  527c, 319
  530ab, 307
  530b, 305
  530d, 307
  530e, 308
  531c, 305, 307
  534a, 274
VIII
  547b, 6, 12
  550c–551b, 12
  555bc, 12
  559c3–4, 6
IX
  580e, 12
  580e–581a, 12
  581c3–4, 39
  589d–590a, 12
  591ce, 13
  591e, 12
X
  596a6–8, 42
  613a, 10
  613b9–10, 16, 26
  613c4–5, 11
  613cd, 13
  619a, 13

Sophist
  225a, 268
  237be, 51
  245d1–4, 37
  252e–260b, 22
  256d–257a, 20
  258d–259b, 20
  261d, 22
  263a, 49
  263b, 49
  263b11–12, 20

Symposium
  199d, 126

Theaetetus
  144cd, 27
  152d, 27
  171e5–7, 245
  173e, 312
  181d, 83
  185a8–185d1, 19
  185b10, 21
  188c6, 48
  189b1–2, 51
  189bc, 49
  190e–191a, 51
  191b, 52
  209e8–210a1, 243

Timaeus
  17c, 285
  20ab, 280, 285
  22bd, 266
  22c7, 266
  26ce, 266
  27d–28a, 35
  27d6, 79
  28a4–6, 35
  28b, 279
  28c–29a, 270
  29a, 284
  29b1–d3, 269
  29b2–5, 269
  29b5–c1, 272
  29c1–3, 269
  29c2, 268

Plato (cont.)
  29c4–d3, 270
  29c6, 277
  29d2, 265
  29d–30c, 281
  30b5, 282
  30b7, 284
  31a4–8, 283
  37d, 90
  37d–38b, 79
  37e–38a, 83
  40de, 273
  40e, 274
  44d, 279
  45b, 318
  45c, 318
  46a, 319
  46b, 319
  47ac, 320
  47b4–5, 320
  48d, 272, 277
  48d3, 277
  53c, 285
  53d, 277
  55c, 279
  55cd, 283
  59c6, 277
  59cd, 280
  67d1–2, 269
  75bc, 279, 282
  90e, 284
[Plato]
  Eryxias
    402de, 6
Plotinus
  Enneads
    II.5, 109
    III.7, 81, 83
    [45] 6, 22–36, 88–9
    VI.1, 109
    [42] 15–22, 148
    [42] 25, 9–10, 23
    [42] 29, 18, 34
Plutarch
  De Tranquillitate Animi
    466d, 327
  On the E at Delphi
    392a, 75
    393a, 83
    393b, 77
Porphyry
  Life of Pythagoras
    53, 69
Posidonius, 351

Proclus
  On the Timaeus
    343.18277
Ptolemy
  Optics, 321
Putnam, Hilary
  'The meaning of "meaning"', 246

Quintilian
  VI.2.29–30, 349
  X.7.15, 348

Ross, David
  Aristotle's Metaphysics
    clxiv–clxv, 111
Ryle, Gilbert
  Dilemmas, 93
  'Knowing how and knowing that', 236
  'Logical atomism in Plato's *Theaetetus*', 48, 236
  '*Plato's Parmenides*', 236
  'Taking sides in philosophy', 235
  The Concept of Mind, 236

Scheffler, Israel
  Conditions of Knowledge: An Introduction to Epistemology and Education, 236
Seneca
  Epistle 58, 77
Sepúlveda
  Alexandri Aphrodisiei commentaria in duodecim Aristotelis libros de prima philosophia, 108
Sextus Empiricus
  Against the Mathematicians
    VII.137, 357
    VII.137–40, 349
    VII.87–8, 326
    VII.90, 353
    VII.139, 356
    VIII.5, 327
    VIII.338, 34
    IX.141–2, 33
  Outlines of Pyrrhonism
    I.138, 352
Simplicius
  On Aristotle's Categories
    303.32 ff. Kalbfleisch, 148
    303.35–304.10 Kalbfleisch, 150
    307.1–6 Kalbfleisch, 151
  On Aristotle's Physics
    1.12.14–13.13, 251
Sophonias
  In Libros Aristotelis De Anima Paraphrasis
    66.38–67.4, 208

Sorabji, Richard
  Time, Creation, and the Continuum, 80

Tale of the Eloquent Peasant, 339
Themistius
  On Aristotle's De Anima
    55.25, 207
Theophrastus
  Fragment 307d FHS & G, 142
Thucydides
  IV.65, 312
  IV.76.2, 285
  VIII.72.2, 285

Valerius Maximus
  VII.14 ext. 2, 327
Vitruvius
  1.2.2, 346

1.7, 362
VII
  praef 10–12, 329–30
  praef. 11, 346–7
  praef. 14, 333
  praef. 16, 342

William of Moerbeke
  Aristoteles Metaphysica, 101
Woodger, J. H.
  Biological Principles: A Critical Study, 302

Xeniades, 327
Xenophon
  Symposium
    4.34–44, 6